Sketches in Dordogne

UPPER PLEISTOCENE PREHISTORY OF WESTERN EURASIA

University Museum Monograph 54

UNIVERSITY MUSEUM SYMPOSIUM SERIES
VOLUME I

UPPER PLEISTOCENE PREHISTORY OF WESTERN EURASIA

Harold L. Dibble
Anta Montet-White
Editors

Published by
The University Museum
University of Pennsylvania
1988

Design, editing, typesetting, production
Scholarly Publications, The University Museum

Printing
Science Press
Ephrata, Pennsylvania

Library of Congress Cataloging-in-Publication Data
Upper Pleistocene prehistory of Western Eurasia / Harold L. Dibble, Anta Montet-White, editors.
xx + 462 p. 28½ cm. -- (University Museum monograph ; 54) (University Museum symposium series ; v. 1)
  "Contains the proceedings of a symposium held at The University Museum, University of Pennsylvania, for five days in January 1987": p. xvii
  Bibliography: p. 431-461
  ISBN 0-09-471853-9
  1. Paleolithic period--Europe--Congresses. 2. Paleolithic period--Eurasia--Congresses. 3. Europe--Antiquities--Congresses. 4. Eurasia--Antiquities--Congresses.
  I. Dibble, Harold Lewis, 1951- II. Montet-White, Anta, 1933- III. Series. IV. Series: University Museum symposium series ; v. 1.
GN772.2.A1U66 1988   88-14119
936--dc19   CIP

Colophon drawn by Georgianna Grentzenberg (after Arlette Leroi-Gourhan and Jacques Allain, *Lascaux inconnu. Gallia préhistoire* Supplément 12. Paris: CNRS, 1979; p. 276, pl. 18a).
Endpapers, "Grotte des Eysies," by W. Tipping (from Edouard Lartet and Henry Christy, *Reliquiae Aquitanicae; Being Contributions to the Archaeology and Palaeontology of Périgord and the Adjoining Provinces of Southern France*, ed. T. R. Jones. London: Williams & Norgate, 1875; between pp. 170 and 171).
Frontispiece, "Château des Eysies," by W. Tipping (from Lartet and Christy, *Reliquiae Aquitanicae*, between pp. 172 and 173).
Laurel-leaf point device from Gabriel de Mortillet, "Evolution quaternaire de la pierre." *Revue mensuelle de l'Ecole d'Anthropologie de Paris* 7 (1897), p. 23, fig. 4.

Copyright © 1988
THE UNIVERSITY MUSEUM
University of Pennsylvania
Philadelphia
All rights reserved
Printed in the United States of America

TABLE OF CONTENTS

LIST OF ILLUSTRATIONS ix
EDITORS' PREFACE xvii
ACKNOWLEDGMENTS xix
PART 1 1

    I.   Dimensions of Research at El Juyo: An Earlier Magdalenian Site in Cantabrian Spain 3
          Leslie G. Freeman, Joaquín González Echegaray, Richard G. Klein, and William T. Crowe

    II.   The Uppermost Pleistocene in Gascony: A View from Abri Dufaure (Sorde-l'Abbaye, Les Landes, France) 41
          Lawrence Guy Straus

    III. The Neuvic Group: Upper Paleolithic Open-Air Sites in the Perigord 61
          James R. Sackett

    IV. Recent Thoughts on the Riss and Early Würm Lithic Assemblages of La Chaise de Vouthon (Charente, France) 85
          André Debénath

    V.   Interprétation d'un habitat au Paléolithique moyen: la grotte de Sclayn, Belgique 95
          Marcel Otte, Jean-Marcel Evrard, and Alain Mathis

    VI. Flint Exploitation and Production at Monte Avena in the Dolomitic Region of the Italian East Alps 125
          Michele Lanzinger

    VII. Une mine de silex paléolithique à Budapest, Hongrie 141
          Veronika Gábori-Csánk

PART 2 145

    VIII. Recent Developments on the Chronostratigraphy of the Paleolithic in the Perigord 147
          Henri Laville

    IX. Observations on Some Middle Paleolithic Time Series in Southern France 161
          Nicolas Rolland

    X.   Typological Aspects of Reduction and Intensity of Utilization of Lithic Resources in the French Mousterian ... 181
          Harold L. Dibble

    XI. Technology, Typology, and Culture in the Middle Paleolithic 199
          Arthur J. Jelinek

XII.	Functional Variability of Lithic Sets in the Middle Paleolithic .... Sylvie Beyries	213
XIII.	Scavenging and Hunting in the Middle Paleolithic: The Evidence from Europe .... Philip G. Chase	225
XIV.	The Ecosystem of the "Middle Paleolithic" (Late Lower Paleolithic) in the Upper Danube Region: A Stepping-Stone to the Upper Paleolithic .... Hansjürgen Müller-Beck	233
XV.	Core Reduction, Flake Production, and the Middle Paleolithic Industry of Zobiste (Yugoslavia) .... Mark F. Baumler	255
XVI.	The Curation of Stone Tools during the Upper Pleistocene: A View from the Central Negev, Israel .... Anthony E. Marks	275
XVII.	Nouvelles découvertes dans le Paléolithique d'Asie centrale soviétique .... Miklós Gábori	287
XVIII.	The Implications of Improved Chronological Determinations for the Soviet Central Asian Paleolithic .... Richard S. Davis	297
PART 3	....	303
XIX.	Integration of Late Quaternary Climatic Records From France and Greece: Cave Sediments, Pollen, and Marine Events .... William R. Farrand	305
XX.	Changing Assemblage Diversity in Perigord Archaeofaunas .... Jan F. Simek and Lynn M. Snyder	321
XXI.	Technological Change in the Upper Paleolithic of the Negev .... C. Reid Ferring	333
XXII.	Problems of Continuity and Discontinuity Between the Middle and Upper Paleolithic of Central Europe .... Janusz Kozlowski	349
XXIII.	Raw-Material Economy among Medium-Sized Late Paleolithic Campsites of Central Europe .... Anta Montet-White	361
XXIV.	Upper and Final Paleolithic Settlement Patterns in the Rhineland, West Germany .... Gerhard Bosinski	375
XXV.	The Gravettian Peopling of Southwestern France: Taxonomic Problems .... Jean-Philippe Rigaud	387

XXVI.	Le Magdalénien ancien en Gironde: conditions de gisement, variabilité typologique et technique .... Michel Lenoir	397
XXVII.	Frontières européennes au Paléolithique supérieur: enregistrements et significations—le cas du Sud-Ouest français .... Denise de Sonneville-Bordes	411
XXVIII.	The Mousterian and Its Aftermath: A View From the Upper Paleolithic .... James R. Sackett	413

PARTICIPANTS IN THE SYMPOSIUM 427
OTHER CONTRIBUTORS TO THIS VOLUME 428
ABBREVIATIONS 429
BIBLIOGRAPHY 431

LIST OF ILLUSTRATIONS

Frontispiece		The ruined chateau at Les Eyzies	ii
Figure	1.1	Magdalenian sites in the Cantabrian region	20
	1.2	Chronological settings of Cantabrian industries and occupations	21
	1.3	El Juyo and surrounding topography	22
	1.4	El Juyo: map of excavated area	23
	1.5	El Juyo: selected sections	24
	1.6	El Juyo: pollen diagram	25
	1.7	El Juyo: botanical yield	26
	1.8	El Juyo: Magdalenian plant parts	27
	1.9	Measurements of *Patella* from El Juyo and Altamira	28
	1.10	Faunal species at El Juyo and Altamira	29
	1.11	Stone tools from El Juyo	30
	1.12	Bone artifacts from El Juyo	31
	1.13	Characteristics of El Juyo lithic assemblage	32
	1.14	Cumulative percentage graphs of the El Juyo Magdalenian assemblages	33
	1.15	Topographic maps of El Juyo Levels 4 and 6	34
	1.16	El Juyo Level 6: limits of dugouts	35
	1.17	El Juyo Level 4: sanctuary in early stage of construction	36
	1.18	El Juyo Level 4: sanctuary in later stage of construction	37
	1.19	El Juyo Level 4: face from sanctuary	38
	1.20	El Juyo Level 6: structures with seed-density map	39
	2.1	Map of extreme southwestern France	42
	2.2	Plan of Dufaure site	43
	2.3	Dufaure: stratigraphic section at western end of terrace-slope excavation area	45
	2.4	Dufaure: Stratum IV "pseudo-pavement"	47
	2.5	Dufaure: stratigraphic section at break-in-slope	49
	2.6	Dufaure: Stratum 4 cobblestone pavement: manuports	53

LIST OF ILLUSTRATIONS

2.7	Dufaure: Stratum 4 cobblestone pavement: artifacts and faunal remains	54
3.1	Map showing the Neuvic group	62
3.2	Chronology of the Neuvic sites	63
3.3	Guillassou rock plan	66
3.4	Plateau Parrain rock plan	67
3.5	Le Cerisier	69
3.6	Le Breuil rock plans	70
3.7	Solvieux site plan	72
3.8	Solvieux: Locality 3, Couche A rock plan	73
3.9	Solvieux: Couche III rock plan	75
3.10	Solvieux: Locality 6, Couche M rock and tool plan	77
3.11	Solvieux: Couche IV industry, burins and retouched bladelets	78
3.12	Solvieux: Couche IV industry, Solvieux truncations	79
3.13	Solvieux: Locality 2, Couche IV rock plan	80
4.1	Map showing location of La Chaise sites	85
4.2	Technique of platform rejuvenation	90
4.3	Lithic typology	91
4.4	Lithic typology	92
4.5	Bifaces from La Chaise	93
5.1	Carte: situation générale des grottes de Sclayn	101
5.2	Vues des trois grottes principales de Sclayn	102
5.3	Sclayn CAS 2: coupe transversale à l'intérieur de la première salle	103
5.4	Sclayn CAS 2: dispersion verticale de l'ensemble des artéfacts dans la couche 5 selon l'axe transversal 15	104
5.5	Sclayn CAS 2: dispersion verticale de l'ensemble des artéfacts dans la couche 5 selon l'axe longitudinal G	105
5.6	Sclayn CAS 2: répartition verticale et latérale des éléments remontés sur le même bloc	106
5.7	Sclayn CAS 2: vue verticale du carré E14	107
5.8	Proportions des différentes catégories de matériaux utilisés dans l'industrie lithique	108
5.9	Nucléus à débitage centripète remonté à l'aide d'une série d'éclats	109
5.10	Différentes phases des débitage du bloc de la Figure 5.9	110

LIST OF ILLUSTRATIONS

5.11	Série d'enlèvements à orientation préférentielle remontés	111
5.12	Sclayn: éclats et racloirs	112
5.13	Sclayn: racloirs et denticulé	113
5.14	Sclayn: couteau et racloirs	114
5.15	Sclayn: racloirs et petit biface	115
5.16	Sclayn: racloirs et éclats	116
5.17	Sclayn: denticulé et racloir	117
5.18	Sclayn: corrélation spatiale entre les esquilles de quartz et de silex	118
5.19	Sclayn: corrélation spatiale entre les éclats et les esquilles de tous les matériaux	119
5.20	Sclayn: répartition des principales classes d'outils lithiques par mètre carré	120
5.21	Sclayn: corrélation spatiale entre les outils et les nucléus	120
5.22	Sclayn: corrélation spatiale entre les nucléus et les éclats	121
5.23	Sclayn: courbes d'iso-densité pour les quartz et les silex	121
5.24	Sclayn: courbes d'iso-densité pour les quartzites et les cherts	122
5.25	Sclayn: courbes d'iso-densité pour les nucléus	122
5.26	Sclayn: courbes d'iso-densité de l'ensemble des documents lithiques	123
5.27	Sclayn: courbes d'iso-densité pour les restes osseux déterminables	123
5.28	Sclayn: plan des liaisons des documents lithiques de la couche 5	124
6.1	Map showing Monte Avena's location	126
6.2	View of limestone outcrop during excavation	127
6.3	Monte Avena stratigraphic sequence, sedimentological parameters, and weathering index	128
6.4	Monte Avena deposits: granulometric grain-size distribution	129
6.5	Monte Avena soil horizons: synthesis of micromorphological characteristics	130
6.6	Monte Avena: three types of cores and refitted flakes	133
6.7	Monte Avena: assorted stone tools	134
6.8	Monte Avena: trench plan showing distribution of flint products	136

6.9	Monte Avena: view of artifact distribution	137
7.1	Plan de la localité de Budapest-Farkasrét	142
9.1	Frequency distribution of Levallois index for large Western European assemblage collection	165
9.2A	Combe-Grenal and Pech de l'Azé: evolution of Levallois indices	166
9.2B	Riss and Early Würm site sequences	167
9.2C	Early Würm sites in southwestern France	168
9.3	Evolution of implements and major implement classes	171
9.4	Evolution of minor implement classes (points)	175
9.5	Comparison of Levallois indices for some assemblages in Combe-Grenal succession	177
10.1	Mean and standard deviation of percentages of major tool classes	183
10.2	Mean and standard deviations for each Mousterian assemblage group (Scraper Index; percentage of denticulates and notches)	185
10.3	Mean and standard deviations for each Mousterian assemblage group (various tool groups)	187
10.4	Mean and standard deviations for each Mousterian assemblage group (various tool groups)	188
10.5	Histogram of assemblage frequency for intervals of Scraper Reduction Index	190
10.6	Mean and standard deviations for the two indices of reduction, related to scrapers and notches	191
10.7	Scatter diagram of all Mousterian assemblages according to the two indices of reduction	192
11.1	Combe-Grenal: relationship between absolute frequencies of all *racloirs* and of denticulates and notches in 31 samples	202
11.2	Combe-Grenal: relative frequencies of bones of large herbivores	203
11.3	Combe-Grenal, Pech de l'Azé, and Corbiac: relative frequencies of three categories of reduction intensity on retouched tools	205
11.4	Combe-Grenal, Pech de l'Azé, and Corbiac: relative frequencies of bifaces	206
11.5	Combe-Grenal: ratios of major retouched tool classes and utilized flakes and of Levallois among all flakes in 31 samples	207

12.1	Core from Corbehem	214
12.2-4	Sidescrapers from Marillac	216
12.5	Sidescraper from Vaufrey	216
12.6-10	Hafted sidescrapers from Biache-St.-Vaast	220
13.1	Combe-Grenal: skeletal portions of equids and large bovids bearing tool marks	228
13.2	Combe-Grenal: relative portions of equids and large bovids compared to percentage of arboreal pollen and to climatic stages	230
14.1	Chronostratigraphy of the "Middle Paleolithic" along the Upper Danube	235
14.2	Cimatic sequence in the Upper Pleistocene	236
14.3	Middle Paleolithic sites along the Upper Danube	238
14.4	Remains of hunted animals at Grosse Grotte	241
14.5	Distribution of artifact types at Grosse Grotte	243
14.6	Bone point from Level II of Grosse Grotte	244
14.7	Lithic artifacts from lower level of Weinberg Caves	245
14.8	Lithic artifacts from upper Middle Paleolithic level of Weinberg Caves	246
14.9	Vegetation profile of Mauern I	247
14.10	The Upper Danube in the Middle Paleolithic	248
14.11	Hypothetical use of ecosystem by herbivores in Beringia	249
14.12	Blade cores of late "Middle" and early Upper Paleolithic	253
15.1	Map of Yugoslavia and surrounding countries	259
15.2	Map of northern Bosnia showing towns and major Paleolithic sites	259
15.3	Zobište: miscellaneous retouched flakes	260
15.4	Zobište: radially flaked cores	261
15.5	Method for recording exterior surfaces of complete flakes	263
15.6	Zobište: types and relative frequencies of complete partially cortical flakes and flake tools >2 cm	267
15.7	Zobište: relative percentage of exterior flake-scar angles on partially cortical and noncortical flakes and flake tools <2 cm	268
15.8	Zobište: mean dimensional data and exterior flake-scar angles on complete naturally backed knife blanks <2 cm	268

15.9	Zobište: mean dimensional data and exterior flake-scar angles on complete noncortical flakes and flake tools <2 cm	269
15.10	Zobište: scattergram of length and width for complete radially prepared flakes and cores	270
15.11	Zobište: reconstructed model for core reduction sequence	272
17.1	Karataou en Tadjikistan	288
17.2	Lakhouti en Tadjikistan	289
17.3	Kaira-Koumi: gisement moustérien de type d'Asie centrale en surface	290
17.4	La grotte Abi-Rakhmat (Tien-Chan)	290
17.5	L'entrée de la grotte Abi-Rakhmat	291
17.6	Le méandre du fleuve Vakhs, avec le gisement Toutkaoul I	292
17.7	Le méandre du fleuve Vakhs, avec le gisement Toutkaoul I	292
17.8	Toutkaoul I pendant les premières fouilles	293
17.9	La grotte Ogzi-Kitchik: fouilles 1972	294
17.10	La grotte Ogzi-Kitchik: fouilles 1977	294
17.11	Le gisement à Karaboura	295
19.1	Paleolithic sites in France in relation to climatic phases, arboreal pollen counts, and radiocarbon dates	307
19.2	Stratigraphic columns for five of the sites shown in Fig. 19.1	309
19.3	Correlations of Grande Pile pollen curve with deep-sea cores	312
19.4	Correlations of exposed strata in Franchthi Cave, along with key radiocarbon dates	313
19.5	Schematic summary of Franchthi sedimentation and variations in environmental conditions, 15,000-5000 B.P.	316
20.1	Simulated random relations between faunal-assemblage richness and sample size	324
20.2	Simulated random relations between faunal-assemblage evenness and sample size	325
20.3	Cubic polynomial regression model for Upper Paleolithic faunal-assemblage diversity over time	326
20.4	Residual plot for function shown in Fig. 20.3	327
20.5	Regression line derived for Upper Paleolithic faunal diversity plotted with Grande Pile pollen profile	329

LIST OF ILLUSTRATIONS

20.6	Cubic polynomial regression model for Upper Paleolithic small-animal assemblage diversity over time	330
21.1	Map of Avdat area, central Negev, showing locations of Upper Paleolithic sites	333
21.2	Metric variability for single-reduction-strategy Ahmarian assemblages	338
21.3	Metric variability for multiple-reduction-strategy Upper Paleolithic assemblages	339
21.4	Lithic artifacts from D100A, an Early Ahmarian site in the central Negev	340
21.5	Lithic artifacts from Sde Divshon, an Early Ahmarian site in the central Negev	341
21.6	Plot of point frequencies and blade/flake ratios for Lagaman and Negev Ahmarian assemblages	342
21.7	Lithic artifacts from Ein Aqev East, a Late Ahmarian site in the central Negev	344
21.8	Lithic artifacts from Ein Aqev, a Late Levantine Aurignacian site in the central Negev	346
22.1	Map of Central Europe at end of Early Würm	350
22.2	Blade index in several early Upper Paleolithic industries in Central Europe	352
22.3	Map of Central Europe in early Interpleniglacial	354
22.4	Evolution of late Middle Paleolithic and early Upper Paleolithic leaf-point industries in Central Europe	356
23.1	Histogram of maximum dimension for sample of Ukrina River cobbles	363
23.2	Cortical blades and byproducts of core preparation from Kadar	364
23.3	Radiolarite cores from Kadar	365
23.4	Histograms displaying medians of length, width, and thickness for a sample of river cobbles and four core samples	366
23.5	Kadar cobble: manner of division and expected return	367
23.6	Histogram illustrating variability in use rate for different blank types	368
23.7	Histogram of width measurements illustrating blank selection for different types of tools	369
23.8	Endscrapers from Kadar	370
23.9	Difference between median lengths of blade blanks and endscrapers	371

23.10	Scrapers and retouched blades illustrating breakage patterns	371
23.11	Processes of blade selection and tool use	372
24.1	Upper Paleolithic sites in the Rhineland	376
24.2	Upper and Final Paleolithic chronology in the Rhineland	378
24.3	Final Paleolithic sites in the Rhineland	380
26.1	Carte de répartition des gisements de Magdalénien ancien en Gironde	398
26.2	Pièces de La Bertonne du site éponyme	399
26.3	Grattoirs de Birac III	402
26.4	Petits éclats courts de Birac III	404
26.5	Représentation des grattoirs, burins et raclettes dans diverses séries de Magdalénien ancien	405
28.1	The stone tool as monument	414
28.2	Upper Paleolithic sequence of the Perigord	418

EDITORS' PREFACE

Modern Paleolithic prehistory emerged in the decade following World War II marked by the transformation of field methods and the inception of interdisciplinary field projects. At the same time, the introduction of systematics in the study of lithic assemblages contributed to the development of a very different understanding of the Paleolithic world. Much of the credit for promoting these changes goes to the individuals who undertook the major field projects of that time: François Bordes at Combe-Grenal and Pech de l'Azé, André Leroi-Gourhan at Arcy-sur-Cure, and Hallam Movius at La Colombière and Abri Pataud. The deep stratigraphy recorded at these sites provided the information upon which environmental and cultural sequences were built, and the data that were generated continue to be at the center of today's debates. Perhaps more important, these field projects have served as training grounds for a generation of prehistorians and, as a result, continue to have a dominant influence on the field today.

During the last two decades there has been a tremendous proliferation of field projects in many parts of Western Eurasia. Vigorous and innovative research has continued in the Franco-Cantabrian area, and also in Central and Eastern Europe and the Eastern Mediterranean, where large excavation projects have brought to light an abundance of new and systematically collected data. The people involved in these more recent projects have introduced into the field a new set of perspectives and methodologies. Not only has the size of the data sets increased, but the quality and nature of those data changed as recovery techniques underwent drastic improvements. These new methods spread quickly, so it seems that archaeologists do not have great difficulty in communicating with each other on the subject of new recovery techniques. On the other hand, they are often less aware of the scope of projects conducted in different geographic areas, with less understanding of the different research goals and less acceptance of different interpretive models. It was the lack of communication and understanding at this level that was the primary impetus for the presentations and discussions brought together here.

This volume contains the proceedings of a symposium held at The University Museum, University of Pennsylvania, Philadelphia, for five days in January 1987. The topic of discussions—The Upper Pleistocene Prehistory of Western Eurasia—was deliberately kept broad to avoid giving the symposium a centralized focus. On the contrary, an attempt was made to bring together specialists representing several newly developed interests and perspectives. Participants came from North America, Western Europe, and Eastern Europe; they have worked on Middle as well as Upper Paleolithic sites; they have experience with different kinds of data, including lithics, fauna, and geochronology; they included senior members of the profession as well as people at the beginning of their careers. However, all participants shared a strong field orientation (most having directed large field projects) and all have in recent years confronted the problems of sorting through and interpreting the mass of data that modern, systematic excavations generate.

It was our aim to bring together a diverse group of prehistorians and to create an atmosphere that encouraged discussions among them. The primary objective of the Philadelphia symposium was to examine the diversity in data, methodologies, and interpretive models that has emerged from recent fieldwork. The symposium was not meant to be a confrontation, but rather an opportunity for participants to express their own views and understand the views of others. The number of presentations per day was kept small, which enabled considerable time to be devoted to discussion following each. To the extent possible, the main points of these discussions are preserved at the end of each paper in this volume.

The volume is composed of three parts. In the first, seven contributions focus on the excavation and interpretation of a single site or a restricted group of sites. Much of the discussion that follows these presentations addresses problems in the recognition of manmade features, postdepositional alterations of archaeological levels, and the effects of local environments on site use. They explore various means of reaching clearer understanding of the nature of the archaeological record. The order of the papers is determined by geography, from the Atlantic to the Hungarian Plain. The first paper, by Freeman et al., is on the excavations at El Juyo, in the hilly flanks of the Atlantic Cantabrian coastal plain of Spain. This is followed by Straus's discussion of the Abri Dufaure, in the French Pyrenees; by Sackett's review of Solvieux and other sites from the Neuvic area in the Perigord; and by Debénath's description of La Chaise in the Charente. Otte's excavations at Sclayn provide an example of the prehistoric occupation of the plain/plateau ecotone in Northern Europe. Lanzinger's excavations at Monte Avena, a quarry site in the Dolomitic Alps, raise issues relating to modes of human occupation at high-altitude localities. The last chapter of this section, by Gábori-Csánk, is devoted to another possible quarry site, this one located in the low-lying periphery of the Central European Plain.

Part two of the volume contains papers dealing with several issues concerning the Middle Paleolithic. This section begins with a discussion by Laville on Perigord chronology and intersite correlations, and the relationship between terrestrial and marine depositional records and the recently published series of absolute dates. Following this are several papers, by Rolland, Dibble, Jelinek, and Beyries, all dealing with various aspects of Middle Paleolithic lithic assemblage variability. These approaches shed new light on an issue that has been under debate for many years and demonstrate the tremendously complex interplay of technological, raw-material, and functional factors underlying these assemblages. These papers also touch on the question of the significance of the nature of behavior seen during the Middle Paleolithic as compared with the later Upper Paleolithic. This problem, aspects of which are discussed further by Chase, Müller-Beck, and Marks, is at the heart of much of the discussion. A related topic that emerges in many of these papers, as well that of Baumler on core reduction, is the question of conscious intent versus simple technological constraints in producing Middle Paleolithic assemblages. (These issues are taken up again by Sackett in his final overview.) Rounding out this part are synthetic reviews by Gábori and Davis on new findings and developments in Soviet Central Asia.

The third and last part of the volume deals with aspects of variability in the Upper Paleolithic. In the opening chapter of this section, Farrand discusses the timing and amplitude of climatic signals of the second half of the last glacial. Points are raised here concerning regional trends and localized variations. In the next chapter, Simek and Snyder examine the question of faunal assemblage diversity. The data they use are from sites in the Perigord, but the model they present has general implications. The following two chapters deal with new methods and models of lithic analysis. The first, that of Ferring, discusses variability in lithic industries of the Levant. In the second, Montet-White presents a model of raw-material economy using data from a site in Central Europe, though her model relates to a relatively common form of settlement pattern. Discussions of these chapters raise general questions concerning the nature and interpretive level of different lithic reduction models of Upper Paleolithic assemblages. In chapter 22, Kozlowski considers one of the most important problems of the European Paleolithic from a broad, interregional perspective. In contrast to most of the other participants, who concentrate on data sets having much more limited spatial and temporal boundaries, he attempts to integrate a vast amount of data. In fact, a number of European research teams have established long-range research programs directed at elucidating a particular form of adaptation of settlement for a given geographic area. Bosinski's work in the Neuwied Basin exemplifies the impressive results that this kind of approach can yield.

Upper Paleolithic systematics have long been dominated by work done in southwestern France. The detail, abundance, and relative completeness of the record in that part of Europe have contributed to the pre-eminence that this area has attained, and continues to enjoy, in Paleolithic research. Several chapters in this part of the volume are concerned with re-evaluation of the Upper Paleolithic systematics in the Perigord. Rigaud presents the revised and currently accepted interpretation of the cultural sequence. De Sonneville-Bordes discusses the question of cultural boundaries. In the last chapter Sackett outlines some of the problems relating to the interpretation of Upper Paleolithic variability with what he himself describes as a "Perigord-centric" viewpoint. In fact, comparisons and contrasts between the Perigord record and that of Northern and Central Europe were emphasized throughout the meeting. As Otte, Bosinski, and Kozlowski pointed out in turn, the Late Pleistocene prehistory of Europe must be considered on a broad continental scale.

Harold L. Dibble
Anta Montet-White

June 1988

ACKNOWLEDGMENTS

For financial assistance in producing this symposium and its publication, we wish to thank the Wenner-Gren Foundation; the Office of International Programs, The University Museum, and the Department of Anthropology at the University of Pennsylvania; and private donors.

Five graduate students from the Department of Anthropology at Penn who were especially helpful during the symposium deserve special recognition: Bong Dizon, Elizabeth Hamilton, Simon Holdaway, Helen Loney, and Steve Mertens. We are grateful to Philip Chase, Veerle Thielemans, and Claudia Suter for their translations of chapters originally written in French and German; and to Anita Liebman, Georgianna Grentzenberg, and Linny Schenck for their work on the layout. Other individuals who have helped in various capacities are Catherine Ambrose, Sophie Luzecky, Toni Montague, Kathy Moreau, Barbara Murray, Peggy Pugh, Patricia Seabolt, and Karen Vellucci. And a very special thanks to Laurie Tiede for her careful attention to all of the details involved in the preparation of this volume.

PART 1

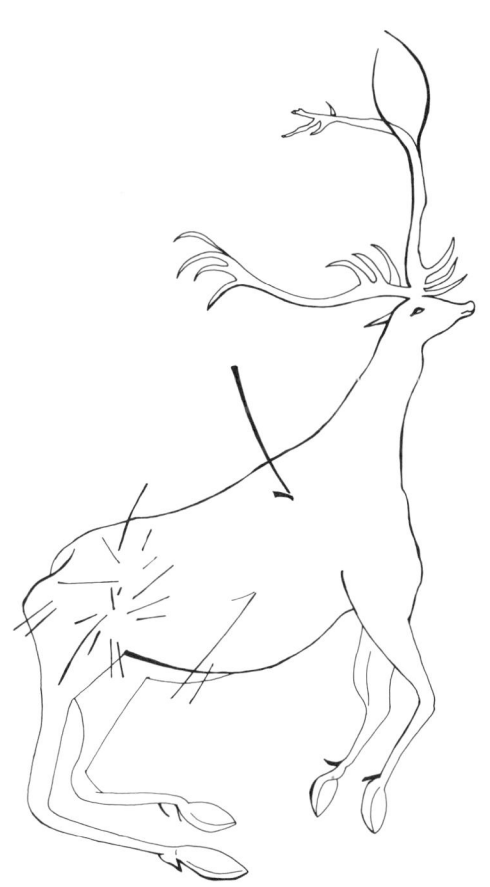

I
Dimensions of Research at El Juyo
An Earlier Magdalenian Site in Cantabrian Spain

Leslie G. Freeman
Joaquín González Echegaray
Richard G. Klein
William T. Crowe

INTRODUCTION

The Upper Paleolithic is a phase of great transitions. Characteristic of Upper Paleolithic complexes are: more consistent patterning of artifact types and metrical attributes, resulting in more obvious differentiation of implement classes; an interest in counting; increased diversity and specialization of tool types, assemblages, and occupations; more marked differentiation of site space; increased variety and complexity of cultural features; marked regional differentiation of assemblages; rapid turnover of industrial complexes; ability to cope with environment in more sophisticated ways; and the appearance of graphic symbolism, musical instruments, and other clear reflections of expressive culture and ideology (Freeman 1975b, 1980; Klein 1980). One may justifiably say that some Upper Paleolithic adaptations reflect the operation of cultural systems as complex as those of some ethnographically known food-collecting peoples.

Upper Paleolithic sites are more numerous and better preserved than is the case for any earlier period. They have received the attention of the most skilled prehistorians. Yet despite the inherent interest of the period, we still have no coherent picture of the lifeways of members of any particular Upper Paleolithic society. We have learned much about climatic change, assemblages of artifacts in bone and stone, and the succession of industries, but we still cannot reconstruct anything like the general outlines of the total subsistence and settlement system of any Upper Paleolithic group.

Sites occupied during a single short phase of Upper Paleolithic industrial development are numerous enough in some parts of the world to warrant an attempt at such reconstructions. One richly endowed region where such investigations are possible is Cantabrian Spain. In recent years, a number of investigators interested in a similar problem set—committed to the regular discussion of goals and working hypotheses, to the development and adoption of the very best tools possible, and to continuous exchange of information about the latest research results—have begun to attack these problems.

Much of their research has been focused on the Cantabrian Earlier Magdalenian. Occupations of this complex are regionally more numerous (and richer) than those representing any earlier Upper Paleolithic manifestation, and more of them are still substantially intact than is the case for Later Magdalenian occupations in Cantabria. Magdalenian cave occupations have proved to be excellent sources of data about Upper Paleolithic cultural elaboration. Structural features are abundant, faunal remains and other biotic materials are well preserved, artifact assemblages are varied, decorated objects are frequent, and the occupations coincide with the maximum flowering of Franco-Cantabrian cave art. Cantabrian Magdalenian occupations provide fundamental evidence for the study of developing cultural complexity and its correlates.

THE CANTABRIAN SETTING

The Cantabrian natural region extends some 600 km along Spain's north coast, from the French border to Cape Finisterre (Fig. 1.1). This region compresses substantial environmental diversity into a small space. It is bounded by two geographic features that significantly affect its character: the shore of the Cantabrian Sea (or Bay of Biscay), whose waters are tempered by a branch of the Gulf Stream, and the crest of the Cantabrian Cordillera, a westward extension of the Pyrenees, with peaks rising to 2640 m above sea level. Between these two bands runs Cantabria, an irregular ribbon of land some 40 km wide, cut by the small isolated valleys of rivers whose waters are as abundant as their courses are short. In the east, the Basque mountain slopes descend right to the sea; in the former province of Santander (now the Autonomous Region of Cantabria), there are more extensive karstic lowlands, broken by limestone outliers and riddled with caves. In the western part of the province of Asturias, limestone bedrock gives way to sandstones, quartzites, and shales, changing the character of landscape again. The coast is ordinarily rocky but is broken by estuaries with beaches and dunes. There is little continental shelf. Cantabria is ever humid—there is no dry season, and more than 1100 mm of precipitation fall on the region each year, mostly as rain. Mean temperature in August is generally below 19° C., while in January averages are above 8° over most of the region—annual averages are between 10 and 15°—and winds are predominantly off the Atlantic.

Under undisturbed conditions, Cantabrian vegetation is lush. There are many large alpine meadows. Disturbed slopes and high valleys are covered with a matorral of heather, gorse, and broom. From treeline to 800 m, there are still preserved a few large stands of deciduous beech woodlands. Below this elevation spread the oak/birch forests that have now been decimated by clearing for pasturage. These give way in turn to shoreland plant communities and the algae-rich waters of the bay.

Important members of the wild fauna are chamois (and formerly ibex) in the mountains, red and roe deer, boar, fox, wolf, bear, wildcat, and capercaillie in the forests. In past centuries rivers teemed with trout and salmon, and flatfish and eels entered their waters in numbers. On the coasts were large populations of limpets (*Patella*), winkles (*Littorina*), clams, mussels, oysters, and such crustaceans as spider crabs, crawfish, and spiny lobster, as well as a variety of fish. In prehistoric times, elephants, Merck's rhinoceros, bison, wild cattle, horses, cave bears, and cave lions were also among the local animal communities.

During the colder episodes of the Pleistocene, most of these species survived despite a decrease of mean annual land-surface temperature on the order of 10° C. There were, of course, changes in both vegetation makeup and distribution, and lower sea levels exposed a fringe of land up to 5 or 6 km wide along the coast. But unpublished reconstructions of Pleistocene vegetation patterns produced by the Small Fractions Laboratories of the Institute for Prehistoric Investigations (IPI)[1] in Chicago suggest that, despite these changes, relative extents of alpine meadow, forest, and grassland were not altered as drastically as was formerly believed, and forest faunas could apparently find adequate forage and shelter throughout. Cold-tolerant species such as the woolly mammoth and rhino, the wolverine and the reindeer, were able to establish themselves in the region, but apparently their foothold was never very solid; they did not come to dominate Pleistocene faunas here as they did elsewhere in Western Europe (Lautensach 1967; de Terán et al. 1969; González Echegaray and Freeman 1978).

With many sites scattered over a great variety of different habitats, all compressed into a narrow belt that can be traversed afoot from coast to mountaintops in a day or two, Cantabria is an almost ideal setting in which to investigate the nature and correlates of changing Paleolithic adaptations in detail. The only deficiency of the prehistoric record is the rarity of stratified, more or less undisturbed open-air sites. Attempts to remedy this lack are now under way, but meanwhile we must attempt to make the maximum use of information available.

THE REGIONAL PALEOLITHIC RECORD

There is so far no indisputable trace of human presence in Cantabria before about 200,000 years ago (Fig. 1.2). Surface finds of handaxes and choppers on the gravels of terraces and beaches have prompted suggestions of earlier occupation, but the evidence is not persuasive. Convincing Late Acheulian horizons, perhaps as old as the Penultimate Glacial, do occur in the base of the Castillo stratigraphy (Cabrera 1984; Freeman 1975a; González Sainz and González Morales

1986) but are not directly datable. The lowest levels at El Pendo (where finds are too few to be diagnostic) may also be Acheulian. The evidence is so limited that little can be said other than to report its occurrence.

Mousterian occupations are well represented in Last Glacial sediments. At Castillo, El Pendo, and Morín, Denticulate Mousterian horizons are found intercalated with deposits containing Typical Mousterian or Charentian Mousterian artifacts. In some Typical Mousterian horizons, rich in sidescrapers, there are also tools called cleaver-flakes, with characteristics peculiar to the Mousterian of Cantabria. Nondiagnostic human remains occur sporadically (as at Lezetxiki), and all are thought to represent Neandertals. There is only one certain structural feature—an area in Morín Upper 17 delimited by an arcuate wall of rubble piles—in a Cantabrian Mousterian site.

Fauna recovered from Morín Mousterian horizons consist predominantly of horses and large bovines, with red deer in a secondary position and traces of other animals. At Castillo, there are very abundant red deer and large bovines, many horses, and good numbers of rhinoceros in one level (22). The list of other species includes wolf, hyena, cave bear, and cave lion, a few roe deer, and rare ibex and chamois. There are also birds, but they may all be either raptors that perched above the site, or their prey. At El Pendo, Mousterian faunas consist mostly of large bovines and red deer. Usually no single species constitutes more than 50% of individuals. Only in sites on the more mountainous Basque coast are ibex ever a major constituent, and there they were undoubtedly abundant in the very near vicinity of the sites. (Some "Mousterian" levels in Basque sites are probably hyena or bear dens where only a scarce and sporadic human presence is indicated.) Marine shellfish are never represented by more than traces, and wild boars are notably rare.

Sites, almost all caves, are usually located on slopes near the coast in Basque country or the midpart of the more open hilly lowlands to the west, and the exploited resources seem to have been sought primarily in the immediate neighborhood, with minimal use of coastal or alpine resources. Cantabrian Mousterians have been characterized as opportunistic large-mammal hunters, taking whatever was easy, not terribly dangerous, and ready to hand (Altuna 1972; Cabrera 1984; Freeman 1980, 1981; González Echegaray and Freeman 1978; González Echegaray et al. 1980).

Upper Paleolithic levels are better represented in the region. Long stratigraphic sequences at Castillo, Morín, and El Pendo document the succession of all major Upper Paleolithic divisions known for France, and in the infancy of our discipline, the Castillo sequence was a central argument for the proper sequential placement of Aurignacian and Solutrean industries. The Chatelperronian is represented in two sites: Morín, where it is below the Aurignacian, and El Pendo, where it overlies an Archaic Aurignacian horizon (González Echegaray and Freeman 1978; González Echegaray et al. 1980). There are no diagnostic human remains from Chatelperronian levels in Spain.

Cueva Morín documents the development of Aurignacian industries, particularly its earlier stages, as richly as any French site. One of its earliest Aurignacian levels produced a rectangular dugout hut foundation, a posthole alignment, and several human burials, one of them preserved as a three-dimensional "soil shadow." Aurignacian and Perigordian occupations are also represented at Castillo and El Pendo, though Perigordian horizons are better known from sites in Basque country. "Stylistic" variation from region to region exists, but the regions are very large and the contrasts between neighboring regions are not striking. Where human remains are found, they are attributable to fully modern *Homo sapiens sapiens*. Most faunal collections are a mix of large ungulates in which red deer, bovines, and horses are represented, but no single element is so disproportionately abundant as to suggest its selection at the expense of the rest. There are levels, however, in which red deer are considerably better represented than other animals. The faunal spectra are often considerably broader than they were in Mousterian times, including small furbearers and birds; there are more frequent shellfish (but no true middens), and alpine animals are regularly found in lowland sites. Otherwise, opportunistic exploitative strategies seem to continue. Engraved animal outlines and geometric designs appear on bones and on the walls near the cave entries. Most of the caves chosen for occupation are still well down in the lowland zone (Bernaldo de Quirós Guidotti 1980, 1982; Freeman 1973, 1975b; McCullough 1971; Straus 1977).

This picture of continued development of subsistence and settlement strategies along the lines already known in the Mousterian, gradually expanding the resource base and adapting technological features, is in marked contrast to later Upper Paleolithic developments. Beginning 18,000-20,000 years ago, with the appearance of Late Solutrean/Earlier Magdalenian industries, some occupation levels indicate technological innovations, increased structural complexity, different uses for decoration, new subsistence strategies, and changed man-environment relations (Freeman 1973, 1975b; Straus 1977). Such a marked discrepancy between earlier and later Upper Paleolithic developments is unexpected: the disjunction, if present, is less notable in France and does not exist in Eastern Europe. Accounting for this difference remains one of the challenging problems of Cantabrian prehistory.

Solutrean assemblages are markedly more regionally differentiated than Aurignacian/Perigordian ones (Corchón 1971; Straus 1983b). In both France and Spain, small regional clusters of contemporary Solutrean occupations share tool-making styles that contrast with the techniques of other close neighbors. There are hints of the standardization of weapon-point sizes to closer tolerances than ever before. One occupation at El Cierro and others at La Riera suggest the selective exploitation of red deer (Straus 1977, 1983b; Straus et al. 1981; Straus and Clark 1986). During the Magdalenian, at sites like El Juyo, Rascaño, and Erralla, these suggestions are confirmed as evident realities (González Echegaray and Barandiarán 1981; Moure 1974; Utrilla 1981, 1982; Altuna and Merino 1984; Altuna, Baldeón, and Mariezkurrena 1985; Barandiarán et al. 1987). Tiny microblades and pointed bladelets, evidently interchangeable replacement points and edge segments of compound tools, appear in large numbers. The variety of represented structural features increases dramatically. Decorations appear that can probably be interpreted as identifying "property marks" on tools or "signatures" on cave paintings, and cave art is at its best and most abundant. Several occupations in Cantabria contain shell middens or accumulations of bones from a single species that indicate the intensive cropping of particular wild resources. Sites now tend to be found dispersed among the different ecological zones, as bases for the periodic harvesting of locally abundant resources (ibex at Erralla and Rascaño, red deer at El Juyo). The distribution of decorative elements has suggested that settlement strategies involve small social units living dispersed most of the year, but periodically aggregating in larger sites such as the great decorated caves, perhaps to conduct seasonal rituals (Conkey 1980; Freeman 1973, 1981; González Sainz and González Morales 1986; Moure 1975; Moure and Cano 1976; Straus 1977).

THE PLACE OF THE EL JUYO RESEARCH

Since the Magdalenian cave site of El Juyo (Fig. 1.3) was first discovered in the early 1950s, its importance for understanding regional Magdalenian adaptations has been evident. At the time of its discovery, the site could be entered only by following a subterranean stream for some meters, then worming through a long, narrow clay "funnel" well above the streambed. The funnel appears only at very rare intervals. For practical purposes, the cave had been almost hermetically sealed at the collapse of the prehistoric entry some 14,000 years ago. At discovery, Magdalenian deposits were found protected by solid flowstone overlying much of the cave vestibule's floor. Sporadic penetration of the cave, first by what seems to have been a single Bronze Age explorer, and later by a little band of people, perhaps native Cantabrian tribesmen seeking refuge from invading Romans, scarcely disturbed the sealed Magdalenian horizons.

Excavations from 1955 through 1957 showed that El Juyo contained a long sequence of earlier Magdalenian levels, including a true shell midden, and suggested at least occasional harvesting of a particular mammalian resource: the herds of red deer (*Cervus elaphus*). The main occupation "level" (actually, several levels) was a rich shell midden, attesting selective exploitation of coastal limpet populations (Janssens and González Echegaray 1958). The site seemed likely to evidence a major shift in subsistence strategies that coincided temporally with the florescence of Paleolithic art in the Cantabrian region. Looking back at those excavations some 20 years later, we thought we saw suggestions that the two phenomena were correlated; that increased efficiency in exploitation of the local food resources might have catalyzed the great development of cave art. The nature of these "wild harvesting" adaptations and their correlates warranted further investigation.

Renewed research at El Juyo was sponsored and principally financed by National Science Foundation grants to the University of Chicago in 1978-79 and again in 1982-83. Supplementary support was provided by the Spanish Ministry of Culture during all field seasons, the Excmo. Ayuntamiento of Camargo in 1979, the Excmo. Ayuntamiento of Santander in 1979-83, and by IPI in 1983. Fieldwork was jointly directed by Freeman, González Echegaray, Klein, and Barandiarán in 1978 and by Freeman and González Echegaray in subsequent years (Freeman and González Echegaray 1981a, b, 1983, 1984; Freeman, Klein, and González Echegaray 1983).

Since that work began, El Juyo has become a central site for understanding late Pleistocene adaptations in Cantabria. Fieldwork at El Juyo has been conducted on a larger scale than is the case for any other Cantabrian Magdalenian site excavated in recent years. In nine months of fieldwork, large, multidisciplinary teams have exposed Magdalenian deposits over more than 40 sq. m (Fig. 1.4). The excavations have been a testing ground for new and improved facilities and procedures for data recovery and analysis. These include the comprehensive retrieval process with its on-site physical and chemical laboratory, foam flotation facility, and macrobotanical identification lab, and on-site electronic data recording and analysis. These procedures have been so productive that the richness of the documentation recovered from the site is exceptional.

METHODS OF DATA GATHERING AT EL JUYO

Techniques employed during the excavation of the site are described in detail in the first volume of the site report (Barandiarán et al. 1987). After preliminary mapping, the site surface was gridded in 1-m squares, the units of excavation. Squares were dug checkerboard fashion. Excavators worked from platforms suspended above the site surface except where thick flowstone layers were available to bear their weight without damaging underlying materials. Within each square, excavation proceeded by sectors 33.3 cm on a side, following the inclination of the strata being excavated, to provide close control of stratigraphy and provenience. Where an apparently homogeneous natural level was more than 5 cm thick, the level was subdivided into 5-cm-deep units. Additional control over depth was provided by at least one vertical measurement to the base of each plotted item from an arbitrary datum plane, using an optical level. Finds within a stratum, including all apparently "natural" stones at least 5 cm in major dimension, were piece-plotted by measurement from two adjacent square walls. The inclination of items that did not lie conformable to the stratigraphy was measured. Stratigraphic sections (the square walls) were drawn at 1-m intervals throughout the site. These procedures are no more than ordinary good practice and are in general use.

The earth from each natural layer or 5-cm subdivision thereof, from a single sector, was then processed separately with all its other contents. (After 1982-83, this operation was the responsibility of personnel of IPI's Comprehensive Retrieval Team.) These procedures provide adequate stratigraphic and horizontal control for tiny artifacts and contextual materials that could not be detected and individually plotted by the excavators.

When the base of a natural level was reached in a sector—i.e., when contact with the underlying natural level was exposed—the depth below datum of the center of the sector was recorded. Wherever structural remnants or suspicious irregularities broke the ordinary lie of the sediments, as many additional depth measurements as necessary were taken at recorded positions to map the changing slope of the surface with acceptable precision. These measurements were complemented with the three-dimensional coordinates of selected objects found lying at the base of each level. All measurements were transformed to general site coordinates (a simple BASIC program handles the conversion automatically) and the data used as input to a computerized mapping program. Topographic maps and three-dimensional graphic representations of any excavated surface can now be produced and updated during the course of excavation, as fast as the data become available.

We have not yet input three-dimensional coordinates of recovered items and features directly from electronic distance-measuring devices to the mapping program, but that is quite possible, and the practicality of virtually instantaneous on-site mapping will be obvious to anyone familiar with the recent work of Jelinek and Dibble at La Quina (Dibble 1987b). We are only beginning to tap the potential of electronic devices for producing excavation maps and plans, and foresee great advances in this direction even in the next year.

COMPREHENSIVE RETRIEVAL PROCEDURES

Samples of earth from promising areas were set aside for flotation during the 1978-79 campaigns. Every grain of earth excavated at El Juyo after the second week of the 1982 field season has been submitted to special processing procedures. The earth from each sector and level (or subdivision) is bagged separately by the excavator, appropriately labeled, and stored just inside the cave entry. Each sample is removed from this temporary storage to the processing area just outside the cave entrance by designated members of the Comprehensive Retrieval Team. One purpose of these procedures is to keep movement of personnel between the excavated area and the environment outside the cave to a minimum. The sample and all bulked finds from the same unit ("natural" stone, unretouched flaking debris, unidentifiable bone splinters, etc.) are logged in an inventory.

A 150-g subsample is removed from the sediments and placed in a sterile plastic pack. This small sample will serve for off-site laboratory analyses including qualitative and quantitative soil chemistry and the extraction of plant opal, pollen, spores, bacteria, and viruses. Two or more subsamples are taken from really large lots of earth. These subsamples are also used for some on-site studies.

Ten cu. cm of dirt from each subsample are examined by an on-site sediment chemistry team, usually consisting of one trained specialist and one assistant. (The equipment needed by the site physicist/chemist is not terribly expensive and can all be carried in a single small suitcase.) That team evaluates the color of the sediments when uniformly moistened, and measures the acidity (wet pH and Delta pH), humic acid, starch, fat, protein, and total and relative soil-phosphate content for each sample, as well as measuring some inorganic values such as iron content. Other measurements are made on only selected samples in the field. Maps of the surface distribution of these values over each level are prepared at intervals each day for use by the research directors in evaluating progress and planning excavation tactics. In tricky situations, the maps have been updated for crucial areas at half-hour intervals. We have found such information can be invaluable to a director when it arrives fresh while excavation is still in progress. If the results of these analyses become available only after much delay, their greatest potential is essentially lost.

Before our experience of the benefits of performing such analyses on-site, the potential of sediment chemistry in archaeological application seemed to us to lie primarily in postexcavation climatic/environmental reconstruction. Most published applications did not show them to be particularly valuable in cultural interpretation; they suggested that analysis of a small number of samples would permit one to judge whether a level had or had not been intensively occupied in comparison with other levels in the same stratigraphic column. But postdepositional leaching and the inability of the techniques to distinguish between short, intensive occupation and long-lasting, less intensive occupation were obvious and ever-present complications. Procedures with more obvious potential seemed to us to deserve priority.

During the 1983 excavations, however, it was repeatedly demonstrated that these physical and chemical parameters provide priceless indications of otherwise masked cultural or depositional processes. For example, anomalously low phosphate levels and higher-than-normal pH values revealed still-buried rubble walls on various occasions, roughly indicating the position of features before the excavators uncovered them. Regular alignments of abrupt changes in these values more than once distinguished rubble walls of dugout structures from rockfalls well before any stone alignments became visible. After experiencing the practical benefits of systematic on-site chemical and physical analyses that keep pace with excavation, we are convinced that they are not just useful but absolutely indispensable to cultural interpretation and the day-to-day planning of excavation tactics.

While the physics/chemistry laboratory worked through its subsamples, recording results in its own separate log, the Comprehensive Retrieval Team began its treatment of the remainder of the recovered material. All bulked finds from an individual sector and sublevel were first soaked in a buffered solution of sodium hexametaphosphate in water. The surface of this liquid was initially skimmed with a 1-mm mesh sieve, and the floated fraction rinsed and set aside to shade-dry in filter paper or paper toweling. In a moist site such as El Juyo, macrobotanicals and other materials of interest are not always buoyant enough for simple water flotation to yield them all, but some always rise at this stage. The cleaned bulked finds were removed, rinsed, and set aside to dry on newspaper-lined trays. Next, the sediments from the unit were slaked in the same water, repeating the skimming, rinsing, and drying of the floated fraction. After the presoak, the slurry of sediments was poured off through a tower of graduated plastic screens, the largest of which had a 1-cm mesh, the smallest a mesh of 250 microns. Often, a third 2-mm mesh screen was added between these. In special circumstances, as when microbes were of interest, the liquid and the contained solids smaller than 250 microns were passed through even finer filters, including ceramic filters. Otherwise, after flotation the liquid and solids that passed the smallest screen were discarded.

The material caught atop the fine screen was then processed by foam flotation in an emulsified paraffin solution (during 1983 the surfactant Triton X-45 was employed) to increase the buoyancy of waterlogged finds. Bubbles of compressed air, introduced at the base of the flotation bath, produced and maintained the desired foam. The fragments that rise to the top of the foam may be hand-skimmed, but it is quicker and more satisfactory to skim the foam with a vacuum, discharging the floating portion atop a filter. Crowe, director of IPI's Small Fraction Laboratories, has designed an extremely effective and very compact apparatus for this purpose. It incorporates a standard small laboratory compressor/vacuum pump to draw the float into a nozzle made of a cut-down funnel and through eighth-inch plastic tubing to the filter in a funnel atop a plastic Erlenmeyer flask with a vacuum port. The floated materials are rinsed as the system is flushed with clean water. Liquid from the flotation process is collected in the Erlenmeyer flask for later examination. The same pump that provides the vacuum simultaneously compresses the air that makes the foam. The coarse residues are floated in similar fashion, but the concentration of wetting agent must be greater to yield a "heavier" suds.

The floated fraction was packed, in its dry filter paper, either in small plastic envelopes or in folded squares of aluminum foil, each appropriately identified. El Juyo samples were then carried to the Small Fraction Laboratories in Chicago for identification and further processing. More recently, at the Castillo excavations, the float from each sample was hand picked in the field laboratory to separate macrobotanicals; seeds and plant remains were photographed and measured, and gross or preliminary identifications made, before Crowe's team left the field.

After flotation, the heavier fraction was everted on drying trays. When dry, the coarse fraction was hand sorted and recovered materials sent to be separately inventoried. The heavy fines were scanned, and any small retouched artifacts in stone or bone removed. After this sort, materials smaller than 2 mm were packaged in sample lots and sent to the microfaunal analyst. When that specialist had removed the identifiable small bones, the remainder of the sample was returned to IPI for warehousing. That mass of well-provenienced detritus includes much potentially informative material such as small shatter from stone-knapping, but until sediments from other sites have been processed in similar fashion, there is no way of determining what it may tell us on a supra-site level, and at present we have not given it analytical priority.

ELECTRONIC RECORDING AND DATA MANAGEMENT

A written inventory was kept of all finds and samples during our first three seasons at El Juyo. At the conclusion of each season, we and other investigators transferred selected parts of the written information to computer files for analysis. Only limited statistical analyses were performed on-site; multivariate testing was done at night and on weekends. In 1983 we began to record parallel sample inventories electronically, using a laptop computer. Trials of electronic data recording were further elaborated by IPI at the Castillo site in 1986. The handwritten inventory has now been eliminated; a printout of the entry is made as each sample is electronically recorded. Although some of our colleagues have been hard to convince, as long as concurrent hard copy is produced, electronic data recording is as reliable as writing: in fact, more so, since impermissible or unreasonable entries can be "trapped." Each evening the day's inventory is copied from the laptop computer to cassette in duplicate, one cassette to be kept by the Comprehensive Retrieval Team, the other to be stored in our offices in Santander after the data are transferred to a larger computer for archiving (on floppy disk) and analysis.[2]

The availability of portable computers on-site makes it possible to document an excavation more thoroughly than ever before, and to retrieve data faster than was previously possible. Searching procedures or indexing programs such as ZyINDEX make it possible to find information in an electronic file much faster than when written documents must be visually scanned. Very sophisticated analytical procedures can now be done on the site itself, during the course of excavation.

A major benefit of electronic data management is, of course, that it infinitely lessens the effort and time that must be spent culling data from the written inventory for specific analyses, and absolutely eliminates copying errors. Any good database management program can quickly sort all items in an inventory in any number of ways, can select for consideration any desired set of data, and can count and add, calculate means and standard deviations, and print out lists and summary data for any subset of data desired. Some will also do regression and correlation analyses or produce graphs and diagrams. Another major advantage is compactness. The written inventory for 1982 and 1983 excavations at El Juyo (some 20,000 entries) covers about 700 large pages. The same information (compressed) can be stored on three 5¼-inch floppy disks. This is not to say that our research now generates less paper than before. On the contrary, we find that it produces many more documents than it did previously, if only because we do so many more analyses, each of which produces some printed output; and we can present their results in graphic form, which requires still more print.

The capacity and speed of today's personal computers is so great that we find ourselves making very little use of mainframe computers for our analyses. With the sophisticated software already available, one can do on a personal computer just about anything that required a mainframe in the late 1970s. Many elaborate programs are extremely fast: as an example, it is now possible to generate rank-order correlation coefficients for a matrix of 50 variables, save the matrix in a file and use it as input for a principal-components analysis with Varimax rotation, and finish all stages of analysis in just under four minutes from the time the last data entry is completed. Because programs are so fast, the analyst can try many different data transformations to determine which is most suitable, can test different data sets, can subject the same data to a wide range of different tests, etc. The better programs are completely interactive, permitting errors to be caught and rectified without stopping analysis. Mechanical drawing tasks are also more effectively handled with computers and drafting programs than by trained draftsmen. These features free the analyst's brain and the technician's hands for productive uses that were out of the question less than a decade ago.

Personal computers are now thoroughly integrated in IPI-affiliated research projects. Nevertheless, we are far from utilizing their full potential and we are only beginning to understand the revolutionary changes they will bring to our discipline in the immediate future. When all analysts have access to desktop computers and peripheral devices and learn to use their power to best advantage, it will be possible to analyze archaeological data more thoroughly than ever before, in no more time than was expended in the process of excavation itself, and to produce a finished monographic publication in no more time than was formerly required to type the manuscript. These are not dreams but present realities.

RESULTS TO DATE

Results of the El Juyo research so far inform us on three levels. First, we have gathered a great deal of information about what went on in the specific occupation levels investigated. Second, there is more broadly relevant information on: 1) the nature of site-formation processes; 2) changing regional environments; and 3) the nature of Upper Paleolithic industrial variants both within and beyond the Cantabrian region. Third, much of what we have learned has the very broadest implications for the future conduct of research in prehistoric archaeology and allied fields, and bears on widely or universally held assumptions about archaeological sites and strata and appropriate research methods.

El Juyo is almost unique in presenting a deep stratified deposit of materials all from a single Upper Paleolithic industrial "phase": there are some 3.5 m of stratigraphy containing perhaps 20 different Upper Paleolithic levels, and every occupation represents the same industrial "subcomplex," the Cantabrian Lower Magdalenian—the local typological equivalent of the Magdalenian III in southwest France (Fig. 1.5). The evidence suggests that these deposits took no more than 1000 years to form.

From the outset, we have held that microstratigraphic work at the site can provide extremely detailed evidence for environmental and climatic change and the evolution of toolkits; we hoped to sample these changes as they occurred over very short—perhaps ten-year—intervals. Though we are still optimistic about the reconstruction of a picture of fine-grained microenvironmental evolution at El Juyo, producing that reconstruction is a complicated process, since most of the sedimentation is anthropogenic. Prehistoric human interference with the orderly course of sediment deposition has been intense. Magdalenian builders dug the foundations of large semi-subterranean huts into older occupation layers, piling the earth elsewhere, thus inverting or otherwise disturbing the "natural" stratigraphy. Stone rubble and other building material was brought from other parts of the cave or from outside to wall the structures. Gaps in deposition occur where house floors were dug. Intact stratigraphic columns are rare indeed.

This situation, also noted twenty years ago at Cueva Morín, and since remarked at Rascaño, Chufín, and Tito Bustillo, seems to be the rule rather than the exception in Cantabria. Where there is so much anthropogenic disturbance, the usual practice of cleaning and sampling a single vertical stratigraphic column at some convenient place, as though the site deposits were everywhere the same and always a faithful reflection of changing external environment, is obviously mistaken. So, from the beginning we have taken multiple samples from all parts of the exposure of every sedimentary unit at the site, whether "natural" or cultural in origin. This extensive suite supplements the samples taken in areas where cultural disturbance seems minimal.

While samples of sediments and biotic materials were taken through the entire depositional sequence, so far the excavation proper—opening large contiguous "horizontal" areas in each occupation with abundant regular "vertical" control—has only penetrated the top meter or so of sediments. Substantial exposures are so far available only for the top five Paleolithic levels. We find marked differences between the Juyo Magdalenian occupation levels in spatial utilization, the construction of features, the nature and condition of recovered biotic materials, and the proportions of artifact types in stone and bone. These seem to reflect differential functions of the various occupations, however, and no consistent temporal trends can be discerned.

The lowest occupation levels extensively excavated, 9 and 8, are successive aspects of a deep shell midden containing thousands of shells of the common limpet (*Patella vulgata*). Occupation Levels 7 and 6 are the earlier and later moments respectively of a massive accumulation of literally thousands of selected red deer remains, representing almost 80 individuals. The western part of the next occupation, Level 4, is a thin seam of much-trampled material resting directly on the flowstone; on the east, the cave inhabitants built a large and elaborate rubble-walled sanctuary containing mounds, trenches, pits, stone slabs, and a sculpted stone face. Even the most grossly superficial evaluation of the characteristics of the El Juyo levels indicates that they were the scenes of very different activity-sets. The site is an ideal locale in which to attempt to understand those activities. It is essentially undisturbed. After the entrance collapsed 14,000 years ago, the site was abandoned and the floor sealed with a thick layer of stalagmite.

Extensive suites of sediment samples were taken in 1978 and 1979 by Dr. Stephen Porter and in 1982 and 1983 by Dr. Manuel Hoyos. Though complete results of their analyses are still unavailable, the sediments document a long earlier period of relatively temperate conditions followed by a sudden deterioration. The series begins with deposits attesting temperate and relatively dry climatic conditions (Occupations 13-7). During Occupation 6, the water table rose in the cave. The rise was gentle, causing no detectable erosion, but depositing over the site a veneer of sterile silts that were particularly thick inside the large dugout structure in this level. Analogous gradual flooding of the cave occurred at the end of our fieldwork in 1983. Flooding may indicate that rainfall distribution had become more concentrated seasonally than it was earlier or has been until present. Level 5 is a stalagmite, attesting periodic shifts between periods of high moisture and accelerated evaporation within the cave interior, and includes large thermifract blocks. Level 4 sediments incorporate more *éboulis* as building material. The cave entrance collapsed and was sealed by stalagmite in Level 3. These upper layers suggest high humidity, perhaps seasonally concentrated, and episodic (perhaps seasonal) drying and evaporite formation in a regimen that had turned quite cold. Later layers are post-Paleolithic and document the reestablishment of interglacial conditions. There are good carbon-14 dates for Level 7 (14,440 B.P. ± 180) and Level 4 (13,920 B.P. ± 240). The onset of stadial conditions in Level 6 was apparently very rapid.

A total of 106 pollen samples were taken at 5-cm intervals through the strata in an area of the site carefully chosen to be as little disturbed by Paleolithic building as possible. Other samples were taken in other parts of the site as excavation progressed. Dr. Arlette Leroi-Gourhan analyzed a subset of these (Fig. 1.6). She also paints a consistent picture of local vegetation evolving from more temperate interstadial conditions that last through Level 7 (her "Pre-Bölling") to the markedly colder Dryas I stadial. Despite the agreement between sediments and palynology, a potential richness of detailed information not available in the sediments alone about finely tuned microclimatic oscillations and areal differences in pollen fallout over the occupation surface was obviously missed, since only 39 of the samples were analyzed. A superficial examination of the pollen content of samples from different parts of the site suggests that spatial differences in pollen drop are probably important. Since 1982, we have taken samples that may be used for palynology as well as other kinds of analysis, from every 33.3 × 33.3-cm sector and every natural level or 5-cm subdivision excavated; this will continue to be our standard practice.

While carbon-14 dates from El Juyo agree chronologically with climatic events assigned to the levels by Leroi-Gourhan, they pose one of the major problems that must be resolved by future research. In France, the Magdalenian III is thought to be a chronologically restricted stage in a sequence of industrial development. The dates on El Juyo's Magdalenian III equivalent assemblages are 1000 to 2000 years later than dates conventionally accepted for this phase in France, and in fact are contemporary with the Late Magdalenian at the nearby cave of Tito Bustillo. Equally late dates have been reported for some French Magdalenian III sites but are usually dismissed as unreliable. If they are reliable, what we conventionally regard as sequential stages of Magdalenian industrial development may prove to be synchronous functional or stylistic variants. Further dates for the Juyo levels should clarify this issue.

Beginning in 1982, all sediment from each excavated sector and sublevel was subjected to flotation. The floated fraction has been found to contain macrobotanicals identified by Crowe. Preservation is excellent. Numerous identifiable plant specimens as well as a great deal of charcoal were recovered from almost 1000 samples floated in the 1982-83 field seasons (Table 1.1, Fig. 1.7). Recovered charcoal is mostly from *Pinus, Salix,* and *Populus*.

Macrobotanicals (even uncarbonized ones) and other delicate biotics were preserved from oxidation by encapsulation in clayey sediments and sealed into the site by the flowstone that caps the Magdalenian horizons, preventing disturbance until the site was discovered in the 1950s. Flotation recovered insect parts of *Homeoptera, Diptera, Coleoptera,* and *Orthoptera,* a great deal of microfaunal material, rare fish scales, and over 400 tiny mollusks, more than 50 of which are marine species.

Seed and stem fragments from El Juyo include several from plants that lack airborne pollen, adding a number of taxa to the vegetation implied by the pollen diagram. The macrobotanical assemblage is remarkable for its diversity. The 853 identified seeds and plant parts recognized to date represent 21 families and 51 genera (Fig. 1.8). The majority are grasses, followed in abundance by *Rosaceae* and *Compositae*. There are some fragments of nuts of *Quercus* and *Corylus* and 31 raspberry pits (*Rubus*). Commonly occurring genera include *Holcus, Senecio, Viola, Agrostis, Silene, Polygonum,* and *Sambucus*. There are a few specimens each of *Chenopodium, Picris, Lepidium, Erica, Trifolium, Nardus, Alyssum, Statice, Carex, Galium, Rumex, Medicago, Allium,* and *Poa*. Sticktights (*Bidens*), horsetail stems (*Equisetum*), and *Ulex* thorns are very well represented (Crowe in Barandiarán et al. 1987; Crowe n.d.).

Every attempt has been made to control modern contamination, and the condition of the prehistoric plant parts is generally quite distinctive and different

TABLE 1.1
EL JUYO BOTANICAL SAMPLES: 1982-83

Year	Level	Samples	Plant Parts	Charcoal	Seed Total
1982	4	193	61	128	119
	6	8	2	2	4
	7	13	2	7	1
	8	67	18	24	35
1983	4	320	27	410.50	260
	6	84	11	1.25	53
	7	50	7	0	20
	8	103	7	7.95	80
	9	36	2	0.20	6
	11	15	2	5.25	34
	12	2	2	0	18
	13	5	4	4.00	78

For 1982, charcoal = counts; for 1983, weight in g.

from that of modern specimens. Greatest seed abundance does not coincide with the areas most traveled or most intensively excavated by our crews—in fact, we were surprised to find that patches of high seed density are instead related to particular cultural features (see below). What is more, many of the genera recovered from the Magdalenian occupations no longer occur near the site, and some are not part of the modern Cantabrian flora. Level 4, for example, yielded some seeds of dwarf northern varieties of plants that have not been represented locally since the Pleistocene. This evidence supports suggestions of a deterioration of climate in the upper part of the Juyo sequence.

An interpretation of the seeds as "ecofacts" is strengthened by the fact that seed representation in any level seems to parallel aspects of human/environment interactions reflected by the mammal and mollusk remains in that level. For example, marsh plants are proportionally very abundant in Level 8. This level is a shell midden, where tiny marine mollusks are also numerous; they must have been brought to the site adhering to algae. The list of sampled plant associations is more varied, and the number of plants from distant mountain slopes more abundant, for Level 4 than the other levels. Seeds from Levels 6/7, on the other hand, could mostly have been collected in the near vicinity of the cave.

Remains of mollusks and fish bones are abundant in the El Juyo levels, particularly Level 8. Benito Madariaga and Klein have studied and measured the Mollusca; most of these are *Patella vulgata*. There are smaller numbers of the winkle (*Littorina littorea*), traces of other mollusks, and some crustaceans as well. Figure 1.9, using Klein's measurements, shows that El Juyo limpet shells tend to be smaller than those from somewhat earlier Magdalenian occupations such as the midden at Altamira. Some think the size decrease reflects climatic deterioration, while others think that pressure on the limpet populations by humans harvesting the largest specimens is the more likely explanation. We hope to resolve the debate by oxygen-isotope analysis of specimens from our excavations at Altamira and from the different Juyo levels. Individual fish are not very numerous in any level and thus not terribly informative at present. Most are salmonids (represented by vertebrae) though a few perch-like freshwater fish and some small coastal shellfish-eaters are also present; some of the fish are minnow-sized and might have been taken from tidal pools. They have been examined by R. Casteel and G. García-Castrillo.

The Magdalenian large mammal fauna, studied by Klein, includes more than 22,000 identifiable skeletal parts of which more than 8600 can be used in estimates of minimum numbers of individuals (Fig. 1.10). Bones from Levels 4 and 8/9 are much more fragmented than are those from Levels 6/7. Apparently there was less trampling of the bones discarded in the dugout in Level 6—perhaps there was standing mud or water in the dugout—than was usually the case for bones on an ordinary occupation surface. Measurements on molar teeth indicate that the Juyo red deer were very large compared with interglacial ones, suggesting that foraging conditions were optimal in Magdalenian times. In Levels 8/9, red deer are somewhat less abundant than in later levels. At the moment, numbers of individuals for Levels 8/9 are too small to demonstrate a statistically significant difference, but if such a difference emerges in the larger samples we anticipate, it might well reflect an environmental change not evident in the pollen record.

Red deer predominate in all levels, but especially in Level 6, where the 78 red deer are 84% of all individual mammals and 88% of all large mammals. There is no clear indication of seasonal occupation, from either sectioned teeth or tooth-wear modes. It was not possible to determine season of death from cementum annuli, because in all but a single specimen of teeth from El Juyo that were hard-sectioned, annuli were simply not visible (Klein, pers. comm.). What is more, studies of dentitions of *Cervus elaphus* from animals whose age and season of death are precisely known suggest so much overlap in degree of abrasion that wear studies of cervid dentitions cannot be expected to provide clear indications of seasonality, even with much larger samples than any archaeologist is likely to gather from a single occupation level. Age profiles for the deer in Levels 6/7 and 4 are catastrophic, indicating the harvesting of whole herds (Klein et al. 1981; Klein, Allwarden, and Wolf 1983; Klein and Cruz-Uribe 1984).

During Level 6 times, red deer were probably the most abundant large animals in the vicinity of El Juyo, so while we can affirm that the cave inhabitants were harvesting red deer, we cannot say that these animals were specially selected out of proportion to their abundance in the local fauna. It is of course possible that the Magdalenians selected El Juyo as a base for red-deer harvesting just because its surroundings teemed with that species—just as they seem to have chosen the upland Rascaño site as a base from which to harvest ibex. Probably choice of settlement location is never purely a "settlement strategy"; it was likely as much a part of Magdalenian subsistence strategies as was the choice of resources to be extracted. What we cannot affirm is that combined subsistence/settlement strategies were an innovation. At best later Upper Paleolithic peoples systematized and intensified preexisting patterns.

Part of the microfauna has been examined by Klein, and the rest is now being studied by José Rey. Klein notes the abundance of cold-climate voles, also reported in other north Spanish Magdalenian sites.

Some 40,000 artifacts have been recovered during the four field seasons at El Juyo. Most are unretouched stone flakes, blades, and debris. The El Juyo artifact series are characterized by keeled and nosed scrapers, backed and retouched bladelets (Fig. 1.11), square-sectioned bone spearpoints (*sagaies*) and shaft segments, and eyed needles (Fig. 1.12), all familiar from Magdalenian III levels and their equivalents in southwest France and Spain. The bone artifact collection is remarkably rich: there are more than 100 whole and partial *sagaies* from Level 4 alone. Decorated bone is common: the most striking bone art object recovered is the cut-out contour of a hind's head, found in the "foundation pit" in the Level 4 sanctuary (Freeman and González Echegaray 1983). It ranks among the masterpieces of Cantabrian Upper Paleolithic art. Another unique discovery was that of three carefully shaped, nearly identical short sections of red-deer metapodial, found neatly stacked atop the north edge of a paved "walkway" leading to the cave entrance from the large structure in Level 6. These are interpreted as dice or divining pieces by analogy with similar artifacts from aboriginal America (Freeman and González Echegaray, in press).

Despite the fact that all the El Juyo levels represent one single Magdalenian industrial complex, there are considerable differences in the relative abundance of artifact classes from level to level. The differences show no consistent temporal trend. Figure 1.13 shows the proportional representation of finished tools, blades, 1982 and 1983 from each of the major levels excavated, and Table 1.2 shows Kolmogorov/Smirnov values for comparisons between the retouched tool series. The "offering levels" in the Level 4 sanctuary are distinctive in having overwhelming proportions of retouched pieces, very few backed and retouched bladelets, and a large proportion of whole *sagaies*. Level 6, packed with red-deer bone, has very high proportions of bladelet tools compared to the "endscrapers" that dominate most other levels (Fig. 1.14). A new tool type, the "Juyo bladelet," has been proposed for a category of microblade with marginal abrupt retouch that is too peripheral to be considered

TABLE 1.2

EL JUYO: RELATIONSHIPS BETWEEN RETOUCHED STONE TOOL ASSEMBLAGES,
MEASURED BY THE KOLMOGOROV-SMIRNOV STATISTIC

	JUYO4	JUYO4S	JUYO6	JUYO7	JUYO8	JUYO9
JUYO4	xxxxx					
JUYO4S	1.81059	xxxxx				
JUYO6	3.18965	3.41642	xxxxx			
JUYO7	2.30505	2.88469	*1.58203*	xxxxx		
JUYO8	*1.32871*	2.10676	2.87587	*1.49865*	xxxxx	
JUYO9	*1.45083*	1.98272	*1.03684*	*0.55501*	*1.21530*	xxxxx

Values greater than 1.63 indicate difference at the < 0.01 level. Pairs of levels exhibiting smaller values (italicized) are considered similar. JUYO4S = sanctuary in Level 4. JUYO4 = remainder of level.

backing, and too abrupt to fit the Dufour category; scores occur in Cantabrian Magdalenian levels. L. Keeley and Carmen Gutierrez (pers. comm.) have studied substantial samples of the Juyo tools, observing that many of the backed and Juyo bladelets were used as projectile points, and others as meat-slicing implements. They found virtually no wear polish on any of the keeled, steep, or nucleiform endscrapers, supporting suggestions that these pieces may have served primarily as bladelet cores.

STRUCTURAL REMNANTS AND SPATIAL DISTRIBUTIONS

El Juyo has already provided more large, well-preserved structural vestiges than any other cave site of comparable age (see Freeman and González Echegaray 1984). A large, semi-subterranean dugout whose dimensions are still incompletely known contains most of the shell midden in Level 8. Another large structure in Level 6 is a complex of four elements (Figs. 1.15 and 1.16). First, there is a small quadrangular room measuring 1.3 × 1.4 m, dug some 25 cm into the sediments and walled with slabs and rubble. It contained many large fragments of coloring material, grindstones, whole or partly worked antler racks, and a large stone lamp. Abutting it to the north is Structure 2, a rubble-walled dugout with rounded north wall and squared-off south wall, some 25-30 cm deep and measuring 2.5 × 2.25 m. Both were built within an earlier, large excavated depression. Structure 2 was filled with selected red-deer skeletal parts, though whether it was built as a waste-disposal tank or simply used that way after abandonment cannot yet be ascertained. A 1.5-m-wide rubble-paved walk or platform leads from Structure 2 towards the old cave entry. There are two small basin-shaped hearths outside the structure, in Level 7.

Some time before the occupation of Level 4, a series of posts was emplaced below the area of the sanctuary (Fig. 1.17). Five have been revealed so far. They are part of an organized arrangement, but the nature of the building represented and its size cannot be determined.

Level 4 had more structures than any other level. The two latest are a pair of rectangular dugout rooms 15-25 cm deep, with rounded corners; the first is 1.4 m on a side and the other measures 1.2 × 1.1 m. These were refilled after abandonment with rubble containing much stone-chipping debris. The major and constructionally earlier complex in this level is the sanctuary (Figs. 1.17, 1.18). As a first step in its construction, the inhabitants excavated a large, "D"-shaped depression about 6.5 sq. m in extent through Level 5 stalagmite to a depth of about 1 m, removing earlier cultural deposit in the process, and banking it up into a sloping "ramp" along the south wall of the chamber. Toward the center of the curved east or "back" wall they dug a shallow pit 65 to 70 cm wide, depositing in it ocher, shells, spearpoints, bones, needles, and the cut-out contour mentioned earlier (Fig. 1.17). The foundation pit was filled, and the dugout wall sheathed with a veneer of rubble 20 to 25 cm thick in a clean clay mortar. Three shallow trenches were dug and filled with assorted materials in a sand and ocher matrix. Atop these were constructed three earthen mounds. Each consists of a series of thin continuous sheets of burnt vegetation, red ocher, spearpoints, and long narrow skeletal parts of red deer, including fetal bones, alternating with deeper layers of indifferent fill that was everted in carefully controlled and clearly cultural patterns from cylindrical containers almost invariably 10 cm wide (Fig. 1.18). Cylinder-lots of earth in the fill layers were disposed in "hexagonal" groups of seven, and in some layers, each distinct rosette of 10-cm cylinders was separately plastered over with colored sandy clay (sometimes incorporating whole limpet shells) so as to form colorful large-scale patterns. Each of the mounds had somewhat different and highly unusual contents: groups of antler tines, white or red coloring matter, special stone tools, etc. Each mound was encased in a clay plaster, and the partly engraved, partly sculpted stone face of a being half human, half large cat, was set in a dominant position atop the front mound (Fig. 1.19). In the space between the mounds were two localized accumulations of fossil shellfish and a pair of whistles made of hollowed and polished iron-oxide nodules. Four smallish pits complete the complex. Their major contents were ocher, shellfish, and eyed needles, sometimes thrust vertically into the pit fill. Before abandonment, the complex was paved with large slabs and rubble, and two hearths set atop the pavement, pointing to the now-hidden stone face.

The El Juyo structures are so numerous and varied that a preliminary classification based on formal characteristics and contents is possible. There are two small square structures in Level 4 and one in 6. Both 6 and 8 (probably) contain large oval dugouts. The D-shaped sanctuary area is similar in shape to Structure 2 in Level 6. There are pavements in Levels 6 and 4, and hearths in Levels 7 and 4. Pits include four small features inside and another outside the sanctuary in 4, and the formally different "foundation pit." The three mound/trench complexes also share certain features and contrast in others. Further excavation at El Juyo will undoubtedly recover the rest of the structure in Level 8 and probably several earlier structural remnants whose presence is suspected.

A study of the forms, constructional details, interior appointments, and content of structures combined with a study of materials found outside them can provide precious information on functional differentiation of space within the site, and suggestions about the nature of the social units that used the space. The study of spatial distributions is not yet complete but already promises new insights. As should be evident, at El Juyo the analyst can compare distributions not just of artifacts, animal bones, shells, and structural remnants, but also of seeds and plant parts, and spatial variations in such chemical values as phosphate content and acidity over the surface of every excavated level. At the time of writing, El Juyo is the only Paleolithic site in the world where so many different kinds of data are available for comparison. The few examples that follow are provided just to give the reader an impression of the yield to be expected.

Distribution patterns in Levels 4 and 6 are more completely analyzed than those from lower levels. In Level 4, patterning is clearest in the area of the sanctuary. Where Level 4 is a thin seam atop a hard flowstone layer, original cultural patterns have been somewhat obscured by trampling and scuffing of materials in prehistoric times. Principal-components analysis of materials from squares above the flowstone suggests that much of the variance in skeletal elements is related to their relative durability. Distribution patterns of artifacts and body parts are blurred, with many squares having similar contents. When the sanctuary area is included, spatial distinctions emerge more clearly. The sanctuary itself is quite distinctive, having far fewer unretouched stone artifacts and much larger numbers of bone *sagaies* than are proportionally expectable. One of the small square structures outside the sanctuary was apparently used as a flaking area or, more likely, a dump for unretouched flakes and stone-knapping debris. In addition to unretouched pieces, it yielded anomalously high quantities of denticulates, nucleiform scrapers, and backed and "Juyo" bladelets. There are at least three other areas with distinctive contents in this level. There is enough coincidence between spatial distributions of recovered artifacts and structural remnants so that plots of different constellations of related artifacts betray the presence of structures even when their walls are not shown. We wish to make it clear that it is not patterns in the relative or absolute density of all finds that betray the presence of structural features, but that specific recurrent constellations of a few similarly covarying types coincide in space with particular structures.

Again in Level 6 we find that distribution patterns show an obvious relationship to structural vestiges, and in this case the patterns are less blurred by postdepositional trampling. Squares in the middle of the large cervid room are virtually devoid of stone artifacts but instead yield anomalously high densities of bone, particularly whole or nearly complete red-deer scapulae and tarsal bones. Just inside the west wall of the cervid room and atop the adjacent stone pavement in Square 7M there are unexpectedly high proportions of red-deer metapodials, hindlimbs, and especially maxillae and mandible fragments. Stone artifacts are moderately represented in the same area. Endscrapers of all kinds except nucleiform, Juyo bladelets, unretouched pieces, and bone needles are exceptionally abundant in Squares 8M (on the pavement) and 8P. The highest densities of these types are always found outside the structure walls. The lamp room produced anomalously high quantities of burin types otherwise rare at El Juyo, colorants, grindstones, and red-deer antler, as well as the only stone lamp found at the site. These examples should indicate the sorts of relationships that have been detected via use of multivariate techniques on the distributions of materials in the El Juyo levels, and they demonstrate the not unexpected fact that surface distributions of finds bear recognizable relationships to the presence of structural remnants.

One more example will be given, due to the unusual nature of the data involved.

While in prehistoric times many macrobotanicals were probably introduced to the site accidentally on clothing, muddy feet, or animal skins, or imported by animals when humans were absent, the distribution of seeds in the levels where they are most abundant indicates that their placement was at least conditioned by humans. Figure 1.20 shows the topography of a part of Level 6 containing structures (dugout rooms) and the density-gradient map for seed distributions for the same area. (The seeds in this structure antedate the rising waters: there is virtually no plant material in the flood silts that make up the bulk of the structures' fill.) When the two are superimposed, it is seen that in the rubble of the walls seed densities are low, while high seed densities are found on the floor next to the walls; this is consonant with an interpretation that the floors were periodically "swept," and that the seeds we recovered, hidden in the corners, escaped the housecleaning process. (The seed distributions in other levels have analogous characteristics.) The areas of highest seed distribution in the fill of the cervid room also contained higher-than-average concentrations of maxillae and hemi-mandibles. Stone artifacts, however, are always twice to four times as abundant as bones in areas where seeds are present in this structure. The distributions of seeds in Levels 4 and 8—the only other levels where data are now abundant enough to justify study—are as clearly patterned and as obviously related to structural features as are those in Level 6. The seed distributions seem to indicate substantial human intervention, though it may have been largely indirect and even unconscious.

We must still complete the analysis of covariation of the different artifact types with other categories of contextual and positional data derived from the analyses of biotic materials and structural features, and with other information. Further data must be gathered from the earlier occupations at El Juyo. We still need more data to determine, for example, what the particular industrial correlates of the shell midden in Level 8 may be, and whether particular tools are related to specific vegetal remains.

Detailed comparisons between the Juyo structures and other features—"cooking pits" at Altamira, pavements at Tito Bustillo, and trenches at Rascaño—are still to be made. When all these analyses are finished, as they will be within the next year or two, we will have a much clearer and more trustworthy outline of the nature and functions of earlier Magdalenian buildings and their place in the larger mosaic of contemporary regional subsistence and settlement strategies. This will help fill out the picture of activities and occupation differentiation provided by the study of portable artifacts and contextual materials such as flora and fauna. The El Juyo research will provide detailed reconstructions of environmental change and illuminate subsistence/settlement strategies, and can additionally provide unique reflections of social organization and ideology that, taken with other data, should establish some landmarks on the broader highway of cultural elaboration in the Cantabrian Upper Paleolithic.

NOTES

1. All authors are members of the Institute for Prehistoric Investigations, 105 Madison, Chicago IL. 60602 USA and Avenida de Pontejos, 9, Santander (Cantabria), Spain.

2. Many of the tables, figures, and diagrams that accompany this paper were electronically produced on personal computers. Computers and software used in our analyses were provided by IPI. Readers may be interested in the nature of this equipment and our experience with it.

All inventories made in the field are recorded on Tandy TRS-80/100 laptop computers with a minimum of 32 K of user-available memory. IPI now has a number of these machines in service, and their low price, small size, features, and durability make them ideal for such applications as ours. (They have recently been discontinued, but the new Model 102 is in all essential respects equivalent.) The TRS-80/100 has a built-in modem making transmission to the PCs in our Santander offices a matter of a telephone call. Since the site is less than 20 km from Santander, and there is always a spare laptop in the office, when there is no rush it is just as convenient to cable the Model 100 to the larger machine and upload the data directly.

The simplest means of transmitting data from one computer to another is by a direct cable link. A communications program must be used to facilitate the transfer. That program is built into the TRS-80/100. IPI uses PC-TALK 3 for cabled transfers to the PC and CROSSTALK XVI for transfers using a modem.

We have had to deal with two problems in using laptop computers on site. Any excavation is dirty, and dirt could damage the machines. Wrapping the computer in a sheet of transparent plastic (or enclosing it in a large, heavy-gauge plastic bag) solves this potential problem. The keys can be depressed and the display read quite readily through the clear plastic. Santander's climate is humid, and the interior of the El Juyo cave is cool as well. Some maneuvering is necessary to keep condensation from getting into the computer's works. When it is cooler and dryer outside the cave than in, the computer is sealed into its bag before it is taken inside. Otherwise, it should be allowed to acclimatize in the cave before it is bagged. Envelopes of silica gel crystals (but not loose crystals) can be enclosed with the computer. Even the best batteries will drain rapidly and may need to be replaced as frequently as twice a day. Alkaline batteries are recommended. Incidentally, the button on the positive end of some kinds of batteries (Memorex, for example) is too short to ensure good contact with the TRS-100's circuitry.

Our main office in Santander uses an IBM portable personal computer with a 20-megabyte hard disk. We also use Corona personal computers in Spain. In our U.S. laboratories, Epson Equity II computers with 20-megabyte hard disks and Hercules-compatible graphics are standard. We have never had the least trouble transferring data between these computers, although certain graphics programs require special drivers to be used with Hercules graphics, and graph-drawing programs written in BASIC must be rescaled for different displays (anyone with a little experience with BASIC can do this for most programs in a matter of minutes). IPI also uses an Apple Macintosh Plus, primarily for graphics work.

There are many fine programs available for both IBM-compatible machines and the Macintosh. IPI makes extensive use of commercial software packages, relying on dedicated software produced in-house only where no comparable commercial program is available. We have not found the commercially available dedicated archaeological software packages that are supposed to do everything for the archaeologist to be anywhere near as useful as the best commercial programs written for a broader audience. IPI uses two database programs for laptop inventory. One was rewritten by Crowe from a public-domain program. The other is T-BASE, commercially available from Travelling Software. Both produce straight ASCII files that can be imported directly by the two relational database management programs, Infocom's CORNERSTONE and Ashton-Tate's DBASE III+, that we find most practical on the PCs. T-BASE uses so little memory for each data entry that 300-400 entries can be made before the 32 K of laptop memory are nearly full and data must be transferred to cassette. (Two to three additional 32-K banks of memory can be obtained—but not from Tandy—and installed, but this is not essential, and we have not had unqualified good results with supplementary memory chips.)

Where large numbers of relatively straightforward calculations must be generated, we find LOTUS 1-2-3 most suitable. We recommend MINITAB and SYSTAT for statistical analysis. Graphs are easily produced with Microsoft CHART. Golden Graphics Corporation produces superb mapping programs for IBM-compatible personal computers: QGRID, TOPO, and SURF. These programs can be used with most dot-matrix printers. Klein has published programs for the analysis of animal bones from archaeological sites (Klein and Cruz-Uribe 1984), and IPI has developed its own BASIC programs, IPOLOGY and IPOLOGYH, for calculation of artifact percentages and indices and cumulative percentage graphing.

DISCUSSION

RIGAUD: What kind of information are you expecting from the spatial analysis of the chemicals, especially iron oxide?

FREEMAN: We do not really know. We are working with a site physical chemist who is analyzing a battery of materials, including iron oxide, for her own interests. I don't know of any case in which the iron oxide, or the ash analysis, has told us anything. Originally, I saw very little utility when she began doing phosphate analysis, since the only applications I knew were well after the excavations had taken place. But we suddenly began to see gradients and abrupt steps in these values on the site when we were in a layer a few centimeters above structures. So, the phosphates and pH turned out to be extremely useful. It is true that we could have found the structures without these techniques. But sometimes questions arise whether you have a linear arrangement of stones underlying a series of rubble or whether it is all just éboulis. In this case it turned out that the Delta pH values, the pH values, and the phosphate values showed us linear arrangements of changes before we were down where we could see the alignments in the stone.

KOZLOWSKI: What are the differences in the dosage of phosphate or pH between the bones inside and outside the walls?

FREEMAN: They are minor but they are constant and regular and show these alignments. Our changes in pH do not go from acid to totally alkaline; in fact, they go from acid to slightly less acid and so on.

SCHRIRE: I am interested in how much material you remove.

FREEMAN: The excavation is not very big. In nine months we have excavated a surface of 40 sq. m down about a meter and a half.

STRAUS: The complex arrangements in the Magdelenian are certainly not unknown and there are a number of other cases elsewhere. El Juyo is the most complex to date of this sort of thing. The excavation of this site is encouraging, I think, because it confirms what we have found at La Riera concerning the intensive utilization of red deer in certain environments. Another comment concerns the fact that your radiocarbon dates overlap with the generally accepted radiocarbon dates from the Upper Magdalenian at Tito Bustillo. We are finding the overlap of the radiocarbon dates and some of the *fossiles directeurs* between Lower and Middle Upper Cantabrian Magdalenian in well-controlled excavations.

FREEMAN: But we have only two good dates, so I really want a lot more before I begin to say with certainty that that is what is happening.

JELINEK: You talk about a pavement. Is there any chance that it is simply roof fall?

FREEMAN: It is not the same material and was apparently brought into the site from several hundred meters away.

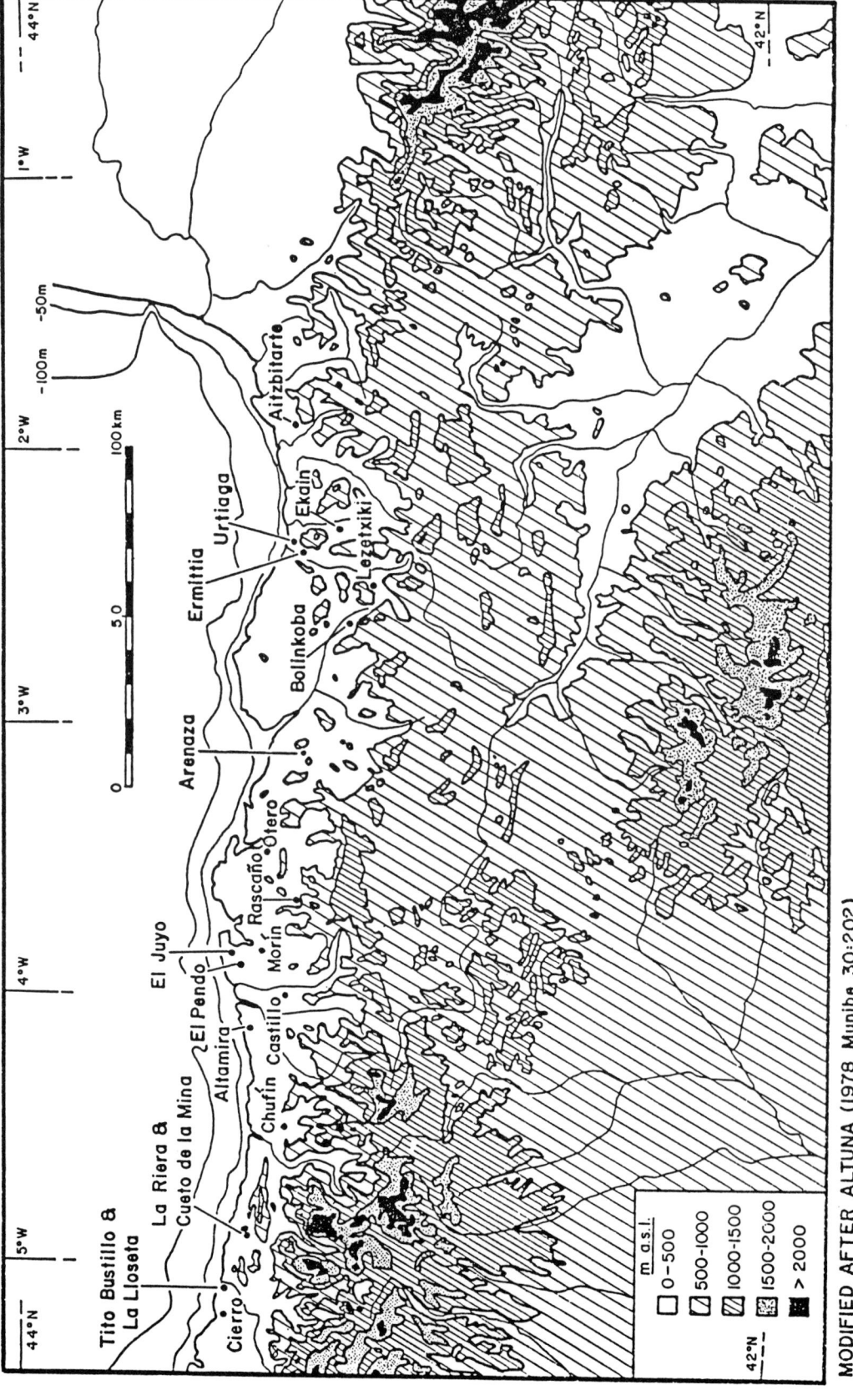

Figure 1.1 Magdalenian sites in the Cantabrian region.

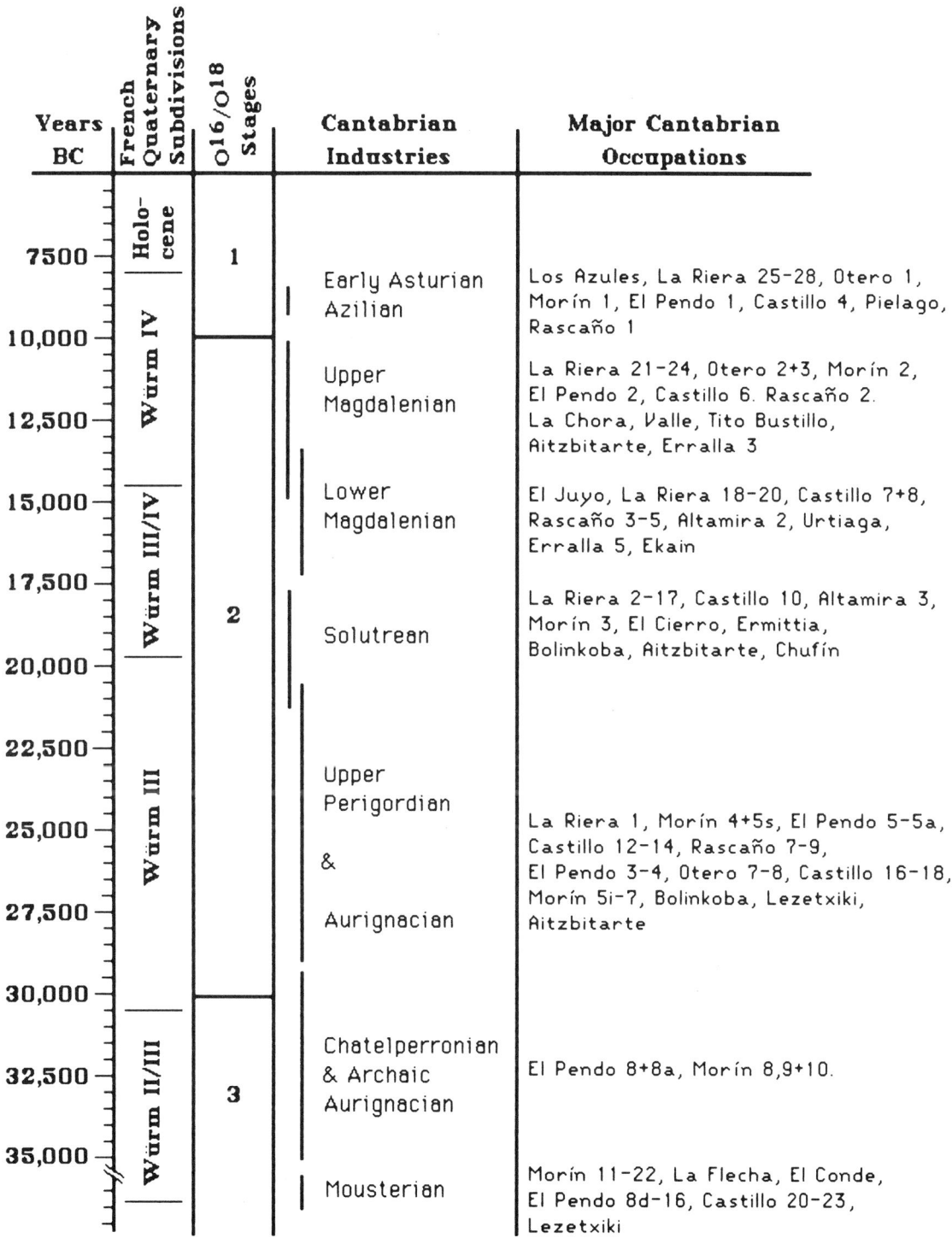

Figure 1.2 Chart showing chronological settings of Cantabrian industries and occupations.

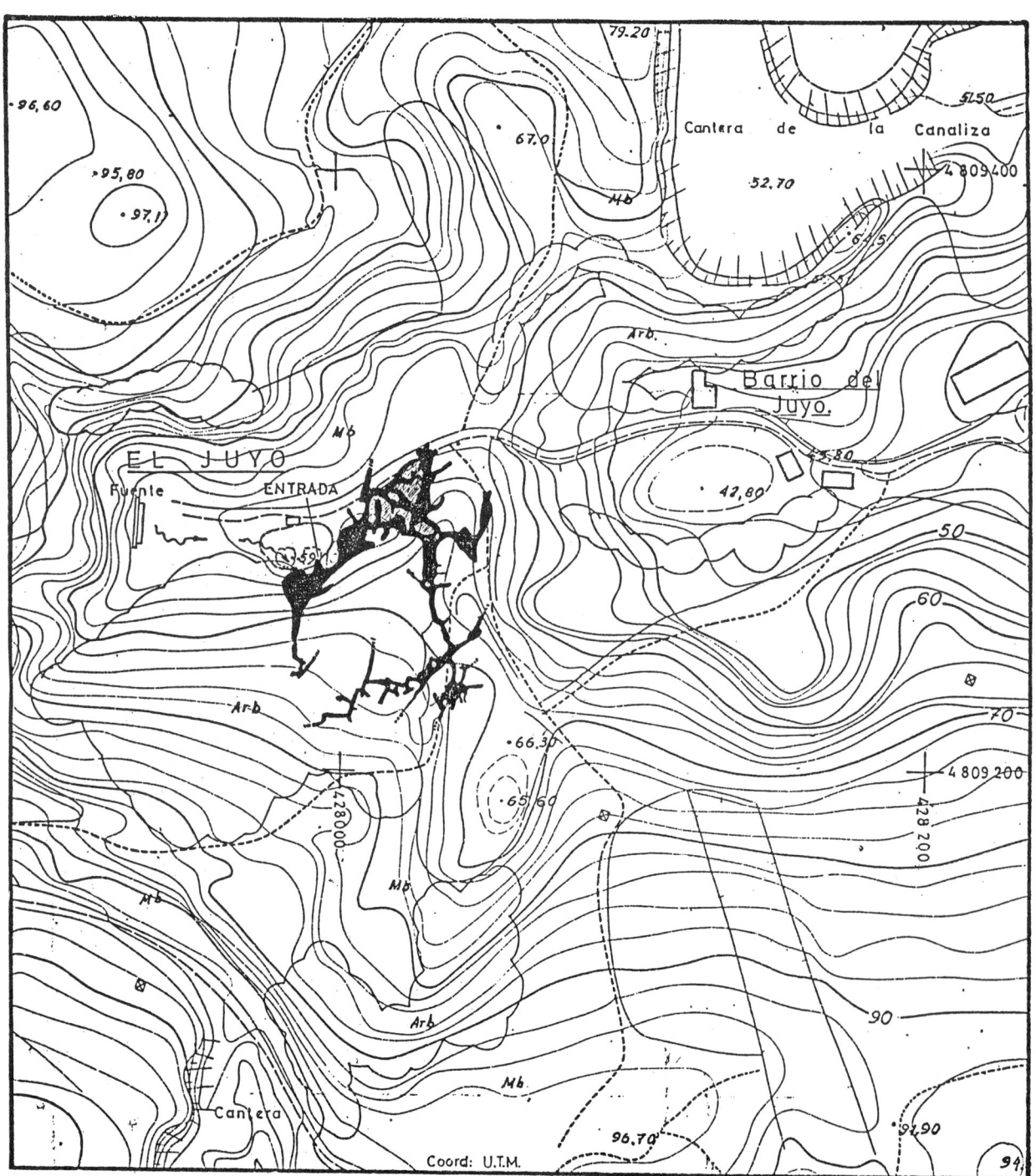

Figure 1.3 El Juyo and surrounding topography.

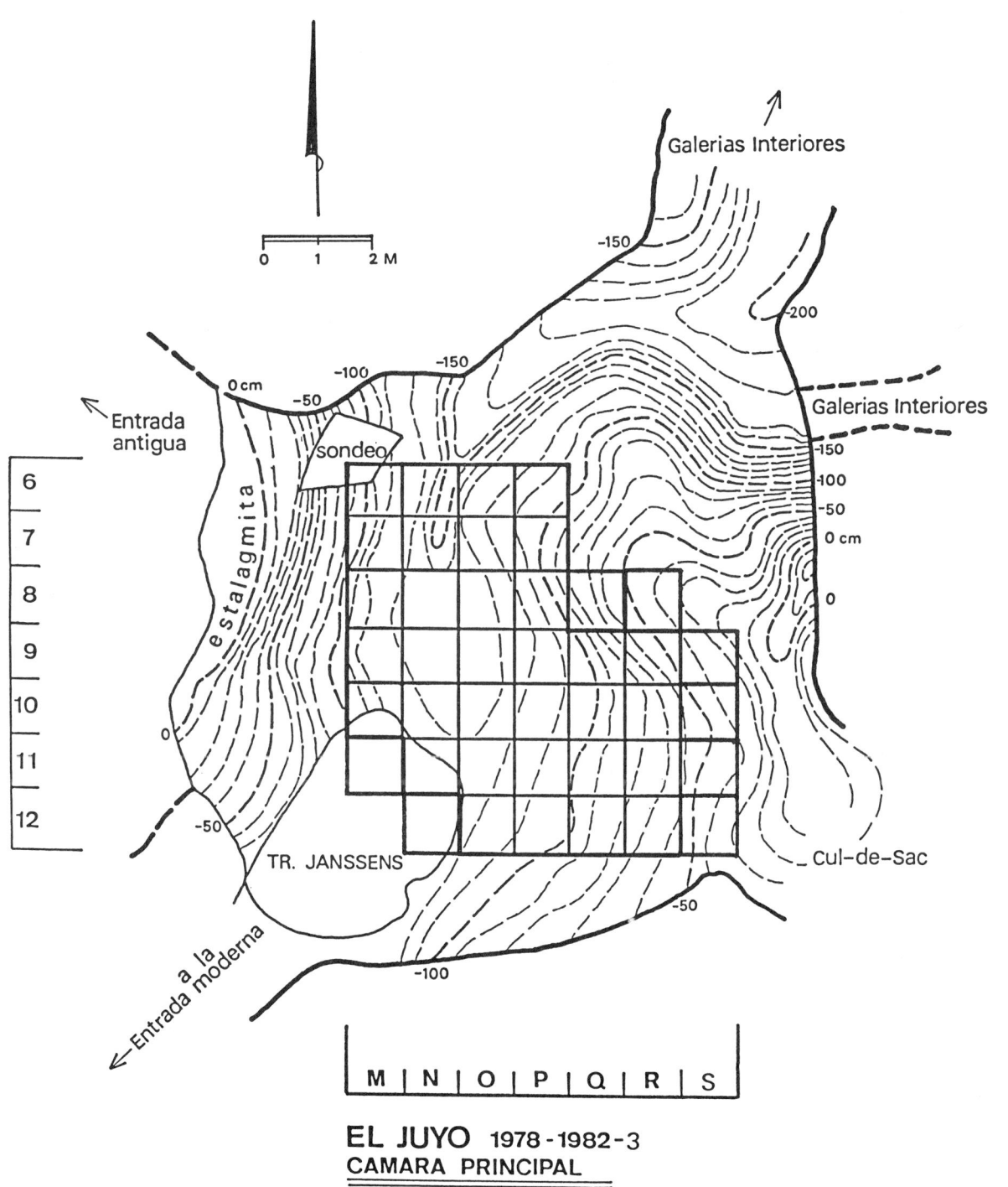

Figure 1.4 Map of excavated area.

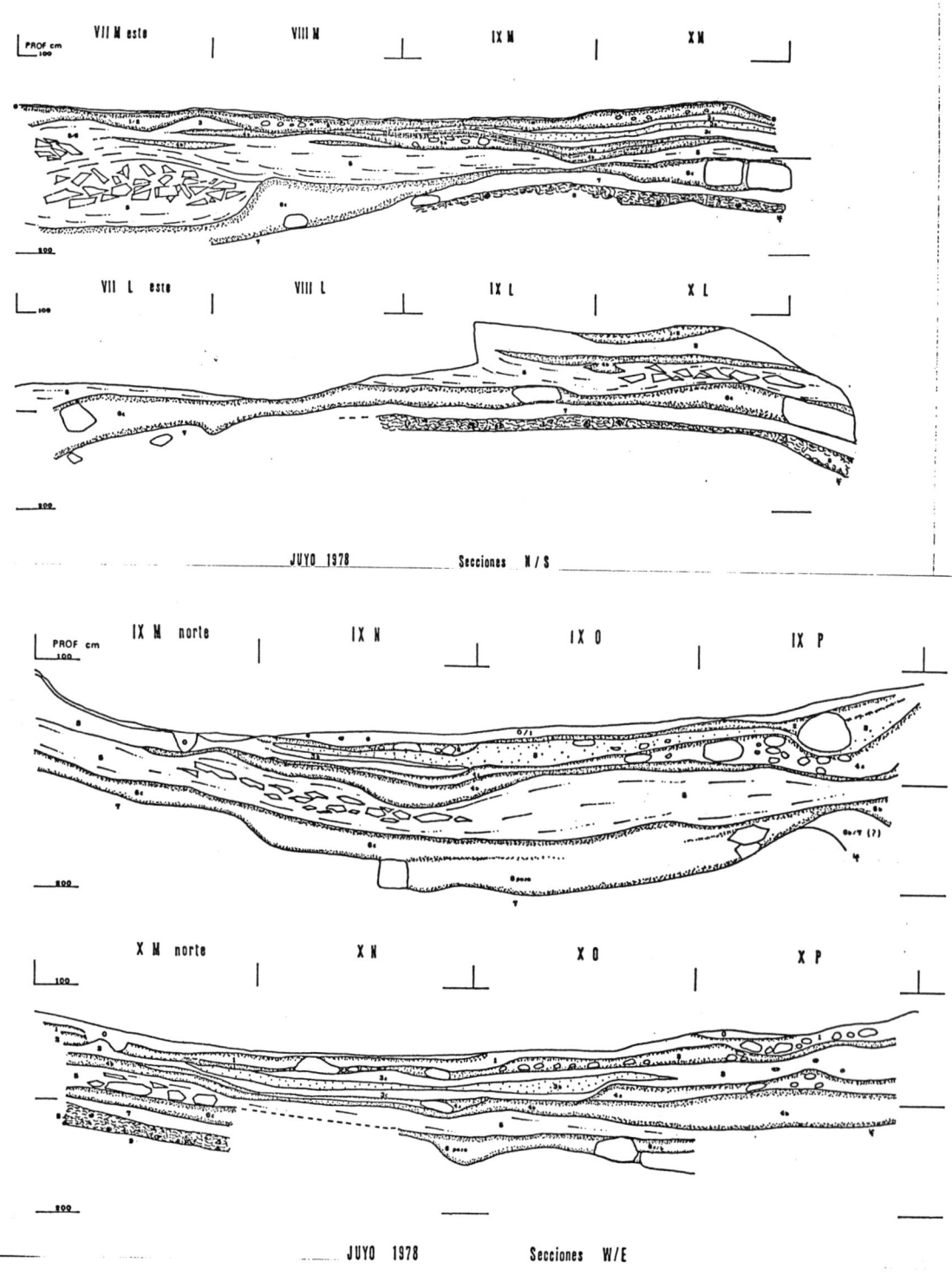

Figure 1.5 Selected El Juyo sections.

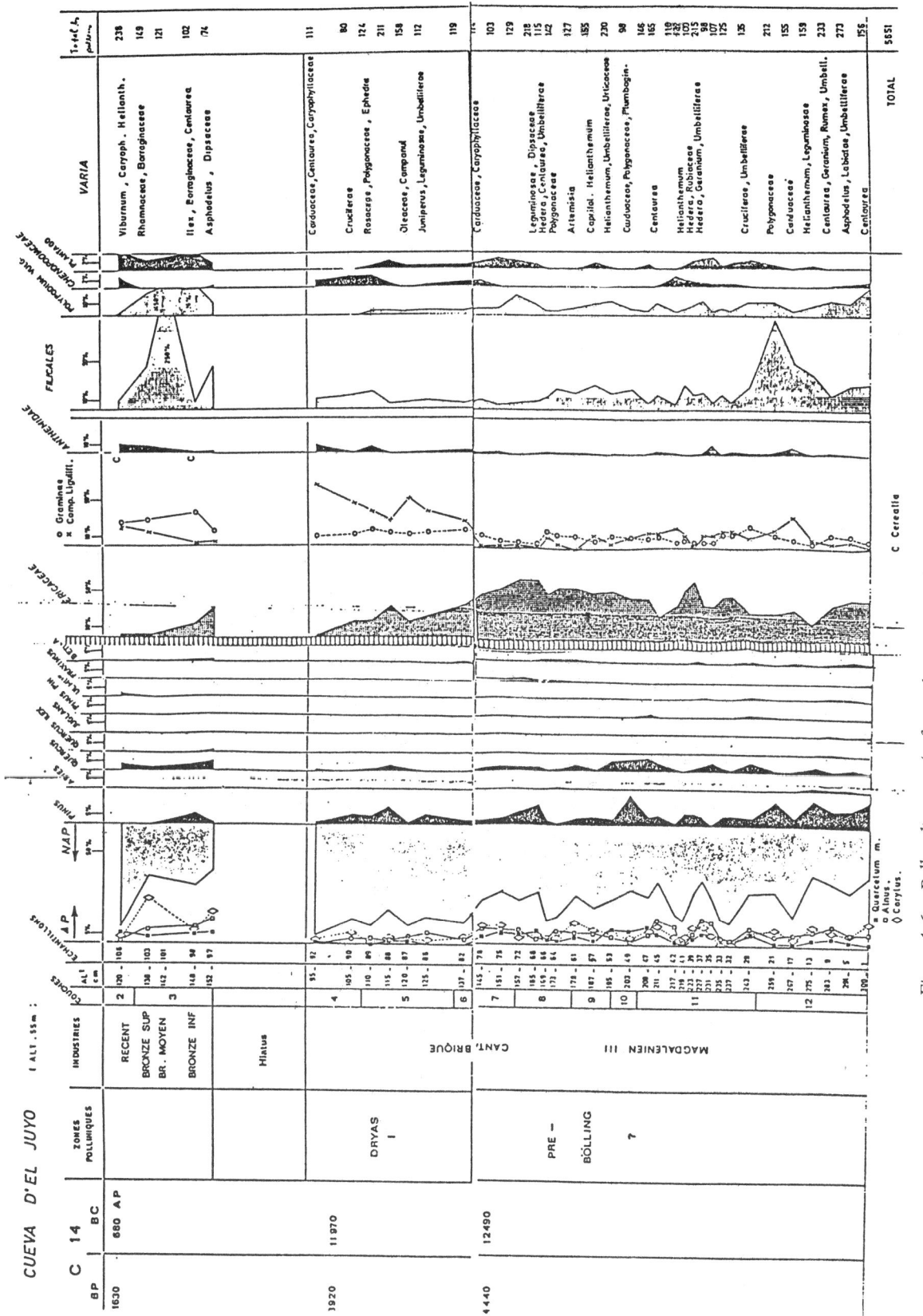

Figure 1.6 Pollen diagram. (After Arl. Leroi-Gourhan in Barandiarán et al. 1987)

El Juyo Botanical Samples: 1982 - 83
For 1982, charcoal = counts; for 1983, gm wt.

Year	Level	Samples	Plant pa	Charcoal	Total se	Ave seed
82	4	193	61	128	119	1.7
82	6	8	2	2	4	1.33
82	7	13	2	7	1	1
82	8	67	18	24	35	1.75
83	4	320	27	410.5	260	2.57
83	6	84	11	1.25	53	2.04
83	7	50	7	0	20	1.33
83	8	103	7	7.95	80	2.29
83	9	36	2	0.2	6	1.2
83	11	15	2	5.25	34	3.4
83	12	2	2	0	18	9
83	13	5	4	4	78	26

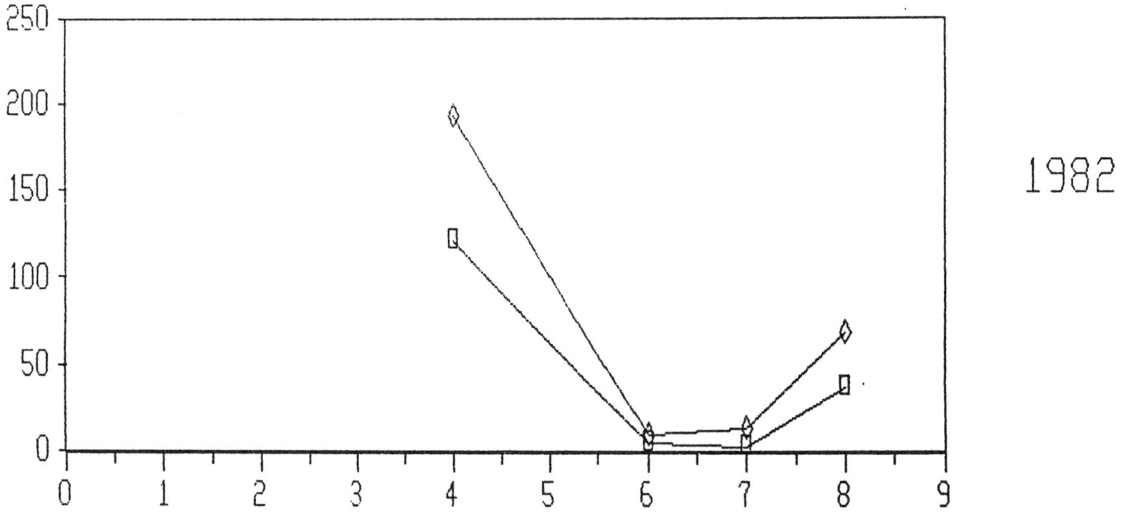

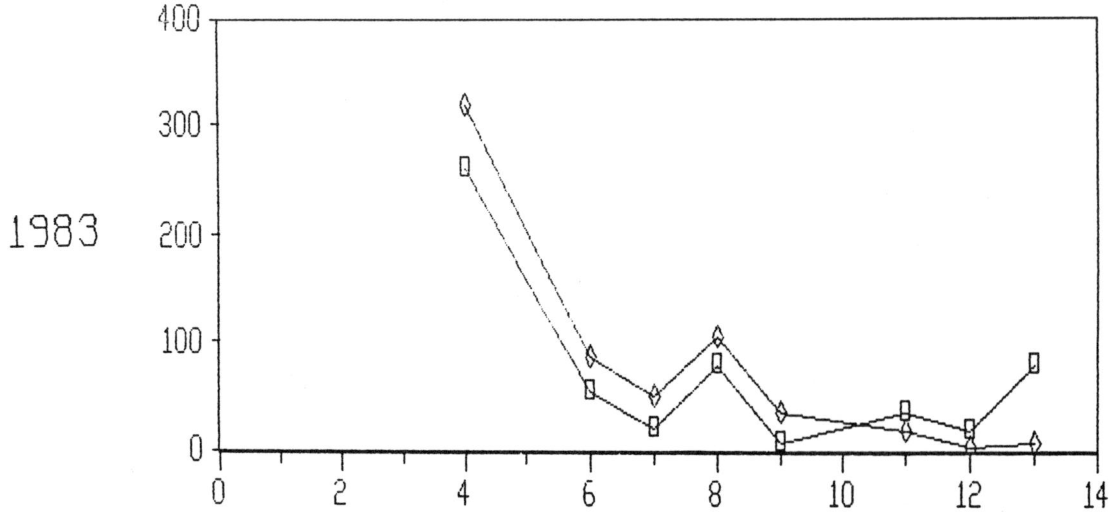

Figure 1.7   Botanical yield, El Juyo excavations.

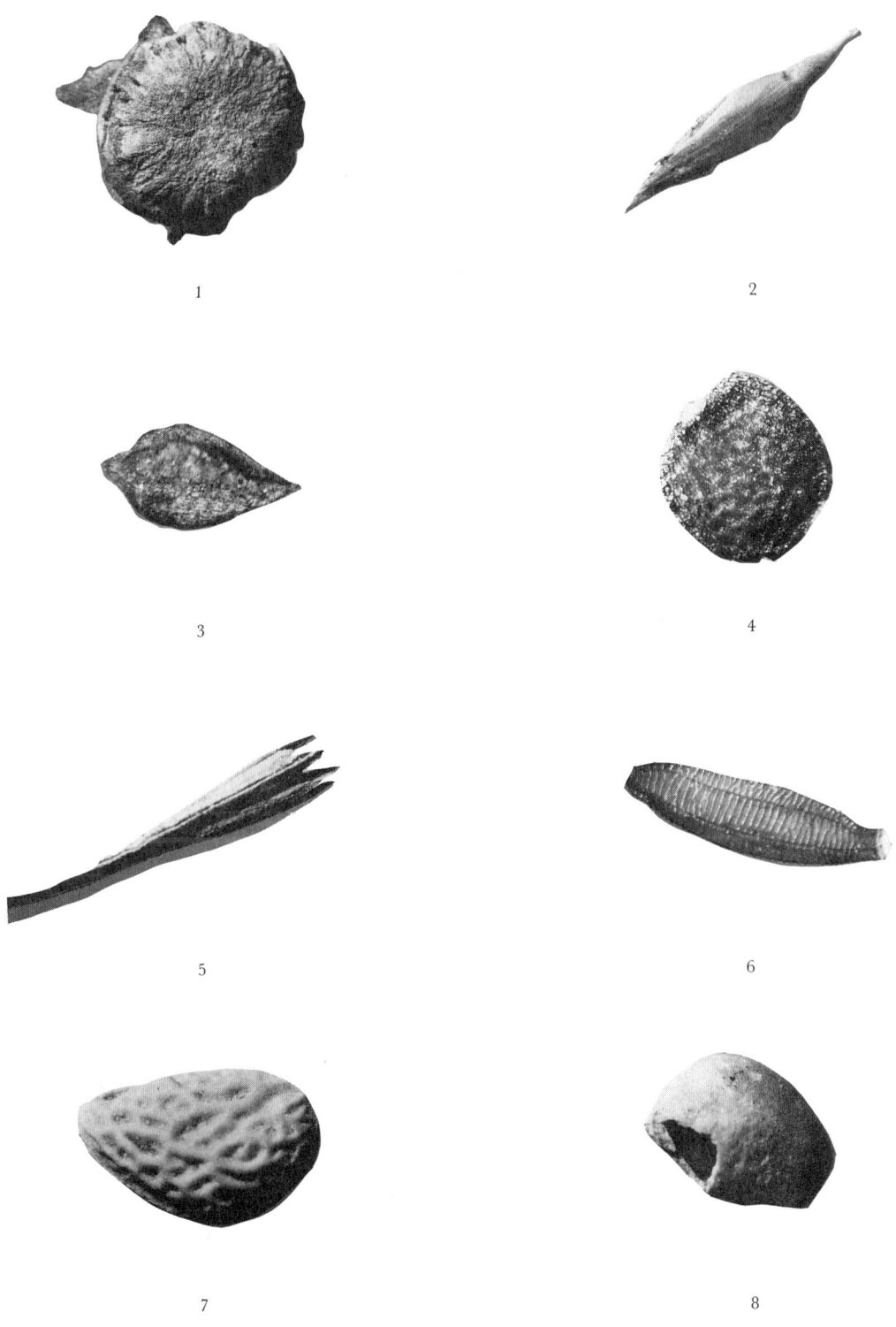

Figure 1.8   Magdalenian plant parts from El Juyo. Measurements are in mm. 1) Quercus, max. L. 7.5; 2) Grass cf. Agrostis, max. L. 2.1; 3) Rumex, max. L. 1.75; 4) Lens, max. L. 0.94; 5) Bidens, max. L. 4.0, max. W. 1.22; 6) Picris, max. L. 4.0; 7) Rubus, max. L. 2.4; 8) Viola (insect damage), max. L. 0.73. Specimens 3 and 6 are from Level 4; others are from Level 6.

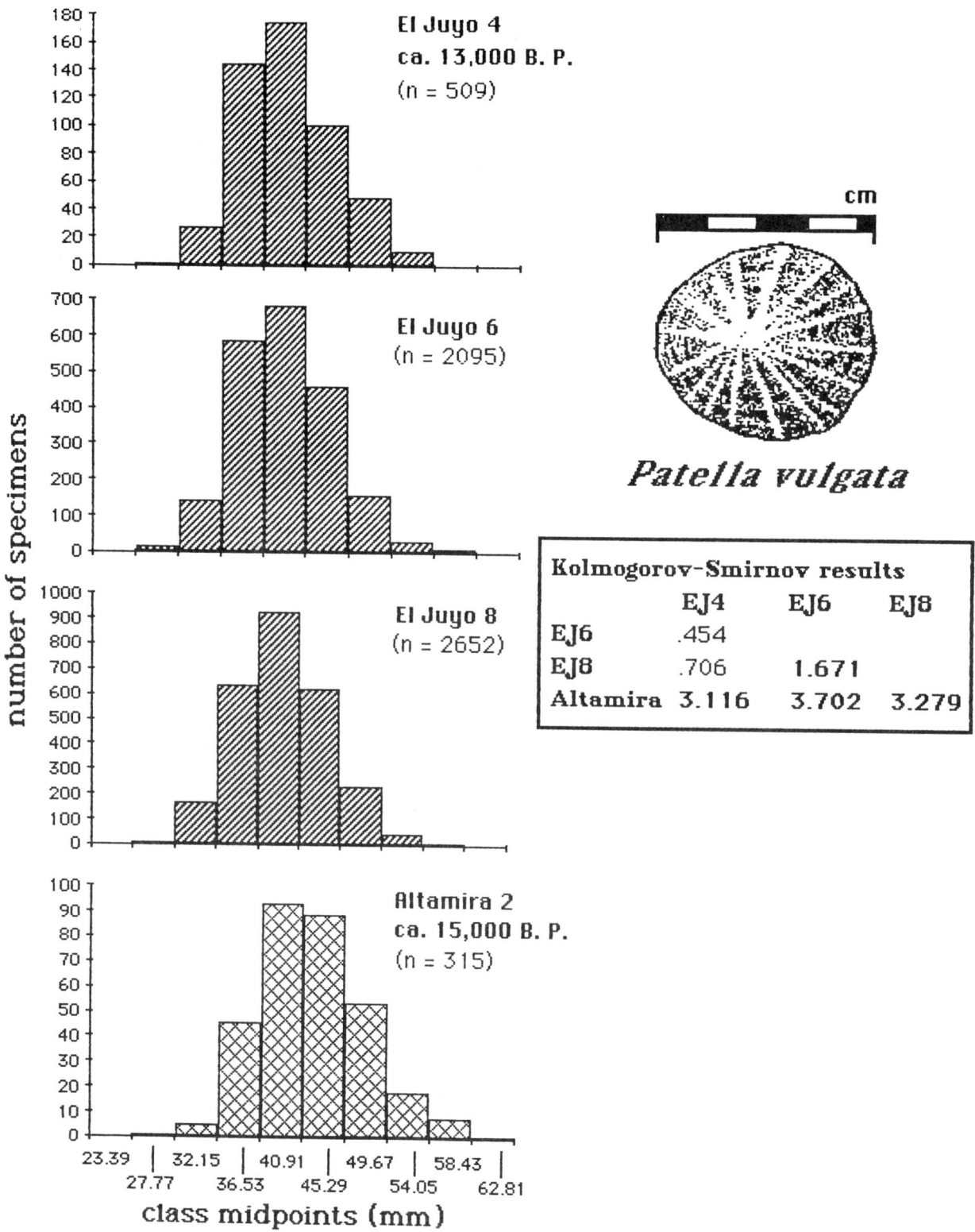

Figure 1.9 Measurements of Patella *from El Juyo and Altamira.*

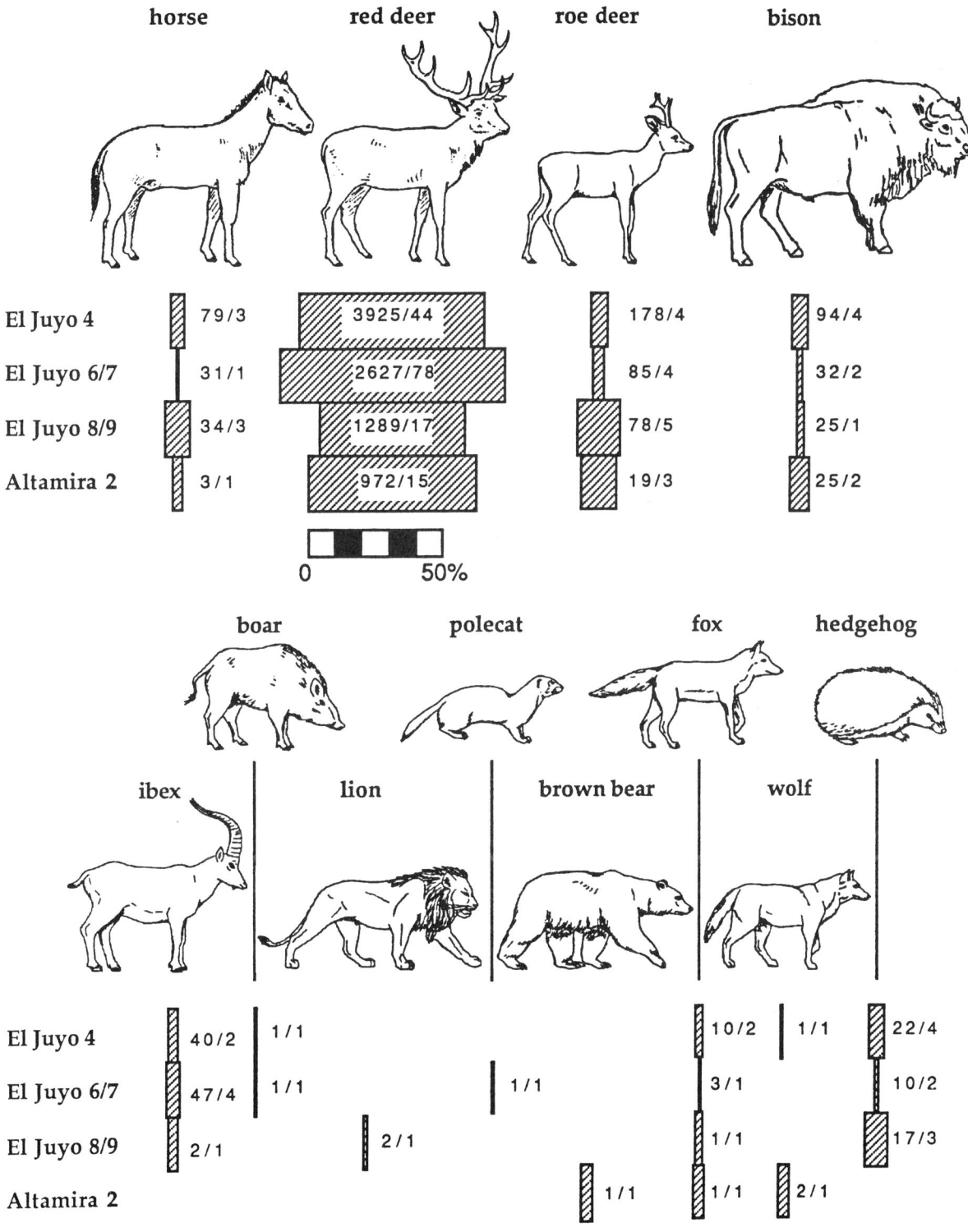

Figure 1.10 *Representations of faunal species at El Juyo and Altamira. n/n = NISP/MNI; the bars represent the percentages of each species in each level, as measured by the MNI.*

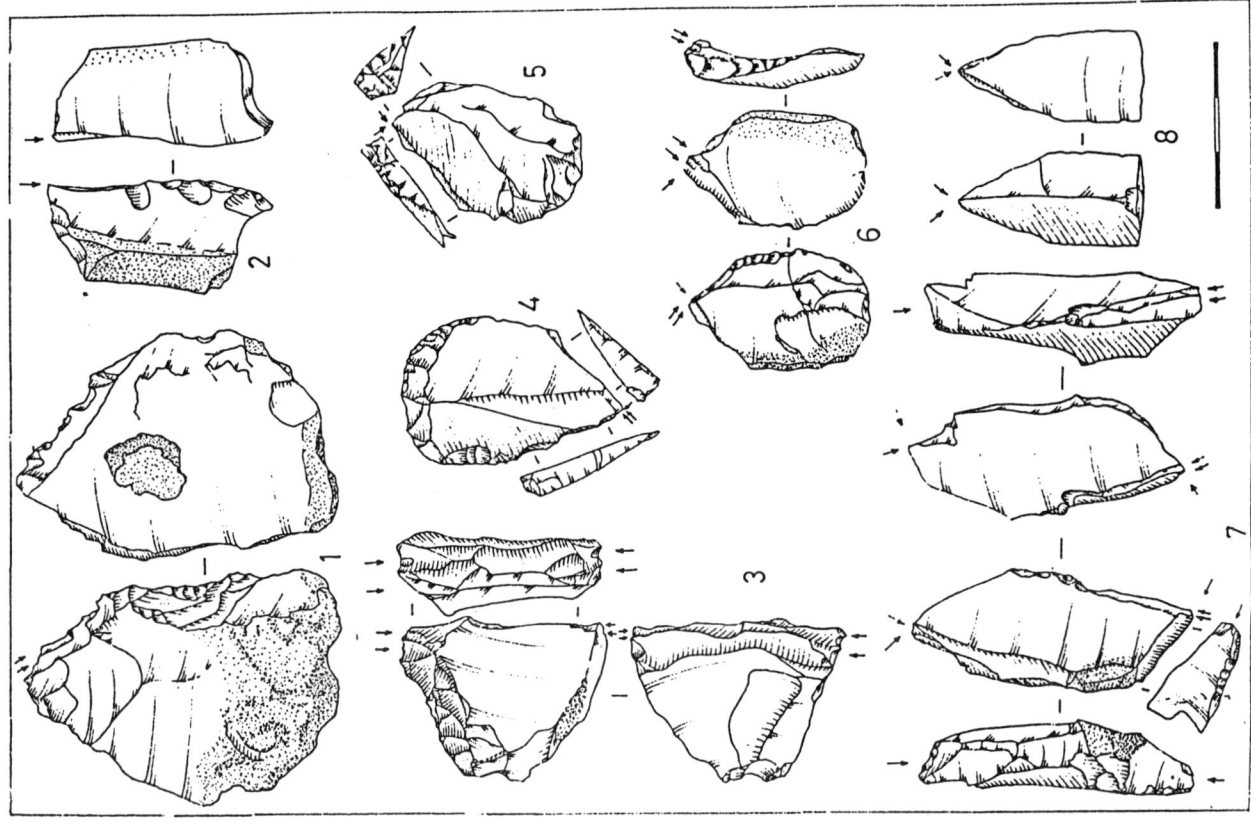
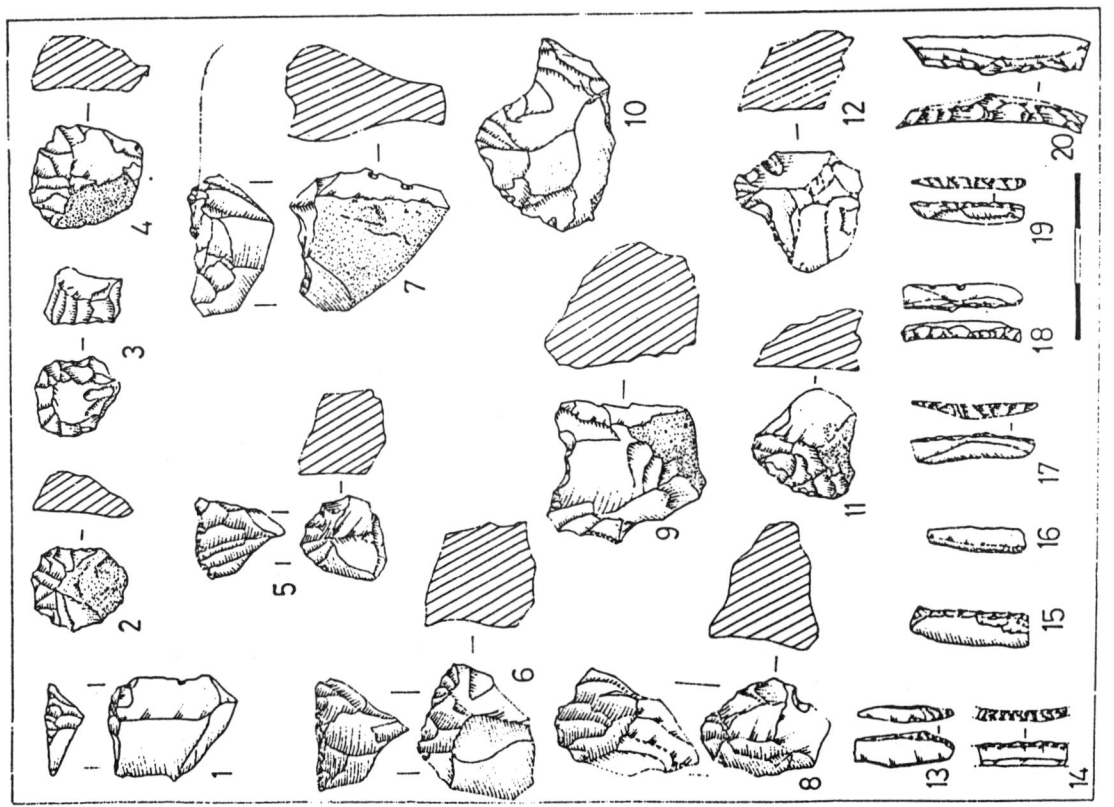

Figure 1.11 Left: stone tools from Level 4; right: stone tools from Levels 6, 7, and 8.

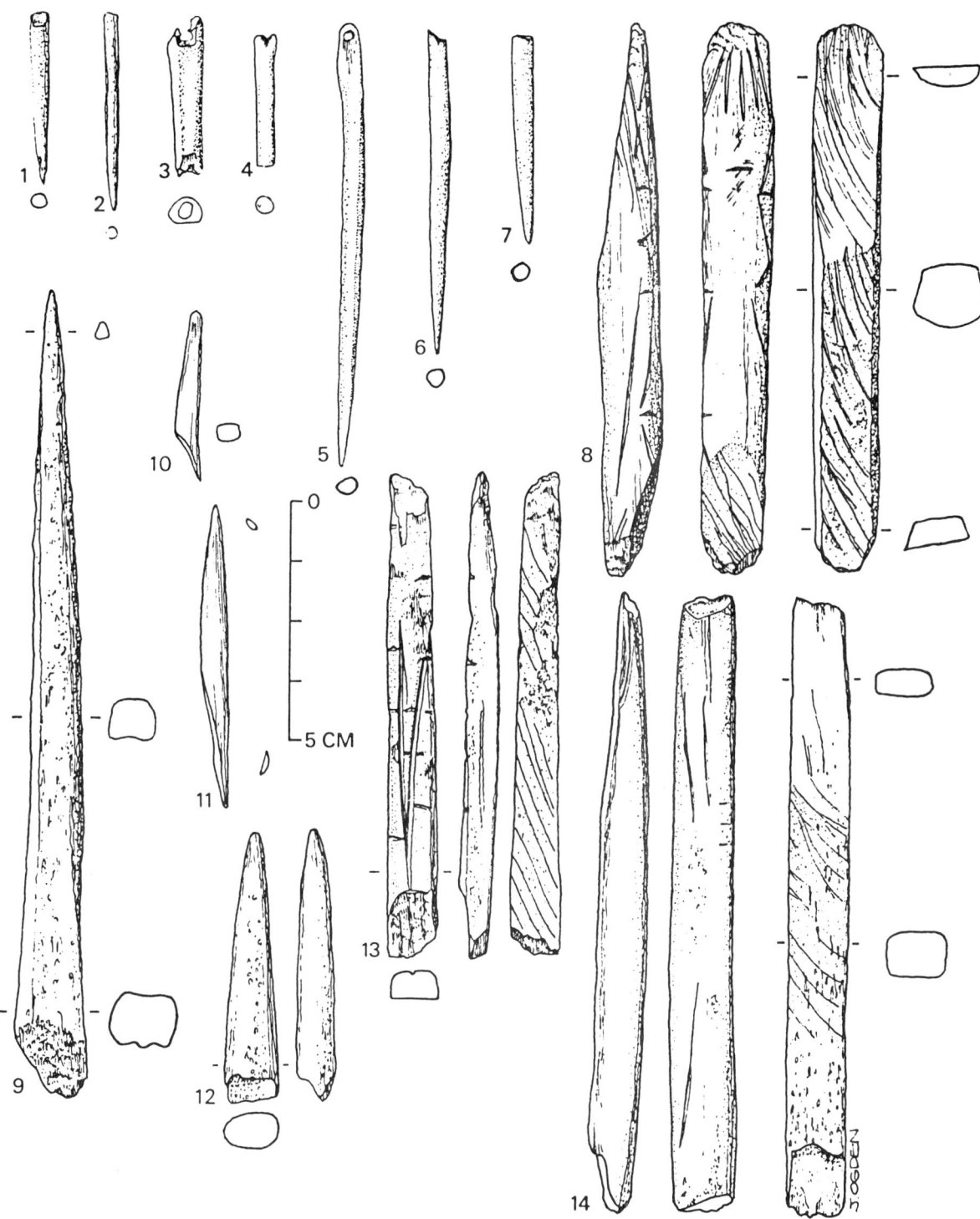

Figure 1.12 Bone artifacts.

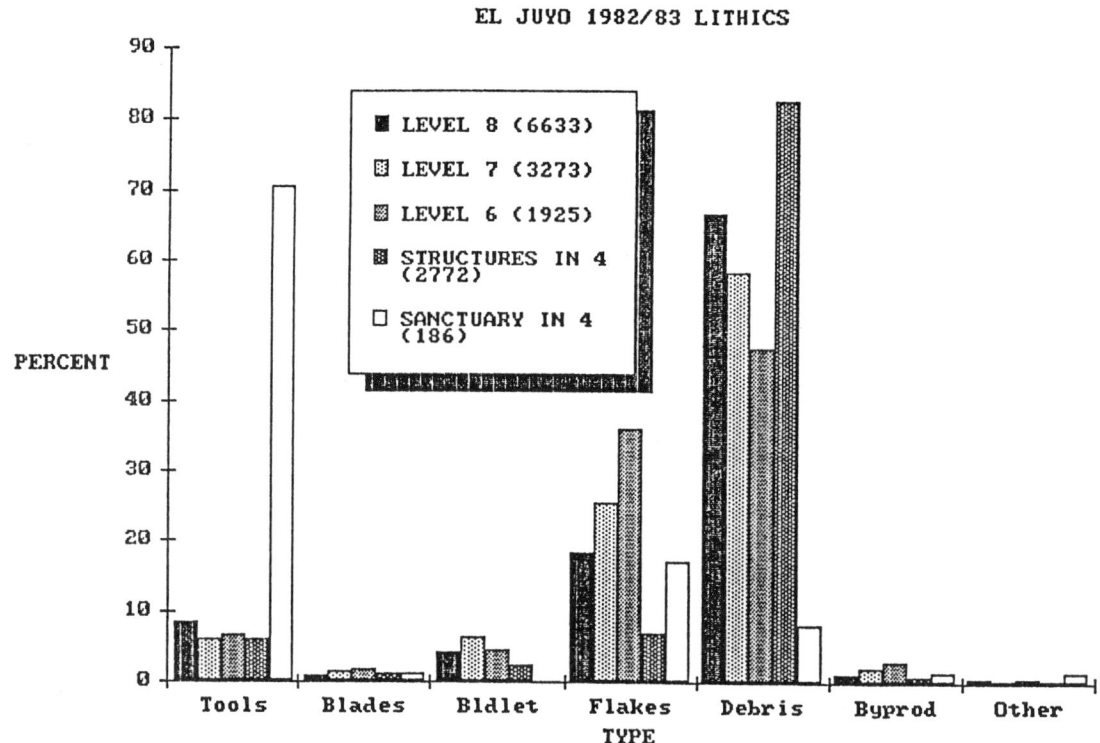

EL JUYO KOLMOGOROV SMIRNOV VALUES: 1983 COLLECTIONS

	JUYO4	JUYO4S	JUYO6	JUYO7	JUYO8	JUYO9
JUYO4	xxxxxxx					
JUYO4S	1.81059	xxxxxxx				
JUYO6	3.18965	3.41642	xxxxxxx			
JUYO7	2.30505	2.88469	<u>1.58203</u>	xxxxxxx		
JUYO8	<u>1.32871</u>	2.10676	2.87587	<u>1.49865</u>	xxxxxxx	
JUYO9	<u>1.45083</u>	1.98272	<u>1.03684</u>	<u>0.55501</u>	<u>1.21530</u>	xxxxxxx

Values greater than 1.63 significant at the <.01 level. Pairs of levels exhibiting smaller values (underlined) are considered similar. Calculations based on the de Sonneville-Bordes cumulative percentage list of retouched tools.

Figure 1.13 Characteristics of the lithic assemblages.

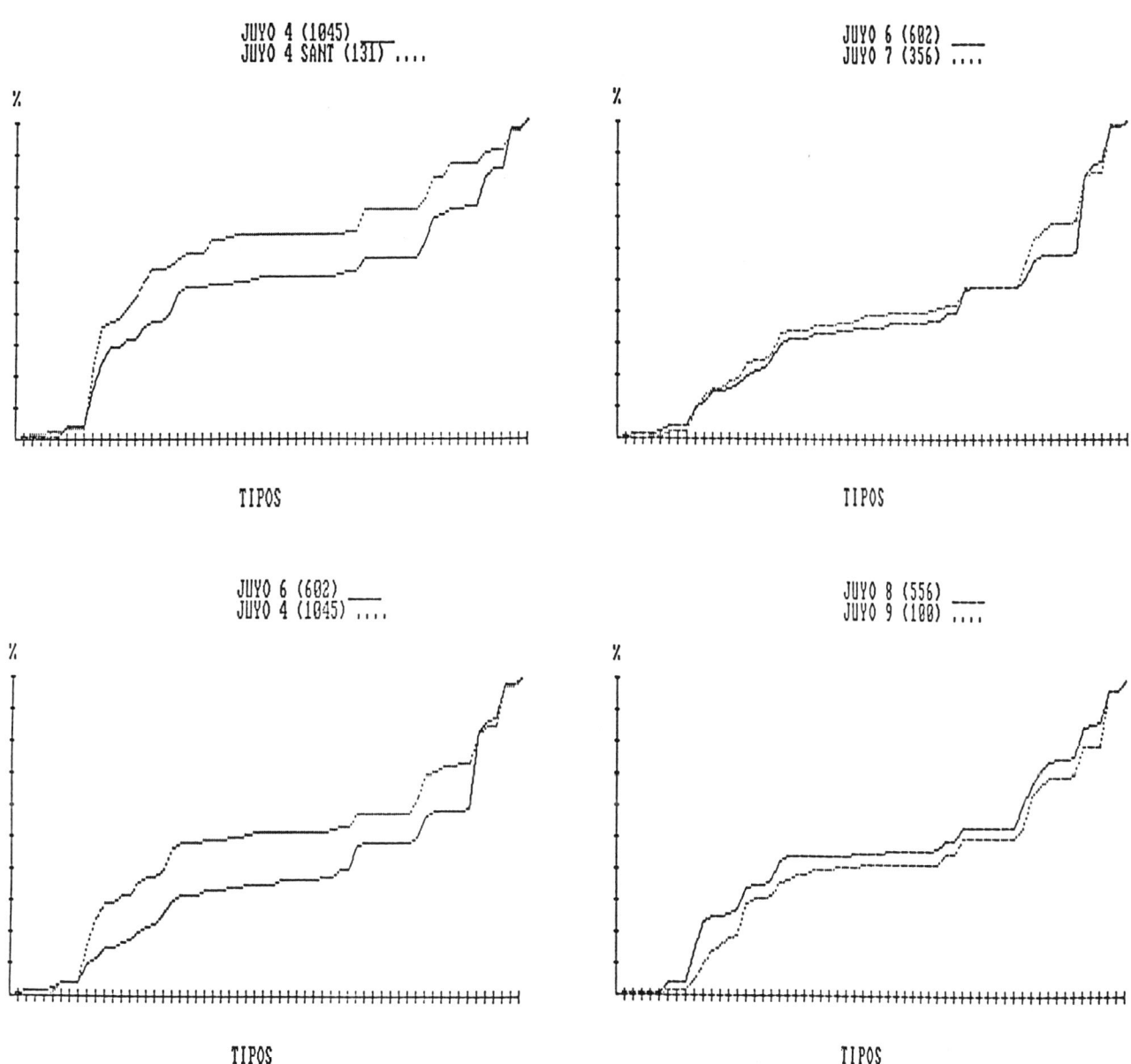

Figure 1.14 Cumulative percentage graphs of the El Juyo Magdalenian assemblages.

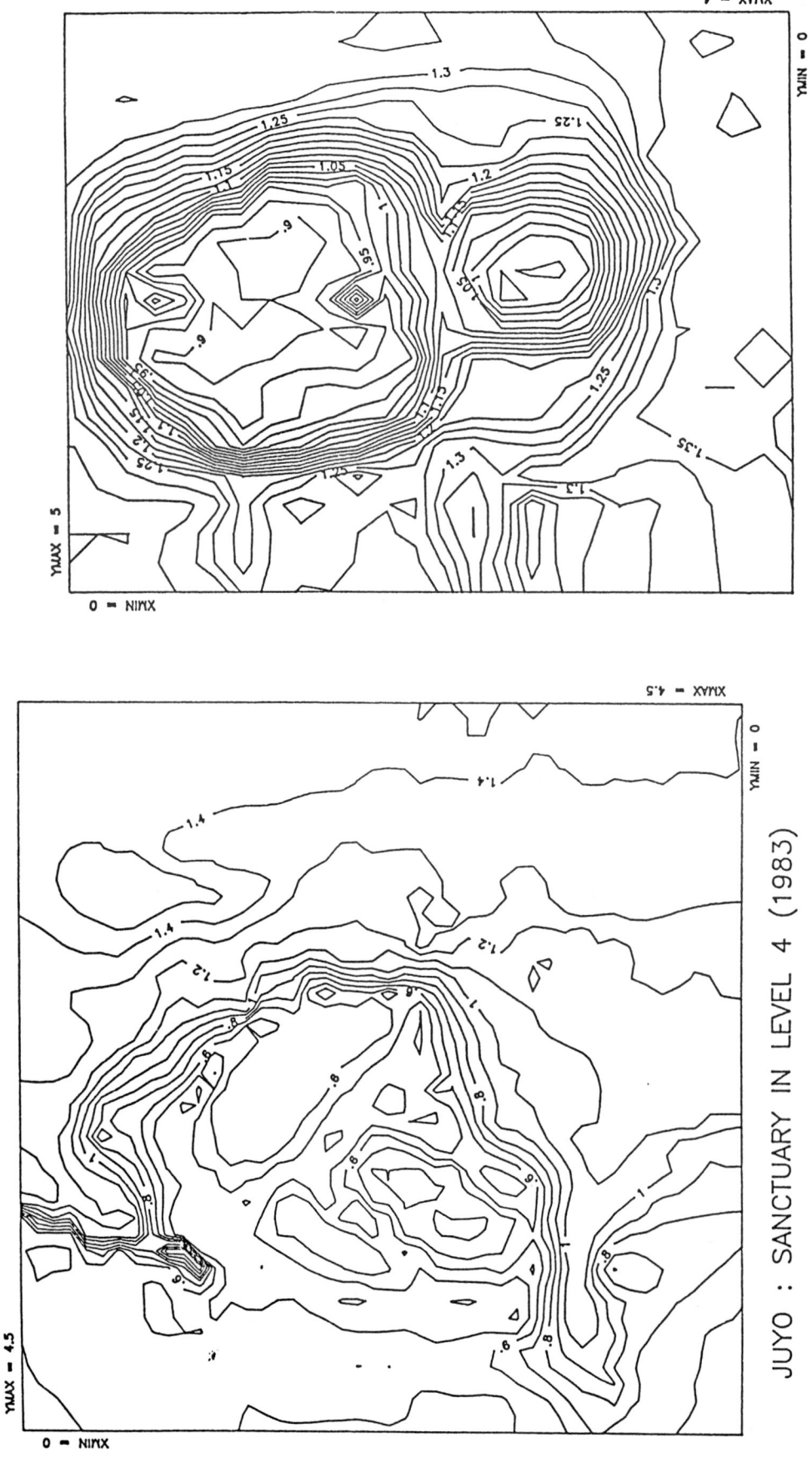

Figure 1.15 Topographic maps of Levels 4 and 6, with structures. Scale and datum are not identical. North is up.

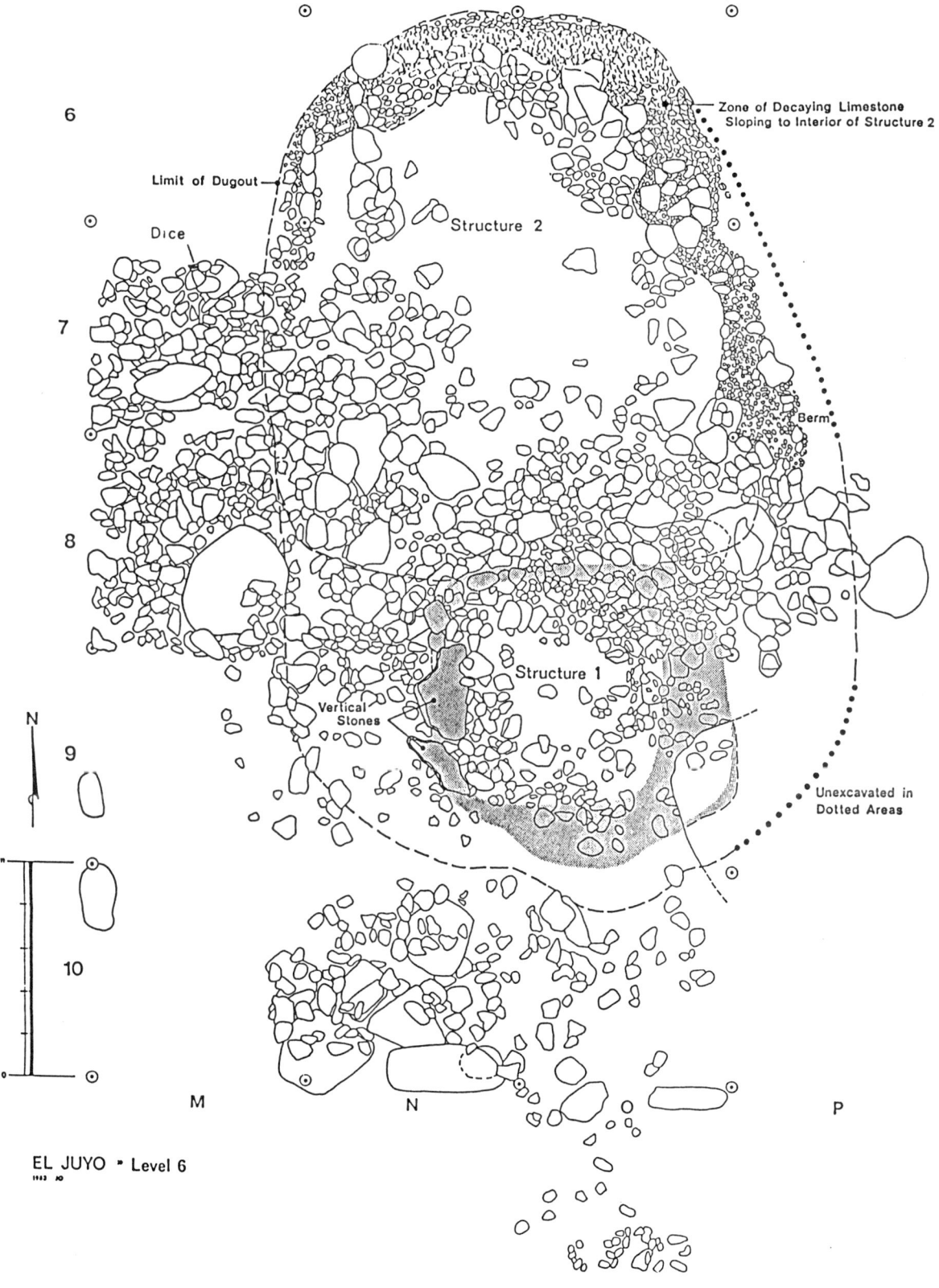

Figure 1.16 Limits of dugouts, with rubble walls and platform, Level 6.

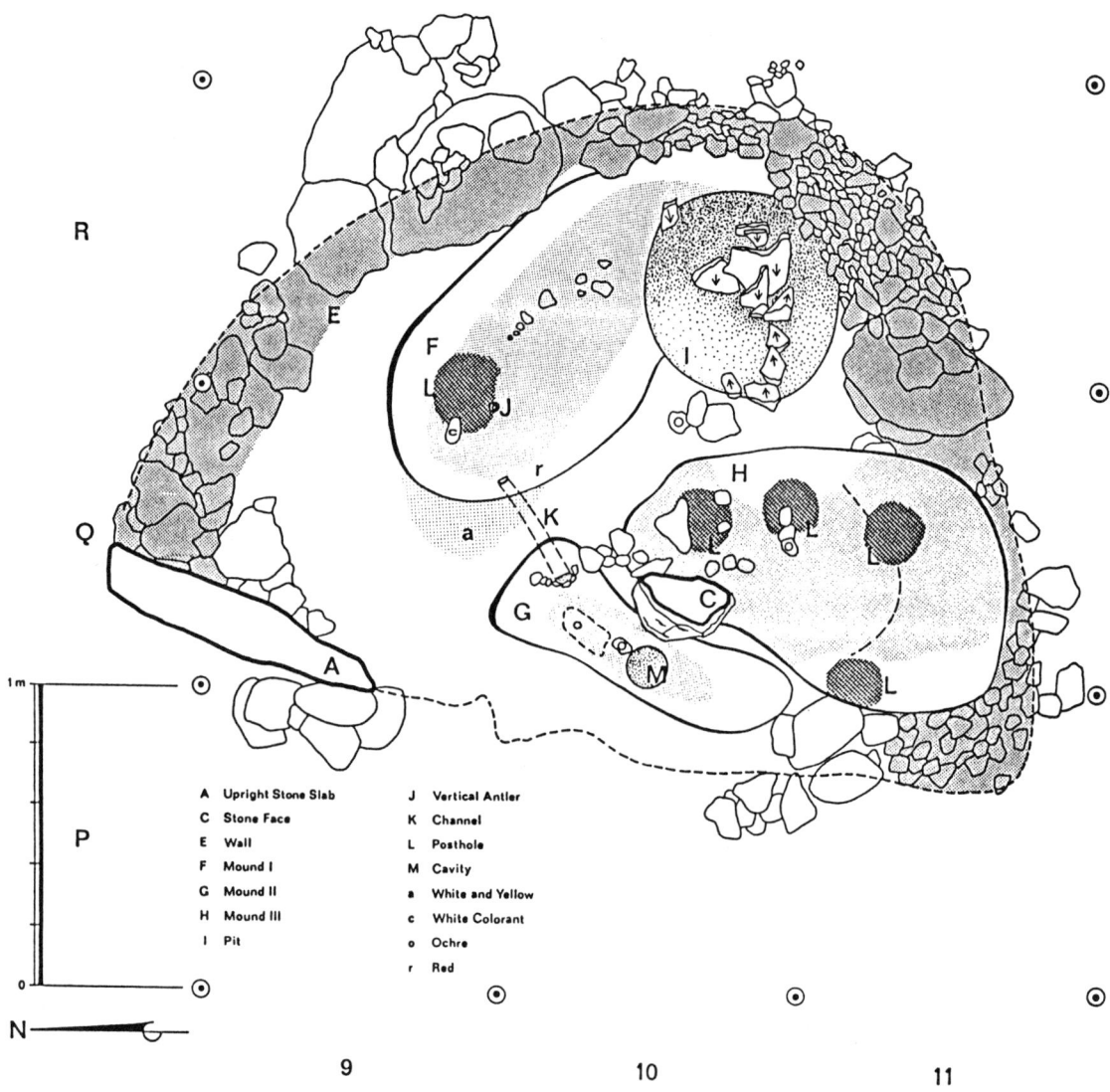

Figure 1.17 Level 4 sanctuary: an early stage of construction.

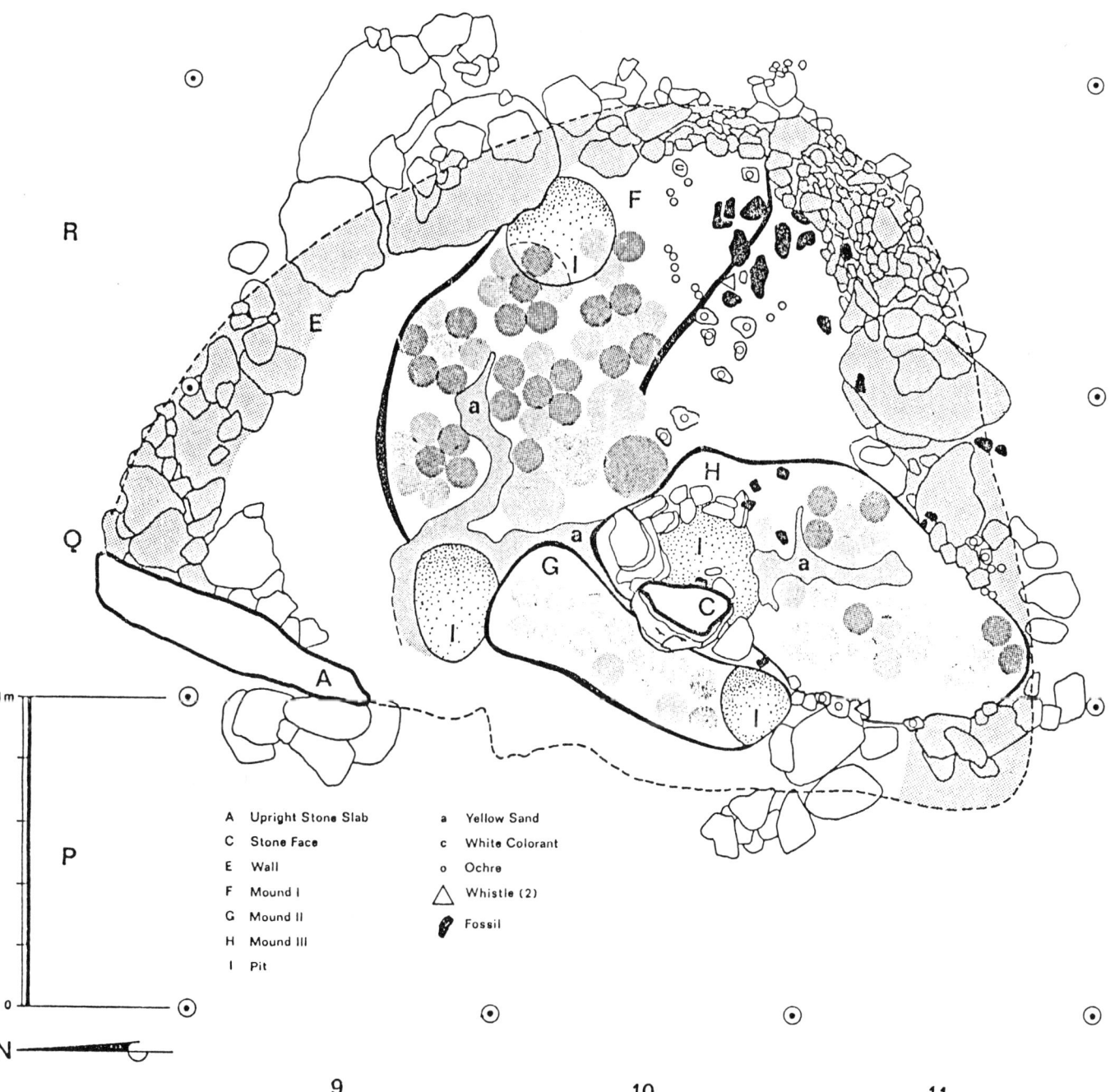

Figure 1.18   Level 4 sanctuary: a later stage of construction.

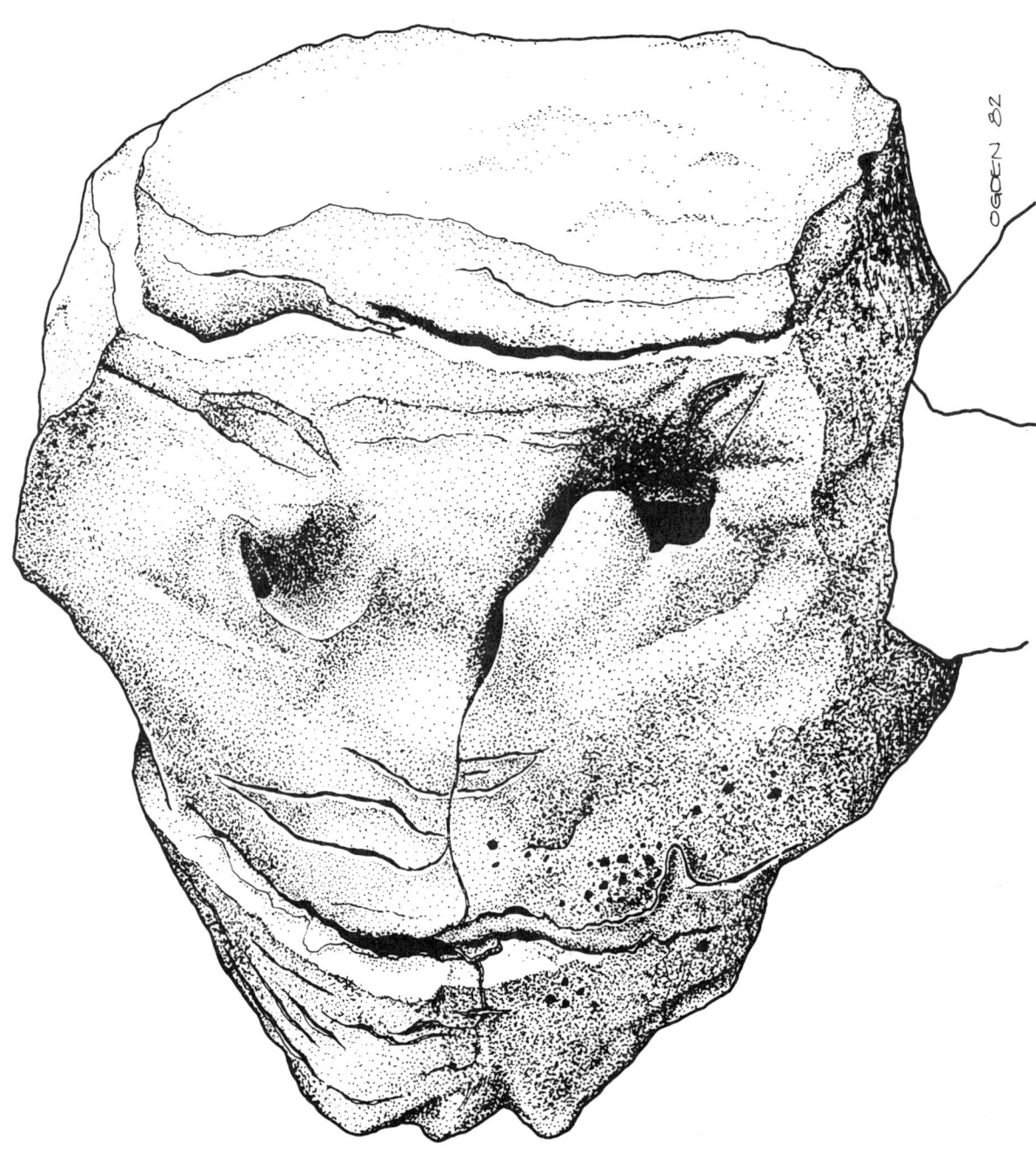

Figure 1.19 The face from the Level 4 sanctuary (35 cm tall).

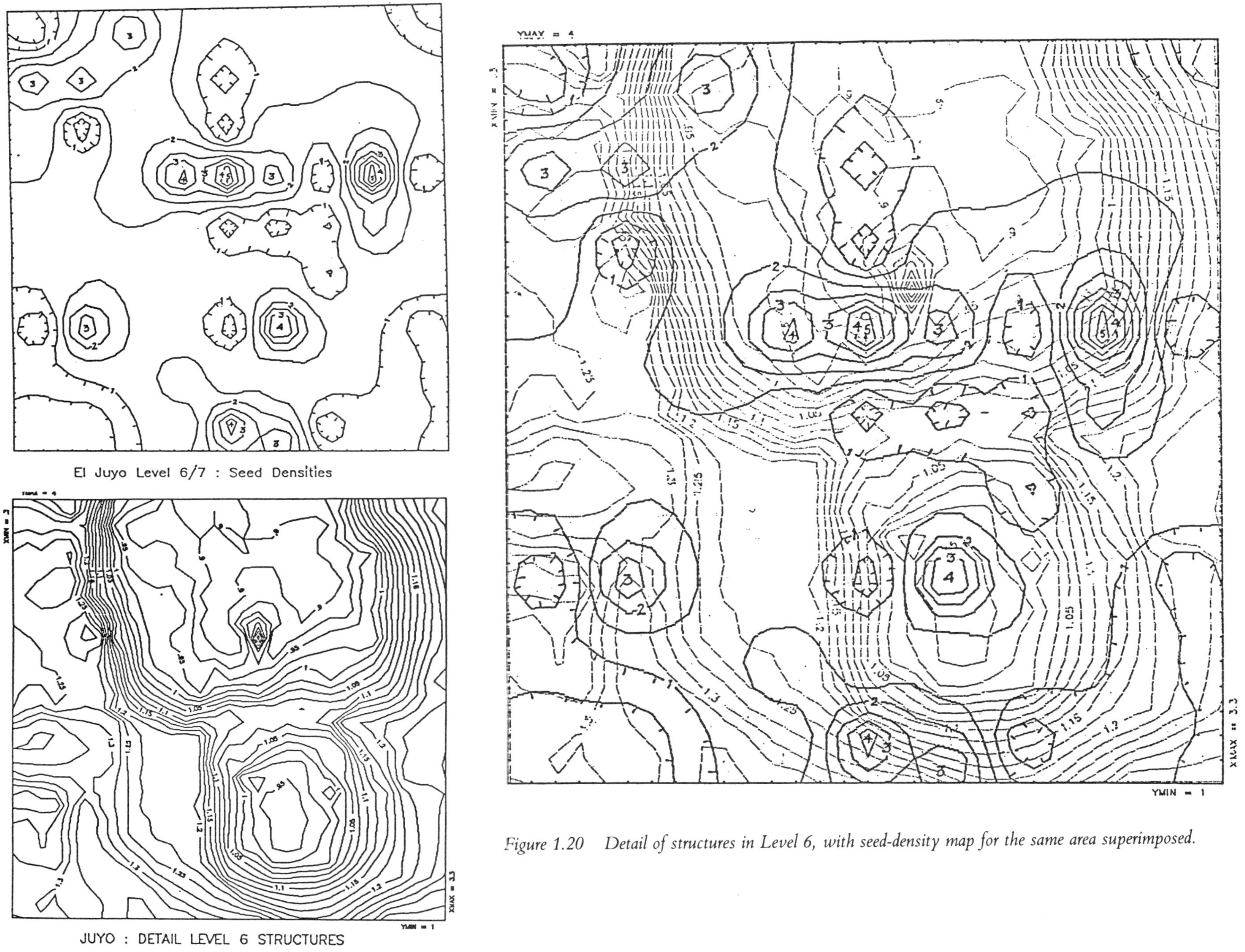

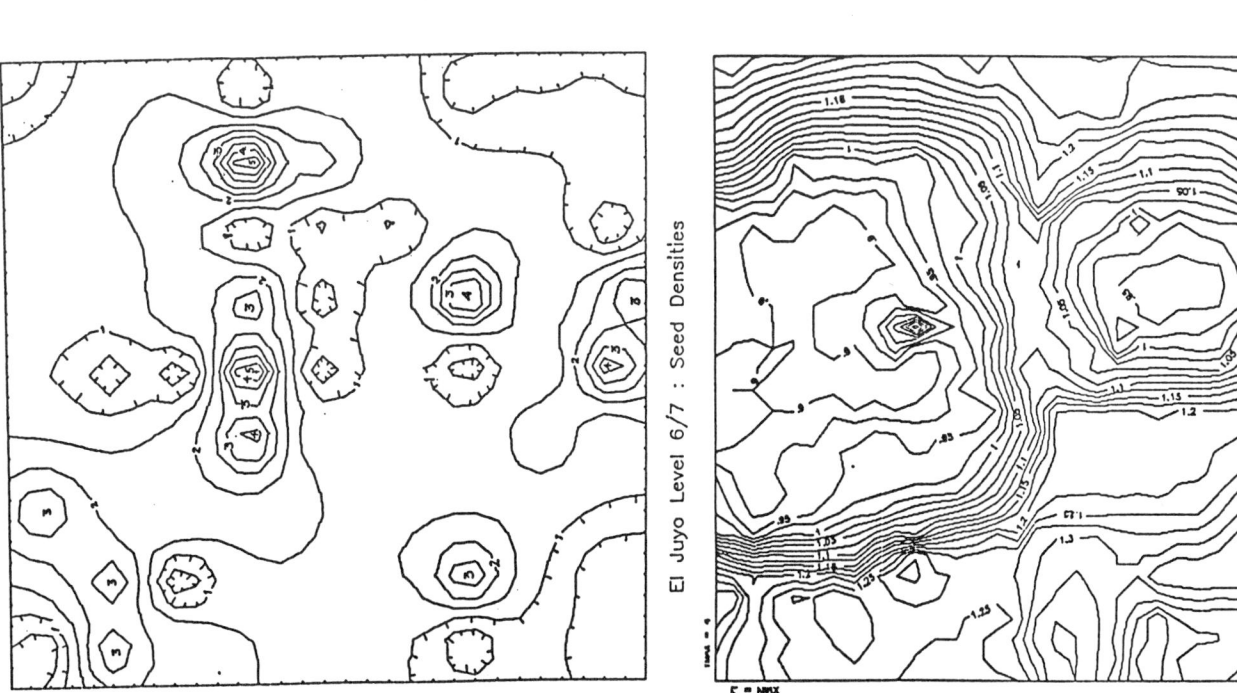

Figure 1.20 Detail of structures in Level 6, with seed-density map for the same area superimposed.

II

The Uppermost Pleistocene in Gascony
A View from Abri Dufaure
(Sorde-l'Abbaye, Les Landes, France)

Lawrence Guy Straus

INTRODUCTION

The excavation of Abri Dufaure, located at the base of the Pastou Cliff some 35 km east of Bayonne and 70 km west of Pau (Fig. 2.1), was undertaken to make detailed comparisons with the nearby site of Duruthy, to study the role of the Pastou sites in terminal Paleolithic adaptations along the northern flank of the Pyrenees, and to contribute substantive information relevant to interregional studies of the Magdalenian/Azilian—notably between southwest France and Cantabrian Spain.

From the results of the 1900 excavation of the rockshelter itself by H. Breuil and P. Dubalen (1901), it was known that Dufaure contained a cultural sequence including at least the traditionally defined Azilian and Upper Magdalenian units. From the excavations of R. Arambourou (1978) at the vast site of Duruthy, 230 m to the west-northwest, it was known that the base of the Pastou Cliff was a major focus of human occupation from ca. 14,500 B.P. through ca. 10,000 B.P. Two other sites, Le Grand Pastou and Le Petit Pastou, which lie between Duruthy and Dufaure, provided further, albeit fragmentary, information on Magdalenian occupations. The Pastou Cliff is an ideal location for terminal Paleolithic hunter-gatherers, with its south-southwest exposure (perfect for solar heating and shelter from north winds), panoramic view of the Gave d'Oloron (a natural axis of communication between the western Pyrenees and the southern Aquitaine Basin), and small rockshelters, together with the nearby ford formed by an ophite outcrop (the first ford upstream from the mouth of the Adour-Gaves fluvial system) and easy access to water, firewood, and plant foods. Seasonality information, principally from the vast, cobblestone-paved "Magdalenian VI" occupations of Alleröd age (ca. 12,000-11,000 B.P.) at Duruthy, indicate use of at least that locus as a winter camp (Arambourou 1978; Delpech 1983). Metric paleontological data suggest, furthermore, that the reindeer of Duruthy were physically larger than their Alleröd contemporaries in Guyenne (Delpech 1983). This suggests the existence of separate Pyrenean and northern Aquitaine reindeer herds, the former migrating between high summer pastures in the mountains and low winter grounds in the southern Aquitaine Basin and coastal zone. Framed as propositions, these tentative conclusions were among the ideas to be tested by the Dufaure Prehistoric Project.

More immediate goals, however, were to compare the stratigraphies, absolute chronologies, paleoenvironmental indicators, structural features, artifact and faunal assemblages of Dufaure and Duruthy. Such comparisons could shed light on functional similarities and differences between the two sites. Then, together with seasonality indicators, analysis of all these data could help determine whether the Pastou was part of a regular, repeated pattern of human settlement and subsistence activities related to the structured availability of major food sources (reindeer, bison, horse, salmon). In short, were the findings at Duruthy replicated at Dufaure? If so, then the Pastou was indeed a major "place" (consisting of several contiguous settlement loci) within the routine Magdalenian settlement system (annual round) in the Pyrenean region. In this case, shifting use of the shelters and terraces at Duruthy, Dufaure, Le Grand and Le Petit Pastou could have been a matter determined by the build-up of trash and vermin or by such

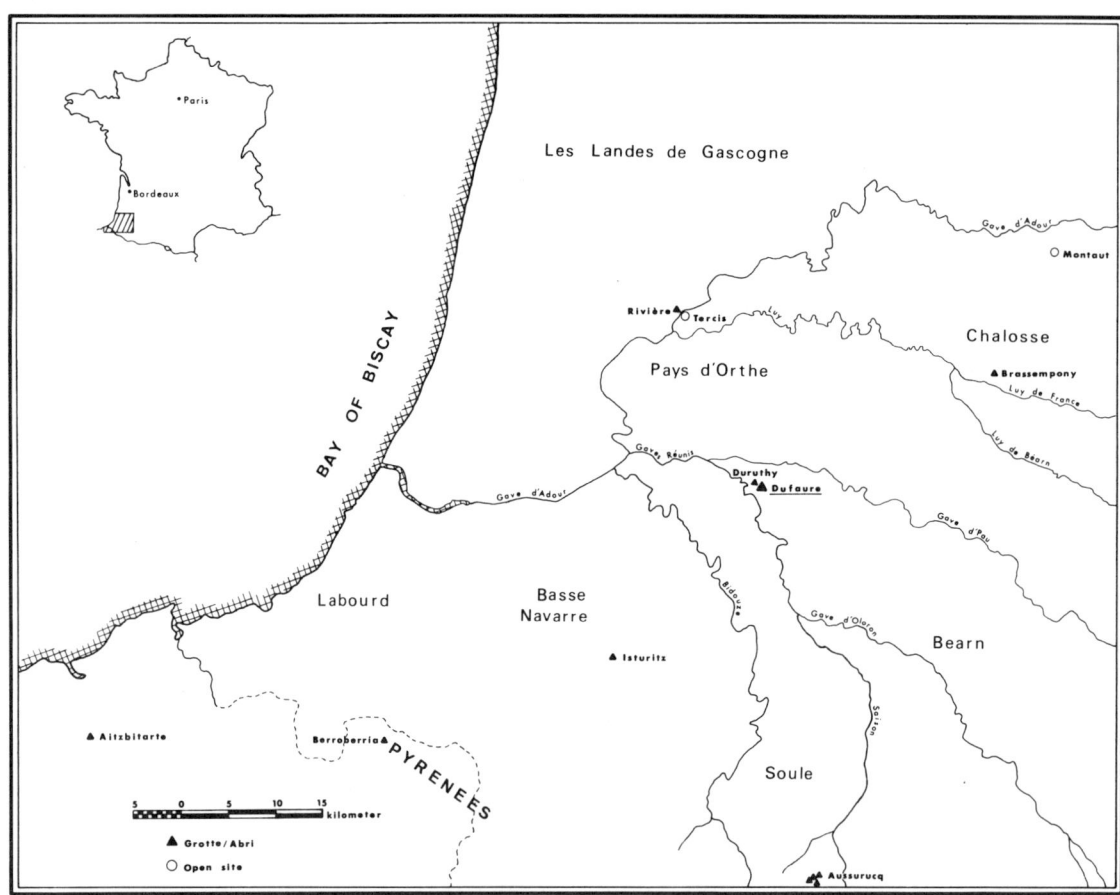

Figure 2.1 Map of extreme southwestern France showing the location of Dufaure and other sites.

intangibles as taboos on sites of disease or death. The re-excavation of Dufaure is thus in part an attempt to replicate an "experiment," namely the excavation of Duruthy. The controls established in this experimental study of site function and human behavior are spatial ("place" is essentially held constant) and temporal (comparisons can be made on the basis of *independent* chronological indicators).

A major goal of Upper Paleolithic research should be the comparison of *regional* adaptive systems which coexisted during particular chronoclimatic phases of the late Last Glacial. Present indications suggest the existence of several late Upper Paleolithic regional adaptive systems in southwest Europe alone (based on fundamental topographical and zoological differences). These include the regions formed by the present-day Charentes-Dordogne-Lot-Corrèze, Provence, the Pyrenees, Languedoc-Catalonia, Levantine Spain, north-central Portugal, and Vasco-Cantabrian Spain.

Each region, while sharing basic technological, chronostratigraphic, and artistic similarities with the others, seems to have had distinctive characteristics as manifested in subsistence and settlement patterns, and possibly differences in art style. Very different human mobility strategies were followed, based on the differing resource structures of these regions (e.g., Straus 1986c). The Pyrenees were a region of major Magdalenian occupation based heavily upon the exploitation of broadly migratory ungulate herd species (plus salmon and ibex), with a distinctive suite of "mobile art" types and motifs, particularly in its "Middle" phase, ca. 14,000 B.P. Despite identical latitude (43° N) along the northern edge of the same mountain chain, there seem to have been significant differences between the Pyrenean and Cantabrian culture areas in the last few millennia of the Last Glacial.

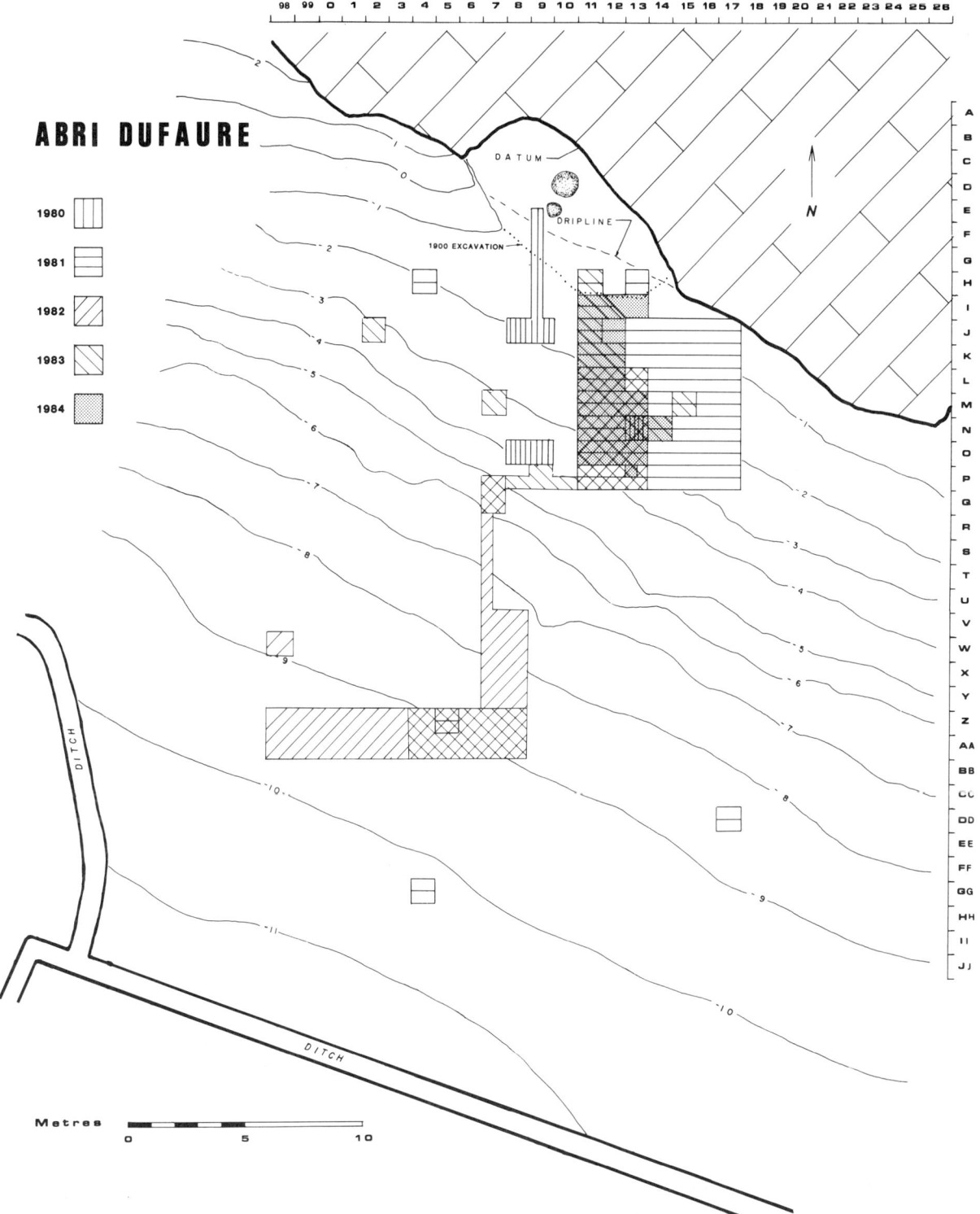

Figure 2.2   Plan of the Dufaure site showing 1-m contours and excavation areas.

BACKGROUND

The site of Abri Dufaure consists of a small rockshelter; a narrow, level terrace area in front of the shelter; a relatively gentle upper slope; a steep break-in-slope; and a footslope area that flattens and grades into the "Würm II" alluvial terrace of the Gave d'Oloron (Fig. 2.2). The site was tested in July 1980; an apparently intact cobblestone pavement surface was discovered in the center of the slope area in front of the eastern side of the shelter, whereas the archaeological deposits were shown to be either disturbed or totally eroded in the western sector of the slope. The cobblestone pavement was clearly a continuation of the one found by Breuil and Dubalen in the shelter and seemed directly homologous to the Couche 3 pavements of Duruthy. Both had yielded Upper Magdalenian harpoons.

THE TERRACE AND UPPER SLOPE

Full-scale excavations were conducted for a total of 12 months in 1981-84. They revealed the following stratigraphy (Fig. 2.3) in the terrace and upper slope area (the rectangle between the I-P and 11-13 or 17 rows):

Stratum 1: dark gray humus and backdirt from the previous excavations.

Stratum 2: yellowish brown colluvial silt and comminuted, nummulitic limestone éboulis (debris) with recent ceramics.

Stratum 3: an éboulis-rich, wedge-shaped layer (thick toward the east, thinner and then absent toward the west and downslope [southward]) with a colluvial silt matrix and low-density, patchy cultural remains. Stratum 3 is thus essentially absent in the 10/11 section. Bone-collagen dates from this stratum are: middle 9600 ± 290 B.P. (Ly-4224), lower-middle $10,310 \pm 270$ B.P. (Ly-4223). Radiocarbon dates from mid-stratum: 9750 ± 110 (AA-2477), 9810 ± 100 (AA-2478).

Stratum 4: a highly anthropogenic horizon formed of cobblestone pavements, with very large quantities of artifacts and faunal remains, in a colluvial silt matrix often forming lenses between pavements. Radiocarbon dates: top $10,910 \pm 220$ B.P. (Ly-1666), middle $11,750 \pm 300$ B.P. (Ly-3181), $12,030 \pm 280$ B.P. (Ly-3245), base $12,260 \pm 400$ B.P. (Ly-3182).

Stratum 5: a deposit also composed of silt, comminuted éboulis, and large limestone blocks with abundant but patchy, discontinuous cultural remains including burnt sandstone plaquettes. The stratum is absent (due to erosion?) on the terrace. There may have been remnants of it in the rockshelter. Radiocarbon dates: $12,690 \pm 230$ B.P. (Ly-3591), $12,990 \pm 270$ B.P. (Ly-2923), base $14,570 \pm 390$ B.P. (Ly-3582).

Stratum 6: a yellowish brown silty clay deposit enveloping very large limestone blocks and containing sparse cultural remains. This deposit is in direct contact with bedrock at least at the upper edge of the slope. It is absent on the terrace. Radiocarbon date: top $14,020 \pm 340$ B.P. (Ly-3583). The presence of saiga antelope coincides with the population "explosion" of this species in Aquitaine during Dryas I (Delpech 1983).

THE FOOTSLOPE

In 1981, a test pit was dug at the foot of the talus slope. Beneath surficial layers containing rolled éboulis, some cobbles, and cultural remains—including both Upper Paleolithic flint tools and ceramics of a variety of ages—a layer of densely packed cobbles was encountered. This layer was initially interpreted as a continuation of the Stratum 4 pavements, a hypothesis made reasonable by the continuous extension of such pavements in Couche 3 down the length of the slope at Duruthy. Other test pits, however, confirmed the disturbed character or absence of the pavements at the eastern and far southern ends of the footslope area.

An area of 10 sq. m of cobble pavement surface was subsequently excavated at the footslope. Ceramics were found down to contact with it in 1982, and they continued to be found among and beneath the cobbles in 1983. The excavation area was reduced to 4 sq. m upon recognition of the disturbed nature of the cobblestone layers, now renamed "Stratum IV." The first few layers of cobbles ("pseudo-pavements") yielded 113 sherds; this is in striking contrast to the cobble pavements of Stratum 4 on the terrace and upper slope, which contained not a single intrusive artifact (the case also with Strata 3, 5, and 6). Stratum IV sherds are Gallo-Roman in age. Their discovery required an explanation and a detailed investigation of the process of site formation and disturbance at Abri Dufaure.

SITE FORMATION/DISTURBANCE PROCESSES

Pending the results of ongoing research by H. Laville, D. Marguerie, and M. Petraglia, I will give a

Figure 2.3 Stratigraphic section at the western end of the terrace-slope excavation area (between the 10 and 11 rows).

brief discussion of the arguments for varying degrees of intactness of the archaeological deposits in the central excavation area on the terrace and slope and for redeposition of the footslope deposits.

Stratum 3, like Couche 2 at Duruthy, shows evidence of a limited Azilian occupation within the rockshelter (indicated by the 1900 discovery of a fragment of a flat-section harpoon and engraved and painted pebbles) and on the terrace immediately in front of the dripline, where a remnant of an apparent living surface was found. Flakes in this small area tend to be heavier than those found on the slope. Elsewhere, in the upper slope area, artifacts and generally comminuted bones are scattered in patches amongst the éboulis blocks and may have washed or been tossed down from the habitation area along the cliff's base. Computer back-plotting of all piece-plotted cultural remains found no evidence of *continuous* lenses within the whole area of Stratum 3. There are no constructed features in Stratum 3 on the terrace or slope.

Stratum 4 is composed of layer after layer of densely packed cobblestones, forming distinct "pavements" like those at Duruthy and at the open-air sites of the Isle Valley in Dordogne (Gaussen 1980). The remnant area of intact pavements has definite boundaries in the east-central part of the upper slope beyond which the cobbles are increasingly dispersed and ultimately absent. Faunal remains are well preserved, and there are instances of several vertebrae and phalanges found in anatomical connection. *Sagaies* (spearpoints) and other delicate antler artifacts were also well preserved, and there are cases of refittable fragments (including one harpoon) found in direct contiguity. Lithic refitting supplies further evidence of Stratum 4's intactness. In Square I11 two nodules of petrographically distinct chalcedony were reduced in situ, producing large numbers of debitage items that remained within a radius of less than a meter of the cores. Many of the over 100 flakes refit. Chalcedony is otherwise extremely rare in Stratum 4, having *not* moved downslope from the terrace knapping locus. Another group of over 100 items of a distinctive green spotted flint (some of which refit) was also localized in the terrace area. A core, four large flakes, and several other pieces of debris that refit to form a nearly complete block were also found together in the terrace area. Numerous other refits of broken artifacts (or examples of objects from very distinctive, rare lithic raw materials which do not directly refit) indicate little vertical or horizontal movement within Stratum 4 (Straus and Petraglia 1985). There is no tendency for the lighter lithics or bones to be accumulated downslope, as would be the case with transport by running water. Computer analyses found some tendency for a north-northeast orientation among the elongated artifacts and bones (i.e., roughly parallel to the slope), although this indicator of possible displacement by flow processes is not very marked. Inclinations basically follow the lay of the land, showing no evidence of significant jumbling by solifluction, cryoturbation, etc. There are, however, definite clusters of burned *éboulis*, cobbles, and artifacts, suggesting the presence of in situ burning areas whose lithic products have not moved since their alteration by fire. These areas of burning are in different locations within the 30- to 50-cm-thick internal stratigraphy of Stratum 4, but each area is composed of burned lithics from two or more contiguous spits (vertical excavation subdivisions of the stratum corresponding here to single layers of cobbles). Thus the stratum has structural integrity in an area of at least 25 sq. m (see Petraglia 1987).

Stratum 5 begins abruptly at the edge of the foot of the previous cliff line in the J row; it is absent in the area of the bedrock threshold of the rockshelter where the cobblestones of Stratum 4 were laid down on bare rock. It is probable that Stratum 5, formed in late Dryas I and early Bölling, had earlier been eroded from this area (and disturbed downslope) at the end of the humid Bölling oscillation. There are no broadly continuous "occupation surfaces" within Stratum 5, but there are areas of evident intactness. In N11 a "cache" of unusually large flakes of good-quality flint was found surrounded and covered by *éboulis* blocks. The flakes all refit. This cache had clearly survived erosion, but so too had localized clusters of scores of rare quartz crystal artifacts (including cores and retouched pieces) found within a couple of squares on the slope. Stratum 5 is typified by the presence of burnt sandstone slabs. In penecontemporaneous Couche 4 at Duruthy, these "plaquettes" formed consistent pavements in the areas excavated by Arambourou (1978). At Dufaure the "plaquettes" are jumbled and tend to be accumulated in the lower squares of the slope area. Thus Stratum 5 seems to be characterized by variably *patchy* and generally only *relative* intactness.

Stratum 6 was excavated in only a few squares on the slope. Artifacts and bones are few and scattered within the yellowish silty clay matrix and seem to form no occupation surfaces. It was probably formed in mid-Dryas I and pre-Bölling times.

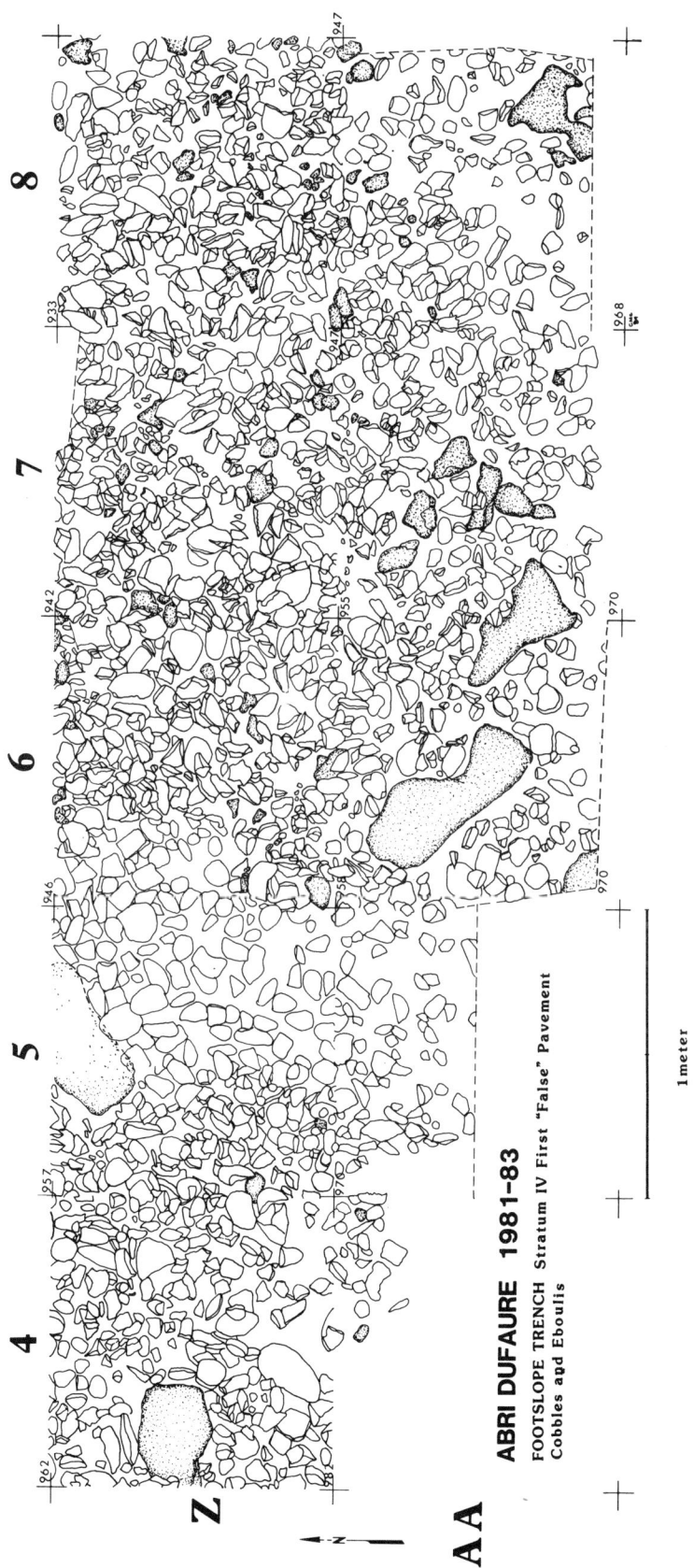

Figure 2.4 Stratum IV "pseudo-pavement" (footslope area).

Stratum IV can best be described in relationship to Stratum 4, since its principal constituents (cobbles, Magdalenian-type lithic artifacts, terminal Pleistocene faunal remains) seem to have originated in the deposits of the terrace and slope (Fig. 2.4). Not only do the Stratum IV pseudo-pavements contain ceramics, but the lithic artifacts are far more generally and heavily patinated than in Stratum 4. The faunal remains in Stratum IV include no mandibles (so abundant in Stratum 4) and few other fragile elements, and are dominated by the densest, most massive elements (all heavily rolled and battered). The cobbles seem to be distributed in lobelike formations, and fanlike lenses of "fines" (bone splinters and debitage) were observed in the upslope row of squares. There are no clusters of artifacts, bones, or burned items that could be interpreted as residues of activity areas. The preferred orientations of elongated objects are *parallel* to the axis of the slope, suggesting that some flow mechanism was involved in the redeposition of these materials at the basal inflection point of the talus slope, whose profile is of typical sinusoidal form. Inclinations tend to be jumbled despite the fairly level lay of the land at the footslope. Furthermore, there is evidence of a greater degree of fragmentation of the Stratum IV artifacts than of those of Stratum 4. The substantial presence of Gallo-Roman sherds mixed in with these materials clearly suggests that their erosion from the top of the talus (probably in a massive solifluction event from the eastern part of the upper slope, where *no* remains of Strata 3 or 4 are currently present) took place in the early centuries of the modern era, when there were Roman villas nearby in the Gave d'Oloron valley and an earthwork directly above the Pastou sites on the plateau summit. The upper and lower excavation areas were connected by a stratigraphic trench dug to clarify the sequence of events leading to the destruction of archaeological deposits on the eastern terrace and slope and their redeposition at the footslope. The abrupt end of the intact cobblestone pavements is well documented at the break-in-slope, where the erosional scar is filled with disturbed sediments rich in derived Magdalenian artifacts, overlying intact Stratum 6 (Fig. 2.5). At this point begin the surficial redeposited footslope layers (including Strata IIIa-c). A small sondage was dug all the way through the pseudo-pavements of Stratum IV (about 60 cm thick). At their base was uncovered a yellowish silty clay layer with a magnificently preserved bovine hemi-mandible and Magdalenian artifacts, apparent testimony to the continuity of at least Stratum 6 throughout the whole length of the talus slope. It had been overlain by several "generations" of solifluction and colluviation deposits.

RÉSUMÉ OF THE CULTURAL STRATIGRAPHY

STRATUM 3

Stratum 3, formed during the Dryas III and Preboreal (according to palynological data), is contemporary with the remnant Azilian deposit at Duruthy, Couche 2 (Paquereau 1978a, n.d.). Stratum 3 yielded 322 retouched tools and 12,274 lithic debris items (cores and debitage), giving a ratio of one tool per 38.1 pieces of debris. (Stratum 4's ratio, on the other hand, was one tool per 18.0 debris items). On average the flakes and blades from Stratum 3 are relatively short (16.5 mm and 36.6 mm respectively, vs. 30.1 mm and 39.5 mm for Stratum 4). Tool group indices are presented in Table 2.1. As can be seen, the Stratum 3 assemblage is typically Azilian in having many more endscrapers than burins. The former are shorter (28.25 mm) than those of Stratum 4 (36.6 mm); about half of the Stratum 3 endscrapers are made on flakes. Backed bladelets make up nearly half the assemblage, while the 21 Azilian points represent 6.5%. The Duruthy Couche 2 assemblage yielded only 106 lithic tools—the principal occupation area in the rockshelter having been dug out in 1874 (Arambourou 1978). No bone tools were found in the recent excavations of the small, thin Azilian remnant deposit. Again endscrapers (40.6%—many on flakes) outnum-

TABLE 2.1
ABRI DUFAURE TOOL-GROUP INDICES

Indices	Stratum				
	3	4	5	6	IV
IG	15.3	8.9	7.7	8.6	7.6
IB	9.7	12.4	13.8	24.7	14.0
IBd	7.8	8.6	11.5	11.5	7.7
IP	0.6	2.4	1.8	4.9	2.3
I1d*	44.7	44.8	43.7	28.4	50.3
ID+	6.3	5.1	5.7	8.6	7.1

* backed bladelets
+ denticulates & notches

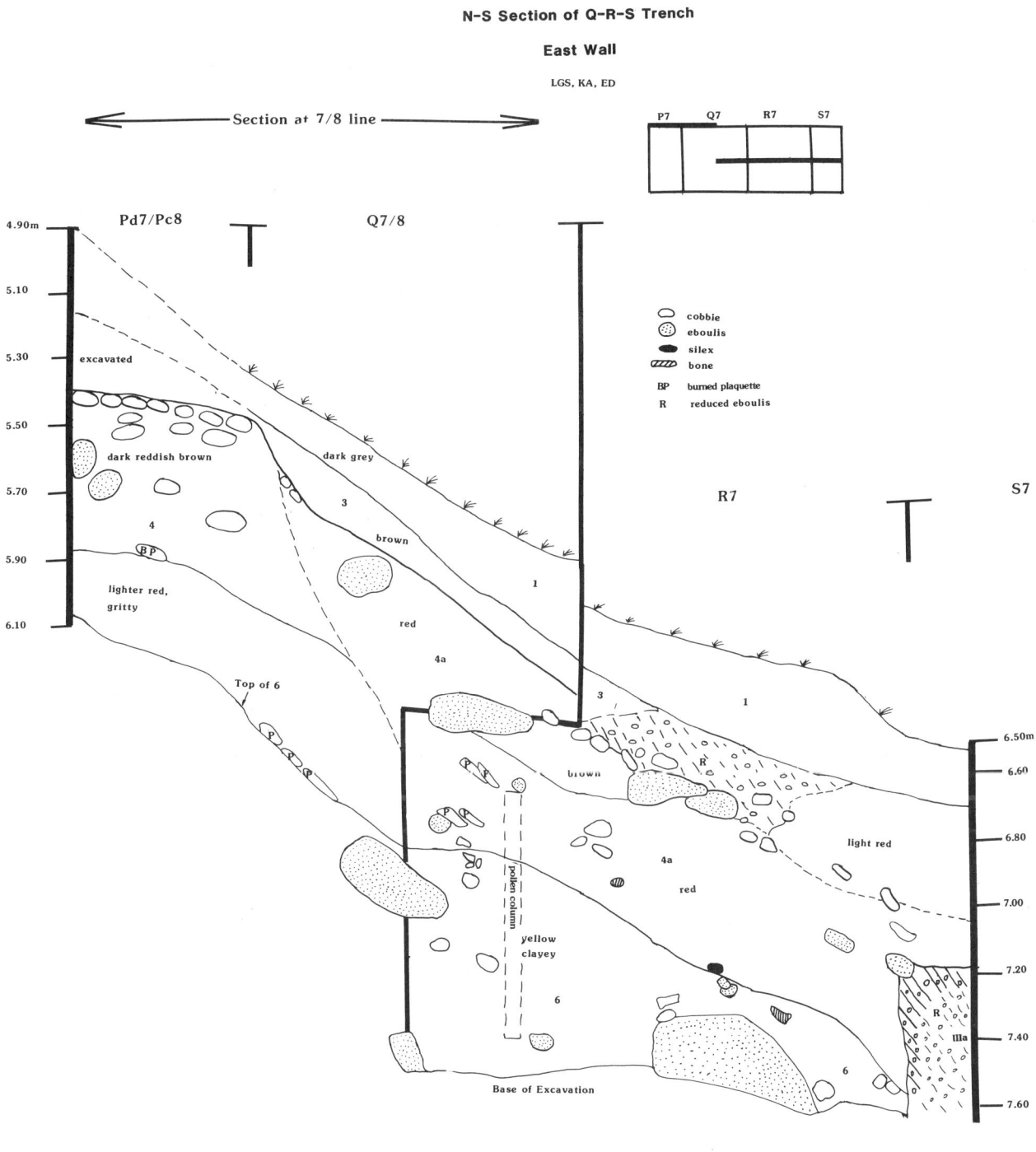

Figure 2.5 Stratigraphic section at the break-in-slope (P-S/7).

ber burins (18.9%—mostly dihedrals). There are 5.7% Azilian points, but backed bladelets make up only 7.5% of the assemblage—a major difference *vis-à-vis* Dufaure Stratum 3. The data from both sites point to a decrease in the diversity and quality of tool types present in the Azilian relative to the underlying Final Magdalenian, although the knapping debris remains abundant and diverse. In both sites, the occupation area shrank radically to include only the small rockshelters and immediate terraces at the cliff base. This shift is dramatic when one considers the very large areas repeatedly paved and used on the talus slope by "Magdalenian" site occupants during the Alleröd. The Azilian was clearly a time of significant adaptive transition, although it spanned *both* rigorous and more temperate climatic conditions at the Pleistocene-Holocene boundary and is technologically similar to the Magdalenian (e.g., Straus 1986b).

STRATUM 4

The principal artifact assemblages at both Dufaure and Duruthy were deposited during the humid Alleröd oscillation and possibly the brief, cold Dryas II phase (Paquereau 1978a, n.d.), during which time vast cobblestone pavements were repeatedly constructed at both sites (presumably to stabilize the slope, providing dry, clean habitation and work surfaces). At Dufaure, Stratum 4 yielded 2545 retouched tools and 45,923 pieces of knapping debris (one tool for every 18.0 debris items). The debitage is somewhat laminar (13.7% of the unretouched debris are blades and 12.9% are bladelets). Burins moderately outnumber endscrapers, as is standard among many (but not all) Upper Magdalenian assemblages. Truncation burins (including Lacan burins, which are frequent at Duruthy) are not uncommon, although outnumbered by dihedral types. Again, backed bladelets make up just under half of the assemblage, though most are broken so that their "minimum number of individuals" is about 440. Pieces with continuous retouch are common (13.3%); large backed and truncated pieces, denticulates, notches, sidescrapers are found in low frequencies (each 2-4% of the total). Azilian points are present in small numbers (0.6%). There are one microlithic triangle, one rectangle, and five trapezes along with a Teyjat point, two Magdalenian shouldered points, 22 pointed blades, and a possible Hamburgian point (to which one can add at least two in the Breuil/Dubalen collections). A Laugerie-Basse point was found in disturbed sediments in one of the 1980 sondages.

This lithic assemblage bears strong typological and general compositional similarities to that of Duruthy Couche 3, although the burin index is over twice as high at Duruthy and the backed bladelet index 10% lower. The higher percentage of burins at Duruthy is intriguing due to that site's very large quantities of worked bone/antler artifacts, including *sagaies* and harpoons. Despite excellent faunal preservation in Stratum 4, the Dufaure assemblage contains only 30 *sagaie* fragments, seven needle fragments, one unilaterally barbed harpoon, two harpoon bases, and a few other miscellaneous pieces. Breuil and Dubalen (1901) had found only six harpoon fragments. Preliminary microwear analyses show that the sample of burin facets studied were not used at Dufaure, although burin *edges* were used in transversal (planing) motion on bone/antler. The paucity of harpoons at Dufaure is accompanied by the virtual absence of salmon remains, in sharp contrast to Duruthy, where in Couche 3 harpoons and salmon remains are abundant and often physically associated (Arambourou, Straus, and Merlet 1985). Specific activity differences between the two penecontemporaneous Alleröd occupation sequences may then be suggested.

STRATUM 5

Stratum 5 was excavated in an area of 15 sq. m. The ratio of lithic tools (1000) to debris (19,376) is 1:19, almost the same as in Stratum 4. The proportions of the various general core and debitage classes are also much like those of the overlying layer. The assemblage of tools compositionally resembles that of Stratum 4, but specialized Final Magdalenian types (including harpoons) are absent and Azilian points are extremely rare. Burins are slightly more abundant relative to endscrapers, while the proportions of dihedral and truncation burins are identical in Strata 4 and 5. There are 14 *sagaie* fragments and one whole bipointed *sagaie*, plus three needles, an awl, two wands, and several miscellaneous pieces of worked antler and bone. Yet there are no works of art, so abundant in penecontemporaneous Couche 4 at Duruthy and at other Pyrenean "Magdalenian IV" deposits, all dating to around 14,000 B.P. This again suggests a significant functional difference between the two sites despite a *general* similarity of their lithic assemblages. Burins, however, are more than twice as abundant (29.9% vs. 13.8%) at Duruthy as at Dufaure, a statistic perhaps in some way related to the far richer bone industry at the former site.

STRATUM 6

The Stratum 6 lithic assemblage is naturally small (81 tools and 974 debris items), due at least in part to the small area excavated. Notable is the fact that burins and backed bladelets each make up about one-quarter of the tools, which are clearly of Magdalenian type—probably temporally equivalent to Couche 5 at Duruthy. There are in fact broad compositional similarities with the "Magdalenian III" of Duruthy, although there burins are even more abundant (45.5%). Both levels lack lithic or osseous fossil directors.

Thus there are essential stratigraphic, chronological, assemblage-compositional, and structural parallelisms between Dufaure and Duruthy, but with interesting detailed differences in bone/antler artifacts (and art works) and burin and backed-bladelet percentages that may indicate differences in primary activity (and/or disposal) between the occupations of the two sites. Even given the erosion at Dufaure, the open-air part of this site was certainly never as large as Duruthy.

STRATUM IV

Finally, it is worth drawing attention to the fact that the composition of the redeposited assemblage of 737 tools associated with the Stratum IV footslope pseudo-pavements is virtually identical to that of Stratum 4, from which Stratum IV probably derived most of its constituents. (The somewhat higher percentage of notches and denticulates in Stratum IV [6.9% vs. 4.2% for Stratum 4] *could* be due in part to edge crushing during slope movement.) There are 15,853 pieces of lithic debris (20.15 for every tool, a ratio very similar to those of Strata 4 and 5).

PRELIMINARY EVIDENCE FOR SUBSISTENCE AND SEASONALITY

The faunal remains are currently under study, so we can present only preliminary indications of the subsistence of Dufaure's occupants. As at Duruthy, the Azilian level (Stratum 3) contains at least red deer, some boar, roe deer, *and reindeer*. The Dufaure reindeer remains confirm the presence of *Rangifer* in Gascony during the rigorous Dryas III period (Delpech 1983). This indicates the existence of a separate western Pyrenean herd, which did not migrate northward during the end of the Würm Tardiglacial, but went extinct in situ. Similar evidence for late survival of reindeer along the central Pyrenees was found in old excavations at Le Mas d'Azil and Le Trou Violet in Ariège (Bahn 1984). The largest faunal assemblage from Dufaure—that of Stratum 4—is dominated by reindeer, together with significant amounts of horse and bovines (probably mostly bison) and some red deer. In this respect, the Final Magdalenian deposits of Dufaure and Duruthy are very similar: reindeer seems to have been the principal game species, despite the relatively temperate, humid, wooded environmental conditions of the Alleröd oscillation. Cranial elements (except mandibles) are scarce at Dufaure, suggesting that the kill and primary butchery loci were not at Dufaure itself, since heavy anatomical elements would have been abandoned prior to transport to the base camp. Such kill loci could have been along the banks of the Gave, as suggested by the site of La Barthe Claverie 3.5 km upstream from Dufaure, where reindeer remains and Magdalenian artifacts were found in the 19th century. As noted above, a notable faunistic difference between Dufaure Stratum 4 and Duruthy Couche 3 is the abundance of fish remains at the latter site and their scarcity at the former. Hundreds of vertebrae (mostly of salmon) have been found in the recent excavations at Duruthy (Delpech 1979; Arambourou, Straus, and Normand 1986: 126). Seasonality data from ungulate teeth demonstrate congruence between the Duruthy and Dufaure Final Magdalenian occupations. All seven of the Dufaure teeth whose sections could be "read" (five reindeer teeth and one each of a bovine and a red deer) indicated cold-season kills (fall, winter, or early spring). Two other reindeer teeth and one red deer tooth gave less secure results also pointing to death in winter (Straus and Spiess 1985). One Dufaure pike vertebra studied by O. LeGall proves spring fishing. Thus, as at Duruthy, there is no evidence for Final Magdalenian occupation in summer.

The Stratum 5 faunal remains suggest a greater abundance of bovines and horses than in Stratum 4. (Such remains also seem to be relatively important in the small Stratum 6 collection.) This pattern, if confirmed, would correspond to Duruthy, where in Couche 4, 45% of the ungulate remains are of bovines and 28% are of horses (31% and 62% respectively in Couche 5), versus 72% reindeer remains in Couche 3 (Delpech 1979). This would suggest either a different pattern of human use of the Pastou Cliff or a different pattern of ungulate availability in Middle Magdalenian (Dryas I-Bolling) times. Unfortunately we thus far lack seasonality data for Stratum 5 at Dufaure; the few data from Duruthy (antlers) also suggest winter occupations. No fish remains were found in the lower Dufaure strata; nor have they been found in the Middle Magdalenian levels at Duruthy. This is a further argument for the functional relationship between salmon and harpoons. Such a conclusion is supported by B. Hayden's (pers. comm.) recent carbon-isotope analyses of French Paleolithic human remains (including those of Duruthy Couche 3), indicating a diet containing a significant fish component only in the *Upper* Magdalenian. The functional relationship is also suggested by the strong geographic correlation of harpoons and sites near the salmon rivers which flow into the Bay of Biscay (see Julien 1982).

The Pastou Cliff thus seems to have been a major focus of winter (or fall/early spring) occupation by Magdalenian and Azilian (= "Epi-Magdalenian") bands whose range probably included the western Pyrenees and southern Aquitaine Basin. The cliff base and its several rockshelter/terrace loci were repeatedly utilized, probably as residential camps in the lowland part of the annual range. The people based at the cliff sites first procured bovines and horses in the adjacent broad valley of the Gave d'Oloron. Later they hunted large quantities of reindeer (in mass kills at traditional water-crossing spots?), sometimes supplemented by salmon as well as occasional horses, bovines, and red deer. And finally, at the very end of the Pleistocene and beginning of the Holocene, they killed red deer, together with boar, roe deer, and a few of the last reindeer to survive in southern France. By this time, the hunting of *individual* ungulates may have become more important. As noted earlier, the Pastou was a preferred setting for major camps because of its variety of rockshelters, excellent views and solar exposure, strategic location (the ford, the natural migration route and game-funneling features of the Gave valley and its steep-sided side valleys just upstream of the sites, etc.), and access to resources (fuel, water, plant and animal foods). It was a favored venue *under a variety of environmental conditions*, as the stratified evidence from Duruthy and Dufaure demonstrates. Yet there were significant differences among the specific occupations of the Pastou sites, even when these were demonstrably penecontemporaneous.

FEATURES AND ACTIVITIES

STRATUM 3

Only one cultural horizon at Dufaure (Stratum 4) has yielded substantial evidence of features and activity areas. As noted above, a remnant Stratum 3 occupation surface (no more than 4 sq. m) on the terrace provides scanty information (Straus 1986a). It contains small, dispersed cobbles (the only evidence of a "paved" surface in any part of Stratum 3), several cores, flakes and blades, a couple of backed bladelets, a burin, several bones, and a couple of boar teeth. This surface certainly gives the impression of a low-intensity, short-duration Azilian occupation consonant with the relative poverty of Stratum 3 as a whole. This is also suggested by the facts rather vaguely reported by Breuil and Dubalen (1901) for their "foyer supérieur," as well as by analogous information from Duruthy Couche 2. One of the striking aspects of the Stratum 3 lithic assemblage is the scarcity of retouched tools (particularly once the 144 backed bladelets are subtracted) and the relatively large quantity of knapping debris, suggesting that lithic reduction was a particularly important activity during these occupations of the site.

STRATUM 5

Stratum 5, while relatively rich in artifacts, manuports, and faunal remains, is apparently low in structural integrity, as discussed above. It is nonetheless clear that much of the site area during Middle Magdalenian times had originally been paved with sandstone slabs. These manuports are almost all reddened by burning and may have been heated to roast meat and/or to retain heat for the human occupants of the site. It is possible that extensive processing and cooking of meat (notably horse and bovine) was carried out during the occupations of Stratum 5. The large numbers of backed bladelets could have been armatures in compound weapons used in hunting. But *sagaies* are also relatively abundant, though by no means as frequent as in Couche 4 at Duruthy. There is some good evidence of the in situ working of antler (e.g., beam pieces with splinters removed for the manufacture of *sagaies*, needles, etc.). Along with the abundant knapping of flint (attested by the numerous cores and both primary and secondary debitage), Stratum 5 is uniquely characterized by a large quantity of crystal quartz debris and even retouched pieces and a "cache" of large flakes.

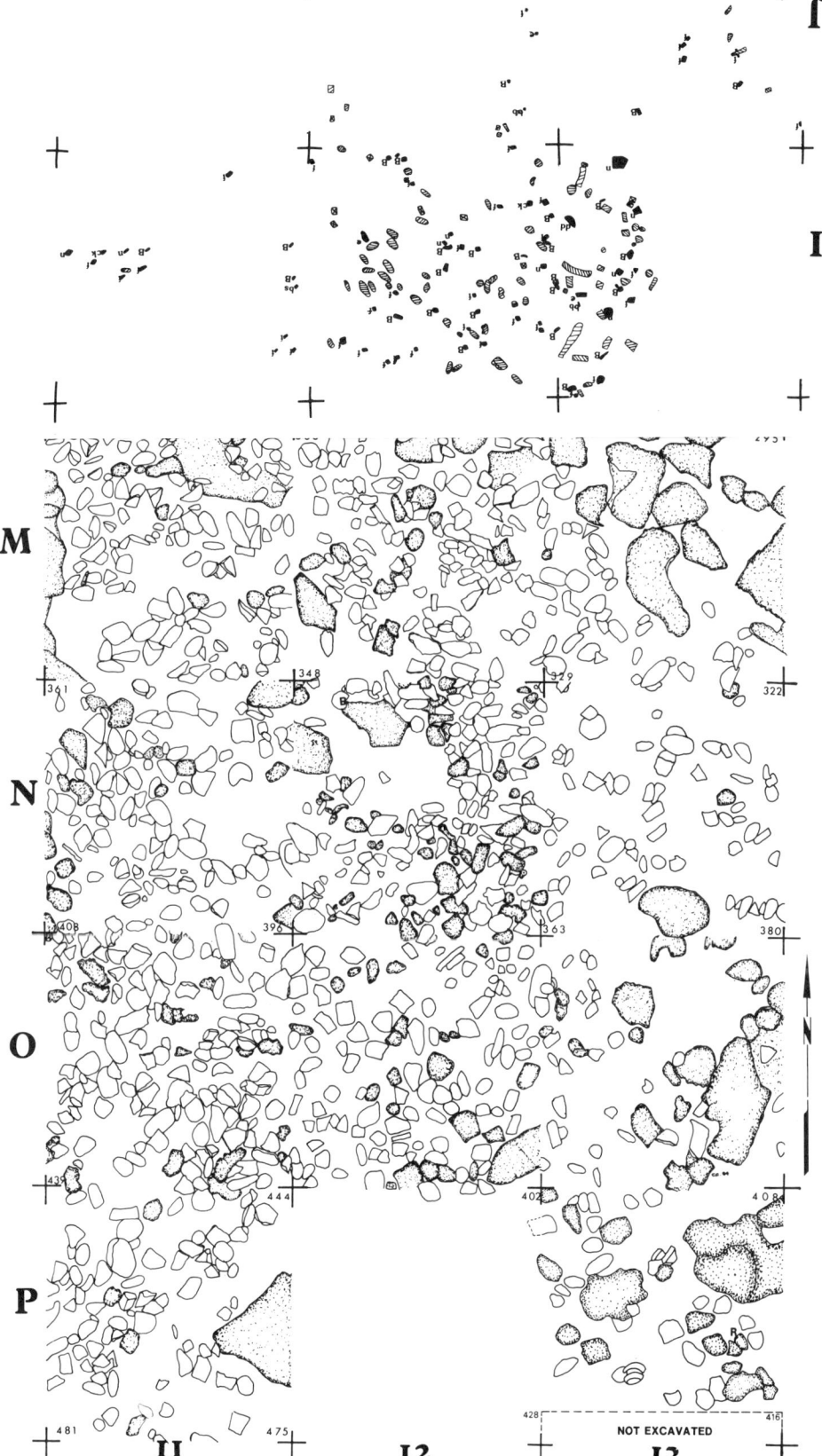

Figure 2.6 A Stratum 4 cobblestone pavement: manuports.

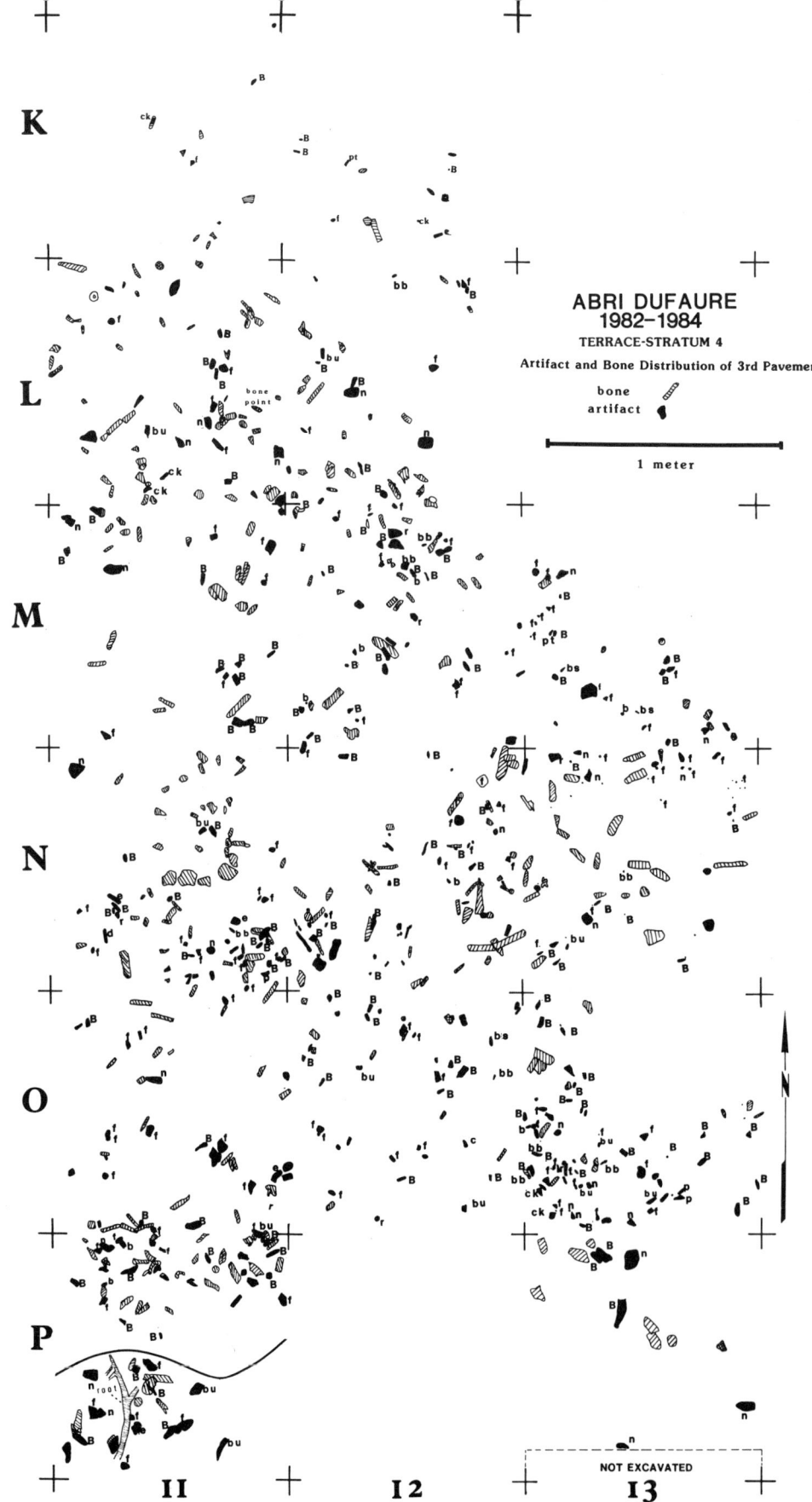

Figure 2.7 A Stratum 4 cobblestone pavement: artifacts and faunal remains.

STRATUM 4

The most substantial intact features and evidence of activities come, of course, from Stratum 4. Before we describe the pavements uncovered in 1980-84 in the terrace and slope, mention should be made of the 1900 description of the "foyer inférieur" (or lower cultural stratum) within the rockshelters per se. Breuil and Dubalen (1901: 251-253) believed that the western sector of the shelter was deliberately separated from the rest by two large blocks set into place by humans and joined by smaller rocks to form a wall. There is a third huge block that did not form a part of this supposed wall. It is possible that all were the natural result of roof fall, and their supposedly deliberate placement must be viewed with caution, although the "completion" of an otherwise natural wall with smaller rocks is entirely conceivable. The large rocks were apparently in contact with bedrock. Breuil and Dubalen also believed that there was an artificial arrangement of rocks below the dripline atop the natural bedrock threshold of the rockshelter. This could simply be a line of *éboulis* fallen from the cliff overhang, as large blocks were found to be most abundant near the cliff in the recent excavations. The "foyer inférieur" of Breuil and Dubalen (1901: 255-257) was capped by a pavement formed of large cobbles and limestone *éboulis*. The stratum contained ashes and wood charcoal, along with abundant artifacts and faunal remains. The thickness of the layer generally ranged between 25 and 55 cm. The eastern part of the lower stratum, however, contained a 30- to 45-cm-thick layer of white ash and black charcoal filled with bones and mandibles of reindeer, red deer, bovine and horse, as well as a worked antler, a harpoon base, and flint artifacts. The wood charcoal of this apparent hearth was all identified as birch in 1900 by a forestry specialist. Breuil and Dubalen (1901: 258) mention other hearths in passing and point out that wood must have been relatively abundant in the vicinity of the Pastou Cliff, in comparison to the then-known Magdalenian sites of the central Pyrenees, where they claim *bone* was burned as fuel. (Indeed, in the Alleröd period there were open woodlands in the valleys of the Gaves. *Betula* is well represented in the Stratum 4 pollen spectra, according to Paquereau [n.d.].)

The eastern hearth lay atop a layer of wet, greenish black clay with blocks and scattered cobbles. This basal level was found in depressions in the bedrock at both the eastern and western ends of the shelter, and *might* be remnants of Stratum 5 or 6 that had survived the erosion (or human removal) affecting the threshold and terrace in front of the shelter.

Thus it seems clear that the occupation residues in the rockshelter corresponding to Stratum 4, while poorly documented, included at least one major hearth (perhaps of "bonfire" type, as there is no evidence that it was dug out or stone-lined) and probably others. Burned wood was abundant. These hearths would have provided warmth (for sleeping?), light, and cooking facilities. The shelter being small, such fires could have heated the limestone roof and walls to retain warmth throughout the winter nights. The hearths would have been foci of sheltered, seated activities, as well as sleeping. There exists, in addition, the possibility of structures built of naturally occurring rocks within the rockshelter. The Stratum 4 pavements on the terrace continue right to the edge of the old excavation.

The remaining area of cobble pavement consists of three sections: the flat southern edge of the terrace, a zone of large rockfall blocks with only scattered cobbles and other cultural remains at a first break-in-slope, and the slope per se down to the abrupt, main break-in-slope along the P row. The eastern edge of intact pavement is clearly evident in the 13 row; the western edge lies within the 10 row. A total of 10 cu. m of Stratum 4 sediments was excavated.

In most squares we uncovered and recorded eight layers of cobbles ("pavements"), sometimes separated by thin lenses of silt. In a few squares we distinguished as many as 14 layers within Stratum 4 (Figs. 2.6-7). The sector consistently having the greatest number of cobble layers is the terrace (I row), where the other cultural remains are also densest, reflecting probably a higher intensity of in situ activities in this level area adjacent to the rockshelter. It is indeed probable that much of the terrace was sheltered by rock overhang in Alleröd times, judging by the mass of *éboulis* blocks that typifies the upslope area of Stratum 3—evidence of major rockfall episodes beginning soon after abandonment of the uppermost Stratum 4 pavement, probably in early Dryas III.

The area of intact to semi-intact pavements on the terrace and slope yielded 10,405 cobbles (6716 of which were piece-plotted) weighing a total of about 2050 kg. On average there are 38.7 completely or nearly whole cobbles per pavement layer per square (vs. 90.4 for the redeposited "pseudo-pavements" aggregated at the footslope). The Stratum 4 pavements had an overall density of 212.9 kg of cobbles per cubic meter excavated (vs. 368.1 kg/cu. m for Stratum IV).

The pavements do not slope evenly downward but rather are arranged into three relatively flat areas divided by steeper sloping bands. Such a micro-topography is also found at Duruthy and is controlled by rows of underlying *éboulis* blocks and the bedrock sill. The slope was definitely and repeatedly paved with some specific purpose(s) in mind. The slope was not, in short, used just as an area for tossing garbage from the shelter area.

Until faunal body-part data are available, it is impossible to speak in great detail of the activities conducted on these pavements. Faunal remains are abundant, so secondary butchering, processing, and consumption are distinct possibilities. All the endscrapers that could be analyzed by K. Akoshima for traces of microwear seem to have been used in hide scraping. There are no signs of constructed hearths, nor are any significant amounts of charcoal preserved outside of the rockshelter. One small area of ash was found in Square O12. Obviously charcoal and ash were leached or eroded away on the exposed slope. As noted earlier, however, there are masses of reddened, cracked, burnt cobbles and *éboulis* in every pavement layer. The burnt manuports are accompanied by potlidded, crackled, discolored flints and some burned bones, and the lot are not randomly scattered across the surfaces. Instead, according to computer plotting and the field notes, the burned objects are concentrated. There are, among the eight pavement layers analyzed, three distinct patterns of burning areas. It is suggested that fires were built atop the pavement, intensely heating the cobbles and *éboulis*, which could then be used to roast meat in large quantities (see Petraglia 1987).

In contrast to Duruthy, where apparent postholes were found in the cobblestone pavements of Couche 3 (Arambourou 1978), none were found at Dufaure, perhaps simply because of the much smaller surface area exposed. Thus, while the entire set of pavements *is a structure*, the only structures discernible within the pavements are usually of the "latent" form as defined by Leroi-Gourhan (1972: 325).

The abundant lithic artifacts (tools and debris) are distributed throughout the pavements, being relatively sparse only in the J-K rows. Spatial analyses currently under way suggest that burins tend to be clustered on the terrace, while some other tool types and cores often seem to be scattered without obvious clusters, despite the existence of definite chipping areas.

The lithic knapping debris found amidst the cobbles of Stratum 4 is abundant and varied: 45,923 classified items divided among all 21 types recognized by the Dufaure Project. Cores make up 0.80% of the total, but there are an additional 2.28% "chunks" (mostly angular core fragments) and 0.02% *pièces esquillées*. Primary and secondary decortication flakes and blades together constitute 4.71% of the total, while crested blades constitute 0.50% and platform renewal flakes, 0.18%. The lion's share of the debris is made up of trimming flakes (chips of 1 cm or less) (31.65%), shatter (angular debris of 1 cm or less) (6.87%), plain flakes with no cortex (26.35%), plain blades (11.83%), and bladelets (12.95%). Burin spalls make up 1.87% of the total. Surprisingly, this statistical distribution of debris types is in general not substantially different from those of overlying Stratum 3 or underlying Stratum 5. Stratum 3 has relatively more chunks and bits of shatter, while having fewer burin spalls and bladelets. Stratum 5 has fewer blades but even more bladelets than Stratum 4, fewer cores but more burin spalls. The differences are seldom great, however. All this suggests a high degree of redundancy in the (diverse) lithic manufacturing activities that were conducted at Dufaure over a period of more than 5,000 years. Not surprisingly, the redeposited assemblage of debris in Stratum IV is also basically similar, although trimming flakes are fewer and plain flakes are relatively more abundant than in intact Stratum 4 or in Strata 3 and 5. Clearly the full range of lithic reduction activities from initial core preparation to tool retouching was carried out in situ.

LITHIC PROCUREMENT

Information on the sources of the main raw materials provides support for this conclusion. We located several sources of flint in the area around the Pastou Cliff. Samples of flint types from Dufaure and samples from the known flint sources were then analyzed petrographically by M. Séronie-Vivien (n.d.). She concludes that our major archaeological flint types are likely to have come from local sources. The source locations we had sampled are in fact no more than 9 km (two-hour walks) in different directions from the site. Other, more distant known sources are apparently not represented (at least among the major Dufaure flints). Even some of the rare raw materials at Dufaure could have been procured locally, either at actual outcrops (chalcedony near Orthez) or in the nearby riverbed (e.g., quartz and quartzite washed down from the Pyrenees). The *local* procurement of lithic raw materials is a good indication that Dufaure (like Duruthy) was a locus of relatively long-term residential occupations. It was certainly not just a specialized hunting camp to which parties came supplied with their lithics from distant sources. Thus the sources and compositional diversity of the Dufaure lithic assemblages, together with the Stratum 4 pavements (and probable Stratum 5 pavements) and the indications of large-scale hunting of major ungulate species, combine with the seasonality data to suggest the role of Dufaure (and the other Pastou sites) in the context of the Pyrenees.

DUFAURE AND THE PASTOU SITE CLUSTER IN THE PYRENEAN CONTEXT

Evidence of Upper Paleolithic occupation of the northern flank of the Pyrenees before the Middle Magdalenian is relatively scarce (although there are some major Aurignacian and Perigordian sites; see Clottes 1976), as is evidence of Mousterian occupation. Solutrean sites—in contrast to both the Perigord and Cantabria—are relatively few in the Pyrenean region and most are minor. Certainly it is only in the Magdalenian that humans began making *systematic* use of high montane and mountain-edge habitats (particularly in Ariège).

THE MIDDLE MAGDALENIAN

It is in the so-called Magdalenian IV, dated by numerous radiocarbon determinations to the two millennia centered on 14,000 B.P. (see Bahn 1984), that a definite pattern of regional settlement develops in and right along the Pyrenees. Middle Magdalenian sites form a linear distribution pattern stretching about 350 km from Isturitz in the west to Gazel in the east. That the Pyrenean group of sites represents something like a distinct regional band territory is suggested by two factors, geography and mobile art. Beyond a line running 60-80 km north of the Pyrenean crestline, there is a wide zone essentially devoid of Middle Magdalenian sites. Sites of this and other Upper Paleolithic periods are once again abundant to the north of the lower Garonne, Avéyron, and Gard Rivers. In terms of mobile art, the Middle Magdalenian in the Pyrenees is characterized first and foremost by *contours découpés*. Less abundant but no less characteristic are the "spiral-motif" antler wands found exclusively in Pyrenean "Magdalenian IV" deposits. Circular engraved and perforated discs cut out of scapula blades are also typical of Pyrenean mobile art in the period around 14,000 B.P. Thus, despite a rather banal lithic industry, the Pyrenean Middle Magdalenian has distinct geographic and artistic unity. Many Middle Magdalenian levels are extremely rich in works of art and bone industry, but Dufaure is not among them and thus its Stratum 5 is definitely "atypical" (functionally distinctive?) in the context of sites in this time period.

To date, the specific distribution of "Magdalenian IV" sites seems to indicate that most major settlements were located in relatively low areas in front of the Pyrenees, not in high mountain valleys per se. Many sites, however, are located right at the point where such valleys break out onto the pre-Pyrenean plains and basins. There are hints of some Middle Magdalenian use of montane habitats per se. Two complementary hypotheses suggest themselves from the patterns of Middle (and Upper) Magdalenian sites and the distribution of exotic objects. The Pyrenees mountain chain provided major food resources for hunter-gatherer bands. The migratory adaptations of several key ungulate species (reindeer, bovines, horse, red deer) probably took advantage of seasonal differences in fodder between lowlands and highlands. In addition, montane habitats contained particular species (ibex, lagopeds) that could be efficiently exploited with the use of appropriate tactics. Human movements between the lowlands and highlands all along the mountain chain would thus permit the efficient exploitation of the full range of the region's resources at different seasons of the year.

On the other hand, there is significant evidence for cultural similarity and contacts along the east-west axis from the Mediterranean to the Atlantic. Besides the distinctive mobile art of the "Magdalenian IV" discussed earlier, Bahn (1977, 1982, 1984) has compiled evidence of the widespread distribution of seashells from the Atlantic in sites near the Mediterranean and vice versa, together with other indications of lengthy band movements and/or intergroup contacts (e.g., seal representations in mobile art, sea-mammal teeth, fossils, etc.). It is significant to note that there are relatively easy avenues of communication *both* between the lowlands and highlands (via the upper valleys of the rivers of southern France) *and* along the east-west axis (via basins, low plateaus, and the lower and middle valleys of such rivers as the

Aude, the Garonne, the Adour, and the Gaves de Pau and d'Oloron). At least in the western and central sectors of the region, there seem to be grouped Middle Magdalenian sites in the lowlands opposite each group of sites at the edge of or in the mountains per se. This pattern suggests that major winter sites were located in the lowlands and that the highlands were exploited by human residential groups which moved to bases nearer the mountains in summer, or by logistical parties based in the lowlands or the mountain-edge sites in either summer or winter.

THE UPPER MAGDALENIAN

The Upper Magdalenian of the Pyrenees is defined by the usual presence of round-section antler harpoons and, sometimes, by certain diagnostic lithic tool types (but see Rigaud 1979). It is generally radiocarbon dated between about 13,000 and 11,000 B.P. The Pyrenean sites of this period lack the regionally distinctive types of art works which characterize the "Magdalenian IV." As in that period, though, there is an apparent gap in the distribution of "Magdalenian V-VI" sites to the north of the string of Pyrenean loci. Upper Magdalenian sites stretch along the Pyrenees all the way from Berroberréa, on the Franco-Hispanic border at the junction of the Pyrenees and Cantabrian Cordillera, to La Teulera in French Catalonia. Deposits dating to this period are somewhat more numerous than those of the Middle Magdalenian, but many sites have strata pertaining to both stages. These are often major residential base camps, either in the lowlands or right at the edge of the mountains.

The settlement pattern suggested for the Middle Magdalenian is even clearer in the Upper Magdalenian, with a notable increase in sites located in high mountain valleys, perhaps in part because of the retreat of the Pyrenean glaciers. The greatest concentration of montane sites is near the confluence of the Ariège and Vicdessos Rivers around the town of Tarascon. Here there are nine residential and/or art sites securely or probably assignable to the Upper/Final Magdalenian. By the end of the Würm, humans were utilizing extremely high habitats, as shown by the recent excavation of La Balma Margineda in Andorra (Guilaine et al. 1985). This and other sites were used for the specialized exploitation of ibex.

Aside from the ibex-hunting camps, most sites of the Pyrenean Upper/Final Magdalenian are dominated by reindeer remains. Although bovines and horses continued to supply major portions of the diet (and both fish and plant foods were significant supplements at this time), reindeer is generally numerically very abundant in the assemblages at most sites. Major slaughters of reindeer herds seem to have been carried out in this period, ironically not long before the extirpation of the species in France.

SEASONALITY

Since the work of R. de Saint-Périer (1920), who hypothesized Magdalenian migrations between the Pyrenees and the Atlantic coast, there has been interest in trying to work out the patterns of seasonal mobility for the region during the last few millennia of the Pleistocene. Bahn (1984) has collected all the (mostly old) indications of seasonality and essentially concludes that Magdalenian groups hunted reindeer herds in the lowlands during the winter/early spring and in their upland pastures in summer/early fall. Recently, preliminary results of a comprehensive study of seasonality in the French Magdalenian by Gordon (1986) have become available. Based on the sectioning of teeth to permit analysis of cementum rings, this study utilized samples from several sites in the Pyrenean region. Gordon found the following for lowland sites: Duruthy—winter, spring, and some fall occupation; Brassempouy—spring; Le Mas d'Azil—spring and some winter; Enlène—spring and winter; Le Portel—winter, spring, and some summer; Canecaude—summer. Sites in the mountains or near their edge yielded the following cementum results: Isturitz—spring, summer, and some winter; Espalungue (Arudy)—spring and summer; Espélugues (Lourdes)—summer and fall; Lortet—fall, spring, and some summer; Gourdan—all seasons, but mostly spring and summer; La Vache—spring and summer. As noted earlier, antlers and tooth-eruption data at Duruthy suggested fall and winter occupations (Delpech 1979), thus not contradicting Gordon's evidence for reindeer (and probably human) absence in summer. This is confirmed at Dufaure by evidence of cold-season kills of reindeer, bovines, red deer, and fish. Clot (1984: 34) found independent evidence of at least fall occupation of Espélugues, although at another site located at the edge of the Pyrenees, Espèche, he noted an indication of winter occupation.

While Gordon (1986) has a different interpretation of his results (i.e., reindeer migrations to northern Aquitaine in summer) that seems to be contradicted by some of his own evidence, it is possible to see his results as confirming the basic pattern foreseen by Bahn and Delpech. The only clear-cut anomaly is the case of Canecaude, an isolated sample location very close to the Mediterranean. Some of the near-Pyrenean sites in the areas of Arudy, Lourdes, and Montréjeau (e.g., Gourdan), plus Isturitz, are understandably seasonally less specific than some of the true upland or lowland sites, since reindeer could have passed near them in spring and fall and been accessible in their summer *and* winter pastures to people camped at these centrally located sites. In addition, these sites tend to include mixtures of materials spanning much of the Magdalenian (IV-VI), since the excavations were very early. Even in sites where the collections reflect clear stratigraphies (e.g., Isturitz, Duruthy), Gordon lumped his samples. Many different climatic phases and environmental conditions could be represented in these lumped faunal collections. Nonetheless, it now seems clear that lowland sites located at some distance from the mountains of the western and central Pyrenees were not occupied in summer. On the contrary, sites in or near the high mountain ranges seem to have been occupied for reindeer hunting in the warmer seasons of the year. But the high mountain site of Les Eglises—with faunas overwhelmingly dominated by ibex, plus salmon and lagopeds—has been demonstrated to be a logistical winter site used by specialized hunting parties who ascended to the Tarascon Valley from bases in the lowlands (Clottes 1983; Delpech and LeGall 1983; Simonnet 1985).

CONCLUSIONS

The Pastou sites constitute one of the principal foci of cold-season lowland Magdalenian occupations. They were residential loci employed repeatedly by relatively large human bands for relatively long periods of time (judging from the effort put into the paving of extensive areas of each locus and from the sheer amount and diversity of artifacts and faunal remains). Although it seems unlikely that the sites at the base of the Pastou Cliff were occupied strictly simultaneously in any given cold season, it is clear that the cliff was, for at least five or six millennia, a major assembly point for over-wintering, and that there would have been many associated special-purpose sites (e.g., kill sites such as La Barthe Claverie; flint, fuel, and plant-food procurement loci) within a foraging radius of the cliff. Results from Dufaure should, however, serve as a warning that activity differences (for example in fishing, bone/antler work, artistic creation) are possible even among such closely situated and otherwise similar sites. Within the broad role the Pastou sites played in the Magdalenian system, specific functional distinctions clearly existed and need to be further investigated.

ACKNOWLEDGMENTS

Research at Abri Dufaure is supported by National Science Foundation grant #BNS81-03589, with additional support from the National Geographic Society, the L. S. B. Leakey Foundation, and the University of New Mexico. Excavations were authorized by the Direction des Antiquités Préhistoriques and the S.V.O.M. de Peyrehorade, owner of the site. I gratefully acknowledge the assistance, advice, and hospitality of R. Arambourou, Curator of the Musée d'Arthous, as well as the efforts of the excavation and analysis crews (notably M. Petraglia, K. Akoshima, and D. Amick) and of the natural scientist project members (J. Altuna, C. Couraud, J. Evin, A. Eastham, H. Laville, O. LeGall, D. Marguerie, M. Paquereau, M. Séronie-Vivien, and A. Spiess). Help in locating flint sources was provided by M. Saule and F. Bellocq. Word processing of the final draft was efficiently done by L. Baca. This report is Contribution No. 26 of the Abri Dufaure Prehistoric Project.

DISCUSSION

LANZINGER: Regarding Stratum 4, which has a maximum thickness of around 50 cm and C-14 dates from about 12,260 B.P. to 10,900 B.P.: There are faunal remains in anatomical connection, which testifies to the intactness of the horizon. But what does this mean in terms of the long-range sitting in the site when in this same level there are eight to 14 living floors? We are, in effect, averaging out many discrete events that may be interrupted for long periods of time.

STRAUS: Obviously we have a big sampling problem. But the Pastou cliff base is actually one site with different loci having been identified by archaeologists. I would not attribute a tremendous amount of significance to the possible functional differences between the small sample at Dufaure and the very large average sample at Duruthy. Presumably people are moving laterally back and forth, not just between these two loci. There is evidence of little silt lenses deposited during periods of abandonment, and this is reflected by rebuilding of the pavements, which is done to provide stable footing on the slope. This cliff is being used over and over again for the same sorts of things that, archaeologically, tend to average themselves out. In a way it does not matter to be be able to say that this is a living floor made on a particular day.

KOZLOWSKI: There is also a real problem of seasonality and migration of the fauna. We may not be seeing seasonal migration patterns, but migration patterns related to larger climatic variations. How can we be sure that we are seeing activities within a single year?

STRAUS: Furthermore, there is a great deal of variability within the behaviors of a single migratory species.

JELINEK: Your practical explanation for the pavements, for footing, is an interesting one. But why would they pave the whole slope? Why not just pave trails up to the shelter?

STRAUS: Because they are doing things on the slope. There are chipping areas on the slope and there are the burning concentrations. So, they are creating a stable surface, admittedly a somewhat sloping one. It would be nice to compare the rockshelter activities with the open-air activities at the drip line, and with the slope activities, but unfortunately this will be impossible here. It is still mystifying why they made such tremendous investments of labor to pave these things.

SACKETT: Regarding the burning concentrations, are the cobbles heated after they are put in place?

STRAUS: Presumably so.

LAVILLE: The site presented a number of stratigraphical problems—it was difficult to excavate and there are stratigraphical hiatuses. The sedimentological analyses used by Farrand or me do not provide satisfactory results. Other sets of analyses are needed.

SIMEK: Might there not have been a considerable downslope movement that acted to distributed features downslope, and in the process created the images of a *pavage*? Do you see a continuous variation in densities that might suggest downslope movement?

STRAUS: No, there is an absolute break as well as internal, or local, variability.

MÜLLER-BECK: Is there a chance that you have some part of the higher levels of the Würm terrace in your shelter?

STRAUS: But the cultural material is 7 to 10 m above the top of the Würm terrace. Furthermore, the burning areas, the chipping areas, and the intact artifacts show that it is not purely geological.

MÜLLER-BECK: You mention Dryas I, Dryas III, and Alleröd, but not Dryas II and Bölling. Do you have any idea what had been happening then?

STRAUS: I suspect that there was an erosional episode during the Bölling. Stratum 4 is Alleröd plus probably the end of Dryas II.

LAVILLE: The Dryas II episode is not well marked in southwestern France. There is no record of it in the Gulf of Gascony, whereas Dryas III is very notable.

LANZINGER: About half of the backed bladelets are broken. Do you think that that was being done intentionally?

STRAUS: I am not sure how you could tell whether it was intentional or not. Far more were broken in the downslope area than in the upslope area, so that much of it may be natural breakage as they fell down the slope.

III

The Neuvic Group
Upper Paleolithic Open-Air Sites in the Perigord

James R. Sackett

The fame of the Perigord region of southwestern France derives from the rich and often deeply stratified cave and *abri* ("shelter") sites which occupy cliffs overlooking the region's numerous rivers and streams. Not surprisingly, their complex depositional histories and industrial successions traditionally required that archaeologists adopt an essentially *vertical* perspective, focusing primarily upon stratigraphy and the systematics involved in ordering lithic industries over time. The results of this work have indeed been impressive. The regional sequence wrested from the Perigord's shelters, especially its Upper Paleolithic segment (ca. 34,000-9000 B.C.), is undoubtedly the most detailed and industrially elaborate one available to us from Stone Age times. And it continues to undergo revision, thanks to modern chronostratigraphic research that is bringing to light kinds of complexity in industrial variation and timing which defy the simplistic ordering schemes left to us by our predecessors (see Laville, Rigaud, and Sackett 1980).

Nevertheless, in line with the burgeoning interest modern Stone Age research has shown in paleoethnology, archaeological strategy in the Perigord has seen during the last quarter century at least a partial shift from the vertical to the *horizontal* or "spatial" perspective. The underlying assumption here, of course, is that the activities that made up prehistoric lifeways cannot be inferred simply from artifactual remains themselves, but in addition require knowledge of how they were patterned spatially with respect to one another over occupation surfaces. Excavations like those conducted by Movius (1966) at Abri Pataud and Rigaud (1978) at Le Flageolet I revealed that shelter sites have much to contribute in an era of horizontal research, and their results have stimulated sophisticated advances in both method and theory (e.g., Simek 1987).

Yet shelters do not constitute the only, or even necessarily the best, source of spatial information. For it seems that this may sometimes be obtained more profitably from sites in the open air, both because of the comparative speed with which their archaeological levels can be uncovered and because their artifacts and associated features often seem to display more obvious horizontal organization. The latter trait stems from the likelihood that settlement tended to be shorter in duration and spatially less circumscribed in the open air than in shelters—factors that would have served to decrease the chances that the vestiges of several different activities would be superimposed and hence spatially confused with one another. It also seems reasonable to argue that one of the potentially most informative kinds of horizontal structure—the remains of purposefully constructed habitations—is more likely to appear in the open air than in sites which constitute natural shelters in their own right. Finally, apart from the question of horizontal patterning itself, it is reasonable to expect that open-air occupation may have entailed kinds of settlement and activity—and, hence, kinds of industrial variation—that are lacking in the shelter deposits and consequently overlooked by the accepted regional sequence.

Now, the Perigord's spectacular shelters understandably encouraged a *mentalité de grotte* among traditional prehistorians, who rarely troubled to explore the potential of the region's open-air resources, let alone cultivate the rather special knowledge and skills their excavation calls for. All too often open sites were held to be no more than superficial artifact scatters, so-called *gisements de surface,* more likely than not disturbed by erosion and cultivation and in any case lacking deep stratigraphic sequences like those provided by the shelters. Even today open sites evoke no more than moderate interest, and in only a few sectors is their exploration pursued in a systematic and rigorous fashion. The most important of these lies along the Middle Isle River Valley in north-central Perigord, where is found one of the richest and most intensively investigated complexes of Upper Paleolithic open-air deposits in all of Western Europe. It is this complex, which will here be termed the Neuvic group of sites, that is our concern. The rather inordinate length of the discussion that follows may be excused by the fact that it constitutes the first comprehensive review of the group in English. It will also be seen that, apart from their specific inherent interest, these sites raise questions of method and theory in horizontal research whose relevance extends far beyond the borders of the Perigord itself.

THE NEUVIC GROUP

The Neuvic stations are found along a 15-km stretch of the Isle River between the towns of Saint Léon-sur-l'Isle and Mussidan (Fig. 3.1). Here the river meanders through a fairly sinuous valley never more than 2 km wide, draining a landscape that is considerably less dramatic topographically than many found elsewhere in the Perigord. The limestone bedrock is too friable to hold an edge for any appreciable length of time. As a result, the transition from the Pleistocene stream terraces that cover the valley floor to the Tertiary detritus that mantles the overlying plateaus usually takes the form of a gentle colluvial slope deposit rather than an abrupt face of exposed rock. Thus largely absent are impressive stretches of cliff like those that harbor so many of the classic shelter sites in the drainages of the Vézère and Dordogne Rivers, a day's walk to the southeast. Apart from the celebrated cave of Gabillou (Gaussen 1964),

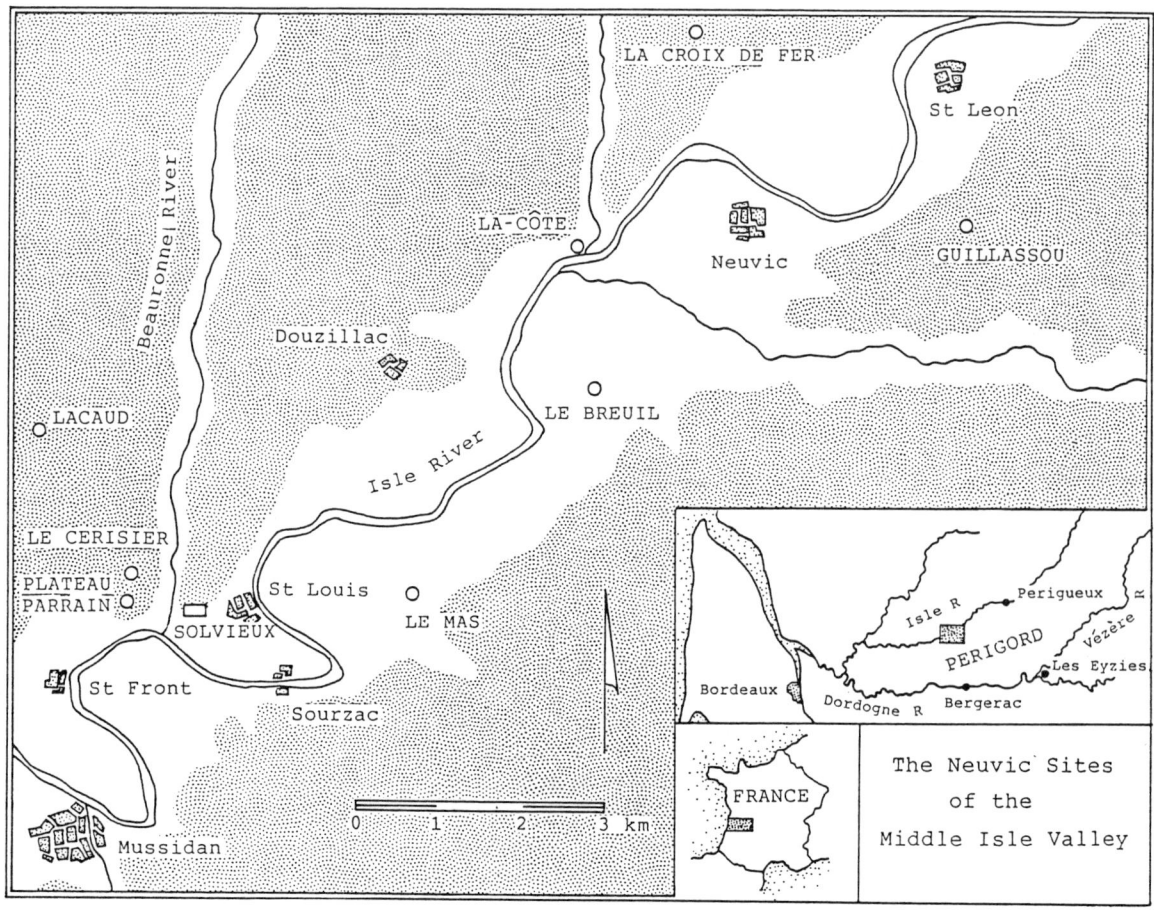

Figure 3.1 The Neuvic group.

the area's known shelter resources comprise only a handful of sites, most of which were long ago dug or destroyed, or both, and now are literally lost (Gaussen 1980: 20-22). Thus it is not surprising that the sector was traditionally regarded as having only minor archaeological importance at best.

But three decades of investigation into its open-air resources have profoundly altered this view. The work began in 1956, with the first systematic excavation conducted at the site of Solvieux by the distinguished amateur prehistorian, Dr. Jean Gaussen of Neuvic-sur-l'Isle. (Solvieux had in fact been discovered in 1938 by Louis Peyrille, who—reflecting the prejudices of his era—assumed he was dealing not with an intact archaeological deposit but instead with the debris from a shelter that itself had long ago been destroyed [see Peyrille and Blanc 1952].) This inaugurated one of the very first sustained programs of horizontal open-air research in France, which Gaussen has pursued in free moments seized from a busy medical practice right down to the present. An important contribution has been made to this effort by Marie-Louise (Mme.) Gaussen and by a Neuvicois trained by Gaussen, Jean-Claude Moissat, whose gift for prospection led to the discovery of many of the Upper Paleolithic sites of interest to us here in addition to several others ranging from Acheulian to Gallo-Roman times. From its beginning this work received valuable support from the late Professor François Bordes and other associates of the Institut du Quaternaire, Université de Bordeaux. But Neuvic has remained both the intellectual and logistic center of gravity for research into the Middle Isle Valley sites, and it is thus as appropriate as it is convenient to refer to this complex of sites after the name of that village.

The scope of activities in the sector expanded considerably in the mid-1960s, when Gaussen and the present writer entered into a warm and fruitful collaboration that continues to this day. It dates to the beginnings of the Solvieux project in 1967, which pursued one of the most intensive programs of excavation yet seen in an open site in Western Europe. The tempo of research soon increased still further due to the efforts of Dr. Jean-Pierre Texier, a Pleistocene geologist at the Institut du Quaternaire, who has

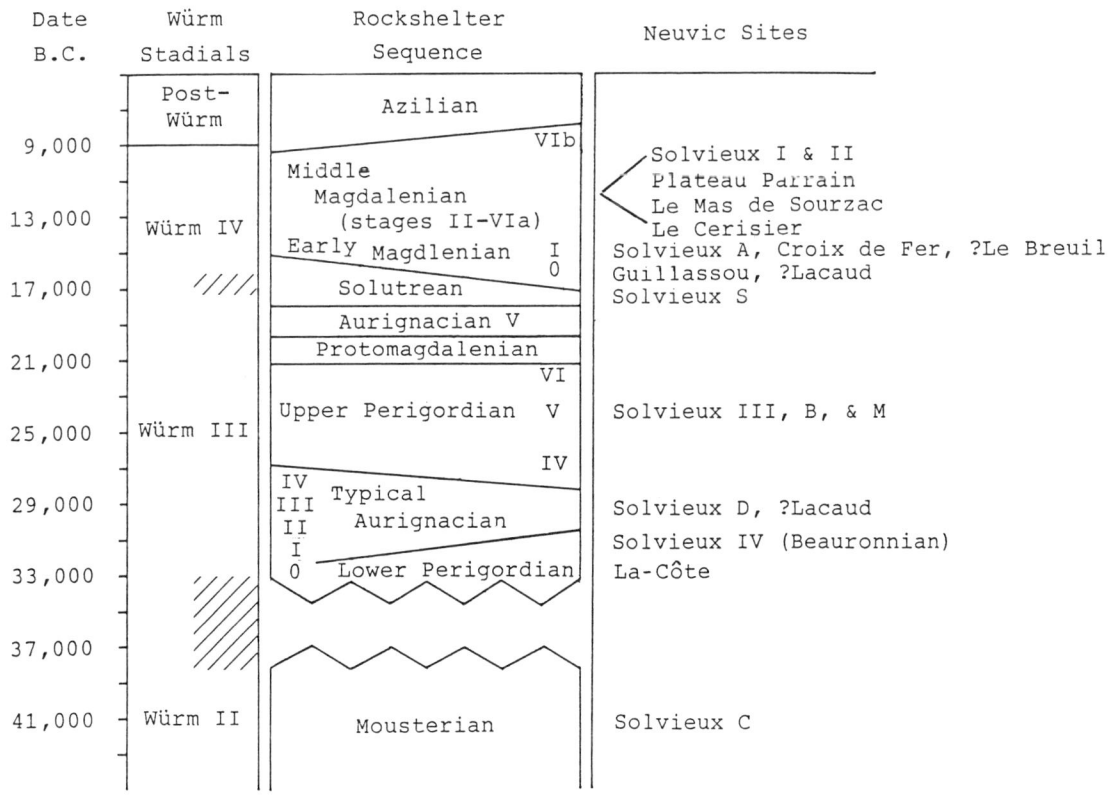

Figure 3.2 Chronology of the Neuvic sites.

undertaken a comprehensive geological study of the Isle Valley as a whole, the analysis of the geology of several individual sites, and the prospection and excavation of additional open-air stations from all epochs of the Paleolithic.

As the last statement implies, open-air resources in the Neuvic sector are not restricted to the Upper Paleolithic alone. Mousterian sites are distributed rather widely, while Lower Paleolithic ones are by no means unknown. Particularly noteworthy in the latter regard is the station of Les Tares, which dates to Riss glacial times and yields one of France's most important "Premousterian" assemblages (Rigaud and Texier 1981). But it is the Upper Paleolithic sites that concern us here. Altogether some 15 of them have seen at least some systematic investigation and an equal number in addition have been provisionally identified by isolated finds of diagnostic stone tools from plowed fields, commercial excavations, and so forth. Our interest here concerns the nine sites indicated in Figure 3.2, which are those that have undergone substantial excavation.

Although its members display much individuality, certain features still typify the Neuvic group as a whole and can be conveniently summarized at the onset. For one thing, they are by no means the light, superficial, and disturbed artifact scatters that typify the *gisements de surface* of traditional archaeological folklore. Their cultural levels (*couches*) are as a rule reasonably intact stratigraphically, and often areally extensive, artifactually rich, and very highly structured horizontally. A distinctive aspect of the couches' structure is their possession of rock features made of cobbles and, occasionally, flagstones and rock slabs. Quartzite, diabase, schist, sandstone, and granite may all appear as "couche rocks," with the first comprising at least 80% of the total. These features never seem to involve the modification of existing gravel beds (whose constituent rocks contrast significantly in morphology and mineralogical composition), but are instead the product of carrying into the sites stones selected from either exposed fluviatile terraces on the valley floor or the detritus that mantles the plateaus and hilly spurs. Couche rocks almost invariably exhibit reddening and fracture due to heating, yet the random orientation of these modifications even among contiguous stones indicates that they must have been heated prior to being arranged in the dispositions in which we find them. Included among these features are dense *pavages* of contiguous rocks, outlining enclosures or *cordons*, certain unique structures of undoubted architectural significance, and more general amorphous scatters.

Apart from their own inherent interest, the rock features provide an organized background to occupation surfaces against which the spatial distributions of stone tools and industrial debris take on enhanced visibility and, in many cases, suggestive patterning. This is of particular importance due to the fact that open-air deposits in the Perigord are highly acidic and thus strongly affected by leaching. Hence virtually absent are the organic remains such as bone and charcoal that furnish so much spatial organization to open-air sites elsewhere in Europe, as are nearly all signs that may once have existed of limestone and of soil features like postholes, pits, and the outline of hearth basins. In this connection, it should be noted that the common French term for living floor, *sol d'habitat*, ought not to be given literal connotation here, since the flint and rock features that make up the Neuvic sites' archaeological couches only very rarely occupy discrete sedimentological units that stand apart from the thick and heavily weathered soil horizons which incorporate them.

The lithic artifacts found associated with the rock features are virtually all fashioned from local flints, whose nodules abound in the sector's limestone and gravel deposits. The specific varieties employed vary significantly from one site to the next; some correlation between them and specific "tool" types (that is, the standardized retouched forms recognized in conventional regional lithic systematics) can also be seen within individual industries. Tools seem always to be accompanied by appropriate amounts and kinds of debitage—unused tool blanks, nuclei, waste flakes, and small chipping debris. There is little then to suggest that the lithic industries represent anything other than expedient technologies, fashioned and presumably used on the occupation surfaces where they are found discarded. The definition of an expedient technology has been provided by L. Binford (e.g., 1973), although for theoretical reasons he might not be happy to find it applied to an Upper Paleolithic context (see Sackett 1982: 89-91).

These tool assemblages display considerable heterogeneity in types and type frequencies, presenting a broad range of comparisons to one another as well as to established industries recognized in the Perigord's shelter sites. While some are nearly identical to those found in the shelters, others are distinctly different; and there are at least a couple for which no shelter has provided even a rough analogue. Thus difficulties are encountered in attempting to bring them into line with the regional sequence, and the Figure 3.2 depiction of the Neuvic sites in the chronological order suggested by their industrial contexts entails some major ambiguities.

The problem of ordering is further compounded by the fact that most of the sites fall into the Magdalenian cultural tradition, where precise attribution can be equivocal even in the case of tool assemblages that exhibit no special idiosyncrasy or ambiguity of their own. The reason for this is that, excepting its earlier and final phases, the definition of temporal subdivisions within the Magdalenian conventionally relies heavily upon bone and antler *fossile directeur* index types (see Laville, Rigaud, and Sackett 1980: 294-297). But, being organic, these of course are not preserved in the open air. The question does not arise with respect to stages "0" and I, the Early Magdalenian or "Badegoulian" industries, since their lithic traits are quite distinct from each other as well as from those that succeed them. But it is reflected in lumping together into a broad "Middle Magdalenian" group (comprising stages III-VIa) the several assemblages that are presumably later than the above but not so late as to possess any of the special lithic *fossiles directeurs* that characterize the Final (stage VIb) Magdalenian.

It is, by the way, surprising that no Final Magdalenian occupations have yet come to light in the Middle Isle Valley, despite the fact that this is the most frequently represented phase of the Magdalenian, and indeed of the Upper Paleolithic as a whole, in the shelters of the Perigord. Neither the size of the Neuvic sample of sites nor its topographic disposition would seem to account for this lack, but depositional factors could be relevant. Thus one might reason that Late Magdalenian levels are absent because, being stratigraphically the most superficial of the Paleolithic series, they have been the first to be destroyed by erosion and cultivation. But the argument can also be made that the diagnostic lithic traits which supposedly signal Final Magdalenian times may in fact represent special activities rather than chronological sequencing (Laville, Rigaud, and Sackett 1980: 340-341; Rigaud 1977). In this case, instead of being temporally significant, their absence in the Neuvic group would be one more indication of the rather special character assumed by industrial variation in the open air.

SITES OTHER THAN SOLVIEUX

Now let us turn to a brief review of the nine principal Neuvic sites that have undergone substantial excavation. This will provide at least a general impression of the very distinctive quality of the group as a whole, as well as illustrate how and in what variety of combinations the features discussed above are expressed in its individual members. All but the last, Solvieux, were investigated principally by Gaussen. The key reference for these is his magisterial *Le Paléolithique supérieur de plein air en Perigord* (1980), which should be considered the basic reference for the Neuvic group as a whole and the main document from which much of the empirical data summarized in this section has been culled. It is hoped that the following sketches of these sites will stimulate the reader to consult this excellent and superbly illustrated volume.

While the distinction seems to have no consistent significance with respect to their form or content, it is convenient for purposes of exposition to divide the Neuvic sites into two groupings according to their topographic situations. Many occupy relatively elevated positions high on the valley rim or on the plateaus that overlook it, while others lie on its lower slope or in soils immediately overlying fluviatile gravel terraces on the valley floor itself.

The highest of the former is Guillassou, which is situated on the crown of a plateau spur 120 m above the floodplain of the Isle. Its archaeological horizon extends over at least a hectare of surface and presumably incorporates several juxtaposed quasi-contemporary zones of habitation, but it has been disturbed in many places both by more recent archaeological features and by cultivation. Apart from extensive testing and surface collecting, a principal exposure of 27 sq. m was dug that revealed a more or less rectangular pavement of contiguous cobbles terminating in, or perhaps simply neighboring, a circular scatter of stones (Fig. 3.3). An assemblage of 142 flint tools accompanied by an appropriately rich collection of debitage concentrates upon this pavement without strictly limiting itself within its margins or showing any marked localizations. (It should be noted that Figure 3.3, like the rest that follow, simply depicts the exposure's rock plan and no more; excellent illustrations of how flint tools and debitage are spatially distributed with respect to the rocks may be found in Gaussen's 1980 monograph.) The tools exhibit the quite special typological and statistical features of the

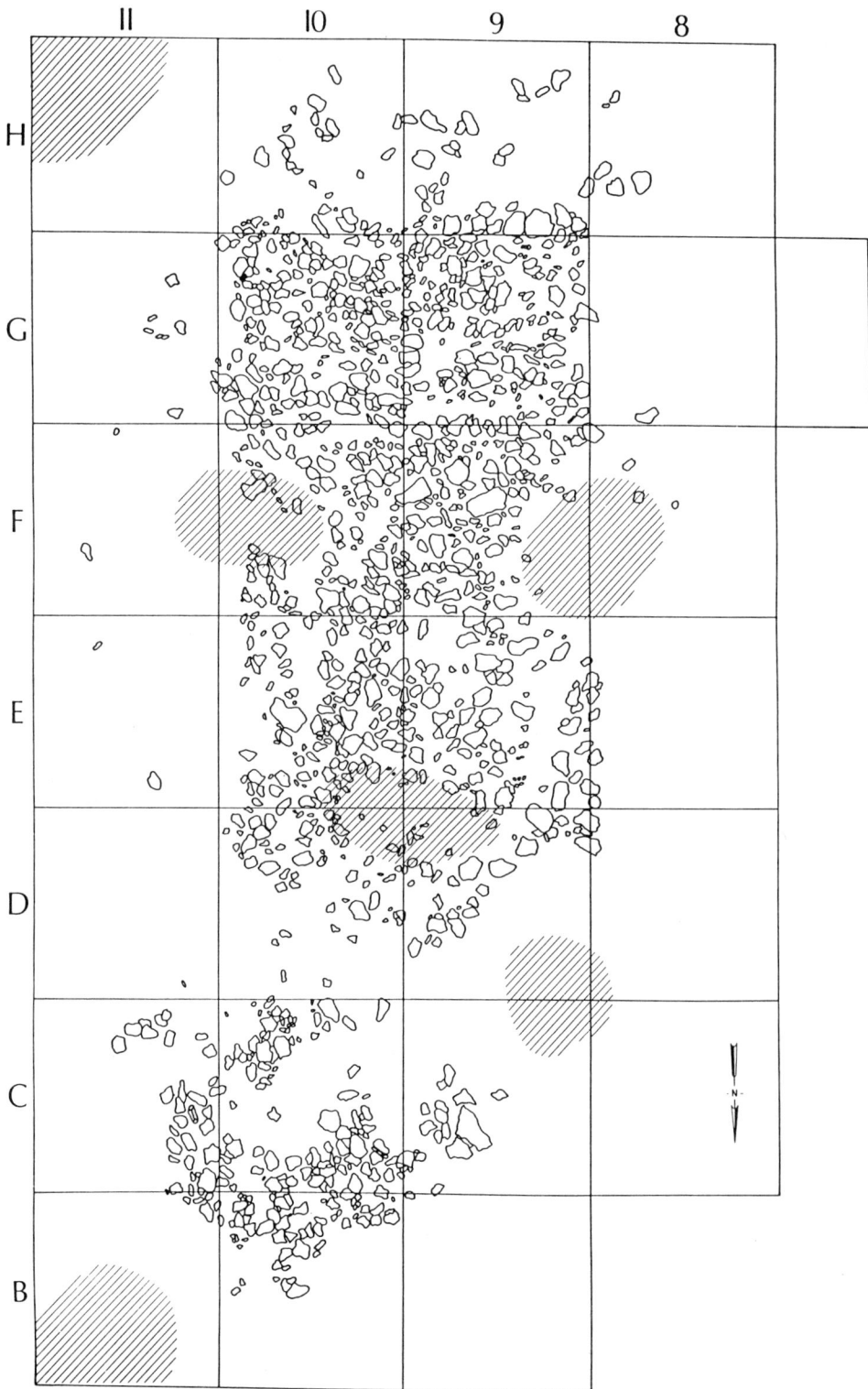

Figure 3.3 Guillassou rock plan (shaded areas indicate zones of disturbance by post-Paleolithic intrusions).

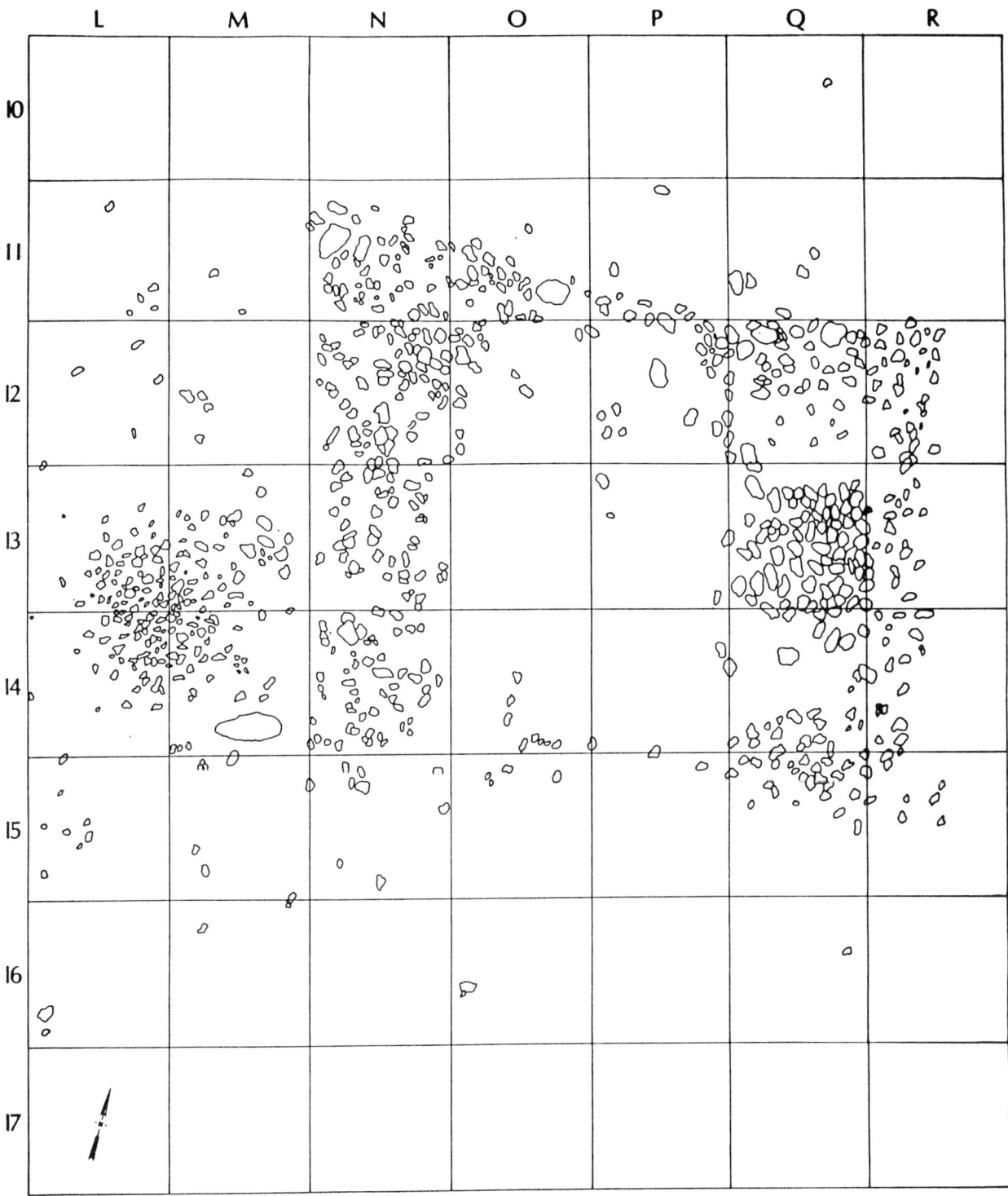

Figure 3.4   Plateau Parrain rock plan.

oldest or "zero" stage of the Early Magdalenian. Although not uncommon in the Charente and the Paris basin, this industry is elsewhere known regionally only from the two shelter sites of Laugerie Haute and Badegoule in the Perigord and, apparently, from one or two stations in the Gironde to the west (see Lenoir, ch. 26).

Occupying a similarly dominating plateau position 100 m above the river floodplain downstream from Guillassou is the station of La Croix de Fer. Again there appear flint tools and debitage, *pavage* rocks, and in addition numerous fragments of red and yellow ocher, in this case extending over several hectares. Here, however, all evidences of spatial organization have seemingly been obliterated by the effects of cryoturbation. A small collection of 50 tools excavated with some difficulty from the site, which came to light only after having been deforested and heavily bulldozed, includes 13 *raclettes* and other typological features characteristic of an Early (stage I) Magdalenian industry. Unlike stage 0 that precedes it, this industry is represented elsewhere in the Neuvic group and in several regional shelters as well. It is of interest, however, that the tool blanks at La Croix de Fer are produced by a discoidal nucleus technique that creates pseudo-Levallois forms quite distinct from those ordinarily encountered in the Magdalenian.

Considerably further downstream is the archaeologically important Plateau Parrain, whose sites lie only some 20 to 30 m above the river but still occupy a similarly commanding position. Two excavations here are of special importance and yield information of considerably greater interest for spatial organization than those considered so far. One is the station itself named Plateau Parrain (Bordes and Gaussen 1970), where a 56-sq.-m exposure revealed a single archaeological horizon which has suffered some vertical dislocation but which nonetheless yields a clearcut organization when its elements are plotted on a horizontal plan. The rock feature consists of a cobblestone cordon that describes a 4 × 4.5 m rectangular enclosure open to the south; a small square *pavage* is located inside the eastern wall of this cordon and a second, more diffuse one lies outside it to the west (Fig. 3.4). Stone tools and debitage are richly represented and concentrate into distinct knapping and work areas, although the tool types themselves show little if any tendency toward nonrandom clustering from one area to the next. It is interesting to note that these artifact concentrations all lie outside the cordon, whereas its interior is comparatively destitute of flint.

The assemblage of 335 retouched tools represents what is the commonest industry encountered in the Neuvic group, a reasonably well made if banal Middle Magdalenian that differs from its counterparts found in regional shelters in terms of only a few local stylistic features.

An attempt in the writer's laboratory to reconstitute the tool and debitage collections from this excavation lends considerable support to Gaussen's impression that it exposed only a small portion of what must be a much larger zone of occupation. Our unpublished joint excavations undertaken in 1984 confirmed that this is indeed the case, that considerably more than a hectare of the plateau's surfaces may be involved, and that other types of rock structures are present as well.

The second site on this plateau lies on its higher step some 250 m to the north of the first, at a spot named Le Cerisier (since it was a single flake protruding from the bole of an uprooted cherry tree that betrayed the presence of the buried archaeological horizon). Here a 30-sq.-m exposure has revealed what is undoubtedly the most extraordinary of the Neuvic cobblestone structures, consisting of a perfectly intact 16-m-square solid *pavage* with an "apse" attached at either end (Fig. 3.5). Flint is much less abundant here than at the site on the lower step, comprising 45 retouched tools and the debitage (16 nuclei and 400 blades and flakes) testifying to their production on the spot. The flint concentrates toward the outer edges of the pavement but in no case extends beyond its margins. The tools consist almost wholly of burins and crude ad hoc notches and denticulations, all showing the stigmata of heavy use and breakage. Although the burins' form and mode of manufacture may be consistent with a Middle Magdalenian assignment, no shelter assemblage of this or any other industrial tradition is known that has a similar quantitative typological makeup. Unhappily, fairly intensive surface exploration and sondaging, including a full week's effort in 1984 by a crew of five, has failed to bring to light any additional evidence of this fascinating occupation.

One additional plateau site contributes a further note of contrast to what we have already seen. This is Lacaud, which is located nearly 3 km from the Isle to the north of Plateau Parrain, at an elevation of 130 m above the floodplain (Gaussen and Moissat 1985). Here, as at Le Cerisier, the occupation seems to be sharply restricted, in this case to a well-delineated oval zone occupying some 28 sq. m. But organized stone features are missing altogether and, equally

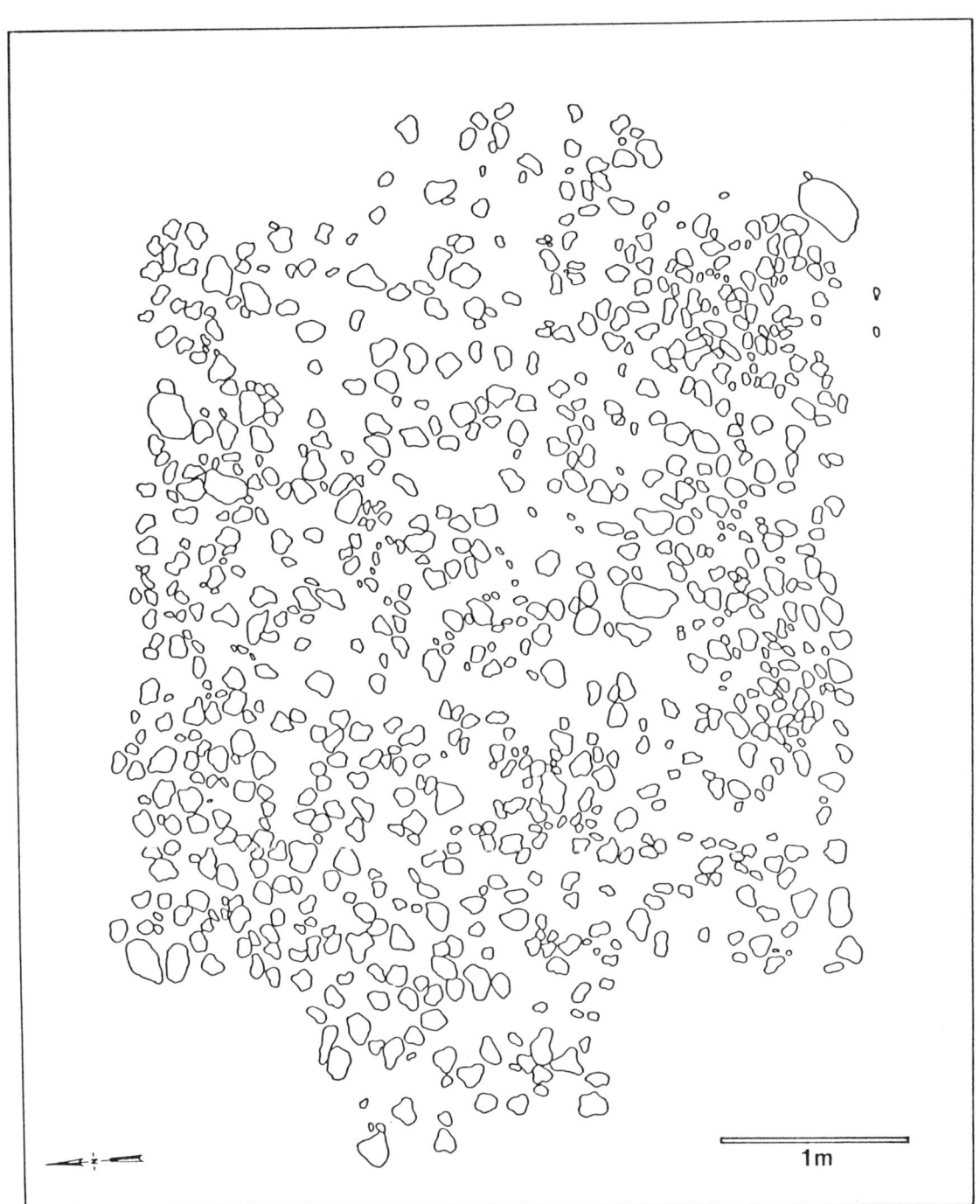

Figure 3.5 Le Cerisier rock plan.

uncharacteristically, there appear quantities of large but seemingly unused nodules of red ocher. Flint tools and debitage are richly represented, and the assemblage of 136 retouched specimens is truly singular. It possesses definite Upper Paleolithic elements such as well-made endscrapers on blades, but its burins are quite atypical specimens made upon flakes. The commonest tools of all make up a *carinate-bec* family of elevated but crude bec and nosed scraper forms that are reminiscent of the Aurignacian. Nonetheless, closely reasoned argument leads Gaussen and Moissat to conclude that the industry most likely represents a hitherto unseen variety of very early Magdalenian. If so, Lacaud, like La Croix de Fer, adds considerable evidence for the presence in the Neuvic group of the same industrial "polymorphism" of the Early Magdalenian industries that Lenoir documents for the neighboring Gironde region (ch. 26). In any event, there is no known shelter assemblage that brings together into one industry the particular ensemble of distinctive traits seen at Lacaud.

Equally great contrasts and novelty are exhibited by those sites located on or near the valley floor. Here again may be found open-air settlements whose tool assemblages differ in no appreciable way from the well-established shelter industries. A typical example is Le Mas de Sourzac, whose occupation extends over at least a hectare of surface area and yields a Middle Magdalenian industry similar to that of Plateau Parrain. Two exposures, yielding nearly identical assemblages numbering 45 and 85 tools respectively, suggest the presence of somewhat loosely organized rectangular pavements like that at Guillassou, but the couche seems nowhere to be free of damage from the plow. The intensive cultivation to which the floodplain has been subjected has brought to light several additional Middle Magdalenian sites, but in none has sufficient testing been pursued to assess the extent and potential of their intact archaeological horizons.

Valley-floor sites can be distinctive as well. Particularly interesting from the industrial point of view is La-Côte, where the beginning of the Upper Paleolithic sequence is represented in the form of a Lower Perigordian (Chatelperronian) industry (Gaussen and Texier 1974). The site may once have been rich, given the fact that 104 tools were recovered just from the vertical stratigraphic section left by the road cut that brought it to light. But much of the zone of occupation seems to have been destroyed, the remainder is currently inaccessible to excavation, and nothing is known of its horizontal organization and possible stone structures.

Finally, a particularly striking valley-floor site is Le Breuil, which furnishes stone structures and flint artifacts that are totally different from those seen anywhere else. Involved are four small rectangular *cabane pavages* about 2 m square each that are disposed at approximately 15-m intervals in a more or less straight line. Two of them are perfectly intact, cabanes 1 and 2 (Fig. 3.6), while the other two have been disturbed by vine cultivation. Of particular interest is the paucity of flint artifacts, comprising

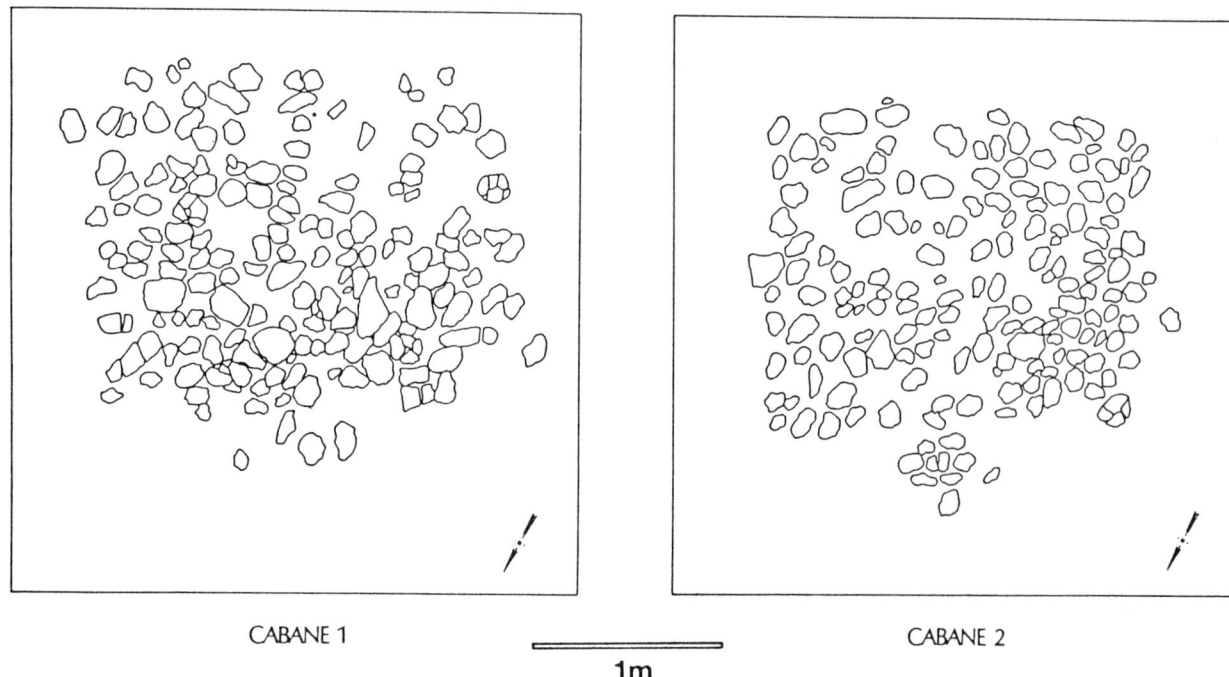

Figure 3.6 Le Breuil rock plans.

only a handful of pieces on each *pavage*; also noteworthy is the fact that the intervals between the *pavages* seem to be totally devoid of artifactual material. Tools are too few to be assigned with precision to an established industry, but their typological range is consistent with the stage I, or *raclette* phase, of the Early Magdalenian.

SOLVIEUX

Finally we come to Solvieux, which for sheer bulk and complexity stands alone. In part this is due to the nature and intensity of excavations there, which—whether measured in terms of work expended or material recovered—considerably exceeds that of all the other Neuvic sites put together. Limitations of time and manpower necessarily restricted Gaussen's attention to archaeological horizons that lie sufficiently close to the plow zone that they can be prospected and directly exposed from the surface. At Solvieux, however, we have been able to go deep, and five large-scale field campaigns under the writer's direction between 1967 and 1974 saw 2500 cu. m of deposit excavated (Fig. 3.7). This effort produced a kilometer of dressed stratigraphic sections, nearly 2000 sq. m of horizontally exposed occupation surfaces, and some 5000 retouched stone tools. That this work still left more than 90% of the site's estimated archaeological resources in the ground indicates bulk and complexity in a more literal sense as well. For in reality Solvieux is not a site but instead a locality incorporating several overlapping sites, a complex of quite diverse settlements occupying a succession of buried topographies where the lower valley slope and floodplain meet. It is a deposit that can attain several meters in depth, that in parts is as complex stratigraphically as a major rockshelter, and that varies markedly in archaeological content from one point to the next over nearly three hectares.

Accounts of Solvieux have appeared in a variety of brief reports in French (of which Sackett and Grimm 1987 is the most comprehensive), but only now is it becoming the subject of a substantial publication. This is the monograph *The Archaeology of Solvieux: Excavations and Industries* (Sackett, forthcoming), which in addition to detailing the substantive results summarized below examines in some depth most of the issues of method and theory that are only very briefly touched upon here. It is anticipated that future monographs in the Solvieux series will report on the stratigraphy and sedimentology of the site's deposits, largely the work of Jean-Pierre Texier and his colleagues at the Institut du Quaternaire, flint reconstitution analyses being conducted by Linda Grimm, and such special topics as Solvieux's rock-tool industries.

More than a score of archaeological horizons have been encountered at Solvieux ranging from Mousterian to Magdalenian times. A few of these remain too poorly known to be identified. Others are identifiable but now consist only of remnants of occupations that were largely lost to erosion during the Pleistocene. These include the Mousterian itself (Couche C) as well as both Aurignacian (Couche D) and Solutrean (Couche S) horizons. The latter two are of special significance because their presence elsewhere in the Middle Isle Valley is attested to only by isolated surface finds. The bulk of Solvieux's archaeological levels, however, make up the principal horizons and secondary lenses of seven major archaeological couches, which will be briefly reviewed in reverse chronological order (see Fig. 3.2).

Couches I and II represent Middle Magdalenian occupations in the western third of the site, whose form and disposition is reminiscent of the several other valley-floor stations attributed to this industry. These horizons may originally have extended from the cliff overlooking Solvieux's northern margin as far south as a buried channel of the Isle River that lies alongside the farm buildings beyond its current southern border. They have been reduced by plowing and erosion, however, to an island of archaeological deposit extending over a few thousand square meters northwards of Locality 1, and even here they have been heavily damaged by post-Pleistocene occupations and the plow. Gaussen's original excavations (1980: 57-102) as well as our own reveal fairly heavily if not contiguously paved surfaces similar to those at Le Mas de Sourzac, accompanied by dense circular concentrations of cobbles that may suggest stone boiling pits. The lower of the two horizons, Couche II, consisting of 218 tools recovered from a 28-sq.-m exposure, is nearly identical to the industry from the neighboring site of Plateau Parrain both in type frequencies and in its possession of a distinctive form known as the Solvieux point, which seems to be an extremely localized horizon marker for the Neuvic's Middle Magdalenian (Gaussen 1980: fig. 21:1, 2).

Couche A is a massive Early (stage I, or *raclette*)

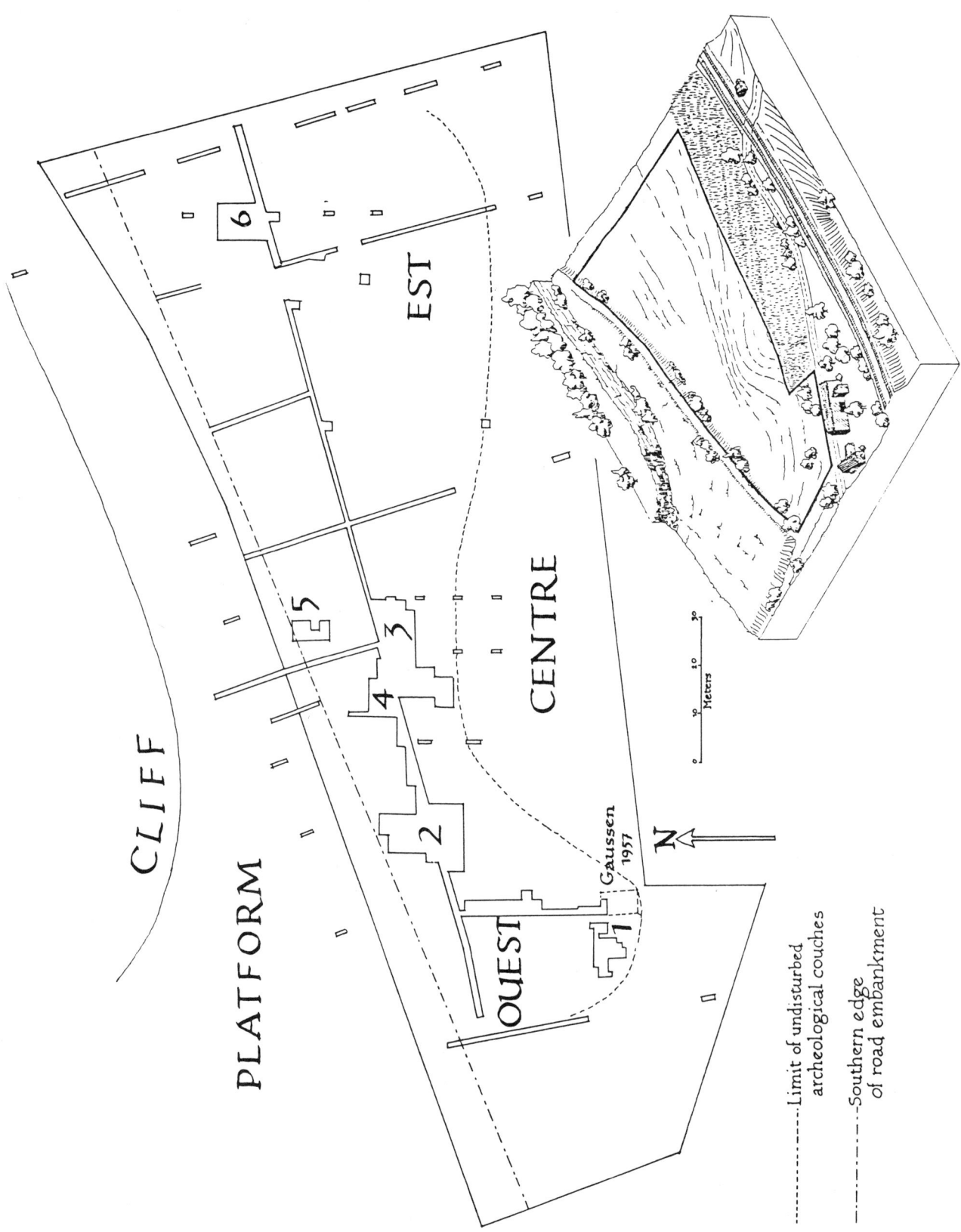

Figure 3.7 Solvieux.

THE NEUVIC GROUP

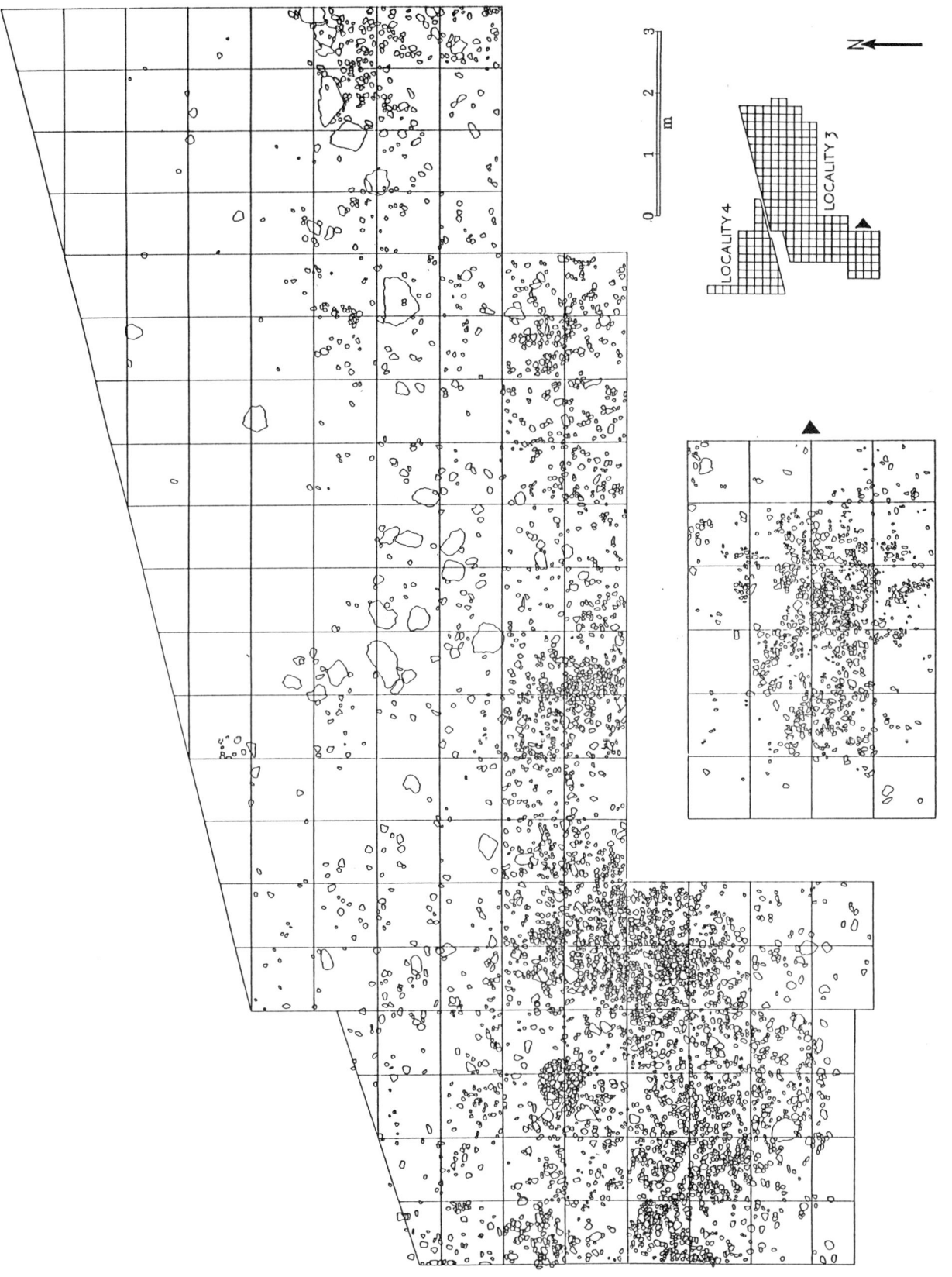

Figure 3.8 Solvieux Locality 3, Couche A (Magdalenian I) rock plan.

Magdalenian occupation that dominates the middle latitudes of the central part of Solvieux. Erosion and cultivation have truncated its extension toward the north, while its southern reach was obliterated when Solvieux's great south-central basin was cut in the last century to obtain material for constructing the railroad embankment. The couche is best known from its principal horizon exposed over 197 sq. m in Locality 3, which yielded an assemblage of 2115 stone tools. The industry is reasonably well made on robust blades and is closely comparable to Magdalenian I assemblages from the regional type-site of Laugerie Haute, save for its extremely strong *raclette* component (34%). The occupation incorporates several thousand couche rocks. Some 300 of the latter make up a "rock-tool" industry that includes hammerstones, anvils, and a variety of bevel-edged forms such as choppers, scraper-planes, and chisels (see Singer 1975). Similar assemblages are known from Solvieux's other couches and seem in fact to appear at most or all of the Neuvic sites. Although they find parallels among Lower Paleolithic pebble-tool industries, it is perhaps more relevant to note that such tools are an integral part of many ethnographically documented lithic technologies, such as those found among California Indians.

But the bulk of the couche rocks have been heated and served as elements in structures that provide a highly diverse and rather striking picture (Fig. 3.8). Dominating the southern and western portions of the locality is a dense if not sharply delineated *pavage* upon which half of the flint tool sample was found, along with a pecked stone lamp bearing a handle. (A second handled lamp, having few rivals in form or state of preservation among the 20-odd specimens of similar type recovered from French sites, appeared in a somewhat higher lens of Couche A in Locality 4 [see de Beaune, Roussot, and Sackett 1986]). Immediately south of it lies a separate pavement that has been damaged by the plow. The removal from its plan of all cobbles bearing the iron-stained marks of the share leaves a 4 × 6 m rectangular feature with clear-cut margins. To the north lies an extremely dense circular mass of cobbles whose vertical profile suggests the outline of a broad pit somewhat wider at the top than the bottom. Many rock fragments in this pit fit together with broken cobbles in the neighboring pavement, suggesting that the construction of the pit may have been responsible for the relative dearth of cobbles now found in its immediate vicinity.

The northern and eastern sectors of the locality are much poorer in flint artifacts and present altogether different structures made up of extremely large blocks that individually may weigh more than 50 kg. These are of special interest because such blocks appear only as isolated anvils and *sièges* in the rest of Solvieux's occupations. The structure suggesting a *fond de cabane* near the center of the locality is composed of rounded diabase boulders which, judging from their elevation relative to the surrounding occupation, may have originally occupied some kind of shallow excavation. Towards the east lies an alignment of tabular blocks of silicified limestone which apparently belongs to a much larger formation extending beyond the limits of the present excavation. Of considerable interest is the fact that upon one of these were found the remains of an engraving of animals (Gaussen and Sackett 1984). Unfortunately, the greater part of the depiction long ago eroded away (which raises the possibility that the neighboring large stones may also once have been engraved). But the vestige that remains—consisting of horse hoofs and the hindquarters of a cervid—is nonetheless of considerable importance, in that it confirms the chronology and industrial association of A. Leroi-Gourhan's style 3, which is abundantly represented at Lascaux as well as at the engraved cave of Gabillou across the river from Solvieux.

Dating appreciably earlier is a vast zone of Upper Perigordian settlement that stretches across the entire middle and upper reaches of Solvieux, incorporating well over a hectare of occupation surface. Three principal areal units are recognized, respectively Couches III (Ouest), B (Centre), and M (Est), all of which are accompanied by one or more satellite horizons. Precise depositional correlations are difficult to establish over such great distances, but all three of the couche systems are quasi-contemporary in stratigraphic terms. The three principal horizons exhibit the diagnostic features common to those Perigordian stage Vc, or "Noaillian," industries dominated by Raysse (Basselar) burins, possess a Gravettian backed blade element that ranges from negligible to only moderate, and display marked differences in blank production strategies despite the fact that they employ the same flint types and possess very similar typological inventories. Their satellite horizons raise anew the highly controversial issue of the stratigraphic relationship Raysse and Noailles burins bear to each other in this highly variable and poorly understood industrial complex (see David 1985; Rigaud, ch. 25).

Although artifactually dense, these "Raysse Perigordian" occupations tend to show only a modest

THE NEUVIC GROUP

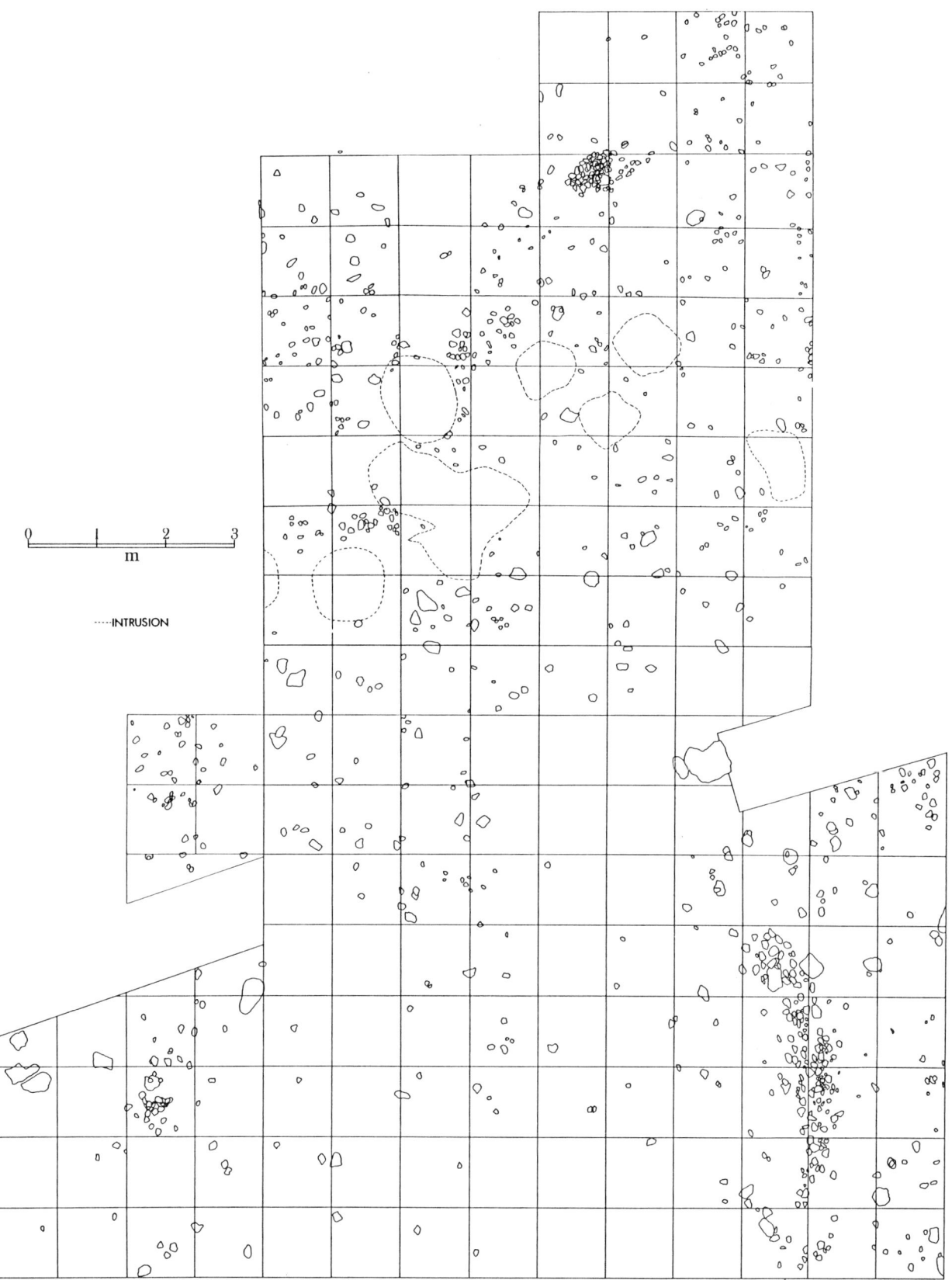

Figure 3.9   Couche III (Raysse Perigordian) rock plan.

degree of obvious spatial organization. Cobblestones and an occasional larger block tend to display fairly light scatters, punctuated occasionally by denser but amorphous concentrations. Typical is the picture revealed by Couche III in Locality 2, whose 180 sq. m of exposure yielded an assemblage of 769 stone tools (Fig. 3.9). The only features of particular interest are the oval mass of cobblestones near its northern edge and the curved "wall" in its southeastern quadrant. Structures like the former are often interpreted as hearths, but here as in most comparable instances in the Neuvic group the evidence is highly equivocal, particularly in the absence of organic residues. Heat-reddened patches are visible on nearly all of the cobbles involved, but they are oriented so randomly with respect to one another as to indicate they were heated prior to the construction of the structure itself. And heat-damaged flint is virtually nonexistent. The "wall" in the southeastern quadrant may possibly belong to a larger feature that extends considerably beyond the confines of the exposure.

Adding the appropriate flint tools and debitage to this or any other of the Raysse Perigordian rock plans would not markedly enhance the impression of patterning. This fact has been brought home particularly in Locality 6, whose 56-m-square exposure yields an assemblage of 456 stone tools from a Couche M occupation which seems to have undergone no movement or disturbance at all. Here a spatial statistical analysis by Winterman (1975) confirms that, despite the obvious concentrations of flint and couche rocks, there seem to be only weak statistical correlations in the horizontal associations among specific varieties of flint artifacts on or between them and the rock concentrations. There may be some tendency for special types such as backed bladelets to be distributed individually (as are *raclettes* in Couche A), and for others, like burins and scrapers, to exhibit somewhat negatively correlated distributions over space. But in general the types are not strongly prone to segregate either in groups or individually into distinct clusterings that stand apart from the more general spatial concentrations exhibited by all tools and debitage viewed in the ensemble. Current work by Linda Grimm, who is conducting a reconstitution analysis of the entire Couche M tool and debitage sample, should throw much additional light upon the horizontal organization of this horizon (Fig. 3.10).

We come finally to Solvieux's most intriguing occupation, Couche IV, which occupies the bank of a buried stream channel in the northwestern quadrant of the site. Its stratigraphic position, sediments, and pollen indicate it must date close to the beginning of the Upper Paleolithic sequence, somewhere in the early Typical Aurignacian/Lower Perigordian range (Texier 1980: 288). This seems to be confirmed by a radiocarbon date of 30,350 B.C. ± 2960 obtained from carbon-charged soil found in one of its hearths (unpublished date provided by Rainer Berger, UCLA Isotope Laboratory).

Couche IV's industry is characterized by an unusual and seemingly primitive method of blade production and a tool inventory that is unique to Solvieux. Burins (36%) are atypical but still highly standardized; the most characteristic type is a quasi-transversal form struck against a steep lateral margin that is regularized by retouch in such a manner as to blur the conventional dihedral-truncation burin distinction (Fig. 3.11). Nearly half (46%) of the assemblage is composed of "Solvieux truncations," a highly variable family of steeply truncated pieces that began their careers as narrow pointed forms but were radically altered by subsequent breakage and rejuvenation into end-products that range from atypical becs through heavily undercut truncations to shouldered endscrapers (Fig. 3.12). Interestingly enough, the only close parallel to this type found in the literature is the *coutelas* described by André Cheynier (1963) at the site of La Cirque de la Patrie in the Ile-de-France, where it forms an integral component of a strongly Gravettian industry that easily may date ten millennia later than Couche IV. In this connection, it should be noted that specimens like the one illustrated, wherein the truncation retouch continues down the margin to simulate a backed point, are extremely rare. While the remainder of the industry includes only a handful of highly atypical endscrapers, there are a considerable number of curved bladelets bearing abrupt inverse retouch (Fig. 3.11).

The Couche IV industry has tentatively been named the "Beauronnian" because the buried channel with which it is associated was presumably left by the Beauronne, a stream that today flows immediately to the west of Solvieux and enters the Isle River just downstream from the site. The Beauronnian must be attributed to either a hitherto unsuspected industrial tradition or an activity complex peculiar to open-air occupation, or both.

It is principally known from Locality 2, where its main horizon has yielded an assemblage of 622 tools. Due to the considerable bulk of archaeological horizons that must be excavated before this deep-lying

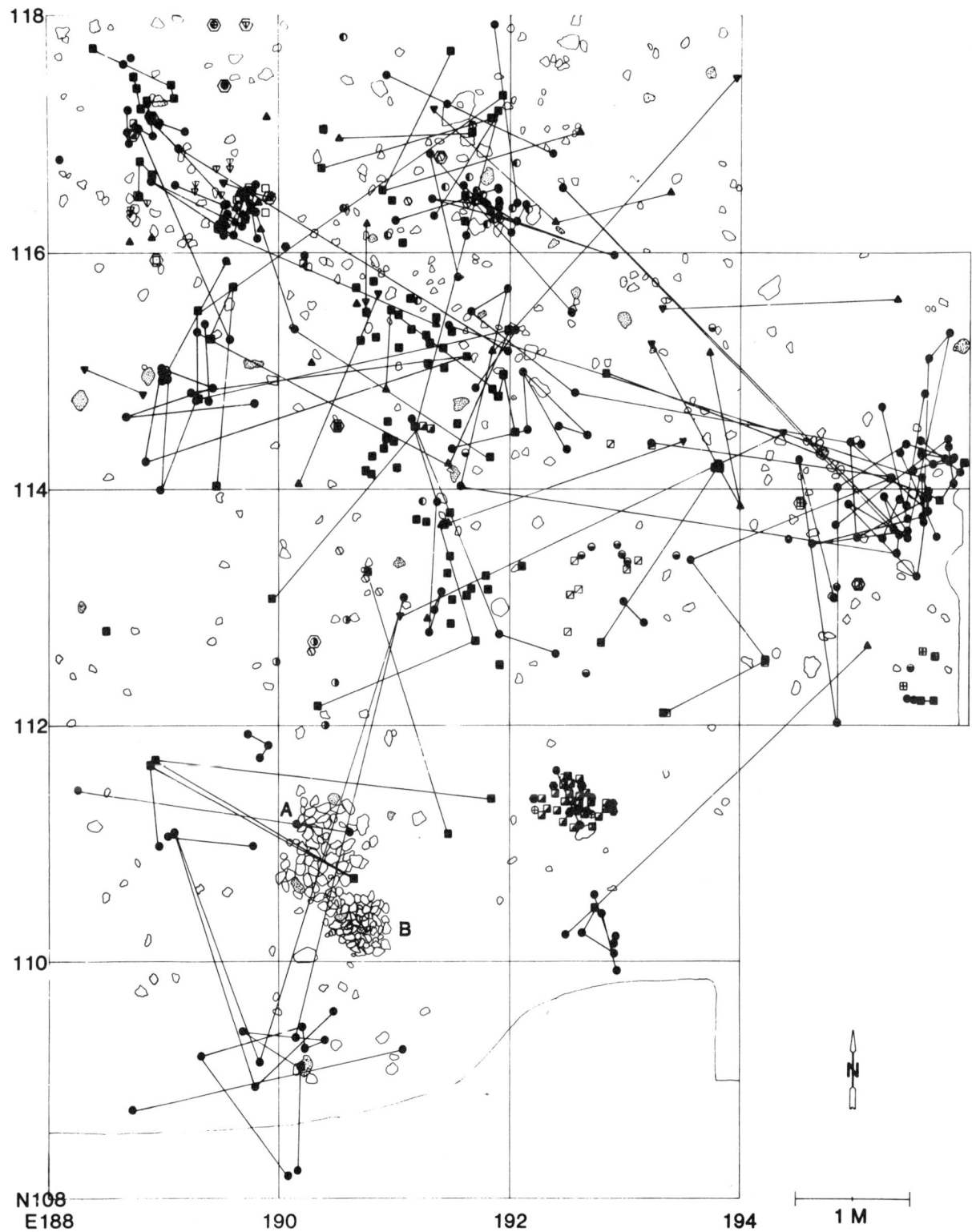

Figure 3.10   Solvieux Locality 6, Couche M (Raysse Perigordian) rock and tool plan. Lines connect refitted pieces. (After Sackett and Grimm 1987: fig. 5)

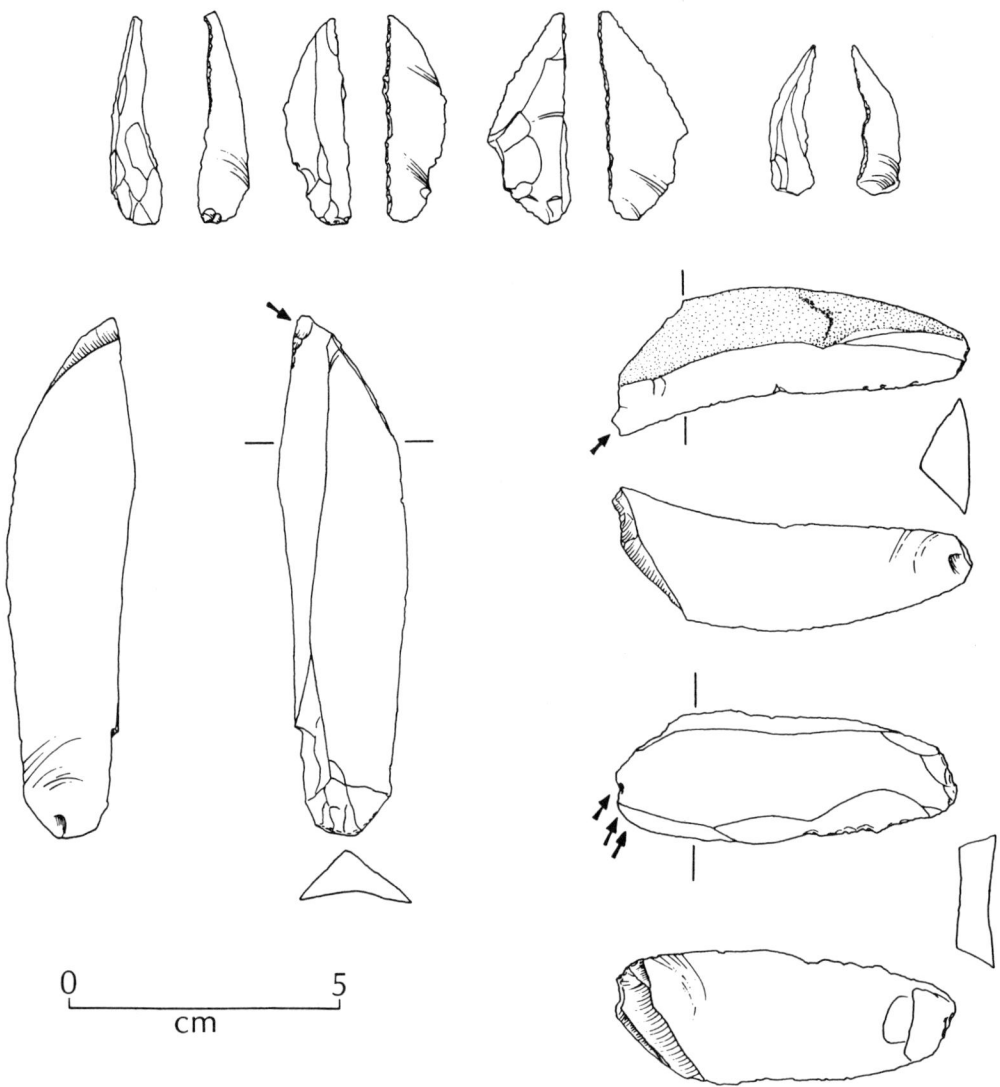

Figure 3.11 Solvieux Couche IV (Beauronnian) industry, burins and retouched bladelets.

occupation is reached, its exposure is frustratingly small (Fig. 3.13). At this depth in the deposit, however, limestone and even small amounts of organic material have escaped dissolution, and there have come to light the Neuvic group's only examples of what appear to be hearths. One lies in the southwestern quadrant of the exposure, consisting of a somewhat dispersed zone of blackened earth associated with a semicircular arrangement of large rocks under which charcoal and small bone fragments have been found. Another, on the eastern margin of the exposure, is characterized by a well-defined circular concentration of what appears to be hearth debris occupying a shallow basin (from which the radiocarbon sample was obtained). A few blocks seem to be associated, and the edge of what may be a related large block feature is visible in the neighboring eastern wall of the exposure. It is tempting to speculate that limestone might have played an important role in the rock features elsewhere at Solvieux and that, had it been preserved, they would exhibit clearer configurations than are now observable. A refitting analysis being pursued by Linda Grimm (see Sackett and Grimm 1987: fig. 9) of all the tools and debitage from this horizon should add much information about its horizontal organization and the technology that underlies this very distinctive industry.

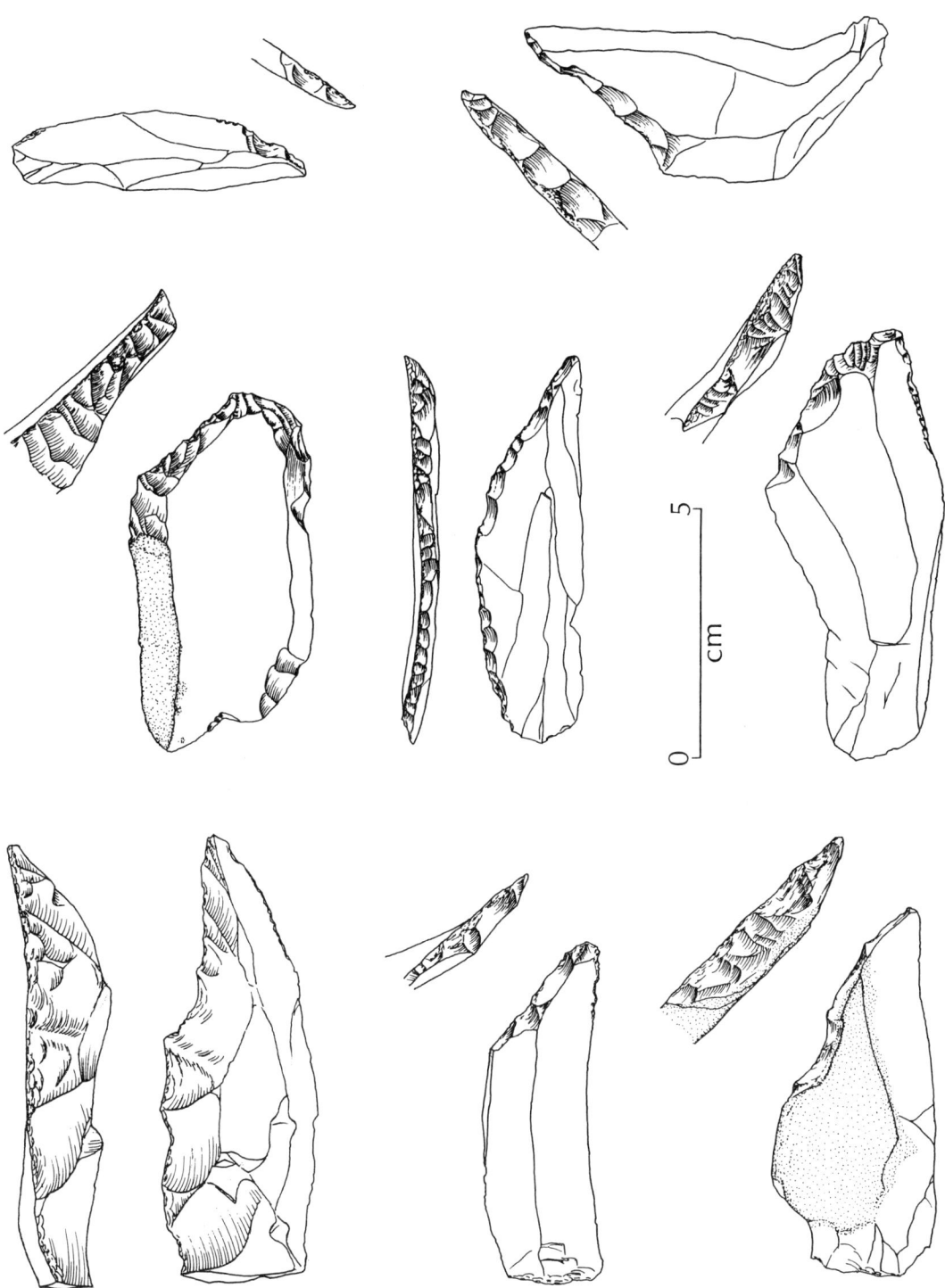

Figure 3.12 Solvieux Couche IV (Beauronian) industry, Solvieux truncations.

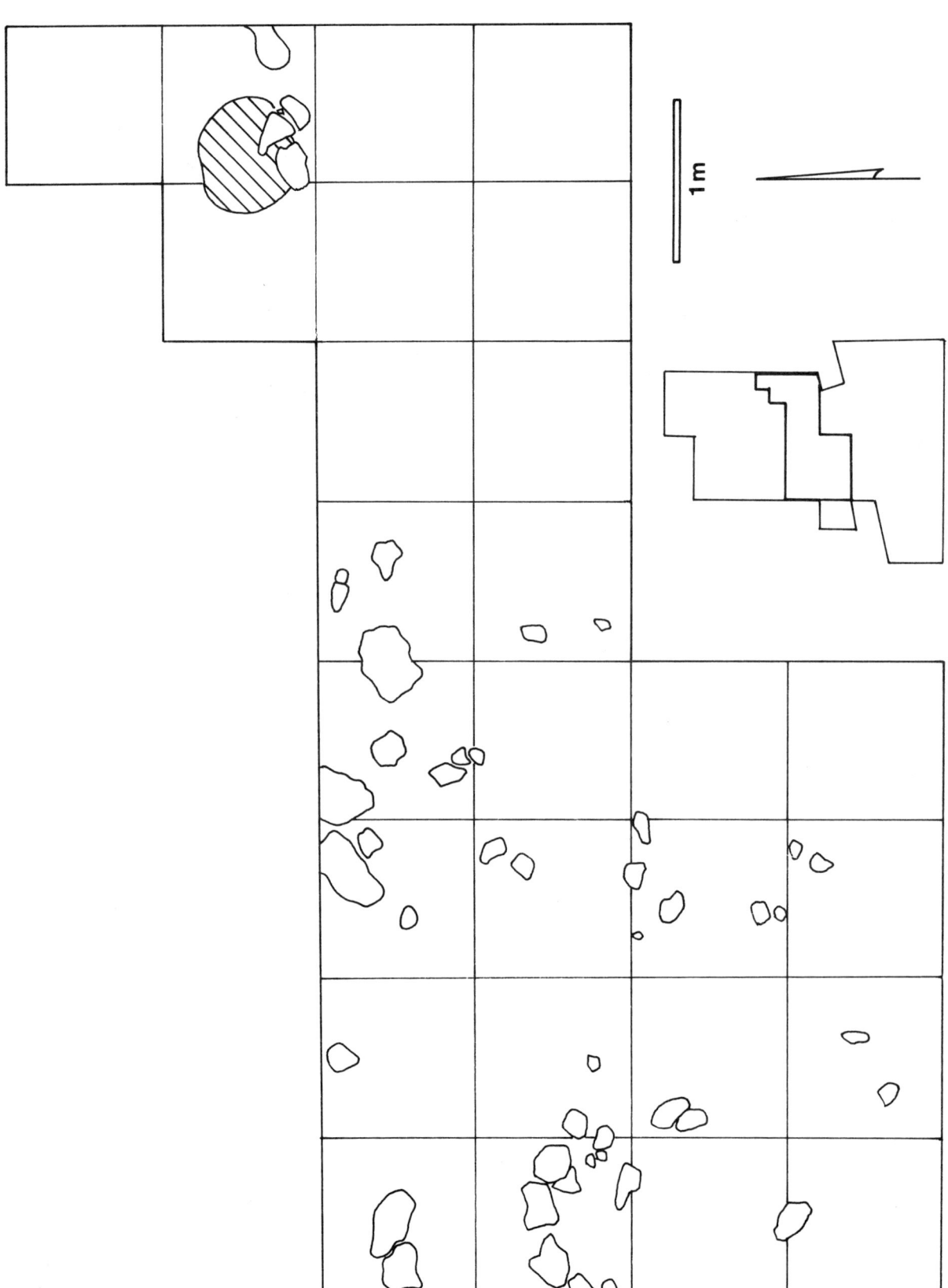

Figure 3.13 Solvieux Locality 2, Couche IV (Beauronnian) rock plan.

OVERVIEW

If one point emerges clearly from the above review it is the great heterogeneity exhibited by the Neuvic sites with respect to size, disposition, structural organization, and industrial makeup. A variety of different kinds of settlements and activities seem to be represented, all of which are by no means likely to be accommodated within any single model of Upper Paleolithic demographic and economic geography. In this they present a challenge to interpretation surpassing that posed by open-air complexes elsewhere in Europe, whose members as often as not tend to exhibit an almost stereotypic homogeneity of organization and content by comparison.

This is not to say that, taken piecemeal, the Neuvic sites fail to provide interesting glimpses into Upper Paleolithic lifeways. For example, their positioning with respect to regional topography and to probable distributions of natural resources in the late Pleistocene is indeed suggestive (see Gaussen 1977). And there is a kind of humanistic immediacy displayed by some of their features that cannot help but evoke pictures of habitation structures in the mind's eye. Surely, for example, the sharply delimited *pavage* at Le Cerisier suggests the confines of a solid-walled structure or perhaps a pit-dwelling. On the other hand, the stone cordon at Plateau Parrain may have served to weigh down the flexible walls of some less substantial, even portable, shelter or tent, outside of which—judging from the flint distribution—most of the activities conducted at the site took place. These and related matters of interpretation are ones to which Gaussen in particular has given much thought (e.g., 1980, 1982), and his often provocative and always enlightening reconstructions of the Neuvic occupations can be read with profit by all students of spatial archaeology.

Specific site reconstructions made by those who do the fieldwork and actually see the substantive data as presented in the ground must always be taken seriously. Nonetheless, their primary function is not to write Stone Age history or even necessarily to generate specific models of site settlement and activity that call for immediate testing. Rather it is to give our paleoethnological skills some exercise, to keep us mindful of the ultimate goals of our research, and to help guide us toward those kinds of sites and data that may ultimately carry us to those goals. The last is of greatest importance. For, in the present still-formative state of the enterprise, it is the immediate and more practical issues of method and theory raised by these sites and their empirical data, and not the cultures which lie behind them, that must command our energies. Some of the more salient issues deserve mention.

To begin with, investigation of the Neuvic sites is strongly colored by two major types of ambiguity. One stems from their lack of organic remains, such as charcoal and bone, whose presence would be so helpful in identifying specific kinds of structures like hearths and, more generally, in giving spatial definition to the activities around which human settlement revolved. It is this organic component, of course, that lends such striking quality of life to the exposures at Pincevent (Leroi-Gourhan and Brézillon 1972) and many of the splendid open stations of Central and Eastern Europe (e.g., Bosinski, ch. 24). The second type of ambiguity is caused, paradoxically enough, by the very wealth and diversity of the Neuvic sites. The ability to talk confidently about patterning in the spatial organization of occupation surfaces stems not only from the explicitness of the relevant data but as well from their redundancy. In other words, one needs to deal with a familiar pattern that repeats itself and is seemingly not to be contradicted by other, potentially rival, patterns. This situation clearly does not exist in the Neuvic sites, whose complex and heterogeneous occupations span nearly the entire Upper Paleolithic, entail several different cultural traditions, and very likely reflect a variety of distinct kinds and aspects of late Stone Age lifeways.

It is therefore of particular importance that the Neuvic group is surrounded by the great bulk of the Perigord's shelter deposits. Neuvicois researchers need not restrict their vision to local resources of information alone, but can instead draw upon a much greater corpus of data relevant to regional Upper Paleolithic ecologies and the demographies, economic strategies, and perhaps even ethnic boundaries of those who exploited them. A new pollen profile from Laugerie Haute or new information about butchering practices or tool localizations at Le Flageolet could prove to be more relevant at any given time to the analysis of a given occupation surface at Solvieux than the discovery of a contemporary archaeological horizon only a kilometer away. In short, when pursuing paleoethnology in the Perigord, open-air and shelter research must be regarded as fully complementary and interpenetrating lines of investigation.

Equating the Neuvic occupations with their shelter counterparts, however, is not a simple business, especially since it has become evident that lithic variation is a subtler and more complex phenomenon when viewed from the perspective of the open air. We have seen that some industries that quantitatively dominate the shelter sequence, such as the Final Magdalenian, do not appear at all in the Neuvic sector. And, while it is true that the established shelter industries often find close counterparts in the open air, this is by no means always the case. Some open-air industries exhibit kinds of atypicality (e.g., the pseudo-Levallois technology at La Croix de Fer) that are not mirrored in the seemingly more stereotyped shelter assemblages. And others, such as Le Cerisier and Le Breuil, may possess altogether typical artifacts but still display such idiosyncratic quantitative makeups that their assignment to the conventional industrial types is tentative indeed. Even more important, there have already come to light in the Neuvic group two industries—that of Lacaud and the Beauronnian industry at Solvieux—that simply have no analogues at all in the shelters.

The significance of the above facts is underlined when one recalls that barely a score of reasonably well defined assemblages have yet been recovered from the Neuvic sites, whereas well over a thousand have been brought to light in the Perigord's shelters. It may well be then that the *mentalité de grotte* has created as much restriction of thought about the nature of Upper Paleolithic industrial variation as it has about the nature of Upper Paleolithic habitation. In short, the special kinds of variation seen in open sites may bear witness to kinds of groups and kinds of activities that are simply not represented in the shelters.

Now let us turn to some more immediate problems presented by the Neuvic sites themselves. Many issues remain unresolved concerning the nature and integrity of their archaeological horizons. Particularly worrisome in this regard is the areal vastness of their occupation zones, which raises the question of when one is dealing with what might fairly be considered a single integral settlement by a specific group of people, and when it is a matter of some sort of depositional composite integrating the remains of repeated, and perhaps only partially overlapping, occupations by several successive groups. Practical means of testing the problem do come to mind, but none is really satisfactory.

For example, one can attempt fitting together flint tools and debitage from widely separated points on the surface, arguing altogether correctly that those which join must truly be contemporary. But given the apparently expedient nature of the technology, it is unreasonable to assume that distant points would be related by significant numbers of successful refittings even if only a single large settlement were involved. In any case, the results would demonstrate only the possible areal extent of a given installation's zone of activities, and not whether this is in fact the only installation actually represented. An alternative line of evidence is provided by areal variations in the typological makeup of tool samples over the surface. But here the same facts can usually be used to argue either side of the question. For example, that an extensive surface yields typologically homogeneous tool assemblages wherever it is sampled might argue as much for recurring passages of culturally similar groups as for the massive installation of a single one. At the same time, areal differences in typology over that same surface would lend themselves to interpretation as spatially segregated activity variations within a single group of occupants as easily as to cultural variations among many. There is, in short, no procedural or doctrinaire solution to the problem and it has to be dealt with on a case-by-case basis. At present it remains unanswerable for the Neuvic group, where anything approaching total exposure of vast archaeological horizons like Guillassou's Badegoulian, Plateau Parrain's Middle Magdalenian, or Solvieux's Raysse Perigordian couches is a practical impossibility, and where no surface presents itself with anything like the self-evident clarity of a prehistoric Pompeii.

Much remains to be learned about the extent and nature of spatial patterning within the surface exposures we already possess. Some of the answers will come from new techniques of laboratory analysis similar to those being developed by spatial archaeologists working on related problems elsewhere. For example, flint tools and debitage, as well as broken rocks and their chips, are being reconstituted in order both better to understand how artifacts are vertically dispersed within and between archaeological horizons and, on the horizontal plane, to define the nature of variability in the spatial contexts in which artifacts were manufactured, used, and discarded. The notion of "tool" itself is being extended beyond the conventional retouched forms to those ad hoc implements that bear the stigmata of use as well as to the rock-tool inventory noted previously. And considerable energy is being expended upon clarifying the patterning that lies behind the conventional morphological typologies used in defining stone tool industries. This enterprise among other things calls for re-examination of the theoretical distinction between style and function that so often plagues lithic archaeologists (e.g., Sackett 1982, 1985). It also calls for the design of new methods of codifying and analyzing formal variation among flint artifacts in order to illuminate the dynamic interaction among tool form, blank production, and reduction strategies (e.g., Sackett 1988a, forthcoming). Unfortunately, the variation analyzed in the latter endeavor does not include the stigmata of usewear, which seem to be masked by the types of patination fostered in the Neuvic sector's soils (Helle Juel-Jensen, pers. comm.).

Such attempts to stretch out methodologically and realize more of the potential of the substantive data will surely enhance our grasp of spatial patterning in the Neuvic sites. But there still remains the question of the scale of our excavations, which of course has much to do with whether one sees patterning at all and, if so, the form it assumes. It may be, for example, that the patterned organization of Solvieux's occupation surfaces is on a scale truly commensurate with their often great areal extent and that our currently available exposures provide windows much too small to perceive it. In other words, despite its size and fascinating diversity, the exposure of Couche A in Locality 3 is still too inadequate to support generalizations about the vast occupation it samples. Coarse patterns cannot be retrieved through fine screens.

Yet it remains true that many Paleolithic occupations for which a high degree of spatial patterning is claimed are known from exposures considerably smaller than those at Solvieux. In some cases, like Le Cerisier and Le Breuil, the organization is so explicit as to be undeniable. But often the question might reasonably be asked, Is not the apparent pattern one observes on a given occupation surface the artificial product of viewing that surface at too fine a scale? For example, the extremely diverse rock features in Couche A's exposure in Locality 3 (Fig. 3.8) would in fact give a much greater appearance of organization were they viewed in more piecemeal fashion. Superimposing on the Locality 3 rock plan cut-out rectangles and squares of various sizes akin to picture mattes could frame specific rock configurations (such as the central *fond de cabane*), lending them a distinctiveness they altogether lack when viewed in the broad focus of the exposure as a whole. Had the excavation itself been more restricted areally and framed them individually, the impression of pattern and organization would have been greatly enhanced. Perhaps our Neuvic experience gives us the right to inquire whether the claims for clear-cut horizontal patterning made by spatial archaeologists working in open-air sites elsewhere in France (and, indeed, in Europe as a whole) may not also be affected by issues of scale. In other words, what is sometimes perceived as pattern may be in reality no more than simplicity born of seeing too little.

In any event, we obviously need more occupation surface—which means more sites and more people to dig them. Good open sites may well be ubiquitous in the Perigord, but open-air research calls for new kinds of knowledge and new skills, and there are few excavators qualified to wrestle with the special stratigraphic and taphonomic problems they pose. Simply to identify an open site and successfully determine the nature and extent of its archaeological horizons calls for dealing with couches that may extend over a hectare and that occupy soils whose depositional history is totally masked by leaching. These soils may be profoundly modified by such agencies as cryoturbation, solifluction, and loss of fine fraction through washing. Even when accessible to probing directly through the plow zone, rich horizons can still be difficult to define because—if they are highly structured horizontally—they consist largely of empty space. The problem is further compounded when one has to grapple with voluminous deposits like those at Solvieux. Sondaging in this case calls for deep stratigraphic trenching, which is an altogether different business from surface probing both in magnitude and in that the amount of artifactual material one encounters in passing through archaeological couches vertically is but a minute fraction of what would appear were they tested from above over a broad area. The problem is illustrated by noting how few stars are actually intersected by a straight edge tossed at random on a map of the heavens.

In particular we need more sites with the volume and complexity of Solvieux. That we presently know of no others does not necessarily mean they do not exist. More likely it reflects the fact that prehistorians are not sufficiently aware of the kinds of deposits they should be looking for or, more frankly, do not recognize them when they see them. We have frequently been reminded at Solvieux of the need for continual refinement in this artisanal domain of research strategy by discovering multiple rich occupations in areas of the site where work in earlier seasons had revealed nothing at all. Indeed, among the major conclusions generated by the Solvieux project is the maxim that, while the pursuit of horizontal archaeology may ultimately end in paleoethnology, necessity dictates that it begin with stratigraphy and taphonomy.

DISCUSSION

JELINEK: In later periods, in the Mesolithic for instance, there are sites with a very limited and restricted inventory of implements which are interpreted as short-term task-specific sites, and large sites which are interpreted as more general base camps. How do you think that fits with the record that you see?

SACKETT: I don't know. I don't want to use the term "site hierarchy," because that has already been taken by people who are interested in the rise of chiefdoms and so forth. Obviously we are looking for a terminology that separates specialized sites and larger home-base camps.

SIMEK: It seems to me the scale of variation implied by these kinds of data, both chronological and cultural, suggests that the problems we are able to address may not be on the precise paleoethnological scale of analysis that is often desired.

IV

Recent Thoughts on the Riss and Early Würm Lithic Assemblages of La Chaise de Vouthon (Charente, France)

André Debénath

The prehistoric sites of La Chaise de Vouthon comprise several caves and shelters in the Jurassic dolomitic limestones of the Tardoire Valley, a tributary of the Charente River (Fig. 4.1). They are situated in the center of a heavily karstic region that contains a number of Paleolithic sites—Fontéchevade, Montgaudier, La Cave, Le Bois du Roc, Marillac—which in turn contain industries spanning the time from the Riss to the Recent Würm. At some distance are the sites of d'Artenac, which contains Mousterian and an industry with bifaces associated with a sabertooth cat, and the well-known site of La Quina.

Two of the shelters of La Chaise warrant our attention here. These are the Abris Bourgeois-Delaunay and Suard, named after the people who first excavated them in the 19th century. These two shelters are part of a large and complex karstic network and, in fact, communicate with other. A lower network is actually functional. Systematic excavations were undertaken here by P. David in the 1950s, and by myself from 1967 to 1983.

Briefly, the stratigraphy of Abri Bourgeois-Delaunay is as follows:

1) Disturbed.
2) Aurignacian.
3) Red sterile layer.
4) Layer with large animal bones, but no industry.
5) Another red sterile layer.
6) "Mousterian" level.
7) Stalagmitic floor.

The above layers were excavated by David.

8) A sandy-clayey bed containing some altered gravels, which can be locally subdivided into four levels.

8') An archaeological level rich in deposits of iron

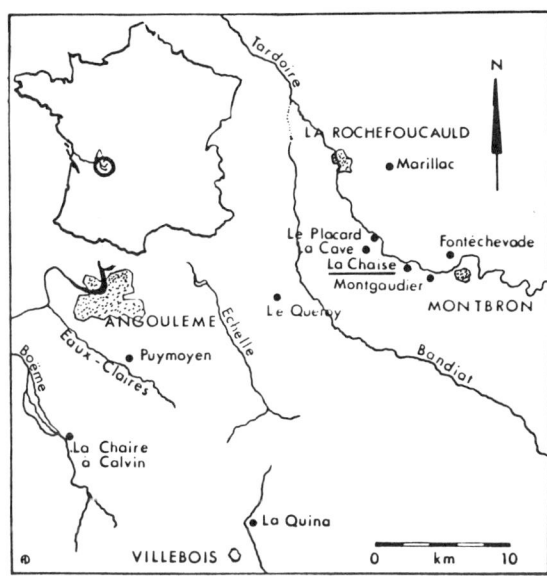

Figure 4.1 Location of the sites of La Chaise.

oxides and manganese, which were earlier mistakenly called Mousterian hearths (corresponding to Level 9 of David).

9) A sandy-clayey layer containing some rounded gravels which is locally subdivided into two levels.

9') A thin level containing some artifacts.

10) A brownish clayey layer, characterized by an abundance of remains of *Ursus spelaeus* (cave bear).

11) Stalagmitic floor.

12) Large ceiling blocks, many of which are encrusted with manganese.

13) Very large deposit ($\simeq 8$ m thick) of sands and clays, sometimes intercalated with gravel beds. In places, this part of the sequence from Layers 8 to 13, excavated by myself, attains a total thickness of 12 m.

The stratigraphy of Abri Suard is more complex, as follows:

Above the sandy-clayey sediments which probably represent the second glacial phase of the Riss (Couche 54), and separated from them by a stalagmitic floor, is a cryoclastic ensemble representing all or at least part of the Riss III (David's Couches III to VIII, or what I have called Couches 48 to 53). The upper part of this ensemble is sealed by a stalagmitic floor of variable thickness, corresponding chronologically, in part, to Couche 11 of Abri Bourgeois-Delaunay. These formations are overlain by David's Couches I and II, which correspond sedimentologically and chronologically to Couches 9 and 10 of Abri Bourgeois-Delaunay.

It is difficult to establish precise stratigraphic correlations between the areas excavated by David and those excavated by myself, since there are no notes concerning the stratigraphy for these two areas available from the earlier excavations.

The deposits of Abri Bourgeois-Delaunay were attributed (Debénath 1974) to the Riss II (Couche 13), Riss III (Couche 12), Early Würm (Couches 10 to 3), and the beginning of the Recent Würm (Couche 2). It is important to recall that the Riss-Würm Interglacial is represented in this shelter by the major polygenic stalagmitic floor (Debénath, Raynal, and Schwarcz 1980). A series of uranium/thorium dates indicate that this stalagmitic layer was essentially formed between 150 and 112 Kyr. Couche 7 was dated by the same method to 106 Kyr ± 10,000.

Abri Suard also contains Rissian sediments. The Riss II is represented by sandy-clayey sediments (Couche 54) reminiscent of those of Couche 13 of Abri Bourgeois-Delaunay. These sediments are separated from cryoclastic *éboulis* of the Riss III (Couches 53 to 48 in my sequence, Couches VIII to III in that of David) by a stalagmitic floor dated by uranium/thorium to 185,000 ± 10,000 B.P. The later *éboulis* were themselves sealed by stalagmitic formations of the Riss-Würm. Overlying these *éboulis* were David's Couches I and II, which correspond to Couches 8 to 10 of Abri Bourgeois-Delaunay.

The techno-typological attribution of these two shelters' industries poses a number of problems. An early study by Bordes (1953e) concluded that there was evidence "d'au moins deux industries différentes: un Moustérien de tradition acheuléenne atténuée . . . et un Moustérien à denticulés . . . Le point important est que ces deux industries sont complètement différentes du 'Moustérien' habituel en Charente, qui est de type La Quina." This diagnosis was important because Abri Suard had already yielded human remains—remains that were thought to represent the first known from the Denticulate Mousterian.

Since then, a number of other human remains have been recovered in good stratigraphic context. Of these, as many were derived from Rissian levels as from levels of the Riss/Würm Interglacial (Debénath 1977, 1980).

Sedimentological studies conducted in 1965 led us to modify some of the earlier conceptions regarding the chronology of La Chaise. Instead of finding that Abri Bourgeois-Delaunay was older than Abri Suard, we arrived at the opposite conclusion (Debénath 1965). At the same time, F. Prat identified Rissian elements in the faunal assemblages of Abri Suard (Bordes and Prat 1965), and Bordes reconsidered the question of the La Chaise industries (Bordes 1965).

If it is impossible to compare these industries with those of the Acheulian technocomplex of the Charente Basin, it is even more difficult to make comparisons with those of Fontéchevade, a site near La Chaise in which the Tayacian is also very poorly defined. Moreover, there is a continuum between the Rissian and Early Würm (Couches I and II) industries of Abri Suard and the Early Würm layers of Abri Bourgeois-Delaunay. These industries of La Chaise give an impression of homogeneity and originality. The originality is due in part to the rather poor quality of the core and flake tools. This poor workmanship probably owes more to the quality of the raw material than to the techniques themselves.

The raw material is highly variable: various flints, including some local (Bathonian-Bajocian) types which often are frost-cracked and of bad quality, and various metamorphic and igneous rocks. A significant portion (ca. 30%) of the industry is composed of nodules of older rocks from the Massif Central that were collected from the Tardoire gravels. Most of these are either unworked or only tested, in which case the flakes are also found.

In terms of technology, the industries of the lower beds of Abri Suard are Levallois, with a Levallois index (for definitions of this and other indices, see Bordes 1950b) of around 20. This index decreases regularly in the layers corresponding to the end of the Riss at Abri Suard and continues to decline during the Early Würm at this locality and at Abri Bourgeois-Delaunay. At La Chaise, no industry can be assigned to the Riss/Würm Interglacial. Faceting is well developed during both the Riss and Würm industries, with an unrestricted faceting index of between 50 and 60. The restricted faceting index, however, is more variable. This index is below 50 both in the lower layers of Abri Suard and during the time of the Early Würm, but above 50 in the later Rissian levels of Abri Suard. The flakes themselves are not very elongated, except again in the later Rissian levels where the blade index is greater than 10.

Without a doubt, the most interesting technological characteristic is what we have called platform rejuvenation (*la technique de reprise du talon*; Debénath 1974, 1983), though it is easily distinguished from actual platform preparation that takes place prior to flake removal. This technique involves the removal of the platform, usually obliquely relative to the axis of the flake. These platform removals, obtained by soft hammer, are not abrupt or very flat. At this point it is called a "simple" or "partial" platform rejuvenation. Occasionally, however, this removed platform then serves as a striking platform for other flake removals from the exterior surface of the flake. In this case we speak of a "total" rejuvenation (Fig. 4.2). This platform rejuvenation is sometimes associated with a more-or-less scalar retouch on the distal part of the flake, thus grading into a Kostenki knife, as defined by de Heinzelin (1962).

This technique has been observed on many different types of platforms (with the exception of cortical platforms) and on different types of tools: scrapers, denticulates, Mousterian points, pieces with inverse retouch, endscrapers, backed knives, and notches. In the lower layers of Riss III (Couches 51 and 52), this technique occurs on 18% and 14% of the industry, respectively.

On the other hand, there are a number of scrapers that are formed on the exterior side of the flake platform, usually on flakes with plain platform whose surface forms a high angle with respect to the interior of the flake. This type of tool is not to be confused with either a particular method of core preparation or the resharpening of Quina scrapers (the Quina index is virtually zero or very low in all these levels, although some pieces do exhibit an atypical Quina retouch), nor does it represent the final reduced form of any other type of scraper.

Thus, we are led to differentiate three industrial facies at La Chaise (Debénath 1974, 1983):

Facies A—Levallois, with a high unrestricted faceting index and well-developed use of platform rejuvenation (the lower Riss III levels, Couches 51-53).

Facies B—Less use of Levallois, a similar unrestricted faceting index but higher restricted one, and a reduction in the use of platform rejuvenation (upper Riss III levels, Couches III-VIII).

Facies C—Weak use of Levallois and rare platform rejuvenation. In this facies, only the unrestricted faceting index is similar to that seen in the other facies (Early Würm layers of Abri Suard Couches I and II, and, by comparison, Couches 9 and 10 of Abri Bourgeois-Delaunay).

Typologically, the Charentian index is moderate in Facies A and B (17 and 15, respectively), though clearly much higher in Facies C (30). As stated earlier, however, the Quina index is weak in all three facies. Regarding other aspects of typology, the first observation concerns the small number of bifaces (the highest biface index is 8, though in general it increases from Facies A to Facies C at Abri Suard, and practically disappears during the Early Würm series at Abri Bourgeois-Delaunay) and the poor quality of manufacture. They are generally atypical, fragmentary, and often backed. Moreover, they are almost always very small.

The scrapers constitute the dominant tool group, with a high proportion of simple convex scrapers. The proportion of denticulates varies inversely with that of the scrapers.

The originality of the La Chaise industries is due to the presence of tools that are infrequent in other European assemblages during the Final Riss and Early Würm: pedunculated tools, bifacial foliate pieces, a number of (sometimes atypical) Kostenki knives. There also exist one Chatelperron knife and a number of composite tools, principally scrapers, which do not fit easily into the system of classification (see Figs. 4.3-5).

Finally, it should also be noted that from the Rissian levels of Abri Suard were recovered several examples of worked bones bearing notches, parallel marks, and scratches (Debénath and Duport 1971).

So, during the Rissian glaciation there continued an evolution of the Acheulian toward industries with bifaces in northern France; the gravel beds of the Charente Valley show a parallel development of very different industries characterized by an absence or extreme rarity of bifaces. When bifaces do occur, they sometimes recall backed forms such as more recent ones from Germany.

The definition of the Acheulian as an industry with bifaces is not very precise. In this part of the Charente these assemblages are essentially Rissian in age (though some forms are lost until the Early Würm) and therefore would be Acheulian. But the typological peculiarities prevent us from assigning them to an Acheulian technocomplex.

We have established an in situ evolution of different industrial facies, from the Riss III to the beginning of the Early Würm. Among the kinds of changes we see are a decrease in the use of Levallois, decrease in platform rejuvenation, variations in the association of denticulates and other kinds of tools (principally scrapers and Upper Paleolithic types which are, now and then, well represented), and the appearance of other tools that are only infrequently seen during this period. These Rissian industries were evolving toward a Mousterian industry, one that is poorly defined at the end of the Early Würm at Abri Bourgeois-Delaunay.

Thus, at La Chaise we are confronted with an industry that does not compare well with either Classic Acheulian, or even the Meridional Acheulian defined by Bordes. Instead, its dominant characteristic is Mousterian.

DISCUSSION

ROLLAND: Among the recently excavated sites attributed to the late Middle Pleistocene, La Chaise has yielded the widest range of documentation. It raises several issues. It was mentioned that the handaxes are few and atypical, and difficult to relate to the Meridional Acheulian. This issue of the Meridional Acheulian is one that has puzzled me quite a bit, and more so now. Bordes was the first one to propose it in the early 1950s as something that was morphologically different from the loess site stations of the Seine and Somme Valleys. Generally it is defined as a type of handaxe industry which occasionally includes either bifacial cleavers or African-type flake cleavers, and handaxes which at times have rather more elaborate classic forms. In addition, the flake tools have a more complex typology, for example in the so-called Rissian layers at Pech de l'Azé. Based on the description by Debénath and my own experience with the Combe-Grenal material, the handaxes and other tools of these two sites seem to show some similarity. It has been suggested that the concept of a Meridional Acheulian was artificially created in the absence of more thorough comparative data on Acheulian handaxe assemblages throughout Western Europe. You do find bifacial cleavers north of the Perigord, and it may have something to do with raw material—in other words, you cannot have flake cleavers in a flint-rich area. But, the contrast in handaxe morphology between the Ante-Würmian industries and the Mousterian of Acheulian Tradition is quite striking. It is difficult to explain that strictly in terms of raw-material properties because they were utilizing the same raw material sources.

Another issue raised concerns the decrease in the Levallois and faceting indices over time at this site. I wonder whether this is connected with a depletion of the source of material over time. Perhaps this could be verified by looking at the number of raw-material pieces found in the industries over time?

An important element noted by Debénath is the appearance of rare tools, deviant forms, which become statistically significant at later times, e.g., the Kostenki knives.

DIBBLE: The Kostenki knives and pieces with the *reprise du talon* are interesting and are similar to pieces that are common in the Near East. There they are called "sinew frayers," Nahr Ibrahim cores, or truncated-faceted pieces. They represent a real typological problem that should be dealt with in more detail. At Bisitun, this kind of retouch occurs randomly on all different types of tools: single, double, and convergent scrapers, points, denticulates, etc., so it does not seem to be a hafting modification just for the points.

LENOIR: There are some also in Combe-Grenal Rissian and Würm I industries, the Würm II from Ruisseau de Graviers, and there are some in Corbiac and other sites. They are distinct from *pièces esquillées*.

KOZLOWSKI: I have examined a series of these kinds of pieces under a microscope and have found wear traces in different places on the tools. We cannot say that it is only a thinning of the tool for hafting.

MÜLLER-BECK: I have two points. First, I think it is very dangerous to use the term Kostenki knife for these pieces. There is a tendency to use such a label and then start to think there is some genesis behind it. Second, I am impressed now that people are finding more and more similarities in the earlier material in order to push back the conception of Middle Paleolithic. How reliable are those dates? Is there *Elephas antiquus* in the lower levels?

DEBÉNATH: No. We need more evidence.

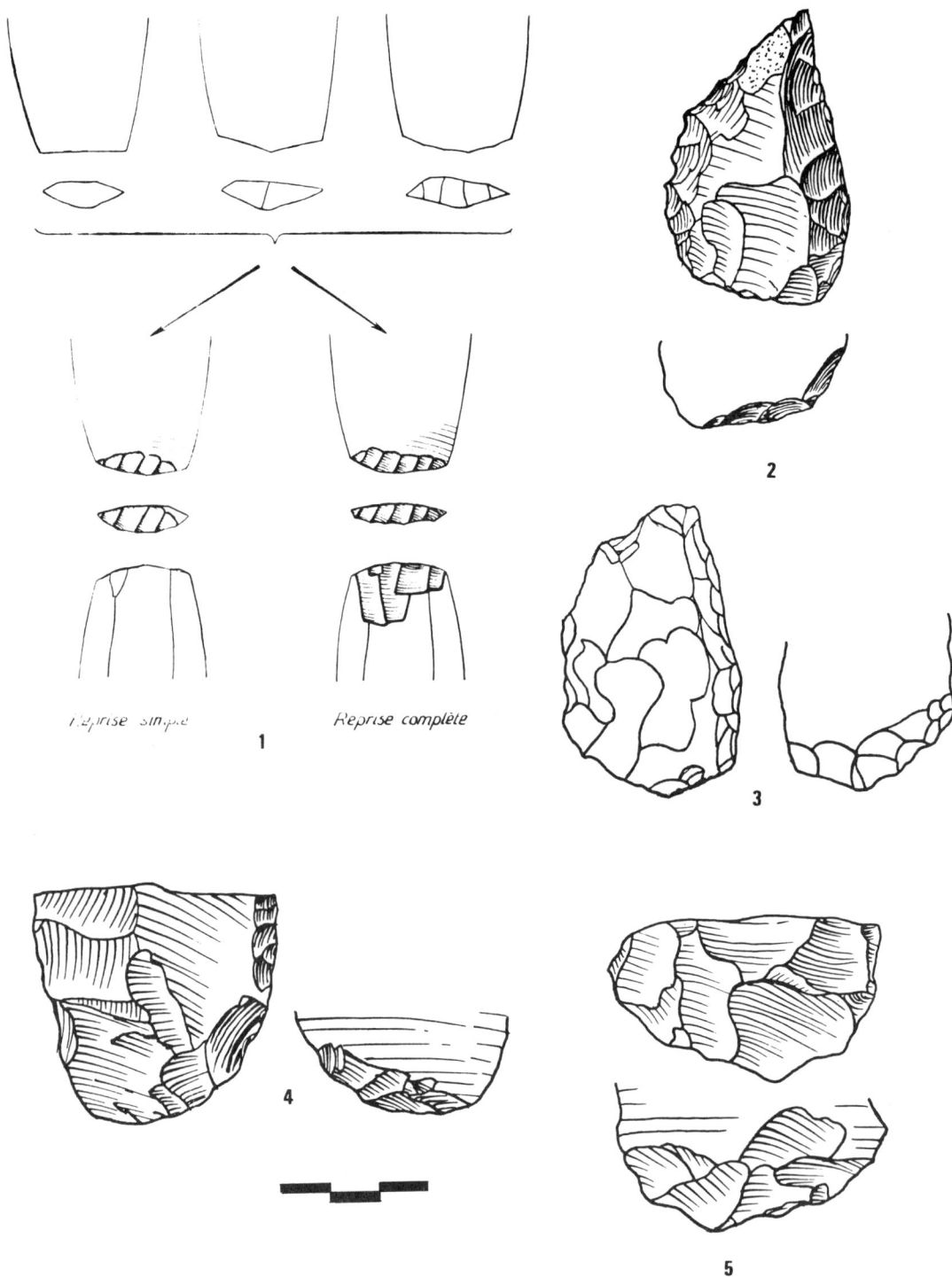

Figure 4.2 Technique of platform rejuvenation—1: schematic view of method; 2: Mousterian point (Suard, Couche 51, Riss III); 3-4: scrapers (Bourgeois-Delaunay, Couche 8, Early Würm; Suard, Couche 51, Riss III); 5: piece with the platform removed by inverse retouch, a technique that is different from platform rejuvenation (Suard, Couche II, Early Würm).

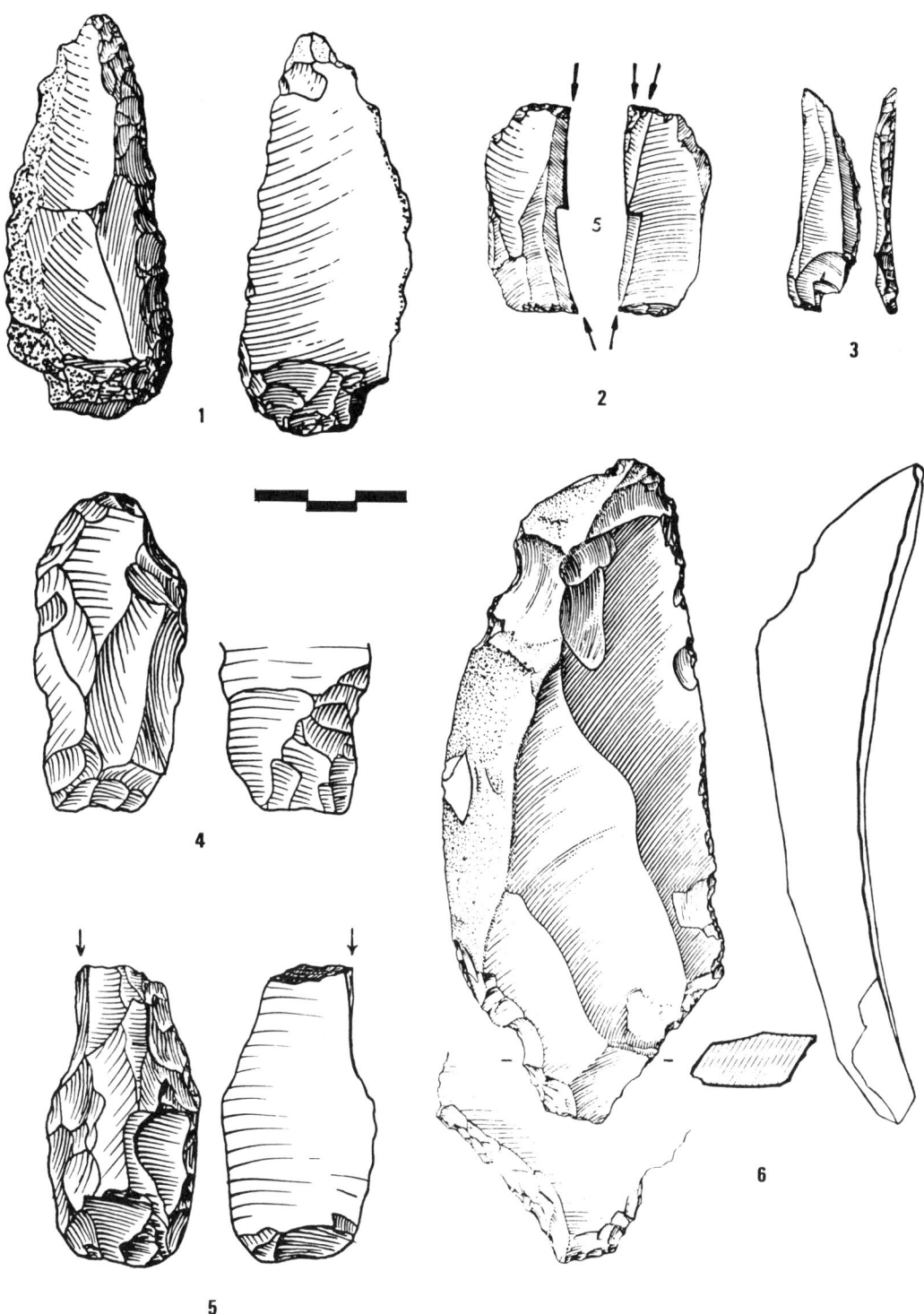

Figure 4.3 Typology—1: simple straight scrapers with thinned back (Suard, Couche 1, Early Würm); 2: multiple burin (Suard, Couche I); 3: Chatelperron point (Suard, Couche IV, Riss III); 4: "diverse" (Suard, Couche 51, Riss III); 5: scraper with a burin on a snap (Suard, Couche 51); 6: pedunculated piece (Suard, Couche 51).

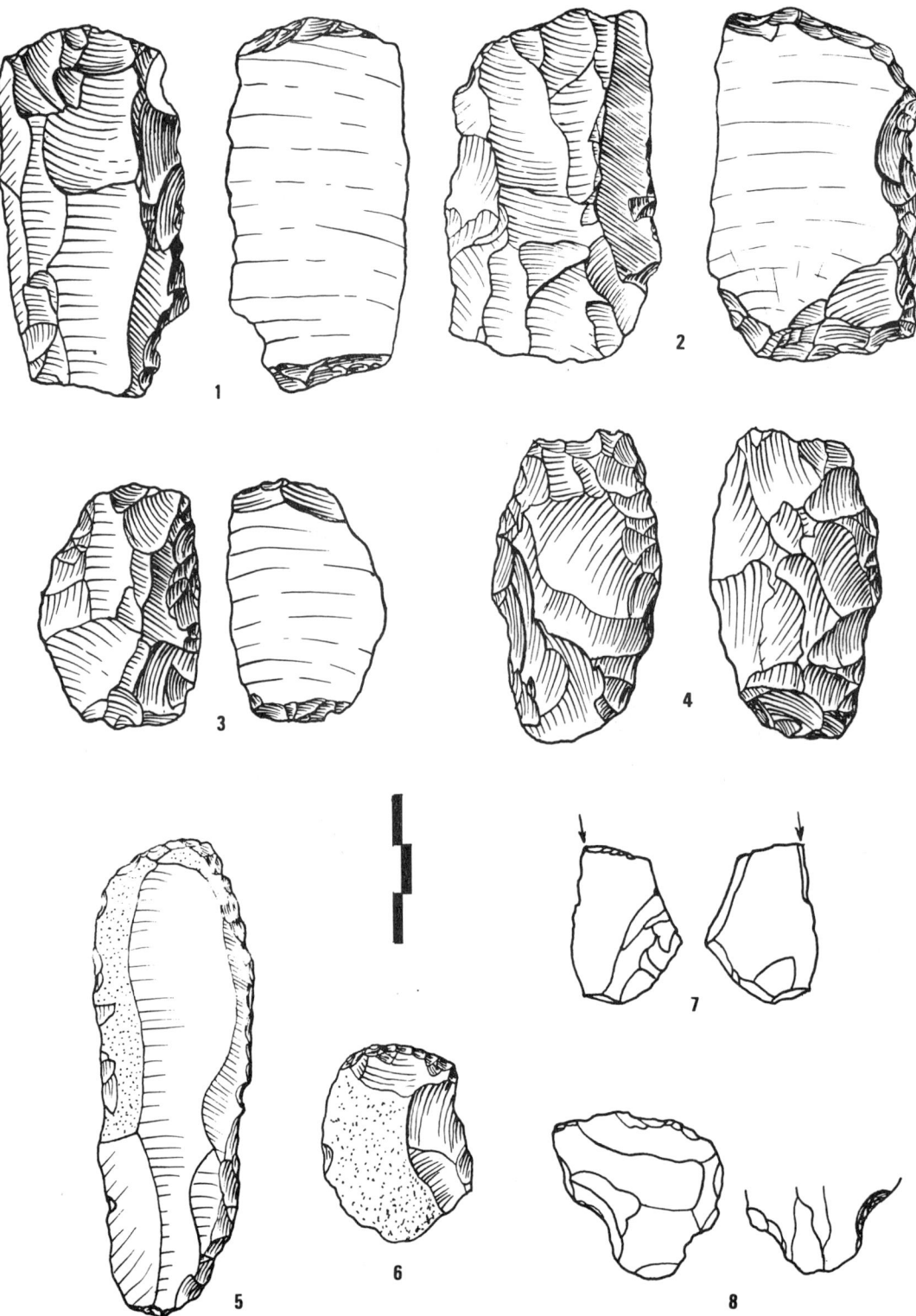

Figure 4.4 Typology—*1-3: Kostenki knives (Suard, Couche 51); 4: bifacial foliated piece (Bourgeois-Delaunay, Couche 9, Early Würm); 5: endscraper on a blade (Bourgeois-Delaunay, Couche 9); 6: endscraper on a flake (Bourgeois-Delaunay, Couche 9); 7: burin (Bourgeois-Delaunay, Couche 8, Early Würm); 8: pedunculated piece (Bourgeois-Delaunay, Couche 8).*

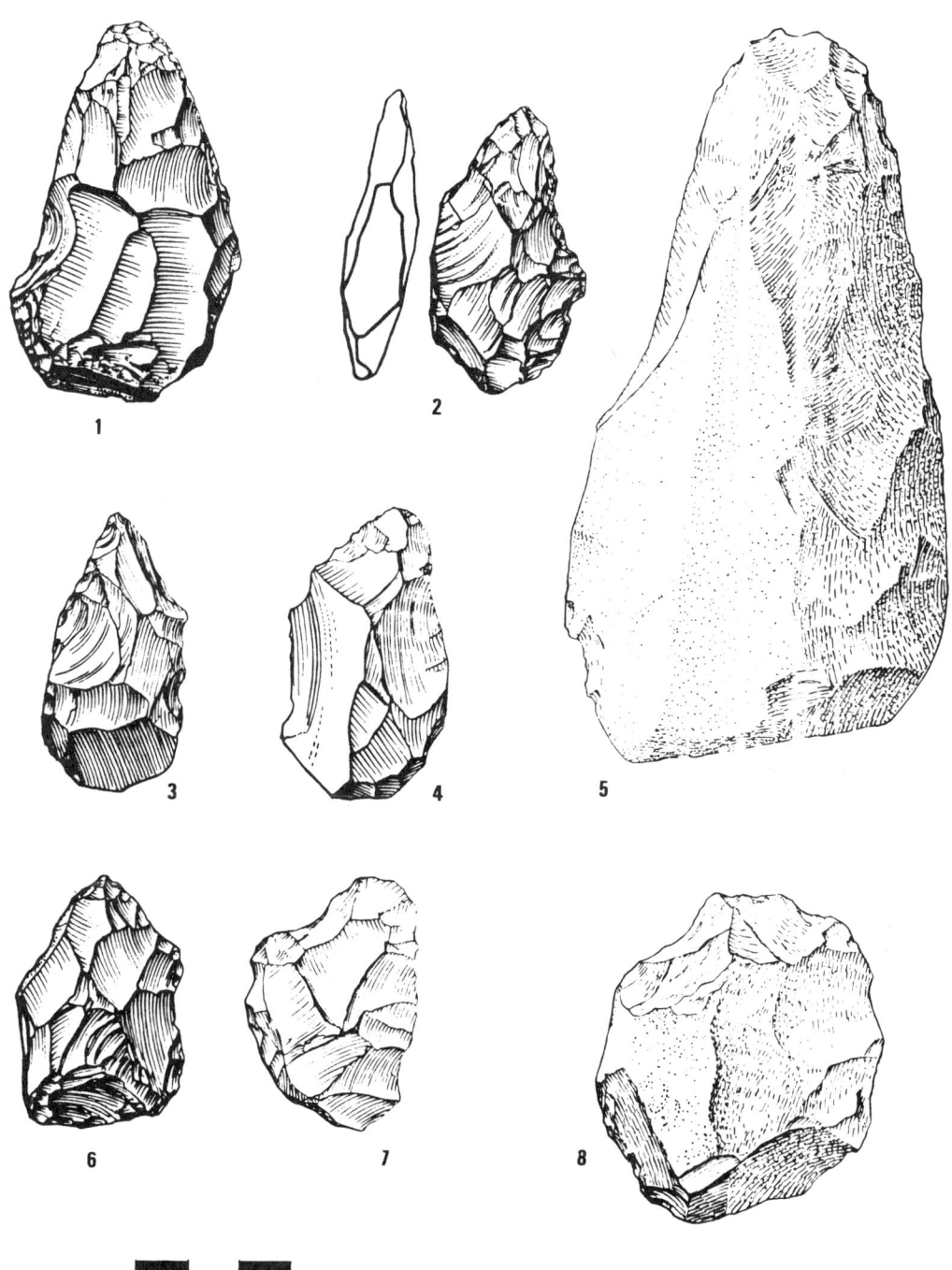

Figure 4.5   Bifaces from La Chaise—1-2: Suard, Couche 1, Early Würm; 3-5: Suard, Couche II, Early Würm; 6: Suard, Couche III, Riss III; 7-8: Suard, Couche V, Riss III.

V

Interprétation d'un habitat au Paléolithique moyen
La grotte de Sclayn, Belgique

Marcel Otte
Jean-Marcel Evrard
Alain Mathis

INTRODUCTION

"STRUCTURE D'ACCUEIL"

La grotte se situe dans un petit vallon adjacent à la Meuse, en Haute-Belgique de direction NE-SW qui entaille des formations de calcaire primaire traversé par un important réseau karstique. Celle qui nous occupe ici correspond à la sortie de la galerie supérieure, largement ouverte vers le sud-est. Deux autres réseaux au moins de galeries horizontales sous-jacentes sont connus; elles ont joué un rôle important dans la sédimentation de la grotte supérieure (Figs. 5.1-2).

La salle d'entrée était entièrement comblée lorsqu'elle fut découverte en 1971 par le Cercle Archéologique de Sclayn. Dans l'état restitué au Paléolithique moyen, l'aire occupée s'étendait à la salle d'entrée et à la terrasse, couverte d'un auvent aujourd'hui effondré. La longueur de cette salle est d'une quinzaine de mètres pour une largeur d'environ 6 m; elle n'est fouillée, à ce niveau, que sur environ les deux tiers de sa superficie. La voûte surplombe actuellement cette salle à plus de 4 m de cette surface mais il est vraisemblable qu'une partie des éboulis cryoclastiques en provienne et aient donc accentué cette hauteur.

Telle quelle, cette vaste salle, à surface sensiblement horizontale, se prêtait donc bien à l'étude de la répartition des traces d'activités éventuellement conservées.

CONTEXTE STRATIGRAPHIQUE

Sur la terrasse, un effondrement partiel du plafond de la galerie inférieure a provoqué une perturbation dans la disposition des couches rendant l'analyse spatiale plus délicate dans cette partie.

Avant l'effondrement de l'auvent (fin du Würm probablement), la grotte largement ouverte, permettait une sédimentation éolienne sur la terrasse et dans la première salle, entrecoupée d'importants éboulis cryoclastiques, de formations calcitiques et d'horizons pédologiques. Des phases d'épanchement de graviers ou de galets provenant des terrasses marines ou fluviales des plateaux sus-jacents, par les cheminées ou directement par la falaise, parsèment ces dépôts (Fig. 5.3).

Les traces de l'occupation humaine principale concernée par cette étude se trouvent mêlées à une couche d'éboulis calcaires d'origine cryoclastique et légèrement érodés par des actions chimiques sur place. Ce dépôt, de disposition sub-horizontale, d'une quarantaine de centimètres d'épaisseur contient le maximum d'artéfacts dans les 20 cm supérieurs et se trouve intercalé entre deux couches de loess ruisselé.

On peut donc être assuré que l'occupation humaine a été contemporaine de la formation du dépôt de plaquettes calcaires. Celui-ci a d'abord été scellé par la couverture de loess superposée (environ 80 cm) puis par une croûte de calcite qui la recouvre et enfin par les importants éboulis calcaires mêlés aux graviers de la dernière glaciation (3 m environ).

MODE DE PRÉSERVATION

D'après l'étude sédimentaire (Gullentops et Deblaere), les éboulis calcaires n'auraient guère subi de déplacements latéraux depuis leur mise en place: aucune trace de ruissellement ne les affecte ni latérallement ni dans l'axe de la galerie.

D'autre part, les artéfacts lithiques ont conservé la fraicheur de leurs arêtes; ils étaient souvent disposés d'une manière sub-horizontale et accompagnés de très nombreuses petites esquilles qu'un courant, même très faible, aurait dû emporter. Cette fraicheur se retrouve également sur les ossements fracturés, eux-aussi entourés de menues esquilles.

Ces éboulis calcaires et ces artéfacts sont mêlés à une faible matrice sableuse originaire, soit de l'altération des calcaires, soit des sédiments éoliens superposés.

Les diagrammes de dispersion verticale montrent une concentration nette qui semble indiquer une occupation unique mais de durée et d'intensité indéterminées (Figs. 5.4-5).

Les remontages verticaux réalisés entre les différentes profondeurs renforcent cette impression (Fig. 5.6).

En résumé, l'étude du contexte sédimentaire (Fig. 5.7) nous amène à restituer une occupation contemporaine de la formation du dépôt cryoclastique (phase finale) de longue durée ou de fréquentations répétées et très rapprochées (pas de séparation verticale) dont une partie des documents auraient pénétré légèrement au travers de ce cailloutis sans apparemment qu'il y ait eu de déplacements horizontaux importants.

POSITION CHRONOLOGIQUE

Deux cycles sédimentaires principaux se distinguent à la fois sur la terrasse et dans la salle d'entrée: *le supérieur,* superposé à la croûte de calcite principale, surtout formé d'éboulis cryoclastiques correspond probablement à la dernière période glaciaire; et *l'inférieur,* beaucoup plus complexe, où alternent les dépôts de loess, d'éboulis et de graviers et que les différentes méthodes d'analyse concourrent à attribuer à la dernière période interglaciaire (de 130,000 à 75,000 approximativement).

En résumant très schématiquement les résultats atteints par l'application des méthodes radiométriques (Schwarcz; Szabo; Aitken; Gewelt [cf. planche]), micropaléontologiques (Cordy) et, surtout, palynologiques (Bastin), on peut considérer que la phase d'occupation principale présentée ici appartient à une période froide intermédiaire entre les deux plus récentes oscillations tempérées du dernier interglaciaire (dénommées Saint Germain I et Saint Germain II [Woillard et Mook 1982]). Cette phase climatique froide correspondrait au stade isotopique 5 (Shackleton et Opdyke 1976) et se situerait vers 80,000 ans (Bastin 1986; Schneider 1983; Otte et Gob 1983).

MATÉRIAUX

Une grande variété de matières lithiques différentes a été utilisée par les occupants de la couche 5. Elles sont cependant toutes d'origine locale: galets de la Meuse et de ses affluents, ou même roches du substrat (chert et calcaires).

Elles présentent toutes des caractéristiques techniques particulières et l'on peut se demander si cette diversité mécanique correspondait à des utilisations différentes ou résultait simplement du hasard des récoltes par les hommes du Paléolithique moyen.

On constate en tous cas une nette différence selon les matériaux quant aux techniques appliquées et à l'abondance des outils (Fig. 5.8).

TABLEAU 5.1

Décomptes totaux: (nombre de pièces)	n	%
silex	1300	26,22
quartz	2909	58,67
quartzite	477	9,62
chert	219	4,42
calcaire	48	0,97
grès	5	0,10
	4958	

On constate que les outils "retouchés" sont principalement en silex et en chert, tandis que le quartzite, le calcaire et le grès ont surtout livré des éclats, apparemment non aménagés (Fig. 5.8). Des différences importantes apparaissent également dans les processus de débitage (cf. ci-dessous) et soulignent une fois de plus le déterminisme exercé par le matériau sur l'aspect d'une industrie, particulièrement au paléolithique moyen, masquant quelques fois des aspects typologiques pertinents (voir à ce sujet Girard 1978).

Incidemment, cette variété de roches utilisées, fréquente à cette période dans le bassin mosan, s'oppose à l'emploi systématique, au Paléolithique supérieur de cette même région, de roches plus homogènes impliquant une recherche à longue distance (Otte 1979).

Dans le deuxième niveau moustérien de la grotte de Sclayn elle-même (couche 1A), on constate déjà l'emploi, supplémentairement aux roches du niveau 5, d'un grès lustré tertiaire dont les affleurements sont distants d'une cinquantaine de kilomètres vers le nord.

L'exploitation des roches de la couche 5 est donc particulièrement orientée vers la récolte de *matériaux locaux*.

TECHNOLOGIE

Les techniques sont approchées, dans cette partie, à la fois par l'observation des stigmates de préparation et au travers des remontages (Figs. 5.9-11).

Un seul *éclat levallois* en grès fin représente cette catégorie réalisé à l'extérieur du site, peut-être au lieu d'exploitation, et démontre la connaissance technique poussée, éventuellement appliquée aux blocs de dimension et aux propriétés mécaniques adéquates.

Les nodules de *silex* (galets marins probablement) de dimensions réduites et de texture grenue ont été traités selon deux procédés différents:

—*débitage centripète* après préparation du dos en vue de l'extraction d'éclats courts et d'éclats préparés dits "para-levallois." On y retrouve les traces de préparation des bords de nucléus et les éclats d'ablation de ces bords destinés à accentuer le bombement de la surface de débitage (Boëda et Pelegrin 1979-80).

—Le *quartz*, par sa nature même, a livré de très nombreuses esquilles, de grands éclats irréguliers et des nucléus globuleux sans orientation préférentielle.

—Le *quartzite* a été débité à partir de galets ovoïdes transversalement livrant des éclats en tranches de saucisson ou en quartiers d'orange (dos cortical opposé au bord tranchant). Les esquilles sont, en cette matière, nettement moins abondantes.

—Les *cherts* sont représentés par des éclats allongés à débitage très irrégulier et de nombreux blocs à peine préparés.

—Les *calcaires* montrent les même techniques de préparation centripète que les silex sous la forme de plus grands enlèvements.

Les quelques enlèvements de *grès* semblent avoir été débités de la même manière que les quartzites.

Par l'abondance des esquilles et des éclats de préparation, il est en tous cas indéniable que les activités de débitage et de préparation d'outils ont été réalisées sur place pour toutes les matières sauf le grès fin de l'éclat levallois.

OUTILLAGE (Figs. 5.12-17)

La plupart des outils sont réalisés en silex, roche se prêtant particulièrement bien à l'aménagement précis par retouches postérieures au débitage. Les enlèvements en autres matériaux peuvent avoir été utilisés tels quels ou avoir subi des modifications non discernables à l'observation macroscopique (Tabl. 5.2).

Sur le plan morphologique et technique, trois grands classes se distinguent nettement dans l'outillage: les racloirs, les couteaux et les denticulés. Nous y ajoutons la classe des "éclats retouchés," de morphologie très aléatoire et sans régularité technique.

A l'intérieur de ces classes très générales, il ne nous a pas été possible de distinguer des "types" dont les caractères eussent été récurrents: angles de la retouche, disposition du front, type du support et rapport à son axe de débitage, forme de la ligne de retouches. Nous n'avons donc pas pu y distinguer les classes habituelles (p. ex.: "racloirs transversaux, à retouches écailleuses, à front courbe, rectiligne ou déjeté"). Toutes ces classes paraissaient se recouvrir mutuellement.

Il semble plutôt qu'un processus particulier a prévalu pour l'aménagement des outils qui furent réalisés et conçus à mesure des besoins et de leurs utilisations et en tenant compte des caractères du support (Tabl. 5.3). Cet aspect "aléatoire" de l'outillage retouché au Paléolithique moyen, déjà mis en évidence (Jelinek 1977; Dibble 1984a; Cahen 1985) semble une caractéristique propre à cette période et semble lié aux procédés de débitage et à la fonctionnologie tout autant aléatoire (Beyries 1984).

TABLEAU 5.2

INDUSTRIE COUCHE 5

	Quartz	Chert	Quartzite	Silex	Calcaire	Grès	Totaux n	%
Nucléus	196	4	22	26	2	1	251	5,06%
Outils	12	14	7	110	-	-	143	2,90%
Eclats	569	26	303	418	46	4	1366	27,55%
Esquilles	2129	5	124	745	-	-	3003	60,57%
Galets	3	169	21	-	-	-	193	3,89%
Totaux	2909	218	477	1299	48	5	4956	

TABLEAU 5.3

	Silex	Quartz	Quartzite	Chert	Totaux n	%
Couteaux	22	2	2	2	28	20
Denticulés	25	4	3	4	36	25
Racloirs & pointes	37	6	1	3	47	33
Eclats retouchés	26	-	1	5	32	22
Totaux	110	12	7	14	143	100

REPARTITION

Une analyse statistique (menée dans l'esprit de Whallon n.d.) montre que les répartitions des documents lithiques des deux matières principaux (silex et quartz) sont équivalentes (Fig. 5.18). Ceci est surtout net pour les esquilles qui constituent l'échantillon le plus abondant dans les deux matériaux.

On retrouve la même corrélation très marquée entre les éclats et les esquilles des différentes roches (Fig. 5.19). Il apparaît donc que les documents lithiques auraient reçu le même traitement aux mêmes emplacements.

Aucune corrélation spatiale n'est évidente entre les outils ou les nucléus et le reste des vestiges lithiques (Tabl. 5.4-5, Figs. 5.20-22). La répartition très uniforme de ces éléments ne renseigne donc nullement sur des localisations d'activités qui y seraient éventuellement associées (Figs. 5.23-25).

Par contre, on peut opposer les aires de concentration de l'ensemble des documents lithiques (Fig. 5.26) à celles des vestiges osseux déterminables (Fig. 5.27).

A l'intérieur de cette dernière catégorie, on constate entre autres la concentration de fragments de côtes vers le fond de la salle et celle de menues esquilles brûlées vers la terrasse. Aucune répartition très nette ou explicite n'est cependant discernée.

De la même manière, le plan de répartition tracé à partir des remontages n'indique guère de concentration particulière bien que de nombreuses liaisons rassemblent les différentes aires de la surface fouillée (Fig. 5.28).

TABLEAU 5.4
INDICES DE CORRÉLATION SPATIALE
ENTRE LES PRINCIPALES CLASSES
TECHNIQUES

	Esquilles	Eclats	Nucléus	Outils
Esquilles	1	0.90604	0.64243	0.66838
Eclats		1	0.71249	0.76485
Nucléus			1	0.70468
Outils				1

TABLEAU 5.5
CORRÉLATION DES PRINCIPALES CLASSES LITHIQUES

	Sx Esq.	Sx Ecl.	Sx Nucl.	Sx Out.	Qz Esq.	Qz Ecl.	Qz Nucl.	Qz Out.
Sx Esq.	1	0.89887	0.43186	0.63702	0.90636	0.91495	0.60184	0.14466
Sx Ecl.		1	0.47707	0.74762	0.85285	0.90581	0.71351	0.26042
Sx Nucl.			1	0.43702	0.47341	0.43681	0.44257	0.12709
Sx Out.				1	0.59864	0.59582	0.40586	0.10734
Qz Esq.					1	0.88202	0.58261	0.27303
Qz Ecl.						1	0.67661	0.16113
Qz Nucl.							1	0.38449
Qz Out.								1

CONCLUSION ET INTERPRÉTATION GÉNÉRALE

Sur la surface actuellement fouillée, il n'apparaît guère de répartition explicite des documents nous permettant d'appréhender un aspect de l'organisation des activités au Paléolithique moyen.

Dans l'hypothèse où, comme nos observations tendent à le démontrer, il y aurait eu peu de déplacements latéraux mais seulement une pénétration verticale et différentielle des documents selon leur densité, leur forme ou leur inclinaison, comment peut-on expliquer cette carence des "structures évidentes" si fréquentes au Paléolithique supérieur?

Peut-être nos modèles explicatifs créés pour des périodes différentes, ne sont-ils pas adaptés au Moustérien (Cahen 1985; Patou 1984) et sans doute devons-nous concevoir une méthodologie apte à mettre en évidence des relations spatiales que notre esprit n'est pas porté à rechercher (Girard-Farizy 1982: 193; Villa 1975-76).

Dans le cas de Sclayn, on peut par exemple concevoir qu'une occupation longue et *permanente* ait été à l'origine du dépôt de ces vestiges. La répartition spatiale des activités semble dans ce cas extrêmement limitée.

S'il s'agit d'installations épisodiques très rapprochées dans le temps (pas de sédimentation intermédiaire) les localisations d'activités peuvent alors avoir été modifiées selon les occupations.

Cette déficience apparente dans l'organisation spatiale a plusieurs fois été soulignée dans les sites du Paléolithique moyen (A. Leroi-Gourhan 1982; Hours et Karlin 1982) et justifie quelquefois la tentative de recherches fondées sur la proximité d'éléments de nature différente (Kozlowski 1984; Whallon n.d.).

Il est en tous cas frappant de constater que la même incohérence semble apparaître dans la classification typologique de cette époque (Dibble 1984a) et dans les résultats d'analyse fonctionnelle qui leur est appliquée (Beyries 1984, in press).

DISCUSSION

SIMEK: What is interesting about the material from Sclayn is the distance that these raw materials have traveled to this particular location, sometimes tens or hundreds of kilometers. In the Perigord, to my knowledge, we have very few Middle Paleolithic sites with movement of raw materials anywhere near that scale. This would suggest a fairly high degree of complexity for this particular lithic technology, which does not agree with notions of dumb Neandertals or dumb Middle Paleolithic peoples restricted in space and using their environment in very simple ways. Also, the fact that these data vary so considerably from the Perigord materials also suggests an even larger degree of variation that needs to be explained.

One point I would like to make is that the interpretation of spatial patterns is essentially independent of the analytic system that we're going to use. Otte states towards the end of his paper that the spatial analysis does not allow him to interpret these materials as the result of human deposition. I would argue that in both an empirical and methodological sense, spatial analysis is not designed to allow one to interpret. The interpretations of these materials have to come from somewhere else. The process of site formation is not one that can be addressed statistically, and therefore the problem of assigning meaning to any pattern we see in the prehistoric past is not going to be answered by our methodologies. We have developed fairly sophisticated data-collection techniques, and are capable of examining the technological and functional characteristics very closely. This has led us to believe that we will therefore be capable of far more sophisticated interpretations. But that is not necessarily so, simply because meaning is not inherent in the analytic techniques that we are employing, whether those techniques are technological, functional, or statistical. We must use other kinds of information available from a variety of different places to explain the patterns that we see, in other words, what Binford called middle-range theory.

HOWELL: Jan said that direct coassociation or coincidences are not enough to arrive at a conclusion of causal relationships. What is the kind of middle-range theory that would satisfy you in this regard?

SIMEK: In dealing with any distribution of materials, there is more than one dimension of variation that has to be considered. There are spatial patterns that can be coincidental. There is also the content of that pattern which can vary independently of the spatial pattern itself. When we do spatial analysis, we are analyzing space and locations; we are not analyzing the things. I think we need to develop a means for relating content with structure. Binford, working on the Alaskan material, has concentrated most predominately on content and has not concentrated at all on space. So I think that he is generating middle-range theory.

HOWELL: I think he was in open space, but you are in a constrained situation. Binford argues, as he has elsewhere, that there are carnivore-accumulated residues which were then perhaps assembled, reworked, accumulated, and exploited by humans. Now, how do you arrive at that conclusion, in terms of finding some set of demonstrable methods that will allow you to make those inferences?

SIMEK: I agree.

BAUMLER: The site of Sclayn also provides a very good opportunity to look at how one group deals with different raw materials.

INTERPRÉTATION D'UN HABITAT AU PALÉOLITHIQUE MOYEN

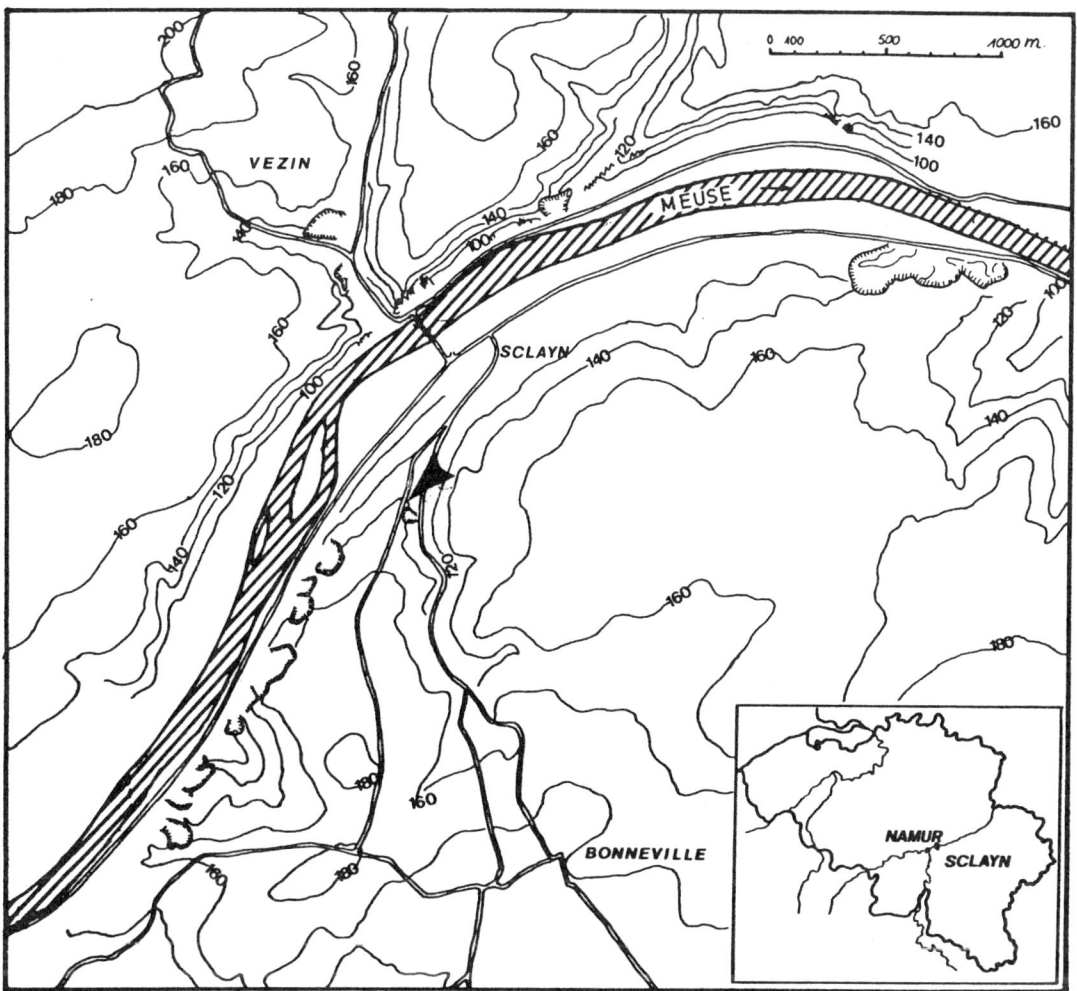

Figure 5.1   Situation générale des grottes de Sclayn (pointe du triangle).

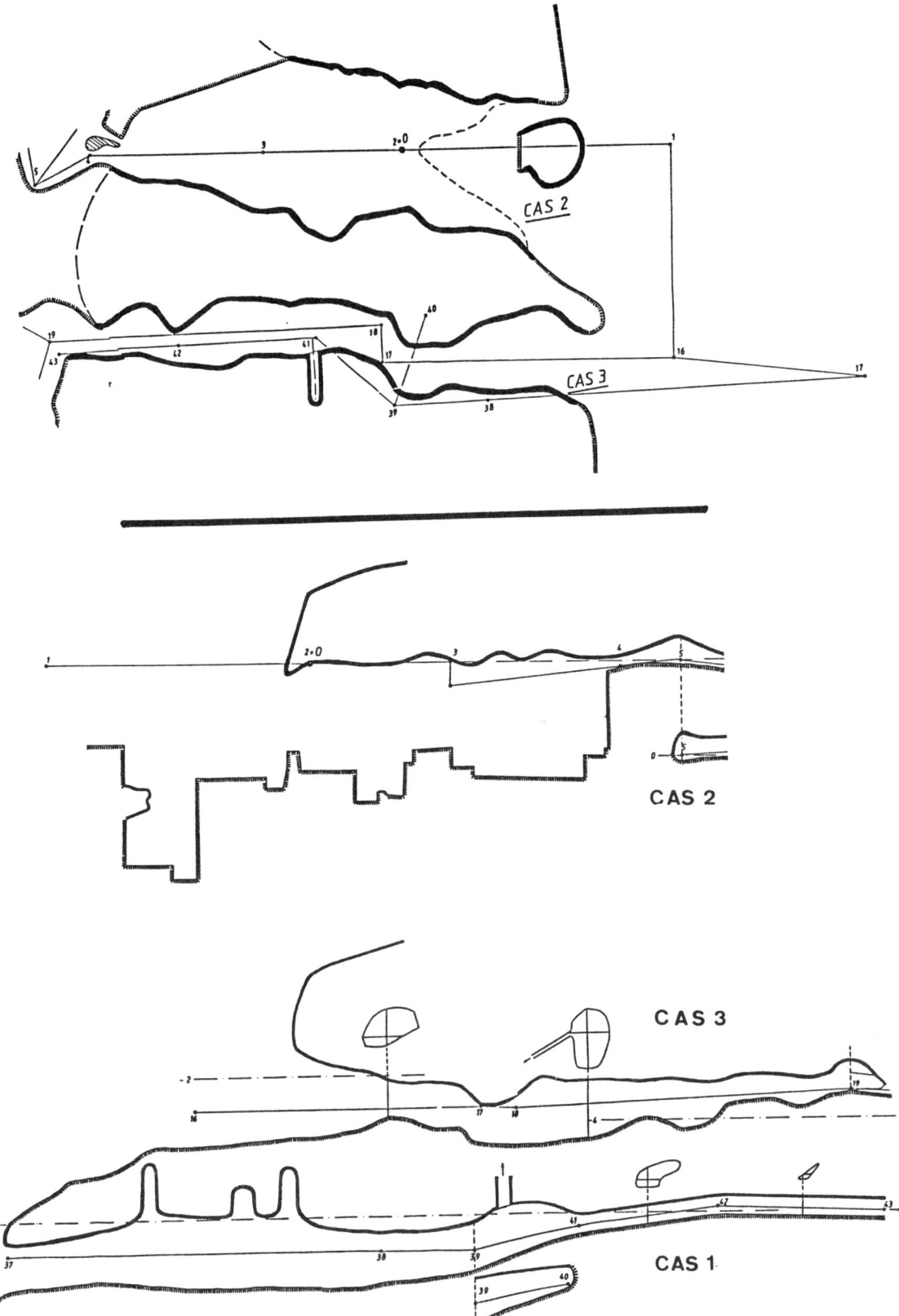

Figure 5.2 Vue en plan (haut) et en coupe (parties médiane et inférieure) des trois grottes principales de Sclayn. Celle concernée par cette étude est la CAS 2. (Relevé Ch. Deblaere)

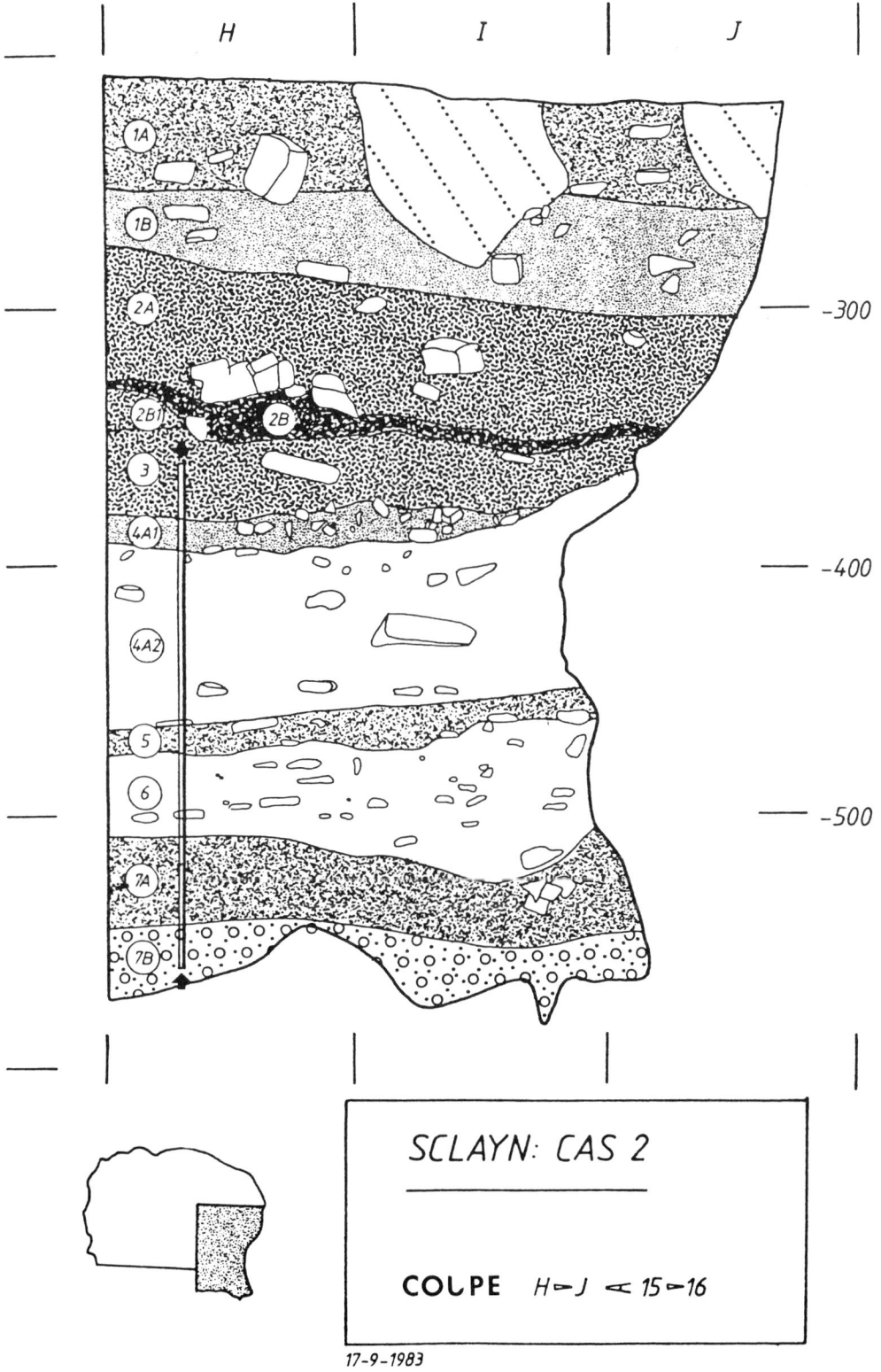

Figure 5.3 Coupe transversale à l'intérieur de la première salle. Les dépôts cryoclastiques vont de 1A à 3. La croûte calcitique est en 4A1. Les deux dépôts de loess sont 4A2 et 6. L'occupation humaine principale est comprise dans le cailloutis 5. (Relevé Ch. Deblaere)

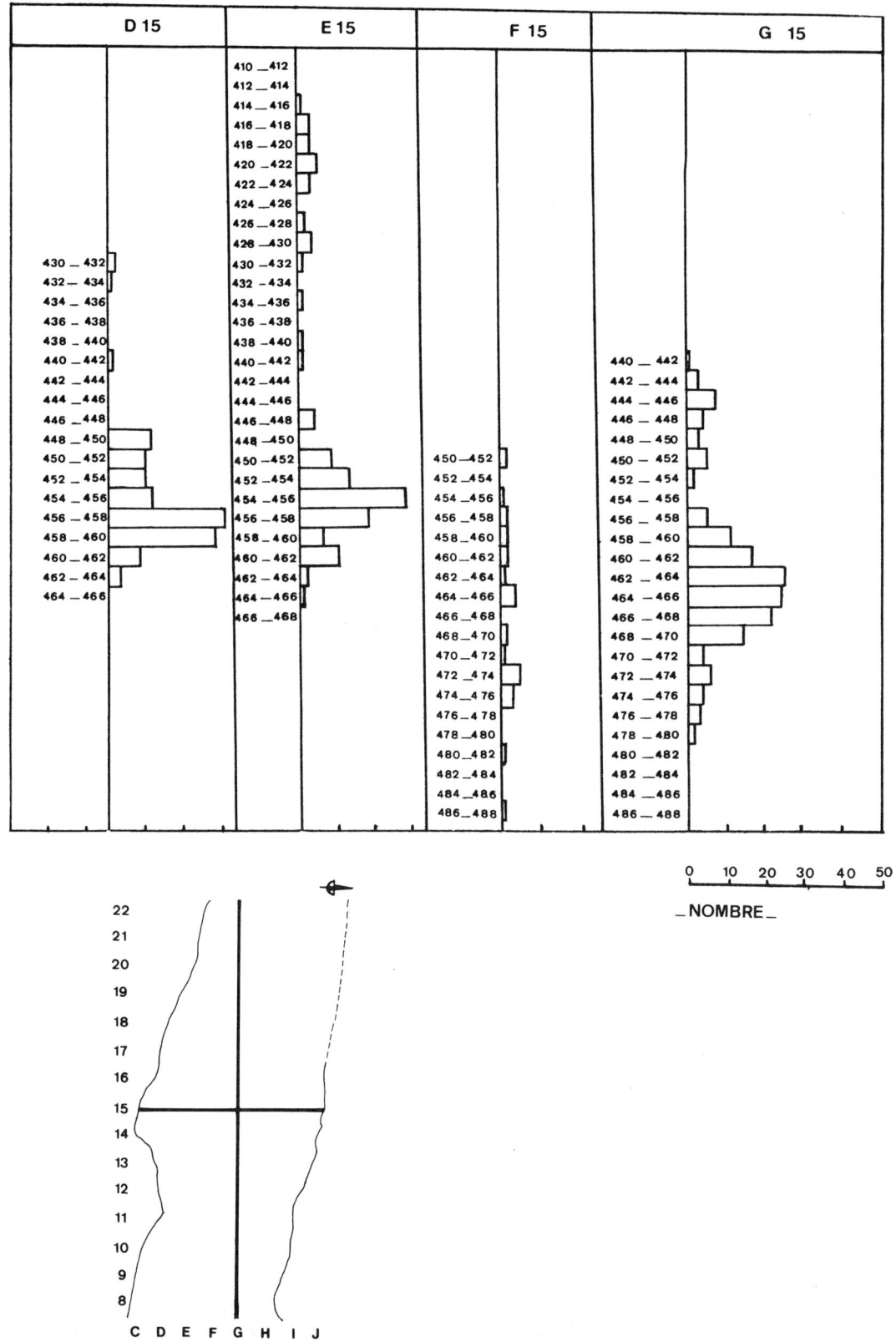

Figure 5.4 Dispersion verticale de l'ensemble des artéfacts dans la couche 5 selon l'axe transversal 15 (intervalle de classe = 2 cm).

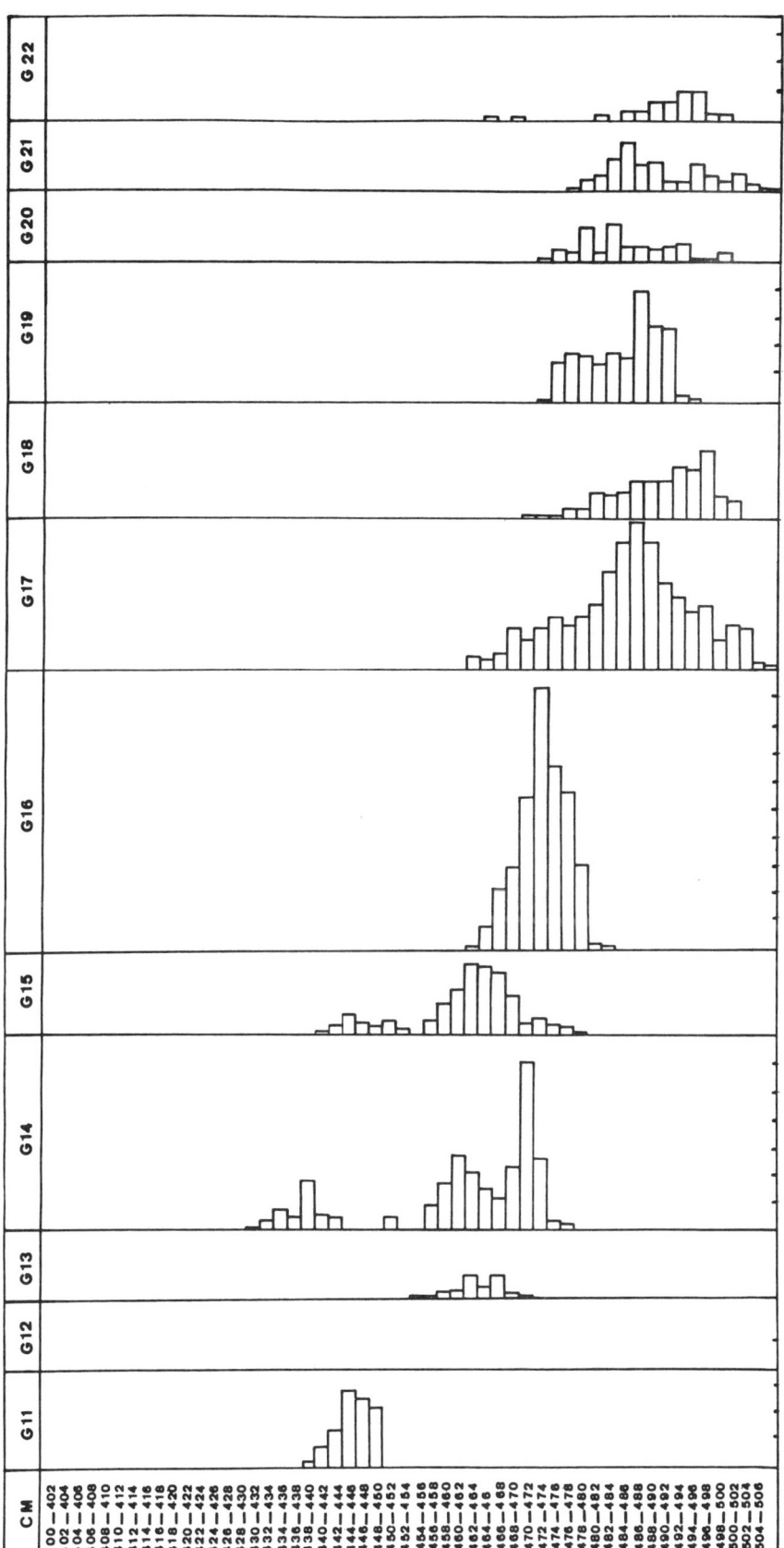

Figure 5.5 Dispersion verticale de l'ensemble des artéfacts dans la couche 5 selon l'axe longitudinal G (intervalle de classe = 2 cm).

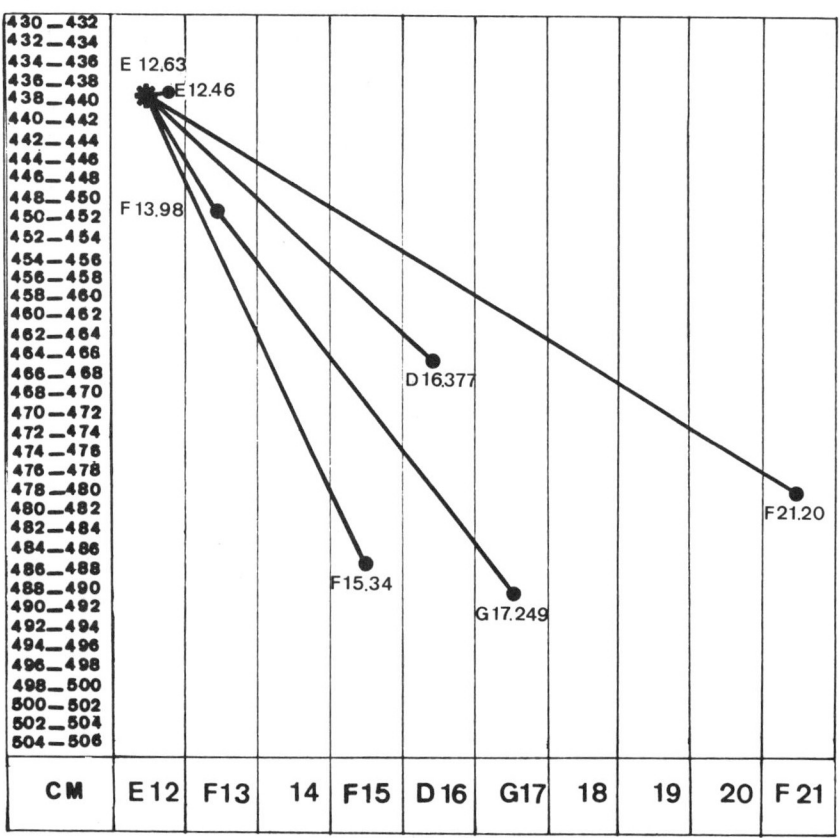

Figure 5.6 Répartition verticale et latérale des éléments remontés sur le même bloc (astérisque = nucléus). La répartition en profondeur ne se justifie pas uniquement par la pente de la couche (cf. Fig. 5.5), mais démontre également un enfouissement différentiel des éléments contemporains.

Figure 5.7 Vue verticale du carré E14 décapé à la surface de la partie supérieure de la concentration.

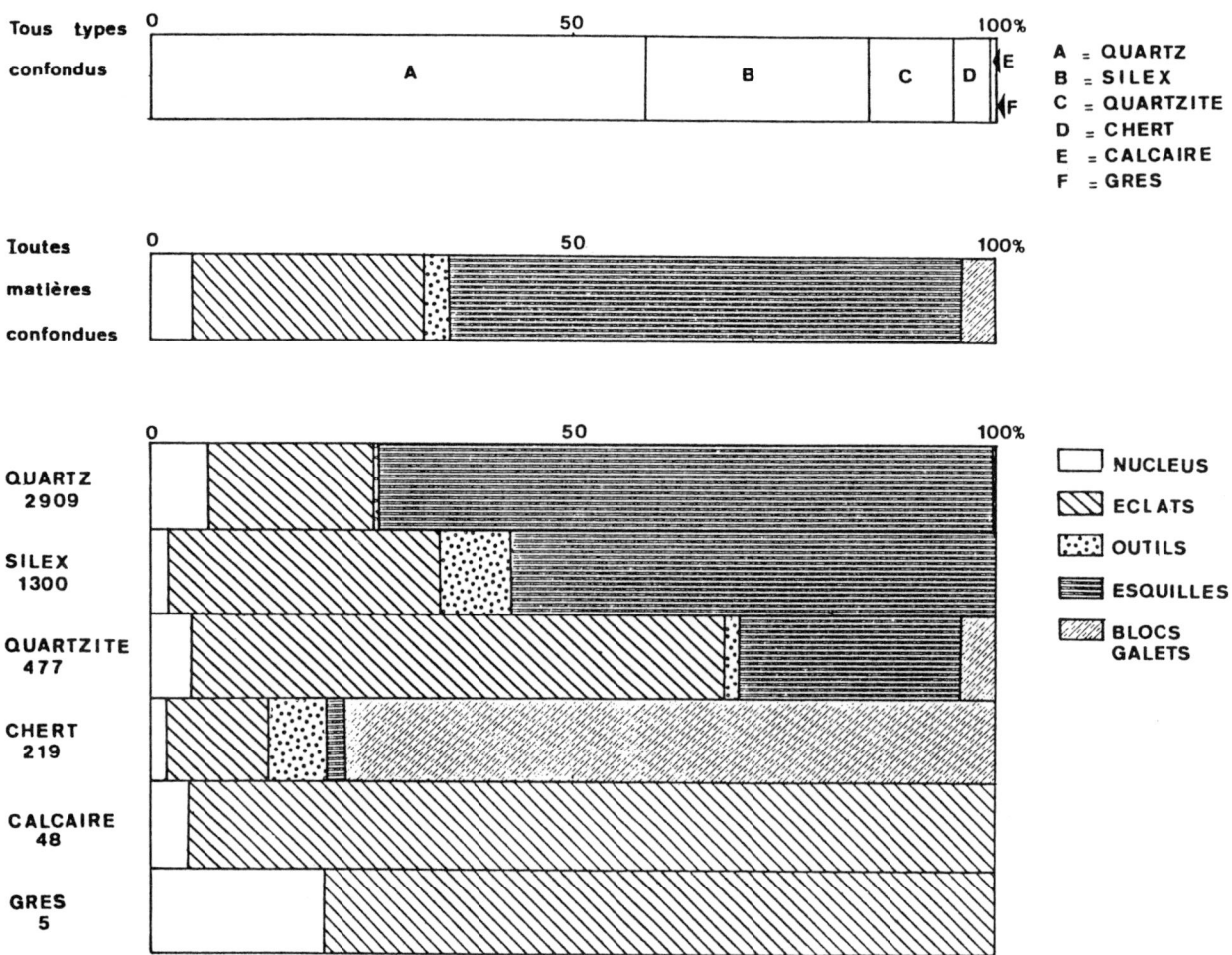

Figure 5.8 Proportions des différentes catégories de matériaux utilisés dans l'industrie lithique exprimées en nombre de pièces (diagramme supérieur). Répartition des différentes catégories de documents lithiques par matériaux (bas) et pour l'ensemble des roches (milieu). On observe des différences quantitatives considérables apparemment dues aux caractéristiques mécaniques de chaque confection d'outils: grands nombre d'esquilles en quartzite et fréquence des outils en silex et en chert.

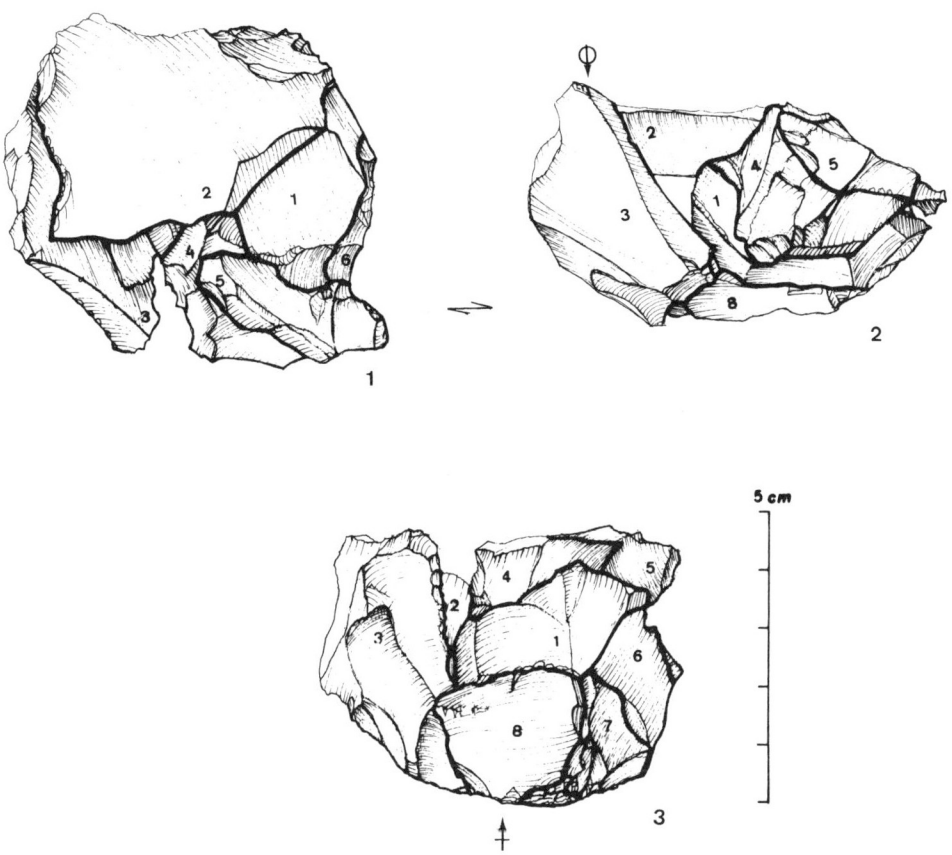

Figure 5.9   Nucléus à débitage centripète remonté à l'aide d'une série d'éclats.

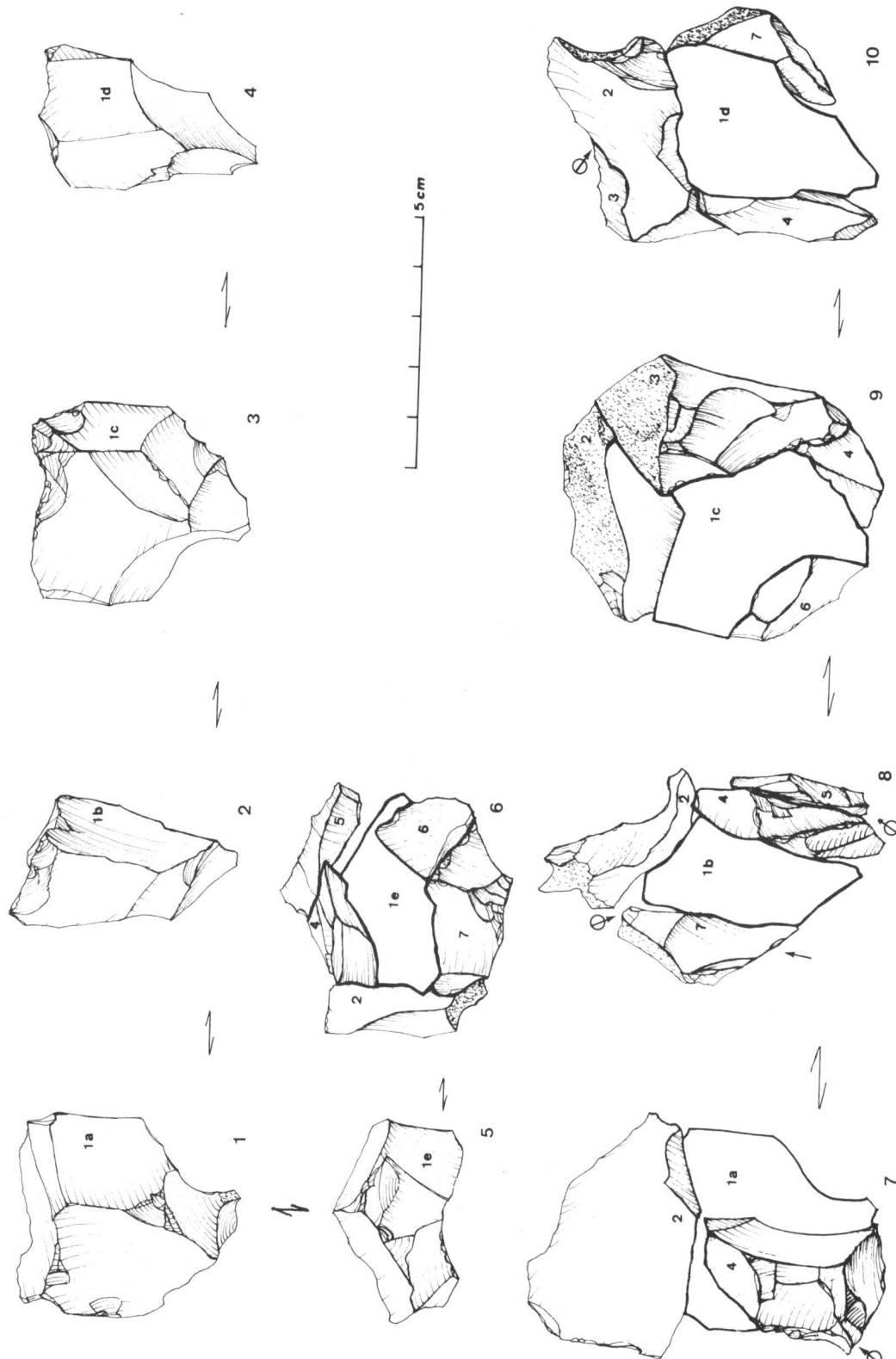

Figure 5.10 Différentes phases des débitage du bloc de la Figure 5.9 à partir du nucléus centripète abandonné (nos. 1 à 5). Les différents éclats sont débités préférentiellement au départ des arêtes du bloc.

INTERPRÉTATION D'UN HABITAT AU PALÉOLITHIQUE MOYEN

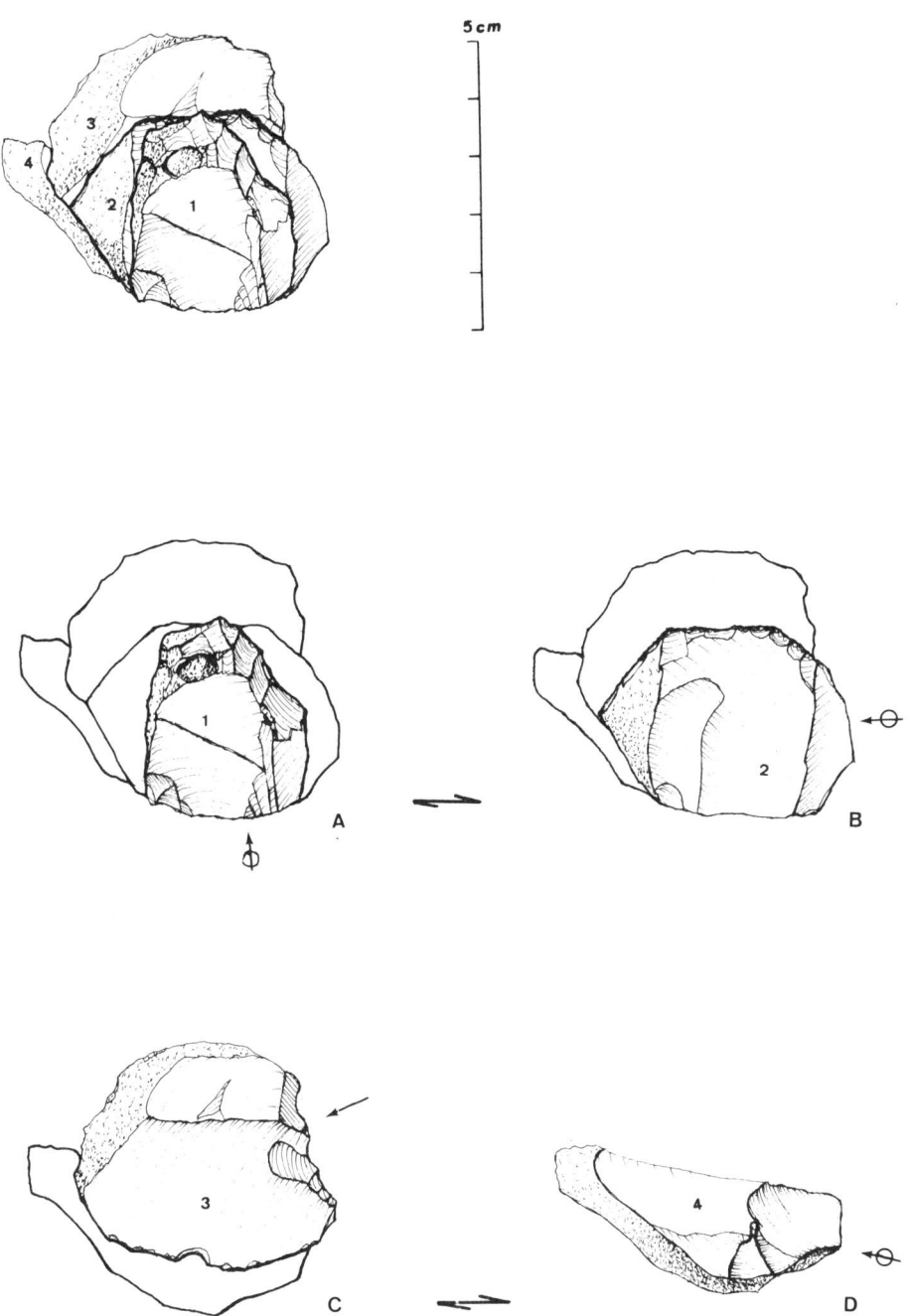

Figure 5.11 Série d'enlèvements à orientation préférentielle remontés dans leur succession technique et incluant deux racloirs.

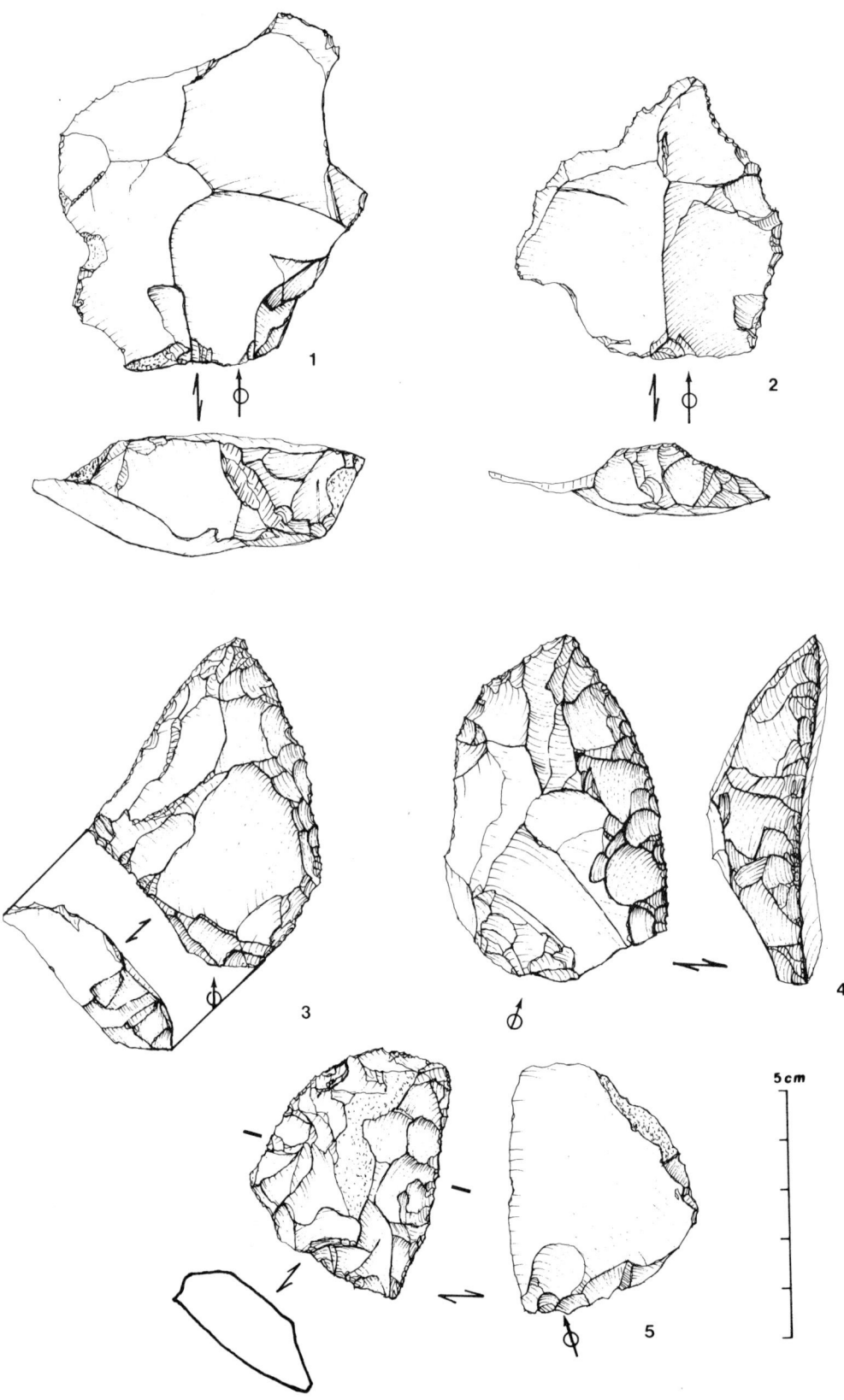

Figure 5.12   1-2: Eclats à débitage centripète; 3-4: racloirs doubles convergents; 5: racloir latéral à dos.

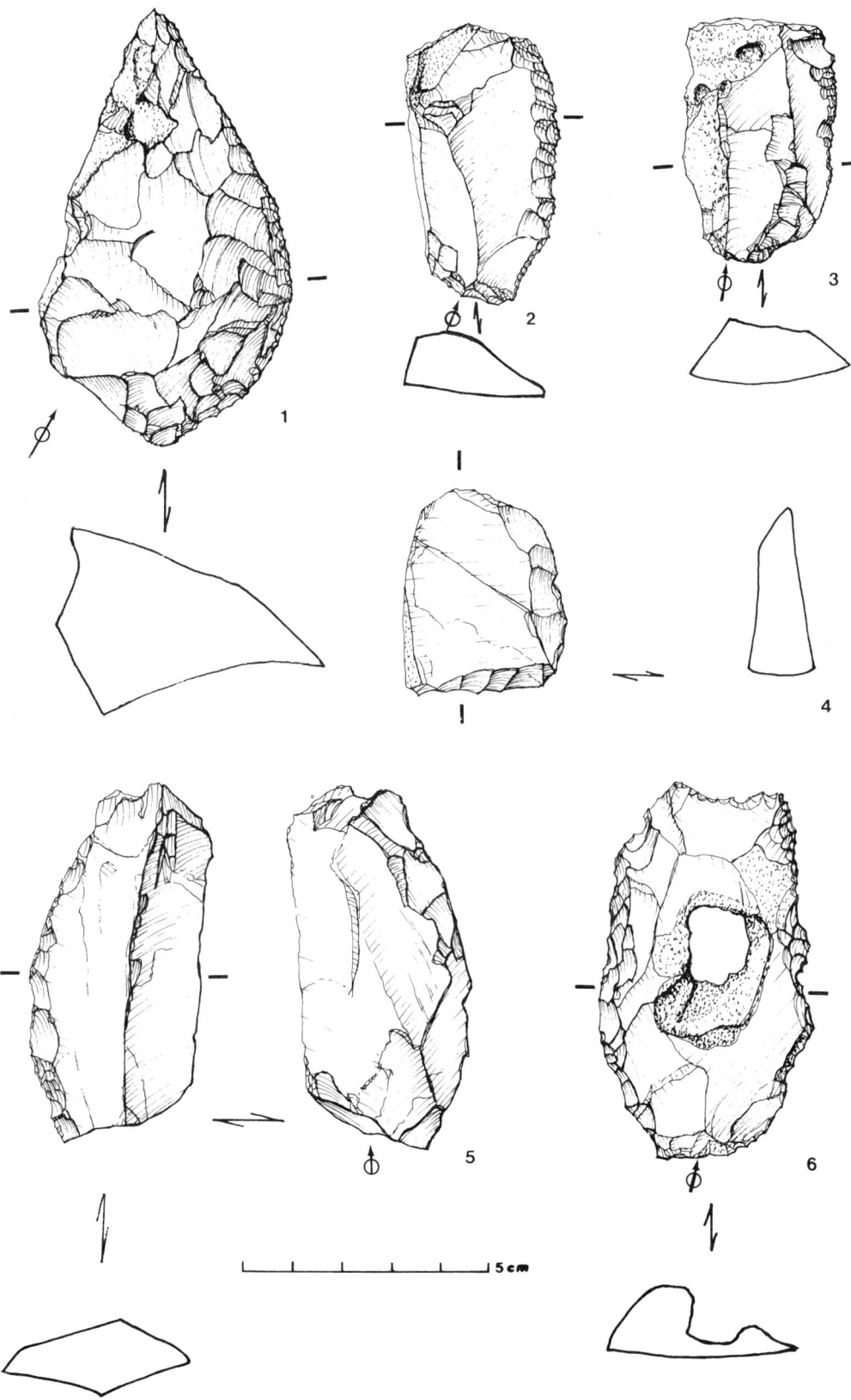

Figure 5.13 1: Racloir latéral convexe à dos; 2: denticulé à dos; 3: racloir à dos naturel; 4: racloir latéral en quartz; 5: racloir latéral en chert; 6: racloir latéral simple.

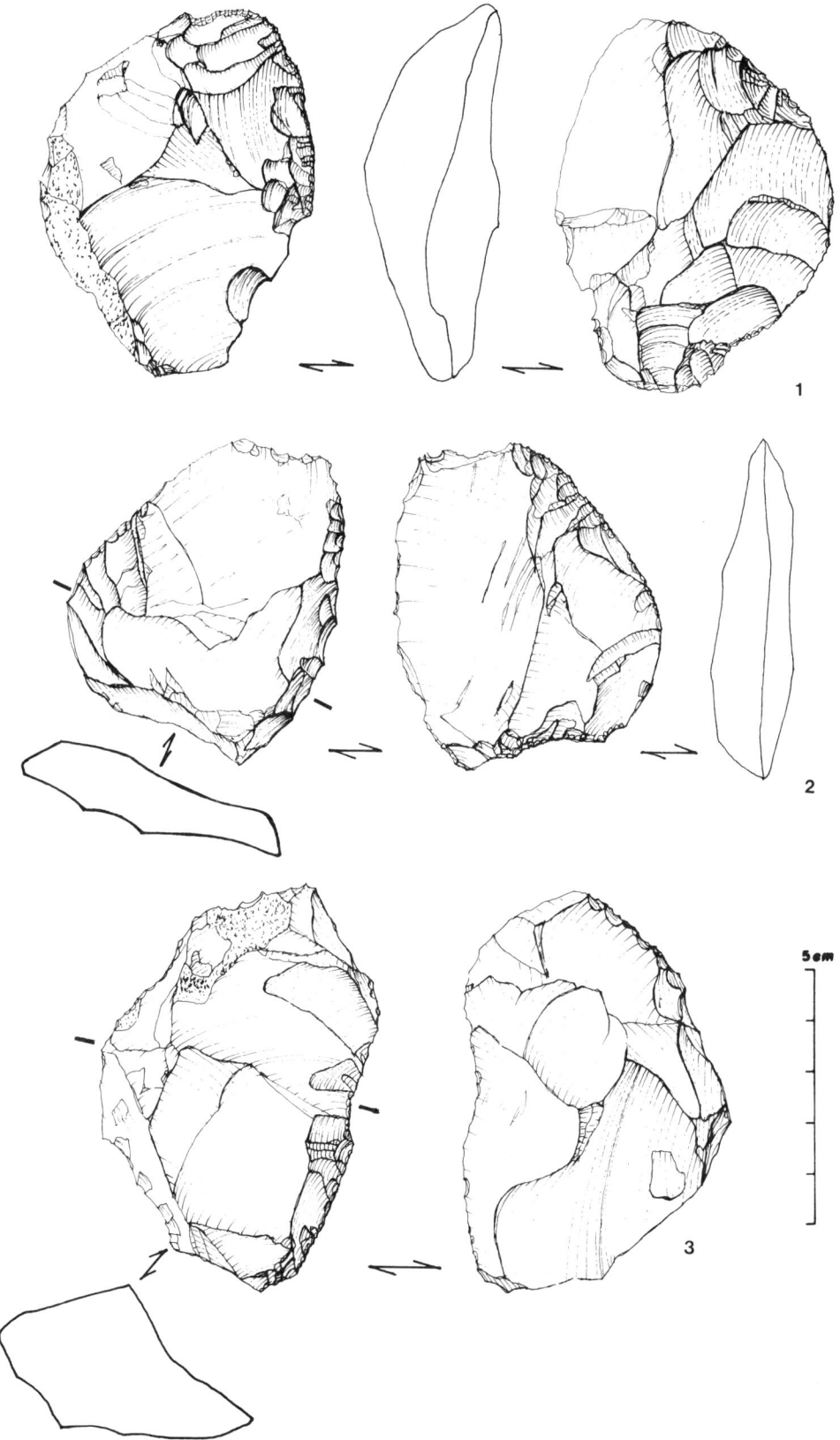

Figure 5.14 1: Couteau biface; 2-3: racloirs bifaces.

INTERPRÉTATION D'UN HABITAT AU PALÉOLITHIQUE MOYEN

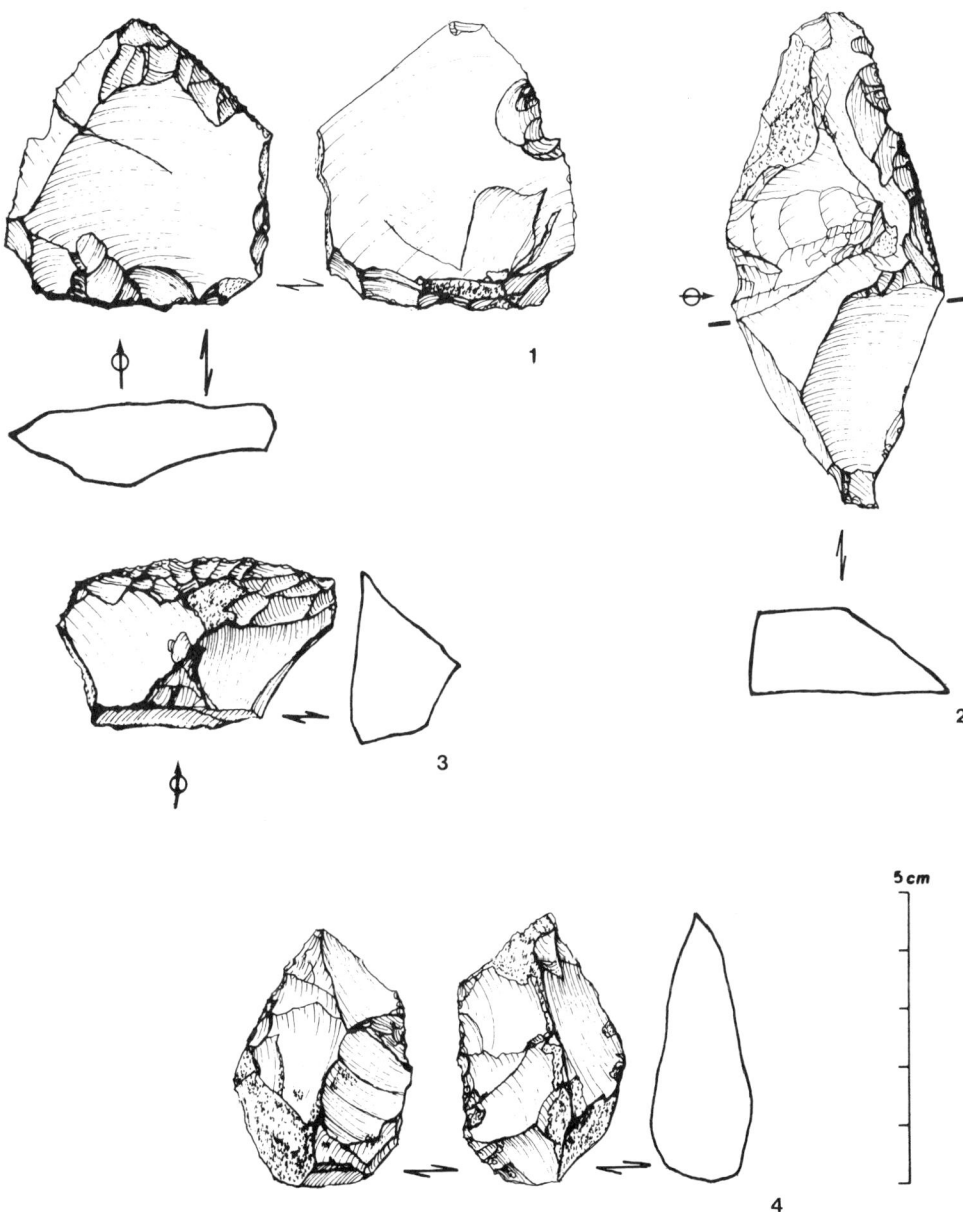

Figure 5.15 1: Racloir à front rectiligne et à retouche alterne; 2: racloir transversal à dos; 3: racloir transversal à retouche Quina; 4: petit biface à bout tronqué.

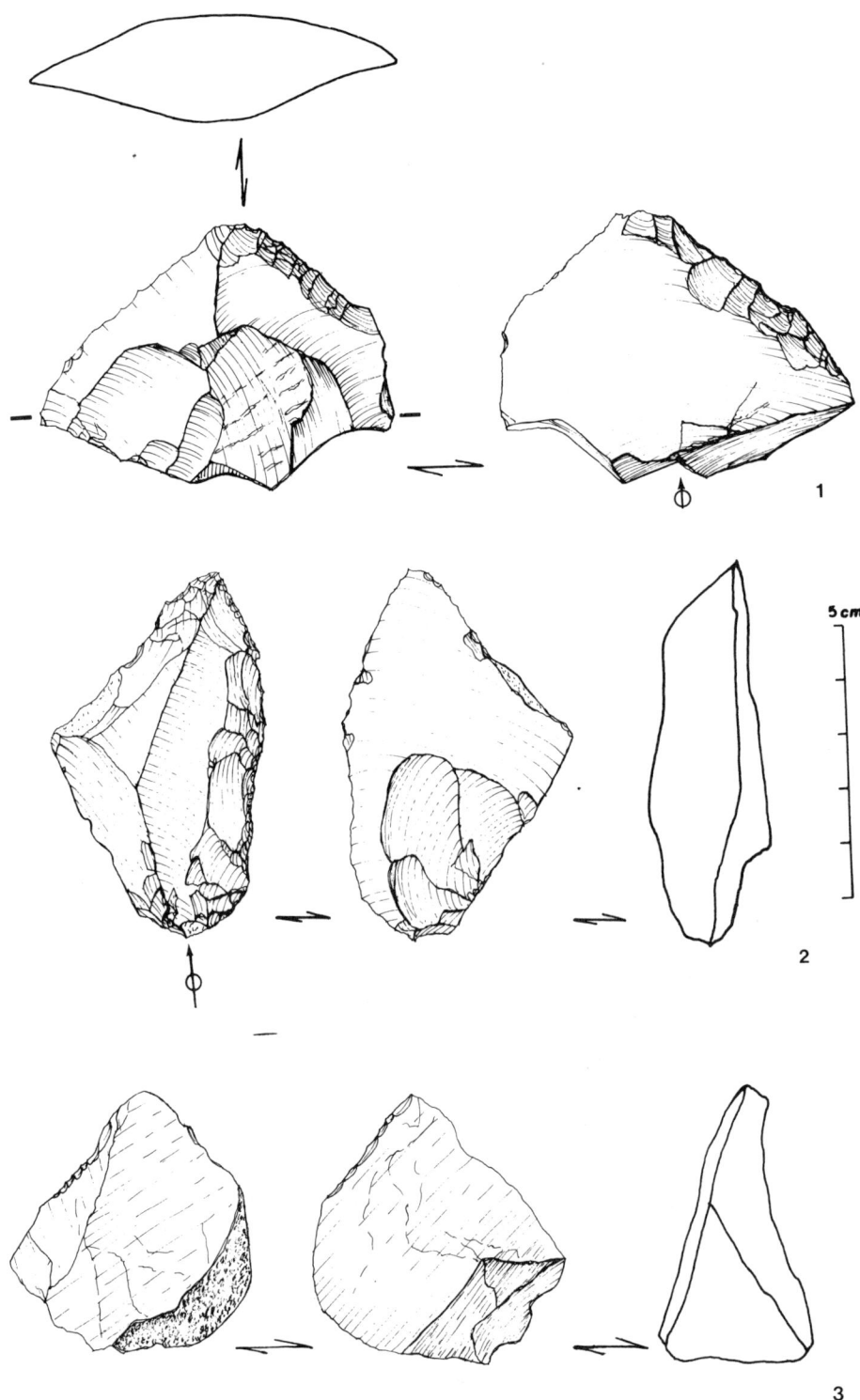

Figure 5.16 1: Racloir à retouche alterne en chert; 2: racloir double convergent denticulé; 3: éclats de quartz appointé par retouche alterne.

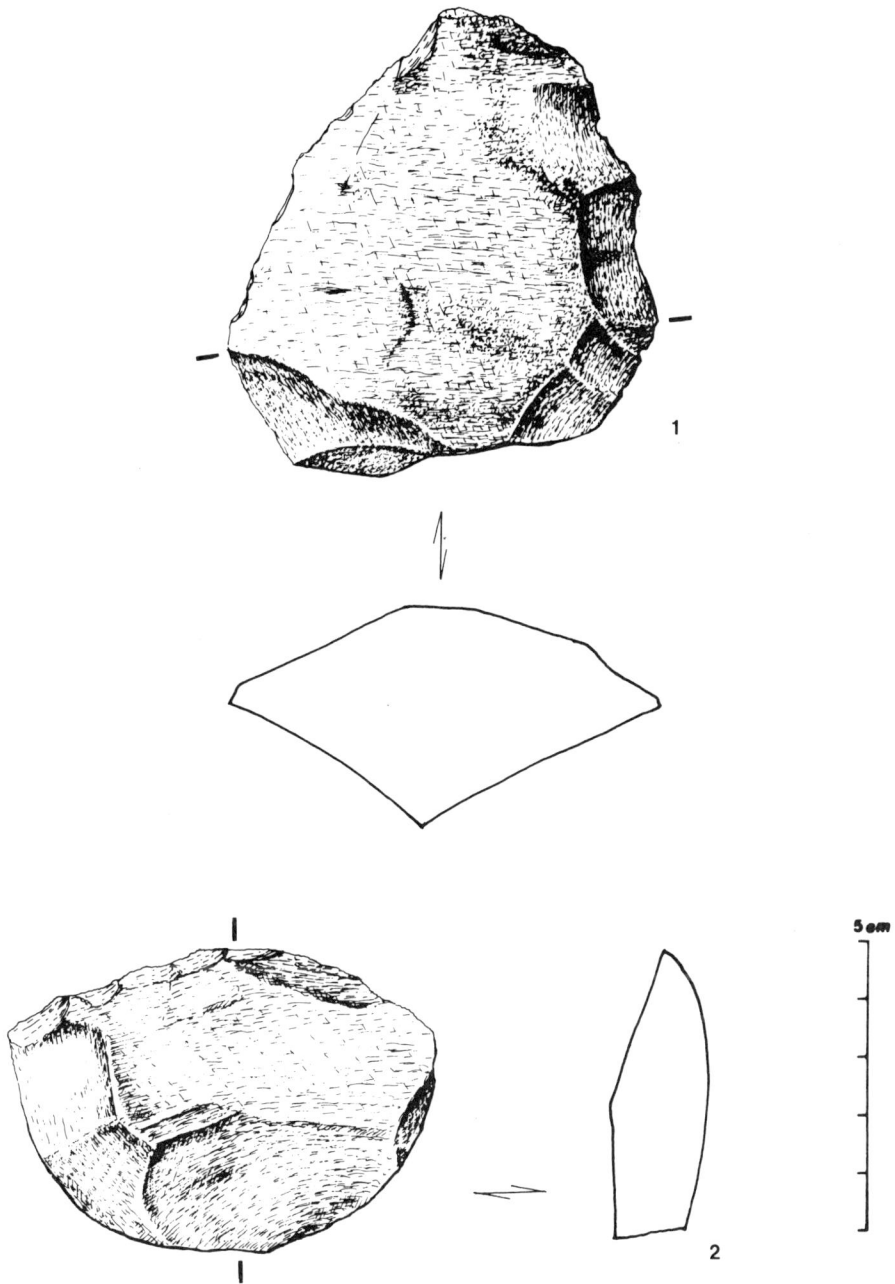

Figure 5.17   1: Denticulé massif en quartzite; 2: racloir transversal en quartzite.

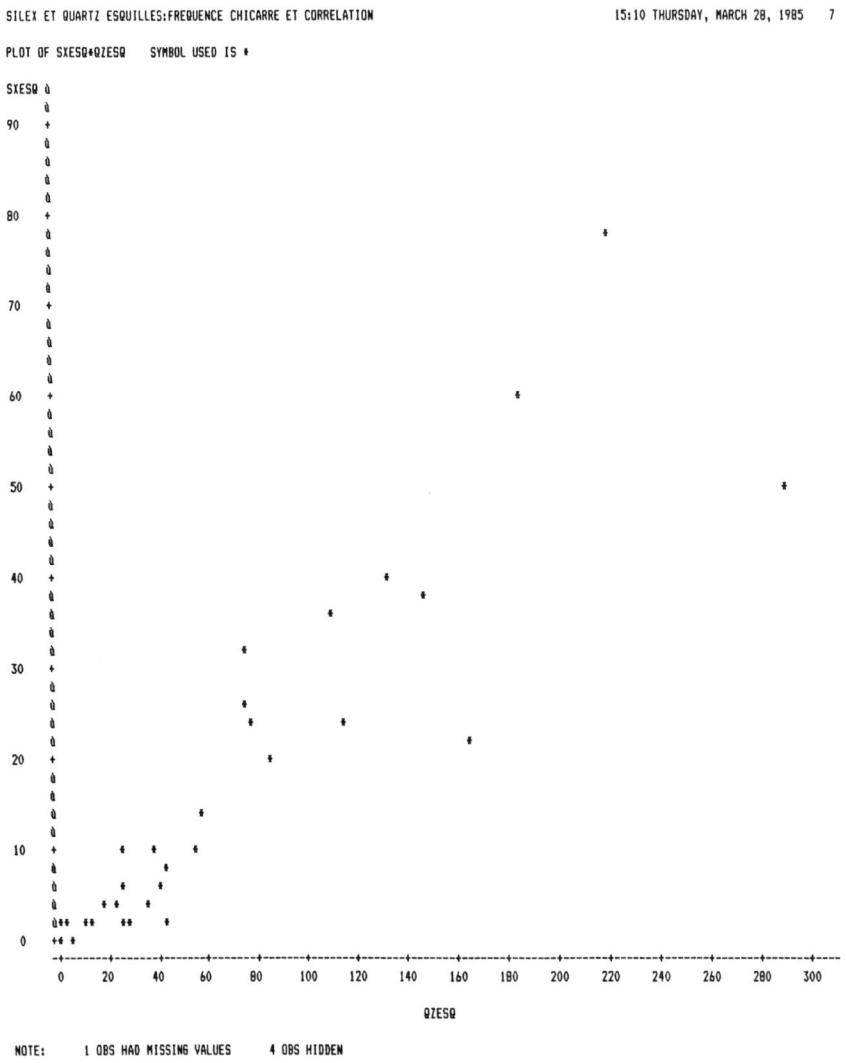

Figure 5.18   Diagramme de corrélation spatiale entre les esquilles de quartz et de silex, apparemment de répartition analogue.

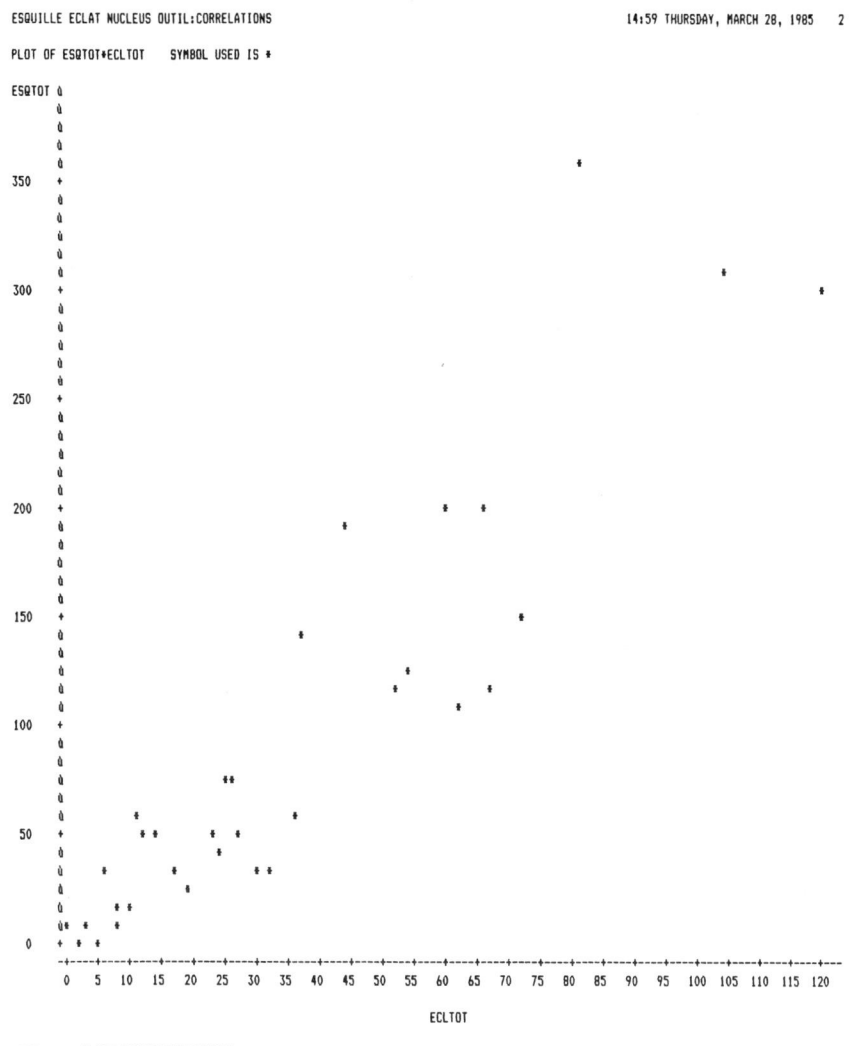

Figure 5.19   Diagramme de corrélation spatiale entre les éclats et les esquilles de tous les matériaux.

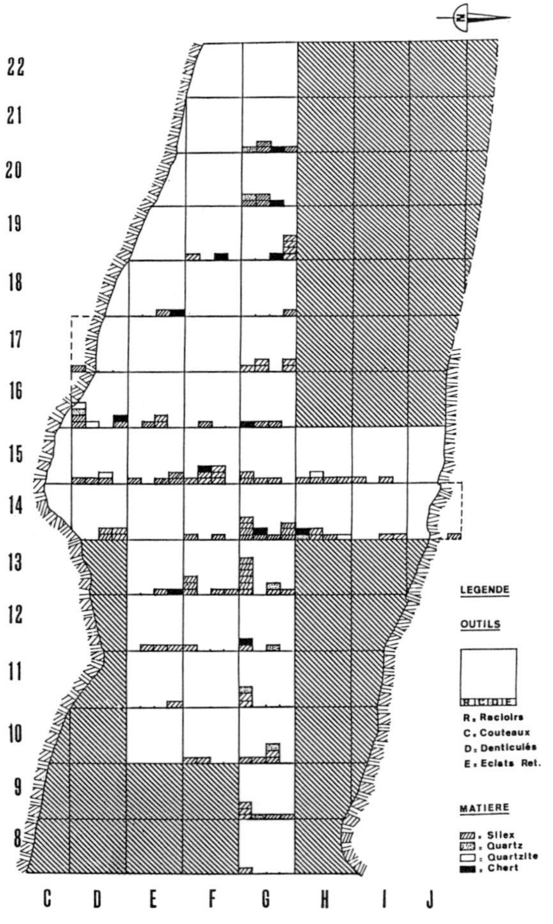

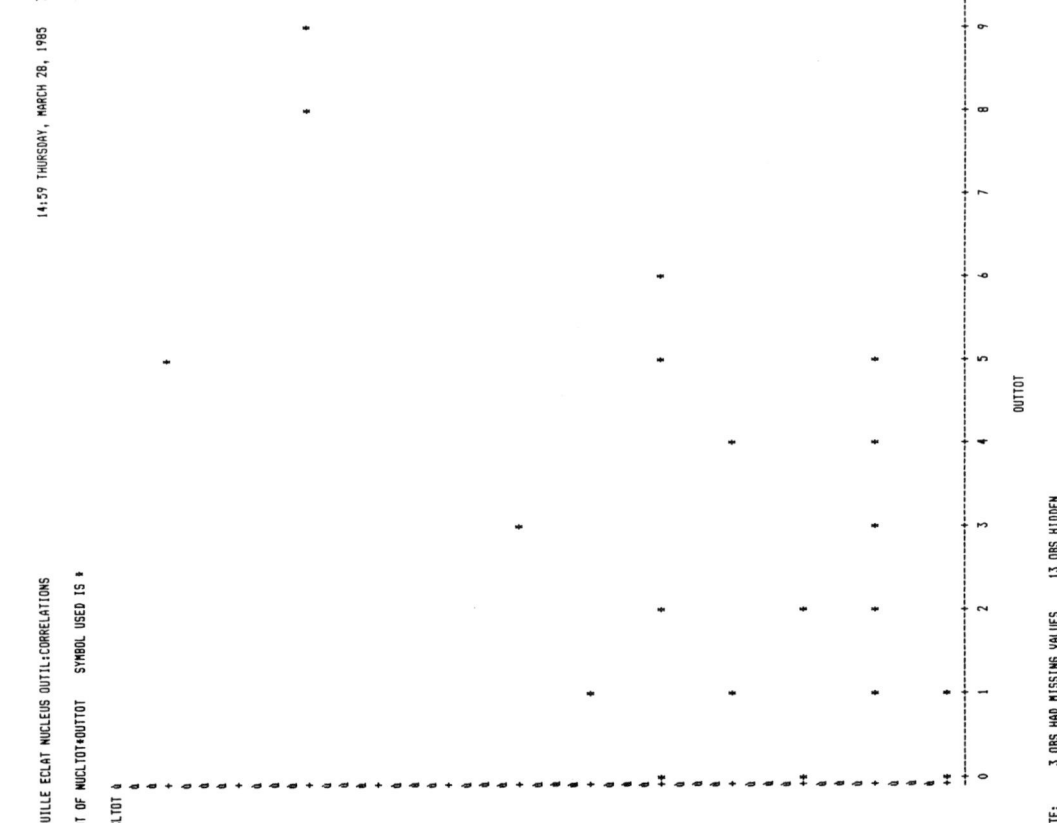

Figure 5.20 *Répartition des principales classes d'outils lithiques par mètre carré. Une concentration de racloirs semble se dessiner dans la partie centrale de la salle.*

Figure 5.21 *Diagramme de corrélation spatiale entre les outils et les nucléus, indiquant l'absence de relation entre leur répartition.*

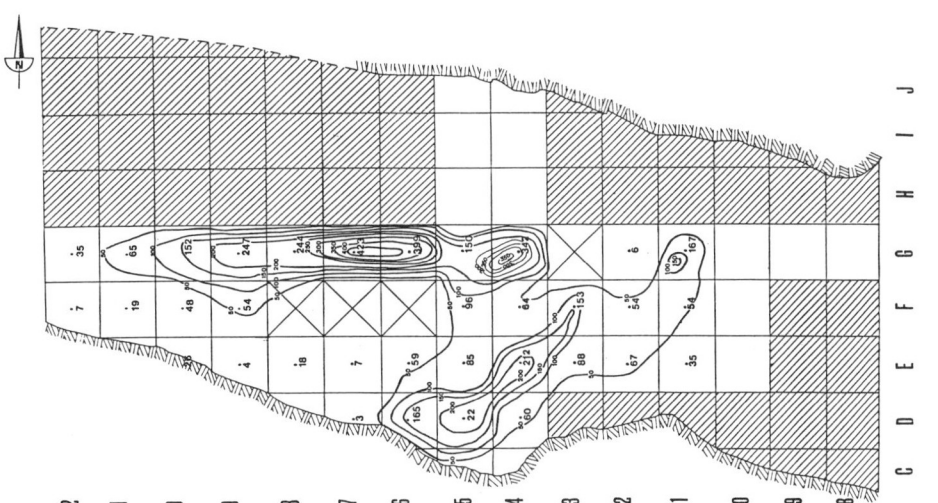

Figure 5.23 Courbes d'iso-densité pour les quartz et les silex.

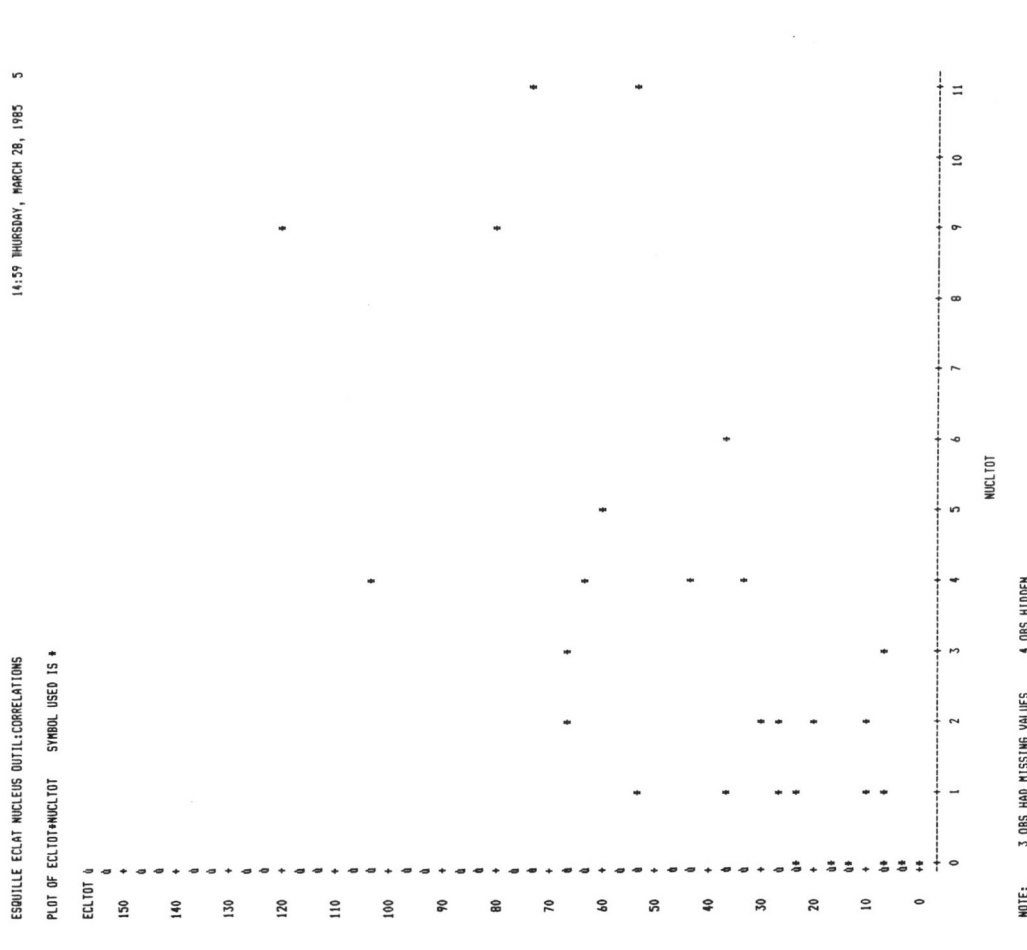

Figure 5.22 Diagramme de corrélation spatiale entre les nucléus et les éclats. Aucune relation nette n'apparaît dans la répartition de ces deux catégories.

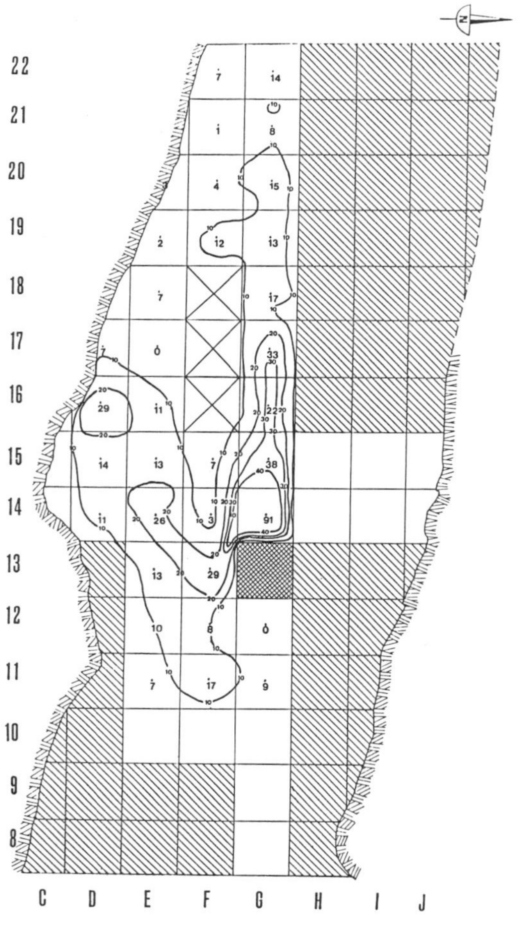

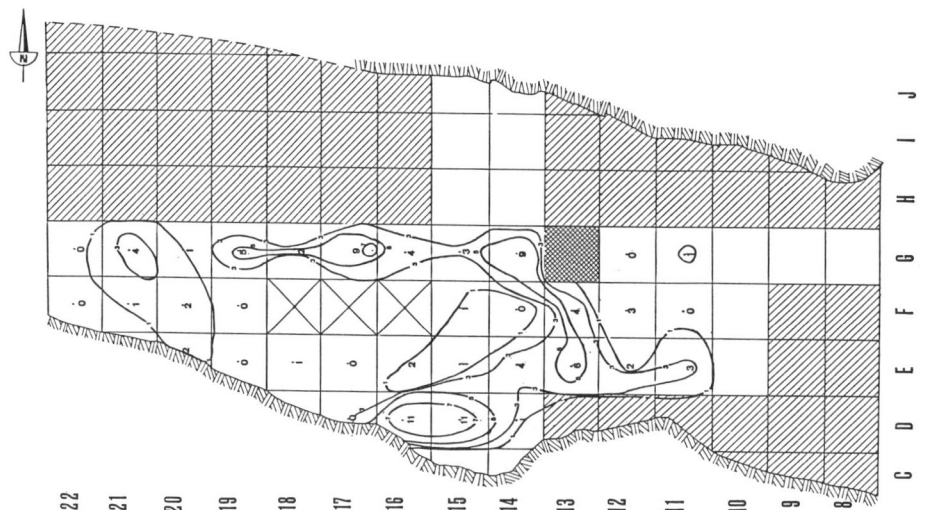

Figure 5.25 *Courbes d'iso-densité pour les nucléus.*

Figure 5.24 *Courbes d'iso-densité pour les quartzites et les cherts.*

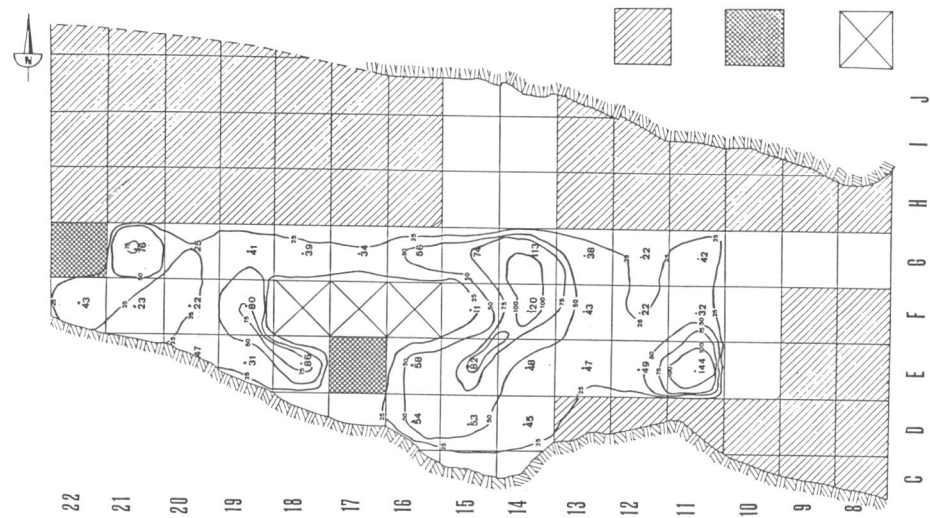

Figure 5.27 *Courbes d'iso-densité pour les restes osseux déterminables. La répartition définit ici deux zones de concentration distinctes de celles du lithique: à l'avant et à l'arrière de la salle.*

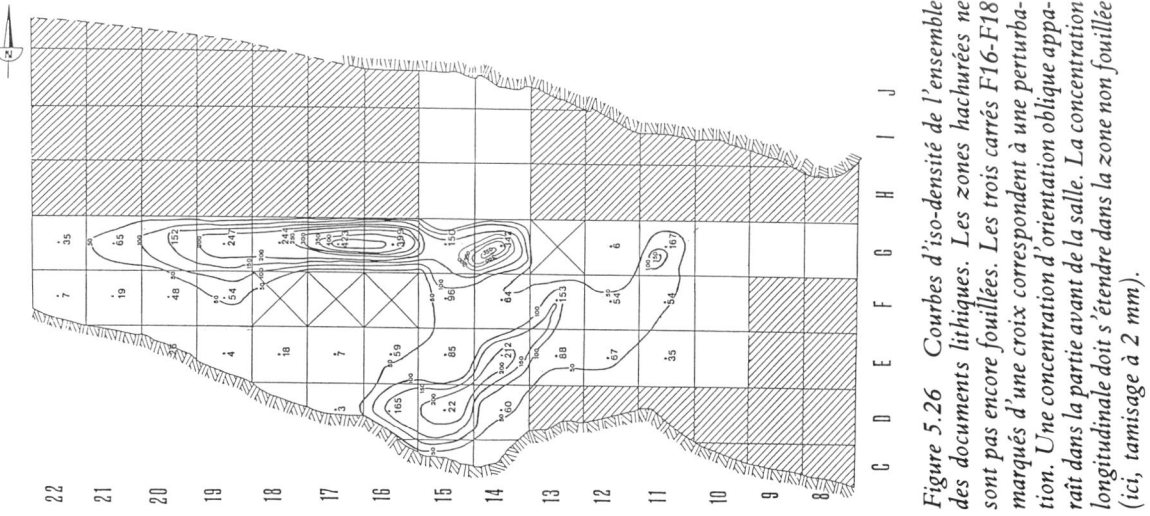

Figure 5.26 *Courbes d'iso-densité de l'ensemble des documents lithiques. Les zones hachurées ne sont pas encore fouillées. Les trois carrés F16-F18 marqués d'une croix correspondent à une perturbation. Une concentration d'orientation oblique apparaît dans la partie avant de la salle. La concentration longitudinale doit s'étendre dans la zone non fouillée (ici, tamisage à 2 mm).*

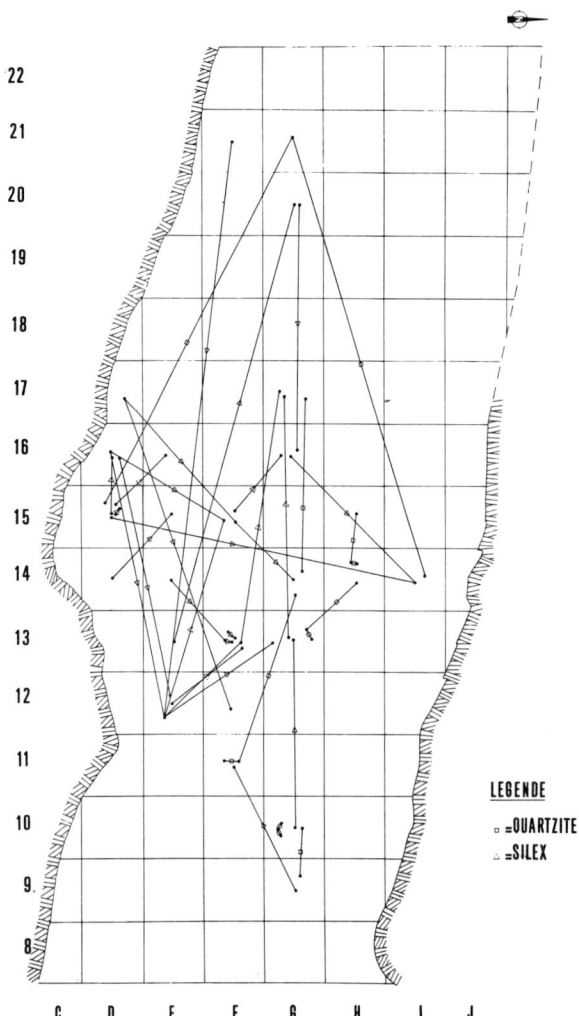

Figure 5.28 Plan des liaisons établies à partir des remontages de documents lithiques de la couche 5 (état provisoire).

VI

Flint Exploitation and Production at Monte Avena in the Dolomitic Region of the Italian East Alps

Lithic Industry, Site Pattern, and Paleoenvironmental Context

Michele Lanzinger

Mauro Cremaschi

INTRODUCTION

Monte Avena is situated in the Dolomite region of the eastern Alps, near the town of Feltre (Fig. 6.1). The summit (1450 m) is a broad plateau modeled by shallowly cut valleys truncated by slope erosion. Artifacts have recently been found here, exhibiting typological characteristics attributable to the Aurignacian technocomplex. The rarity of finds referable to the Aurignacian in Italy, however, and the unusually high altitude of the site (one of the highest of this age), prompted the organization of a systematic excavation carried out over three seasons (1984-85-86). This work, together with a field survey, is still in progress. The aim of this paper is to describe the industry, the spatial organization, and the activities performed on the site. A geological study of the profile, focused mainly on the micromorphology of the soils, describes the evolution of the paleoenvironmental history of the site area.

THE SITE

Although in Pleistocene times this region was intensely glaciated, the summit plateau of Monte Avena was above the valley glaciers even during the maximum glacial phases. These glaciers left their lateral moraines on the mountain slope around 800-1000 m above sea level. The altitude of the mountaintop itself was not sufficient to be the source of a local glacier. At the study area, the peak of the mountain has preserved a soil profile 2.5 m thick.

The archaeological locality is at the head of one of the valleys, which is about 50 m wide at the southern edge of the plateau. The surface area so far excavated (ca. 50 sq. m) connects the central part of the valley to a lateral outcrop of Cretaceous limestone containing flint nodules and bands (known as the *Scaglia rossa* Formation). The outcrop forms a low rockface about a meter high and bounds the valley on its eastern side (Fig. 6.2).

The homogeneous silty sediment has not preserved the original living surfaces and other clear stratigraphical evidence, and so it has been necessary to dig in artificial spits. As they were excavated, the artifacts were left in situ and plotted with a computer-aided procedure. Unfortunately, the physical and chemical activity of the soil has destroyed all bone and pollen remains.

The following stratigraphical succession refers to a section located near the axis of the valley.

—Cuts 1-4 (0-35 cm): Loess beneath a grassy turf. At this level the lithic industry consists predominantly of thick unretouched flakes that probably represent Holocene industries previously recognized in field surveys. In cut 4, a distal fragment of a double-backed microlithic point suggests some sporadic

Figure 6.1 Topography of the southeast Alpine region and localization of the Monte Avena site (1940 m a.s.l.).

Figure 6.2 View of the limestone outcrop during the excavation.

occupation of the area in the Lower Mesolithic (Sauveterrian) period.

—Cuts 5-7 (35-55 cm): The Aurignacian industry described in greater detail below was found within this cut. Sometimes the artifacts show clastic support, but more often they are embedded in the silty matrix without any possibility of recognizing isochronic surfaces.

—Cut 8 and the following (55-220 cm): A few flint artifacts testify to an even older occupation of the site attributable to the Middle Paleolithic. The more relevant artifacts are: four flakes, one with a faceted platform (cuts 14-15); one exhausted Levallois blade core with a prepared striking platform (cut 8); one denticulated scraper on a thick flake with a plain platform (cut 8); one notch on a flake and one carinate notch on a cortical flake with inverse scars (cut 8).

RECONSTRUCTION OF THE PALEOENVIRONMENT

DESCRIPTION OF THE PROFILE

The following description concerns a geological trench dug near the axis of the little site-valley at the western edge of the excavation (Fig. 6.3).

0-5 cm, Horizon A1: dark brown (10YR 3/3); grassy turf.

5-20 cm, B11: dark yellowish brown (10YR 4/4); silty loam, laminar structure poorly developed, weakly granular, charcoal in fragments, clear boundary.

20-42 cm, B12: dark yellowish brown (10YR 4/4); silt loam, fine subangular blocky structure, soft, friable, charcoal in fragments, common Fe-Mn nodules; gradual smooth boundary. Highest concentration of Aurignacian artifacts at the base.

42-65 cm, IIB1: brown to dark brown (7.5YR 4/4);

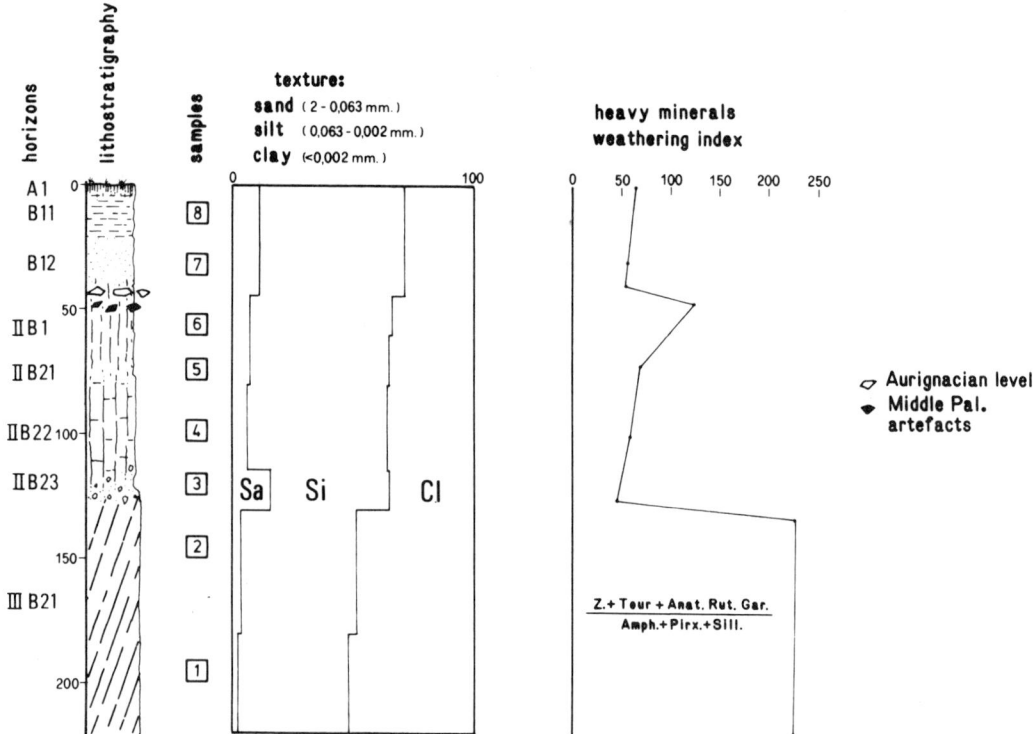

Figure 6.3 Monte Avena stratigraphic sequence, sedimentological parameters, and weathering index (according to Brewer 1976).

silty clay loam, fine and medium subangular blocky, friable; gradual boundary; Aurignacian artifacts are decreasing in rate at the base, beneath which a few Middle Paleolithic pieces were found.

65-78 cm, IIB21: brown to reddish brown (7.5YR 4/4-5YR 4/3); silty clay loam, well-developed medium and fine subangular blocky, slightly hard, some thin Fe-Mn coatings and some slikensides, rare chert fragments, gradual boundary.

78-118 cm, IIB22: brown to dark brown (7.5YR 4/4); silty clay loam, well-developed medium angular blocky, hard, many slikensides, gradual boundary.

118-128 cm, IIB23: reddish brown (7YR 4/4); silty clay loam, strongly developed medium and fine angular blocky, hard, many Fe-Mn coatings, many little slikensides, very gradual boundary.

128-220 cm, IIIB21: dark reddish brown at the top (5YR3/3), yellowish red at the base (5YR 4/6); weak fine angular, friable, not stony, slightly hard, boundary not exposed to the bedrock.

TEXTURAL AND MINERALOGICAL ANALYSES

Textural analyses, according to the field evidences, led to the distinction of three lithostratigraphic units:

1. Upper loess cover, including the pedogenetic horizons A1, B11, B12;
2. Lower loess, including the pedogenetic horizons IIB1, IIB21, IIB22, IIB23;
3. Relict paleosol, in which only the IIIB21 horizon is preserved.

The grain-size distributions of the two loessic covers define unimodal curves, moderately sorted with a well-marked peak in medium and fine silt (Fig. 6.4), and show similarities with the other loesses of the north Italian pre-alpine plateaus (Cremaschi 1987). The sand content is low and the clay increases slightly, from 28 to 35% in the lower loess. The sand peak and the unsorted grain-size distribution of sample 3 point to a colluvial origin for the base of the lower loess sheet.

The uppermost unit 3 consists of a relict paleosol (terra rossa), developed on limestone and very rich in clay (about 50%) (see Fig. 6.3).

Heavy-mineral ($d > 2.9$) composition has been regarded as a source of information about the provenience of sediments in each lithostratigraphic unit, helping to estimate the degree of weathering of the soil horizons and the main pedological and lithologic discontinuities. The heavy minerals of the sandy

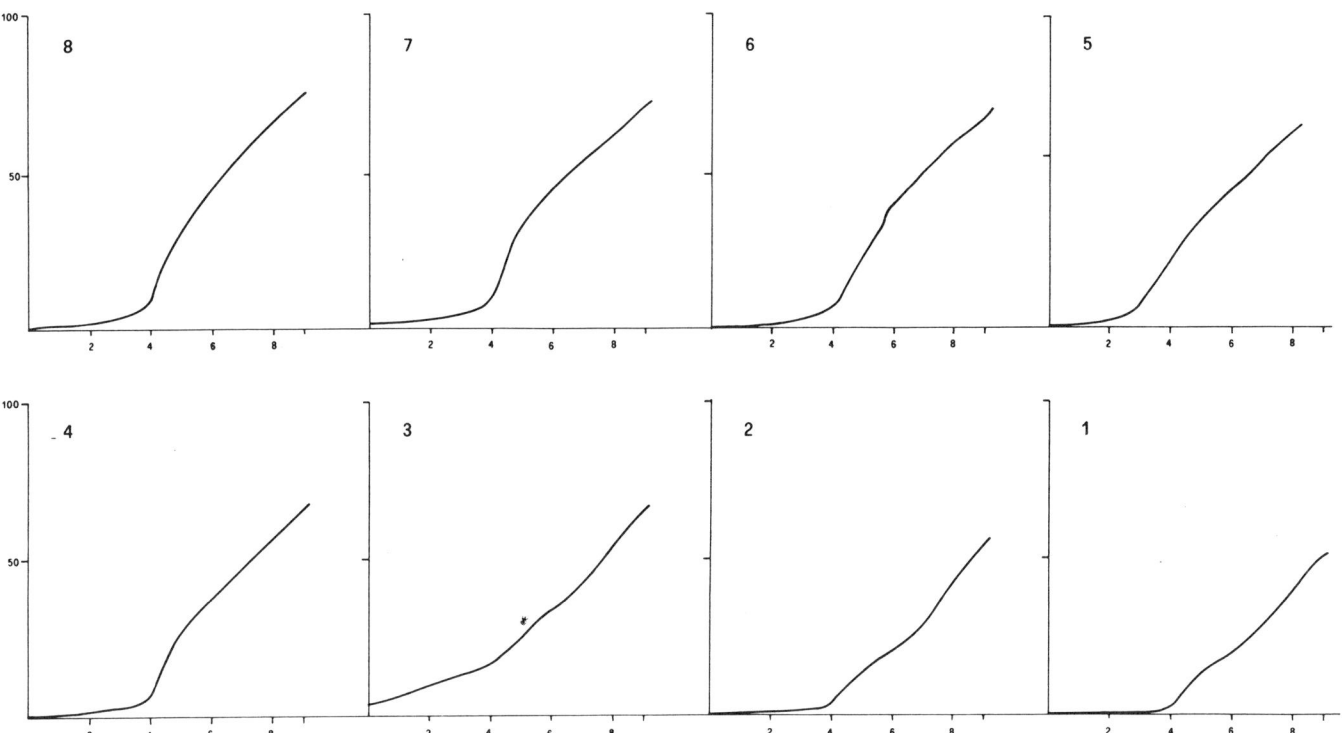

Figure 6.4 Granulometric grain-size distribution of the two loessic covers (samples 8-4); colluvial level (3); relict paleosol (8).

fraction (250-63 microns) have been selected in order of decreasing stability; the weathering index (WI) has been calculated according to Brewer (1976)—that is, the ratio of stable minerals (zircon, tourmaline, anatase, garnet) to unstable minerals (amphiboles, pyroxenes, sillimanite).

The loess deposits in the first two units are mainly composed of eruptive paragenesis which did not originate from the nearby limestone outcrops. That means they have been deflated from the glacial deposits of the nearby Piave Valley and from the fluvio-glacial sediments of the Po plain (Cremaschi 1987).

The terra rossa lower unit (IIIB21) has prevalent stable heavy-mineral composition (anatase, tourmaline, and zircon) in respect to the unstable metamorphic minerals (especially amphiboles) and thus shows a more intense pedogenesis. The trend expressed by the weathering index (Fig. 6.3) highlights the very different compositions of the loessic covers and the paleosol. The peak at the top of the IIB1 horizon points to the effect of another pedogenetic phase; it shows decreasing effects between the top of the lower loess unit and the bottom of the profile.

MICROMORPHOLOGICAL CHARACTERISTICS

The micromorphological characteristics of the Monte Avena profile's soil horizons are described in Figure 6.5, according to Brewer (1976), with references to Fedoroff and Goldsberg (1982) and Van Vliet and Lanoe (1985). The horizons B11 and B12 (samples 8 and 7) have similar patterns; the matrix is slightly birefringent and the cutanic features are rare, but pedorelicts, allochthonous Fe-Mn nodules, and papulae are common. In the IIB21 horizon (sample 5) the cutanic features increase slightly in number; they consist of "complex cutans" (composed of alternating ferriargillans, siltans, skeletons and matrans, sometimes broken and embedded in the matrix) with thin and continuous argillans related to voids. Skeleton grains show a clear wavy distribution of the muscovite flakes (fluidal patterns). In the IIB22 and IIB23 horizons (samples 4 and 3), well-developed cutanic features increase markedly in number; the main pedologic pattern is due to round aggregates in sediment of loess.

The characteristics of the IIIB21 horizon are the high sepicity of the matrix and the high incidence of

Samples	8	7	6	5	4	3	2
Horizons	B 11	B 12	II B1	II B21	II B22	II B23	III B21
Skelton grains	Quartz + Mich. + Feld. Fine sand. silt	-do-	-do-	-do-	-do-	-do-	Quartz (FF)
Lithorelicts	Quartz (F) Charcoals (F)	—	Chert (F) Charcoals (FF)	Charcoals (C)	Chert (F) Feldspar (F)	Chert (F)	Quartz (FF)
Pedorelicts	from III B 21 (C)	from III B21 (C)	—	—	—	—	—
Voids	channels (C) large chambers (C)	-do-	channels (F) very large chambers (C)	channels (C) vughs (C)	branching channels	-do-	Planes (C) Channels (C) Vughs (F)
Plasmic	silasepic	silasepic	masepic	insepic	masepic	masepic – bimasepic	omnisepic
Basic	porphyroschelic	-do-	-do-	-do-	-do-	-do-	—
Cutanic features	—	—	complex cutans (F) argillans	complex cutans (C) Ferriargillans (C) Thin ferriargillans (F) in voids	-do- but (CC)	Ferrri-mangans Quasi-mangans	Stress-cutans (M) Ferriargillans (C) Complex-cutans (C) Quasi-mangans (C)
Glabulae	alloctonous Fe-Mn nodules (C) papulae (C)	-do-	alloctonous Fe-Mn nodules (M) papules (C)	-do- papules (CC)	-do- but (F)	Fe-Mn nodules (C)	Fe-Mn nodules (C)
Other features	—	—	fluidal patterns of mica grains	—	—	Fluidal patterns of mica grains Perigla- cial rounded aggr.	—

Figure 6.5 *Synthesis of the micromorphological characteristics of the soil horizons:* (C) *common,* (M) *medium,* (F) *few.*

stress cutans. Ferriargillans are also well preserved; interpedal accumulations of loess material illuviated from the overlying horizons have also been observed.

DISCUSSION

The rubefaction, the high clay content, and the very stable heavy-mineral association of the IIIB21 horizon are attributed to part of a relict terra rossa-like paleosol. Until now it has not been possible to produce a direct chronometric age, but similar paleosols, well known along the meridional fringe of the Alps, are commonly attributed to nonglacial climatic periods of the Early Pleistocene and Late Tertiary.

The uppermost IIB23, IIB21, and IIB1 horizons, with in situ Mousterian and Aurignacian implements at the top, are dated to a loessic cover of Upper Pleistocene age. The clear gap, in stratigraphy and time, that separates the two lithological units is connected by the presence of the "round aggregates" layer, which is to be interpreted as the result of ice lensing and slope gelifluction (Van Vliet and Lanoe 1985).

The pedogenesis of the Upper Pleistocene loess cover is attested by the matrix illuviation in the form of "complex cutans." The same pedological features are observed in modern soil under conditions of a continental climate with seasonally contrasted water regime (Fedoroff and Goldsberg 1982). The top of this unit (IIB1), with papulized, broken cutanic features and fluidal patterns of the skeleton grains, is interpreted as the result of a heavy climatic deterioration connected with frequent freeze-and-thaw cycles (Cremaschi and Lanzinger 1983, in press).

The superimposed, more recent loess cover (B12 and B11) is younger than the Aurignacian occupation of the area and is connected to the last glacial stade of the region. A certain number of thin and continuous argillans and ferriargillans in the voids of the IIB1, IIB21, and IIB22 horizons are the products of the postglacial pedogenesis.

From the top of the terra rossa soil, the sequence of the climatic events recorded in the Monte Avena profile is summarized as follows:

—cold with alternating phases of wet and dry: base of the earlier loess deposition with freeze-and-thaw cycles;
—dry cold: early loess deposition;
—slightly temperate in seasonally contrasted climate: pedogenesis of the early loess;
—cold and wet: degradation of the top of the soil developed on the loess;
—dry cold: later loess sedimentation;
—temperate: pedogenesis of the two loess covers.

The two eolian deposition phases are dated without better specification to the first and second Würm Pleniglacials; the pedogenesis with a curbing effect on deposition of the early loess is connected to the Würm Interpleniglacial climatic heating.

Because of its stratigraphical position, the Aurignacian assemblage is dated to the time between the two loess sedimentations. In the European continental stratigraphy, it would correspond to the Hengelo-Arcy and the following temperate phase of Arcy and the successive climatic deterioration due to the beginning of the cold phase of the second Würm Pleniglacial.

THE AURIGNACIAN INDUSTRY

The following part of the report is intended as a preliminary description of the products coming from the Aurignacian level.

BLOCKS

These are fragments of different sizes (up to 15 cm), nodules or bands of the local flint. The surfaces of these blocks generally show pre-existing planes of discontinuity or fissures, thus making it difficult to determine whether these are the products of natural fracture (gelifraction) or of rough knapping.

PRE-CORES

These were obtained from small blocks or carinate flint flakes. They are divided into three types.

Type 1: without a standardized form, shows one or more scars. This could be an initial stage in the formation of the other, more elaborate types of pre-cores.

Type 2: on block or thick flake. The preparation is obtained by means of unidirectional adjacent scars forming a subrectilinear, slightly curved or very curved margin.

Type 3: the block is carinate (approaching a pyramidal form) and generally cortical; the majority of the scars are the negatives of blades and bladelets that removed the original cortex.

It is not always easy to distinguish between the three types of pre-cores and the forms of cores derived from them, especially with some of the more elaborate forms. Many broken pieces with scars are interpreted as pre-core fragments.

CORES

The cores are classified on the basis of their form, the localization of flake scars, and the type of intended product, as follows.

Type 1: Discoid, obtained from small fragments. They show centripetal scars related to the production of flakes. There are some examples that show little or no preparation that derive from the second type of pre-core described above. An example of this type, reconstructed to the pre-core stage through refitting of five flakes, shows stages of rejuvenation obtained by a process of platform preparation similar to that on the corresponding pre-cores (Fig. 6.6:1).

Type 2: Prismatic, obtained from small blocks with two or three percussion planes in the production of blades and bladelets (Fig. 6.6:2-3). This is a rare form that has already been described for the Aurignacian.

Type 3: Subpyramidal with laminar scars, originating from the third type of pre-core described above (Fig. 6.6:4-7). A few of the very regular pyramidal forms fall in the category of *rabots*, with typical forms that have already been described for the Aurignacian (Fig. 6.7:1-2).

KNAPPING PRODUCTS

Laminar products are not well represented at this site except for a few bladelets 2-3 cm long, with triangular section and outline with parallel or subparallel edges, which are most probably obtained from pyramidal cores. Almost all of these examples are complete, many are carinate, and frequently they have a cortex that, in certain cases (first-order flakes), covers the whole dorsal surface. Their sections are irregular, often with undulations on the dorsal side caused by the structural unevenness of the original block. Their striking platforms are mainly smooth and, in the first-order flakes, can be cortical. Faceting is rare, but is present among flakes coming from a reconstructed nucleus (Fig. 6.6:1). Most of the flakes with cortex tend to be carinate with irregular section and outline. Often they seem to be products resulting from the initial reduction phases of the blocks and flint fragments present on the site. This operation seems to have been intended for the production of the pre-cores rather than the blanks.

TOOLS

Very few flint tools were found but some of them, including the *rabots*, carinate endscrapers, and the *Dufour*-like bladelets, are elements diagnostic of the Aurignacian complex.

Burins—There are two doubtful examples of typical carinate burins. The first is a simple burin on a laminar flake with transversal scars starting from a single platform (Fig. 6.7:5). The other is a multiple burin on a very thick flake. At one end is a series of transversal scars on the flat face, and at the other end a burin with transverse and single lateral scar (Fig. 6.7:4).

Endscrapers—These tools are carinate, or thick tending towards the carinate type, on flattened blocks or on thick, short flakes (Fig. 6.7:6-7, 10-11). Among these are one carinate scraper that is flattened with shoulder and lamellar scars (Fig. 6.7:8) and one carinate scraper with another inverse-carinate, shouldered endscraper at the opposite end (Fig. 6.7:9).

Troncature-endscrapers—One example is on a small thick and narrow block. At one end is a carinate endscraper with lamellar scars, at the other a very thick transverse truncation.

Bladelets—There are four examples of these tools, all of which occur on lamellar blanks chipped from pyramidal cores with steep marginal retouch. They have a very fine retouch toward the inframarginal type. The retouch is direct in two cases and inverse in the others (Fig. 6.7:12-15).

Retouched flakes—There are 25 examples, including one elongated form with deep, steep, and direct retouch (Fig. 6.7:3).

These assemblage data, summarized in Table 6.1, reflect only the first three field seasons, but some interpretations are suggested.

The flint blocks form the largest group. Their spatial distribution is not limited to the area at the limestone outcrop base, where they are present in maximum number, but they continue to span toward the axis of the small valley, where they are mixed together with other artifacts. This suggests that the blocks are not a colluvial deposit but have instead been intentionally placed on the site area. A few of those that were broken and scattered have been refitted.

It is significant that there is such an abundance of pre-cores and cores (226) compared with tools (69), and that among the pre-cores there is such a high incidence of blocks with one or more non-organized

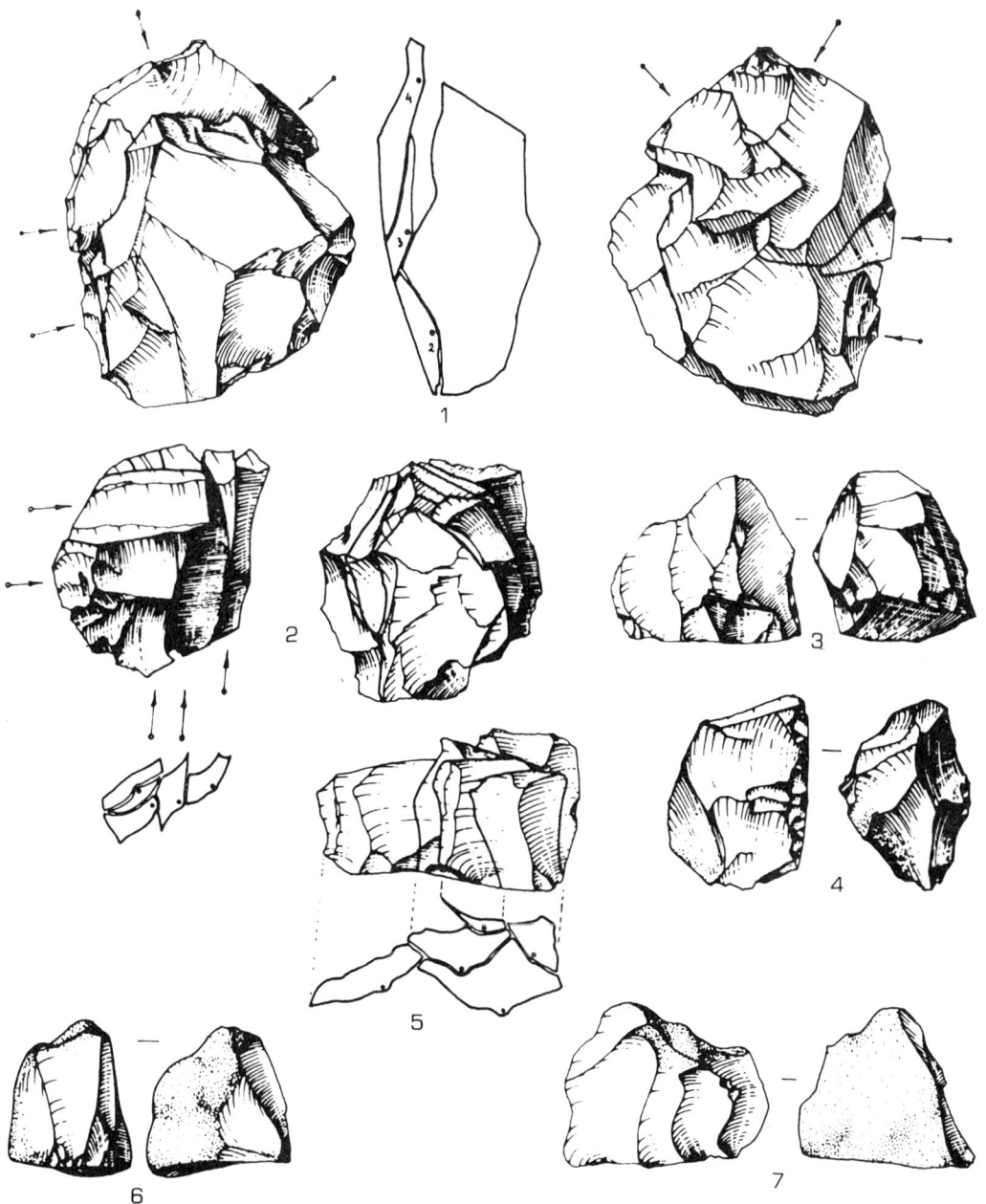

Figure 6.6 1: Refitted core (type 1) with four of the flakes resulting from its reduction, with the dorsal face on the left and ventral face on the right. The knapping was accomplished by means of relatively random centripetal detachment starting from a prepared platform, which was then renewed during the operation; 2-3: refitted core and one prismatic core (type 2); 4-7: subpyramidal cores (type 3). (Drawings by G. Almerigogna)

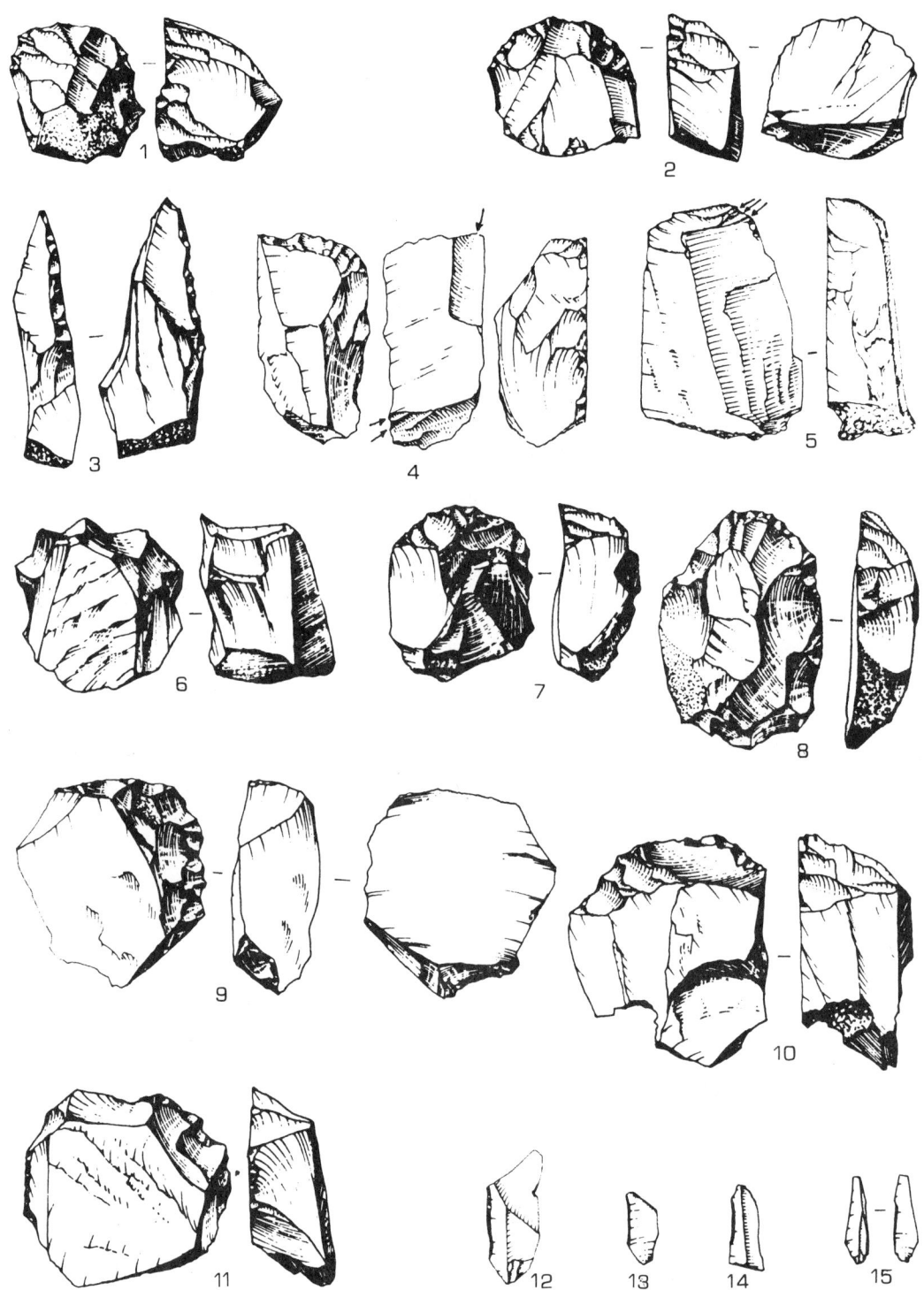

Figure 6.7 1-2: Rabots; *3*: retouched flake; *4*: multiple burin on a very thick flake; at one end is a series of transversal detachments on the flat face, at the other end a burin with transversal preparation and single lateral scar; *5*: simple burin on laminar flake with transversal scars starting from a single knapping surface; *6-7, 10-11*: carinate short endscrapers; *8*: carinate flattened endscraper with shoulder and lamellar scars; *9*: carinate endscraper with an inverse carinate shouldered endscraper at one end; *12,14*: bladelets with steep marginal retouch; *13,15*: bladelets with steep inverse marginal retouch. (Drawing by G. Almerigogna)

TABLE 6.1
PRIMARY BREAKDOWN OF THE LITHIC ASSEMBLAGE

Blocks	1753	51.2%	Scrapers/Endscr.	40	
Flakes	1374	40.2	Retouched flakes	25	
Pre-cores and Cores	226	6.6	cf. *Dufours*	4	
Tools	69	2.0			
Pre-cores 1	102	61.1%	Cores 1	25	42.2%
Pre-cores 2	45	27.0	Cores 2	13	22.2
Pre-cores 3	20	11.9	Cores 3	21	35.6

scars (61.1%), i.e., pre-core type 1. It is reasonable to suppose that such a composition of the assemblage depends on the functional specialization of the site and perhaps it reflects open-cast mining of the flint with preliminary reduction and selection prior to the tool manufacture.

It is also possible to advance a few considerations with regard to the nature of the flint on the site. There are two flint-bearing geological formations in the pre-Quaternary stratigraphy of Monte Avena. The Biancone Formation (the uppermost Jurassic formation in the area) is characterized by white to grayish white limestone, heavily stratified with bands and nodules of black flint. The more recent Cretaceous formation, known as the Scaglia rossa, consists of well-stratified red-pink marly limestones containing frequent beds of red-ocher-colored flint (Munsell 5YR 6/4). The older formation outcrops throughout the Monte Avena area, while the Scaglia rossa is typical of the summit area at the locality of the dig. With the exception of three fragments of Jurassic flint, the entire lithic assemblage of the site originates from this type of Cretaceous flint.

The flint distribution within the outcrop is not uniform. In the area near the rockface were large flint flakes and blocks together with a debris of corroded limestone chips. The end products and waste flakes are concentrated in the central part of the valley. In this latter area the limestone chips were not present, but there were blocks and fractured bands. This difference in areal distribution suggests that the area immediately in front of the rockface was used for the extraction and initial reduction of the flint blocks.

In the area nearer the axis of the valley a few refittings were possible, starting with about 20 flakes and laminar elements scattered over a very limited area (about 1 sq. m). This assemblage constitutes a "latent structure" of a flint workshop, where each series of core reconstructions reflects a single knapping sequence. On the basis of these refittings, the most extensive concentrations identified on the site could be interpreted as the superimposition of several structures (Fig. 6.8:6).

As already mentioned, the eolian sediment forms a homogeneous blanket in which structural elements such as postholes are not preserved. An indirect indication of a hearth, however, results from the presence of numerous burned flints clustered over a 2-sq.-m area (Fig. 6.9).

Thus, the operational sequence of activities performed at the site includes extraction of the flint; rough knapping for pre-core manufacture and selection; tool preparation; discard of exhausted cores or unusable pre-cores; and eventual export of pre-cores, cores, and blanks. As for the flint mining, it is still impossible to say whether the flint nodules were extracted directly from the limestone outcrop or were gathered from the cryoclastic debris of the rockface foot, or both.

In general the quality of the local flint is rather poor due to the presence of microfractures. Because of this, it is likely that a preliminary selection of nodules was done by means of a rough shattering. The selection of suitable material was then extended to the chipping phase of the pre-cores. The high number of the first group of pre-cores, those that were only outlined and then discarded, would support the notion that this stage of reduction was a sort of test of the raw material. It has also been noticed that the quality of the material in this stage is usually worse in comparison with the exploited cores. As previously mentioned, the knapping products of the pre-core preparation are very numerous. A more careful exploitation of the flint and the production of lamellar blanks are also documented, and a few of these products have been refitted.

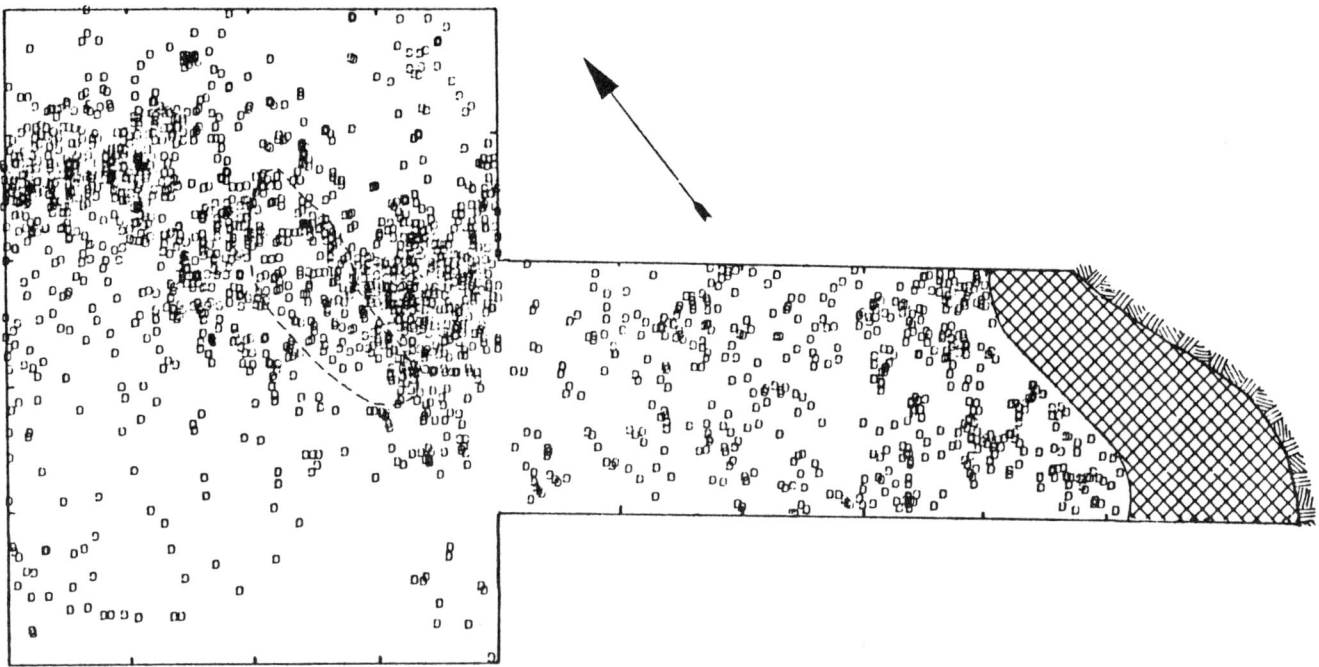

Figure 6.8   Plan of a trench showing the distribution of the flint products. Calcareous debris in the crossed area; the dashed line delimits the scatter of the products with thermoclastic alteration.

From an overall perspective it seems clear that the high numbers of broken pieces, pre-cores, and cores are out of proportion with the low frequency of tools. The rarity of tools could reflect the kind of maintenance tasks carried out in the site or, alternatively, a limit of reduction that was carried out at this site. It would seem reasonable that a part of the fine-quality pre-cores, unexhausted cores, and probably a selection of the best blanks (including, perhaps, some of the tools) were thus exported to some area beyond that investigated so far. Without any other site assignable to this complex in the nearby region, it is impossible to comment on the range of this exportation.

At the moment it is thus possible to propose two interpretations of the settlement pattern of this Aurignacian site:

—The site was specialized for flint exploitation and early stages of reduction. This strategy would seem to be oriented toward the export of preformed material to other camps.

—The settlement shows a sophisticated relationship with the territory. The geological analysis (see above) suggests that during the time of the Aurignacian occupation the plateau was covered by a temperate vegetation such as a mountain forested grassland. Since this same environment was well known to have been exploited in the Late Pleistocene Epigravettian and Early Holocene Sauveterrian, the site of Monte Avena may be an older example of the same type of exploitation of the alpine environment. The location of the site in the middle of a hollow of the plateau, sheltered from the mountain winds and near several karstic springs, made it a desirable place to camp. The exploitation and reduction of the flint from the rockface and the cryoclastic debris is not surprising.

Figure 6.9 View of an artifact distribution.

CONCLUSIONS

The finding of this Aurignacian site on Monte Avena allows us to begin to understand a technocomplex that is poorly known in the region. There are data relevant to studies of exploitation and stages of reduction of raw material, including the preparation of the pre-cores and subsequent knapping, all of which are scarcely documented for the Aurignacian. It is probable that continued excavation will add further information on interpretation of this lithic industry's spatial concentrations.

The main importance of this site, however, lies in the rarity of Aurignacian mountain sites: the only other known examples are the caves of Potocka (1700 m) and Mokriska (1500 m) in the Caravanche Mountains. The combination of the study of the lithic industry with the paleoclimatic data gained from the geological analysis should help to clarify the manner and character of the peopling of the Alpine region during the Würm Interpleniglacial.

ACKNOWLEDGMENTS

This research was performed in the Istituto di Geologia di Ferrara, Chair of Human Paleontology. It was sponsored by the Popolamento umano in Italia—Uomo ambiente nel passato: censimento ed analisi—Ministry of Public Instruction 40%, and Loess e paleosuoli centroalpini of CNR—Centro per la Stratigrafia e Petrografia delle Alpi Centrali.

M. Lanzinger conducted the field research and the studies of the lithic industry and site pattern; the paleoenvironmental study was carried out in collaboration with M. Cremaschi. The authors thank Ms. C. Christopher for kindly correcting the English translation of the text.

DISCUSSION

FARRAND: The fact that there are two different loesses with the Aurignacian in between them and associated with at least a weak pedogenesis is suggestive that the Aurignacian might have been occupying this area during somewhat milder conditions. It raises a general question: Where did the loess come from? Was it just a local product, was it being produced as the glaciers were in the adjacent valleys, or was it produced before the glaciers came or after they retreated on the bare ground, or on the moraine that remained when the glacials were actively there? The site is only about a hundred meters below the crest. This means that we were into a periglacial ground. There is probably very little vegetation and loess could in fact be generated in that vicinity at that time. That situation may have postdated the Aurignacian settlement, which itself may have taken place during an interstadial of some sort. You mentioned that there are some other Aurignacian sites known, but not in the immediate area. I wonder, how close are those other sites and do they have have any typological similarity?

LANZINGER: No. The other two sites are quite different and are located about 250 kilometers away.

FARRAND: Is there any chance that the pre-nuclei are just nodules that were broken naturally?

LANZINGER: No, we think that the people were breaking up the materials.

MARKS: Were they using any kind of large hammers to knock the flint out?

LANZINGER: We have no evidence of that. It seems that they were collecting the blocks and perhaps breaking down some.

MARKS: Can you take a piece of the rather bad-quality flint yourself and knock out other pieces of flint by hitting the limestone right around them? Does that work?

LANZINGER: Yes. It works but it is not a good solution to the problem.

BAUMLER: Do you have any idea how common such outcrops are?

LANZINGER: On the top of the mountain we have not so many outcrops. But in fact, the whole region around is very rich. I agree with Montet-White that there is no particular reason to go that far up in the mountains.

MONTET-WHITE: The situation you describe may be very similar to that of sites located in the Dinaric Alps. It could well be a hunting camp with the exploitation of raw-material sources being somewhat incidental. Why, for example, would people move all the way up the mountain to get this material, even if it is specially good? Your site presents similarities with Luščić, which is an Aurignacian workshop. And although the raw material is very different, there are similar patterns to the ones you are discussing with a lot of preparation flakes. The pattern of core preparation seems to be very similar. There is a very small artifact inventory with a few little carinates, one or two endscrapers, and burins. As in the case of your site, the good blades and the good cores are just not there. They may be taken out somewhere else.

And by the way, the Aurignacian level at Luščić is stratified in an altered loess deposit and corresponds to a period of climatic amelioration.

Do you have any kind of burnt flint?

LANZINGER: Yes, we do.

MONTET-WHITE: In Yugoslavia, Bosnia especially, Aurignacian sites are rare and there is a stratigraphic gap. In many of the sites a prolonged period of erosion seemed to separate the Mousterian from the Gravettian. And in some cases, the sediments are there but there is no occupation. So it is very difficult to know what the Aurignacian occupation might have been. And in Croatia, where there are some Aurignacian sites, the tool inventory is very small. So whenever there is Aurignacian, it's a very ephemeral kind of occupation.

STRAUS: Does not the possibility exist that the lower loess underneath your "Aurignacian" could, for example, be Dryas 1 and the upper loess be Dryas 3? In the Pyrenees, in Cantabria, and probably in the Alps, it is in the Magdalenian that you get the penetration of the mountains. Maybe the situation is entirely different in the southern Alps, where there was maybe an earlier penetration of the high mountains. Obviously the thermoluminescence dates of the flint will be crucial.

MÜLLER-BECK: I think that there was a late Middle Paleolithic or early Upper Paleolithic in the Alps. We have in Switzerland sites with bone points and some stone tools. Typically, we find endscrapers and also some blade tools which are very often quite crude. But it is evident that the last cold period was definitely afterwards.

KOZLOWSKI: This occurrence of sites at very high altitude, up to 2000 m or more in the eastern and perhaps northern Alps, is one of the very enigmatic events in archaeology. I think that there is a possible climatic interpretation of the traces of this early Upper Paleolithic in these very high mountains. In the lowlands of Northern Europe we have an impression that the Interpleniglacial was really cold and we have in North-Central Europe evidence of permafrost during the Interpleniglacial. But charcoal from the southern Alps indicates at the same time, during the Interpleniglacial, the presence of not only the conifers but also some deciduous trees, at high altitudes. Further ecological study of this region will be very important.

FERRING: Did you find any exotic flints at the site?

LANZINGER: No.

FERRING: Well, the reason I asked you is that there is a model of hunter/gatherer site formation with very mobile groups which suggests that hunter/gatherers bring tools with them to get things started when they set up a new site. These exotic pieces will get discarded. At the quarry site where we have been working lately, there is less than 1% of material that appears to have been introduced from elsewhere. Perhaps it is important to ask, for your case, with very mobile groups moving very quickly and frequently, Are they taking raw material with them when they go to the new camp site?

KOZLOWSKI: It seems that in Gravettian quarry sites in Central Europe they have used only a very small amount of imported raw materials.

OTTE: The cultural attribution is important, of course, but what I think is much more important is the kind of quarrying behavior that you have illustrated today. As Kozlowski has just mentioned, there is good comparative material in Central Europe, mostly in Gravettian, and also there are good comparisons to be made with Upper Paleolithic from Egypt, more than 32,000 years old. Are there pits or traces of broken limestone from which flint nodules could have been extracted?

LANZINGER: We cannot be sure, since it is difficult to distinguish the effects of flint extraction from the natural alteration of the limestone.

COMMENTS

OTTE: Il serait probablement très fructueux de comparer le mode d'exploitation de ces mines de silex du nord de l'Italie avec celui que l'on peut tirer de l'étude des autres sites miniers paléolithiques, tel que Piekary en Pologne, les sites de la vallée du Vag en Slovaquie et les sites de Haute Egypte (32.000 B.P.) fouillés par P. Vermeerch et son équipe à laquelle je participais. Quelles furent les méthodes d'extraction utilisées sur le site et surtout quels sont les fragments de la chaîne opératoire qui sont restés sur place, liés aux zones d'affleurement?

Bien qu'on ne puisse exclure l'idée d'une exploitation paléolithique, l'attribution du site italien à l'Aurignacien est assurément problématique sur la base d'une aussi faible documentation typologique.

VII
Une mine de silex paléolithique à Budapest, Hongrie

Veronika Gábori-Csánk

Le gisement paléolithique le plus nouveau de la Hongrie se trouve à Farkasrét ("champ de loup"), dans un arrondissement occidental de Budapest, qui est heureusement aujourd'hui encore peu habité. Le nom officiel du gisement est Budapest-Farkasrét et j'ai commencé les fouilles en 1984.

La région est couverte d'un dolomite poreux de l'époque de la Trias supérieure. Un long vallon principal se tailla dans ce dolomite—c'est la rue Denevér aujourd'hui—qui est, au gisement, d'une profondeur de 10 m. Il est très incliné vers l'ouest et va en s'élargissant, plus loin il y a un affaissement tectonique, ce qui signifie conjointement une grande énergie de relief.

Un petit vallon latéral—une tête de vallon—s'ouvre dans la partie supérieure du vallon principal, qui est complètement rempli. Son remplissage jaunâtrerouge, fort stratifié est bien visible dans le dolomite. Dans le Pléistocène supérieur, ce petit vallon était vide: c'est le gisement, la mine de silex, est une exploitation à ciel ouvert, donnée par la nature. C'est que le dolomite poreux est plein de grands rognons de silex et de débris de silex bleuâtres-gris. C'est ce dernier qui fut exploité par l'homme du mur du petit vallon, tandisqu'il laissa beaucoup d'outils de bois de cerf, d'outils de mineur, et quelques outils de pierre au fond du terrain de la mine.

L'âge de la mine est tout à fait clair par sa situation morphologique aussi, parce que le vallon principal se forma à partir du commencement du Holocène. (Sur la Figure 7.1, la situation à l'âge pléistocène est marquée par une ligne interrompue. En haut, marqué par un flèche, on voit la petite tête de vallon, le terrain de la mine.) Le petit vallon latéral ne pouvait s'ouvrir qu'avant l'affaissement du vallon principal, c'est-à-dire, durant le Pléistocène.

Au cours des fouilles, on a pu constater qu'au sommet de la colline il n'y a pas de fosse de mine. Nous avons fait des mensurations géographiques détaillés. Ces mensurations n'ont indiqué d'autres anomalies que le remplissage évident du vallon, sa forme, sa direction et sa profondeur. Par quelques sondages, nous avons constaté qu'il n'y avait pas de couche pléistocène au dessous du sol de redzina; c'est le dolomite qui apparaît immédiatement. Mais entretemps, dans la couche inférieure du remplissage du vallon, on trouvait des outils en bois de cerf en grande quantité.

En ce qui concerne la stratigraphie, nous avons sur cette région et notamment sur ce point du vallon des observations stratigraphiques détaillées. En 1929 déjà, des géologues renommés ont constaté que ce lieu était célèbre de ce qu'ici une sédimentation de sable mêlée de débris de pente venus du vallon se situait stratigraphiquement entre le Pannonien et le Pléistocène supérieur. Ils ont décrit les phénomènes torrentiels, les affluences d'eau, c'est-à-dire tout ce qu'on peut voir, aujourd'hui aussi, dans la coupe stratigraphique. Naturellement, ils ne savaient pas encore qu'il s'agissait d'un gisement archéologique.

La sédimentation n'est pas d'origine locale. Elle se compose de loess, de sable et des débris de pente. Dans la coupe stratigraphique, on voit d'anciens sols fossiles, de minces horizons sablonneux, parfois de minces horizons de cailloutis. Ils se sont déposés durant le Pléistocène—après qu'on a exploité le silex, et les outils en bois de cerf sont restés à leur place.

Il est important que ces affluences d'eau, ces couches torrentielles n'ont troublé nulle part le niveau archéologique. La cause en est simple. Quand, de temps à autre, il y avait de l'eau dans la tête de vallon, on n'y travaillait pas. La conséquence en est que les bois de cerf ont apparu dans un état intacte et frais. L'eau descendant dans les couches, avec la poudre de dolomite (carbonate) les a conservés très bien.

Le premier gisement est long de 7 m, large de 1,5 m,

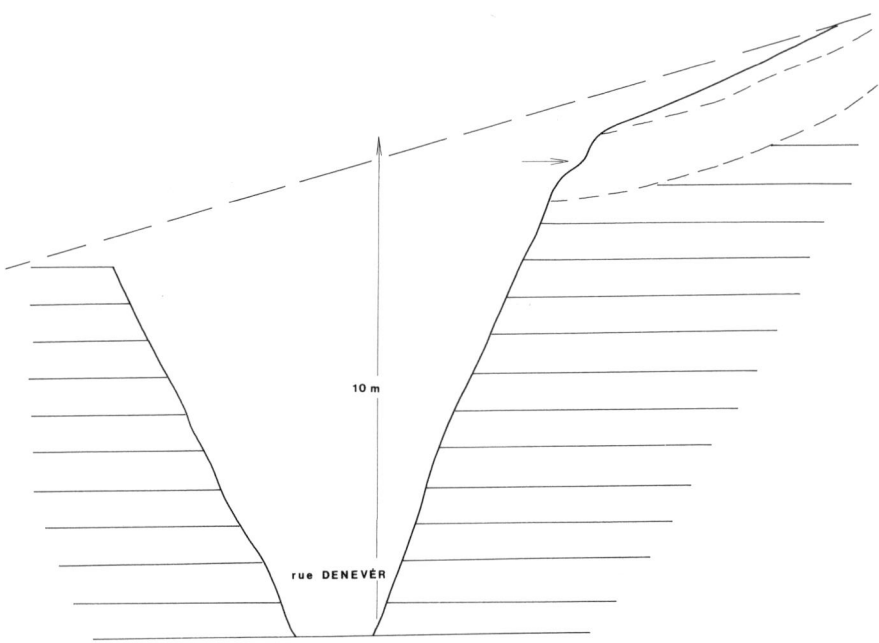

Figure 7.1   Plan de la localité de Budapest-Farkasrét.

et profond de 4,2 m. Sur ce petit terrain on a trouvé 58 outils en bois de cerf façonnés; in situ, horizontalement, les uns à côté les autres, parfois l'un sur l'autre, tout comme ils ont été abandonnés là.

La matière archéologique se situe en trois horizons. Il y a une différence de profondeur de 20 à 30 cm, et tous les trois horizons ont été retrouvés au fond du remplissage.

La plupart des outils sont préparés à partir de l'andouiller d'oeil et de l'andouiller moyen du bois de cerf. Ce sont des tendeurs, des marteaux et des outils analogues à une pioche. Ils sont fabriqués tous de la ramure du *Cervus elaphus*; ils sont tous coupés ou limés. Il n'y a pas d'autres os d'animaux du tout: dans ce sens, il n'y a donc pas une faune déterminante. Il ne s'agit pas d'un habitat; ici on a extrait du silex, on a entamé les blocs, abandonné les outils, puis emporté la matière première.

Dans le niveau le plus inférieur, parmi les outils en bois de cerf, nous avons trouvé un racloir de type moustérien, et un chopping-tool. Autour d'eux, dans de petits "nids," il y avait des déchets d'atelier caractéristiques et de petits déchets de fabrication dans de plus petites caches encore. Ces derniers se produisaient quand on testait la qualité du silex; mais ils ne sont pas des débris de fabrication. Au cours du tamisage, nous avons trouvé, dans la même couche mince et du même mètre carré, quelques éclats tronqués, deux racloirs simples, et quelques couteaux à dos. Il y a encore quelques éclats triangulaires avec bulbe.

Tout cet outillage lithique très restreint est d'un caractère paléolithique moyen, et représente, parmi les industries de Hongrie, le même horizon typologique, un horizon ancien.

Toutes ces pièces mentionnées sont cassées, gâtées; la matière première était défectueuse, difficile à tailler: elles restaient là comme par hazard, elles ont été abandonnées. C'est que la mine elle-même n'est pas un atelier. Outre le terrain qui occupe à peine un mètre carré, il n'y a pas de débris d'atelier véritable, et les éclats de 2 à 3 mm sont aussi très rares.

En revenant aux bois de cerf, ce qui est important, c'est la technique, la typologie et les directions ultérieures des études.

A chaque pièce, on peut observer très bien la manière de fabrication; on peut voir bien si un outil s'est fendu, s'est brisé et on a recommencé à le travailler; les coupures, les limages, etc. La perlure des bois est toujours coupée. Il est à supposer que les bois n'appartenaient pas à des animaux abattus à la chasse, mais qu'ils provenaient de ramures tombées.

La ramure du cerf est déterminée par la nature, est une "constante," mais pas toujours, et pas à chaque individu. Les possibilités de l'utilisation sont aussi différentes. Si l'on prend une ramure régulière, bien évoluée (celle d'un mâle à 18 mois), on trouve, du bas en haut: 1) l'andouiller d'oeil; 2) l'andouiller de glace;

3) l'andouiller moyen, qui manque souvent à l'animal; et 4) l'empaumure.

Dans cet ensemble des ramures, la première possibilité de l'utilisation est l'andouiller d'oeil. C'est le plus rare. C'est là que la ramure est plus épaisse, et elle doit être sciée à deux endroits. De cette partie du bois on fabrique un outil analogue à un marteau, à une pioche. La deuxième possibilité est la deuxième partie, l'andouiller de glace qui deviendra aussi un outil analogue à un marteau, avec deux surfaces battantes (avec une tête double). Mais il est plus simple d'enlever à la scie cette branche. Dans notre matière, c'est l'utilisation de la troisième branche qui est assez fréquente, ce qui signifie que cette branche ne manquait pas aussi souvent à l'animal, qu'aujourd'hui, grâce à la sélection de la chasse ou par suite des causes biologiques. La quatrième partie de la ramure n'était pas utilisée: ces branches sont courtes.

Mais ce ne sont que les premiers "pas typologiques." Les directions ultérieures des études sont: la définition de l'âge des animaux, et l'établissement du nombre des individus, puis la détermination des espèces différentes des *C. elaphus* (qui ne sont pas les mêmes au Pléistocène et à l'Holocène), ou p. ex. la "science des trophées" qui, sur notre territoire et aujourd'hui, connaît plus de quarante déformations biologo-oecologiques, etc. Dans la matière de Farkasrét, les ramures déformées sont assez fréquentes.

Sur la chronologie de la mine, voici ce qu'on peut dire pour le moment:

En Hongrie, le Paléolithique moyen dure à partir de la fin de l'interglacial Riss-Würm à peu près jusqu'à la fin du Würm I (d'après la périodisation glaciologique alpin). Le *C. elaphus* n'est pas un indicateur climatologique. Il est général au cours de tout le Pléistocène supérieur: il peut être trouvé dans le Würm ancien, il est le plus fréquent durant l'interstade Würm I-II, et il est encore fréquent au début du Würm ancien, dans la phase paléontologique de Varbó, d'un autre nom dans "l'horizon hystrix."

La station d'Érd est à peine à 20 km de Budapest-Farkasrét. Sa couche inférieure peut être datée de la fin de l'interglacial, du début du Würm ancien; sa couche supérieure est proche du Würm I (datations de C-14: 50,000 ans; celles des niveaux de la couche supérieure: 44,300, 38,100 et 35,000 ans). Les couches de la grotte de Subalyuk, avec deux squelettes de Palaeoanthropus et avec une industrie d'un caractère différent que celle d'Érd, sont du même âge que celle d'Érd. Les gisements du Bassin des Carpathes et d'autres territoires sont en général du même âge.

Ce qui est beaucoup plus important, c'est l'époque de l'exploitation minière du silex. En examinant la littérature des mines préhistoriques, nous pouvons constater que les plus anciennes sont du Néolithique ou un peu plus jeunes encore. Il est probable dans quelques régions de l'Allemagne et de la Suisse, que certaines mines ou lieux d'exploitation ont été utilisés déjà dans le Paléolithique supérieur.

Dans le Paléolithique moyen, nous connaissons beaucoup d'ateliers de silex, surtout en France et en Belgique, mais ce sont des ateliers de fabrication d'outils. C'est donc Budapest-Farkasrét qui peut être considéré le premier site où on connaît, incontestablement, une mine, une exploitation à ciel ouvert, et surtout des outils de mineurs à cette époque.

Il faut mentionner un seul gisement encore: la mine d'ocre de Lovas en Hongrie. Là, dans les creux du dolomite, on a trouvé plus de cent outils en os et en bois de cerf, bien polis. Leur datation est pour le moment problématique; d'après les analyses nouvelles, à cause de la prédominance de l'Alces, ce serait la dernière phase chaude du Riss-Würm(?). Mais la mine de Lovas, indépendamment de son âge, n'est pas une analogie pour nous. C'est qu'une mine d'ocre a un rôle, une signification tout à fait différents que ceux d'une mine de silex.

La seule mine de silex qui remonte à la même époque que celle de Budapest, est en Suisse, à Löwenburg, près de Bâle. Dans cette mine, on a trouvé les mêmes outils moustériens de type levallois que sur la crête de colline au dessus d'elle. Cette mine a été gâtée par l'exploitation néolithique, et c'est comme ça qu'elle est devenue une "mine néolithique." D'après mon opinion, il est presque certain que l'exploitation commençait là dans le Paléolithique moyen, et qu'elle continuait en deux ou trois périodes. J'ai vu Löwenburg, au cours des fouilles de contrôle, avec Mme E. Schmid. J'espère que mes fouilles vérifieront ses premiers résultats aussi.

PART 2

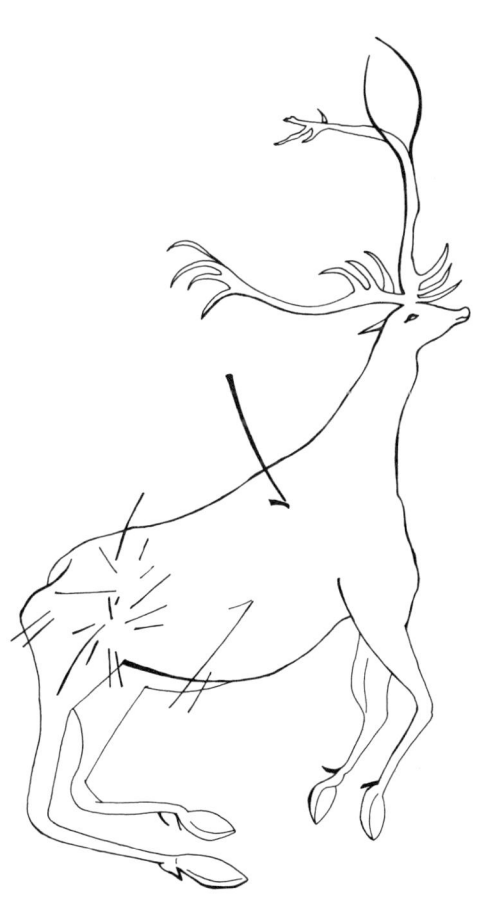

VIII

Recent Developments on the Chronostratigraphy of the Paleolithic in the Perigord

Henri Laville

The sedimentological analysis of the deposits of some 20 caves and rockshelters of the Perigord has provided the basis for a coherent chrono-climatic interpretive system of the Paleolithic period. While the publication, in English, of short notes concerning the implications of these research results on the sequence of the lithic industries in the Perigord (Laville and Rigaud 1973a, b) and that of *Rock Shelters of the Perigord* (Laville, Rigaud, and Sackett 1980) occasioned few commentaries (Bradley 1982; Bricker 1981; Klein 1982; Mellars 1982), the TL (thermoluminescence) dates recently obtained for Combe-Grenal and Le Moustier (Bowman and Sieveking 1983; Valladas et al. 1986), on the other hand, have generated new questions concerning the chronostratigraphy of the Middle Paleolithic industries of the Perigord (Bowman and Sieveking 1983; Mellars 1986a, b).

The call to question was based on radiometric data only, to the exclusion of evidence derived from the natural sciences; but it is in the light of the latest multidisciplinary research completed within the Perigord and adjacent areas that the questions should be discussed. We cannot ignore the fact that, since the chrono-climatic system of the Paleolithic period was first established, new sedimentological, paleontological, and palynological studies have come to complete previously acquired results. The system's validity has been confirmed by recent work done on the deep-sea cores in the Gulf of Gascony as well as by the correlations that we have been able to establish with the long palynological sequences of La Grande Pile and Les Echets.

Syntheses derived from these different kinds of information have been published recently (Laville et al. 1983; Laville, Raynal, and Texier 1985b, 1986; Delpech, Laville, and Rigaud, in press), presented at specialized symposia (Delpech, Laville, and Paquereau 1986; Laville, Delpech, and Rigaud 1985; Laville, Raynal, and Texier 1986) or as part of monographs (Delpech and Laville, in press). These publications present the research advances as well as the revised interpretations these advances have suggested. Our latest views concerning the time periods traditionally designated as Riss and Würm, during which are placed the sequences of Paleolithic industries known in the Perigord, will be considered here. Problems related to the contribution of TL dates to the chronology of Middle Paleolithic industries and, in more general terms, the contribution of radiometric data to the chronology of the Paleolithic will be raised in the course of this discussion.

THE RISSIAN PERIOD

THE TRADITIONAL CHRONOLOGICAL FRAMEWORK

It is largely through analysis of the deposit sequences from the cave of Pech de l'Azé II and the Combe-Grenal rockshelter, and that of their paleontological and palynological content, that the chronological framework of the time period traditionally attributed to the Riss in the Perigord was established (Bordes and Prat 1965; Bordes, Laville, and Paquereau 1966; Bordes 1972; Laville 1973a, 1975). This research brought to light a certain degree of complexity within the Rissian stages. Two distinct climatic phases were identified within Riss I, four within Riss II, and seven within Riss III. Except for the beginning of Riss I and the end of Riss III, which are clearly cold, the first two stadials are marked by relatively mild conditions. In contrast, Riss III as a whole is characterized by a major climatic deterioration with short and poorly marked episodes of cold recession.

DATA FROM THE ABRI VAUFREY AND THEIR IMPLICATIONS

Recently acquired data from the Abri Vaufrey, which has yielded typical Mousterian industries of Rissian age (Rigaud, in press) tend to alter the chronoclimatic framework based solely upon the study of Pech de l'Azé and Combe-Grenal. In particular, the major stratigraphic breaks as well as the deposits' sedimentological (Kervazo and Laville, in press) and paleontological (Delpech, in press) characteristics suggest that the four Rissian stadials (Riss 0, I, II, III) and the three interstadials, identified elsewhere (Texier 1982), may well be represented at the Abri Vaufrey. The attribution of the Rissian series of stadials and interstadials to isotope stages 12 to 6 seems confirmed.

Most important is the recognition of a climatic reversal during the Riss III (isotope stage 6) that was of sufficient amplitude to produce a modification of the faunal assemblage and a change in the spatial distribution of ungulates. *Saiga tatarica*, *Capra* sp., and *Rangifer tarandus* make their appearance in the Abri Vaufrey sequence at the very end of the Riss. Most likely, the faunal change coincided with the rapid drop in temperature manifested during the second part of isotope stage 6. The three taxa, unknown in the Perigord within the older Riss deposits, have been identified at Combe-Grenal within deposits attributed to Riss III. In all likelihood, only the very end of Riss III is represented at the site. The applicability of the Combe-Grenal results to the whole region needs, therefore, to be reconsidered, at least insofar as the Riss III is concerned (Delpech and Laville, in press; Delpech, Laville, and Paquereau 1986).

THE WÜRMIAN PERIOD

New data on the chronostratigraphy of the time period designated under the "Würm" label have to do with:
a—revision of the hierarchic ordering of climatic events, and establishment of new divisions within the traditional chronological system, to take into account the new natural-science data;
b—reinterpretation of climatic dynamics;
c—identification of climatic markers;
d—establishment of correlations with ocean-core data and continental palynological sequences; and
e—integration of radiometric data.

TRADITIONAL REGIONAL CHRONOLOGY

Within the traditional chronological system used in the Perigord, the time period designated Würm includes four stadials (Würm I, II, III, IV) separated by three interstadials (Würm I-II, II-III, III-IV). According to this system, the Würm I and the Würm II, which correspond to the main developmental phases of Middle Paleolithic cultures, comprise eight and nine climatic phases respectively. The Würm II-III Interstadial, which corresponds to the transition between Middle and Upper Paleolithic, is defined as a sequence of climatic events taking place within a generally temperate context. Würm III, during which the development of the Aurignacian-Perigordian sequence and the Early Solutrean took place, comprises 14 climatic phases. The Würm III-IV Interstadial is viewed as a climatic break corresponding to the end of the Solutrean and the beginning of the Magdalenian. As for Würm IV, it is subdivided into nine phases during which developed the Magdalenian and Azilian industries.

NEW DIVISIONS

The former interpretation of the climatic episodes that were traditionally considered major breaks, and designated Würm I-II Interstadial and Würm II-III Interstadial, is under review. These events are now seen as climatic crises—as defined by Rognon (1983)—marked by an increase in humidity; as a result, the chronological system of the Würmian period has been modified. In this revised system, the episode known as Würm II-III is the only one to be considered an interstadial. Nowadays it is designated the Würmian Interstadial. Würm I and II are grouped under the label of Early Würm, and Würm III and IV together form the Late Würm (Table 8.1).

THE EARLY WÜRM

Climatic Sequence and Chronological Markers

In the proposed new system, 18 distinct climatic phases have been identified within the Early Würm, Phase X corresponding to the I-II Interstadial of the traditional system.

After a well-marked cold episode regarded as the signal of the Würm Glacial (Phase I), a series of milder episodes alternate with colder phases until, and including, Phase VIII. In the context of this climatic evolution, the ameliorations in temperature of Phases II, IV, VI, VIII decrease progressively, and Phases III, V, VII become progressively colder and dryer. The fauna is dominated by forest-adapted species, including a small red deer markedly different from the large red deer of the later Riss. Reindeer seldom appears, and then only during the coldest episodes.

Phase IX, which follows, is marked by very rigorous conditions. This phase constitutes a climatic threshold which resulted in deep and durable changes of the paleoenvironments. During Phase IX, the large red deer reappears along with reindeer and ibex, which constitute the principal elements of the fauna. At the same time appears a new type of flora dominated by steppic taxa, *Ephedra*, *Armeria*, and *Poterium*. Following the Phase IX climatic break, climatic conditions remain cold (Phases X, XII, XIV, XVI, XVIII), interrupted by brief, more humid oscillations. The floral assemblage remains identical to that of Phase IX during the coldest episodes. Reindeer remains predominant, associated with a large red deer. In that context, Phase X—the Würm I-II Interstadial of the traditional system—appears only as the expression of a climatic crisis marked by greater humidity. It is intrusive, not sufficiently marked to break the climatic equilibrium achieved during Phase IX; flora and fauna remain identical before and after Phase X.

Correlations with Isotopic Stages and Palynological Sequences

The sharply cold episode that constitutes Phase I of the Early Würm has been found with the same characteristics in the nearby region of the Gulf of

TABLE 8.1
EQUIVALENCE OF TRADITIONAL AND REVISED CHRONOLOGICAL SYSTEMS

NOMENCLATURE			
Traditional		New	
WÜRM IV	IX	XXIV	LATE WÜRM
	VIII	XXIII	
	VII	XXII	
	VI	XXI	
	V	XX	
	IV	XIX	
	III	XVIII	
	II	XVII	
	I	XVI	
Würm Interstadial III-IV		XV	
WÜRM III	XIV	XIV	
	XIII	XIII	
	XII	XII	
	XI	XI	
	X	X	
	IX	IX	
	VIII	VIII	
	VII	VII	
	VI	VI	
	V	V	
	IV	IV	
	III	III	
	II	II	
	I	I	
Würm Interstadial II-III		Würm Interstadial	
WÜRM II	VIII	XVIII	EARLY WÜRM
	VII	XVII	
	VI	XVI	
	V	XV	
	IV	XIV	
	III	XIII	
	II	XII	
	I	XI	
Würm Interstadial I-II		X	
WÜRM I	IX	IX	
	VIII	VIII	
	VII	VII	
	VI	VI	
	V	V	
	IV	IV	
	III	III	
	II	II	
	I	I	

Gascony (Turon 1984). Following the Riss-Würm Interglacial, which can be correlated with the Eemian and the isotope substage 5e, Phase I must then be attributed to 5d, the following cold substage. Phase I should therefore fall between 115,000 and 95,000 B.P. An equally brusque climatic deterioration appears also on the pollen diagrams of La Grande Pile and Les Echets (de Beaulieu and Reille 1984; Woillard 1978, 1980). It corresponds to zone C of these diagrams and has been designated locally as Phase Melisey I (see Table 8.2).

A climatic evolution similar to that of the Perigord's Phases II-VIII has been found not only in the sediments of the Gulf of Gascony but within the pollen sequences of La Grande Pile and Les Echets as well. The temperate Phases II and IV may be viewed as parallel to zones D and F respectively, that is to say, with the phases Saint Germain I and Saint Germain II, where arboreal species are affected by changes similar to the ones taking place in the Perigord. Phase III is the logical equivalent of the Melisey II phase. Similarly, Phases V and VII, which correspond to the progressive advance of pleniglacial conditions, find their counterparts in the phases Ognon I-II and III (= Lanterne I).

From Phase IX on, the institution of rigorous climatic conditions is paralleled in zone G of the Les Echets sequence and the upper part of zone Lanterne I of La Grande Pile. Phases X-XVII correlate in turn with zones II and I of the Les Echets sequence and the lower part of La Grande Pile's zone Lanterne II (up to the Pile amelioration). Phase X thus finds its equivalent in the Goulotte phase, while Phases XI-XVIII correspond to Stadial 2 of the Lanterne II zone.

The climatic characteristics of the phases described above, along with the dates obtained for Pech de l'Azé and La Chaise (Charente) (Schwarcz and Blackwell 1983; Schwarcz, Blackwell, and Debénath 1983) support the following correlations with the oxygen isotope curve:

Temperate Phase II = substage 5c (105,000 to 95,000 B.P.)
Cold Phase III = substage 5b (95,000 to 85,000 B.P.)
Temperate Phase IV = substage 5a (*pro parte*) (85,000 to 75,000 B.P.)
Phases V to VIII, corresponding to a relative climatic instability, could be placed at the boundary between substage 5a and stage 4
Cold Phase IX = stage 4 (75,000 to 65,000 B.P.)
Phases X to XVIII = parts of isotope stage 3 (65,000 to 40,000 B.P.).

Radiometric Dates from Combe-Grenal and Le Moustier and Their Implications

Combe-Grenal

The results of TL dating of burnt flint samples from the site of Combe-Grenal (Bowman and Sieveking 1983) raise doubts concerning the chronological position of the site deposits and of the industries these deposits contain. They also put in question correlations already established between stratigraphic sequences attributed to the Final Riss and the Early Würm on the basis of multidisciplinary studies (Table 8.3). According to Bowman and Sieveking, the dates would place Layer 60 between 100,000 and 120,000 B.P. (1 standard deviation), that is to say, at the level of substages 5e and 5d of the isotopic curve. With an error of 2 standard deviations, the same layer could be placed within isotopic stage 6 (Riss III).

According to the same authors, the lower section of the sequence, Levels 55 to 49, would date around 63,000 B.P. with a 4% error, corresponding to isotopic stage 4. If the placement of Level 60 within stage 6 were accepted, it would mean that the episodes of pedogenesis and erosion that affected Levels 56 to 59 should represent the whole of isotope stage 5 rather than substage 5e only. The identification of the Riss-Würm Interglacial with 5e would imply that the TL dates for Levels 55 to 36 are too low. If, on the other hand, the dates are correct, they suggest that the pedological events and the erosion affecting Levels 56-59 should correspond to substages 5c and 5a both. This argument gives absolute priority to radiometric data without consideration of the different sedimentological, palynological, paleontological, and archaeological data which have been used to place the Combe-Grenal sequence within a regional context and to propose correlations with other chronological systems.

The evolution of faunal and floral assemblages identified within Levels 64 to 49 at Combe-Grenal is in every respect identical to that recognized within the nearby sequences of Pech de l'Azé (Dordogne) and La Chaise (Charente), for which other dates have been obtained (Schvoerer et al. 1977; Schwarcz and Blackwell 1983; Schwarcz, Blackwell, and Debénath 1983). In spite of their statistical margin of error, these results also must be taken into account (Table 8.4).

The evolution of floral assemblages identified within Levels 55 to 38 at Combe-Grenal, and assigned to substages 5d to 5a, is identical to that uncovered from ocean cores taken from the Gulf of Gascony, which is

TABLE 8.2
ATTEMPT TO CORRELATE THE CHRONOCLIMATIC SUCCESSION IN PERIGORD WITH
LA GRANDE PILE AND LES ECHETS POLLINIC SEQUENCES, THE STANDARD POLLINIC
ZONATION, AND THE OCEANIC ISOTOPIC STAGES
(AFTER LAVILLE, RAYNAL, AND TEXIER 1986)

	GRANDE PILE	LES ECHETS	SUD-OUEST + MASSIF CENTRAL	POLLEN SEQUENCE	Isotop. Stages	
I	MARCOUDAN I		XVII	LASCAUX	2	
	MARCOUDAN II		XV PLENIGLACIAL	LAUGERIE		
	MARCOUDAN III		VIII SEUIL	TURSAC		30,000
	GRAND BOIS C B A		VII INSTABILITY	"KESSELT"		
			V	ARCY		
	STADIAL IV		IV			
			III			
H	CHARBON 40,000	L base	II SIGNAL?		3	
	STADIAL III	K	I 34,000 WÜRM			
	PILE 50,000	J	SIGNAL? INTERSTADIAL 43,000	LES COTTÉS		
			2 1 TAMBOURETS. ROYAT			
	STADIAL II	I	XI-XVIII PLENIGLACIAL			60,000
	GOULOTTE 60,000	H	X		4	
	STADIAL I	G	IX SEUIL			
G	OGNON II III 70,000 I	F upper	V-VII		5a	75,000
F	SAINT GERMAIN II	F	IV INSTABILITY		5b	85,000
E	MELISEY II	E	III			95,000
D	SAINT GERMAIN I	D	II		5c	105,000
C	MELISEY I	C	I SIGNAL		5d	115,000
B	EEMIAN	B	RISS - WÜRM	EEMIAN	5e	
A	LINEXERT	A	RISS		6	128,000

TABLE 8.3
CLIMATIC CORRELATIONS AND TL DATINGS AT COMBE-GRENAL

Isotopic Curve		Grande Pile		Phases		Layers	TL Dates
— 75,000	Stage 5a	St. Germain II	WÜRM ANCIEN	IV	MOUSTERIAN		
— 85,000	Stage 5b	Melisey II		III			
	Stage 5c	St. Germain I		II		49	68,000 ± 7000
— 105,000						50	62,000 ± 7000
	Stage 5d	Melisey I		I		55	61,000 ± 7000
— 115,000	Stage 5e	Eemian			Pedogen.		
— 128,000				7	ACHEULIAN	56	
				6			
	Stage 6		RISS III	5			
				4			
				3		60	105,000 ± 14,000
				2		60	113,000 ± 13,000
				1			

settled by isotope analysis and securely correlated with the Grande Pile sequence.

If the phenomena of pedogenesis and erosion affecting Levels 59-56 represent all of stage 5, or even stages 5c and 5a, to which isotope stages should the notable climatic ameliorations attested in Levels 52 to 47, 43 to 42, and 41 be attributed? Our present knowledge of stages 4 and 3 climatology leaves no room for ameliorations of that amplitude. The industries of Levels 64 to 56 are attributed to a southern variant of the Acheulian, and industries from the overlying levels to the Mousterian (Bordes 1972). If the pedogenesis affecting Levels 59 to 56 is attributed to substages 5c and 5a, the Acheulian industries are of post-Eemian age.

There is no mention of dosimetry for Levels 49 to 55, from which came the flints that were analyzed. Flints from Level 20 have also been used for dating, even though the dosimeter was destroyed; dosimetry was not conducted at the dated samples' place of origin (de Sonneville-Bordes, pers. comm. from F. Bordes archives).

On the basis of these arguments, it would be difficult for us to accept Bowman and Sieveking's results. In no way do they constitute sufficiently reliable arguments to question the chronological interpretation of the Combe-Grenal sequence.

TABLE 8.4
TL AND U/TH DATINGS AT PECH DE L'AZÉ AND LA CHAISE

RISS III (stage 6):

    La Chaise, Suard, c. 51 TL .... 126,000 ± 15,000
    La Chaise, Bourgeois-Delaunay, c. 11 lower U/Th .... 151,000 ± 15,000

RISS-WÜRM (stage 5e):

    La Chaise, Bourgeois-Delaunay, c. 11 upper U/Th .... 123,000 ± 17,000
                                                                                                                          117,000 ± 8,000
                                                                                                           112,000 ± 5,000

EARLY WÜRM:

    —phase II (stage 5c):
        Pech de l'Azé II, c. 4 U/Th .... 123,000 ± 15,000
    —phase IV (stage 5a):
        Pech de l'Azé II, c. 3 U/Th .... 103,000 ± 27,000
        La Chaise, Bourgeois-Delaunay, c. 7 U/Th .... 101,000 ± 12,000
    —phases II-IV (stages 5c to 5a):
        La Chaise, Bourgeois-Delaunay, stalagmite overlying c. 7 U/Th .... 114,000 ± 7,000
                                                                                                           89,500 ± 5,000
                                                                                                           71,000 ± 6,000
        La Chaise, Suard, upper stalagmitic floor, U/Th .... 101,000 ± 7,000
                                                                                                            94,000 ± 22,000

Le Moustier

A series of TL dates for Le Moustier, derived from burnt flint samples taken under well-controlled conditions, provide new and valuable information on the chronological placement of the sedimentary units of Le Moustier's lower shelter sequence (Valladas et al. 1986). Table 8.5 summarizes the stratigraphic sequence derived from sedimentological and palynological studies (Laville 1973a,b; Laville and Rigaud 1973a; Paquereau 1974-75). The TL dates obtained by Valladas have been integrated in the table. Some discrepancies appear when the two data sets are compared:

First, Levels G4 and G1 are attributed to Phases VII and IX of the regional chronological system as a result of the natural-science data. The two phases correspond to the end of isotope substage 5a and the beginning of stage 4, between 85,000 and 53,000 B.P., and are put in parallel with Lanterne I (Phase VII) and the beginning of the Lanterne II ("Stadial 1") pollen zones of La Grande Pile (Phase VII). This attribution is substantiated, among other arguments, by palynological evidence; the presence of heliophilic, steppic grasses (*Ephedra, Gallium, Poterium*), which are clearly indicative of a climatic threshold within the Early Würm, are noted for the first time in the Le Moustier sequence within Level G4.

According to the results of TL dating, the same levels are placed within isotope stage 3; they would then coincide rather precisely with two well-marked episodes of climatic deterioration of the Tyrrhenian Sea isotope curve, core KET 8004.

Two hypotheses can be advanced to explain the discrepancies:

1) The TL dates for Levels G1 and G4 are too young by some 5000 years, which *a priori* is not inconceivable since the dating is derived from a single measurement.

One might add that, while the numerous dates for the underlying deposits—the H9-H2 series in particular—remain relatively coherent within themselves, discrepancies of 5000 years or so do exist. For example, three measurements derived from samples from Levels H2E and H4 each give dates of about 40,000 ± 4000; these fit between the dates of 48,100 ± 5800 for the deepest level of H2E and 46,900 ± 3000 for Level H7B, immediately above.

2) Levels G1 and G4 could be more recent than is indicated by natural-science data; in that case, the erosional phenomena attributed to Phase X (former Würm I-II Interstadial) would in fact be more recent. The floral assemblages identified within Levels G4 and G1 are compatible with a more recent date, since the steppic grasses which appear with Phase IX persist in the Perigord until the end of the Early Würm.

Levels H1 and J are attributed to the Early Würm Phases X to XIV by sedimentology and to Phases X-XII by palynology. Both interpretations assume the existence of a long hiatus between Level J and Level K. We interpreted this hiatus as corresponding to the last moments of the Early Würm, following the erosional phase of the Würmian Interstadial, and attributed Level K to the last episodes of the Interstadial.

TL dates place Levels H1 and J between 45,000 and 39,000 B.P., that is, at the end of the Early Würm. Given the overall coherence of the TL dates and in spite of the above-mentioned inversions, we are compelled to question earlier correlations and to consider the existence of a several-millennia hiatus between Levels G4 and H1. The hiatus could be the result of erosional processes noted at the top of Level G4 (whatever the age of the latter) that were formerly attributed to an episode of Phase X (old Würm I-II Interstadial) but could well be more recent—contemporaneous, for example, with more humid episodes such as the Early Würm Phase XIII or Phase XV. There again, the floral assemblages associated with Levels H1-J are compatible with a younger date.

As indicated above, the publications of TL dates from Le Moustier's lower shelter prompted Mellars (1986a, b) to revive for a time the old debate concerning the chronological position of the Mousterian industries of the Perigord, an effort on his part to re-establish the viewpoint that our work had called into question. According to Mellars (1965, 1969), at least three of the five major Mousterian groups have specific chronological placement within the Early Würm: the Ferrassie Mousterian precedes the Quina Mousterian, which in turn is followed by the Mousterian of Acheulian Tradition. The chronostratigraphic correlations that we have established between the stratigraphic sequences of Combe-Grenal, Pech de l'Azé, Caminade, and Le Moustier disprove that interpretative scheme, showing the contemporaneity of these industries at several different time periods of the chronological sequence.

Mellars (1982) presented a critical assessment of the correlation system shortly after its publication (Laville, Rigaud, and Sackett 1980). In his review, the author questioned the validity of the correlations based on natural-science data, focusing on two points that, in his view, we had not taken into consideration. First, the chronological framework derived from environmental data assumes—according to Mellars—that on the one hand, the complete range of climatic events of the time period under consideration is registered; and on the other hand, the possible existence of hiatuses or lacunae within the stratigraphic sequences under study has been rejected. Second, the scheme implies that every single one of the identified events is sufficiently well defined to permit only one possible correlation within the overall scheme. One more major criticism is directed to the scheme I proposed; the sequence of climatic events attributed to the first part of the Last Glacial (a span of about 45,000 years, according to Mellars) must necessarily be incomplete, since only 17 episodes have been identified within that time period, whereas 24 oscillations have been described for the second part of the Last Glacial.

As to the first point, it is obvious that the identification of possible stratigraphic lacunae remains the stratigrapher's major concern. The knowledge of the field during excavations, the descriptive study of the deposits, the study of profiles are, for the geologist as well as for the prehistorian, the only means of identifying stratigraphic gaps. Still, the magnitude of these lacunae, once they have been recognized, remains difficult to evaluate. The example of stratigraphic lacunae identified at Le Moustier between Levels G4 and H1 and between J and K is significant in that respect. As for the second point, we must point out that the proposed correlations are not based exclusively upon the characteristic traits of each event. Correlations are established primarily on the basis of comparisons between sequences of events. The characteristics of some specific climatic events, particularly the biological characteristics, may be taken as chronological markers utilized in establishing intersite correlations.

As for the number of climatic oscillations that took place during the Early Würm, 115,000-45,000 B.P. (a span of 70,000 rather than 45,000 years), and during the Late Würm, 35,000-10,000 B.P., it must be said that the number and magnitude of climatic fluctuations suggest that natural phenomena do not always agree with the prehistorian's view.

We will not review in detail the arguments advanced by Mellars (1986a, b) in support of the interpretation he proposed when the TL dates from Le Moustier were published, dates which, according to Mellars, disprove the system of correlation I have proposed. The rebuttals these arguments suggest have been presented for the most part by Ashton and Cook (1986). We regret, as they did, the excessive haste that led Mellars to exploit the radiometric results from Le Moustier to reaffirm his position without taking other elements into account. Mellars's response (1986c) to Ashton and Cook does not seem convincing. Even though we do not follow these authors when they attribute great importance to the Combe-Grenal radiometric results, we are surprised, as they were, that Mellars makes no mention of Bowman and Sieveking's (1983) contribution to the subject. We are surprised, as they were, that the pollen diagram from Combe-Grenal rather than the one from Le Moustier, published by Paquereau (1974-75), was correlated to the isotopic curve in a publication otherwise devoted to Le Moustier.

We regret that, in his haste to exploit the radiometric documents, Mellars has neglected information derived from multidisciplinary research conducted at Caminade, Pech de l'Azé, and other sites in southwestern France. Lastly, we regret that the weak increase in arboreal pollens noted in Level 38 at Combe-Grenal (Mellars 1986a: fig.1, 410) is presented as the manifestation of the Würm I-II Interstadial of the traditional system (Phase X of the Early Würm), when the Interstadial, there as elsewhere, is marked by processes of alteration and erosion clearly seen in Levels 35 and 36. The increase in arboreal pollens corresponds to Phase VIII of the Early Würm. Details certainly, transcription errors perhaps, these flaws tend to discredit a publication which could have initiated a constructive debate.

The facts remain and, in spite of minor reservations concerning the dates of Levels G4 and G1, it now seems established that the levels containing MTA industries at Combe-Grenal and at Le Moustier's lower shelter were deposited during the same period and that, therefore, the Quina Mousterian from Combe-Grenal is anterior to the MTA of Le Moustier. This established fact, however, is insufficient to draw generalized conclusions about the chronology of Mousterian industries in the Perigord. Other data sets need to be taken into account.

Even though Le Moustier's upper shelter deposits have been completely removed by Peyrony's (1930) and Bourlon's (1910, 1911) excavations, the observations they made are still useful; and Bordes's interpretation (1969) of the industries must be taken into consideration. According to Bordes, who was referring to Bourlon's observation at the front of the upper shelter, three Mousterian levels were interstratified between the Upper Paleolithic and a level of Typical Mousterian, the stratigraphic equivalent to Level J in the lower shelter. Above the Typical Mousterian were, first, a Mousterian assemblage too small to be identified, then a complex level with Quina Mousterian at its base and at the top nine handaxes or bifacial scrapers, which—according to Bordes—represented either the reappearance of an MTA industry or Quina-type bifacial scrapers. An indeterminate Mousterian industry underlay the Upper Paleolithic levels. Bordes's observations indicate that, at least locally, Quina Mousterian occupations may have occurred above the MTA occupations.

This point is substantiated in no uncertain terms by the results of excavations recently conducted in Dordogne and the neighboring department of Lot-et-Garonne:

—At Fonseigner (commune de Bourdeille, Dordogne), J.-M. Geneste (1985) described the presence of Quina Mousterian industries associated with a fireplace built with pebbles (Level A) above several MTA levels.

—At Le Moulin du Milieu (commune de Gavaudun, Lot-et-Garonne), work by A. Turq (1982) has shown the superposition of various Quina Mousterian occupations (Couches VII-I) over several MTA levels (Couches XI-VIII) in a stratigraphic context that leaves no doubt as to the primary position of the material.

One thus cannot question, solely on the basis of dates derived from Le Moustier's lower shelter, the chronoclimatic correlations heretofore proposed. The MTA of Pech de l'Azé remains contemporaneous with the Quina industries from Combe-Grenal, and the Quina Mousterian of Caminade remains posterior to the MTA of Pech de l'Azé. Furthermore, the sedimentological study of the Roc-de-Marsal sequence (Assassi 1986) indicates that the latest Quina levels of that site are contemporaneous with the Early Würm Phases XIV to XVI, that is to say, with the last MTA levels of Pech de l'Azé.

THE WÜRMIAN INTERSTADIAL

On the basis of the analysis of several sites, cave entrances, and rockshelters, I have identified in the Perigord three successive stages within the Interstadial (Laville 1969a, 1975):

1) sediment alteration and soil formation during the climatic optimum;
2) erosional phase;
3) slope wash and accumulation of colluvial deposits at the end of the Interstadial.

As a result of alteration and erosional processes, the fauna and flora of the Interstadial's earlier episodes are not known in the Perigord. But palynological data from Les Tambourets, Haute-Garonne (Laville, Paquereau, and Bricker 1985), and from the Massif Central (Raynal et al. 1985) indicate that the first stage of the Interstadial was marked by a significant increase in temperature and greater humidity, whereas the second stage was cooler but more humid. In contrast, the pollen spectrum of the third stage, in the Perigord as well as in neighboring areas, indicates the presence of a forested landscape which can be related to the amelioration of Les Cottés (Bastin, Levêque, and Pradel 1976). These observations along with C-14 dates from Camiac, Gironde (Lenoir 1983), and TL dates from Royat, Puy-de-Dome, justify the definition of the Würmian Interstadial as a major climatic event whose three stages took place between 43,000 and 34,000 B.P.

Taking into account the date of 34,000 B.P. obtained for Zone L at Les Echets, the following correlations are proposed:

Stage 1 = Les Echets Zone J
Stage 2 = Les Echets Zone K
Stage 3 = Les Echets Zone L, bottom.

Correlations are not so easily established with La Grande Pile. Stage 1 of the Interstadial, however, may be viewed as the equivalent of the Pile Oscillation even though the C-14 date of 49,800 B.P. is too high (Woillard 1980). Stage 3 may be related to the Charbon Oscillation. Data from the Gulf of Gascony place the Würmian Interstadial within the second half of isotope stage 3 (Laville et al. 1983).

THE LATE WÜRM

Climatic Sequence and Chronological Markers

Natural-science data converge to substantiate the definition of 24 climatic phases within the Late Würm, with Phase XV corresponding to the Würm III-IV Interstadial of the traditional system. During the time period corresponding to Phases I-X, the series of climatic events, although shorter, follows a developmental trend identical to the one described for the Early Würm. After a period of climatic instability during which milder episodes (Phases III, V, VII) alternate with more rigorous ones (Phases IV, VI, VIII), pleniglacial conditions are established following the threshold which occurred during Phase VIII. The thermophilic, deciduous trees which reappeared with each milder episode until Phase VII disappear then, not to reappear until Phase XXI. Furthermore, a decrease in the stature of the reindeer population, notable after Phase VIII, may be viewed as a phenomenon related to the less favorable environmental conditions which prevailed until Phase XX inclusively. In this Pleniglacial context, Phases XV (formerly the Würm III-IV Interstadial), XVII, and XIX appear as crises marked by increases in humidity but little temperature change. Reindeer of small stature constitute the main element of the faunal assemblage. Phases XVI, XVIII, and XX are colder and dry episodes. The appearance of the saiga antelope during Phase XVI is a chronological marker in the Perigord.

The Pleniglacial ends with Phase XX. In the temperate context of Phases XXI and XXIII, Phase XXII is weakly marked. As for Phase XXIV, it presents the brutal and intrusive characteristics of a cold climatic crisis in the context of previously improved conditions.

Correlations

Taking into account the characteristics of the various climatic episodes described above, the three episodes of higher temperature and greater humidity—Phases III, V, and VII of the Late Würm—can be correlated with the Arcy, Kesselt, and Tursac episodes of the pollen sequence established by Arl. Leroi-Gourhan (1977).

It should be pointed out, however, that the series of C-14 dates, obtained not only in the Perigord but also in the rest of southwestern France, raise questions concerning the validity of the chronological boundaries set by Arl. Leroi-Gourhan for each climatic episode, especially for the periods before 20,000 B.P. Table 8.6 indicates that the radiometric dates can only place Phases I to XIV within a 1000-year margin. The pollen sequence does not contain the equivalent of Phases IX, XI, and XIII.

Correlations can also be proposed between the chronoclimatic sequence of the Late Würm in the Perigord and the long continental pollen sequences.

The Late Würm is the equivalent of Zones L (top), M, N, O, and P of the Les Echets sequence. In the Grande Pile sequence, the Late Würm starts with Lanterne II, stage 4, and continues with Grand Bois II and III, the possible equivalent of Arcy and Kesselt and of Phases III and V of the regional system. Phases VII (Tursac), XV (Laugerie), and XVII (Lascaux) could be placed in parallel with substages Marcoudan I, Marcoudan II, and Marcoudan III of the Lanterne III stage, even though these episodes are not so well marked in the Perigord.

CONCLUSIONS

Our intent was to bring together in this chapter conclusions derived from the most recent research on the chronology of the Paleolithic period in the Perigord. The object was to underline the fact that questions about the relative chronological placement of the Paleolithic industries cannot be addressed by referring to older works, some of them published more than 15 years ago. Results and interpretations have been complemented by the more recent natural-science data, paleontological and palynological data especially. Radiometric studies have also contributed to our knowledge of Paleolithic chronology. Some authors give radiometric dates the priority in their discussions. My intent is not to minimize the importance of radiometric dates or the contribution of research conducted in these fields. The examples mentioned above for the Middle as well as for the Upper Paleolithic emphasize that radiometric dates can only be interpreted in the context of, and along with, the results of sedimentological, paleontological, and palynological research.

The examples of Combe-Grenal and Le Moustier demonstrate that Middle Paleolithic industries need to be studied and interpreted in the context of multidisciplinary research. The same is probably true of Upper Paleolithic industries.

ACKNOWLEDGMENTS

I wish to express my thanks to A. Montet-White, who kindly translated this paper; to all my colleagues of the Institut du Quaternaire; and to F. Delpech, J.-P. Raynal, and J.-P. Texier in particular, who have allowed me to use information which is the result of teamwork.

TABLE 8.5
CLIMATIC CORRELATIONS AND TL DATINGS AT LE MOUSTIER LOWER SHELTER

ISOTOPE STAGE	LA GRANDE PILE	PERIGORD CHRONOLOGY (traditional)	PERIGORD CHRONOLOGY (new)	LE MOUSTIER levels	LE MOUSTIER TL dates
stage 3	CHARBON PILE / LANTERNE 2	INT. WÜRM II-III / WÜRM II	WÜRMIAN INTERSTADIAL	K	K : 42,600 ± 3700
	stadial 2	IV / III / II / I	XIV / XIII / XII / XI	J / I / H4-H9 / H1-H3	J : 40,300 ± 2600 / I : 40,900 ± 5000 / H2-H9 : 42,500 ± 2000 / H1 : 46,300 ± 3000
	GOULOTTE / LANT. 1	INT. WÜRM I-II	X		
stage 4	stadial 1 / OGNON III / OGNON II / OGNON I	IX / VII / V / VIII / VI	IX / VII / V / VIII / VI	G4 / G3 / G1 G2	G4 : 50,300 ± 5500 / G1 : 55,800 ± 5000
stage 5a	ST. GERMAIN II	IV	IV	F / E	
stage 5b	MELISEY 2	III	III	D	
stage 5c	ST. GERMAIN I	II	II	C / B / A	

(WÜRM I / EARLY WÜRM covering stages 4–5c)

Isotope stage scale: 40, 50, 60, 70, 80, 90, 100

TABLE 8.6
DISTRIBUTION OF C-14 DATES (± 1 SIGMA) OBTAINED FOR DEPOSITS REPRESENTING THE VARIOUS CLIMATIC PHASES OF THE LATE WÜRM IN SOUTHWESTERN FRANCE: COMPARISON WITH THE CHRONOLOGICAL LIMITS ESTABLISHED BY ARL. LEROI-GOURHAN (1977) (AFTER LAVILLE, DELPECH, AND RIGAUD 1985)

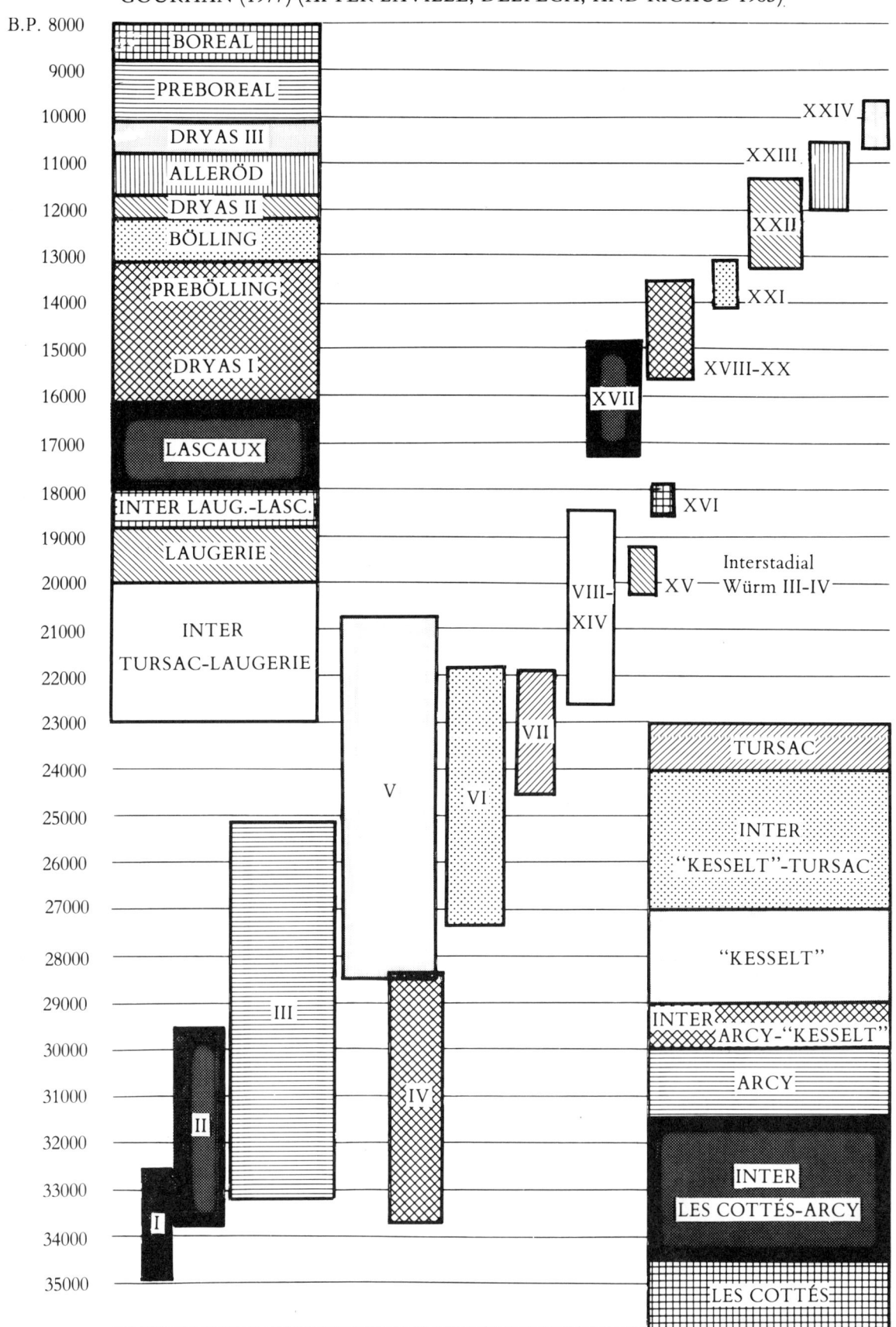

The size of the rectangles is proportional to the number of C-14 dates available for each phase.

DISCUSSION

BAUMLER: The correlation of the terrestrial evidence with that of the deep-sea cores is of fundamental importance in allowing us to discuss interregional developments in the Mousterian. But I am sure that in the years to come we are going to continue to debate exactly where the various subphases 4 and 3 fit in the French sequence. Würm II is a good candidate for stage 4. An important implication of placing the Riss-Würm into stage 5e is that it pushes the Mousterian in France back to 120,000 years ago, or quite a bit earlier than what was previously assumed. Moreover, this means that there was a major global climatic change within the Mousterian. We might want to consider what effect this change may have had on the use of rockshelters and caves, for example, from the period in stage 5 to the period in stage 4.

STRAUS: That is, a major interglacial within the Mousterian without change in the technology.

RIGAUD: I think we are mixing different things, i.e., Mousterian, Neandertal, and glacial chronology. We have to separate the different topics in different domains. We have dates for a Mousterian, what has been called the "Pre-Mousterian," not Acheulian, beginning at 250,000 B.P. Whether there were Neandertals at that time or not, I do not know. As for the climatic break, we have virtually no change between the very old Typical Mousterian and quite recent examples of the same industries.

STRAUS: This lack of change is fascinating. It may say something about Neandertal behavior.

BOSINSKI: We have some TL dates of loess of about 130,000 for the end of the Riss, so this fits rather well for the Riss 6. And for us, it is obvious that the Middle Paleolithic begins before stage 5, at least to about 200,000 and there may be some Quina- or Ferrassie-like industries back to 300,000. There are few sites before 300,000 but quite a few for the 200,000 period.

JELINEK: Which, again, reflects the notion of how little change there was for such a very long time.

MÜLLER-BECK: There are three different dating techniques being employed here—Uranium/Thorium, C-14, and thermoluminescence—each with different scales and problems. Given the standard deviation ranges that are published with these dates, the interpretation for correlations with specific glacial stages is difficult. For example, can you separate the Arcy Oscillation chronologically?

LAVILLE: Yes, based on fauna and pollen as well. But we always try to correlate not just a single event, but a series of them.

MÜLLER-BECK: But you cannot really date a single event. It may be possible to see it stratigraphically, but you cannot necessarily place it within a range much less than 4000 years.

KOZLOWSKI: In southern Poland, the inland is extended south far into the Vistula Valley. The date of the glacial maximum is well indicated. Recent excavations by Schild south of Warsaw indicate that a change in climate and hydrography related to the glacial advance took place between 70,000 and 73,000. And a series of TL dates from northern Poland obtained from sands overlying the glacial moraine cluster between 50,000 and 45,000. The pleniglacial can therefore be dated rather precisely between 68,000 and 53/52,000. This major change must have had important consequences on the life of Mousterian groups.

IX
Observations on Some Middle Paleolithic Time Series in Southern France

Nicolas Rolland

TOPIC AND ISSUES

In this paper I present and discuss data on lithic toolmaking repertoires from stratified Middle Paleolithic occurrences in southern France that have a bearing on diachronic variations. The time span involved ranges from the beginning of the Riss glacial complex up to the end of Early Würm, following the French Alpine chronology applied to the region, perhaps from 200-500 Kyr up to 38 Kyr.

The Middle Paleolithic, as understood here, represents the final stage of the Early Paleolithic in Western Europe (Combier 1962). It consists of a predominantly flake-tool technocomplex made with prepared-core, or mode 3 (Clark 1969: 31), primary flaking techniques (Levallois or disc-core), resulting in more standardized toolkits. This broad definition encompasses pre-Würmian, later Acheulian, Premousterian, and "Tayacian" occurrences.

The present focus on time series follows up themes covered in previous studies on Middle Paleolithic emergence and variability (Rolland 1975, 1981, 1986). Admittedly, a diachronic approach runs into forbidding practical difficulties, given the enormous time duration involved and the low density of archaeological documentation. It deserves, nevertheless, exploratory consideration. Findings may point more clearly to future avenues of research.

Time-series models include "random walk" (Isaac 1969: fig. 4), "cumulative" (i.e., nonrecurrent or statistical), and "cyclical" (i.e., nonrecurrent or mechanical) patterns (Lévi-Strauss 1958: 314-315). The evidence considered here consists of lithic artifact assemblages, presented descriptively through class and metrical attribute analyses, with reference to named industrial entities. Tentative interpretations follow, adopting—whenever feasible—a holistic approach to integrate lithic repertoires in their paleoenvironmental and sociohistorical contexts.

Lithic repertoires remain the most regularly available line of Paleolithic documentation, but their intrinsic information content is limited or ambiguous. Earlier researches concentrated on describing and classifying stone artifact collections in their chronostratigraphic framework with little reference to their anthropological significance. Some workers, further on, moved deliberately away from this towards paleoecological themes. Present research designs consider the interplay among all lines of evidence, including lithics, an approach providing more meaningful reconstructions of ancient hominid behavior and lifeways.

PRESENTATION OF DATA

The sites selected for analysis comprise two groups: those yielding the main body of evidence and those complementing it. The first includes: Combe-Grenal, La Micoque, Pech de l'Azé I and II, Bouheben, La Baume-Bonne, and Le Rigabe. The sites in the second group are Roc de Marsal, Hauteroche, Abri Chadourne, Caminade, Roc en Pail, Petit-Puymoyen, Le Maras, La Baume des Peyrards, and Orgnac III. All except Bouheben represent enclosed sites (caves, rockshelters, *aven*). The first group contains occurrences covering most of the Middle Paleolithic duration, although only Combe-Grenal possesses a rich and detailed succession, particularly for the Early Würm Mousterian complex of industries, as well as

Quaternary collateral evidence.

The observation units in this analysis are (a) *sites* representing culture-stratigraphic units; (b) *archaeological layers* defined by microstratigraphic methods or ancient living surfaces, e.g., Combe-Grenal layers 42-3, 38, 29, 27, 25, 14, 12 or Pech de l'Azé II layer 4F, with extensive hearths and ashbands; (c) *named industrial entities* or taxonomic units such as the pre-Würmian Acheulian, Premousterian, and "Tayacian"; and the Early Würm Mousterian complex consisting of the Mousterian of Acheulian Tradition (MTA) types A and B, Typical Mousterian (MT), Denticulate Mousterian (MD), Ferrassie (F) and Quina (Q) variants of the Charentian (Bordes 1953a).

In terms of chronology, this paper will follow the French Alpine chronological system and its subdivisions based on climate-stratigraphic criteria. The major units—i.e., Riss glacial, Riss-Würm interglacial, and Early Würm glacial—are tentatively assumed to correspond with similar units elsewhere in Europe—i.e., Saale, Eemian, and Weichsel. Problems emerge when one attempts to correlate stadials, interstadials, and oscillations between and even within regions. Space does not allow discussion in detail of these interesting issues or various correlation schemes proposed by Quaternary researchers and prehistorians. It should be added that several workers (Isaac 1975; Kukla 1978; Cordy 1982) recommend rejecting the traditional European glaciation schemes altogether. A useful summary for much of the time span covered by the Middle Paleolithic is found in Labeyrie (1984).

Two important limitations inherent in the material covered by our study must be acknowledged. The first of these is the scarcity of radiometric calibrations for sites under consideration. In view of the considerable time span involved, fine-grained measurements of Middle Paleolithic time series will become viable only after a detailed chronostratigraphic framework has been developed for southern France. Valuable guidelines are becoming available for the Early Würm (Schwarcz and Blackwell 1983; Dennell 1983; Valladas et al. 1986; Mellars 1986a; Laville, ch. 8). They confirm that previous estimates and certain correlation schemes (e.g., Waterbolk 1971) compressed unduly the Early Würm succession. The Würm I duration becomes substantially protracted, with a low density of occurrences. The second limitation is that cross-dating with other regions with references to calibrated marine paleotemperature studies points to good resolution in the future (see Laville, ch. 8) but must be regarded as hypothetical for the time being, as far as the region under consideration is concerned.

It should be added that: (a) numerous depositional gaps probably exist, even in detailed successions such as Combe-Grenal; (b) the La Micoque sequence remains highly schematic and provisional, requiring numerous further subdivisions, as indicated by revisions (Laville 1973a: pl. 70). Recent fieldwork also suggests a greater antiquity than assumed before for that site (Rigaud 1984); (c) because numerous difficulties persist in matching stratigraphic columns within the region itself, reliance will be placed on the better-established datum lines, based on recent calibrations and on broad patterns for environmental changes and biostratigraphy and culture-stratigraphy (Bordes and Prat 1965; Bordes, Laville, and Paquereau 1966; Bordes 1972; Laville 1973a; Paquereau 1974-75; Mellars 1969; Le Tensorer 1978). Site densities improve with Early Würm (Würm II especially), although it is realized that rock-stratigraphic and biostratigraphic correlations (Bordes 1972; Laville 1973a, ch. 8) are at variance with culture-stratigraphic patterns (Mellars 1969, 1970, 1986a, b).

The analytical procedures used here will consist of grapho-statistical tabulations for certain major and minor artifact classes, as well as metrical attributes for whole assemblages and certain artifact classes.

Class-frequency data include the following:
1. Levallois technical index (IL);
2. Percentage frequencies of different relict margin types (i.e., *talons* or platform);
3. Implement percentage frequencies (Is);
4. *Racloir* percentage frequencies (Rs);
5. Denticulate and notch percentage frequencies (D + Ns);
6. Mousterian-point percentage frequencies (type nos. 6-7 in the Bordes type-list);
7. Tayac-point percentage frequencies (no. 51 of the list).

Implements are defined as all regularly retouched tools in Bordes's type-list. Their frequencies, as well as those of *racloirs*, denticulates and notches, and Tayac and Mousterian points, are calculated according to the procedure outlined in Rolland (1977, 1981), i.e., against a total that also includes all unretouched Levallois and non-Levallois flakes and blades, rather than by using real indices. Including non-Levallois flakes and blades in the total is justified by microwear analysis and by ethnoarchaeological and archaeological observations indicating that these pieces may often have functioned as tools, as well as often represented actual or potential blanks. They also display frequency variations of their own, with significant patterns such as the covariations with separate Mousterian-complex industries (Rolland 1977).

Metrical data include size, shape, and mechanical attributes obtained from linear and ratio measurements. Definitions and procedures, outlined in Rolland (1972, 1986), comprise the following attributes:

1. *Size variates*
    L_1, morphological axis linear length for flakes or flake tools;
    CL, morphological axis linear length for cores;
    CB, morphological axis linear breadth for cores;
    CT, morphological axis linear thickness for cores.
2. *Shape variates*, including
    T/B_1, cross-sectional ratio of morphological linear thickness over breadth;
    $L_1 + B_1/T$, relative morphological thickness index.
3. *Mechanical or percussion variates*
    RMA, percussion angle of relict margin (or flaking angle);
    RMW, surface width of relict flaking margin (or *talon*);
    L_2, percussion axis linear length;
    B_2, percussion axis linear breadth;
    B_2/L_2, cross-sectional ratio of percussion breadth over length (or relative mechanical elongation);
    θ_2, cotangent of L_2 and B_2 (or relative mechanical elongation).

Statistical manipulations will be restricted to simple descriptive procedures, such as frequency histograms and polygons, and to measures of central tendencies (arithmetic mean). More elaborate descriptive and inferential methods have been applied to the same data in previous studies (Rolland 1975, 1986). The collections analyzed here represent availability rather than random samples. Sophisticated quantitative treatments of time series are available (Allen 1966: ch. 8) but usually presuppose random sampling. Further exploration into such methods nevertheless remains desirable (see Simek and Snyder, ch. 20).

A further limitation results from the fact that certain archaeological layers from different sites contained insufficient material and so had to be excluded from data presentation in order to avoid meaningless random variations. This also introduces a degree of discontinuity in the time series.

PREPARED-CORE TECHNIQUES

Prepared-core techniques, Levallois and disc-core, constitute a key element in the Middle Paleolithic. Both require skill and illustrate basic technological innovations.

The Levallois technique itself constitutes a decisive innovation underlying many of the Middle Paleolithic's main characteristics (Leroi-Gourhan 1966: 95). The technique is defined as a control of primary flaking through special core preparation, producing pre-shaped blanks or tools (Bordes 1961b: 17). This definition, perhaps too broad to be operational, is supplemented by useful descriptions (Bordes 1950b, 1961b: 13-16, 1970: 31-36; Kelley 1954; McBurney 1960: 130-133). Characteristic Levallois products are flat, relatively large flakes whose contours conform to the core's outline. They could be used as natural cutting tools or as *supports* (blanks) for implements (Leroi-Gourhan 1966: 98-99). The notion of a "Levalloisian" industry or tradition has become redundant. Most so-called "Levalloisian" occurrences actually coincide with quarry situations where pieces are utilized and discarded in a profligate manner, with fewer trimmed tools, by contrast with cave or rockshelter settlements containing heavily retouched "Mousterian" assemblages (Bordes 1953b).

Disc-core flaking represents a special case of Levallois technique, involving much of the same reduction sequence. Many Levallois cores in fact ended up as disc cores (Bordes and Bourgon 1951: 4; Leroi-Gourhan 1966: 100-106). The purpose here is to obtain series of mass-produced centripetally flaked, smaller, pointed, centrally ridged products, asymmetrical with their percussion axis, until the core is reduced to flattened, more or less rounded byproducts (Breuil and Lantier 1959: 74; McBurney 1960: 133-135; Bordes 1961b: 72-73). Both techniques overlap geographically but some clumping seems to emerge in parts of Western Eurasia, e.g., the Levant and Kurdistan (Skinner 1965; Crew 1975; McBurney 1975; but see Dibble 1984b).

The question of origins remains obscure. Lack of detailed and radiometrically calibrated regional sequences precludes stating whether Levallois flaking was monocentric or polycentric (Leroi-Gourhan 1966: 99). Most agree, however, that the genesis of this technique was rooted in handaxe bifacial trimming: "le glissement du biface-outils avec ses éclats-déchets au biface-nucléus avec ses éclats-outils" (Leroi-Gourhan 1966: 112). Emergence processes point to differences between Europe and Africa (Bordes 1971: 3). In Western Europe, it appears in the record just prior to or at the beginning of the Riss/Saale glacial complex (Waechter 1968; Tuffreau 1971; Bonifay 1981).

The broad definition of Levallois technique (but see Baumler, ch. 15) and exclusive reliance on morphological criteria for identifying different techniques mean that assemblage sorting must include, at times, pieces obtained by different techniques or for other purposes, such as handaxe bifacial trimming flakes and some decortication flakes (Bordes and Bourgon 1951: 4). Even so, descriptions based on reconstruction of Levallois reduction sequence through refitting of prehistoric assemblages (Kelley 1954) or replicative experiments (Bradley and Sampson 1986), as well as metrical attribute analysis (Rolland 1972, 1975), compensate for this.

FACETING AND LEVALLOIS TECHNIQUE

Ambiguity persists in establishing to what extent these two technical aspects are interrelated. Faceting, while often present in Levallois technique, remains insufficiently diagnostic (Bordes 1961b: 14). Confusion about this has arisen when attempts are made to identify the earliest evidence for Levallois technique in the record (Kelley 1949; Breuil and Kelley 1956; Bordes 1966). Quantitative sorting of Levallois and non-Levallois pieces' relict margins (i.e., platforms) can help us assess the relative importance of faceting in Levallois technique.

Table 9.1A shows frequency distributions for unsorted Early Paleolithic collections from France. Strict faceting does not dominate. Table 9.1B gives frequency distributions after sorting into Levallois and non-Levallois flakes or blades. The patterns here show that although faceting is not a sufficient criterion for diagnosis of Levallois, it remains a dominant

TABLE 9.1A
RELICT MARGIN TYPES WITHIN EARLY PALEOLITHIC UNSORTED FLAKE ASSEMBLAGES

	Plain	Faceted SS	Dihedral
%	52.7	31.8	15.2
n	103	103	102

TABLE 9.1B
RELICT MARGIN TYPES WITHIN EARLY PALEOLITHIC SORTED FLAKE ASSEMBLAGES

	Plain	Faceted SS	Dihedral
Levallois %	33.8	53.8	12.4
Non-Levallois %	58.1	25.5	16.2
n	103	103	102

attribute. The majority of other faceted pieces probably correspond with disc-core flaking, otherwise not isolated as a technical index.

LEVALLOIS INDEX

The frequency histogram in Figure 9.1 summarizes the distribution for Levallois index (IL) for a large assemblage collection from Western Europe. The exponential pattern suggests that Levallois flaking was a relatively "improbable" event, implying a degree of technological elaboration on behalf of Middle Paleolithic toolmakers.

Figure 9.2 compares Levallois indices among several site sequences throughout southern France. In Figure 9.2A, we observe two separate modal tendencies at Combe-Grenal: a gradual Late Riss rise until mid-Würm II; a decline and subsequent rise during later Würm II. The decline coincides with the Ferrassie to Quina transition, already observed in southwestern France (Mellars 1969: fig. 4). It persists among most Denticulate Mousterian (MD) layers, although less consistently. The Pech de l'Azé sequence, while less detailed or complete, also shows a gradual Levallois index rise—a sharp jump was reported for layer 7b (Bordes 1972), but assemblage size here was too small to be included in the graphic. Levallois technique peaks during Würm I. Following another stratigraphic gap (after the late Riss I at the site), Levallois indices decline somewhat during later Würm II.

Figure 9.2B contains less detailed or complete site sequence series. Most of them range from Riss to the end of Early Würm. We note again a Riss to Early Würm rise, suggesting that this time span corresponded with gradual unfolding of prepared-core techniques throughout southern France. Würm patterns in Mediterranean France, on the other hand, remain more consistently uniform, on the whole, than in the southwest. Orgnac III contains one of the rare last-interglacial occurrences.

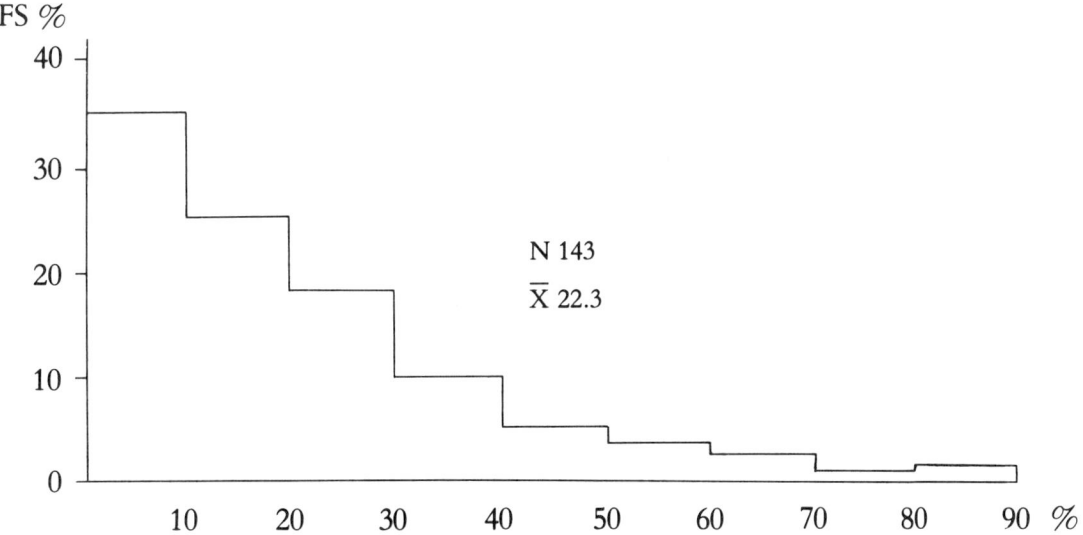

Figure 9.1 Frequency distribution of Levallois index: distribution approximates an exponential model.

Figure 9.2C shows patterns during Würm II (although the first two layers at Roc de Marsal could be Würm I) in southwestern France. Each of the site successions documents independently the trend toward decline noted above for Combe-Grenal, coinciding again with the Ferrassie/Quina transition and prolonged into the MD layers. The Typical Mousterian (MT) Würm II layer at Bouheben (Fig. 9.2B) also showed a similar pattern. This recurrence, in the case of Charentian industries, could provide a useful culture-stratigraphic marker for that region, unless invalidated by some hitherto unreported trend reversals.

In summary, with respect to Levallois-technique time series, both regions display similarities at first but diverge during Würm II, the southwest displaying more complex patterns, with both cumulative and recurrent series. It is also conceivable that some instances, such as Orgnac III and La Baume-Bonne, will need more chronostratigraphic details and larger samples. The latter site may also illustrate a facies variant. Raw material came from small pebbles brought into the site, implying a degree of simple curation. Its "Mousterian" appearance may also imply a later chronostratigraphic position, closer to the Late Riss Combe-Grenal layers.

LEVALLOIS INDEX AND METRICAL ATTRIBUTES

Table 9.2 compares Levallois indices' variations with metrical attributes such as flaking angles, relative thickness, and dorsal preparation for whole (unsorted) assemblages. Central tendency values for these attributes point to a degree of cohesion between

TABLE 9.2
Comparisons Between Levallois Indices and Metrical Attributes

Assemblage	IL	RMA	B_1+L_1/T	D
(1) Bouheben				
Layer 1	19.4	108.4	7.2	4.9
2	11.9	110.4	6.7	5.0
(2) Combe-Grenal				
21	1.7	117.3	6.2	3.6
38	19.7	108.6	8.4	5.4
42-3	16.9	105.8	7.4	5.8
50	10.6	107.5	6.7	5.4
52	13.6	107.8	6.7	5.1
58	5.8	112.5	6.7	4.6
59	4.2	111.3	6.9	4.9
(3) Le Rigabe				
G	29.6	107.9	9.4	4.5
X	-	110.2	8.6	4.3
(4) La Baume-Bonne				
D	11.5	114.8	5.8	3.5
30-2	9.6	115.6	5.9	3.1

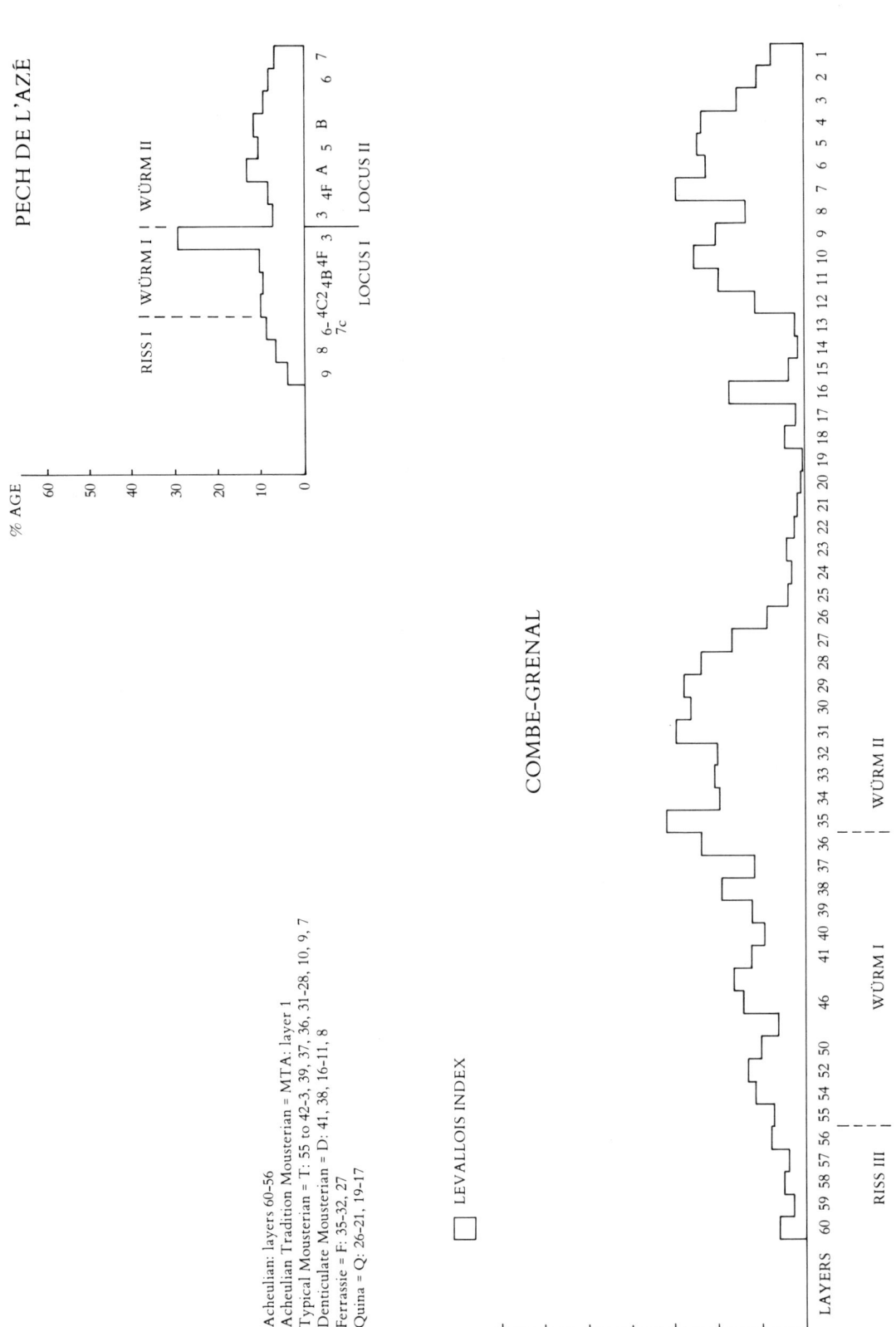

Figure 9.2A Evolution of Levallois indices.

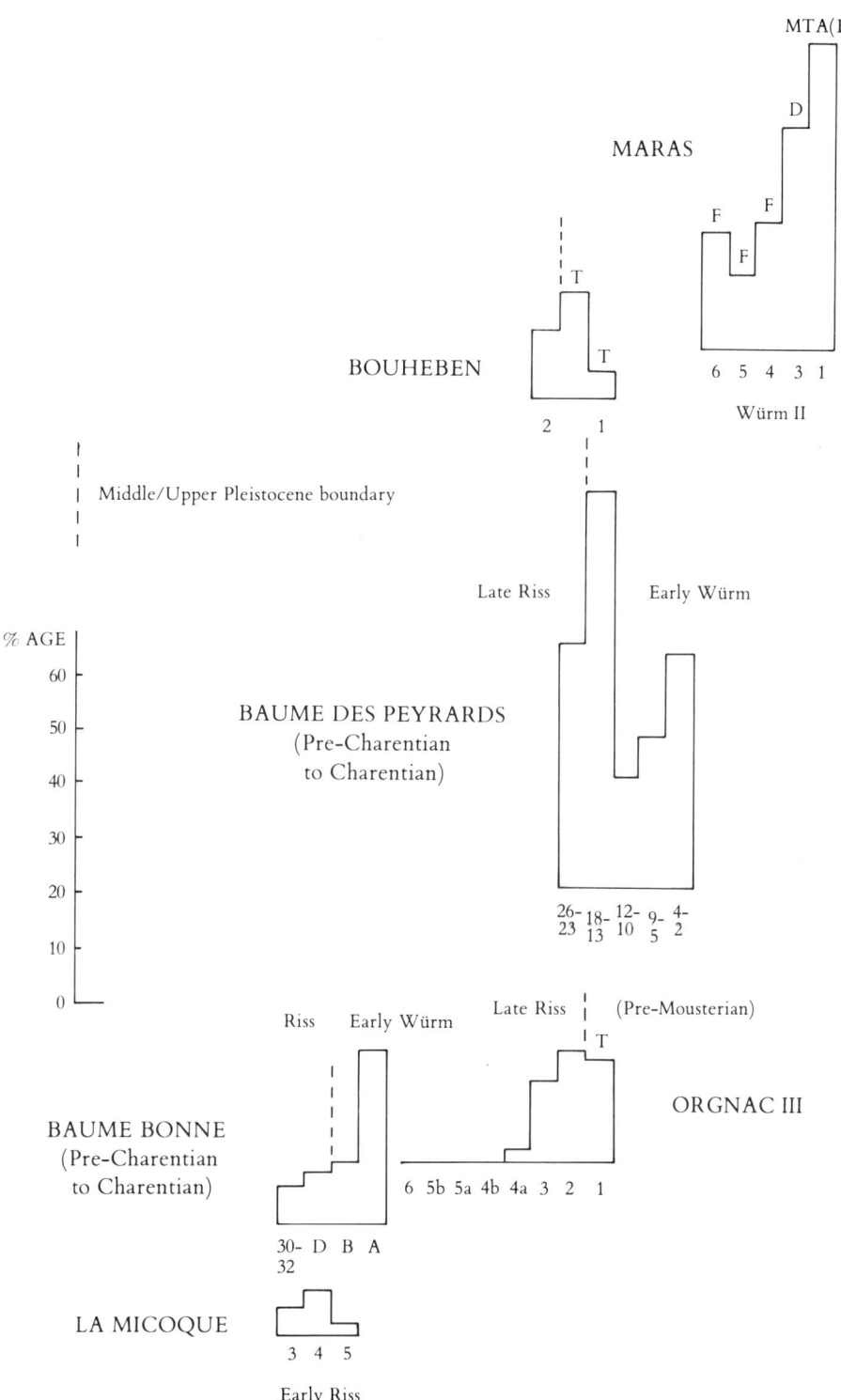

Figure 9.2B Riss and Early Würm site sequences.

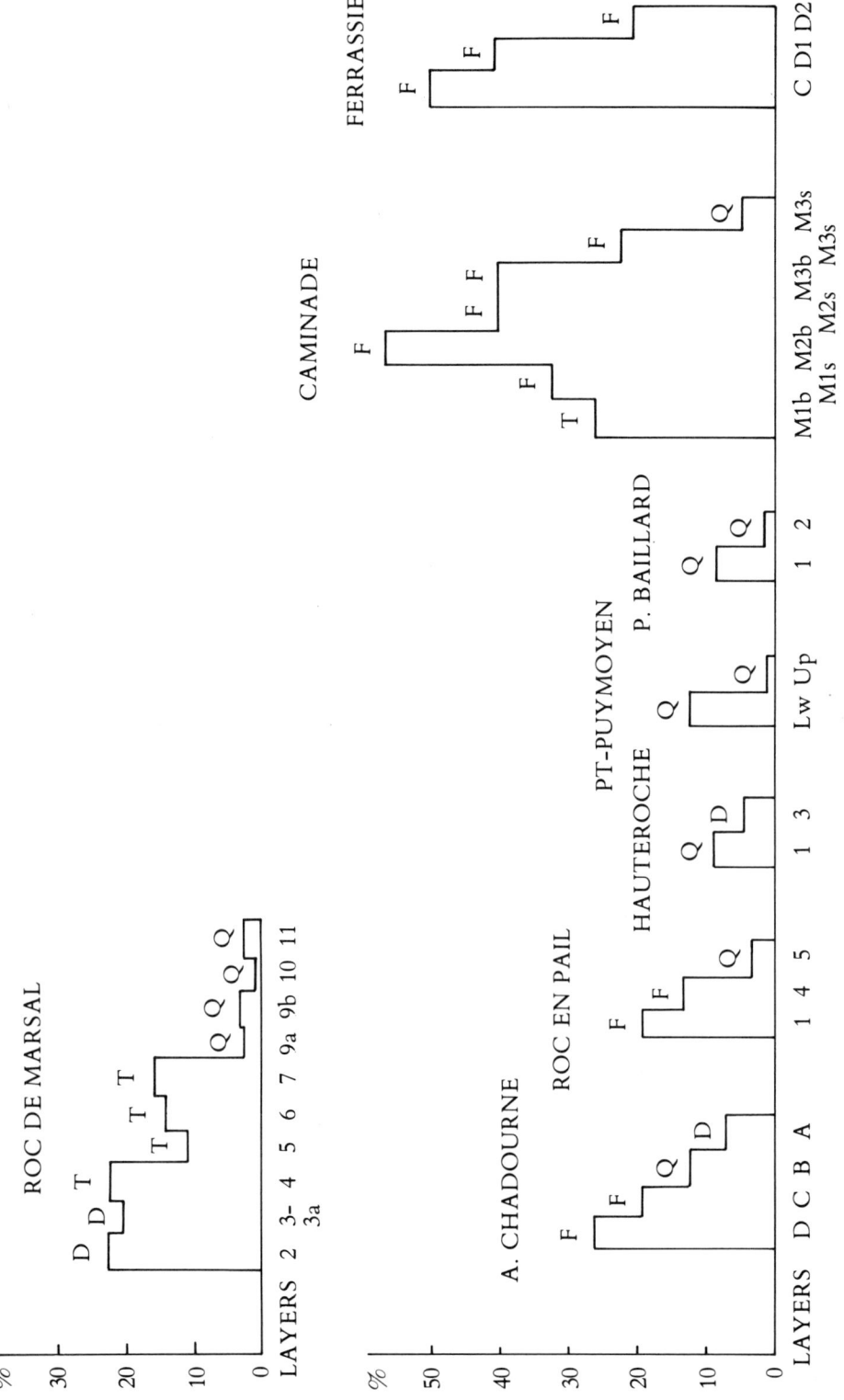

Figure 9.2C Early Würm sites in southwestern France.

the two lines of data: as IL increases, so does the proportion of assemblage flakes with more acute flaking angles, more dorsal scars, and reduced thickness, thus measuring the technique's influence on assemblage morphology. Similarly, the trend toward decline within the Charentian succession becomes apparent in the Quina assemblage in Combe-Grenal layer 21.

TRENDS WITHIN THE LEVALLOIS ASSEMBLAGE COMPONENTS

Table 9.3 compares time series for the same metrical attributes, with the addition of flake release axis (θ_2), for assemblages and sites where Levallois components offered sample sizes adequate for such a purpose. Each site sequence displays repeatedly a moderate tendency, expressed among Levallois pieces' attributes, toward increasingly refined Levallois toolmaking from Riss to early Würm II, corresponding roughly with a rise in that technique's importance.

SUMMARY

Prepared-core technique becomes gradually more important and more refined throughout southern France from Riss to early Würm II, when regional divergences emerge. The record of the southwest, a region with a richer and more detailed documentation, becomes more complex. We hypothesize a succession by joining La Micoque's earlier Riss layers with Combe-Grenal's whole sequence, supplemented for late Würm II by Pech de l'Azé I. Segments for the three sequences probably overlap, with possible stratigraphic gaps. Metrical attributes apparently confirm the influence on assemblage characteristics of introducing Levallois technique and suggest gradual refinements in that technique until its Würm II phase of expression. This approach explores new aspects that cannot be detected from class analysis alone.

IMPLEMENTS AND IMPLEMENT CLASSES

IMPLEMENTS

This term refers to any tools regularly modified by intentional trimming. Secondary retouch may result from design, task-specificity, or successive modification from repeated use and resharpening. Most Middle Paleolithic implements in Europe were manufactured on flake or blade *supports*. The main interest in isolating such a broad category lies in evaluating

TABLE 9.3
METRICAL ATTRIBUTE TRENDS FOR ASSEMBLAGE LEVALLOIS COMPONENTS

Assemblage	IL	RMA	B_1+L_1/T	D	θ_2
(1) Bouheben					
Layer 1	19.4	106.7	7.7	6.2	0.98
2	11.9	108.8	7.4	6.7	1.06
(2) Combe-Grenal					
38	19.7	106.6	9.8	6.3	1.20
42-3	16.9	105.3	7.7	6.2	0.98
50	10.6	105.5	7.3	6.4	0.90
52	13.6	108.3	7.1	5.4	0.90
58	5.8	110.2	8.1	5.9	0.90
59	4.2	110.5	7.9	6.3	0.80
(3) Le Rigabe					
G	29.6	104.5	10.8	5.7	0.98
X	-	105.9	9.9	6.3	0.91
(4) La Baume-Bonne					
D	11.5	111.2	7.6	5.8	0.86
30-2	9.6	114.5	6.9	5.1	0.93

how many *supports* were transformed into regularly retouched tools among different assemblages and industry types. Major Paleolithic implement classes are *racloirs*, denticulates, and notches. Other tool types such as small handaxes and points, while significant designs on their own, remain quantitatively less important. Implement classes examined separately in this study include *racloirs*, denticulates and notches, Tayac and Mousterian points.

RACLOIRS

Racloirs represent the most common Middle Paleolithic implement group and are subdivided into some 20 types in the Bordes type-list. Their relative frequencies, calculated by real or essential indices, provide the basis for partitioning the Mousterian complex into separate taxonomic units (Bordes 1953a; Bordes and de Sonneville-Bordes 1970). *Racloirs* constitute essentially very simple tool forms whose variations depend on retouch lines, positions of morphological axis and *support* types, intensity and types of trimming. Many may represent repeatedly used and rejuvenated tools, with gradual size reduction (Leroi-Gourhan 1961: 5, 1968; Brézillon 1968: 268; Dibble 1984a). Trimming is positioned on the piece's main axis, forming a continuous line, at times prolonging or regulating natural cutting edges. The determination of function remains an open question; *racloirs* may have been used for diverse tasks. Many researchers regard *racloir* morphology as fitting the kinetic actions involved in cutting tools, particularly softer materials (Mellars 1964: 231; Leroi-Gourhan 1966: 998, 1969). Certain worn pieces may have also been used for woodworking purposes, in their latest stages of utilization.

DENTICULATES AND NOTCHES

These represent the most frequent implement group, next to *racloirs*, during the Middle Paleolithic. They constitute virtually the only implement type in certain industries such as the MD. They possess fine or bolder serrations or single and multiple notches, positioned mostly laterally. Some denticulates probably served as *racloirs* at first. Many pieces display evidence of heavy use and retrimming (Leroi-Gourhan 1956). Although their function has not been definitely determined, ethnographic observations, experimentation, and microscopic examination have led many to conclude that denticulates and notches served mainly for woodworking or hard-material processing, involving sawing, pokeshaving, scraping (Clark 1958a, b; Bordes 1962, 1970: 201; Kantman 1970a, b, c). Harder wood induces rapid wear (Crabtree and Davis 1968); perhaps this explains why harder-grained lithic material was often preferred for the manufacture of these tools.

TAYAC POINTS

These are convergent denticulates, identified for the first time at La Micoque (Bordes 1961b: 36). They occur throughout the Middle Paleolithic, although in low frequencies.

MOUSTERIAN POINTS

These pieces are more or less elongated, thin or retouched, triangular or lozenge-shaped in outline, with an acuminated tip (Bordes 1961b: 22), not infrequently bearing evidence of possible impact damage, made often on Levallois or disc-core flake *support* types. Their litho-mechanical properties may illustrate a major design advance, with increased cutting-edge length reducing stress concentration when these points were employed as spearheads (Kopper 1981). The occupants of Fontmaure consequently preferred a hard flint over the local fine-grained opaline-jasper for manufacturing points (Pradel and Pradel 1970: 488-489).

IMPLEMENTS AND MAJOR IMPLEMENT-CLASS TIME SERIES

IMPLEMENT FREQUENCIES

Figure 9.3 combines frequency variations from several site sequences; a number of patterns emerge. Implement frequencies remain generally low or moderate during Riss and Würm I, with the exception of La Baume-Bonne, and increase during Würm II (the Bouheben open-air site excepted). High implement frequencies coincide with "Precharentian" (La Baume-Bonne) and Charentian occurrences. The lowest frequencies are found during Würm I.

RACLOIR FREQUENCIES

These follow closely those for implements, except for Pech de l'Azé I (late Würm II) where they coincide with the MTA industry. It has been shown before (Rolland 1977) that increases in *racloir* manufacture account for most instances of high implement frequencies.

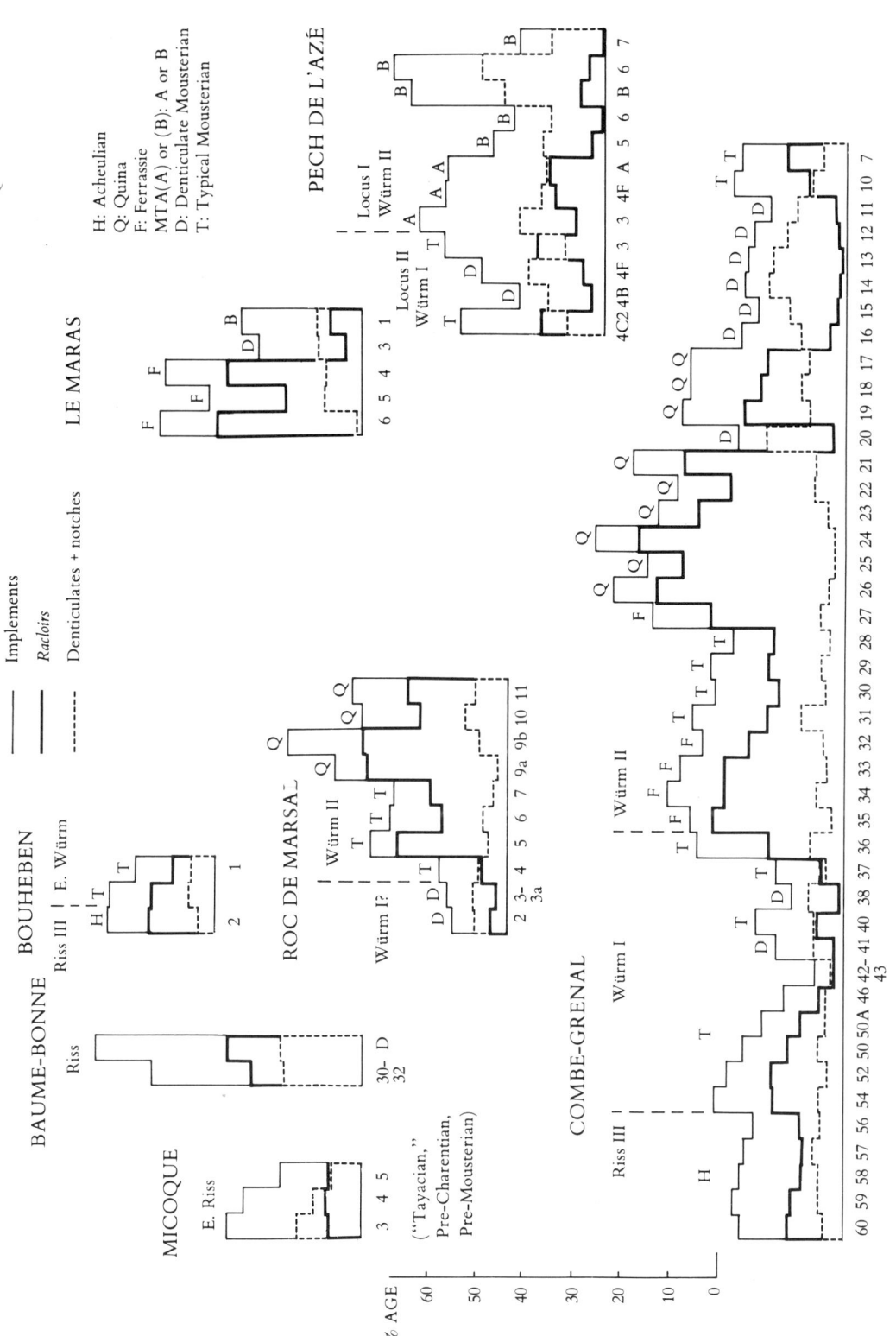

Figure 9.3 Evolution of implements and major implement classes.

DENTICULATES AND NOTCHES

Two main observations apply to this category: frequencies remain generally low or lower than for *racloirs* and generally coincide with low implement frequencies whenever they become dominant. A gradual rise appears during late Würm II, beginning with the last phase of the Charentian (Quina) succession, e.g., at Combe-Grenal, Roc de Marsal, and other sites not included in this study; and these types dominate in the MD and MTA (especially type B) layers.

MAJOR ARTIFACT CLASSES' AVERAGE SIZES

Table 9.4 presents size attributes (mean length or $L\bar{X}_1$) for whole assemblages, implements, unretouched or utilized flakes or blades, *racloirs*, denticulates and notches. Table 9.4A compares mean size values for pre-Würmian occurrences. No particular tendencies appear, except that *racloir* sizes more frequently exceed those for other artifact classes.

Table 9.4B compares similar data for the Early Würm, with occurrences arranged according to Mousterian-complex taxonomic diagnosis:

(a) mean sizes form moderate but definite patterns among different artifact classes. A majority of implement components are larger than whole assemblages (in 18 out of 24 instances) or unretouched flakes (18/24). *Racloirs* also seem larger than any other categories (14/24);

(b) size variations between artifact classes, however, are not spread uniformly. They covary somewhat with named industrial entities. MD assemblages contain most instances where the size of unretouched pieces exceeds that for implements. Denticulates and notches tend to be smaller implements.

Another qualification is that absolute values for denticulates and notches in the Charentian remain generally low, except for the last Quina occurrences. *Racloirs* also become very scarce in MD assemblages. Mean size values here more probably reflect random variations, which could explain why most of the few instances where denticulates' and notches' mean sizes exceed those of *racloirs* (5/24) happen there.

The most significant generalization from these comparisons is that while size ranges overlap substantially and mean differences remain modest, the latter recur consistently among separate artifact

TABLE 9.4A

MEAN LENGTH (L_1) COMPARISONS FOR IMPLEMENTS AND MAJOR IMPLEMENT CLASSES AMONG PRE-WÜRMIAN ASSEMBLAGES

Assemblage	Whole Assemblage	Implements[1]	Unretouched Flakes	Racloirs[2]	Denticulates & Notches[3]
Combe-Grenal					
Layer 58	47.2	*49.1*	44.9	49.9	48.0
59	51.3	51.2	51.4	50.8	*52.0*
60	50.3	*52.5*	46.9	*53.9*	49.0
Bouheben					
2	61.9	61.6	62.4	61.8	58.7
La Baume-Bonne					
D	43.0	43.5	46.5	44.0	42.5
30-2	42.9	*46.6*	40.7	*49.6*	42.9
La Micoque					
4	51.1	*51.1*	50.7	*52.0*	48.4
3	51.0	*51.7*	47.5	50.2	49.1

[1] Instances when implements' lengths exceed those of unretouched flakes are italicized.
[2] Instances when *racloirs'* lengths exceed those of other artifact classes are italicized.
[3] The only instance when denticulates' and notches' lengths exceed those of other artifact classes is italicized.

TABLE 9.4B

MEAN LENGTH (L_1) COMPARISONS FOR IMPLEMENTS AND MAJOR IMPLEMENT CLASSES AMONG EARLY WÜRM INDUSTRY TYPES

Assemblage	Whole Assemblage	Implements[1]	Unretouched Flakes	Racloirs[2]	Denticulates & Notches[3]
A. Typical Mousterian					
Combe-Grenal					
Layer 29	57.1	*60.6*	52.7	*63.5*	57.1
42-3	48.2	*53.1*	47.4	52.4	48.0
50	47.3	*48.9*	45.6	*49.3*	48.0
52	47.7	*50.2*	45.1	*51.0*	49.5
Pech de l'Azé II 4C2	47.6	46.2	49.2	47.6	47.6
Bouheben 1'	56.0	*56.2*	55.8	51.0	49.5
Hortus	40.9	*46.1*	38.4	*51.3*	47.7
Le Rigabe (G)	42.0	*48.0*	40.1	49.1	*49.3*
B. Charentian					
Combe-Grenal					
17	47.7	*48.4*	45.4	*49.6*	48.4
21	50.7	*51.6*	45.5	*52.2*	48.4
23	55.1	*56.4*	48.4	*56.9*	54.7
25	51.8	*53.0*	45.8	*53.6*	45.1
27	52.7	*54.6*	47.6	*55.7*	48.9
35	52.8	*54.9*	47.9	*56.2*	45.3
C. Denticulate Mousterian					
Combe-Grenal					
11	48.0	46.2	47.3	*52.5*[4]	50.2
13	40.4	40.2	40.8	40.7	39.8
14	40.1	39.7	40.9	39.5	39.7
16	51.6	50.5	52.6	46.4	52.1
20	24.8	46.9	43.1	*48.5*	46.9
38	56.3	*59.1*	55.5	56.7	*59.9*
Pech de l'Azé II 4B	45.9	48.7	49.1	*50.7*	48.4
Pech de l'Azé II 4F	44.6	*48.2*	44.0	48.6	*48.8*
D. Mousterian of Acheulian Tradition					
Pech de l'Azé I 4F	49.9	*50.0*	38.9	-	-
Le Dau	63.9	63.4	63.1	*68.7*	59.5

[1] Instances when implements' lengths exceed those of unretouched flakes are italicized.
[2] Instances when *racloirs'* lengths exceed those of other artifact classes are italicized.
[3] Instances when denticulates' and notches' lengths exceed those of other artifact classes are italicized.
[4] Relative and absolute values for this implement class are very low in this industry type.

classes and Mousterian industry types where "random noise" would be expected.

MINOR ARTIFACT CLASSES' FREQUENCY VARIATIONS

Any possible time-related trends among Tayac and Mousterian points can be evaluated more realistically in terms of presence/absence clusters, given the fact that both categories appear in low frequencies.

Figure 9.4 compares frequencies for Mousterian and Tayac points among four site sequences covering most of the Middle Paleolithic duration when joined together.

Mousterian points appear during the late Riss at Combe-Grenal and Bouheben. They are regularly present until late Würm I. They become common, after a gap, during Würm II, coinciding closely with the Ferrassie industry, after which they decline and disappear entirely. Mousterian points are lacking entirely at La Micoque and La Baume-Bonne. The richer collections from earlier excavations by Hauser and by Peyrony also contained few or none, except for the Micoquian horizon (layer 6). These collections were not included in the study because the lack of adequate excavation standards ruled out reliable quantitative analyses.

Tayac points appear somewhat earlier in the Riss at La Micoque, La Baume-Bonne, and Combe-Grenal but become scarce or absent during Würm I. They reappear gradually during later Würm II at Combe-Grenal. They are entirely absent throughout the Bouheben sequence, an open-air site where denticulates and notches also tend to be scarce.

GENERAL DISCUSSION

The objective in this section will be to transcend description and consider theoretical aspects, searching for possible causal connections, and identify some of the factors involved in the time series. These may include, depending on the situations: (1) toolmaking repertoires in their multiple dimensions, ranging from artifact manufacture, design, and functional requirements to wear and rejuvenation; (2) long-term historical antecedents, such as motor habits or other idiosyncrasies offering alternative preferences among lithic material properties likely to influence or modify toolmaking repertoires; (3) indirect circumstances, such as environmental change acting through land use and settlement strategies, that would have repercussions on the expressions of repertoires.

This objective—namely, identifying behavioral or contextual parameters—remains more tentative, limited by the scarcity of, and gaps in, collateral evidence. The discussion will revolve around the following themes: (1) emergence and diachronic variations in prepared-core techniques; (2) diachronic variations in implements and implement classes, looking for possible correlates; (3) the question of the "Tayacian"/Charentian megacycle. Whenever some of these have already been tackled in detail through previous publications, the main points are merely summarized. Further discussion will be restricted to new observations or modifications of earlier conclusions. Greater focus is given to southwestern France because of its richer documentation.

PREPARED-CORE TECHNIQUES

Levallois technique appears for the first time in the Mediterranean late during the "great" or Mindel-Riss interglacial, at the Mas des Caves (Lunel-Viel) site complex (Bonifay 1981) and, during Riss glacial, at Le Rigabe layer X (Bonifay 1964-65), on the basis of biostratigraphic assessments. New research at La Micoque (Rigaud 1984) also suggests a greater antiquity than previously estimated.

Table 9.5 gives a Riss-complex succession for the emergence of prepared-core techniques in southwestern France, with reference to diagnostic core types from La Micoque and Combe-Grenal. An additional trend appears, as previously with Levallois technique. It may correspond with a technical idiosyncratic development which, as we shall see further on, may set this region apart.

The Late Riss presence of Mousterian points, as we observed earlier, was probably contingent on the prior existence of prepared-core techniques and may represent a new and more efficient extractive device (hunting spear?). A similar development is suggested by evidence from La Cotte de St. Brelade (Jersey), with the late Saale appearance of elongated points with damaged tips (Callow 1986). The notion referred to before, that the Levallois technique's intent was to obtain preshaped cutting tools with optimal-size edges, is now examined against the record for Levallois technique during Würm II in southwestern France.

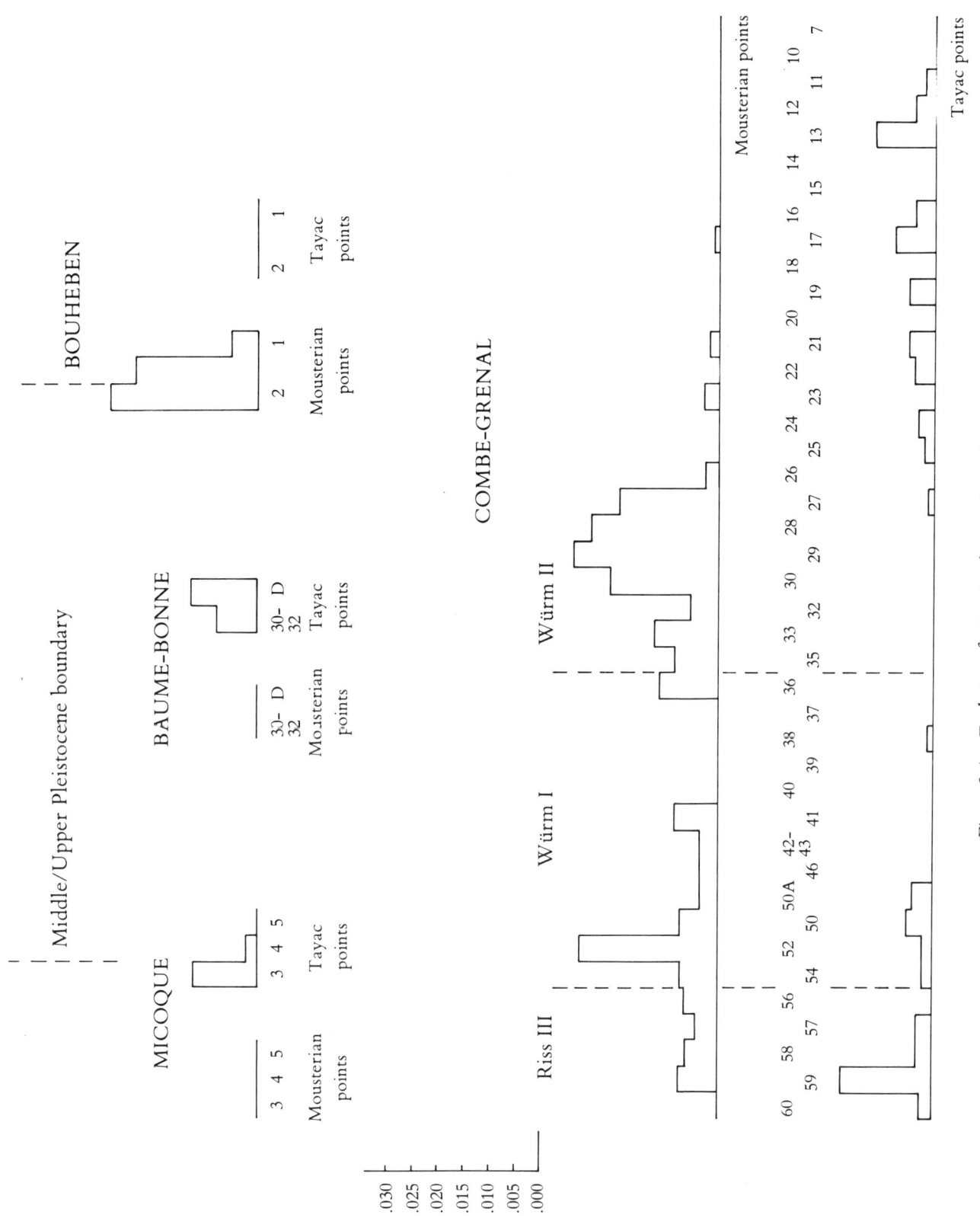

Figure 9.4 Evolution of minor implement classes (points).

TABLE 9.5
EMERGENCE OF PREPARED-CORE FLAKING AS SHOWN BY CORE-TYPE PERCENTAGES IN SOUTHWESTERN FRANCE

Assemblage	% Prepared Cores	% Levallois Cores	% Disc Cores
Combe-Grenal			
Layer 57	25.0	2.5	22.5
58	33.6	7.0	26.6
59	40.2	25.0	15.2
60	24.2	6.5	17.7
La Micoque			
5	12.5	3.1	9.4
4	22.5	5.0	17.5
3	10.0	-	10.0

Figure 9.5 compares diachronic variations between Levallois indices and assemblage mean lengths at Combe-Grenal. Most layers present a fair degree of covariation between both variables, with the exception of Quina industry layers, where mean length remains high despite sharp drops in IL. This relative independence suggests that other primary flaking devices—such as the so-called salami slices (Bordes and de Sonneville-Bordes 1970: 61)—effectively replaced Levallois technique, if size remained the preferred outcome. This preference implies a deliberate choice, rather than a loss or a case of devolution, since the largest Levallois piece in the entire Combe-Grenal sequence occurs in Layer 21, where Levallois index is at its lowest. Mean sizes, by contrast, covary clearly with those for IL in the case of the subsequent MD layers.

THE MEANING OF DIACHRONIC VARIATIONS AMONG IMPLEMENTS AND IMPLEMENT CLASSES

We have discussed in other publications the hypothesis that variations in implement frequencies, which coincide with different Mousterian-complex industries, are due to variations in lithic material economizing or profligacy, by differing degrees of tool rejuvenation and by flaking nodules more or less exhaustively (Rolland 1977, 1981). These decisions arise from several possible circumstances: (a) the contrast, already cited, between flint-rich quarry sites and a profligate attitude in northern France, and the cave or rockshelter winter residences, with a more sparing use of lithic materials in the southwest (Bordes 1953b); (b) sea-level fluctuations, inhibiting access to familiar lithic material sources in a coastal context (Callow 1986). More detailed contextual information for the inland sites in southwestern France, where several site sequences contain polytypic cultural stratification and markedly variable implement frequencies, does not offer such straightforward situations. Combe-Grenal layer 43, for instance, possesses an assemblage with very few implements and mostly unretouched Levallois pieces, reminiscent of open-air occurrences from the loess region and suggesting occupational episodes of short duration.

We have proposed, in order to account for these complex polytypic patterns and implement frequency variations within single site successions, an indirect link between them and paleoclimatic variations (Rolland 1981: table 1). The resulting covariations would imply repercussions on settlement strategies, reflected in varying assemblage structure. Annual flux rhythms among seminomadic Neandertal populations would be expressed by more or less intensive site use, and more or less prolonged duration of seasonal occupation. Communities manufacturing Quina-type assemblages, for instance, could illustrate more extended seasonal occupation at one particular site, contemporaneous with more severe paleoclimatic episodes.

One could screen implement frequency data by reference to paleoclimatic periodization models (Paquereau 1974-75: 123) with such a hypothesis in mind, although this kind of approximation remains relatively crude and must allow for a margin of error. A major practical difficulty facing this undertaking is the scarcity of long and detailed stratified time series with contextual evidence, Combe-Grenal providing

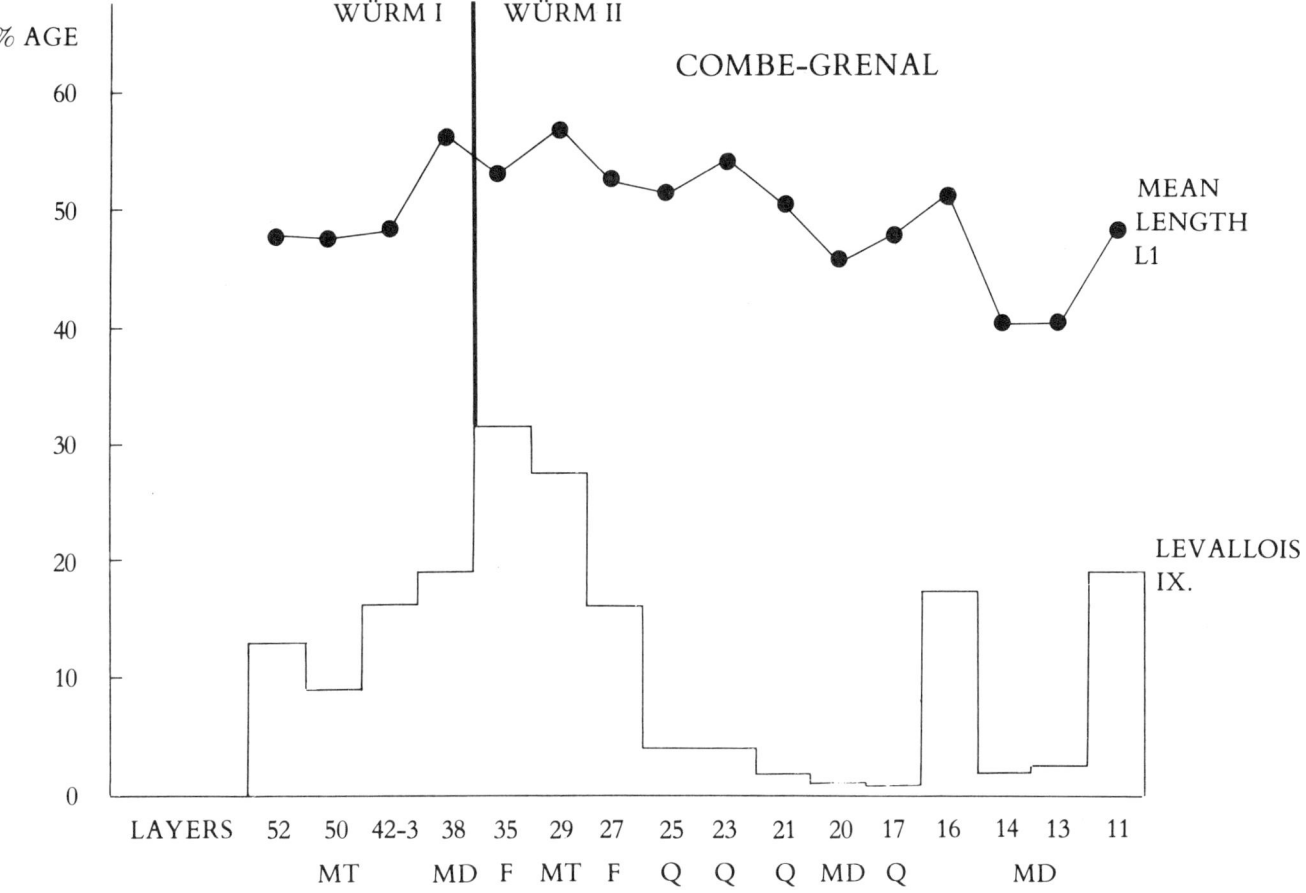

Figure 9.5 Comparison of Levallois indices: time-stratigraphic ordering and mean length for some assemblages in the Combe-Grenal succession. Assemblages are sorted by Mousterian types. Only denticulate assemblages show any indication of covariation between mean flake assemblage size and Levallois index.

a rare exception. Most other sites contain truncated sequences that are more difficult to cross-date with the general paleoclimatic model for the region. Cultural-stratigraphic correlations present risky alternatives, but enough progress has been achieved in refining diachronic patterns among Middle Paleolithic industries that certain provisional conclusions seem, at least, conceivable. The MTA type A into B development, the Ferrassie into Quina transition, the late Quina pattern with increasing manufacture of denticulates and notches (Le Tensorer 1978; Turq 1985), provide examples. We propose here that the MD layers at Combe-Grenal, Pech de l'Azé II, and Roc de Marsal may represent a single Würm I culture-stratigraphic episode (see also Mellars 1969: 160-161) distinct from the later Würm II post-Quina MD series in southwestern France. Several other sites not included here contain stratigraphic columns not incompatible with this.

We note the following trajectories, when inspecting possible covariations between industry types and/or implement-class time series and paleoclimatic changes: (a) assemblages showing lower implement frequencies with denticulates and notches dominant, whether MD or MT, seem usually penecontemporaneous with Würm I mild or temperate phases II, IV, and VI at Combe-Grenal, Pech de l'Azé II, and Roc de Marsal; (b) most assemblages with lower implement frequencies and denticulates and notches dominant (MD in every instance) again overlap entirely or immediately precede the Würm II milder phase V or belong to the milder beginning of phase VI.

These findings do not provide a complete fit—an unrealistic expectation given the limited degree of resolution in Middle Paleolithic research—but do depart from randomness. In a majority of instances, MD assemblages recur cyclically during mild, milder, or temperate episodes, whereas virtually all Charentian occurrences seem penecontemporaneous with more severe paleoclimatic conditions. The MD covariation patterns appear to transcend the boundaries of southwestern France (Rolland 1981), although certainly not absolutely. The Würm II MD episode may illustrate an adaptive cycle, reflected partly by less intensive occupation episodes, partly by some toolkit adjustments. Dominance by denticulates and notches, however, cannot be simply reduced to reactive repertoire modifications during that time span, since we observe that a cumulative trend seems to take place which underlies the late Quina phase, the MD, and the MTA within southwestern France. The MTA type B, with its increased Upper Paleolithic tool component, also precedes immediately the first (or Chatelperronian) Upper Paleolithic horizon. This late trend towards increasing manufacture of denticulates seems widespread in France and beyond, immediately before the Upper Paleolithic, whether in the MTA or other industry types (Leroi-Gourhan 1956, 1966: 106; Combier 1967; Girard 1974; de Lumley 1965). An MTA type B-like industry occurs in the Ardeche, where type B remains unknown. Denticulates and notches become the functional antecedents of Upper Paleolithic endscrapers, burins, and strangulated blades (Leroi-Gourhan 1963, 1966: 115).

THE "TAYACIAN"/CHARENTIAN MEGACYCLE

Several authors have stressed taxonomic and long-range phyletic affinities between pre-Würmian entities variously described as "Tayacian," Proto-Charentian, Pre-Charentian, and Early Würm Charentian industries across southern France, on the basis of similarities in typological and technical indices (Bordes and Bourgon 1951; Bordes and de Sonneville-Bordes 1970; de Lumley 1969: table 18; Le Tensorer 1978).

The term "Tayacian," as originally introduced, was intended to isolate a technological stage representing an incipient form of prepared-core technique in some pre-Micoquian layers at La Micoque (Breuil 1932: 184; Breuil and Lantier 1959: 73). The term, however, lacks a definition and adequate description. No universally accepted definitions have been available since (Rolland 1986: table 1).

Table 9.6 compares a set of assemblages commonly included within this broad "Tayacian"/Charentian complex, with respect to a wide range of characteristics. They show considerable interassemblage variability: La Micoque layer 3 (the type occurrence for the "Tayacian") stands out for traits such as low implement and *racloir* frequencies, largest core sizes, maximum relative flake or flake-tool thickness, percussion margin breadth and relative relict margin breadth to percussion length values. Some of the traits show a gradient towards the Quina industry (Combe-Grenal 21), particularly Levallois index, flake lengths, flaking angle, and relict margin width.

Two aspects set La Micoque apart from the other assemblages: relatively low implement and *racloir* frequencies, by contrast with the Pre-Charentian (La Baume-Bonne layers) and Quina occurrences, where patterns would suggest raw-material economizing and curation (emphasized also by the small cores at La Baume-Bonne); and the prevalence of side-struck rather than prepared-core flakes (expressed by variates B_2/L_2, RMW, RMW/L_2).

Other descriptive characteristics also contribute to the perception of La Micoque 3 as an archaic Middle Paleolithic episode. These include a distinct core type (Rolland 1986: figs. 8.2-4) illustrating perhaps a technological trajectory stage, specific to southwestern France and rooted in the "Southern Acheulian" tradition (Bordes 1966; Guichard 1976). The latter hypothetical variant would share more affinities with

TABLE 9.6

COMPARISONS OF QUANTITATIVE CHARACTERISTICS BETWEEN "TAYACIAN" AND CHARENTIAN ASSEMBLAGES

Assemblage	IL	Is	Rs	Ds+Ns	L_1	CL	CB	CT	T/B_1	L_2	B_2/L_2	RMA	RMW	RMW/L_2
Combe-Grenal 21	1.7	44.2	33.7	5.8	50.7	59.6	45.1	30.1	0.43	44.5	1.00	117.3	22.0	0.54
La Baume-Bonne D	11.5	54.3	27.9	16.3	43.0	40.3	32.4	20.5	0.44	39.6	0.98	114.8	17.4	0.49
La Baume-Bonne 30-2	9.6	42.7	22.0	15.7	42.9	-	-	-	0.48	40.1	0.95	115.6	19.4	0.54
La Micoque 4	7.6	24.0	6.9	9.9	51.1	65.1	52.3	32.1	0.45	47.5	0.91	113.6	18.6	0.41
La Micoque 3	1.1	16.5	6.4	6.2	50.0	69.7	56.6	35.0	0.51	44.0	1.08	115.6	24.0	0.58

the Lower Paleolithic in Iberia and, more remotely, with Northwest Africa (Rolland 1986). La Micoque 3, if the interpretation proves correct, would illustrate a developmental process in which the practice of manufacturing side-struck flake preforms for handaxes or flake cleavers was adapted to the smaller nodules found in the Dordogne River valley and its cave or rockshelter habitats, a point made by Breuil. This motor-habit adjustment to a flint-rich area would in turn set off a multistage technological sequence. It begins with a "Tayacian" side-struck flake stage at La Micoque 3 (anticipating prepared-core technique; e.g., Table 9.5), which is subsequently superseded by the initial prepared-core stages, partly at La Micoque 4 and especially in the Late Riss Combe-Grenal occurrences, with increased IL and faceting indices. This version of the "Tayacian" restores its technological specificity and represents, if correct, an example of regionally based innovation through convergence, distinct from the handaxe bifacial finishing genesis for prepared-core techniques elsewhere in Western Europe. The overlap of certain attributes between the "Tayacian" technique and the Quina industry is more apparent than real. The relatively high B_2L_2 values at Combe-Grenal (21) represent, to a large extent, intensively reduced cutting tools through successive resharpening of an originally large, more elongated raw flake (see Dibble 1987d: fig. 1), rather than side-struck flakes.

CONCLUSIONS

(1) Diachronic variations exist throughout the Middle Paleolithic time range from sites in southern France. Limited documentation, however, makes this conclusion tentative. It remains unlikely nevertheless that these variations can be simply reduced to "noise." Improved documentation may show some of them to be lateral, or facies, variations.

(2) The essentially limited repertoire range and lower specificity level of the Middle Paleolithic, in contrast to the Upper Paleolithic (de Sonneville-Bordes 1966), rule out the possibility of detecting more sharply outlined time series. Prospects are improving, however, throughout Western Europe and beyond, for carrying out more refined investigations of diachronic developments within the Middle Paleolithic, with new and rigorously carried out excavations, growing availability of more diverse on-site and off-site evidence, and improved geochronological resolution. This broadened data base will offer attractive prospects for examining the interplay among technological, sociohistorical, and paleoenvironmental variables and produce better insight into ancient hominid behavioral parameters.

(3) The most basic innovation marking the Middle Paleolithic remains the emergence of prepared-core technique, as far as lithic repertoires are concerned. This made possible further refinements at the level of implement standardization and the development of more effective extractive weapons (Mousterian points). Other less conspicuous changes may also have been set into motion by the possession of flake toolkits. We propose, for future research, the notion that a modest degree of specialization appeared during Würm II. We note sharper alternations between assemblages massively dominated by *racloirs*, with maximum implement frequencies higher than during pre-Würmian phases, and with perhaps more widespread resort to more varied resharpening trimming techniques than those in assemblages marked by denticulates, notches, and low implement frequencies. These patterns, as was hypothesized, could be part of a wider phenomenon, namely, episodic changes in settlement strategies in response to paleoenvironmental fluctuations. Further support for this idea may also be indicated by the later Middle Paleolithic trends discussed in the paper: gradual use of denticulates and notches, increased Upper Paleolithic tooltype manufacture (Veyrier, Beaux, and Combier 1951). Moderate length differences between artifact classes may also reveal such specializing tendencies.

(4) Various conditions or causes appear to have been involved in the time series identified in this paper. They range from preconditioning factors exemplified by regional idiosyncrasies in the development of prepared-core techniques, to indirect influences resulting from paleoenvironmental changes.

DISCUSSION

STRAUS: It seemed to me that there are two premises involved in doing such a paper. One is our ability at this moment in time to arrange sites in valid chronological order for the Early Würm and perhaps earlier. Rolland starts with a few individual stratigraphic sequences such as Combe-Grenal and then tries to place sites into chronological phases which still seem to be very much up in the air, even in such a well-controlled area as the Perigord itself. But to extend it beyond the Perigord at this moment seems to me to be a risky business, and so it may be premature to attempt to establish any time series.

The second premise is an assumption that there should be some long-range trends in Mousterian technology that could be observed across many different sites, under many different environmental conditions, with sites that serve different functions and different roles within settlement/subsistence patterns. Despite all the differences that could come into play due to archaeological sampling and the kind of palimpsests that result from the formation of geological deposits of different thicknesses, Rolland assumes that time trends can be seen. There may be serious problems we have to think about in terms of what controls the variability we are sampling within the sites. Is it due to something that is not just transgenerational, but which lasted for scores and scores of millennia? We are dealing with processes that we cannot conceive of, that transcend glacial and interglacial change, that transcend stadial and interstadial change. What kind of mechanism would one envisage to explain long-term directional change of a purely cultural nature?

JELINEK: I think the points are well taken, especially the issue of internal changes. Similar sequences of internal changes in the physical character of sites perhaps lead to changes in the way the site was used and the resulting industries, giving us similar directional sequences of industrial variability that we spuriously think relate to each other in time.

ROLLAND: I am in agreement with these qualifications because I have asked myself the same questions. We are dealing with very simple technological changes: what we see is the Middle Paleolithic unfolding from the Final Lower Paleolithic; that transition is a very gradual one. You get a trend at Combe-Grenal, or more obviously at La Baume Bonne, marked by a refinement of the techniques and so on. The overall trajectory of the Paleolithic seems to have direction in the midst of considerable natural variation.

STRAUS: If I could just make a comment on something that is buried within your paper, that Freeman pointed out years ago regarding Cantabrian Spain, that the Mousterian really seems to be a bipolar sort of thing. You have the scraper-rich industries and the denticulate-rich industries. Maybe those are the main axes of technological variability in the Mousterian.

ROLLAND: Another point that I would like to make is that not only do you have some cumulative trends but you also may have cyclical trends, such as with the Quina industries and the Levallois index. You also get some stochastic variations, or sharp fluctuations within a given timespan, for example, the Levallois index fluctuating wildly towards the end of the sequence.

X

Typological Aspects of Reduction and Intensity of Utilization of Lithic Resources in the French Mousterian

Harold L. Dibble

One of the more well-known problems in Upper Pleistocene research concerns the nature and interpretation of Middle Paleolithic assemblage variability. This problem, commonly known as the "Bordes-Binford Debate," is the subject of numerous articles and is presented in most introductory texts in archaeology. Yet in spite of so much attention, a satisfactory solution continues to elude Middle Paleolithic scholars. This paper cannot present a comprehensive review of the arguments put forward to date (see Bordes 1961a, 1973, 1981b; Bordes and de Sonneville-Bordes 1970; Binford and Binford 1966; Binford 1973; Mellars 1965, 1969; Rolland 1977, 1981; also chapters by Beyries, Jelinek, and Rolland). Rather, its purpose is to review the basic nature of Mousterian assemblage variability, and to suggest aspects of lithic technology and use that may be contributing to it.

THE NATURE OF MOUSTERIAN VARIABILITY

The Mousterian of France was generally distinguished from other Paleolithic assemblages during the last century (Lartet and Christy 1864; de Mortillet 1883; see Daniel 1975: 99-109). Attempts to organize Middle Paleolithic material chronologically or according to environmental parameters, however, were not generally successful. The real revolution in Middle Paleolithic research was brought on almost 40 years ago by the work of François Bordes and Maurice Bourgon (Bordes 1948, 1950b, 1953a; Bordes and Bourgon 1951; Bourgon 1957). It consisted of two major innovations. The first was the definition of a standardized type-list for describing virtually all Lower and Middle Paleolithic artifacts and the technologies used to manufacture them (Bordes 1961b). The second innovation had to do with how these types were used to organize and analyze separate assemblages. Instead of using simply the presence or absence of particular typological *fossiles directeurs* to classify Mousterian assemblages, scholars based their classifications on the *relative frequency* of major classes of types. As Sackett (1981: 95) points out, it was the separation of description of the individual artifacts (on the basis of the type-list) from the classification of assemblages (on the basis of relative type frequency) that marked the fundamental contribution of what is generally called the Bordian method.

It is important to understand the details of this method. In its modern form, Bordes's type-list for Lower and Middle Paleolithic industries is composed of 63 types, most of which are retouched flakes. Within this list are several major classes, some of which are used to create various typological indices.

The first class is composed of unretouched Levallois flakes (types 1-2) and Levallois points, retouched (type 4) or not (type 3). When divided by the total number of artifacts (types 1-63), this percentage of types 1-4 is known as the Typological Levallois Index (ILty) or the Typological Group I Index. The Technological Levallois Index (IL) is computed as the number of all recognizable Levallois flakes, retouched or not, relative to the total of all flakes and flake tools.

Scrapers, or *racloirs* (types 9-29), make up the second major typological class. These can be divided into four subclasses that differ in terms of the number of retouched edges and the location of those edges relative to the major axis of the flake blank: (1) simple single-edged scrapers (types 9-11) that have one lateral retouched edge; (2) double scrapers (types 12-17), with two nonjoining laterally retouched edges; (3) convergent scrapers (types 18-21), which exhibit two edges that come together to form a point, usually at the distal end of the flake; and (4) transverse scrapers (types 22-24)—those with a single retouched edge opposite the striking platform.

The Scraper Index (IR) is computed by dividing the number of all scrapers by the total of types 1-63. If Mousterian points (types 6-7) and *limaces* (type 8) are included with scrapers in the numerator, the new index is known as the Typological Group II Index, or Mousterian Group Index. The percentage of the total of types 10, 22, 23, and 24 is known as the Charentian Index (IC).

The Upper Paleolithic Group Index, or Typological Group III Index, is defined as the percentage of types 30-37 and type 40 in the total list. This includes end-scrapers (types 30-31), burins (32-33), *perçoirs* (34-35), backed knives (36-37), and truncations (40). Actually, some of the types in this group span both ends of the Paleolithic, for the backed knives are also used to create the Unifacial Acheulian Index (IAu), which is the percentage of these pieces relative to the total list (types 1-63). The Total Acheulian Index (IA) adds the number of bifaces in both the numerator and denominator of the index.

The percentage of denticulates (type 43) is also known as the Typological Group IV Index, although it is standard practice today to compute another index based on both notches (type 42) and denticulates relative to the total number of flake tools.

A large number of types (types 5, 38-39, 41, 44-62) are not normally used in the computation of special indices but do contribute to the total number of tools. But because some do not show signs of intentional modification, the indices described above can alternatively be computed excluding them. Thus, the restricted type list—what Bordes calls the *essentiel* list—does not include types 1-3 and 46-50. As Jelinek (1975: 303-304) points out, two of the remaining types, the naturally backed knives (type 38) and pseudo-Levallois points (type 5), are only reflections of technology and perhaps, at least in the case of the naturally backed knives, raw-material shape and size. As such they too should be excluded from the essential list.

Bordes's type-list encompasses a tremendous amount of variability seen in the flake-tool component of Lower and Middle Paleolithic assemblages throughout the western Old World. To his credit, relatively few pieces that are recovered do not fall into one or another of these categories, although there are some regional varieties that have already been added to the original list (e.g., bifacial foliate points) or should be added (such as truncated-faceted pieces that are common in the Near Eastern Levantine and Zagros Mousterian; see Debénath, ch. 4, and following discussion).

Beyond the flake tools, other major industrial components include bifaces, with several defined types, and cores. Unretouched flakes other than those produced with special technologies noted above (Levallois or disc-core) are counted and observations made on aspects of their shape and platform preparation. These observations are used to compute other technological indices: the Blade Index (ILam), or the percentage of flakes that are more than twice as long as they are wide; and the unrestricted (IF) and restricted Faceting Indices (IFs), which are based on the number of faceted platforms or faceted *plus* dihedral platforms, respectively, divided by the total number of observable platforms.

It is on the basis of these types and the various typological and technological indices that Bordes and Bourgon (1951: 13-14) defined the various groups of Mousterian assemblages that are recognized in Western Europe. Following Bordes (1953a: 460-463), the principal assemblage groups in this region are defined primarily on the basis of the Scraper Index.

Assemblage Group I: The Charentian group, with an essential IR of greater than 55%. Two subgroups are recognized:

A. Quina Mousterian, which has a low IL, low IFs, and low ILam, but very high IC reflecting a high frequency of transverse scrapers. A large number of these scrapers exhibit Quina retouch, which is a heavy retouch with many hinge and step fractures.

B. Ferrassie Mousterian, which has a much higher IL, IFs, and ILam and much lower IC than the Quina subtype.

Assemblage Group II: This group also exhibits two subgroups, though both have an essential IR of between 22 and 37% and variable amounts of Levallois, faceting and blades. In fact, the major difference between the two subgroups is the percentage of bifaces:

A. The Typical Mousterian, which has few or no bifaces.

B. The Mousterian of Acheulian Tradition, Type A (MTA-A), which has a relatively high Total Acheulian Index.

Assemblage Group III: These assemblages all exhibit Scraper Indices of between 3 and 13% and a generally high relative frequency of notches and denticulates. Again, two subgroups are defined:

A. Mousterian of Acheulian Tradition, Type B (MTA-B), which has some bifaces, though fewer and usually smaller and less well made than is true for the MTA-A. However, there are relatively more backed knives and sometimes an elevated ILam.

B. Denticulate Mousterian, with a large number of denticulates and rare scrapers, bifaces, and backed knives.

A FRESH LOOK AT TYPOLOGICAL PATTERNING IN THE MOUSTERIAN OF FRANCE

Since the early work of Bordes, a number of Middle Paleolithic assemblages have been excavated or reported and it is instructive to review some of the typological patterning that occurs among them. The assemblages used in the study are presented in Table 10.1. All of the ones used here have essential counts greater than 100 (to avoid sampling errors), but not all were collected under controlled conditions according to modern excavation standards. Therefore, an important series of assemblages used here are those from Bordes's own excavations at Combe-Grenal, Pech de l'Azé, and Corbiac.

The first step in interpreting patterns of assemblage variability is to determine which types are contributing to the observed assemblage patterns and which are not. There are actually two different, though related, questions: (1) Which types exhibit the most variability over all the Mousterian assemblages? (2) Which types are associated most strongly with the defined assemblage groups? As it turns out, the same tool types are relevant to both questions.

The first question is what tool types vary the most, regardless of assemblage type. As both Rolland (1981) and Jelinek (1984a) have shown, most of the typological variation among French Mousterian assemblages is related to scrapers, denticulates, and notches. A simple way to show this here is by examining the mean and standard deviations of the percentages (relative to the essential count) of the major tool classes. This is done in Figure 10.1. What can be easily seen is that over all the assemblages there is a tremendous amount of variability with respect to all scrapers and to notches and denticulates. There is very little overall variability with respect to the other type classes.

In fact, because scrapers or notches/denticulates comprise so much of assemblage variability, they are inversely correlated themselves at the incredibly high value of $r = .9235$ ($N = 72$, $P < .0001$). In other words,

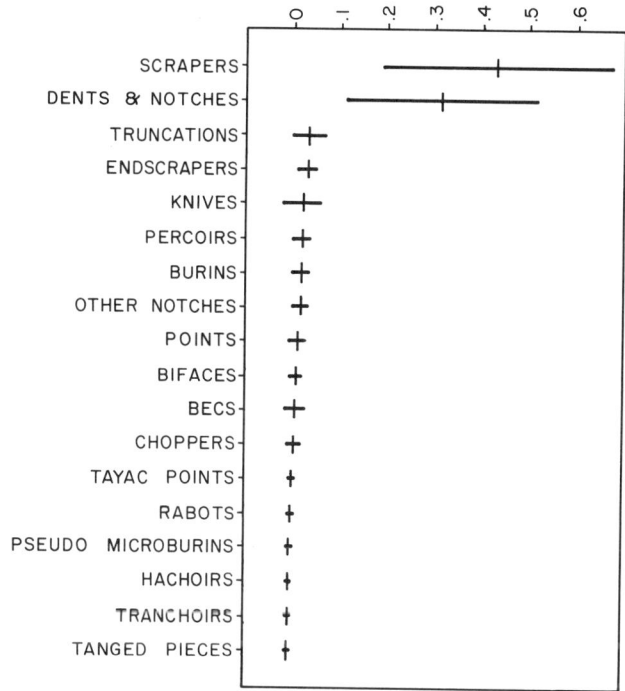

Figure 10.1 Mean (vertical dash) and standard deviation (horizontal bar) of percentages of major tool classes over total number of assemblages. Percentages are based on essential counts minus types 5 and 38.

if more scrapers are introduced into an assemblage, then the relative percentage of that class goes up and forces down the relative percentage of the other class, i.e., notches and denticulates. The difference between this r value and a perfect correlation, where r would equal -1.0, represents the amount of variability due to differences in the relative frequencies of the other types. In statistical terms, over 90% of interassemblage variability is due to different frequencies of scrapers versus notches and denticulates, which in turn means that less than 10% of assemblage variation is related to the other types.

TABLE 10.1
ASSEMBLAGES ANALYZED IN TEXT

Site	Layer	Industry	Source
Combe-Grenal (CG)	11, 12, 13, 14, 15	Denticulate	Bordes, unpub.
Combe-Grenal	17, 19	Quina	Bordes, unpub.
Combe-Grenal	20(J)	Denticulate	Bordes, unpub.
Combe-Grenal	21, 22, 23, 24, 25, 26	Quina	Bordes, unpub.
Combe-Grenal	27(P)	Ferrassie	Bordes, unpub.
Combe-Grenal	28, 29, 30	Typical	Bordes, unpub.
Combe-Grenal	32, 33, 35	Ferrassie	Bordes, unpub.
Combe-Grenal	37(Z)	Typical	Bordes, unpub.
Combe-Grenal	38	Denticulate	Bordes, unpub.
Combe-Grenal	40, 50, 50A, 52, 54	Typical	Bordes, unpub.
Pech de l'Azé I (P1)	NSS, NSM, NS2, NS3	MTA, Type B	Bordes, unpub.
Pech de l'Azé II (P2)	3	Typical	Bordes, unpub.
Pech de l'Azé II	4B	Denticulate	Bordes, unpub.
Pech de l'Azé II	4C2	Typical	Bordes, unpub.
Pech de l'Azé IV (P4)	F1, F2	MTA, Type B	Bordes, unpub.
Pech de l'Azé IV	F4	MTA, Type A	Bordes, unpub.
Pech de l'Azé IV	I2	Typical	Bordes, unpub.
Pech de l'Azé IV	J3B	"Asinipodien"	Bordes, unpub.
Pech de l'Azé IV	X, Z	Typical	Bordes, unpub.
Pech de l'Azé IV	Z	Typical A	Bordes, unpub.
Corbiac (C)	M1, M2	MTA, Type A	Bordes, unpub.
Abri Chadourne (CH)	A (Blanc, Fitte)	Denticulate	Bordes, Fitte, and Blanc 1954
Abri Chadourne	B, C	Quina	Bordes, Fitte, and Blanc 1954
Abri Chadourne	D	Ferrassie	Bordes, Fitte, and Blanc 1954
Mas-Viel (MV)	Série N-L	Quina	Niederlender et al. 1956
Mas-Viel	Série Dr. C	Quina	Niederlender et al. 1956
Grotte de l'Hyène (H)	IVA, IVB1, IVB3	Denticulate	Girard 1978
Roc de Marsal (RM)	IXA, IXB, X, XIA, XI-indet., XII	Quina	Turq 1985
Fonseigner (F)	DS, DMI, E	Typical	Geneste 1985
Brouillaud (B)	C	MTA, Type A	Geneste 1985
Brouillaud	D	Denticulate	Geneste 1985
Sandougne (S)	D	Denticulate	Geneste 1985
Sandougne	F	MTA, Type A	Geneste 1985
Le Roc (LR)		Denticulate	Geneste 1985
Le Dau (LD)	MP	MTA, Type A	Geneste 1985
Vaufrey (V)	VIII	Typical	Geneste 1985
Combe-Capelle (CC)	Abri Peyrony	MTA, Type A	Dibble, unpub.
Puynormand (N)	Série blanche	MTA, Type A	Lenoir 1983
Puynormand	Série grise	MTA, Type A	Lenoir 1983
Ruisseau de Graviers (RG)	1B, 2	Typical	Lenoir 1983

Each layer is treated as a separate case. Initials correspond to those presented in Figure 10.7.

The second question is which types are most strongly associated with the defined Mousterian assemblage groups. It is already known that Bordes recognized the importance of these same two type classes, i.e., scrapers and denticulates/notches, when defining the six Mousterian assemblage groups. Thus, by definition, Mousterian assemblage groups should exhibit significant differences in relative frequencies of these two typological classes. This can be easily seen in Figure 10.2, which shows the means and one standard deviation for each of the six major Mousterian groups for the IR and the percentage of notches and denticulates. Not surprisingly, again because these groups were defined on the basis of these types, the relationship between assemblage group and IR is significant ($F = 56.98$, $df = 5/66$, $P < .0001$), as is the relationship between group and percentage of denticulates and notches ($F = 64.74$, $df = 5/66$, $P < .0001$). Perhaps more important than a simple significance test, however, is a measure of the amount of variability in scraper frequency that is "explained" by the Mousterian assemblage groups. One measure, Eta^2, which is computed by dividing the sums of squares of the intergroup variation by the sums of squares of the total variation, is .8119 for IR and .8306 for the percentage of notches and denticulates. Statistically, this means that over 81% of scraper variability relates to, or is "explained" by, the Mousterian assemblage groups. Likewise, about 83% of denticulate variability is explainable according these groups.

But what about the other types? Are there any significant associations between some of them and the

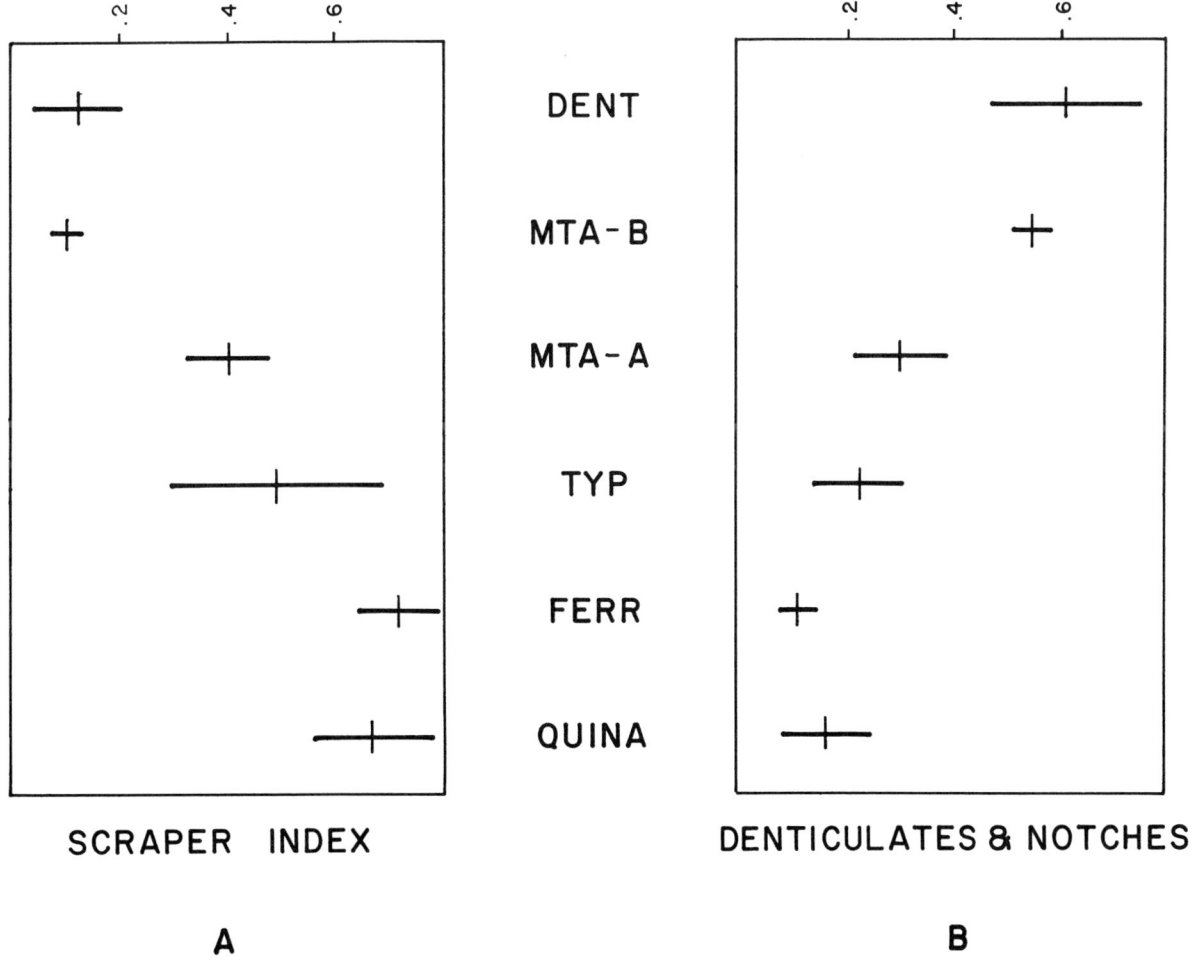

Figure 10.2 Mean and standard deviations for each Mousterian assemblage group for Scraper Index and percentage of denticulates and notches. Both computed on basis of essential counts minus types 5 and 38.

Mousterian assemblage groups? It is difficult to look for such relationships because, as was just shown, variability in the minor types is overwhelmed by variability in the scrapers and denticulates. This effect can be eliminated, however, by examining the percentages of the minor groups relative only to themselves. That is, for the next few comparisons, percentages of tool classes will be calculated relative to the essential total *minus* all scrapers, notches, and denticulates.

By examining the more minor type classes this way (see Figs. 10.3-4), it is possible to see that Quina and Denticulate industries both show significantly higher percentages of *perçoirs*, while Quina industries alone show increased percentages of endscrapers. Not surprisingly because of its definition, the MTA-B shows significantly higher percentages of backed knives but also a significantly lower percentage of truncations. Both the Typical and Ferrassie Mousterian groups show significantly higher percentages of points. Interestingly, the MTA-A does not separate itself from Typical Mousterian according to anything except bifaces, a fact noted also by Bordes and Bourgon. According to the values of Eta^2, not much variability in the other type classes is associated with the Mousterian assemblage groups.

So, while these data clearly support the original definitions of the assemblage groups put forward by Bordes, it is also clear that the problem of Mousterian variability is related to only a few type classes. Overall variability is dominated by scrapers and notches/denticulates and even interassemblage group variability is primarily related to these types.

TOOL REDUCTION AND TYPOLOGICAL VARIABILITY

One of the implications of the preceding analysis is that correct interpretation of Mousterian assemblage variability depends on correct interpretations of the two principal typological classes of scrapers and notches/denticulates. Crucial to this problem is an understanding of relationships that may exist among the separate types in each class.

For the various scraper types, it has already been shown (Dibble 1984a, 1987a, c, d) that variability among them can be understood as stages in the continuous reduction of the tools through resharpening. Two distinct reduction sequences are suggested on the basis of replicative experiments. The first involves a sequence from single-edged sidescrapers through double-edged sidescrapers to convergent scrapers. The second sequence involves the continuing reduction of a single edge. Typologically, this sequence is represented first by the single-edged types which, as the reduction continues, can be transformed into transverse scrapers. *Déjeté* scrapers (type 21) can result from either sequence, depending on the point in the reduction of the first edge at which the second edge is retouched (see Dibble 1987c). But, in either reduction model, single-edged scrapers represent the least-reduced pieces while convergent and transverse scrapers represent those most reduced.

These two continuous reduction sequences could thus account for variability in 16 distinct types of scrapers. That is, scraper typological variability can be interpreted as reflecting reduction according to one or the other of these two sequences. But it is quite likely that these reduction patterns cover more than just the named scrapers dealt with in these analyses, that is, types 9-24. For example, there is no problem in seeing *limaces* (type 8) as a form of convergent scraper, though one that has been heavily reduced on both the proximal and distal ends. Thus *limaces*, like transverse and other convergent forms, probably reflect a long sequence of reduction of the piece.

Another class that may be placed into the scrapers are the Mousterian points (types 6-7). For many years the distinction between Mousterian points and convergent scrapers has been a recognized problem area in the typology (Bordes 1954b, 1961b). Is it possible that these two classes simply partition a continuum of variability in convergent scrapers? In other words, are Mousterian points simply convergent scrapers that fortuitously exhibit a sharper or finer point? Two kinds of evidence suggest that this is the case.

First, there is a strong correlation ($r = .60553$, $N = 72$, $P < .0001$) between the percentage of points and that of convergent scrapers (both computed on the basis of the total essential counts). Such a relationship would be expected if they were functionally and technologically the same tool, but would not necessarily occur if they were being used for completely different tasks. Also as would be expected from the reduction model, Mousterian points *and* convergent scrapers are both highly correlated with double scrapers ($r = .60487$ and $r = .6876$, respectively, both significant at the .0001 level).

A different argument against types 6 and 7 being functional points can be based on the frequency of proximal ends versus distal pointed ends. It has been documented (Flenniken 1985; Flenniken and Raymond 1986) that true point tips usually occur with less

LITHIC RESOURCES IN THE FRENCH MOUSTERIAN 187

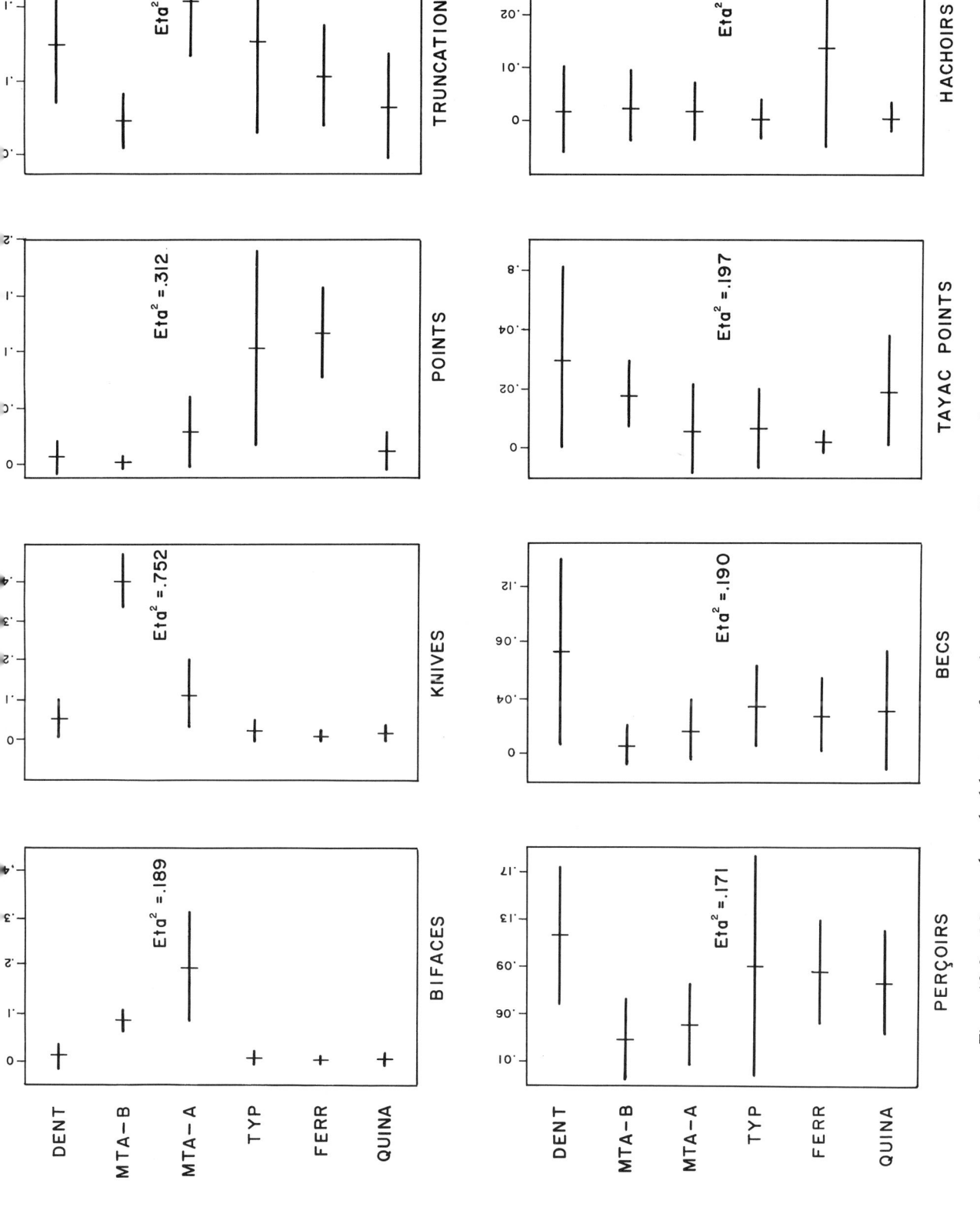

Figure 10.3 Mean and standard deviations for each Mousterian assemblage group for various tool groups. All computed on basis of essential counts minus types 5 and 38 and minus all scrapers and denticulates. Eta^2 represents the percentage of variability of the relative tool frequency "explained" by, or linked to, the Mousterian assemblage groups.

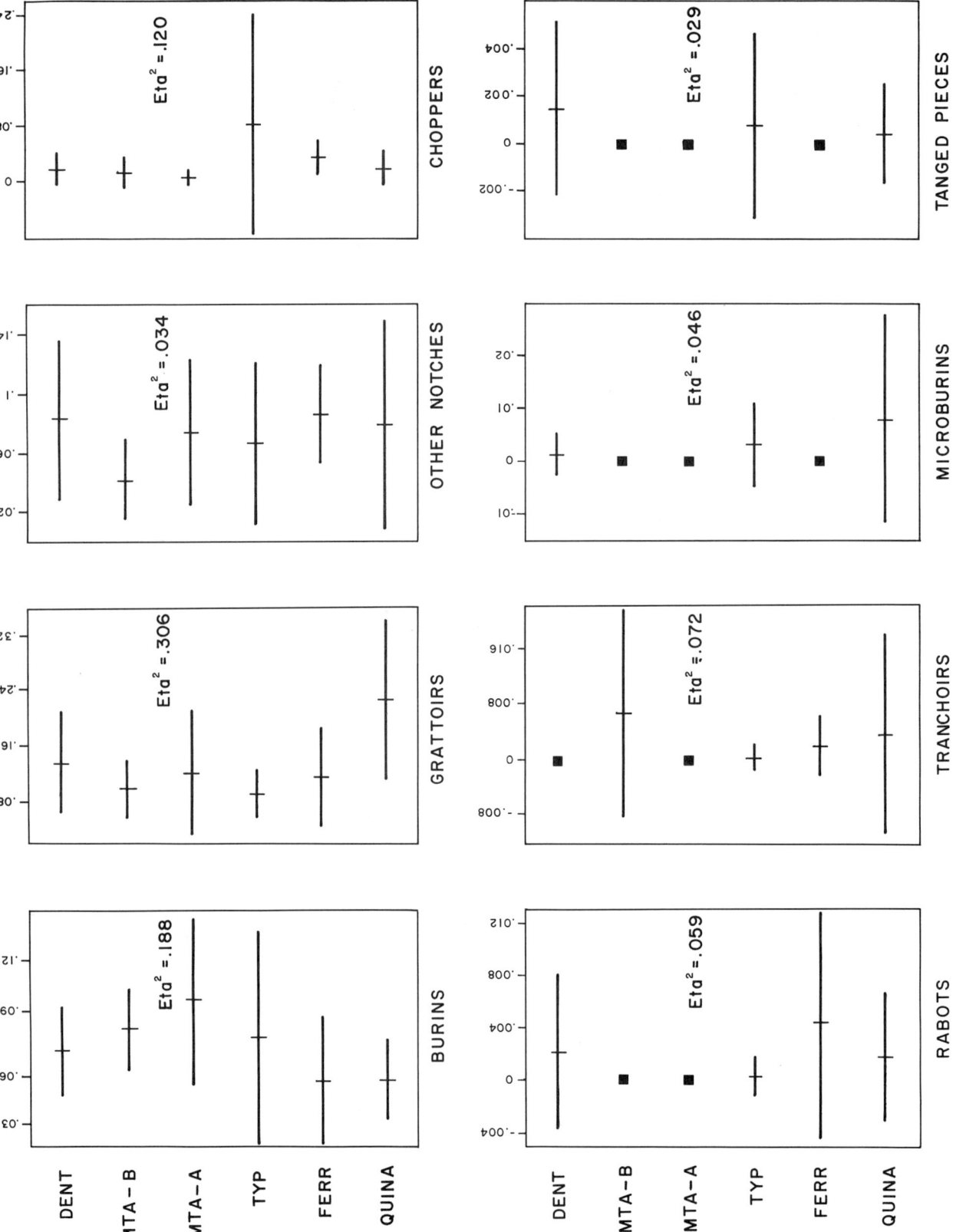

Figure 10.4 Mean and standard deviations for each Mousterian assemblage group for various tool groups. All computed on basis of essential counts minus types 5 and 38 and minus all scrapers and denticulates. Eta² represents the percentage of variability of the relative tool frequency "explained" by, or linked to, the Mousterian assemblage groups.

frequency than point bases. This is because the former are often broken off and lost at the site of use, while the latter can be returned to the habitation area and reworked. Simon Holdaway, a graduate student at the University of Pennsylvania, has recently examined this aspect of two Mousterian assemblages from Iran, Bisitun and Warwasi. Both of these industries are very rich in points and convergent scrapers (Dibble 1984b; Baumler et al. 1986). His work shows that the frequency of distal fragments of all convergent pieces is not lower than that of proximal fragments; in fact, the two frequencies are about the same. At these sites, the pattern of proximal versus distal fragments does not follow what would be expected of true functional points and instead suggests that fragmentation was due to other factors.

Thus, two different lines of reasoning suggest that so-called Mousterian points can be interpreted as types of convergent scrapers. Perhaps detailed microwear analysis could verify or reject this notion. But until such evidence is available, it is not unreasonable to suggest that these "points" also represent an end point of reduction.

Before we compute this index, however, it is important to recall that there are two different scraper-reduction sequences apparent in Mousterian industries: the single-double-convergent sequence and the single-transverse sequence. On the basis of previous studies (Dibble 1987d) it is apparent that both sequences are being followed *within* different kinds of assemblage groups from France. For a particular tool, the choice of one sequence versus the other relates probably to the original shape of the flake blank. But it can also be shown that there are differences *among* assemblages in terms of the overall emphasis of one sequence or another. This can be demonstrated if the index is computed as above, but made negative if there are more double and convergent scrapers than transverse scrapers. In this way, large negative values of this index (which will be called the Scraper Reduction Index) will indicate heavy reduction primarily according to the first model (single-double-convergent); large positive values will indicate heavy reduction primarily according to the second model (single-transverse); and small values in either direction will indicate little overall scraper reduction. Again, *déjeté* scrapers can result from either reduction model and so are excluded from either the convergent or transverse totals for purposes of determining which reduction model is predominant.

It must be emphasized that the aim here is not to eliminate types, but rather to interpret them. Because the various scraper types appear to be the result of more or less reduction, it is possible to use counts based on Bordes's typology to examine assemblages according to the amount of scraper reduction exhibited. To do this, a new index of scraper reduction can be computed by dividing the number of convergent scrapers, transverse scrapers, and Mousterian points (i.e., the classes that reflect heavy reduction) by the number of single and double scrapers (i.e., the lightly reduced types). Industries with a large index computed this way are those with more transverse and convergent forms; thus they are the assemblages that exhibit more scraper reduction. A small value of this index will characterize those industries that do not show as much reduction.

A graph of the distribution of this index (Fig. 10.5) exhibits a bimodality corresponding to the two scraper-reduction models. The mode to the left (negative) represents those industries that reduce the scrapers predominantly according to the first model. The mode on the right corresponds to those industries that reduce scrapers predominantly according to the second model. Interestingly, these modes correspond closely to another variable, the Levallois Index. The industries which show scraper reduction according to the first model have a mean IL of 15.74, while the other group has a mean IL of only 5.57. This difference is significant ($t = 5.70$, $df = 63$, $P < .0001$).

Thus, the choice of one scraper-reduction sequence versus another relates to the technology of blank production. It is most likely that this is because different technologies result in flakes of different shapes, one shape being more suited to a particular kind of reduction than another. The use of Levallois technique often results in more elongated flakes, which would be most suited to retouch on both sides rather than eventual reduction from the end. Unfortunately, no data are available to demonstrate that Levallois pieces in particular are chosen for one reduction model and non-Levallois pieces for another. But one way to look at the effect of blank shape is through the Blade Index (ILam), which will reflect the percentage of long narrow flakes. It is true that assemblages which demonstrate more of the single-double-convergent reduction have a higher mean ILam (9.99) than those assemblages that have predominantly a single-transverse reduction (5.95). The difference in ILam between these two groups is significant ($t = 3.157$, $df = 55.2$, $P = .0026$). It is also interesting that this pattern is repeated in the Near East, where non-Levallois Ya-

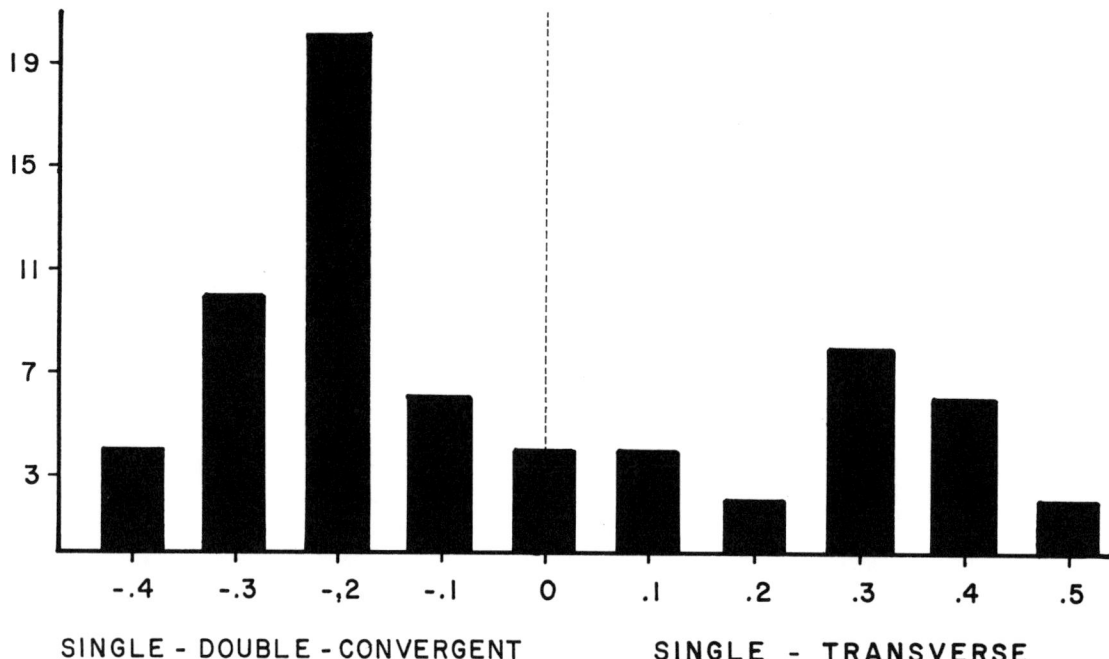

Figure 10.5 Histogram of assemblage frequency for intervals of Scraper Reduction Index. Negative values are assigned to those assemblages that have more double and convergent scrapers than transverse scrapers. The bimodality reflects the difference in kind of reduction sequence, not the degree of reduction, which is normally distributed.

brudian industries also exhibit the single-transverse model, while the so-called Zagros Mousterian, now known to have moderate IL and high ILam (Dibble 1984b; Baumler et al. 1986), exhibits the single-double-convergent model of reduction almost exclusively (Dibble 1984a).

Figure 10.6A displays the relationship between this index of scraper reduction and the various Mousterian assemblage groups. This relationship is significant ($F = 15.61$, $df = 5/66$, $P < .0001$). Quina assemblages exhibit high indices of reduction according to the single-transverse model, while Typical, Ferrassie, and MTA-A have, on average, moderately large negative values indicating more reduction according to the single-double-transverse model. Denticulate and MTA-B exhibit little overall scraper reduction. Thus, to a significant extent, Mousterian assemblage variability is associated with the amount and kind of scraper reduction.

It may also be possible to examine another form of tool reduction, this time related to notches and denticulates. For example, many specimens of denticulates from Middle Paleolithic contexts can be viewed as multiple *notches* on the same flake blank. If this is true, then there may not be a functional difference between notches and most denticulates. Instead the latter may simply be examples that were more worked and reduced. Arguing for this notion are the facts that technologically a denticulate is nothing more than a series of notches, and that the essential percentages of these two types are also strongly correlated ($r = .56158$, $N = 72$, $P < .0001$). It is even possible to identify pieces in the archaeological record that seem to reflect such a resharpening process in these tools (Lenoir 1986).

This would allow us to compute another reduction index related to notches, by dividing the number of denticulates in an assemblage by the number of notches. Like the Scraper Reduction Index computed above, a higher value of this index—i.e., more denticulates than notches—would reflect more reduction and reuse of these tools. A lower value would indicate less reduction. The relationship between this index and the Mousterian assemblage groups, shown in Figure 10.6B, is again significant ($F = 3.67$, $df = 5/66$, $P = .006$).

As was shown earlier, scrapers and notches/denticulates represent the most salient aspects of Mousterian assemblage variability. The two indices just computed represent two different aspects of tool reduction for these two type classes, one related to scrapers and the other to notches. It is interesting to examine the distribution of assemblages according to both of these two indices simultaneously, as is shown

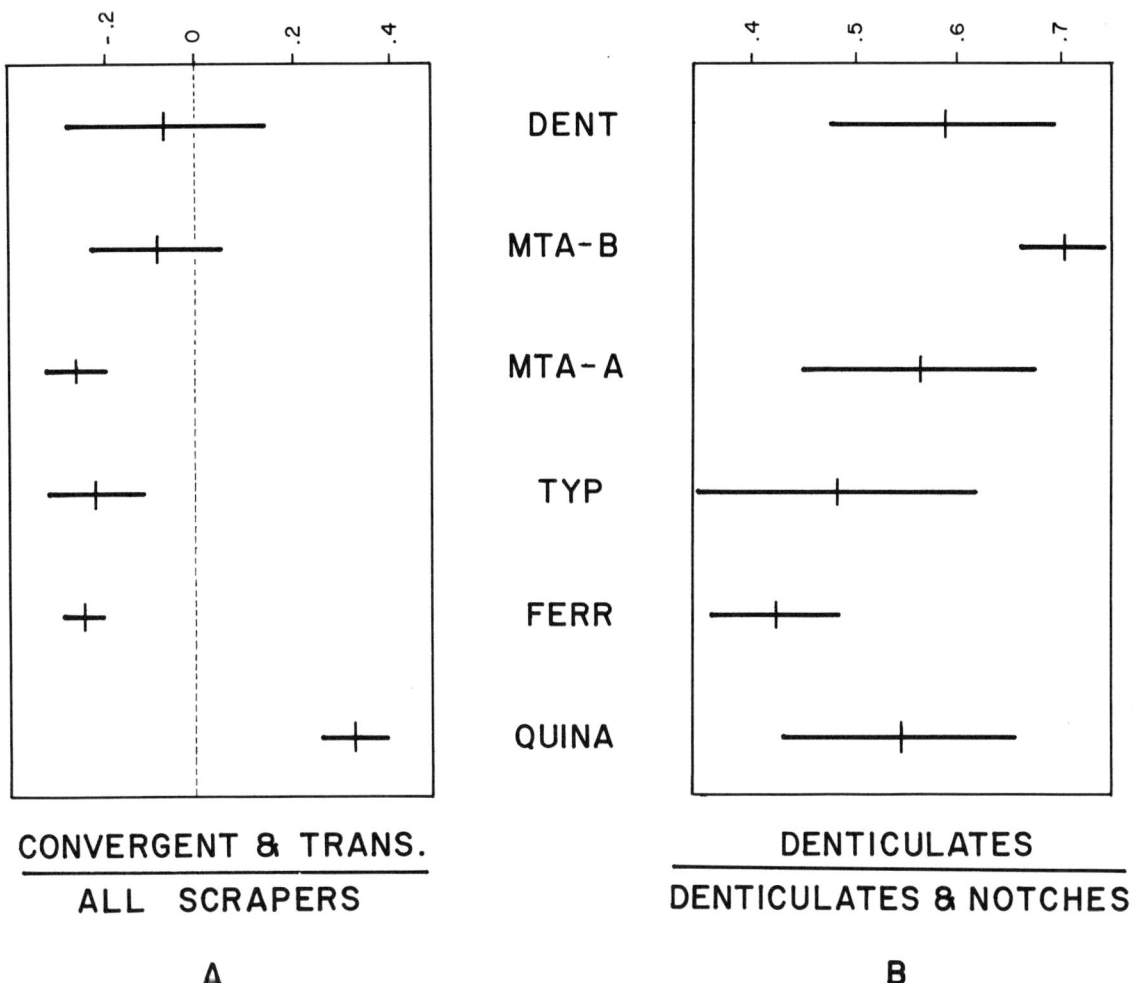

Figure 10.6 Mean and standard deviations for the two indices of reduction, related to (a) scrapers and (b) notches. See text for details.

in Figure 10.7. In this figure, the vertical axis is the Scraper Reduction Index and the horizontal axis is the analogous index relating to notches. The symbols used in the figure reflect the assignment of each industry to one of the six Mousterian groups.

The most interesting feature of this graph is that there is some segregation of the Mousterian groups according to these two indices. Along the vertical axis, Quina industries exhibit a positive value indicating more use of the single-transverse model. This corresponds also to the generally low IL associated with these industries. But Quina industries also exhibit relatively high absolute values of this index, which suggests that the scrapers in those industries are relatively more reduced. On the other end of the scraper-reduction axis, the end corresponding to the single-double-convergent model, are the Typical, Ferrassie, and MTA-A industries, i.e., those with a higher IL and with varying degrees of scraper reduction. Generally, the Denticulate group and the MTA-B are located in the middle of this axis and thus show little reduction of scrapers.

The horizontal axis, corresponding to notch reduction, serves to separate the MTA-B and the Denticulate industries from the others and from one another. Thus, the MTA-B can be seen as a more intensively reduced industry than the Denticulate Mousterian, as seen in the much higher number of denticulates relative to notches. Another feature of this industry that also suggests more reduction is its characteristically small and heavily reduced bifaces.

In the lower right-hand corner of the graph are a

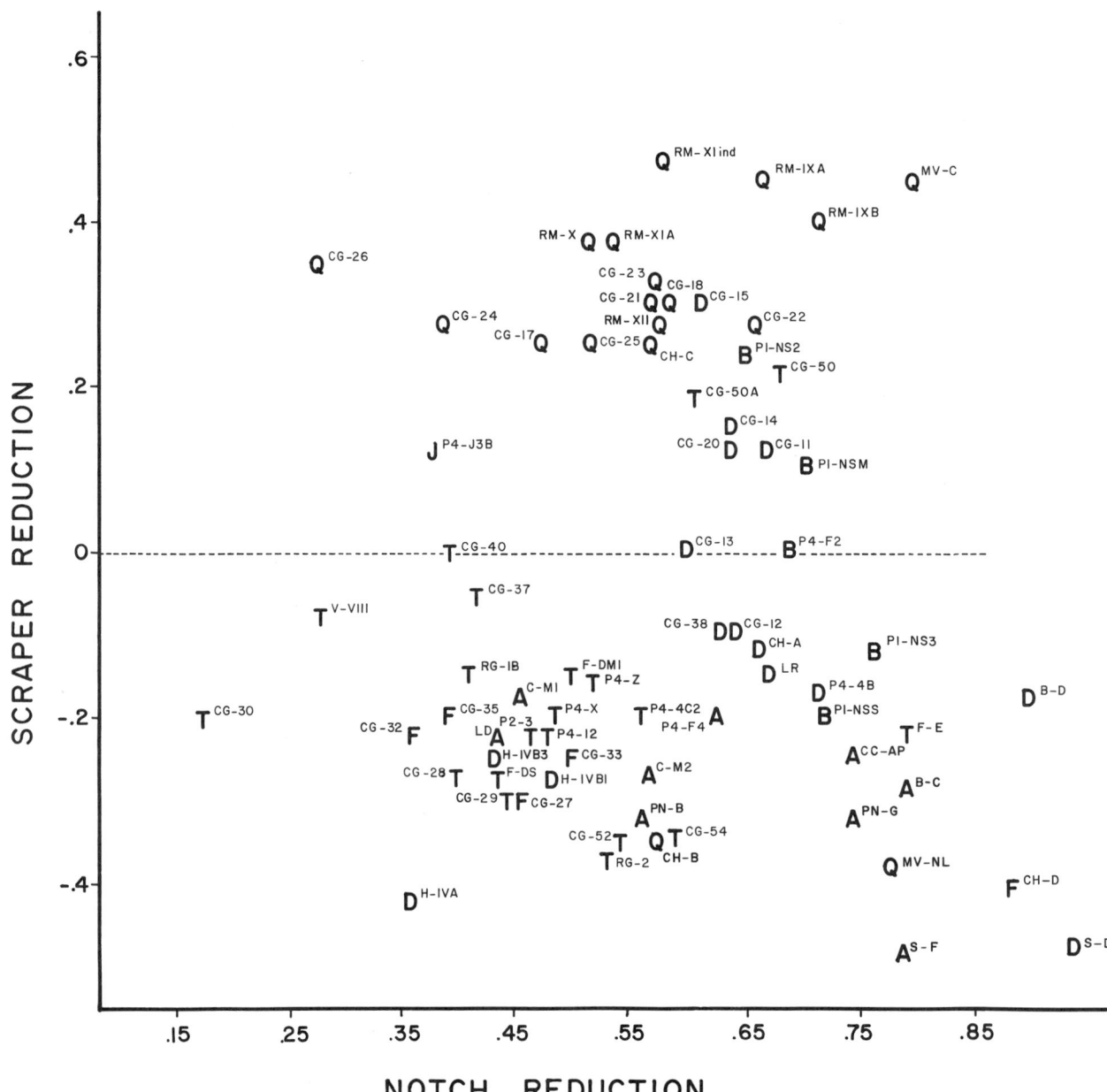

Figure 10.7 Scatter diagram of all Mousterian assemblages according to the two indices of reduction. Negative scraper-reduction values indicate a predominance of the single-double-convergent reduction pattern. Symbols: Q = Quina Mousterian; F = Ferrassie Mousterian; T = Typical Mousterian; D = Denticulate Mousterian; A = Mousterian of Acheulian Tradition, Type A; B = Mousterian of Acheulian Tradition, Type B; J = Asinipodian (Pech de l'Azé, J3B).

number of assemblages that do not fit these patterns. Interestingly, with the exception of Puynormand G and Fonseigner E, all of these "outliers" are from older collections and may suffer to some degree from excavator bias. In fact, the placement of these early collections to the right side could simply be due to a failure to recognize Clactonian notches, which would have the effect of elevating the index relating to denticulates and notches. Other notable exceptions that are not so easy to explain are the three levels from Grotte de l'Hyène (Arcy-sur-Cure), IVA, IVB1, and IVB3 reported by Girard (1978), which show very high absolute values of the Scraper Reduction Index according to the single-double-convergent model; and the two Typical assemblages from Combe-Grenal (50 and 50A) that also seem somewhat out of place.

The segregation into the various Mousterian assemblage groups is not perfect, but these axes do not represent relative frequencies of major tool groups, which is the major criterion for traditional industrial assignment. The axes shown in Figure 10.7 are purely measures of reduction *within* the two major type classes, i.e., scrapers and notch/denticulates, and do not measure the frequency of one type class *relative to* the other. Moreover, some other types that are related to those groups, especially the bifaces and backed knives, are omitted entirely. So, there is no reason to suspect *a priori* that any patterning similar to the traditional distinctions of these groups should be apparent in this graph of the two reduction indices. Yet to the extent that the assemblages are segregated according to these indices, and given that the indices themselves relate to tool reduction, then it clearly follows that the placement of assemblages in Figure 10.7 must also relate to these two aspects of reduction. This would allow us to interpret the Mousterian assemblage groups as relating to tool reduction.

OTHER MEASURES OF REDUCTION AND INTENSITY OF UTILIZATION OF LITHIC RESOURCES

The above analysis focusing on tool-reduction patterns gives an entirely new perspective on the nature of Mousterian assemblage variability. Such reduction probably relates to the overall intensity of utilization of the lithic resources. This notion was first put forward by Rolland (1981) and Jelinek (1976, 1984a), who offer some other aspects of assemblage variability that relate to the same factor.

Two of the more important variables that potentially relate to intensity of utilization are the ratio of tools to unretouched flakes and the ratio of flake tools and unretouched flakes together to cores. Blanks that are selected for retouch come from an original flake population that existed at the site. In turn, this original flake population is a result of core reduction. Under conditions where more intense utilization of the lithic resources is taking place, one would expect to see more flakes produced per core, and the selection of more of those flakes to be made into tools. Data presented by Rolland (1977: table 1; 1981: 22–23) show that this is the case for Quina and Ferrassie assemblage groups, both of which demonstrate a great deal of scraper reduction. In fact, Rolland (1981: 28) himself relates implement and flake ratios to the possibility of repeated resharpening of scrapers.

Other data presented by Rolland also fit well with patterns that would be expected with scraper reduction. For example, he reports (1981: 27) that scraper length exceeds the length of unretouched flakes. This is also the case for Yabrudian levels from Tabun (Dibble 1987a) and clearly relates to selection of the bigger flakes to be made into tools. In fact, it has been argued that reduction of tools continues until a minimum width is achieved; flake blanks that are originally under that size are rarely used at all. Thus, average tool size (with a minimum size related to the need to grasp the tool) should always exceed the average size of the unretouched pieces (whose minimum size is only a question of recovery techniques).

RELATIONSHIP OF THE PATTERNS OF TOOL REDUCTION TO THE ORIGINAL MOUSTERIAN ASSEMBLAGE GROUPS

The basic data used in this paper are counts of Bordes's types, and the resulting patterns are essentially those found by Bordes and Bourgon. Is this is a surprise? In one sense, the answer is no, simply because the data are the same. But what was added in this analysis was an interpretation of certain of those types, an interpretation that was developed in earlier work by looking at patterns of variability within particular assemblages. The next step, taken here, was to relate assemblages according to measures that reflect that interpretation.

There is no *a priori* reason to assume that the assemblage groups defined by Bordes would have any relationship to reduction. So, in this sense, the agreement between the traditional assemblage classification and the one seen on the basis of measures of reduction is surprising, or at least not predicted. To some extent, the continued segregation of the assemblage groups on the basis of the reduction indices supports their existence as defined. At least it seems that the patterns first observed by Bordes truly are fundamental aspects of Mousterian variability.

The agreement is not perfect, however. The first point of disagreement is that Bordes did not view the use of Levallois technique as being of special significance for relating or segregating industries, with the exception being the separation of Quina and

Ferrassie variants. In terms of scraper reduction, though, it has a clear effect on the emphasis of one reduction sequence or the other. The Quina industries are truly isolated from the Ferrassie, Typical, and MTA-A, both typologically and technologically. The three latter groups are very similar in terms of reduction.

A second point of disagreement concerns the bifaces, which represented a primary criterion used by Bordes and Bourgon for assemblage classification. By definition this artifact class does separate the two MTA variants from the others. But as shown earlier, the overall variability in bifaces is not very great. And in terms of the manufacture and reduction of scrapers it is apparent that the MTA-A is more similar to the Typical, and the MTA-B is much more akin to the Denticulate, than either is to the other. Rather than reflecting a major historical tradition and connection between the MTA-A and MTA-B, it may be that bifaces are occurring in varying frequencies independently of other tool classes. Thus, Bordes's (1953a) original grouping of MTA-A with the Typical and MTA-B with the Denticulate (see above) may be preferable to the more recent tendency to stress a historical connection between MTA-A and MTA-B on the basis of what are not, statistically speaking, very important artifact types.

SUMMARY AND CONCLUSIONS

The purpose of this paper has been to review the basic nature of Mousterian assemblage variability, and to suggest aspects of lithic technology and use that may be contributing to it. In reviewing typological variability, we see that relatively few types are of real importance in terms of their association with the named Mousterian variants. This finding, while consistent with the original definitions of the assemblage groups, narrows considerably the focus of attention for interpreting them. Statistically, the two most important type classes for this problem are scrapers and notches/denticulates. Both of these classes exhibit variability interpretable as reduction, and new indices have been computed to best measure the amount and kind of that reduction in an assemblage. The distribution of assemblages along the two new axes of reduction is shown to mirror the original assemblage groups, thus providing an interpretive framework for explaining Mousterian assemblage variability.

This study underlines the importance of scraper versus notch/denticulate tool classes. It has been argued here that typological variation within these classes relates to reduction. What is still uncertain is why some industries exhibit more of one of these tool classes than of the other. Rolland (1981: 28) suggests that it relates to differential rates of attrition and need for rejuvenation between these two classes. This explanation is appealing simply because it relates to the notion of reduction that is being presented here. Replicative and controlled experiments could be of great value in determining whether this notion is correct. Perhaps also, more studies of existing collections should be focused on variation within the notch/denticulate class.

If so much Mousterian assemblage variability can be related to reduction, an important question is what kinds of conditions foster more or less of that behavior. It has been suggested (Rolland 1981; Mellars 1969) that there is an association between some of the Mousterian variants and climate. Perhaps this should be investigated further using continuous measures of reduction and intensity. Among these are the two indices of reduction, one for scrapers and one for notches/denticulates, the ratio of retouched tools to unmodified flakes, and the ratio of blanks to cores.

Another area to be investigated concerns the factors that influence the production of Levallois pieces. As was seen, this technology has clear typological ramifications. What remains to be clarified is the extent to which this technology is influenced by raw-material constraints, climate, or historical tradition. The increased attention that is being paid to this technology (see Boëda 1986; Boëda and Pelegrin 1979-80; Dibble 1985a; Geneste 1985) may help to answer some of these questions by identifying new analytical methods.

There is no doubt that Bordes and Bourgon focused their attention on some of the most fundamental aspects of Mousterian variability. Their revolution in method continues to stimulate thought on the nature of Mousterian assemblage variability and at the same time provides a means of relating that variability to a number of factors. It is hoped that the interpretations offered here build constructively on their work and that of several other researchers and that they suggest other productive avenues of future investigation.

ACKNOWLEDGMENTS

The author wishes to thank Mme. Denise de Sonneville-Bordes for permission to use the unpublished data from Combe-Grenal, Pech de l'Azé, and Corbiac.

DISCUSSION

SACKETT: What is now called traditional systematics was based upon a type-list and a few basic morphological distinctions. Many people contributed to this, though F. Bordes was perhaps the leader and therefore we often refer to Bordesian systematics or Bordesian approach. Some people, theoreticians rather than pragmatists, view these type-lists as models or paradigms, with the effect that these types dictate the way in which they look at the universe. Bordes never meant it that way: he was interested in efficacy, not in truth. A type-list should not dictate the way you think. Rather, it simply gets you to the point where you have something worthwhile to think about. So we are going beyond the type-list, viewing tools not as discrete items in themselves but part of an unfolding of decisions and actions on the part of artisans, something Bordes did intuitively by knapping tools. We tend to do it now in a more formal way.

LENOIR: I'm not sure that Dibble's reduction models are the only possibility. At Combe-Grenal, I have observed different things in *pièces supports* that vary with the different types of scrapers. For example, most of the transverse scrapers are on thick, non-Levallois flakes. Many of the ordinary scrapers are on flakes with cortical backs, which is very useful for hafting. So it seems to me that there are differences in the choice of *pièces supports*, though in some cases I think that reduction plays a big role in the transition from one type to the other. The same is true for Quina retouch, which I have examined experimentally. Like F. Bordes and de Sonneville-Bordes, I believe that Quina retouch must be intentional, but it also depends on the cross-section of the blank. In fact, Quina retouch can be produced by modifying a denticulate made with a series of Clactonian notches. So, there are several ways of explaining this kind of morphology.

BOSINSKI: For me, the difference between Mousterian types Quina and Ferrassie relates to the use of Levallois technique or not, and this also relates to platform size. So, I still think that the differentiation between transverse, simple, and double scrapers, between Quina and Ferrassie Mousterian, is the blank.

DIBBLE: I agree. As I explained, the two models of scraper reduction are related to differences in the *pièces supports*. The industries that are making single, double, and convergent scrapers are the Levallois industries, that have thin and elongated flakes. When an industry is making short and especially thick flakes, then the other reduction model applies. For these reasons, I would emphasize the role of Levallois as being a primary factor in differentiating Mousterian assemblages. It is fundamental in that it gives rise to the differences in typology that we see in the scrapers. So I think that I am in agreement with both you and Lenoir, that to get these kinds of attributes that we see in the heavy Quina scrapers, it takes a different kind of blank, i.e., that it is related very much to technology. It would be good to have data, like Rolland's, that would allow us to examine exactly which pieces were made into convergent scrapers, double scrapers, versus transverse. I might also point out that this distinction between single-double-convergent and single-transverse, and the relationship with Levallois, holds up in the Near East. The non-Levallois Yabrudian industries from Tabun follow the single-transverse model predominantly, while Zagros Mousterian from Bisitun, which has a fair amount of Levallois and many scrapers, shows the single-double-convergent reduction pattern exclusively.

MARKS: It seems to me that you've got two different things involved here: one is somewhat mechanical, how intensity of utilization will result in certain typological changes. But, in all assemblages that I know of, you have a range from thin blanks to thick blanks. It's the choice of which blank to use initially that may come close to the cultural decision.

DIBBLE: And the choice of technology to produce those blanks.

SACKETT: But we do not know at what end the choice was being made, and we do not know the intentions of the artisan.

MARKS: In the Near East, there's a good relationship between the scraper forms and availability of raw material. In the Negev, where we have huge sites with a wide range of variability of blank forms, complicated scraper forms and Mousterian points are extrordinarily rare, and retouch on scrapers is almost always very flat. In short, there's almost no resharpening at all: if they need another piece, they pick up another piece and use it. At Tabun, in a cave where it's a matter of getting up and walking outside, in the same technology you have many more of these.

DIBBLE: Jelinek, Rolland, and I have been focusing on the question of the intensification and re-utilization of lithic resources within a site. It is going to be a function of raw-material variability, a function of intensity of utilization of the site, etc., all of which can be reflected in different ways. If you have a lot of material, with flakes lying all over the place, then even a random selection of a blank will yield one that is unretouched. After it is used, it will be thrown back in with the rest. If you are going back into that cave, time and time again—perhaps over a millennium, and continually picking blanks, using them, and throwing them back down, then eventually the percentage of previously retouched pieces will increase. Now when they come back in and look for something to pick up, even if their choice is random, the chances are higher that they will pick up something that was already a single scraper. If they retouch the other side, then it's a double scraper. So it is as much a function of the amount of raw material in the form of blanks that exist at the site, as it is of the amount of material available in the surrounding area.

SACKETT: One of the issues that bothers me is, again, the intention of the artisan. You demonstrated a relationship between typological result and a technological beginning, but we don't know at what end the choice was being made.

ROLLAND: We moved away, at one point, from a single focus on lithic technology/typology into environmental studies. Now I think it's coming back full circle, but with a gain in knowledge, in that now we are trying to relate the lithics to a variety of environmental and social processes. And decision making probably occurred at the time certain nodules were selected. In the Quina levels at Combe-Grenal, for example, the core sizes are larger than those of any other industries present in that site, and even larger than the flakes and tools from those levels. In other words, they brought in large nodules, and probably also selected blanks, knowing perhaps that they were going to stay there longer.

COMMENTS

DE SONNEVILLE-BORDES: Une *remarque historique* d'abord. La mise en évidence quantitative du *complexe moustérien* s'inscrit dans une démarche méthodologique plus générale, dont les étapes sont antérieures, qu'il s'agisse de la définition et de la quantification de la typologie et des techniques de taille à propos des couches moustériennes du Moustier (Bordes 1948) ou de la conception novatrice et même révolutionnaire de l'*évolution buissonnante* des industries du Paléolithique ancien et moyen (Bordes 1950a), à mettre au compte exclusif de F. Bordes, ce qui justifie parfaitement l'expression *Bordian method*.

Pour les *conclusions* de Dibble, dont les démonstrations statistiques élaborées sont acceptées ici telles que, il est bien évident que racloirs et encoches-denticulés représentent dans les séries moustériennes les éléments principaux, leurs variations apparaissent donc comme presqu'exclusivement responsables des variabilités moustériennes. Mais quelque perpléxité nous arrête dans la mesure où la série moustérienne, et au-delà le groupe moustérien, risquerait de se réduire alors, peu ou prou, à un ou deux outils, indépendamment de leurs variations internes exprimées par les subdivisions du groupe technotypologique. Observable également et davantage, et plus dangereusement, dans les études sur le Paléolithique supérieur, où certaines réduisent l'ensemble du technocomplexe à l'"indice de burin" et à l'"indice de grattoir," cette tendance réductrice actuelle risque de conduire ou tend à orienter vers l'effacement de la notion significative de l'ensemble expressif que représente un outillage, ou encore un type dans ses variétés, au bénéfice de la valorisation d'un objet banalisé, "idée" ou "modèle." Ainsi, par l'abandon de la conception de l'ensemble, expressif global des options ou des choix ou des intentions du fabricant, reviendrait-on au "fossile directeur" du siècle dernier, mais avec une démarche appauvrie. L'analyse quantitative sophistiquée donne priorité à un type d'outil comme facteur éminent de différenciation, mais en même temps le prive de ses caractéristiques particulières regroupées, qui en font pourtant un outillage culturellement expressif, association d'intentions délibérées, à codage privilégié. Il ne nous apparaît pas évident que cette simplification aide au débroussaillage efficace de l'énorme combinatoire chronologique et technotypologique du Paléolithique moyen que les spécialistes s'efforcent de démêler depuis un siècle.

Le reclassement dont les outillages moustériens sont l'objet et auquel Dibble apporte une contribution intéressante peut autoriser des cheminements sur des pistes encore inexplorées. Mais l'hypothèse de la réduction par utilisation et réaiguisage, qui conduit tel racloir à un autre stade technomorphologique, d'ailleurs attesté par des exemples ethnographiques (Australie), n'emporte pas l'adhésion unanime (objection de M. Lenoir, également expérimentateur), en particulier pour des types aussi fortement caractérisés que le racloir type Quina notamment, qui est l'exemple le plus frappant de l'"intention realisée dans la matière" selon la définition du type par F. Bordes (1950b). Ceci concerne aussi le choix préliminaire du support, qu'il s'agisse de la forme de l'éclat brut à aménager ou de la matière première elle-même, dont la récolte participe déjà de la conception préétablie du type à réaliser. Si le réaiguisage ou l'usage ont éventuellement modifié tel ou tel type d'outil, au besoin facilitant le passage du racloir convergent vers la pointe moustérienne par exemple, l'association des contraintes surmontées (matière première, pièce-support/blank, retouches, épaisseur, courbure, etc.) ne laisse à notre avis que peu de possibilités à une transformation morphologique évolutive analogue pour le racloir type Quina—pas plus que pour le biface ou l'éclat Levallois. La volonté de *faire* est initiale.

Reste à expliquer les comportements qui entraînent des différenciations quelles qu'en soient les modalités et les étapes. H. Dibble propose des influences extérieures, climatiques par exemple, sans y insister. C'est un autre problème.

Ces remarques ne doivent pas dissimuler l'intérêt certain du texte de H. Dibble. Elles soulignent seulement le danger de la tentation d'une explication unique qui exclurait la notion que type d'outil comme série lithique ont une signification propre en relation avec la totalité des options qui aboutissent à leur réalisation.

OTTE: Les possibilités de passage d'une forme typologique à l'autre dans les outillages moustériens démontrées par H. Dibble, suggèrent l'absence de stéréotypes préconçus dans la forme achevée de l'outil, emmanché et utilisé. Cet aspect aléatoire rappelle celui observé dans les études tracéologiques que l'aménagement intermittent était plus significatif pour l'emploi et la fabrication d'un objet moustérien que sa conception préalable.

XI
Technology, Typology, and Culture in the Middle Paleolithic

Arthur J. Jelinek

INTRODUCTION

This paper examines some aspects of the current status of the problem of explanation of Mousterian industrial variability in the early last glacial cycle ("Würm I and II"). The focus here is on the Western European industries, and particularly on those of southwest France, where patterns of industrial variability were first defined. Where pertinent, observations are included on the Near Eastern industries, although these are seen as differing from those of Western Europe in several fundamental ways (e.g., occurrence of Levallois technique and biface manufacture in the Levant and intensity of reduction in the Zagros-Taurus region).

The paper begins with a brief interpretive recapitulation of the developments in archaeology that have contributed to an understanding of the problem. This section is followed by an examination of some particular examples of industrial variability, largely drawn from materials from the excavations of Professor François Bordes at the sites of Combe-Grenal and Pech de l'Azé I, II, and IV. The Combe-Grenal sequence is viewed as particularly important since it comprises the most detailed stratigraphic succession of Mousterian described in Western Europe. Some aspects of the nature and uses of typologies are incorporated in this section. The final section includes some general comments on the nature and extent of Middle Paleolithic industrial variability as seen through present evidence and knowledge.

AN INTERPRETATION OF THE DEVELOPMENT OF THE PROBLEM

The discovery of patterning in the relative frequencies of distinctive chipped stone implements in the Mousterian of southwestern France by Bordes and Bourgon (Bordes 1957) marked the beginning of a new phase of research in Paleolithic archaeology. In retrospect we can see that this discovery resulted from the application of a sequence of procedures that are customarily followed in the scientific ('objective') study of observable phenomena. This sequence, which begins with the isolation of a phenomenon, follows a progression of description, classification, and analysis of variability, and concludes with a synthesis. It allows the practitioners of science to formulate explanatory hypotheses about isolable phenomena in a context of investigation in which replicability of methods and results is possible.

The isolation of the Mousterian as a phenomenon was accomplished in the mid-19th century, and the description of implements and assemblages was a characteristic feature of the archaeological literature through the first half of the 20th century. Classification during this period was normally confined to the segregation of general classes of retouched tools. The comparison of collections and definition of distinctive assemblages or industries was based on relative (but not quantified) abundance or scarcity of artifact classes and the presence or absence of particular kinds of tools (e.g., *racloirs* [scrapers], points, bifaces). The revolutionary nature of Bordes and Bourgon's contribution lay in the formulation of a detailed classification (typology) of distinct formal categories of artifacts ('tool types') and of features that reflected techniques of production of flakes and cores. The data derived through the use of this classification were then analyzed with quantitative comparisons of relative frequencies of types in the collections available to them. The explicit exposition of the typology that resulted from their classification (Bordes 1961b) made possible the same kinds of quantitative comparisons of collections by other workers.

The several repeated patterns of assemblage composition that were revealed by the application of this technique to collections of Mousterian artifacts by Bordes and Bourgon have served as a focus for research on the Middle Paleolithic in Europe and Western Asia for more than 30 years. The explanation of these patterns continues to be a dominant theme in most synthetic studies of the Mousterian in this region. The initial interpretation of these patterns by Bordes (1961a) saw them as reflecting distinct sociocultural groups, each with its own preferences for the manufacture of the range of tools necessary for survival. Implicit in this hypothesis is the idea that the Mousterian industrial variability is 'stylistic' (Sackett 1973, 1982, 1986; Jelinek 1976) and that aspects of ethnic awareness and identification associated with the presence of stylistic differentiation among modern *Homo sapiens* were present among the Neandertals who produced these Middle Paleolithic artifacts.

Bordes's interpretation was questioned by L. R. and S. R. Binford (1966), who used a multivariate (factor) analysis of collections from Jabrud I and Shubbabiq in the Levant and a single sample from Houpeville in northern France in an attempt to demonstrate that the industrial differences in the Mousterian were the result of differences in activities carried out at different times by peoples sharing a uniform technology. While the particular study is of questionable value for the interpretation of the Western European Mousterian and of Mousterian variability in general,[1] the idea behind it represents a fundamental alternative to a stylistic explanation of variability.

Another alternative interpretation, also suggested relatively early on, was proposed by Mellars (1969), who saw some repeated patterns of chronological succession of Mousterian industries in stratified sites in southwestern France. In particular, he pointed out evidence for a succession in Würm II from Ferrassie to Quina to Mousterian of Acheulian Tradition (MTA). On the basis of faunal associations with MTA and Quina industries he proposed that the regional habitat was different during these two kinds of occupations, with colder conditions in association with Quina levels (1969: 145). Mellars saw the Ferrassie-Quina-MTA sequence as an evolution within the Mousterian but did not address the causal factors behind these changes. He saw the Denticulate and Typical industries as less clearly related to these time changes and suggested that some aspects of these industries might be the result of " 'functional' mechanisms" (1969: 163).

Additional criticisms and defenses of each of these three interpretations of industrial variability have been presented (e.g., Binford 1973, 1983c: 226-227, 432; Bordes 1973, 1978), but they do not represent substantial changes of views (with the possible exception of the most recent reference by Binford, which states that at that time he believed that "our methods of inference are thus far inadequate" to treat the question [1983c: 432]).

Eventually, a new and stimulating approach to the problem was taken by Rolland (1977, 1981). He proposed, after a study of collections from more than 120 separate contexts, that a primary factor contributing to Mousterian industrial variability was the relative intensity of reduction of lithic raw materials. He saw a number of causal factors as likely contributors to reduction intensity, including quality and availability of raw materials and climatic conditions. He discovered a strong relationship between the relative frequency of *racloirs* and the relative frequency of all retouched tools and a continuous unimodal distribution for the latter category. He interpreted this as evidence favoring a single (as opposed to multiple) cultural phenomenon. His use of metric variability added a qualitatively new dimension to the study and suggested that size of flakes might have been a consideration that determined whether *racloirs* or denticulates were manufactured. His suggestion that rigorous climatic conditions coincided with periods of intensive reduction (Quina industries) introduced a possible causal factor for some of the sequential variation observed by Mellars.

More recently, several studies complementary to Rolland's interpretations have been carried out by Dibble (1984a, 1985a, 1987c). Dibble's work has focused on progressive modification in the manufacture of stone implements (primarily *racloirs* and points) and on the influences of raw-material variability on flake *production*. On the basis of experimental work and the examination of collections from Western Europe and the Levant, he has shown that through repeated reflaking of one or more scraper edges a single flake will successively acquire the form of a series of the different *racloirs* in the typology. He sees two basic alternatives in this succession, probably largely dependent on the initial character of the flake. In one (longer flakes with sharp lateral edges), first one and then both lateral edges are retouched, forming a *racloir double*, and ultimately meet to form a *racloir convergent*. In the other alternative, when shorter flakes are retouched on one lateral edge, the progress of reduction results in a scraper edge that first is oblique to the axis of flaking and ultimately is transverse. Virtually all *racloirs, limaces* (bi-convergent double convex *racloirs*), and probably points as well, separated in the typology can be accounted for by the different stages of reduction in these two models.

Dibble's work is a demonstration of the relevance here of the *Frison effect* (Jelinek 1976), recognized by Rolland as a potential contributor to Mousterian industrial variability (1981: 25). In order to understand the principle of this effect it is necessary to understand that the products of flaked stone technology are fundamentally different from the tools of a modern industrial technology. Each of the flaked stone products is both an object with a particular form suitable for a specific range of tasks, and a piece of raw material whose shape can be easily altered for continuing use for similar or different tasks. If this interpretation is followed, the archaeological record of the Mousterian can be seen as largely composed of associations of lithic materials at various stages in a potentially prolonged sequence of reduction. If this view is correct, one basic question that we should be addressing is why in each instance the reduction was carried to the particular point at which the object was abandoned. One fundamental implication of this approach to the interpretation of the Mousterian record is that it is unlikely that a knapper ever consciously decided to make a transverse convex demi-Quina *racloir* or any of the other extreme end points of sequential reduction, but rather that these forms resulted from the repeated resharpening of the edges of relatively few kinds of implements as they were conceived by their makers.

Thus, while Rolland's study implies that the detailed classification of *racloirs* in Bordes's typology is redundant for purposes of separation of the major groups of Mousterian, Dibble's work provides an explanatory mechanism for most of the patterns observed by Rolland. But while the relative degree of reduction of raw material does appear to be a basic underlying factor contributing to Mousterian industrial variability, it seems not to be the *only* factor. If this were so, we would expect a relatively smooth continuum in the typological composition of the Mousterian collections. Now Rolland has convincingly demonstrated that there are aspects of tool manufacture in the group of 120 collections that he examined that do show continuity (i.e., implement frequencies [Rolland 1981: 23, fig. 2] and *racloir* frequencies [Rolland 1981: 25, fig. 4]). While there does appear to be a strong relationship between the relative frequencies of *racloirs* and all implements, there is no similar relationship between all implements and the other major Mousterian tool category, denticulates and notches (Rolland 1977: 252, fig. 2). What this means is that as more and more flakes were retouched into implements (reduced), a predictable number of those reduction products were *racloirs*, while the number of denticulates and notches produced bore no relationship to the overall amount of reduction taking place. This may illustrate the limits of the utility of the concept of relative raw-material reduction as an explanation of Mousterian industrial variability. It seems to be a relatively powerful tool for the explanation of differences between Typical, Charentian (Quina, Ferrassie), and MTA-A industries, but does not contribute to an explanation of the differences between these industries and MTA-B and Denticulate.[2]

SOME PARTICULAR EXAMPLES OF MOUSTERIAN INDUSTRIAL VARIABILITY

As can be seen in the foregoing discussion, the question of Denticulate Mousterian is one that is of primary concern in the Western European industries. Industries with high frequencies of denticulates appear to be almost absent in Southwest Asia, prominent exceptions being Levels 5 and 9 at Jabrud I, which were classified as Denticulate by Bordes (1955), and the recently reported open site of Far'ah II in the northern Negev of Israel (Gilead and Grigson 1984). The opposition of industries dominated by denticulates to those dominated by *racloirs* in southwest France is well illustrated by samples from the excavations of

Bordes at Combe-Grenal. This site is of particular importance in the study of industrial variability because it comprises the best excavated sample of a long sequence of Middle Paleolithic occupation in Europe. The advantages of such a site are that geographical factors, such as distance to water and lithic raw materials, can be viewed as constant in relation to other variables, such as climatic and industrial differences.

At Combe-Grenal the relationship between absolute frequencies of *racloirs* and denticulates in 31 Early Würm levels clearly illustrates the dichotomy that existed in tool discard at the site (Fig. 11.1). This obvious preference for one implement category or the other does not seem amenable to explanation by distance to raw materials (since this was constant), environmental factors (which vary from cool and humid to cold and dry in Denticulate levels and even more widely in other levels), or size of habitation area (which is comparable in Denticulate and other levels).

Faunal associations at Combe-Grenal, as an indication of possible preferential resource exploitation, do show Denticulate as the only industry associated with high relative frequencies of bones of *Equus* (as was suggested in a general sense by Bordes on several occasions [e.g., Bordes and de Sonneville-Bordes 1970: 71; Bordes 1972: 144]), but this association accounts for only three of the seven Denticulate levels in which sufficient faunal remains were present for a comparison. As is illustrated in Figure 11.2, the remaining four levels include virtually every relative combination of faunal elements present in the site (data from Chase 1983). The findings of Chase, based

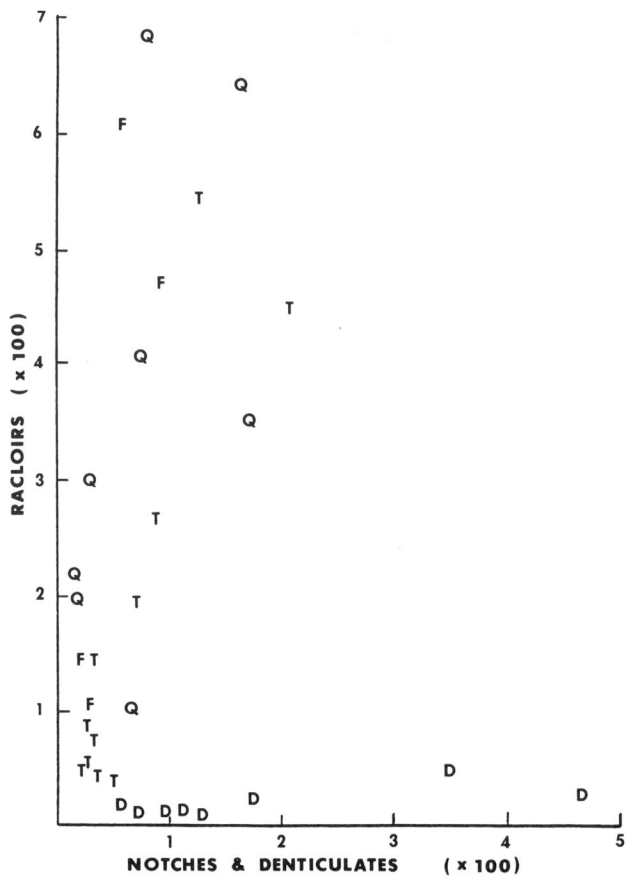

Figure 11.1 *Relationship between absolute frequencies of all* racloirs *and absolute frequencies of denticulates and notches in 31 samples from Combe-Grenal (levels included shown in Fig. 11.5). Industrial designations: D = Denticulate, F = Ferrassie, Q = Quina, T = Typical.*

on a detailed examination of the faunal remains, are significant here; he sees no strong evidence of differences corresponding to industry in the exploitation and processing of animal resources through the sequence at the site, with the exception of the most rigorous climatic conditions, which are primarily associated with Quina industries (1986: 57).

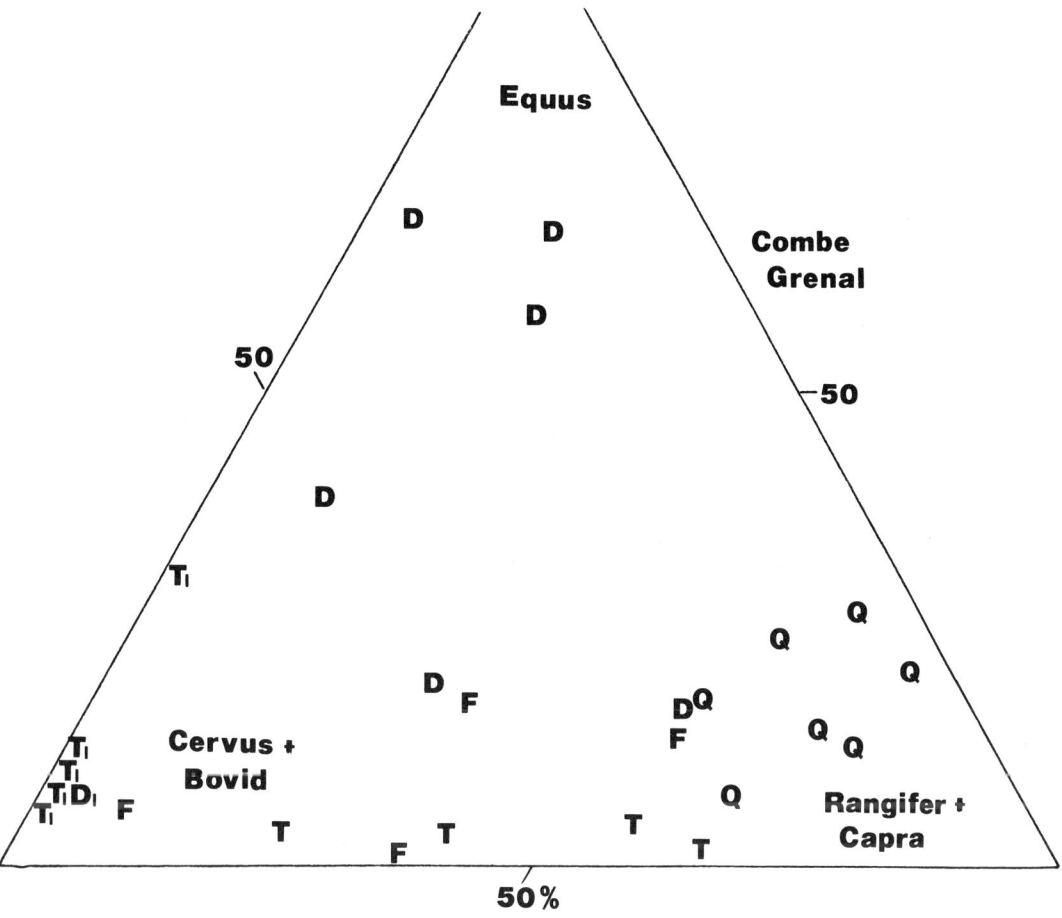

Figure 11.2 *Triangular coordinate diagram showing the relative frequencies of bones of large herbivores in 27 samples from Combe-Grenal. Industrial designations as in Figure 11.1. T1 and D1 designations refer to Würm I levels.*

ALTERNATIVE TYPOLOGICAL VIEWS OF THE MOUSTERIAN

Since the most obvious kinds of variability that can be controlled at Combe-Grenal do not appear to bear any relationship to the occurrence of Denticulate industries at the site, a useful alternative approach might be to re-examine the typological components of the industry based on technological attributes of manufacture to seek more fundamental aspects of behavior that could show relationships to the other Mousterian industries. The rationale for such an examination lies in the nature and purpose of typologies as tools in the scientific processes mentioned at the beginning of this paper. Typologies are products of classification in which materials (or other observed data) with common properties (attributes) are grouped together as 'types'. This kind of ordering makes it possible to formulate generalizations relating to the phenomenon from which the classification is drawn, and from these generalizations to proceed to analytical examination and synthetic statements about the phenomenon. Typological classifications are not normally created in a vacuum; rather the attributes chosen are those that appear relevant in terms of their probable relationship to unanswered questions pertaining to the phenomenon under examination. An ideal typology is one in which the type categories are mutually exclusive (unambiguous); such a typology is derived by treating qualitatively different kinds of variability in separate classifications. Implicit in the foregoing discussion is the fact that no single typology is adequate to treat all of the problems relating to any phenomenon. Relevant typologies must be constructed to address each problem; in ideal circumstances alternative typologies will be constructed to establish which attributes are most useful in answering those questions about the phenomenon that are being addressed.

The typology constructed by Bordes and Bourgon was designed to discover relationships between stratigraphically associated groups of Mousterian artifacts. It sought the maximum meaningful number of categories of attribute association for an exploration of possible patterns in the data. The confidence in each of the attribute associations in the typology was based on the extensive familiarity of Bordes and Bourgon with Middle Paleolithic artifacts from their excavations and in museum collections. This knowledge resulted in an intuitive awareness of artifact variability that was formally coded into the typology. Nobody familiar with Mousterian industries would challenge the repeated occurrence in those industries of any of the morphological categories included in the typology; this in itself is a tribute to the knowledge and awareness of the formulators of a typology that has been in extensive use for more than 30 years. That the typology has admirably served its initial purpose is abundantly illustrated by the fact that a major focus of attention in the discipline is the explanation of those patterns that were exposed through its use. Now a logical continuing step is the examination of the attributes in the typology that appear most relevant to the patterns of variability exposed in the industries, and the re-examination of those industrial assemblages in the light of alternative classifications based on that knowledge.

It is in fact this kind of alternative classification that has already been applied by Rolland in his examination of the Mousterian (1977). He lumped all of the categories with the attribute of "*racloir*-ness" into a single category of "*racloirs*" and demonstrated a meaningful relationship between the relative frequency of this 'type' of artifact and the relative frequency of all retouched pieces to unretouched pieces.

A slightly more detailed alternative approach to restructuring the formal attributes implicit in the Bordes typology can be taken by following Rolland's suggestion that intensity of raw-material utilization plays an important role in determining industrial variability in the Mousterian. The retouched flake tools in the type-list can be roughly classified into four categories on the basis of the intensity of flaking that they exhibit.[3] The relationships of relative frequencies of tools in these categories for industries from Combe-Grenal, Pech de l'Azé I, II, and IV, and Corbiac are shown in a triangular coordinate diagram in Figure 11.3 (the two simplest categories of retouch are combined here). The diagram indicates a polarity between Charentian industries and Denticulate which conforms to the findings of Rolland in the discussions above (and for many of the same reasons since *racloirs* and notches/denticulates are the most numerous contributors to Category 3+4 and Category 1 respectively). One advantage of the diagram beyond Rolland's presentation is that it demonstrates the relationships of all of the industries based on an estimate of reduction intensity and shows some segregation of each kind of Mousterian (i.e., none occurs across the entire distribution). The widest scatter is shown by Typical industries, which are to a large extent characterized typologically by the absence of elements distinctive to the other variants and the presence of elements shared to some extent by all variants. Here a question of sample sizes and nature of occupations may be relevant but has not been explored.

One interesting feature of this arrangement becomes apparent when an additional category of artifactual evidence in the form of frequency of bifaces is considered. Figure 11.4 shows a superposition of these data (relative frequency of bifaces in the sum of retouched flake and core tools) on the arrangement based on retouch intensity. An interesting conclusion that can be drawn from this diagram is that the relative frequencies of retouch intensity are also

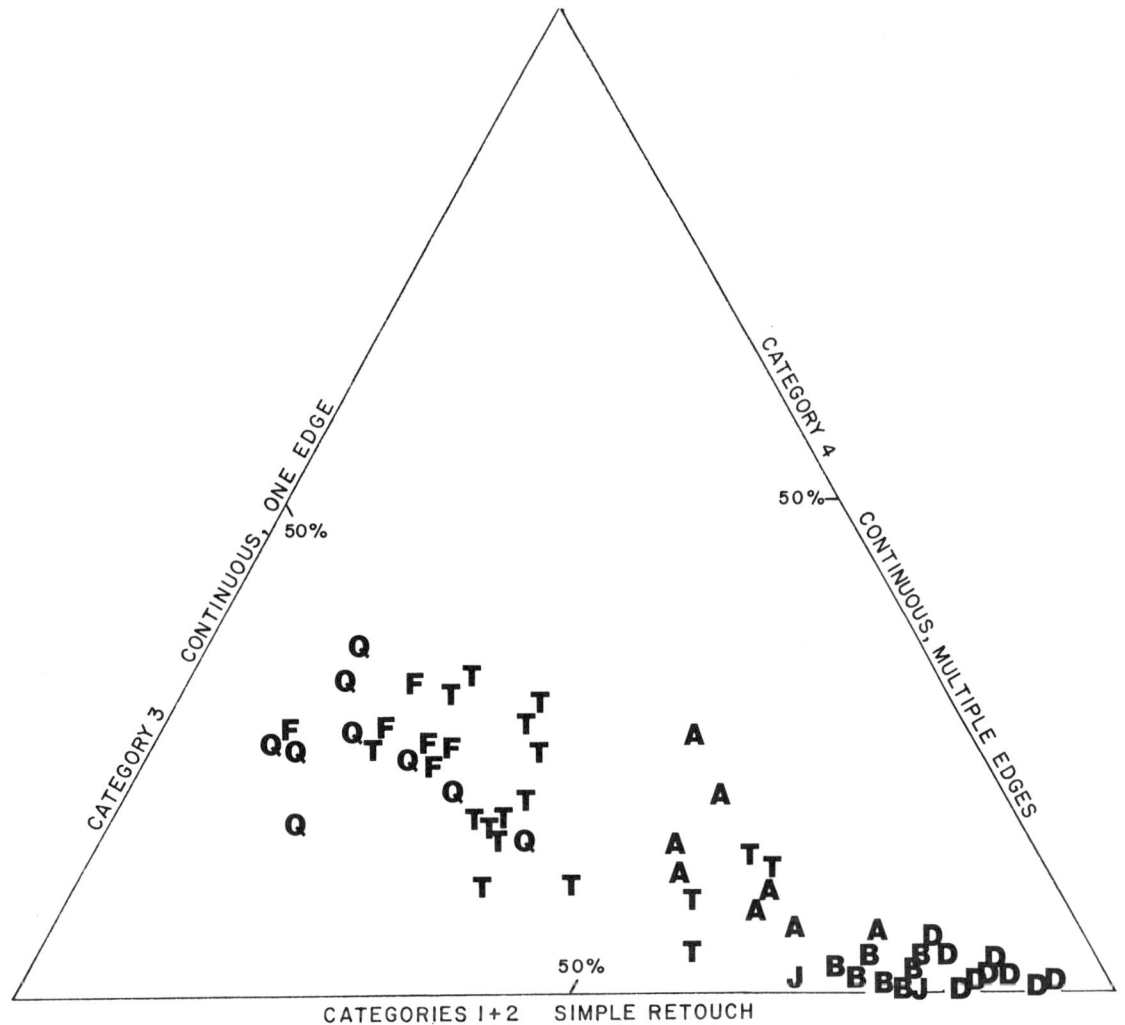

Figure 11.3 Triangular coordinate diagram showing the relative frequencies of three categories of reduction intensity on retouched tools from Combe-Grenal, Pech de l'Azé I, II, and IV, and Corbiac (Mousterian levels). Industrial designations of D, F, Q, and T as in Figure 11.1; A = MTA-A, B = MTA-B, J = Asinipodian.

strong predictors of biface manufacture, an activity that would not otherwise be expected to be associated with particular patterns of flake-tool manufacture. That is, one can say with a considerable degree of confidence that if particular ratios of these reduction categories are present in a collection from this part of the Perigord, bifaces will also be present. An alternative way of interpreting this information is that, aside from the presence of bifaces, MTA industries have a distinctive typological composition that is shared with only a few Typical industries and the enigmatic Asinipodian. This, then, is another dimension in which attributes logically associated with intensity of raw-material exploitation appear to have strong explanatory power in addressing the problem of Mousterian industrial variability, including some relevance for the Denticulate industries.

I would like to include one more example in this discussion of the application of alternate typological categories to the interpretation of industrial variability at Combe-Grenal before turning to a more general discussion of these problems. This example is

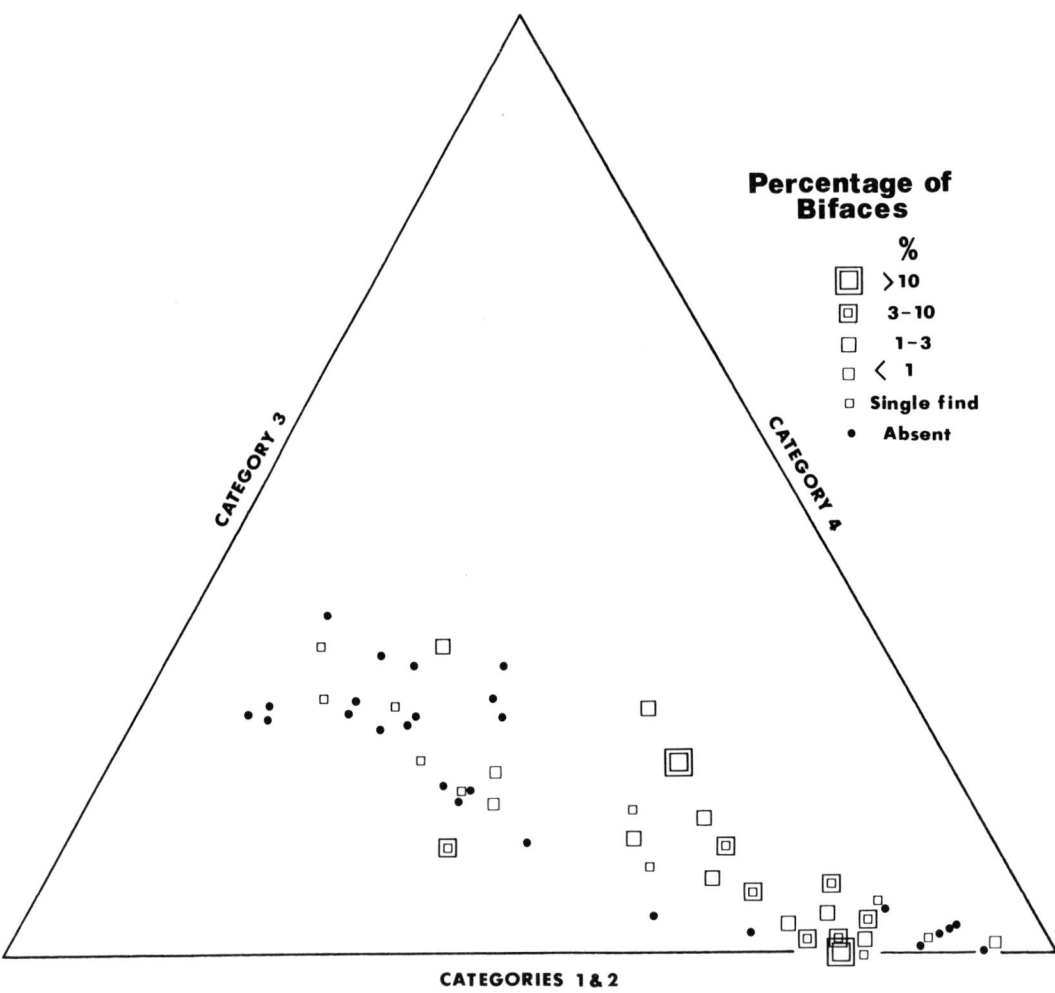

Figure 11.4 Triangular coordinate diagram showing relative frequencies of bifaces as a percentage of all retouched core and flake tools superimposed on distribution of samples in Figure 11.3.

concerned with the nature of changes in the frequency of several major categories of artifacts that are suggested as relevant to this problem by the work of Rolland and Dibble. Here I have separated (A) simple lateral *racloirs*, (B) all other *racloirs*, (C) notches and denticulates, (D) other retouched tools, and (E) utilized flakes, as major typological categories. This information is presented for 31 levels at Combe-Grenal in Figure 11.5, along with the relative frequency of Levallois flaking and a summary of environmental conditions as indicated by paleoclimatic data. The information from the Würm I deposits is relatively scattered, with many discontinuities in cultural occupation. It appears that the site was used relatively infrequently during this period. The Würm II deposits, however, show considerably more continuity in occupation and it is this continuity that is of interest here. It is clear that through virtually all of this sequence, when continuity of occupations is present the changes from one level to the next are gradual rather than abrupt. The frequencies of the predominant artifact categories (and Levallois technique) shift slowly within industries and across industrial boundaries. The single exception is the Denticulate industry of Level 20, which does appear and disappear abruptly. Its appearance is unaccompanied by any strong evidence of environmental change, while its disappearance corresponds to a shift to

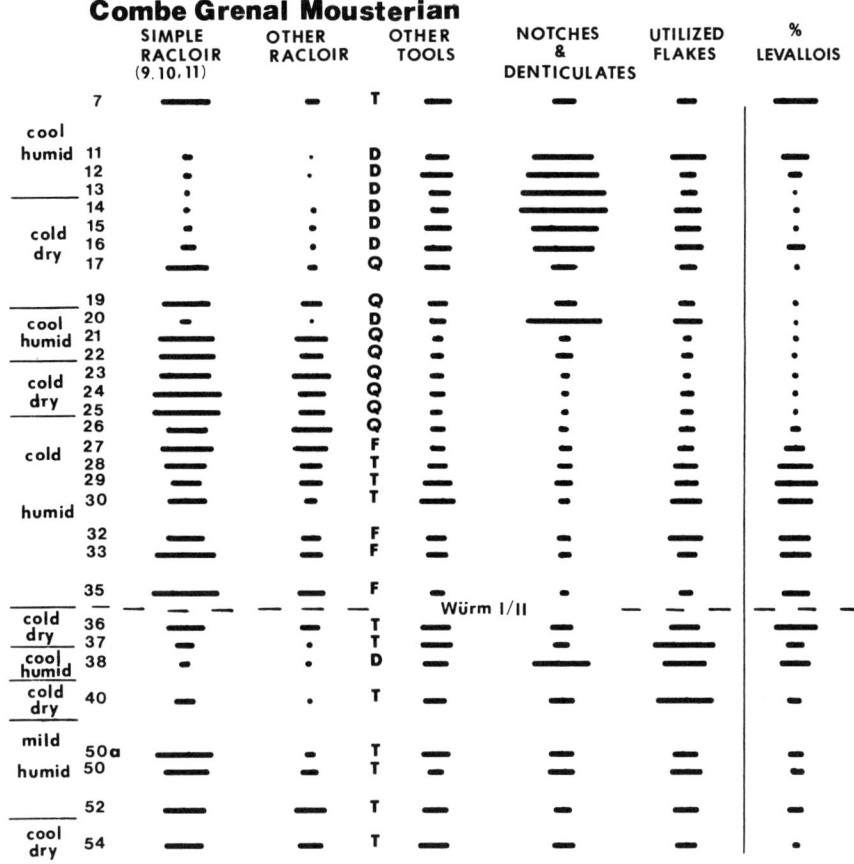

Figure 11.5 Ratios (%) of major retouched tool classes and utilized flakes and ratios of Levallois among all flakes in 31 samples of Mousterian industries from Combe-Grenal. Industrial designations as in Figure 11.1.

colder, drier conditions (during which several succeeding Denticulate layers are found later in the sequence). It appears to me that the overall evidence strongly favors cultural continuity in the occupation of the site and thus a single cultural tradition with shifting emphases in tool manufacture through time.

The one exception here is that of the Denticulate Mousterian of Level 20, but the trends shown in Levels 17 through 11 strongly suggest that under other circumstances Denticulate industries can be demonstrated to be a part of this continuum.

SOME GENERAL OBSERVATIONS ON THE CURRENT STATUS OF THE QUESTION OF MOUSTERIAN INDUSTRIAL VARIABILITY

The most obvious feature of Mousterian industrial variability is that it is clearly a complex phenomenon for which there is no single causal explanation. None of the explanations that have been suggested can be shown to account for all of the variability encountered, nor, conversely, can any be definitely ruled out as a contributing factor.

It is likely that Mousterian social groups were composed of relatively small and mobile populations of highly adaptable individuals. Some of them managed to survive for at least 80,000 years in Western Europe in environmental circumstances that varied from conditions little different from the present to a near permafrost tundra. In order to accomplish this they employed a combination of biological, technological, and social adaptations that were significantly different from those of present-day hunter-gatherers. Our major challenge as archaeologists is the reconstruction of the *paleocultural* patterns (Jelinek 1977) that were employed by those last fossil hominids. The kind of patterning that characterizes Mousterian industries provides us with some of our best clues relating to the nature of Mousterian paleoculture. An outstanding feature of this cultural evidence is the apparent lack of innovation and recombination of ideas into new inventions and techniques; concomitant with this is a general lack of evidence of complex tools. Thus we tend to see the adaptations of the Mousterians as stable and dependable ways of deriving nutrition and shelter from a wide variety of habitats.

Most of our evidence of Mousterian industries, and virtually all of our evidence of sequences of industries, is derived from the depositional contexts of rockshelters and cave entrances. This means that one major question that we will need to answer before we can place these materials in a full cultural perspective relates to the circumstances under which these relatively unusual and special habitats were occupied. There is good reason to believe, on the basis of the location of campsites of modern hunter-gatherers living in regions in which caves and rockshelters are present, that these may not have been seen as particularly desirable locales. That this may have been true in Middle Paleolithic Europe is perhaps attested by the fact that the industries found in shelters that exhibit the most extreme phases of reduction (Quina), and therefore may generally reflect most intensive habitation, are associated with the most rigorous climatic conditions. That is, the shelters were most intensively used when open sites were untenable.

While this may be a reasonable explanation for the presence of Quina occupations in many sites, it seems unlikely that it is the only explanation for the presence of Quina industries. At the eponymous site of La Quina this industry is associated with great quantities of bones of large herbivores, the size and composition of which suggest that a considerable amount of primary butchering of animals driven or frightened off of the cliff above the site was taking place during the deposition of those levels (Jelinek, Debénath, and Dibble 1986). In this instance it seems likely that the intensive reduction of raw materials was a result of prolonged use of tools in circumstances favorable for the butchering of numbers of large animals where it was inconvenient to go off to procure fresh raw material. If we assume, as can be proposed from the studies of Rolland and Dibble, that the number of different kinds of implements recognized by the Mousterians was mainly limited to a few categories of *racloirs*, denticulates and notches, bifaces, and opportunistic sharp flakes, it is likely that the *racloirs*, for instance, served a number of purposes from butchering to hide preparation and may be found in heavily reduced form as a result of a variety of circumstances.

In addition to the problems that we can see in the Western European Middle Paleolithic, as we venture further afield we confront qualitatively different situations whose interpretation in part is compatible with the knowledge derived from the French Mousterian and in part appears to belong to a different world. In the Zagros-Taurus area, where suitable raw material is relatively rare, intensity of utilization in virtually all circumstances appears to be the reason for a uniform industry characterized by high frequencies of retouched tools, most of which represent the final stages of possible reduction (Dibble 1984a, b). In the Levant we are confronted with the need to explain the sudden appearance of a predominance of Levallois flaking in the industries in shelters, when the technique has apparently been known in the region for hundreds of thousands of years. The explanation for the appearance and disappearance of an emphasis on prismatic-blade manufacture and the resultant production of quantities of tools identical to those of the Upper Paleolithic in the Amudian and Pre-Aurignacian industries, perhaps 70-80,000 years ago, is a problem that we do not appear to be any closer to resolving now than at the time that these enigmatic industries were first isolated, over 50 years ago.

In the Levant the opposition in tool manufacture in the early Middle Paleolithic seems to be between *racloirs* and bifaces (which are present in much higher frequencies than in the French Middle Paleolithic). The cyclical nature of the ratio of bifaces to *racloirs* at Tabun suggests a relationship to resources that shifted in response to global patterns of climatic change (Jelinek 1982b), but this hypothesis has yet to be confirmed with environmental evidence from the site. It is tempting to see the same level of time scale for the gradual changes in the major tool categories at Combe-Grenal, but here it is already clear from the detailed environmental studies that no strong overall environmental associations lie behind most of the relationships between *racloirs* and denticulates.

In all of the Mousterian shelter sites, no matter how abundant the cultural evidence, it is certain that we are dealing with immense intervals of time (sufficient in the deeper sites to account for several thousand generations of Mousterians). As we look at the small samples of lithic material retrieved from these atypical habitats and extrapolate to the total amount of material that they may have contained, in relation to the intervals of time over which the deposits were accumulated, and to tool production in other habitats, we can begin to form an idea of the tiny biased fraction of the probable total of technological production upon which we have based our studies. The amazing thing, in view of these extreme limitations, is the relatively clear patterning that is present through the whole Middle Paleolithic sequence. It is cause for hope that the very limited methodical persistence of the Mousterians that is reflected in these patterns will eventually provide the key to a better understanding of their world.

Thus, within the theme of the title of this paper, our present evidence increasingly favors a dominance of routine technological sequences of reduction as a basic factor in the production of the multiple morphological categories that we as modern *Homo sapiens sapiens* can distinguish as products of the Mousterian paleocultural industries. There is some intriguing suggestion of increasing specialization and complexity in the early Late Pleistocene record that may in fact anticipate the more complex patterns of industrial differentiation and fully cultural behavior that are apparent in the Upper Paleolithic, but this remains to be demonstrated.

As we become increasingly aware of the limits and variety of the world inhabited by the Mousterians, we should be better able to isolate the different variables that influenced those restricted aspects of their behavior that are left to us in the archaeological record. It is only when we can isolate *and control for* these different kinds of variability that we can begin to distinguish between the dependent and independent variables that lie at the heart of an explanation of the differences in the Mousterian industries. We have made considerable progress toward an awareness of the complexity of this problem since it was first brought to our attention by François Bordes. Our best opportunity for further progress lies in the open sharing of information and ideas that were such a remarkable feature of his approach to prehistory.

ACKNOWLEDGMENTS

No paper on this topic can result from an individual's working in isolation. I am particularly indebted to my colleagues Harold L. Dibble, Philip G. Chase, Donald A. Graybill, and Gary O. Rollefson for many discussions and exchanges of ideas. We have had so much contact over the years that I think that it would be impossible to trace the origins of many of the ideas expressed in our papers, nor do I think this is particularly important as long as the ideas are useful and stimulating. My deepest debt, however, is to my late friend and colleague, François Bordes, who introduced me to these problems and whose generosity with his materials has made possible some of the small analyses presented in this paper. I am deeply grateful to him and to his heirs for permission to use these data.

NOTES

1. All of the samples in the study but one are drawn from collections from the Levant, where, despite the application of similar labels, the nature of variability is fundamentally different from that encountered in Western Europe. The inferences of function of particular tool types are frequently highly questionable, which brings the Binfords' particular interpretations of the factors isolated into question. The inclusion of unretouched flakes as variables is highly questionable since recovery techniques for these kinds of artifacts at Jabrud I and Shubbabiq were clearly not comparable. Most important, the statistical results of the factor analysis are virtually worthless since one basic condition for such a test is clearly violated in that the number of variables used (40) far exceeds the number of cases (17). This is a classic example of the "garbage in—garbage out" that results from a "cookbook" employment of multivariate statistics.

2. It seems to me that the results of Rolland's studies make a stronger case for the separation of Denticulate and MTA-B on the one hand and the MTA-A, Charentian, and Typical on the other than does his split between Charentian and 'Le Moustier' industries based on what appears to me to be an arbitrary division in total implement frequencies (Rolland 1977: 251, fig. 1). The reliability of this relative frequency of implements (retouched tools) to total artifacts is heavily dependent on uniform recovery techniques (e.g., sieving vs. not sieving, uniform size of unretouched flakes retained and counted, etc.). If, in addition, it is more likely that smaller unretouched flakes

will be overlooked when implements are relatively abundant, then the differences in these ratios between the Charentian and the other industries might be somewhat exaggerated.
3. Category 1—Retouch by one or a few blows: Types 32, 33, 42, 43, 44, 52, 53, 54. Category 2—Retouch limited to short or discontinuous edges: Types 4, 34, 35, 37, 39, 40, 41, 57, 58. Category 3—Extensive continuous retouch on one edge: Types 9-11, 22-25, 30, 31, 36, 55. Category 4—Extensive continuous retouch on multiple edges: Types 6-8, 12-21, 26-29, 60, 63.

DISCUSSION

SACKETT: Regarding paleoculture, the modern view of hominid evolution is as a series of ecological niches, most of which no longer exist. The earlier ecological niches are not only different ways of behaving, or different levels of organization, or different kinds of culture, but also different biologies. But we have some ecological niches which are not, the Neolithic being an example. No one in this room would argue that the people who made a Neolithic way of life were any less human than the Magdalenian. In other words, we are not assuming a one-to-one equation between biology and culture in this sense. Yet once you go back into the Middle Paleolithic, you are. Neandertals do show evidence of symbolic behavior and even an aesthetic sense. They just do not express it in the instrumental form that Upper Paleolithic people did.

CHASE: Dibble and I have reviewed the evidence for symbolic behavior in the Middle Paleolithic with negative conclusions. A lot of the reported cases cannot be defended or they rest on unsupported linkages, for example, between burials and religion or aesthetics and symbolism.

MARKS: But in the Near East, for instance, there is no evidence for any kind of symbolic representation until the Natufian, at about 10,000 B.P.

ROLLAND: Another important dimension of variability is in terms of spatial or geographic variability. We certainly see some regionalism of certain technological elements, going from the North African stemmed tools in the Aterian, flake cleavers in the Iberian Peninsula on both sides of the Pyrenees during the early Würm, the distribution of the Mousterian of Acheulian Tradition near the Atlantic and northwest Germany, and the leaf-point industries of Germany, Hungary, Bulgaria, etc. So, granted that there are qualitative or quantitative features which seem to fall, either by their sheer simplicity and relative monotony, outside the range of material expressions of cultures. But because of this regionalism, I would call them paleocultures in the sense defined by Taylor or Childe, for example.

MÜLLER-BECK: Given the complex regionalism that occurs throughout Western, Central, and Eastern Europe, it is clearly more than just functional differentiations.

BOSINSKI: These other Mousterian groups outside Western Europe are often neglected since the focus is so much on Bordes's defined groups.

STRAUS: Regarding the Mousterian of northern Spain, I think that it is a raw-material difference, and so I would be very reluctant to conclude that it is necessarily a paleocultural regional difference.

ROLLAND: Regarding reduction, what we see is a degree of transformation of unretouched flakes which may have been tools originally, and this is the kind of variation described by Jelinek. Based on my own work it is clear that Levallois pieces were often selected and preferential, but not always. The Quina Mousterian is different, where they produced very large blanks which were then reduced.

SACKETT: I do not agree with the association of style with ethnic awareness and identification, i.e., where style has to be something which is purposely invested by artisans in order to carry social information of some kind.

Second, regarding reduction sequences, it seems that there is an underlying argument of you and Dibble that, since we are talking about mechanical contingencies of lithic manufacture, the artisan himself was somewhat unaware of the consequences of his knapping. But I do believe that artisans were aware of the consequences of their actions, and just talking about the reduction sequence doesn't tell us the motivation to the artisan. In this regard, then, we have to be careful about drawing typological consequences based upon what we think may have been the intentions of the artisan.

JELINEK: During a sequence of reduction of a piece, I do not think that a Neandertal thought ahead to that final end point prior to discard of it. I think that there was a discrimination in terms of the kinds of blanks used for particular purposes, but it is a chicken-and-egg question to try to determine their intentions. For example, in the Quina Mousterian of Combe-Grenal, there are a number of short wide flakes that were unretouched. Now, do we see these short wide flakes as the last manifestation of the kinds of flakes that were not picked up and used by Quina Mousterians—i.e., that they used all of the longer flakes until only these things were left? Or were they deliberately making a lot of short wide flakes because they were better for those transverse thick scrapers? We do not know. The only way to investigate it is to go back and examine technological attributes of flakes so that we can see whether the flakes on which they were making scrapers are likely to have been short wide flakes originally. I agree with you that motivation is a questionable thing, but we do see some basic patterns of manufacture of flakes that was probably intentional, which had to do with the kinds of edges they wanted, which would result in a complete or an intensive sequence of reduction, and which would result in particular end products that were different.

SACKETT: Of which they were aware.

JELINEK: Yes. I think they were aware, but it is a complex problem. It has to do with the kind of raw material that was present, with the kind of flakes they could make on that raw material, with their tradition of extracting flakes—this is really a predeterminant of what the industry is going to look like. I think Dibble's research is probably crucial there, in that without making particular kinds of flakes, they could not make particular kinds of scrapers. So this technological aspect underlies that.

Regarding Paleoculture, I agree with Trinkaus that the profound nature of the differences in the Neandertal skeleton, and the kinds of activities with which they were coping, implies that the Neandertals were behaving in fundamentally different ways. There was much more intercession of physical strength for things that were later compensated for by technology. For example, I think the lack of appreciation of worked bone as a resource throughout the Mousterian is fundamental. And I do not think that there was a very elaborate woodworking industry in the Mousterian either, in spite of the microwear evidence. I do think there is more to the kind of symbolic behavior we see in the UP than in the Mousterian. I have, in fact, remarked that we do not know why the Mousterians were burying their dead. I don't think that there are any very strong instances of association of goods with the deceased.

SACKETT: You could also compare Çatal Hüyük with UP and make the same kind of argument.

JELINEK: No, I don't think so. The case of Teshik-Tash is a good example. First, whether or not there was a circle of goat-horn cores surrounding the burial is questionable. But second, if they did dig a hole, why not use a piece of those ubiquitous goat skulls that have those nice horn cores on them, to scoop out the hole? After you are done, you push the kid in, you push dirt over him, and you throw the horn cores on top.

MARKS: Why do you dig the hole?

JELINEK: Good question. We do not know why they buried the dead, whether it was a question of some feeling of afterlife (which has yet to be demonstrated), or whether it was because they smelled bad and they didn't want to just throw them down the slope, so they covered them up.

I think the monotony of those industries, by itself, and their very general patterns of distribution, are the important points. This is not what happens in the next stage of development with modern *Homo sapiens*. It is something that we have to test with the very narrow line of evidence of the material that is left, primarily stone tools—which is like trying to interpret what is going on in the kitchen by looking at the cutlery.

MARKS: The question of whether the Mousterian was complicated or not depends on how you look at it. Many of the papers here, and my work as well, tend to make observations that are tied to mechanical properties of flint and basic reduction sequences that give one few options. If we looked at the Upper Paleolithic this way, we might not see quite so much difference from the Mousterian.

SCHRIRE: I am disturbed that an explanation for why Neandertals might not have the same capacities as later people is that they were very robust. It struck me that this kind of thinking was the basis of the slave trade.

JELINEK: I think there is a problem in terms of our present social context, whenever it is said that one people or another is or was different. This calls up certain emotions on the part of many of us because we know of injustices, both past and current, that are based on such a fallacious reason. All I can do is try to formulate some context in which to put all of the evidence that I see on the basis of my own experience and my colleagues' experiences, into a framework that accounts for as much of the difference that we can see between ourselves and these last fossil hominids. The weight of evidence, it seems to me, suggests that there is a serious difference. However, it is not a simple difference. For example, these people were not morons—they could not have survived in periglacial Europe if they were.

MANN: I would like to point out that some of the skeletal materials associated with Eastern European Upper Paleolithic are pretty robust as well. There is a complex situation going on biologically, which may not be associated in a simple way with the change in culture.

STRAUS: Jelinek has counted the number of removals it takes to produce a given tool, but it seems to me that the edges involved are functionally very different. Perhaps a denticulate is simpler and quicker to make, but you cannot do the same range of things with that kind of edge that you can with a convex scraper, for example.

JELINEK: You are absolutely right. I think the Neandertals thought about different kinds of tools and that they were aware of using different kinds of edges to do different things. But we can only document two kinds of edges, although there was certainly more underlying all of that. But I do not see that this contradicts what I have been trying to get across. What we are investigating are some of the things that contribute to the morphological patterns, and from here we can proceed with more detailed investigations in other directions.

DIBBLE: I would like to make a point about the selection of blanks to make into tools. Similar to what Marks said in his paper, I think that these sites represent caches, in effect, of raw material—people could come back at any time and pick up flakes to use or modify, and so there are going to be patterns of selection going. When I compared the retouched pieces with the unretouched component at Tabun, I found that all of the unretouched pieces had a mean width and platform size below the average width and platform size of the retouched scrapers, so it does seem that width is a criterion for selection (for retouching)—narrow flakes are not being picked up and reduced. So, this means that the blank component that is left over at the site is an artifact of their selection.

JELINEK: It is a negative picture of what they wanted.

DIBBLE: Exactly. Which means that it is difficult to go from that group of unretouched pieces to statements about what their original intentions were.

XII
Functional Variability of Lithic Sets in the Middle Paleolithic

Sylvie Beyries

INTRODUCTION

The problem of the interpretation of Middle Paleolithic lithic assemblages was raised as soon as their homogeneity and their variability were brought to light through the work of Bordes and Bourgon (Bordes 1950a, 1953d, 1961a; Bordes and Bourgon 1951; Bourgon 1957). They found that these assemblages showed a degree of homogeneity in terms of the types of tools found in each (e.g., scrapers, points, and flakes); and variability in terms of the relative proportions of these types between assemblages. Many attempts have been made to explain this variability. Stated briefly, three of these are that: (1) it is a result of a chronological evolution, with different assemblage types in a site corresponding to different stages of cultural evolution (Mellars 1965, 1969); (2) it reflects the traditions and technological activities of different groups inhabiting a territory at more or less the same time but having few contacts with each other. The very isolation of these groups may have allowed the preservation and the handing down of such traditions (Bordes 1961b, 1972, 1973); and (3) the shape and composition of the different lithic assemblages are directly related to the type and composition of human activities, the variability thus being functional in character (Binford and Binford 1966; Binford 1973).

Because Mellars's hypothesis does not seem convincing according to the latest results, the coexistence of different facies appears to be the most reliable assumption. We are then left with two opposing theories as to why synchronous variability is exhibited in the Middle Paleolithic of France: Bordes's theory that it is related to cultural differences and the Binfords' claim that it is functional.

Recently, I attempted to see if functional analysis through microwear studies would help achieve a better understanding of this problem. This work has proceeded in two stages. The first has sought to relate the typology to various worked materials. The results of this are interesting but, as will be observed, remain unsatisfactory. The second stage has been focused on understanding the full cinematics of the tool. Although this stage has not yet been completed, initial results have been encouraging.

For the first part of this study, materials from five French sites have been observed: Pié Lombard (Alpes Maritimes)—Typical Mousterian; Corbehem (Pas-de-Calais)—Typical Mousterian with a high percentage of Levallois; Layer 13 of Combe-Grenal (Dordogne)—Denticulate Mousterian; Layer 9 of Marillac (Charente)—Charentian Mousterian, Quina type; Arcy-sur-Cure (Yonne)—Typical Mousterian with strong Levallois. Altogether, 481 items have been examined: 330 tools belonging to the type-list established by Bordes, and an additional 14 cores (see Fig. 12.1) and 137 pieces of debitage. The functional determinations have been carried out by using a metallographic Nikon microscope magnifying rate from 100X to 400X.

RESULTS

The most obvious results are the high number of items not showing any traces of use on the one hand, and on the other, the disproportion in the presence of the different materials which were used. Thirty-seven percent of tools (47% of the unretouched tools, 35% of the retouched ones) do not show any working

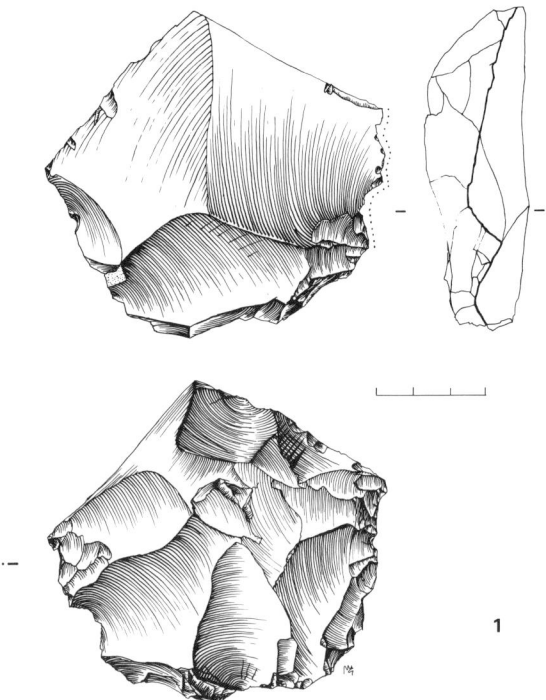

Figure 12.1 Core from Corbehem (Pas-de-Calais); the dots show the side which has worked on wood.

marks. Of the ones that do exhibit wear marks, 64% show traces of usage on wood. This overrepresentation of woodworking is noticeable on all types of tools. The use on animal material is underrepresented: 5% on hide and skins, 3% on antlers, and 8% on meat or bone. The rest of the marks either could not be identified (5%) or were produced by associated materials such as wood with skin or bone with skin.

The observation of particular types of tools yields few general conclusions. Three major type classes were studied and will be discussed in turn.

DENTICULATES AND NOTCHED TOOLS

Two subgroups have been distinguished in the studied material: a) tools with Clactonian notches, and b) irregularly notched and denticulated tools. Bordes (1961a) defines Clactonian notches as "large notches produced by a single hammer strike, sometimes regulated by small secondary retouches that may come from usage." According to the placement of the notch (or notches) on the flake, different types of tools can be obtained: simple notches, denticulates, piercing tools, Tayacian points, and end-notched pieces. Thus, the following analysis will examine the worked portion of each piece that is a notch, regardless of the specific typological class to which it belongs. Thirty-eight such Clactonian tools are included in this work. Among them, only 17 bear traces of wear, as can be seen in Table 12.1.

As mentioned before, there is a tendency toward woodwork specialization in Mousterian tools, and this is clearly seen in the study of Clactonian notches (type 42). Except for one notch from Vaufrey, the polishing of which could not be determined, *all the other items show on the notch a polishing caused by work on wood.* Furthermore, a small, irregular usage retouch, together with a blunting of the edge, can be noted on the area of use.

Irregularly notched and denticulated tools show "small shallow notches" (Bordes 1961a). From the preliminary study of 29 notches and 32 irregularly denticulated tools, no particular specialization of the function stands out (see Tables 12.2 and 12.3). The 22 items not showing any polishing on the characteristic part (first column of the tables) might be pieces that were modified due to geological alteration, trampling, or spontaneous removals during manufacture.

TABLE 12.1
BREAKDOWN OF CLACTONIAN NOTCHES EXHIBITING WEAR TRACES BY TOOL TYPE AND SITE

Type of Tool	Without Working Marks	With Working Marks
piercing-tool		
Combe-Grenal		1
notches		
Corbehem	1	1
Vaufrey	2	5
Marillac	6	4
Arcy-sur-Cure	4	1
denticulates		
Combe-Grenal	2	2
Marillac	1	1
Tayac points		
Combe-Grenal	4	1
Vaufrey	1	1
end-notched tools		
Marillac	1	
Totals	22	17

TABLE 12.2
BREAKDOWN OF IRREGULAR DENTICULATES AND NOTCHES
BY SITE AND MATERIAL WORKED

	None	Wood 1	Wood 2	Skin & Wood 1	Skin & Wood 2	Bone 1	Bone 2	Skin 1	Skin 2	? 1	? 2
Corbehem	1	1	1			1	1				
Vaufrey	5	2				1		1			
Combe-Grenal		3	1								
Pié-Lombard	1										
Marillac	3					1				1	
Arcy-sur-Cure	2		2		1						
Totals	12	6	4	0	1	3	1	1	0	1	0

1—polishing corresponding to characteristic part
2—polishing not corresponding to characteristic part

TABLE 12.3
BREAKDOWN OF IRREGULAR DENTICULATES AND NOTCHES
BY SITE AND MATERIAL WORKED*

	None	Wood 1	Wood 2	Skin 1	Skin 2	Antlers 1	Antlers 2	Meat 1	Meat 2	? 1	? 2
Corbehem	1		1				1			1	
Vaufrey		1	1						2	1	
Combe-Grenal	5	5	2								
Marillac	4	3		1							
Arcy-sur-Cure		2								1	
Totals	10	11	4	1	0	0	1	2	0	3	0

* Excluding those without use on retouched part
1—polishing corresponding to characteristic part
2—polishing not corresponding to characteristic part

TABLE 12.4
BREAKDOWN OF ALL NON-CLACTONIAN NOTCHES AND DENTICULATES
BY SITE AND MATERIAL WORKED

	Wood	Skin	Meat	Bone	?
Corbehem	1			1	1
Vaufrey	3		2	1	1
Combe-Grenal	8				
Marillac	4	1		1	1
Arcy-sur-Cure	2				1
Totals					
notches	6	1		3	
denticulates	12	1	2		

Table 12.4 presents a similar breakdown, excluding the pieces where the use does not correspond to the retouched part (seven notched, five denticulated). More than two-thirds of these pieces are connected to work on wood. But because two of these pieces have been used to carve meat, one to scrape hide, and three to work bone, it is not possible to conclude that there is a true specialization among such types of tools. Yet while both the notches and the denticulated tools seem to have worked on wood and skin, only the notches show traces of bones; marks due to meat carving appear only on denticulated tools. On the other hand, the Clactonian pieces do show more specialization in woodworking, though this will require further confirmation.

SCRAPING TOOLS

A scraping tool is a flake that has been shaped on one or several edges by a continuous retouch. In the strict definition of this tool, this retouch is thought to be purposeful. A certain number of pieces regarded as scraping tools in this study, however, show a retouch which may—in our point of view—be due to use. Perhaps if finer distinctions concerning the retouch were made, the results shown here would be different.

Of the 64 pieces having continuously worked edges, 55 (i.e., 76%) exhibit purposeful retouch (Tables 12.5 and 12.6). In the large majority, these tools have worked on wood. Out of the remaining 25% (scraping tools obtained through use-retouch), work on bone is predominant with eight examples (see Figs. 12.2-5).

The reader should bear in mind that Tables 12.5 and 12.6 deal only with the retouched parts of tools. If a scraping tool exhibited use-wear on only an unretouched portion of the tool, it would be considered here under the next section, dealing with unretouched tools.

UNRETOUCHED PIECES OR USE ON UNRETOUCHED AREAS

The absence of regular or continuous retouch eliminates some pieces from the restricted type-list, but the absence of retouch did not, of course, preclude the use of these flakes in the past. Microwear analysis enables us to determine the proportion of such pieces, as shown in Table 12.7. It can be seen that slightly more than half of the unretouched pieces bear wear traces, with backed knives exhibiting the most. As for Levallois flakes, the results here should be viewed

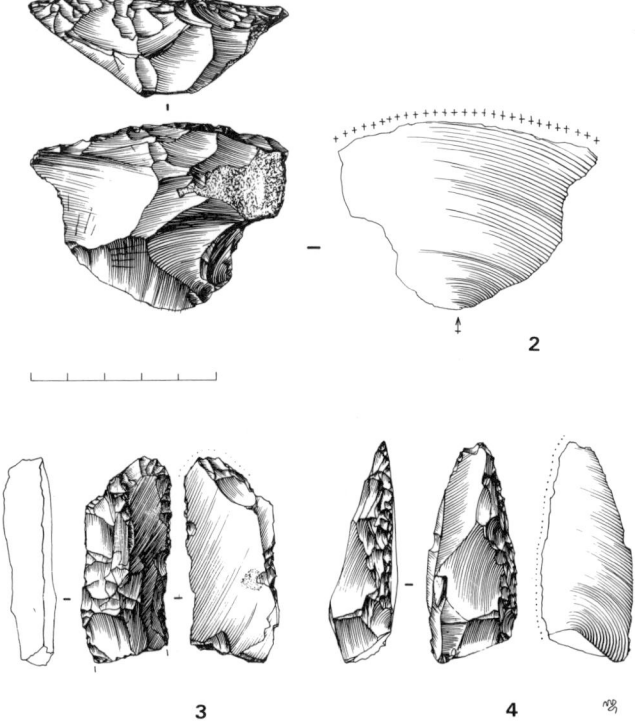

Figures 12.2-4 Sidescrapers from Marillac (Charente). The crosses on no. 2 show the side which has worked on bone; the dots on nos. 3-4 show the sides which have worked on wood.

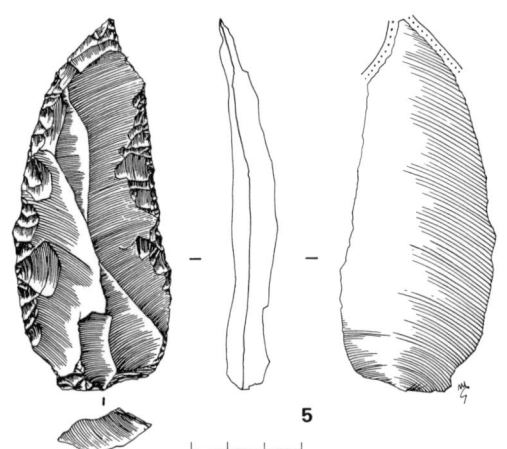

Figure 12.5 Sidescraper from Vaufrey (Dordogne); the dots show the side which has worked on wood, and the line shows the part which has worked on skin.

with caution, since most of the Levallois flakes come from Corbehem, the only site where flakes of this type have been obviously worked. For the Levallois pieces, woodworking predominates. For the backed

TABLE 12.5
USE OF RETOUCHED PARTS ON SCRAPING TOOLS ACCORDING TO SITES

		Wood		Skin		Bone		?		None
Site	Bordes Type	1	2	1	2	1	2	1	2	
Corbehem	9	1					1			
Corbehem	10			1						
Corbehem	11		1							
Corbehem	19	1								
Corbehem	25									1
Corbehem	26	1								
Vaufrey	9	2								1
Vaufrey	10	2	1			1	1			5
Vaufrey	12	1								
Vaufrey	13		2							
Vaufrey	15	2		2						
Vaufrey	17	3	1							1
Vaufrey	19			1						
Vaufrey	21	1								
Vaufrey	25	1								
Combe-Grenal	9	1								
Combe-Grenal	10	1								
Combe-Grenal	11	1								1
Pié-Lombard	9					1				1
Pié-Lombard	10	1								2
Pié-Lombard	13									1
Pié-Lombard	24					1				
Pié-Lombard	27	1								
Marillac	9	1							1	
Marillac	10	10	1			1	3	2		10
Marillac	11	1								1
Marillac	15									1
Marillac	21	1								
Marillac	23	6	1	1						
Marillac	25		1							
Arcy-sur-Cure	9	1	1							1
Arcy-sur-Cure	10	2					1			1
Arcy-sur-Cure	13	1			1					
Arcy-sur-Cure	21								1	
Arcy-sur-Cure	24	1								
	Totals	42	9	5	1	5	8	3	1	27

1—scrapers with purposeful retouch
2—scrapers with usage retouch
Whenever doubt existed whether the retouch was done on purpose or produced by use, it was considered as purposeful.

TABLE 12.6
USE OF SCRAPING-TOOLS' RETOUCHED PARTS ON ALL THE SITES

Scrapers obtained through purposeful retouch					Scrapers obtained through use-retouch				
Bordes Type	Wood	Skin	Bone	?	Bordes Type	Wood	Skin	Bone	?
9	4		2		9	1		2	1
10	16	1	2	2	10	2		6	
11	2				11	1			
12	1				12				
13	1				13	2	1		
15	2	2			15				
17	3				17	1			
19	1	1			19				
21	2			1	21				
23	6	1			23	1			
24	1		1		24				
25	1				25	1			
26	1				26				
27	1				27				
Totals	42	5	5	3	Totals	9	1	8	1

TABLE 12.7
BREAKDOWN OF MATERIALS WORKED WITH UNRETOUCHED TOOLS

Type of Tool	Bone	Wood	Skin and Wood & Skin	Bone & Meat and Antlers	?
1/2	25	13	2	1	1
3	—	1	—	1	—
5	2	1	—	2	1
36	1	—	—	—	—
38	9	9	1	10	3
Totals	37	24	3	14	5

Types shown are Levallois flakes (1/2), Levallois points (3), pseudo-Levallois points (5), backed knives (36), and naturally backed knives (38).

knives, butchering seems to have been emphasized. It is clear, however, that unretouched tools, and particularly backed knives, are real tools and not just waste. Indeed, the proportion of such pieces that exhibit traces of wear is about the same as in the retouched tools.

To summarize the results from these five sites (see Table 12.8), it is possible to conclude that the great majority of retouched tools give evidence of having been used on wood. There are ten exceptions, these being scrapers that appear to have worked animal material (skin, bone, meat, and antler). The unretouched group indicates more diversified activities. While woodworking does appear often on these pieces, use on animal material is apparent on a greater number.

TABLE 12.8
SUMMARY OF POLISHES FOUND ON DIFFERENT TYPOLOGICAL OR USE CLASSES

	Wood	Skin & Wood & Skin	Bone & Meat & Antlers	?
Group 1				
genuine scrapers	42	5	5	3
Clactonian tools	17	—	—	—
Totals	59	5	5	3
Group 2				
usage scrapers	9	1	8	1
notches & irreg. dent.	18	1	5	4
Levallois tools	18	2	4	3
backed knives	9	1	10	3
Totals	54	5	27	11

Group 1 represents deliberately retouched tools, and Group 2 those pieces showing only retouch brought about by use.

BIACHE-ST.-VAAST

In order to obtain more accurate results, a series from the Mousterian site of Biache-St.-Vaast (Pas-de-Calais) was selected. This series has the advantage of having a surface state of exceptional freshness, which permitted a remarkable preservation of various wear traces (see Figs. 12.6-10). The present study deals with 26 scrapers divided into three categories: asymmetrical convergent scrapers (n = 3); symmetrical convergent scrapers (n = 12); and non-convergent scrapers (n = 11).

ASYMMETRICAL CONVERGENT SCRAPERS

These tools are blade-shaped flakes with a slightly cortical proximal zone. The primary retouched edge is slightly concave and lies within the distal third of the tool. It is a low-angle retouch, short and slightly scaled. Wherever its location (i.e., left or right), this zone has been the most active part. Next to this area the blade edge is completely crushed and, near the side, exhibits strong polishing marks due to work on wood. Though no directional striation could be seen, the organization and distribution of the polishing indicate scraping action.

No wear marks on the surfaces of these scrapers allow us to conclude that they were hafted. It would seem that these tools were probably held sideways and had a longitudinal action on the wood.

SYMMETRICAL CONVERGENT SCRAPERS

Five scrapers of this type have been manufactured on blades and eight from smaller flakes. With the exception of one, all of these tools show totally identical marks with the used part being a reduced zone located on each side of the point, and all were used for more or less intensive work on wood. There are, however, three types of marks found on them:

1) Four tools show on their surface, in the proximal two-thirds, an organized striature. This striature covers the whole most proximal one-third; in the mesial portion it covers only elevated zones of the piece. In two cases, the mesial striae are transversal and those on the proximal part are subperpendicular to these. Together with these striae, traces of polishing due to rubbing against skin can be noted. Such marks indicate that the tool was probably bound onto a wooden haft that caused the striature and the

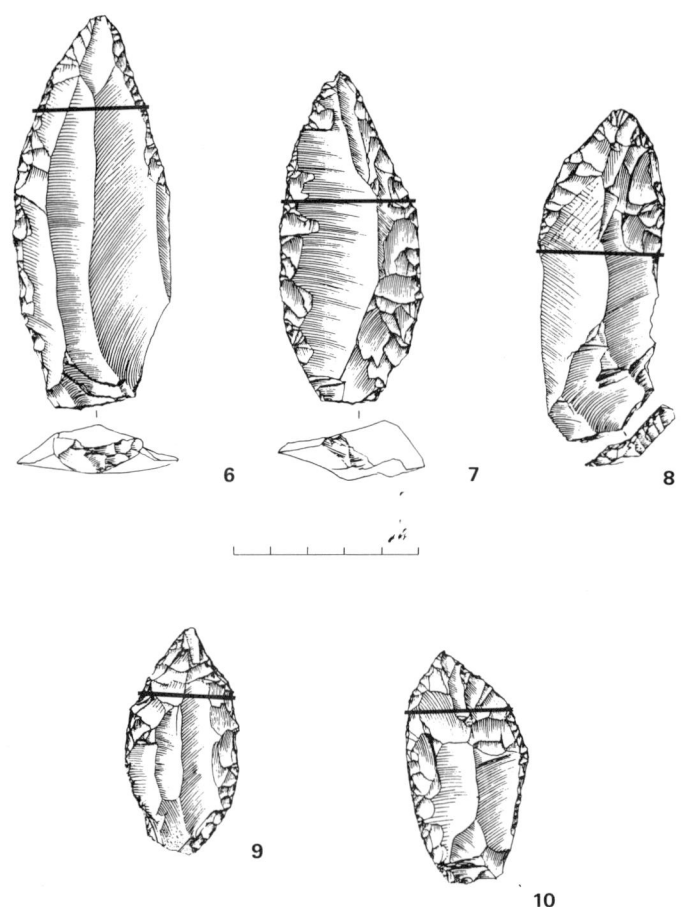

Figures 12.6-10   Hafted sidescrapers from Biache-St.-Vaast (Pas-de-Calais).

micropolish, and either held on with leather strips or encased in a leather sleeve. On the two other scrapers the striae are parallel to the piece's axis; this might indicate a plierlike hafting.

2) Five tools show traces, on both their mesial and proximal surfaces, of polishing due to rubbing against skin or wood. The distal third is absolutely without traces of wear. The difference between the two parts of the tool hints that a zone of the piece was protected by a wood-and-skin haft. As no striature appears, it would seem that the tool was not able to move about in its haft during use; therefore the haft suited the tool well.

3) On both mesial and proximal parts, the ridges of these scrapers display clear signs of crushing, often combined with polishing traces owed to rubbing against skin or wood. This crushing suggests considerable rubbing against a hard material—either directly against a haft or cushioned slightly with a skin sleeve.

These observations—striae, surface polishing, and ridge crushing—add up to certain testimony that these tools were hafted when used.

On its left side, the last scraper shows a highly developed polish coming from work on bone, together with subperpendicular striae indicating meat carving.

NON-CONVERGENT SCRAPERS

On these 11 tools, the retouch is short, subparallel, and low-angled. The active part is always the retouched zone, whatever its location on the edge(s). According to these functional analyses, these pieces may be split into two groups: long scrapers and short scrapers.

Long scrapers' length exceeds their width. On these tools two types of use were found, one indicating work on wood and the other on hide. The active areas were located on two different parts of the cutting edge. Four of this type have been used on wood, one on hide, two on both. Work on wood is not well demonstrated. No preference in the direction of work could be found (three pieces show a longitudinal direction, five show transverse). The zones which were worked on hide, however, are extremely blunt, and small transverse scratches show a scraping action. As with the asymmetrical convergent scrapers, no traces indicate they were hafted.

Short scrapers show butchering marks on their entire retouched parts. Considerable striation, together with the general repartition of the micropolish, indicates that they were used for carving. It seems, as in the preceding cases, that such tools were held in the hand.

CONCLUSIONS

Based on the first group of results presented here concerning the relationship between typology and worked materials, one may reach the conclusion that typological variability is not linked to specific activities. In other words, the same work—for example, on wood—could be accomplished with different types and in different typological assemblages. But if the second group of results is considered (though they are not fully completed), it can be noted that a precise study of tool use tends to show that a relative standardization exists for certain types of tools: convergent scrapers were hafted and were used either to scrape or to strike wood. Non-convergent scrapers were probably not hafted and were used on more diversified material—on wood when their retouch is regular, on animal materials when that retouch is irregular.

Even if the study of the material from Biache-St.-Vaast leads us to think that some tool groups correspond to functional activity groups, the debate concerning the interpretation of Mousterian assemblage variability will not be completely settled, since the cultural hypothesis still cannot be excluded. As a matter of fact, recent technological studies conducted by E. Boëda and J. M. Gouedo demonstrate that absolutely identical tools may be obtained through completely different conceptual schemes. Therefore, morphologically identical tools may have been used for a specific activity, and the cultural choice is seen in the method by which these tools were manufactured.

DISCUSSION

Editors' note: Beyries's paper was read in her absence by Marcel Otte.

JELINEK: A problem that is frequently unrecognized in looking at use-wear is that the effects of soil polish are virtually indistinguishable from woodworking. It leads a lot of people to talk about woodworking on tools when actually it is the result of small but very long-term movement of soil particles around the object.

OTTE: It would not explain why such polish is more frequent compared with the Upper Paleolithic.

JELINEK: It would if they were buried longer and there was more movement of soil. Moreover, the prevalence of woodworking polish may simply be a reflection of the fact that woodworking produces a more pronounced polish that overrides the effects of cutting meat or softer material. So, one would expect that it is the heaviest use of the tool that is going to be reflected here and that there may have been a considerably greater amount of use of these things on softer materials than we can see in the final form.

RIGAUD: We know about the retouched tools, but we do not know about unretouched artifacts, which can be used for other things, including meat. I would like also to comment about the distribution of the wear patterns, not on the tools but on the site, within the intrasite distribution of the artifacts. Beyries has found that there is no distributional pattern and that woodworking occurs everywhere. There are two possible explanations. One is that of Binford: that they were scavengers and that they were not using the stones for cutting meat. And there is another possibility, raised by Jelinek: that because of the geological background, almost all traces of wear on the tools were removed and what is left now is something like a soil polish. So, with Mousterian assemblages, its very difficult to tell what is what.

SACKETT: Is there evidence of high arboreal pollen that would indicate a relationship between wood in the environment and evidence of woodworking?

BOSINSKI: Loess steppe was the predominant environment.

RIGAUD: In the Perigord there is always wood around the sites, even in the coldest climatic episodes.

FREEMAN: We should use caution about making sweeping generalizations concerning woodworking in the Mousterian. The material from Cueva Morín, excavated back in the 1960s and which has been decently curated, seems to show that everything was used on bone. Now we have the same range of artifact types that are mentioned here, so that might suggest that we are looking at sampling differences.

FERRING: I think these conclusions, particularly with respect to the converging pieces, might provide some means to measure or to test Dibble's idea concerning the reduction of those scrapers as a result of resharpening. If you use the Paleo-Indian spearpoints from North America as an analogue, which were clearly hafted, the resharpening of those spearpoints always betrays the fact that they were hafted because the base of the point becomes a shoulder. If these convergent scrapers were, in fact, hafted, and assuming that the hafting was relatively durable, then there should be a break in the lateral profiles of the pieces betraying the part that was hafted as opposed to the part that could be resharpened. In other words, if Dibble is correct that a converging piece evolves through resharpening, then hafting should betray that morphologically.

OTTE: But the pieces could be taken off the haft when they are resharpened.

DIBBLE: Given that we are seeing the last traces of use on a tool, a more definitive test of the resharpening hypotheses would be to try to refit the small retouch flakes onto scrapers and see if we can find traces of wear on them that would indicate earlier uses of that tool before it reached its final form.

MÜLLER-BECK: In the Arctic, in the Pre-Dorset, we see so far that the burins are always used for bone and endscrapers are always used for wood. But the knives can be used, evidently, for everything, like a pocketknife: what you see is the last use. And what has begun before, you cannot see anymore. Another point is that I would like to see reports on use-wear documented by photos. This is difficult and expensive, but necessary.

BOSINSKI: We have to realize that the absence of bone, antler, and ivory in the Middle Paleolithic is made up by the large scale of wooden implements.

MÜLLER-BECK: There are three other points to make. First, this kind of study has to be done on other large samples, since there are some tools which may be used very shortly and show practically no wear and others that are used more heavily and show many more traces. Second, it is important to realize that a tool that is used skillfully is not stressed and may not show as many wear traces. Third, the material that the tool is made from has a tremendous effect on the development of use traces.

FREEMAN: We also have to remember that the artifact types that we're talking about had a wide distribution in space and time, and were widely distributed over such environmental diversity. Thus, it may not be likely that we are going to be able to identify a single material responsible for the wear on all Mousterian tools of a particular category anywhere in the world. There is the distinct possibility that in different places at different times, different materials were being worked with similar sorts of implements.

COMMENTS

OTTE: Puisqu'il semble établi qu'aucune corrélation stricte ne peut être observée entre les fonctions des outils moustériens et les faciès définis selon des critères techno-typologiques, la signification fonctionnelle de ceux-ci présentée par L. Binford doit être sérieusement remise en cause. D'autre part, l'extension géographique très variable de ces différents faciès, considérée à l'échelle européenne rend évidemment très caduque une telle théorie puisque des régions entières ne seraient consacrées qu'à certaines activités! Il apparaît nécessaire une fois de plus de quitter le cadre étroit du Périgord où ces groupes furent jadis définis pour tester toute nouvelle forme d'interprétation.

La dominance du travail des outils de silex sur matières végétales, observée par Sylvie Beyries se retrouvait également au site de Mesvin en Belgique (étude D. Cahen et J. Gijsels). Cela signifie qu'il s'agit d'un phénomène relativement général dont la signification profonde nous échappe encore mais qui doit tenir à l'importance des autres formes d'outils réalisés en matériaux organiques dont de trop rares traces subsistent.

L'organisation, apparemment aléatoire, du fonctionnement des outils moustériens retracée par l'étude de Sylvie Beyries semble correspondre à l'absence de systématique dans la configuration des types d'outils (cf. étude de H. Dibble) et à l'absence de structuration nette dans les surfaces d'occupation moustérienne.

XIII
Scavenging and Hunting in the Middle Paleolithic
The Evidence from Europe

Philip G. Chase

The people of the Upper Paleolithic are the first hominids whose behavior is universally acknowledged to be fully modern. For this reason, gaining a clear picture of the adaptation of their Middle Paleolithic predecessors is of particular importance for understanding our biological and behavioral evolution. The topic has not lacked for attention from either human paleontologists or archaeologists, although there is today no clear consensus. The weight of opinion has shifted through time, from general disregard late in the last century, to a view of Middle Paleolithic hominids—particularly of "Classic" Neandertals—as extremely primitive and unintelligent, to a more recent tendency to minimize differences between them and modern *Homo sapiens*.

Almost throughout the debate, however, one thing has been generally taken for granted—that the animals consumed by Middle Paleolithic peoples were obtained by hunting. It is only recently that this assumption has been challenged or even closely scrutinized.

Lewis Binford, studying the faunal remains from the Middle Stone Age levels of the Klasies River Mouth Sites in South Africa (Binford 1984), found that the assemblage did not reflect his expectations of remains left by hunters. He concluded that whereas the Klasies River Mouth inhabitants had been killing small game, they obtained large animals by scavenging rather than by hunting. The implications for our view of human evolution were, in Binford's view, primarily twofold. First, as late as perhaps 40,000 years ago, people did not have the technological ability to hunt large game; second, they apparently shared food on a much smaller scale than would be expected given traditional notions of Upper Pleistocene hominids. In fact, Binford saw the whole pattern of subsistence at the Klasies River Mouth as indicative of a remarkable lack of foresight and planning.

Binford has more recently expanded his investigations to include the Upper Pleistocene of Europe (Binford 1985). Here he reports something rather different from what he found at the Klasies River Mouth. While he believes that during the Riss, "hunting seems likely for only small animals and rodents" (1985: 319), he argues that "by Würm II times in south-central France, hominids were regularly hunting moderate-body-sized animals. In addition, they were scavenging large-sized animals, such as aurochs and horses" (1985: 320). He is somewhat noncommittal on the extent to which the larger moderate-sized game, particularly red deer (*Cervus elaphus*), was hunted during Würm I times.

His survey of the European data is much less detailed than his study of the Klasies River Mouth material. Given the importance of his ideas to our understanding of human evolution, it will be worthwhile to analyze the Middle Paleolithic evidence from Europe in more detail.

In order to do so, however, we must first review two subjects: (1) exactly what roles are being postulated for hunting and for scavenging in the adaptation of Middle Paleolithic hominids, and (2) the criteria by which one may recognize scavenging in the archaeological record.

The possible roles of scavenging in hominid adaptation can be separated, for our purposes, into five categories:

1) scavenging of carcasses as the primary source of food, so that the hominids filled a scavenger niche;

2) scavenging as the primary or only means of obtaining meat, with the bulk of food coming from plants;

3) scavenging of the carcasses of larger animals as a more or less incidental supplement to hunting of smaller animals;

4) scavenging as incidental, with hunting of both

large and small animals being the primary source of meat;

5) a complete absence of scavenging.

The first alternative has not been proposed for the Middle Paleolithic by Binford, or, to the best of my knowledge, by anyone else. Gamble (1986, 1987), however, has proposed it as the winter adaptation of Middle Pleistocene peoples in Europe, on the grounds that the carcasses of winter-killed animals would have been the food source most readily available to hominids that he describes as unable to compete with (or even to defend themselves from) the carnivores with whom they shared the landscape.

This adaptation seems unlikely. A major problem with scavenging as the primary source of food, particularly the scavenging of winter kills, is the danger of protein poisoning. People forced to rely on flesh for the bulk of their calories are in danger of dying unless they are able to eat large quantities of fat (Speth and Spielmann 1983). This can happen even to modern hunters armed with rifles (see Stefánsson [1962: 143-145] for a firsthand account). Since winter-killed animals will almost always be those individuals in the worst condition among a population already in poor condition, it seems highly unlikely that their carcasses could have provided enough fat relative to lean meat to support hominids who relied upon them for the bulk of their calories.

Because he is concerned more with assessing hominid capabilities than with reconstructing particular subsistence systems, Binford is not entirely explicit about whether the second alternative—that scavenging was the main source of meat but not of food—describes the adaptation of Lower Paleolithic peoples of Europe. By Middle Paleolithic times, though, he describes hominids as hunting species such as reindeer and red deer, which are abundant in Middle Paleolithic sites. It thus seems more likely that he pictures Middle Paleolithic adaptation as better fitting the third alternative, hunting of smaller animals and scavenging of larger ones, with the body-size threshold between the two methods of meat procurement becoming progressively larger through time.

It seems highly likely that Pleistocene hominids occasionally scavenged carcasses (alternative 5), since not to do so would have been to ignore a perfectly good (if often unreliable—see Schaller and Lowther 1969) source of food.

Testing Binford's scavenging hypothesis against the data from the Middle Paleolithic of Europe, then, becomes a matter of choosing between two alternative adaptations: (1) hunting of smaller species by hominids who were able to obtain meat from larger animals only by scavenging, or (2) hunting even of larger species on a regular basis with scavenging occurring only as an incidental supplement to hunting when the opportunity arose (much as most of us willingly pick up a coin lying on the pavement even though we do not expect to make our living in this manner).

In order to choose between these two alternative adaptations, we must be able to distinguish between hunting and scavenging in the archaeological record. In his monograph on the Klasies River Mouth Binford (1984: 65-77) indicates that for him the most important test implications for the scavenging hypothesis are based on the fundamental assumption that the predator who kills an animal will have access to and will consume the best (most meaty) portions of the carcass. The scavenger will be left with only the less productive parts of the carcass. Therefore, at a scavenger consumption site, the portions of the skeleton introduced will be those of least use to carnivores—heads and distal limb bones. Moreover, there will be signs that considerable effort was expended to obtain meat, marrow, etc., from these marginal parts. Finally, since the carcasses available to scavengers will often be partially desiccated and therefore stiff and hard to butcher, they will often show signs of heavy-handed butchering, especially in the form of hack marks made by heavy blows with massive tools, rather than the cut and slice marks characteristic of butchering fresh carcasses.

These criteria for recognizing scavenging in the archaeological records make intuitive sense. We now have in addition, however, a list of criteria based upon Robert Blumenschine's empirical observations of carcasses available to scavengers in the Serengeti Plain and the Ngorongoro Crater:

1) a predominance of adults over juveniles or younger individuals, with most young being those of larger species;

2) a predominance of medium-sized adult and larger carcasses over those of smaller size classes;

3) a predominance of fragmented limb and cranial parts over elements from the axial region of the skeleton;

4) a high proportion of all defleshing and cut marks occurring on head and lower limb bones, with increasingly lower frequencies being found on parts defleshed progressively earlier in the consumption sequence;

5) smaller taxa being represented by a greater predominance of latterly consumed skeletal parts, and displaying defleshing cut marks on a more limited series of body parts than larger taxa. (Blumenschine 1986: 139)

Blumenschine's work showed that carnivores consumed carcasses in very much the way Binford had expected, eating the fleshiest parts first. Thus criterion 4 means that tool marks will be most common on the postcranial axial skeleton and on proximal limb bones, while the "latterly consumed parts" referred to in criterion 5 are those least useful to carnivores and therefore least likely to be consumed by them, i.e., cranial and distal limb bones.

Two things should be noted about the application of Blumenschine's criteria. First, the patterns predicted may also be found in osteological assemblages left behind by human hunters, since hunters may choose mature or larger animals over smaller ones or may leave the least meaty bones behind at a kill site from which the best parts of the carcass have been transported for consumption elsewhere. Second, criteria 2 and 5, which are based on body size, are not usable in a situation such as Binford has postulated for the Klasies River Mouth or for Middle Paleolithic Europe, where smaller species were hunted and only larger ones were scavenged. Granted these limitations, however, Blumenschine's test implications have the advantage of being based on solid empirical observations. It is a tribute to Binford's astuteness that they agree closely with his own expectations.

With these test implications, we may now turn our attention to the European evidence in order to distinguish between our alternative roles for hunting and scavenging in the Middle Paleolithic of Europe.

A reasonable place to start is the site of Combe-Grenal (Dordogne, France), where Binford obtained his Middle Paleolithic data. Binford's first and Blumenschine's third criterion for recognizing scavenging in the archaeological record, the abundance of parts of marginal value (heads and distal limb bones), is met by the remains of red deer from the Würm I. In fact, it is exactly the meatiest parts of the carcass that are missing from the site, and there is a tendency for the frequency of the remaining parts to be positively correlated with the size of the marrow cavity (Chase 1986: 46-50). This is entirely in line with one's expectations of what would be found at a site where the animals were scavenged rather than hunted. As Binford (1984: 69) himself has pointed out, though, such patterns may also be produced by hunters, a fact illustrated at Combe-Grenal itself, where the skulls-plus-distal-limb-bones configuration is characteristic of both red deer and reindeer (*Rangifer tarandus*) remains in the early Würm II (Chase 1986), at a time when Binford agrees they were hunted. In fact, on this criterion alone, there is no reason to think that the Würm I red deer remains do not represent animals killed at or near the site, whose best parts were carried off to be consumed elsewhere, while the parts with the lowest food-to-weight ratios were eaten at the site by the hunters. Thus we must look to other criteria to decide whether or not red deer were hunted during the Würm I.

Before doing so, let us examine the relative abundance of different parts of the skeleton for the two large-animal taxa represented at the site, equids and large bovids (*Bos* and/or *Bison*). Large bovid remains are so few at Combe-Grenal that it is hard to see how one could use them to draw any conclusions about scavenging. In the 31 Würm II beds with sufficient archaeological remains to allow Bordes (Bordes and Prat 1965) to identify the lithic industry, there were an average of only 2.9 *Bos/Bison* postcranial remains per bed, with a mean MAU (the number of individuals represented by each anatomical element [Binford 1984: 51]) of only 0.058 per element per bed. Yet the postcranial elements that yielded the highest MAU were not distal limb bones but rather proximal ulnae and radii (Chase 1986: 204), so that what data there are do not fit the skulls-plus-distal-limb-bones criterion.

Equids are also so poorly represented that it was not possible to draw detailed conclusions concerning butchering from their remains (Chase 1986). In those beds with reasonable numbers of bones, though, the remains definitely do *not* fit the skulls-plus-distal-limb-bones pattern. In Beds 11-19, it is true, the assemblage is dominated by crania, mandibles, proximal radii, and proximal metatarsals; but in Beds 20-22, ulnae, innominates, and distal tibiae are the most common bones; and in Beds 23-25, crania, scapulae, distal humeri, ulnae, distal metacarpals, innominates, and second phalanges (Chase 1986: 38, 201-203). On this basis, there is no evidence that either large bovids or equids were scavenged. In fact, the opposite is true. The data for equids run counter to what is predicted by the scavenging hypothesis.

It is logical that a scavenger, with only the poorer parts of the carcass available to him, would concentrate considerable effort upon extracting edible material from those parts, especially material (such as marrow) which he was better equipped to get at than were the carnivores responsible for the kill (this is why Blumenschine writes of "fragmented limb and cranial parts" in his third criterion). This does not mean, however, that hunters ignore such food sources as marrow. There is abundant evidence to the contrary at Combe-Grenal, where the long bones of all species, including those Binford believes were hunted, were consistently broken for marrow throughout the sequence. Even small bones were broken. In the Würm II, 55% of the first phalanges of reindeer were broken, as were 62% of the second phalanges. For red deer in the Würm II, the percentages were much higher, 93% and 63%, while equids resembled reindeer, with 71% and 55% of these phalanges broken. (Bovid phalanges were too few to provide meaningful evidence.) In fact, Binford (1978: 30-31) has quoted the Nunamiut as saying that, in the old days small bones such as phalanges were often broken for marrow. The breaking open of cervid mandibles for the little edible material they contain is attested from the Upper Paleolithic of Le Flageolet, also in the Dordogne (Ait-Fora 1986). Moreover, the phalanges and metapodials of reindeer and red deer from the Würm II of Combe-Grenal display frequent tool marks (Chase 1986). It is thus clear that hunters as well as scavengers could be expected to exploit skulls and distal limb bones for food, and that evidence of such activity does not constitute evidence for scavenging.

As noted above, Binford proposed evidence of butchering stiffened carcasses as a criterion for recognizing scavenging. In the Pleistocene of Europe this is less reliable evidence than in southern Africa, since the northern climate was such that partially frozen carcasses might have been butchered by hunters. (In fact, Binford [1984: 103-104] used his observations of Nunamiut Eskimo butchering of frozen carcasses as models for recognizing the butchering of stiffened carcasses at the Klasies River Mouth.)

The question is moot for Combe-Grenal, because such evidence is virtually absent (see Chase 1986: 74-78). All of the tool marks on the bones of equids were cut marks such as would be produced by cutting through soft flesh, while none were the kind of hack marks described by Binford for the larger animals at the Klasies River Mouth. The only marks on a *Bos/Bison* bone (on a femoral shaft fragment from Bed 25) that might be interpreted as the result of hacking closely resemble those attributed by Binford (1981: 47-48) to carnivore gnawing, and replicated by Feustel (1973: 178-180, pl. 73) by using bone for flintknapping.

Moreover, the distribution of cut marks on the skeletons of both large bovids and equids is the *opposite* of what one would expect from scavenging according to Blumenschine's fourth criterion. They are very heavily concentrated on the meatiest portions of the carcass (Fig. 13.1). This implies that it was the best parts of these large animals, not the marginal parts, that hominids were exploiting most heavily.

The age profiles of the equids at Combe-Grenal also fail to support the notion that these animals were scavenged. One would expect, given that scavengers can exploit only those animals that die of natural causes, that the population of scavenged carcasses

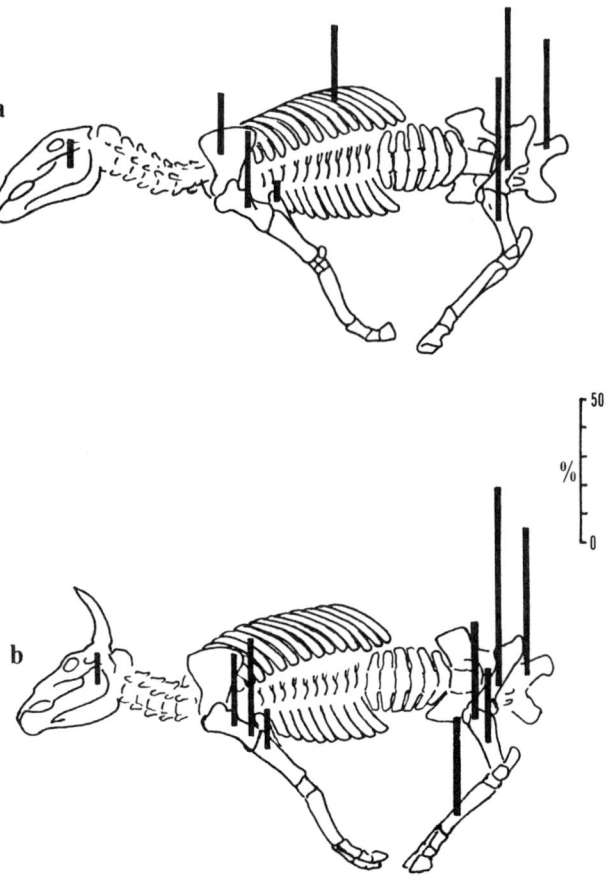

Figure 13.1 Percentage of each portion of the skeletons of equids (a) and of large bovids (b) at Combe-Grenal bearing tool marks. The location of the base of each vertical bar indicates the portion of the skeleton. The height of each bar represents the percentage. Percentages for long bones are calculated separately for proximal and distal ends and for shafts.

would match, in terms of age, the age curve for animals dying from natural attrition. In fact, the failure of the eland (*Taurotragus oryx*) population at the Klasies River Mouth to approximate such a curve was cited by Klein (1986) as one of the main reasons to doubt Binford's conclusions concerning scavenging of that species.

As Blumenschine has shown, however, most small animals are fully consumed, or nearly so, before their carcasses are abandoned by the predators that killed them. As a result, the age curve of a scavenged population will not be dominated by young and old, as might be expected, but by adults, and among the adults one would expect to find the older animals predominating (that is, one would expect to find a curve fitting that of natural attrition, but with the youngest animals removed). In fact, the elands from the Klasies River Mouth show a very different pattern; juveniles and prime-age adults are common—it is only the older individuals that are underrepresented (Klein 1975, 1976).

The assemblage of *Bos/Bison* teeth from Combe-Grenal is heavily dominated by adult as opposed to deciduous teeth (based on my own counts), although only about one in seven is heavily worn. These animals therefore do fit roughly Blumenschine's first criterion. Given that large bovids fit neither his second nor his third criterion, however, one is forced to conclude that an explanation other than scavenging (such as deliberate choice on the part of the Combe-Grenal hunters) must account for this phenomenon.

Marsha Levine (1983) has analyzed the age profiles of horses from the three beds for which adequate samples were available. None of these samples is what one would expect for a scavenged population. All three beds most closely fit either a total life assemblage or a family group (i.e., the entire living population less the bachelor males). Since the age structures of the animals killed are the same as those in a living population, the inescapable conclusion is that they were hunted, almost certainly by driving, and that they did not die by natural attrition.

Binford (1984: 223) has listed some data on horse-tooth lengths from Combe-Grenal that indicate that the sample may be biased by differential transport by hominids of the upper and lower jaws. These data must be used with great caution, however. Length of tooth is equated with age, regardless of which tooth is being measured. But upper teeth are longer than lower teeth of the same age, and within the same jaw the lengths of teeth vary greatly (Levine 1979: app. 6).

The apparent discrepancies between upper and lower jaws in these data therefore may reflect only the relative frequencies of the particular teeth measured, rather than their ages. This may be an especially acute problem, since Binford measured only 62 teeth from Beds 14-16, although Levine was able to measure 340 teeth from Bed 14 alone. Since it is not stated how Binford's sample was drawn, there is no assurance that it is representative.

Up to this point, then, we have seen that the skulls-plus-distal-limb-bones pattern of remains is a necessary part of the evidence for scavenging, since it is the natural result of utilizing the less meaty portions of the carcass. But taken alone it is not sufficient evidence, since hunters also produce such patterns. Empirically, the evidence from Combe-Grenal shows that equid remains were not distributed as one would expect if they had been obtained by scavenging. While they were very few in number, the same is true of the remains of large bovids. Only for red deer in the Würm I and Würm II and for reindeer in the early Würm II was this criterion for scavenging met.

Signs of exploitation of the less desirable portions of the carcass are demonstrably useless for distinguishing between hunting and scavenging. Signs of heavy-handed butchering of partially desiccated carcasses are lacking at Combe-Grenal, for moderate-sized and large species alike.

All this adds up to a complete lack of evidence for scavenging at Combe-Grenal. In fact, because equid remains do not fit the expected skulls-plus-distal-limbs pattern, because large bovids and equids were butchered by cutting rather than by hacking through desiccated tissue, because the cut marks on these animals are concentrated on the meatiest parts of the body and because these equids' ages indicate that they were hunted, there is instead evidence that large animals were being killed regularly. Scavenging, if it occurred, was apparently too rare to leave a recognizable mark in the archaeological record.

There is further, positive evidence for hunting as opposed to scavenging of large animals in the Middle Paleolithic of Europe. One body of evidence comes from Combe-Grenal itself. Scavengers are dependent upon natural deaths for carcasses to scavenge. This means that the availability of a species is determined by natural rather than cultural factors. One would therefore expect to find some correlation between changes and continuities in the natural environment, on the one hand, and changes and continuities in the relative frequencies of scavenged species, on the other.

As can be seen in Figure 13.2, however, this is not the case for the large animals at Combe-Grenal. In fact, there is a remarkable lack of relationship between the proportions of large equids and large bovids and the climatic data. This independence in choosing resources implies hunting rather than scavenging.

If the data from Combe-Grenal indicate that large animals were hunted rather than scavenged, data from elsewhere in Europe are entirely in agreement with this conclusion. There are data that indicate that Middle Paleolithic peoples were capable of killing very dangerous game. In some cases the evidence is indirect. At Hortus in southeastern France, carnivores, especially leopards (*Felis pardus*), were represented almost entirely by crania and the bones of the foot and tail (de Lumley 1972: 608-609). This is not suggestive of natural death, but rather of hunting of carnivores for their hides. A similar pattern characterizes the remains of wild boar (*Sus scrofa*) at San Agostino, Italy (Tozzi 1970; Chase 1986: 102).

Striking direct evidence of hunting of very large game comes from early in the Middle Paleolithic, at Lehringen in Germany, where a wooden spear was found with the skeleton of a butchered elephant (*Hesperoloxodon antiquus*) (Movius 1950; Adam 1951). Gamble (1986, 1987) has interpreted this and a similar spear from Clacton as probes for locating carcasses under the snow. The Lehringen spear, however, was found *under* the bones of an elephant (Adam 1951: 83). Gamble (1987: 94) attributes this location to "natural thawing." It is hard to see how frost action could have moved the wooden shaft under a skeleton that was, for the most part, still in anatomically correct position (Adam 1951: 83). One must conclude, therefore, that it got there either before the animal died or at the time of death. Adam's interpretation of its use, that it was a spear, is thus the most likely.

That the killing of large animals was not rare in the Middle Paleolithic of Europe is attested by sites where they were killed in great numbers. At Mauran in the French Pyrenees, 3500 remains of large animals were recovered, 98% of them from *Bos* and *Bison*, representing a minimum number of 108 individuals[1] (Girard and David 1982). At Volgagrad on the edge of the Crimean Plateau, 78% (366) of the remains were those of bison (*B. priscus*), while at Il'skaya on the eastern littoral of the Black Sea, 70% (a minimum of 30) of the individuals recovered were bison (Gábori 1976a: 205). If the portion of the site excavated was representative of the whole, as many as 1200 bison may have been killed there (Gábori 1979: 245). Finally, one must mention the site of Starosel'e in the Crimea, where the assemblage was dominated by 58,909 remains of the ass (*Equus asinus*)—a minimum of 287 individuals (Klein 1969: 82). Although *E. asinus* is smaller than the horse (*E. caballus*), it is hard to believe that it was significantly easier to hunt.

While there is no proof that these large concentrations represent single hunting episodes, the preponderance of a single species indicates that the animals do not represent a cross-section of carcasses available for scavenging, and the large numbers make it impossible to argue that the predominance of one species is due to sampling error. We are therefore

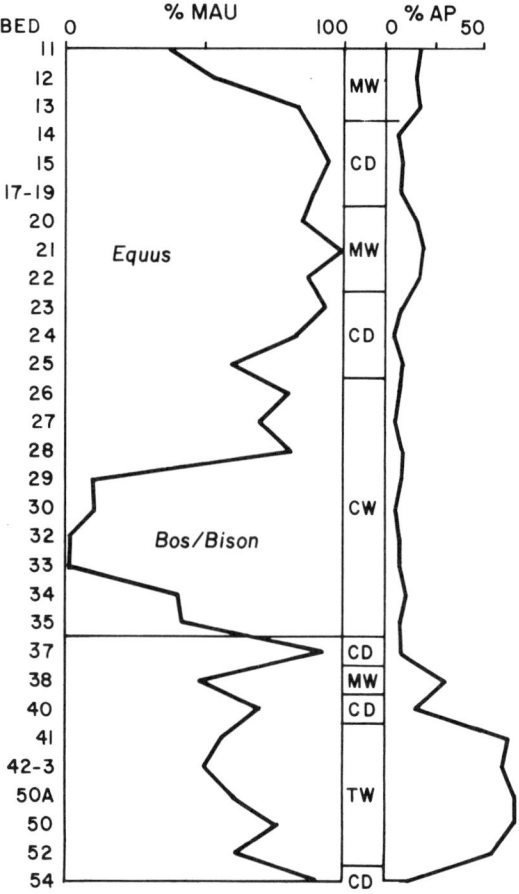

Figure 13.2. Relative proportions of equids (left) and large bovids (right) at Combe-Grenal, compared to percentage of arboreal pollen (from Paquereau 1974-75: 82-83) and to climatic stages defined by Laville (1969a, b) on the basis of sedimentological data. Calculated on the basis of total MAU (from Chase 1986: table A1). (C: cold, D: dry, M: mild, T: temperate, W: wet.)

forced to conclude that the Middle Paleolithic peoples of Europe were fully capable of systematically hunting large animals.

It seems clear that in Europe large game was hunted. In fact, small game was to a very large extent ignored in favor of medium to large species (see Chase 1986: 130-134). Reasons given for this include lack of population pressure (Clark and Straus 1983; Clark and Yi 1983), lack of sufficiently sophisticated technology (Straus 1977: 67), and the possibility that return for effort was greater for large animals than for small ones (Ackerly and Bayham 1984; Gamble 1986).

It would be interesting to test whether or not scavenging of medium-sized and large game was common in Europe at an earlier date, during the Middle Pleistocene. Binford has looked at the data very cursorily and apparently intends to examine them in more detail (Binford 1985: 316). Such a study would be very welcome. One should, perhaps, be somewhat cautious about accepting his preliminary conclusions. A look at the discussion of the remains from Swanscombe (Binford 1984: 316) will illustrate some of the problems.

At Swanscombe, very few bones bore tool marks. There were traces of disarticulation on a mandible, on an atlas, and on a distal tibia. A proximal tibia, a distal tibial shaft, and a distal humeral shaft bore traces of defleshing. (Binford does not specify to what species these bones belonged.) From the low percentage of tool marks, it is logical to conclude as Binford did that most of the animal remains at Swanscombe are there because of nonhuman agents. It does not necessarily follow, however, that that portion of the assemblage for which hominids were responsible was scavenged. A quick look through any set of paleontological data (e.g., Musil's [1980-81] catalog of cave-bear sites) shows that natural assemblages of fauna are common. We also know that hominids accumulated assemblages of animal bones. Given the large amounts of time represented in a Paleolithic site, it would probably be the exception rather than the rule to find a faunal assemblage that was *not* a combination of animals brought in by carnivores and animals introduced by humans. The fact that at one time carnivores brought prey into a site is therefore not *ipso facto* evidence that the animals brought there by humans were scavenged. If this were the case, we would probably have to conclude that humans did little hunting at any time. The problem is not one of determining whether carnivores were responsible for some of the material at a site. It is, rather, one of determining what it was that people were doing with the animals for which *they* were responsible.

Binford concludes, on the basis of evidence such as the distribution of cut marks on the bones at Swanscombe, that the people there were exploiting the meatiest parts of the carcass. As he puts it, "Jumping far ahead in time to the period of the first appearance of hominids in the British Isles we see a very similar pattern but with perhaps a slightly different focus—scavenging appears to be *much more meat oriented*" (1984: 321; emphasis added) and "*scavenging was systematically for meat, not for marginal parts (such as marrow bones)* . . ." (1984: 320; emphasis his).

As Blumenschine has demonstrated, some of the most important criteria for recognizing scavenging are based on the fact that the meatiest portions of the carcass will be unavailable for human exploitation. In fact, the assumption that this is so forms the basis of Binford's own criteria for recognizing scavenging. If this is so, then the discovery of a pattern of human exploitation of the meatiest parts of the carcass must be taken as an indication that people were *not* scavenging. Binford must show how data contrary not only to Blumenschine's empirical observations but also to his own predictions can be taken as evidence for scavenging before we can feel confident in accepting his conclusions.

Nevertheless, the Lower Paleolithic data from Europe are scanty and must still be considered inconclusive. While the evidence from the Middle Paleolithic is quite clear in contradicting the notion of scavenging, we must have much more detailed and extensive studies of Lower Paleolithic assemblages before we can either accept or reject Binford's conclusions concerning this earlier time period. Certainly we cannot continue simply to assume that Middle Pleistocene peoples were hunters. Just as certainly, the question must be answered if we are to understand the evolution of human behavior. Binford has, once again, performed an important service by forcing us to take a closer look at our assumptions.

NOTE

1. Such estimates, based on minimum numbers of individuals, are probably far too low. MNI underrepresents the true number of individuals, and this underrepresentation is more severe the larger the original number of individuals.

DISCUSSION

BOSINSKI: I would like to raise one question concerning the hunting behavior of Middle Paleolithic man. It strikes me that we do not know of hunting places in the Middle Paleolithic. Although Chase mentioned exceptions, the general rule is for there to be mixed game and a very low specialization. Capturing many animals at one time is useful only if they were able to conserve the meat—perhaps this was not possible then. Another possibility is that those people moved around frequently, staying only a very limited time at any one place, so that we do not find traces of their camps. Do you see any differences between settlement and hunting camps?

CHASE: There are a number of things that we have to look at. The Middle Paleolithic spans a huge amount of time and one site may very well represent a series of mixed occupations that cannot be isolated. Moreover, these occupations are not often contemporary in human terms but rather they are contemporary only in geological time. Right now we cannot recognize the more specialized components of the same site, so we may actually have more hunting camps than we think we do. But I do not think that Middle Paleolithic people were specialized in the sense of depending on one species.

FERRING: Your idea that people scavenge opportunistically seems intuitively right. But it also seems to me that your evidence here for the lack of scavenging is extremely strong.

CHASE: The problem is how to recognize scavenging and separate it from hunting in the archaeological record. For example, we should distinguish between primary and secondary scavenging. Primary scavenging is where an animal dies in a nonviolent process and the hominid gets every bone before another carnivore does. In that case, you get a carcass just the same as if you kill it and you will process it in the same manner. In this case, I know of no way of determining from the archaeological record whether you have a scavenged carcass or a hunted carcass. But I do not imagine that happened too often.

RIGAUD: I think that Combe-Grenal does not have the best material for this kind of study, because it was not collected to resolve this kind of archaeological problem.

STRAUS: Also true is the fact that material from the other sites mentioned by Chase have not been studied with the care that he has taken for the Combe-Grenal material. I am not sure that these other sites are well enough understood to allow us to talk about massive slaughter of animals throughout Europe. As Chase pointed out, the deposits at Combe-Grenal and most other Middle Paleolithic sites are formations which in some cases took thousands of years to accumulate. So, perhaps there are levels in Combe-Grenal with 90% reindeer, but what does that represent in terms of hunting behavior? This could represent only one reindeer a month over hundreds of years.

CHASE: But there is a catastrophic age profile for those horses. In other words, it reflects the age distributions of a living population, not animals who died of attrition. I am not saying that Paleolithic people killed animals only by driving enormous herds over cliffs. But when you get a very definite concentration of one species and the frequency of species doesn't change with the climate, then there is a deliberateness, or at least a nonrandomness, in which species were exploited. And it does not look like scavenging.

XIV

The Ecosystem of the "Middle Paleolithic" (Late Lower Paleolithic) in the Upper Danube Region

A Stepping-Stone to the Upper Paleolithic

Hansjürgen Müller-Beck

DEFINITIONS OF CONCEPTS AND CHRONOSTRATIGRAPHY

François Bordes (1954a) correlated his conception of the beginning of the Middle Paleolithic with the start of the Riss-Würm Interglacial as it was conceived of at that time. Although this proved to be a useful demarcation in regard to France, it seemed rather arbitrary for southern Germany. The scarcity of finds in the Upper Danube region (Müller-Beck 1956) made such a delimitation unverifiable. So, a description of those Late Pleistocene assemblages in terms of "Late Lower Paleolithic," not yet possessing the "Upper Paleolithic" characteristics, appeared to be more appropriate. In southern Germany, the Upper Paleolithic started with the evolution of the Aurignacian of the Vogelherd type (Riek 1934; Hahn 1977). Their inventory had more affinities with the classic Mousterian or the developed Micoquian (Late Acheulian). The real "leaf-shaped point inventories" (*Blattspitzen*) of an apparently later date clearly form a distinct feature. Besides, a definition of the beginning of the Late Pleistocene (Müller-Beck 1967) through correlation with the Eemian, which is the most valid way to delimit its boundaries, could not be established at that time because reliable paleobotanical finds at Paleolithic sites were lacking. Even today, we often face the same difficulty.

In the last 30 years, the correlation of the beginning of the Late Pleistocene with that of the Florenstufe Eemian in Central Europe has become generally accepted (Welten 1982). Today, for our area and for Western Europe, we are also aware that nominal categorical distinctions in the morphology between what can be called plausible archaeological inventories before and after the Eemian are minor and rather difficult to pinpoint. They show some differences in composition which may at least partially be attributed to the vegetation of the site environment. But these differences can also arise from direct technological causes. The principal characteristics of the basic industry and the emergent transformations are in any case identical over a broader time span. Hence, in contrast to Bordes, G. Bosinski (1967) and others have considerably broadened the concept of the "Middle Paleolithic" by including also the pre-Eemian period. Their proposal conforms to my observations published in 1956. Departing from this extended notion, the continuation of the "Lower Paleolithic" in the "late Lower Paleolithic" has been described as "Middle Paleolithic." Yet the extension of the concept of the "Middle Paleolithic" to the first occurrence of well-manufactured Levallois cores seems to be as unsatisfactory as the former hypothesis. So, one may either plead for a return to Bordes's more restricted definition of the Middle Paleolithic, or opt to place the Lower Paleolithic within the newly proposed range (Müller-Beck 1956). In the latter case, a more pronounced differentiation of this period and the Upper Paleolithic, initiated by the Vogelherd Aurignacian, must be achieved.

We will demonstrate that the finds from the Upper Danube, which are the focus of this paper, must all be classified as post-Eemian. This means that they belong to the Late Pleistocene. To describe them as "Middle Paleolithic" or "Upper Paleolithic" is of secondary importance. They certainly cannot be attributed to the "early Lower Paleolithic" pre-Eemian period.

Nevertheless, the problems in classifying the chronostratigraphy in relation to its actual manifestation in southern Germany will briefly be discussed. The classic "Holstein," traceable in its regionally differentiated sequence up to the Swiss Alpine frontier, is chronostratigraphically well defined (Welten 1982). It remains uncertain, however, whether the Holstein has to be correlated ultimately with deep-sea isotope stage 11 (Sarntheim, Stremme, and Mangini 1986), ca. 400,000 years B.P. on the long time-scale; or whether it must be associated only with stage 9c, ca. 320,000 B.P. on the short time-scale. Upon the Holstein follows a series of steppe, forest, and tundra isotope stages, analogous to what meanwhile has been attested for the more established sequence of the Late Pleistocene (Welten 1982). The division into a "Lower" and a "Middle" Pleistocene, as proposed by W. Soergel (Grahmann and Müller-Beck 1967), has been proven to be quite useful. Thanks to the site of Bilzingsleben (Mania, Toepfer, and Vlček 1980; Mai et al. 1983; Mania and Weber 1986), we know for certain that during the Dömnitz forest period, which according to Sarntheim, Stremme, and Mangini (1986) is identical with the "Wacken" and is to be distinguished from the smaller Holstein, *Palaeoloxodon antiquus* occurs for the last time in a warm forest environment. In association were found remains of *Homo erectus* and an elementary flake industry, along with a remarkably sophisticated bone- and antler-working technique, marked by incisions ranging from simple geometrical patterns to a genuine rectangle (Mania and Weber 1986). To correlate this Dömnitz (Wacken) phase with isotope stage 9c or 7a, and to date it ca. 300,000 years B.P. in the long chronology or 200,000 years B.P. in the short chronology, remains problematic. It is interesting, however, to note that the advance of the ice cap during the classic Alpine Riss and the synchronic Saale in northern Germany succeeds the Holstein only after a considerable period of time—even in the short chronology. In any case the soil is very rich during the "Treene" (Stremme 1986), perhaps indicating a prominent warm period correlated with isotope stage 7a, as Sarntheim, Stremme, and Mangini (1986) have suggested. As in the stratigraphic model of the two eldest Jungend-moraines in isotope stage 2, the presence of the layers of both "Drenthe" and "Warthe" ice-positions in isotope stage 6 is not to be excluded. Consequently there would be a Treene situated before the morphologically identifiable Drenthe glacial, which is followed in its turn by a third one. We are confronted with similar problems for the chronology of the Late Pleistocene in the vicinity of the levels of the Jungend-moraines. They must have started after the "Denekamp" (and "Paudorf"/"Stillfried B"), instead of before this last period.

According to our definition (Grahmann and Müller-Beck 1967), the progression of the "middle Middle Pleistocene" (Fig. 14.1) may have continued until 220,000 B.P. in the long chronology and have known a highly differentiated evolution. Thus, the corresponding forward movement of the ice cap during the Late Pleistocene, from the end of the Eemian up to the beginning of the "Turicum 6" progression (Welten 1982), must have covered the span of ca. 115,000 to 25,000 B.P., by no means exceeding 100,000 years. Once again, for this estimation the "long chronology," based on C-14 and U/Th data scales, is used. In the "extrapolated C-14 scale," only a difference of approximately 50,000 to 60,000 years could be recorded (Welten 1982; Fig. 14.2).

The dates of deep-sea isotope stage 5e, which meanwhile have been positively correlated with the Eemian, succeed stage 6 in the Atlantic and the Pacific ca. 122,000 to 125,000 B.P. on the U/Th scale. This corresponds to their maximum flooding levels. Next come stage 5c, with a high-water mark around 108,000 to 103,000 B.P., and stage 5a, ca. 82,000 to 81,000 B.P. in the long U/Th scale. The largest ice-advance (in northern Germany the "Brandenburg"-stade, in the Alps the "Outer Jungend-moraines") has been dated to 17,850 B.P. (C-14 scale of the "short" chronology), so barely 8000 years before the beginning of the postglacial period (Martinson et al. 1987). This attribution coincides with the direct C-14 dates of these stages between 20,000 and 16,000 B.P., classed by Welten (1982) under the Turicum 6 (Fig. 14.2). Calibrated solar-year data for this period are not yet available.

The total duration of the Eemian (isotope stage 5e), with its well-known vegetational history, has been estimated on the basis of the varve-layer count at around 15,000 years (Müller 1974). The first succeeding glacial progression in the Alps seems to have had a wide expansion (Turicum 1: Welten 1982; Fig. 14.2), but this fact does not inform us about the ice sheet's duration or force, nor does it give us any indications of the glacial's actual influence on floral and faunal evolution. Recent meas-

Turicum 6		Gravettian	20,000 C-14
		Gravettian	
Turicum 5c			
	Denekamp	Classic Aurignacian	
Turicum 5b		Haldenstein Blattspitzen	
	Hengelo	Mauern Blattspitzen	40,000 C-14
Turicum 5a			
		Schambach Oben Grosse Grotte II	
Turicum 4			
Turicum 3		Grosse Grotte XI	
	Brörup	Schambach Basis	
Turicum 2			
Turicum 1		Vogelherd IX	
	Eem		120,000 Th/U

Figure 14.1 Chronostratigraphy of the "Middle Paleolithic" along the Upper Danube, Turicum 1-6 ice advances. (After Welten 1982; —— most probable time range; ······ possible time range)

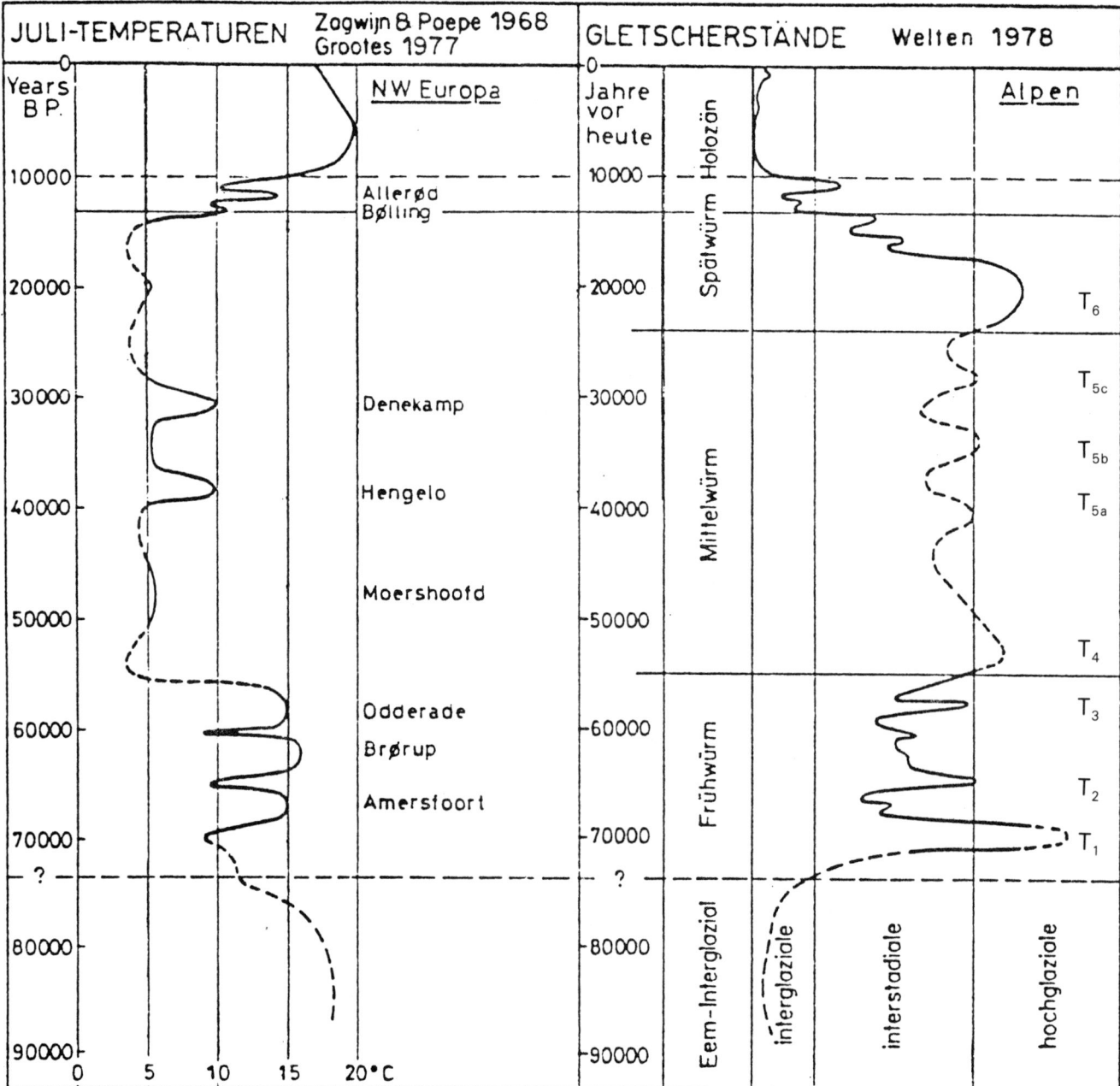

Figure 14.2 Climatic sequence in the Upper Pleistocene after the pollen spectra analyzed by Welten (1982) in Switzerland in comparison with data from the Netherlands:
a) after reconstructed July temperatures (Zagwijn and Paepe 1968, version: Grootes 1977);
b) after hypothetical glacier advances (stages) (Welten 1978) in the northern Alp-forelands of Switzerland. T_{1-6} = Turicum 1-6 = stages of the Würm glaciation (place and magnitude partially hypothetical). The time-scale correlates with the actual opinion of a "short chronology."

urements at smaller glacier streams in the Antarctic have demonstrated that the ice cap covered distances of ca. 800 m a year during times of relatively limited rainfall (Lucchita and Ferguson 1986). This means an increase that can run up to 8 km during the course of ten years and 80 km in one century. At such rates, a progression from the middle of Sweden up to the final layers of the Brandenburg phase must have been barely a matter of a millennium. In the Alps, because of the intense precipitation, a progression period of only a few centuries must be presumed. For the advance of the Turicum 1, two to three centuries may have sufficed. But even then the conditions must show fundamental "glacial" tendencies, similar to those long known for the period after the Eemian, when there still followed a series of more favorable vegetational periods ("Amersfoort," "Brörup," etc. up to Denekamp: Zagwijn and Paepe 1968). On the U/Th scale, the first clear decline in temperature, which can be inferred from the animal species as well, seems to appear ca. 80,000 to 70,000 B.P., before the Brörup. On the C-14 scale this value may lie around 70,000 to 60,000 B.P.; in the short chronology it is situated around 50,000 B.P., after the Brörup. So it remains an open question whether Turicum 5 or Turicum 6 can be associated with the aforementioned U/Th data. There is no doubt, however, that the Brörup caused an important renewed afforestation that continued for some millennia, leaving behind a corresponding soil composition (Welten 1982). Welten dates the end of this vegetation zone to ca. 55,000-53,000 C-14 years B.P. His Turicum 4 would be equivalent to the first Late Pleistocene cold-climate phase in isotope stage 4. The smaller ice progressions Turicum 5a-c would be part of the "Interpleniglacial" as defined by the Dutch authors Zagwijn and Paepe (1968) and Grootes (1977). During this phase the shift from the Middle to the Upper Paleolithic must have occurred around 35,000 to 30,000 B.P., in the form of the southern German Aurignacian. The available C-14 data do not permit a more precise dating. At any rate, the maximal progression of the ice cap during the Alpine Jungend-moraines only took place ca. 20,000 B.P.

These radiometric dates must be interpreted with caution, though, until calibration with a reliable criterion is possible. This may and will be obtained in the near future by a dendrochronological sequence from somewhere in the Rhone Valley or from the Mediterranean. We can therefore regard Welten's assumptions (1982) only as isotope stages valuable for their stratigraphic order. Since the available data do not yet form a complete, continuous chronology, exact correlations based exclusively on these dates cannot be made. Furthermore, the use of two different scales (U/Th and C-14), to which new ones with their own individual statistics will someday be added, poses a serious problem.

THE REGION AND ITS SITES

The area denoted by the term "Upper Danube" shall not be restricted to the upper course of the river above Ehingen, but will also encompass the region above the bursting of the Danube at Kelheim, including the basin of Ingolstadt and the tributaries coming from the Swabian and Franconian Albs. Thereto belong the Danube swamp adjacent to the west, and the ca. 5-km-broad valley from Ulm to Ehingen. From the south the Riss, Iller, Günz, Mindel, and Lech Rivers, and the Isar in part, transport rubble—mostly in the form of glacial gravel—into the valley of the Danube, thereby covering ancient surfaces and Paleolithic stations which must be preserved underneath. Between Ulm and Ingolstadt, a valley track of approximately 100 km, the Danube falls from 466 to 365 m above sea level (Fig. 14.3). The findspots within this area are situated chiefly in caves in the northern alpine valleys (e.g., Haldenstein Cave at the upper end of the Lone Valley, at a height of 585 m above sea level). A series of open-air stations, scattered on the hilltops or within the slip mass, have so far rarely been considered (e.g., Gaimersheim near Ingolstadt, located 380 m above sea level in the loess-colluvium of the valley fill).

The stations under scrutiny can be discussed only in a summary way. Excluded from this survey are a number of singular finds, and the sites near Essing, because of their location near the outlet of the bursting of the Danube. Our overview will also include some critical heuristic remarks and a description of the location of the sites.

The two sites farthest to the west (Fig. 14.3) are located in a wider area of the Lauchert Valley, north of Sigmaringen. This valley runs from the north into the uppermost part of the Danube Valley above

Figure 14.3   Middle Paleolithic sites along the Upper Danube: 1) Göpfelstein Cave; 2) Schafstall; 3) Kogelstein; 4) Sirgenstein; 5) Grosse Grotte; 6) Haldenstein Cave; 7) Bocksteinschmiede; 8) Bocksteinhöhle; 9) Stadel; 10) Vogelherd; 11) Heidenschmiede; 12) Irpfel Cave; 13) Weinberg Caves; 14) Speckberg; 15) Gaimersheim; 16) Hohle Stein bei Schambach.

Ehingen, where it is still narrow and deep. Göpfelstein and Schafstall caves each contained a "Middle Paleolithic" inventory of cutting tools in a single sedimentary level. Below Ehingen, the discoveries at Kogelstein near Schmiechen, a small hilltop, and remains of a cave in the Blaubeurer Valley, formerly a tributary of the Danube, yielded only a very limited assemblage. Planned road constructions in 1988 will necessitate investigations which may provide some definite explanation about the sedimentation of the valley and may reveal more sites. In Grosse Grotte ("big cave"), excavated only after 1960, ten sedimentary levels with Middle Paleolithic inventories were present in the upper part of the slope high above the valley bottom. Sirgenstein Cave, already explored before the First World War, yielded Middle Paleolithic finds in two different sedimentary zones. This site is located on the middle of the slope in the Blaubeurer Valley. From here, a broad panoramic view must have been possible during colder climatic phases when trees were sparser. For the adjoining Lone Valley north of the Danube, Haldenstein Cave should be mentioned. Two pre-Upper Paleolithic levels were found, showing—notwithstanding their limited dimensions—a characteristic composition. This narrow hole lies only at a limited height above the bottom of the valley and the Lone spring. In Bockstein, further downstream, two sites were discovered: Bocksteinhöhle with Middle Paleolithic findings in a lower sedimentary zone, and Bocksteinschmiede containing several findspots. Before and after World War II, two Middle Paleolithic main levels which are spread all over the slope were excavated. The relatively elevated Bocksteinschmiede, especially, offers an overall view of the surroundings. In particular, it looks out on a deer path that still leads into the valley. Still further downstream, Stadel Cave is located almost directly on what is now the ground level of the valley. It seems likely, however, that during the exploitation of the cave in Middle Paleolithic times, the surface level must have been lower. The two occupational strata were uncovered in the last years before 1939. Vogelherd Cave further down, separated only by a flat hilltop from the bed of the Danube River, overlooks a broad branch of the valley and again has a view of a passing path for hoofed animals. Already in 1931 four successive strata belonging to the pre-Upper Paleolithic period were discovered in areally limited sedimentary remains. The Upper Paleolithic period itself is represented by two typical Aurignacian levels in the cave just below the highest preserved hilltop. In the adjacent Brenz Valley to the east, two stations can be named. First is Heidenschmiede, rich in finds, with at least two occupational strata on the upper slope of the Schlossberg. By its location at a branch point of the valley, it enjoys once again a strategic vantage point for hunting. Second is Irpfel Cave, easily accessible because of its position on the middle flat valley slope. Weinberg Caves near Mauern, which belong to Bavarian territory, are stationed in the dry valley at Wellheim. This was probably already deserted by the Danube at that time. Northward they overlook the valley, while southward they view the wide lowland and the river itself. Excavations shortly before and after the Second World War revealed two strata. The finds were scattered at random within a large quadrant. The Aurignacian is barely marked in the sloping strata. The Gravettian level, on the other hand, is more circumscribed and has a relatively high density of finds. Nearby lies the vast open-air station of Speckberg, which owes its existence to the sedimentary decline of a rocky protrusion. It offers a broad panorama on the slightly lower Schutter Valley and the Ingolstadt Basin towards the east. During systematic excavations at Speckberg, many thousands of Middle Paleolithic artifacts were found in relation to three stratigraphic layers. Finally, reference should be made to the small find complex of Gaimersheim, which was discovered at the edge of the eastern basin of Ingolstadt thanks to the attentiveness of an anonymous Russian World War II prisoner. A short distance away, Hohlestein Cave near Schambach revealed—during excavations conducted just after the war and again after 1970—eight Middle Paleolithic find complexes, spread over a sedimentary sequence of approximately 12 m. This site is located on the middle of the valley slope leading from the northern Altmühl to the Danube.

In total, we have here 16 stations with Middle Paleolithic assemblages, though of unequal informational value. Without exception, all lie north of the Danube within ca. 160 km as the crow flies. Obviously they represent only a section of the original exploitation zone of which they must have been part. The main outlines of this zone can be reconstructed by considering the present topographic situation, the substratum, and the vegetational potential of that time, by which also the productivity of the fauna was determined. In general terms, the area stretched from the upper part of the Albs over the sheltered valley of the Danube in its varying width, to the southern counterslopes and hilltops, and to the valleys of the alpine confluents amply providing fish and birds. Starting from the northernmost sites, the distances amount to ca. 10 to 40 km. To simplify our model, let us put forward an average distance of 25 km from the northern to the southern exploitation frontiers. The minimum area would then embrace approximately 4000 sq. km with the Danube itself as an axis. Evidently, the 43 Middle Paleolithic sites discovered so far have yielded only a small selection of the original artifact production, and thus of the preserved but still-unexcavated tools. This ratio is exemplified in particular at Speckberg, where different strata are accumulated. Per square meter of sedimentation, up to 4000 Middle Paleolithic artifacts were recovered. They form the traces of an exploitation period which must have continued for 10,000 to 20,000 years, since the remains belong to the period from the end of the Pleistocene to the Holocene, covering a time span of almost 13,000 years, even when phases of varying length for which no samples were present interrupt this sequence. Almost the total range of artifact types defined by Bordes are encountered at Speckberg, representing different kinds of activities. So we have either one main layer of long-term occupation or several strata of subsequent occupations, offering complete documentation of the entire range of functional variations. Unfortunately, the sedimentary condition does not permit us to distinguish between these two possibilities. Nevertheless a whole spectrum of different uses is illustrated, this on an extremely important spot topographically because of the nearby presence of large reserves of raw material. One finds not only tabular flint, used for the manufacturing of tools with a specific cutting function, but also Cretaceous quartzite for the fabrication of handaxes. The quartzite's higher resistance (compared to the flint) permits heavier labor entailing greater risk of breakage.

For the Middle Paleolithic finds in Weinberg Caves, the average per cubic meter accounted for only eight artifacts, showing a density of 0.2% in comparison to Speckberg. This observation can be put in perspective, though, when observing the assemblage of Hohlestein Cave. Recent excavations at this site have proved that well-retouched lithic tools (scrapers, blades, etc.), isolated during abrupt sedimentation, occur separately as traces of executed labor, while cores and flakes, documented by their denser concentration, form so-called "production units." From a functional point of view, this means that the last-mentioned tools were manufactured over a limited period of time, whereas the intensive re-employment of the "retouched utensils" promoted their long-term usage without major macroscopic modifications, before they were finally abandoned on the spot (at least in regular cases).

ARTIFACTS, PREDATORS, AND CHRONOLOGICAL CLASSIFICATION

An exhaustive discussion of all 43 assemblages would far surpass the scope of this summary review. We shall therefore restrict our attention to the most noteworthy aspects, while focusing our argumentation on the ecological and chronological correlations.

It is evident that the lowest inventory of Vogelherd (Riek's Level IX) belongs to the beginning of the sequence of the Upper Danube region. This assemblage consists of simple, almost unmodified flake tools, found in association with milk teeth from a forest elephant species of the warm period, *Palaeoloxodon antiquus*. The next level (Riek's Level VIII), made up of rubble deposited during a cold period, also contains flints plus the remains of *Equus germanicus*, which is a marker of a steppe environment. Appearing only in the strata above (Riek's Level VII), apart from the horse, are *Rangifer tarandus*, *Cervus elaphus*, *Bos primigenius*, *Mammuthus primigenius*, and *Coelodonta antiquitatis*, in association with a simple assemblage of flakes that includes some scrapers (Müller-Beck 1956). Also present are the remains of mankind's contemporary in the cave, *Crocuta spelaea*, which may have been partly responsible for the portage of prey into the hole (von Koenigswald in von Koenigswald, Müller-Beck, and Pressmar 1974). This inventory is correlated with a fauna of the cooler steppe, but still copses of unknown dimension must have existed. The presence of *Ursus spelaeus* attests to the grass and coppice vegetation of that time. The 40 flake tools in Level VII are linked with at least 23 individuals of *Equus*, seven of *Mammuthus*, four of *Coelodonta*, three of *Bos*, two of *Cervus*, and one of *Rangifer* (for further details, see Müller-Beck

1956 and Bosinski 1967. The same references apply to the stations below, unless noted otherwise). In a smaller area of Level VI—the latest Middle Paleolithic stratum in Vogelherd, which Riek still describes as "Lower Aurignacian"—were found once again a flake inventory of 30 objects, two spearheads made of bone, and faunal remains of which only those of a reindeer and *U. spelaeus* could be identified with certainty. This very simple assemblage, devoid of any bifacial retouch, is part of a sedimentary layer already belonging to the important warming phase of the "Interpleniglacial," which has long since been defined as the "Aurignacian Oscillation" (Müller-Beck 1956).

Faunal elements of a warm environment also occur in the lowest layers of Hohlestein Cave near Schambach, where *Capreolus capreolus* was recovered along with *Cervus* and *Megaceros*. *Rangifer* is not yet present (Rieder 1983) but was discovered in the second-highest stratum (Rieder's B I). This author

Tierarten	Schicht											
	II	III	IV	V	VI	VII	VIII	IX	X	XI	XII	XIII
Ursus spelaeus	●	●	●	●	●	●	●	●		●		•
Capra ibex	●	●	●	●		●		●				
Rangifer tarandus	●	●	•	●								
Bos vel Bison	•											
Coelodonta antiquitatis	•											
Cervus sp.	●				•							
Ovis argaloides	●									•		
Vulpes vel Alopex	●									●	•	
Vulpes vulpes	●		●							•		
Equus sp.	●					•						
Martes sp.	•											
Crocuta spelaea										•		
Lepus sp.	●			●	•							
Aves	●											
Mammonteus primigenius	•											
Felis silvestris	•											
Mustela nivalis		•										
Lemmus lemmus	●	●	●									
Dicrostonyx torquatus	●	●	●									
Arvicola terrestris	●											
Microtus arvalis-agrestis	●	●	●									
Microtus nivalis	●											
Microtus gregalis				●								

● mehr als 4 Belege   ● bis 4 Belege   • 1 Beleg

Figure 14.4 Remains of hunted animals in the archaeological levels of Grosse Grotte. (From Wagner 1983)

cites *Rangifer, Mammuthus, Equus, Crocuta, U. spelaeus,* and *U. arctos.* The assemblages of the third and fourth complexes are identical (C I and II/III), but yield at the same time a great number of lemming remains. All three layers further contained food bones of *Cervus, Capra,* and *Rupicapra.* These species are lacking in the fifth complex (Rieder's N IV), which therefore apparently must have been the coldest phase during the Middle Paleolithic period. Their reappearance in the sixth and last complex (Rieder's S IV) may indicate some climatic improvement. Of importance here are the already-mentioned "tools" (production units): flakes and cores, manufactured out of the same raw material. In most cases they lie close to each other and are composed of up to 19 individual pieces which can also partially be combined. They testify of flaking activities in the cave. The impossibility of making a complete reconstruction of the artifacts suggests that parts must have been removed to be reused on another spot. The three-dimensional retouched tools, on the contrary, were found separately in the sedimentary layer.

A similar long stratigraphy of the fauna is present in Grosse Grotte in the Blaubeurer Valley (Wagner 1983). There, the sedimentation reaches 2.5 m. It does not contain the different hyena and cave-bear levels which could be distinguished in Hohlestein Cave near Schambach. The hyena does not appear frequently, but here also the bear is common. The uppermost zone, where the largest quantity of faunal remains was found (Fig. 14.4:II), provides again the typical cold-steppe fauna with *Mammuthus, Coelodonta,* and *Rangifer.* Apart from them, *Cervus, Capra, Ovis, Equus, Alopex, Lemmus,* and *Dicrostonyx* clearly point to a cold climate. The lithic tools represent mainly flake derivatives (Fig. 14.5). Bifacial retouched objects are rare, but some refinement can nevertheless be noticed on the upper part. A very remarkable fragment of a well-worked bone point of the "Lautscher type" was found in a stratigraphically secure context (Fig. 14.6).

The brief description of these discoveries already covers 22 of the known Middle Paleolithic inventories of the Upper Danube, so about half of the total of 43. They form an intelligible stratigraphic sequence in the three stations under discussion. The grade of deficiency of possible layers between the observed strata, however, remains an open question. The largest gaps seem to occur at Vogelherd, the smallest in Hohlestein Cave near Schambach. We shall have to return to their possible correlation.

In a survey of other stations with several strata, Speckberg should be mentioned first (Müller-Beck 1967). Two separate lower levels there reveal a series of handaxes made of Cretaceous quartzite, while the flake tools are usually fabricated out of Jurassic "Plattenhornstein" from the Malm levels. The upper Middle Paleolithic level yields more flat retouched bifacial forms. Faunal remains are almost completely absent and cannot be associated with certainty with the different Paleolithic levels. Apparently, this condensation of layers is due to the penetration of the artifacts into the subsoil. Hundreds of Middle Paleolithic cores with worn-down edges document the intensive workshop activity on the hilltop.

At Bockstein in the Lone Valley, two well-separated main strata occur, the lower containing only cutting tools and cores, the upper displaying a definite bifacial industry of handaxes and handaxe-scrapers (see Bohmers 1951), besides variants of handaxes and leaf-shaped forms. On the basis of these tools, Bosinski (1967) defined his "inventory type" of Bocksteinschmiede. The hunted fauna here also consists for the most part of *Equus,* but *Rangifer* and *Mammuthus* are likewise present. The opposite is true for Heidenschmiede in the Brenz Valley, where more variants of handaxes are encountered in the lower sedimentation complex than in the upper, flake tools being predominant in these last levels. Documentation, however, remains obscure. The associated fauna suffer from the same shortcoming, since they were not analyzed separately. They include *Equus, Rangifer, Mammuthus, Coelodonta,* and *Dicrostonyx. Cervus* is absent. In the category of birds, one finds willow grouse, eagle owl, goose, and duck. The two levels at Sirgenstein in the Blaubeurer Valley have solely flake tools without bifacial retouching, but nonetheless 56 of the total 700 artifacts are cores. In both layers, the faunal taxa are practically identical: *Equus* and *Rangifer* occur often, *Bison* and *Mammuthus* are less well represented, *Cervus* is omitted completely. *U. spelaeus* is very common. Here also, especially during wintertime, the bear is concurrent with humans in the occupation of the cave. The presence of *Dicrostonyx* once again operates as a marker of a cold climate.

A completely different archaeological sequence is offered by Weinberg Caves near Mauern (von Koenigswald, Müller-Beck, and Pressmar 1974; Brande 1975; Bleich 1975). In the inventory of the

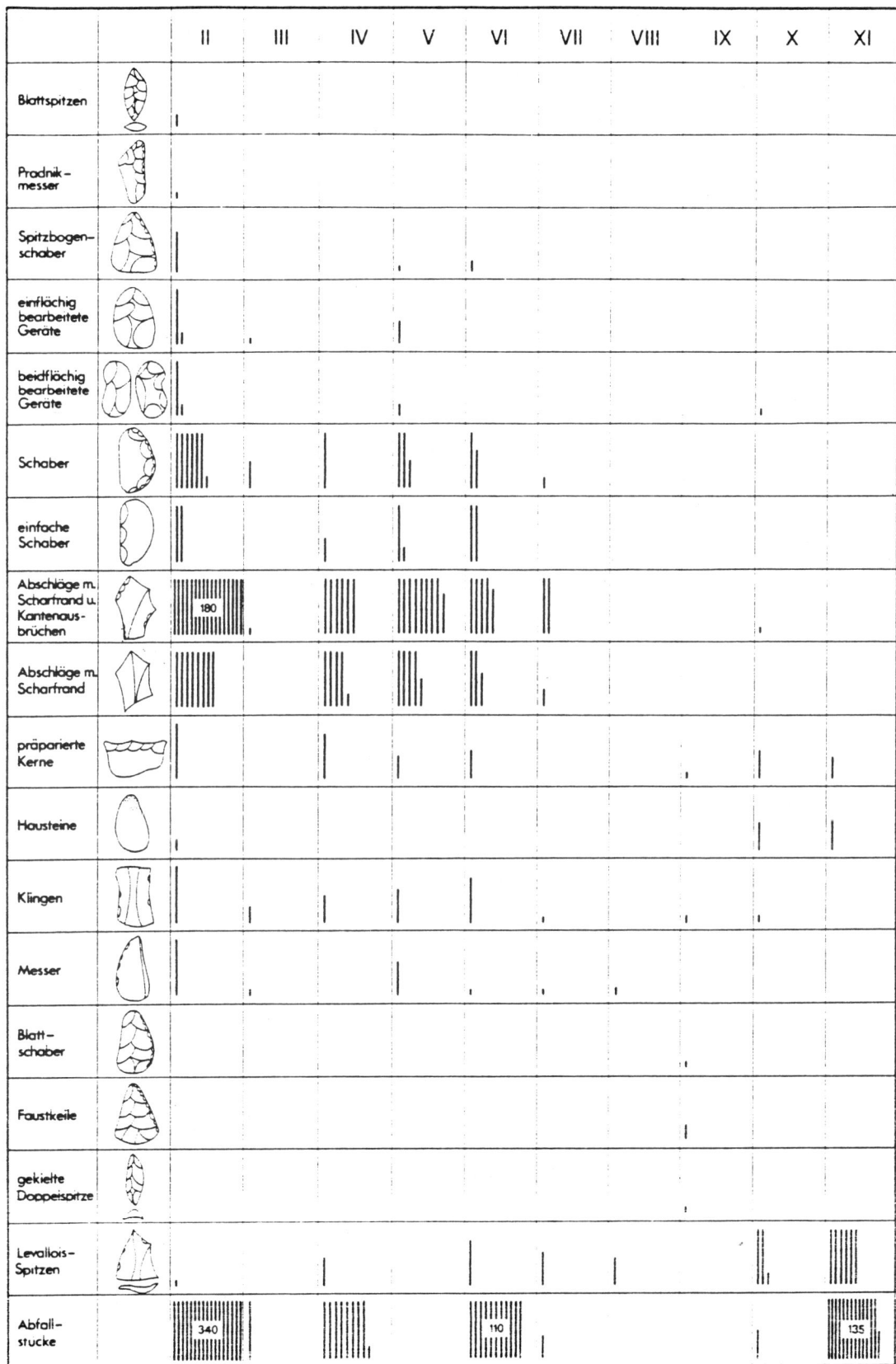

Figure 14.5 Distribution of artifact types in Levels XI (lowest) to II (highest) of Grosse Grotte. One mm line-length is equal to one object. (From Wagner 1983)

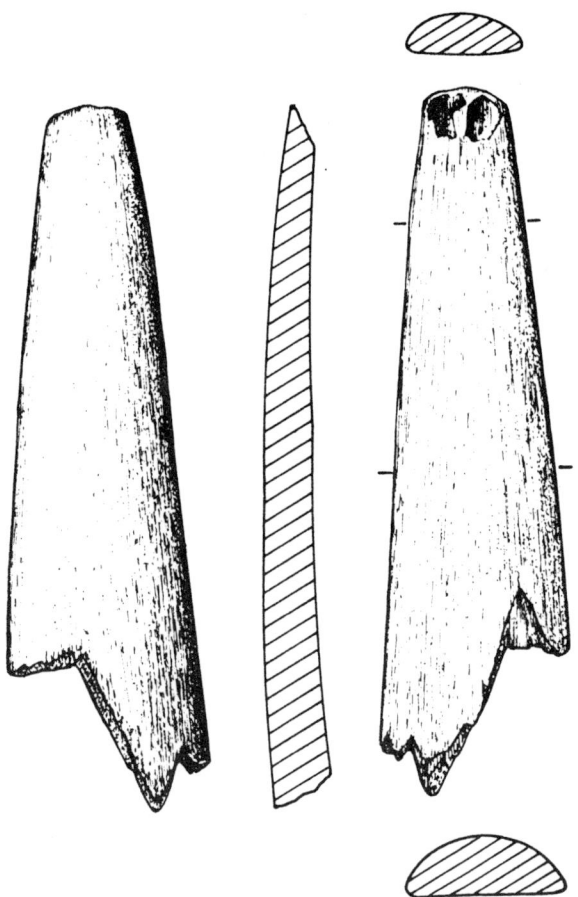

Figure 14.6 Bone point from Level II of Grosse Grotte. Scale 1:1. (From Wagner 1983)

Finally there is the multilayered station of Haldenstein Cave in the upper Lone Valley. A small, simple flake assemblage was found in a lower stratum, together with a great number of toad and frog remains. The layer above contained an inventory of limited size with two very carefully prepared leaf-shaped points and a heavy blade. The associated fauna comprised *Coelodonta, Equus* cf. *germanicus, Equus* cf. *przewalski* (this for the first time in a Middle Paleolithic context), *Cervus, Rangifer, Crocuta,* and *U. spelaeus.*

The other stations provided the following evidence. At Stadel in the Lone Valley, two levels contained cutting tools in association with the standard fauna—*Equus, Rangifer, Mammuthus, Coelodonta, Crocuta,* and *U. spelaeus.* The lowest layer yielded the only positively identified human remains of the Middle Paleolithic period, viz., a 25-cm-long fragment of a femur attributed to *Homo sapiens neanderthalensis.* No further details have yet been reported. In Göpfelstein Cave and in Schafstall in the Lauchert Valley, another level with cutting tools was discovered. The faunal remains of the first cannot be assigned to the Middle Paleolithic without raising some doubt. Those at Schafstall clearly belong to the Middle Paleolithic period, as assured by the presence of *Rangifer, Equus, Mammuthus, Coelodonta, Capra,* and *Bison.* The small flake inventory of Kogelstein near Schmiechen was connected with a large fauna: *Equus, Rangifer, Coelodonta, Bos, Megaceros, Capra, Cervus, Crocuta,* and *Ursus,* plus that indicator of a cold climate, *Dicrostonyx.* Another small stock of flake tools is found at Irpfel Cave in the Brenz Valley, in context with the remains of a real pack of hyenas, comprising at least two cubs, eight fully grown and two elder individuals of *Crocuta.* Their activity is also attested by the major part of the prey fauna: 15 individuals of *Equus,* nine of *Coelodonta,* eight of *U. spelaeus,* seven of *Rangifer,* three of *Bison,* three of *Megaceros,* and one of *Rupicapra* (in each case the minimum number). Finally, the small cutting-tool assemblage of Gaimersheim was associated with *Equus* remains, accentuating once again the importance of this species in the fauna of prey.

lower layer complex, flake tools and typical Middle Paleolithic cores prevail (Fig. 14.7). Additionally, a singular broad, flat handaxe was discovered. In the layer above, on the contrary, once more a colluvium of allochthonous origin with numerous leaf-shaped points and blades was found in association with steep cores (Fig. 14.8). The fauna is composed as before of *Equus, Rangifer, Mammuthus,* and *Coelodonta.* Brande's pollen analysis (1975) has confirmed that the Paleolithic phase with leaf-shaped points of Mauern's upper levels can be situated in the "Interpleniglacial," since the vegetation possesses a distinctive steppe character with reserves of copses present in sheltered areas (Fig. 14.9). Thereafter follows a classic Gravettian in a rubble layer, which was clearly deposited during colder climatic conditions (Bohmers 1951; Zotz 1955). A fragmentary bone point of the Lautscher type also dates from the Paleolithic leaf-shaped-point phase of Weinberg Caves.

In estimating the time range of the find complexes, the situation of Weinberg Caves near Mauern and its connection with the filling of the valley demonstrate that these features, at least, have to be situated around the Late Pleistocene period (Brande 1975). Even without this information, there

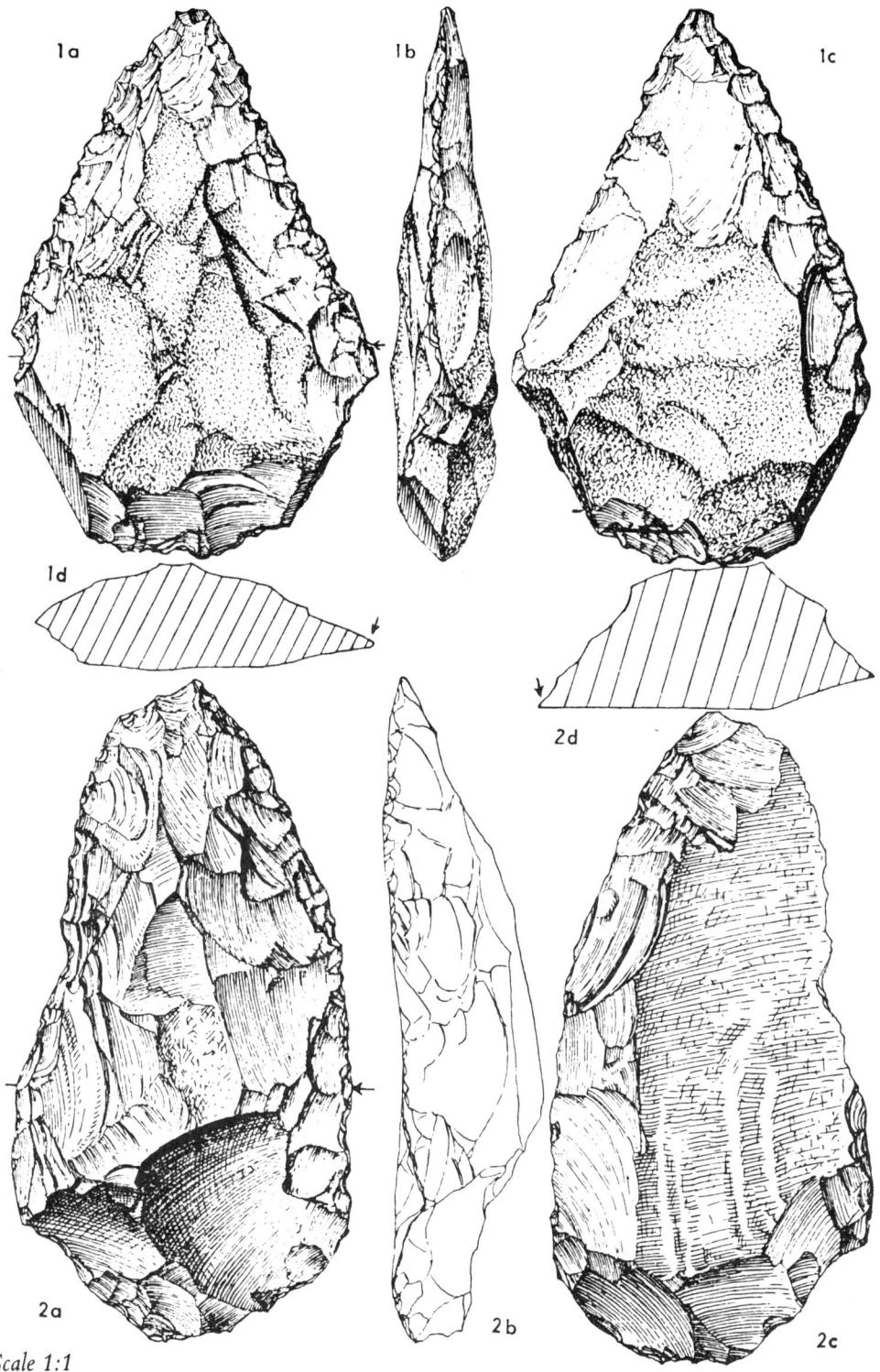

Figure 14.7 Lithic artifacts from the lower level of Weinberg Caves. (From Bohmers 1951)

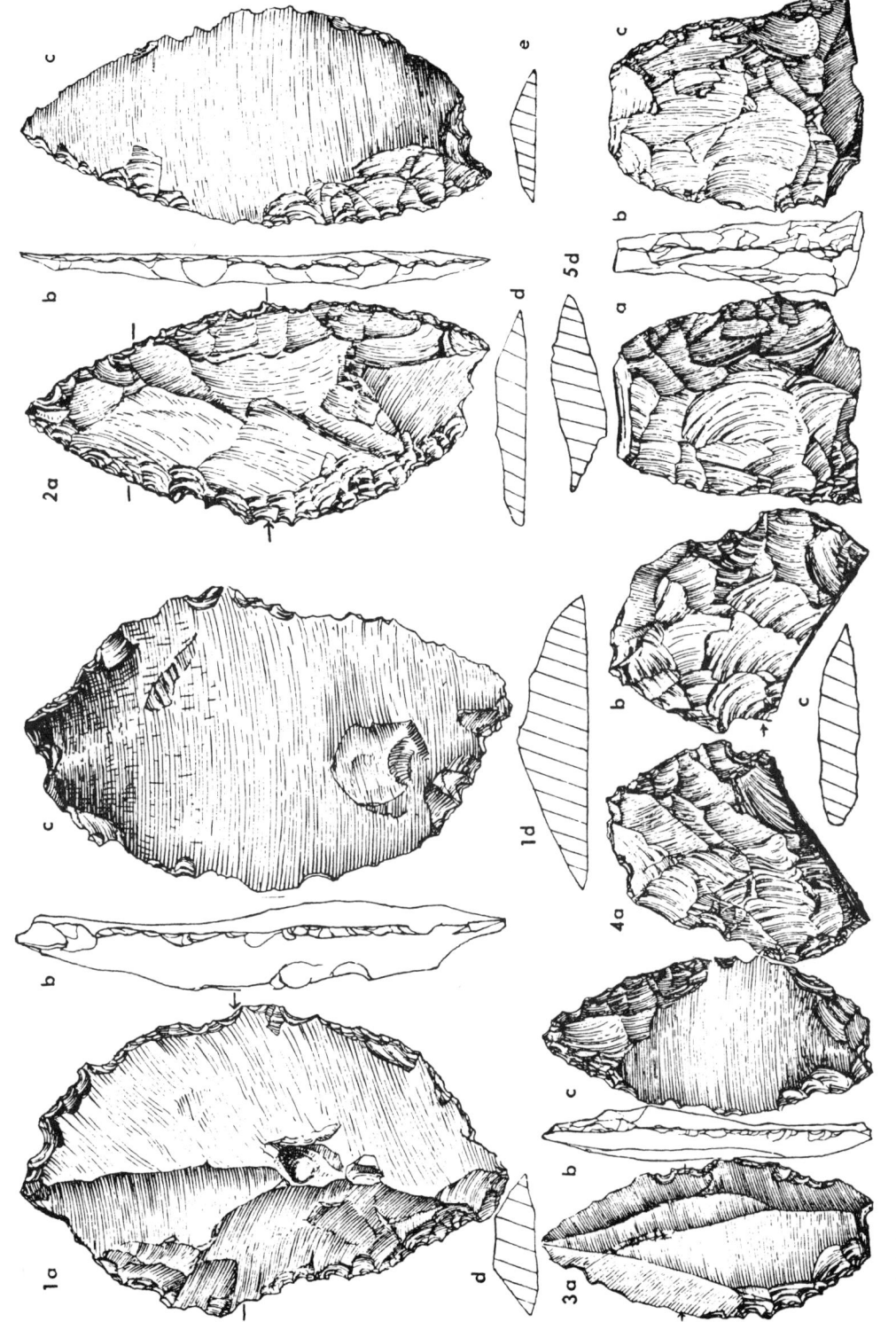

Figure 14.8 Lithic artifacts from the upper Middle Paleolithic level of Weinberg Caves. (From Bohmers 1951)

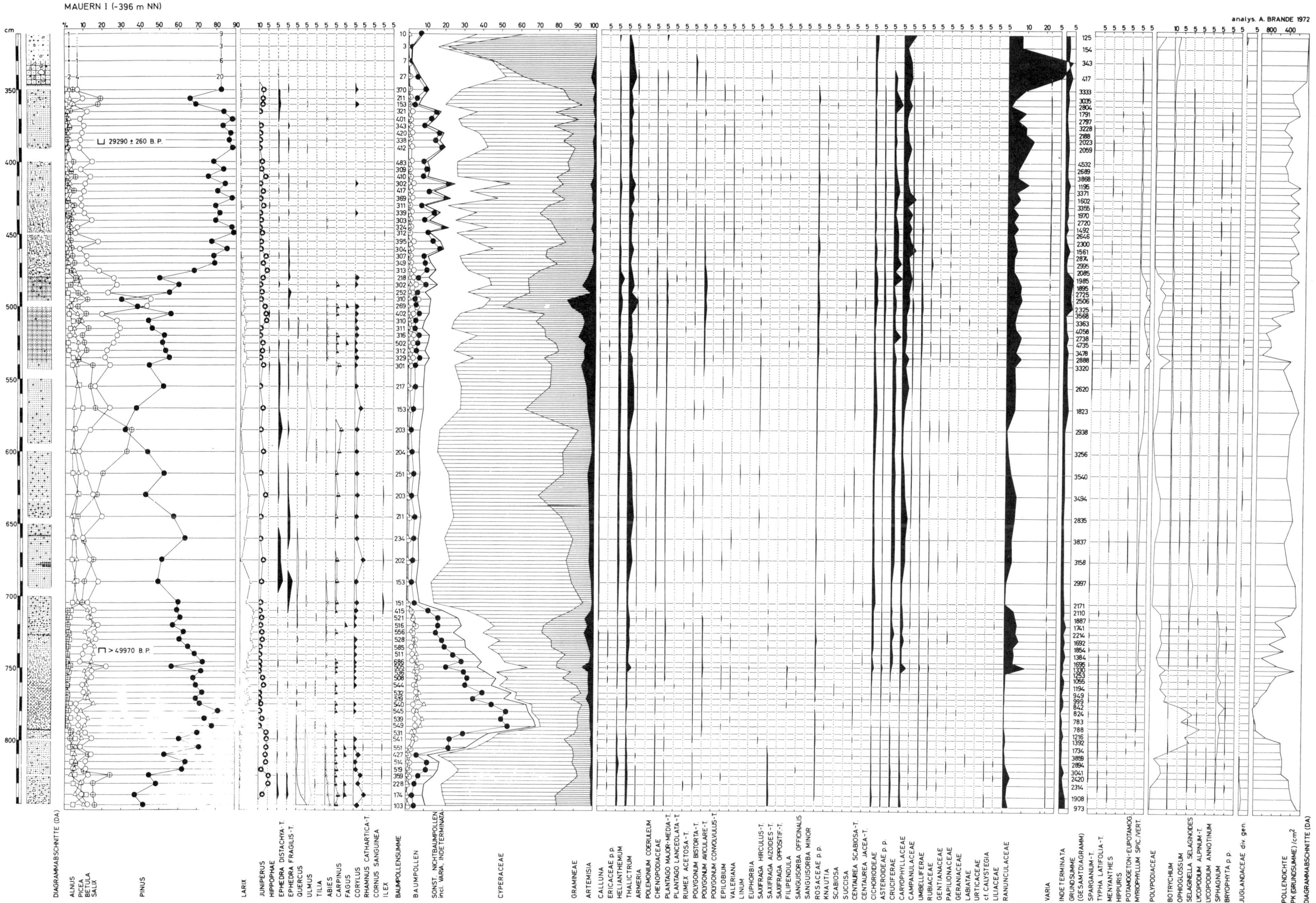

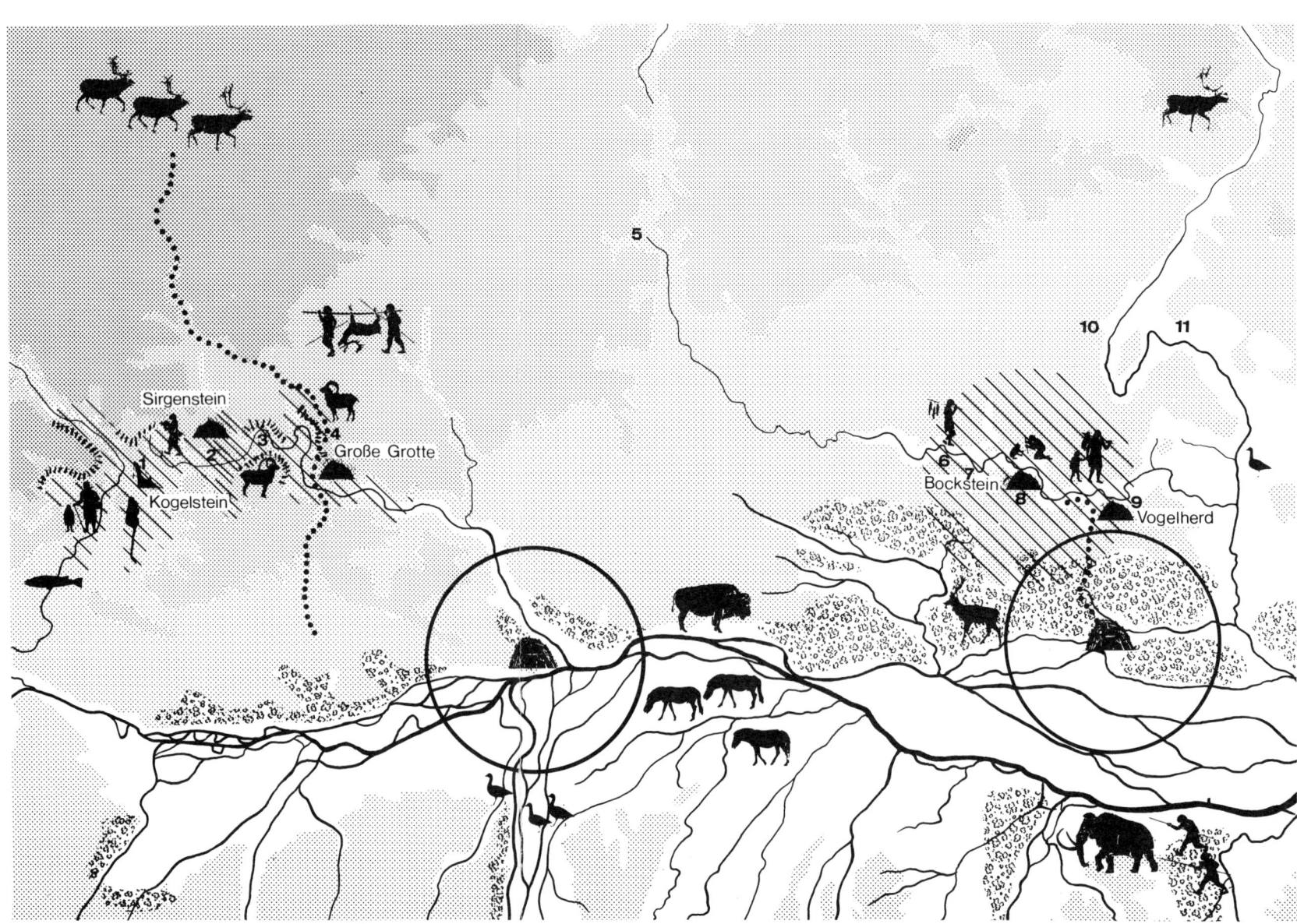

Figure 14.10   The Upper Danube in the Middle Paleolithic, from Ehingen to Lauingen, showing ecological niches and types of occupation: 1) Kogelstein/Schmiechen; 2) Sirgenstein; 3) Geissenklösterle (Aurignacian); 4) Grosse Grotte; 5) Ursprung/Haldenstein; 6) Bocksteinschmiede; 7) Bockstein; 8) Stadel; 9) Vogelherd; 10) Heidenschmiede; 11) Irpfel Cave.

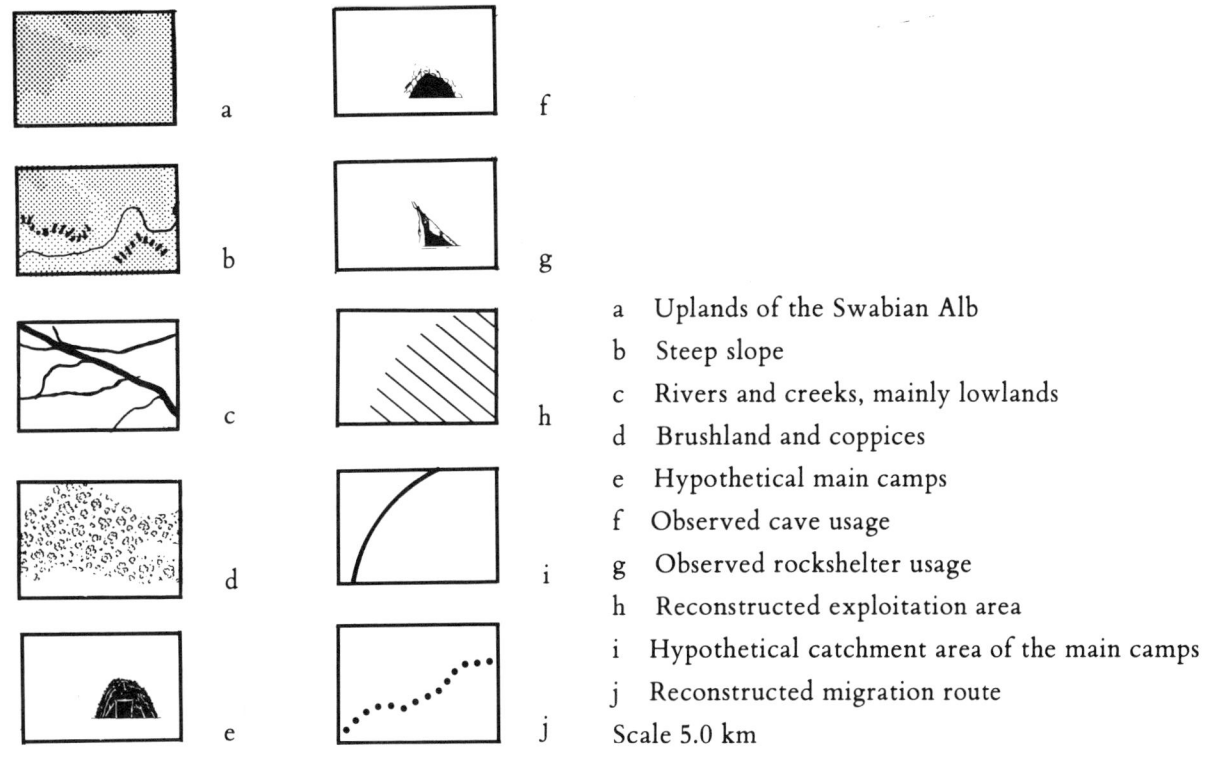

Figure 14.10 Legend.

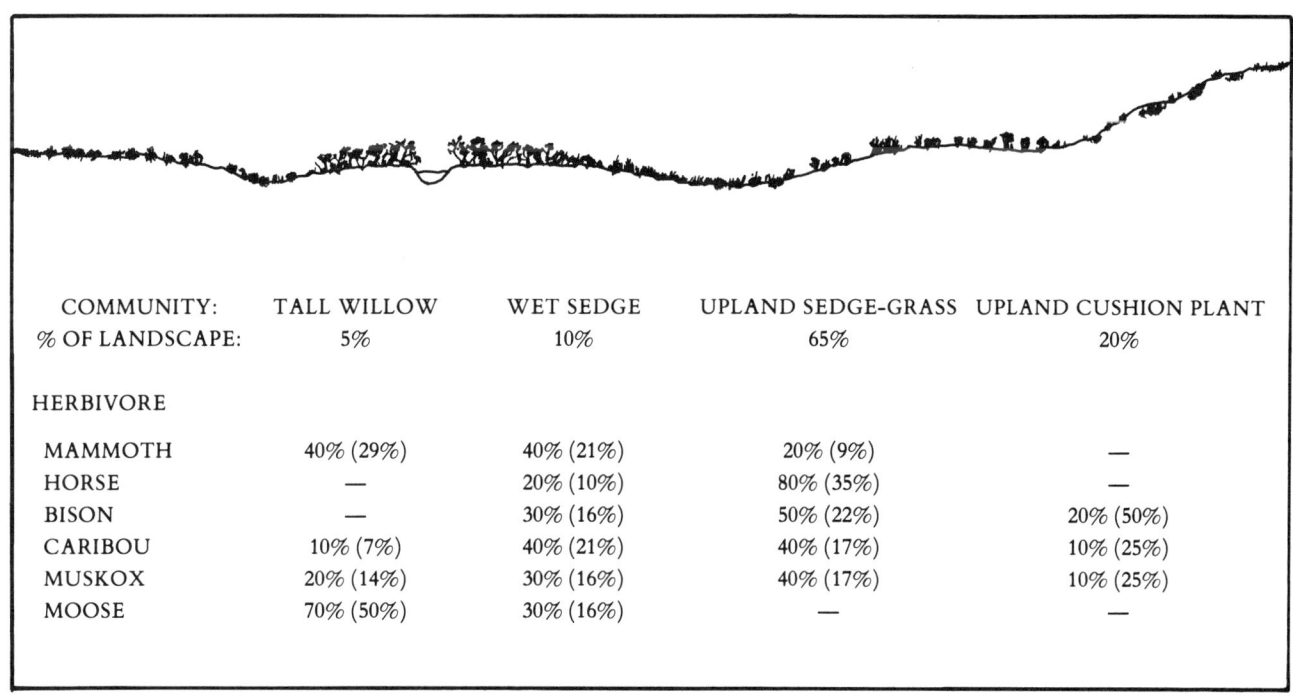

Figure 14.11 Hypothetical use of the ecosystem by herbivores in Beringia 25,000 years ago; % added to right is feeding sum for species. (After Bliss and Richards 1982)

are no indications to place any of the strata in the caves in the full Eemian. Level IX (Riek 1934) of Vogelherd, where *Palaeoloxodon* was found, comes closest to it. This level can thus be assigned at the earliest to the end of the Eemian, before Welten's Turicum 1 (1982), since the faunal remains and the artifacts are considered primarily synsedimentary. It is not impossible, however, that the forest elephant was present in our region during the forest phase between Turicum 1 and 2, since this genus appeared during the Eemian even further northeast, in the vicinity of Warsaw. In the southwest of France, *Palaeoloxodon* seems to have continued to exist long after the Eemian. A different case is *Capreolus capreolus,* whose presence has been documented in southwestern France during the Aurignacian at Abri Pataud (Müller-Beck 1982). It is not impossible, then, that this species still occurred in southern Germany during the forest phases between Turicum 2 and 3 and between 3 and 4 (Fig. 14.2). Consequently, in Hohlestein Cave the cold phase may have fallen only in the Turicum 4. The upper Bocksteinschmiede inventory, Level VIII of Vogelherd, and the base of the sequence in Grosse Grotte may also belong to this period. The lower level of Heidenschmiede and the two lowest strata of Speckberg must be classified as earlier. The upper leaf-shaped-point level of Weinberg Caves, on the other hand, stands above the Turicum 5a according to the "Hengelo equivalent." All Middle Paleolithic inventories containing colder faunal elements are to be ranged before this phase, although it is unclear whether they must be related to Turicum 4 or Turicum 5a. We can suppose that older deposits—from before Turicum 4—are less frequent than later ones. Most of the preserved inventories have been deposited only since Turicum 4. The latest Middle Paleolithic period is represented by the leaf-shaped point of Haldenstein Cave, where a new horse type was discovered for the first time: *Equus* cf. *przewalski,* apparently different from the classic heavy type of Middle Paleolithic horse known as *germanicus/caballus.* The chronostratigraphic distance between the Aurignacian of Vogelherd and Geissenklösterle (Hahn 1983), which can equally be correlated with horses of the *E. przewalski* type (Müller-Beck 1982), has become very small (Fig. 14.2).

SYSTEMS OF EXPLOITATION

Even though the discussed sites, defined by the Alb heights and Malm caves as places of sedimentation, are all located along the northern side of the Danube Valley, they make up only a part of the valley's total ecological system (Fig. 14.10). Naturally the hunted fauna was not confined only to the northern side-valleys of the system. According to the reflections of Bliss and Richards (1982) with respect to the "Arctic Steppe Biome" (Fig. 14.11), a differentiation in the main exploitation areas of the hoofed animals must be taken into consideration for our region, too. They can be ranged in the following distribution pattern:

TABLE 14.1
DISTRIBUTION OF FAUNAL GENERA IN THE DANUBE VALLEY

Animal Genera	Dry Valley Bottom	Wet Valley Bottom	Slope Areas	Plateaus
Mammuthus	bushes	grass, sedge	sedge, copse	herbs (few)
Equus	grass	grass, sedge	sedge	
Bison	grass	grass, sedge	sedge	herbs (few)
Cervus	copse	grass	copse	
Rangifer	copse, grass	grass, sedge	sedge, copse	herbs, lichen

Mammoths graze by preference along the valley bottom. They shift quickly from plateaus where the food supply is sparse, especially during prolonged periods of cold temperatures and scarce vegetation. Horses are still more bound to the valley, since they need a larger blend of nourishment which the plateaus and the higher slopes cannot provide during cold climatic phases. Bison also find grazing land on the plateaus. Because of their dependence on a copse diet, deer would rather browse in the lowland and on the lower slopes. Reindeer, on the contrary, exploit all areas, although they tend not to frequent the copse zones. When competing against deer and mammoths, they are forced to pass to the more barren plateaus, where they still can find food thanks to their mobility. Being highly sensitive to swarming insects (even more so than deer, with their tougher hides), reindeer may have shifted seasonally from windy plateaus during summer to wind-protected valleys, covered by copses, in the winter.

Ibex and chamois occur more often in rocky areas still covered here and there by spots of grass and sedge, which serve them as refuge. The cave bear probably lived in the proximity of small woods, bushes, and grassy areas, but—being a carnivore—it supplied itself also with seasonal hunting and fishing in the valley bottom. For the hyena, the main hunting field and surely the carrion area were the valley and its lower slopes. This species had to compete with other beasts of prey such as the lion and the wolf, but most likely these formed only small groups, as is the case today in the subarctic, e.g, in the subalpine zones (tiger and lion).

Recent excavations have proved that bird hunting and fishing were practiced already during the Aurignacian (Torke 1981). Until now, the exact scale of the plant exploitation could not be documented. When local afforestation was sufficient, hazelnuts and beechnuts were gathered as well as berries and mushrooms. But this certainly does not hold for the periods when the forest elephant and the deer still existed. These periods represented phases during which the relatively dense copse vegetation on the slopes slowed down the dynamics of sedimentation, limiting thereby the formation of new accumulation on the slopes and in the caves, where artifacts could be stored and ultimately preserved.

Basically, we can assume that most of our Middle Paleolithic finds belong to periods characterized by subarctic and arctic faunal biomes, decreasing density of vegetation, and consequently augmented sedimentary activity. Deer do still occur rather frequently. From their presence, we can deduce the availability of copses of a certain height, since these form the necessary protection for the relatively sedentary does. The rhinoceros, too, probably needed access to copses within a moderate distance.

Let us consider as a kind of model the principal findspots on the Upper Danube between Ehingen and Lauingen (Fig. 14.10). The 11 sites known here are located mainly upstream in caves in the adjacent northern creek valleys. Schmiechen (1) lies by a west-east access path used by wild animals, not far from an ascending cross-path leading towards the northern plateaus. Sirgenstein (2) is marked by a similar location. Geissenklösterle (3) and Grosse Grotte (4) are centered exclusively on the main valley, which they overlook from high up the slopes. Urspring (5) is again situated close to a cross-road that conducts northward through the Alb, near the descent to the plains of Neckarland. Bocksteinschmiede (6) and Bocksteinhöhle (7) are stationed in the flatter ancient Lone Valley with its side access to the Alb plateau. Likewise at Stadel in the Lone Valley (8), the secondary valley gives access to the south, away from the Danube. Vogelherd (9) also lies at a valley branch which can be well surveyed from above. Irpfel Cave (10) at the valley edge of the Brenz lowland overlooks the plain from a greater distance, whereas Heidenschmiede controls on one side the Brenz Valley, a strategic position in terms of hunting, while the other side is near an ascent at a steep section of the valley.

Departing from the above-mentioned model, the animal symbols on the map (Fig. 14.10) correspond to a somewhat idealized distribution of the hoofed animals, red deer included. Their exact chronostratigraphic locus is not important here. After all, the reconstruction of the vegetation as a cross-cut over a long period can likewise only be summarized. Our presentation may be correct for ca. 80% of the different periods under discussion. The only open question remains the scale of the copses on the lee side. A heavier growth may be presumed in places where no major floods of the Danube have to be taken into account. Their presence not only can be deduced from the already-mentioned existence of deer, but also can be proven by the results of Brande's research (1975) on the pollen profile of the soil of the valley in Mauern (Fig. 14.9), which covers the progressions Turicum 4 to 5b (after Welten

1982). His analysis revealed *Pinus, Betula, Salix, Picea, Larix,* and *Alnus,* even in relatively cool sections of the profile. Furthermore, steppe elements are well represented by grasses and herbs.

Inasmuch as it is evident that the Middle Paleolithic hunters did not live only in or near the cave stations—discovered thanks to their susceptibility to sedimentation and their high chances of being traced—two hypothetical head stations are added to this map which must have been located in copse zones on relatively dry ground. These camps enabled the hunters to benefit from the *Mammuthus-Rangifer-Cervus* ranges close by. We can assume that one site must have been located at the Blau mouth near the present city of Ulm, and the other where the Lone River flows into the Brenz near the town of Sontheim. In spite of the cooler but dry continental climate, during periods of a relatively high solar position in the Middle Paleolithic Ice Age, primary production must have been greater in Central Europe than in the present arctic, so it seems obvious that both camps were occupied simultaneously. When reconstructing the size of the groups for the winter sojourn, two household nuclei can be supposed at each place, but there may have been three or more. Even as a very cautious estimate two to six families functioning as an economic and production unit must be assumed for the valley section under discussion. This number offers a realistic minimum number of two to six Middle Paleolithic hunters and a total population of eight to 24 individuals who obviously also exploited the middle valley and the ascending slopes in the southern reaches of the valley. It constitutes only a demographic variable which cannot claim a statistical value. In a total area of 4000 sq. km, four or five main stations presumably existed, so reaching a density of 0.01 person per sq. km. This is similar to the percentage of the historical arctic Inuit population, with the difference that the Inuit live in a zone of more limited productivity. Our estimation, therefore, is most likely lower than the real number, especially when long-term periods of favorable climate—underrepresented in the findings because of lower chances of sedimentation—are incorporated within this valuation. Supposing this number is correct, they must have been a very careful people who avoided unnecessary risks. In case we presume a psychologically more stable and venturesome variant, the population would consist of four to twelve households of ca. 16 to 48 individuals with a density factor of more than 0.01 person per sq. km at the maximum.

CONTINUITY OF EXPERIENCE AS FOUNDATION OF THE EARLY UPPER PALEOLITHIC

Finally we shall discuss the problem of the transition from the Middle to the Upper Paleolithic within the restricted perspective of the Upper Danube region. Except for the femur fragment discovered at Stadel, no human remains of the Middle Paleolithic period are known with certainty. It is unclear whether *H. sapiens sapiens* from Mittleren Klause ultimately belongs to a Middle Paleolithic inventory, but the assumption remains valid (Müller-Beck 1956). A radiocarbon dating could clarify this matter. Furthermore, the female skull found at Ehringsdorf (Eemian or even older, certainly not younger) is not considered very typical for *H. s. neanderthalensis*. This is confirmed by the unpublished research of E. Vlček (after Feustel 1986). It is conceivable that *H. s. sapiens* was represented in Middle Paleolithic inventories on the Upper Danube well before the Aurignacian, but this has no more than speculative value. Unfortunately, it is still common to measure cultural and technological skills on the basis of skeletons' morphological features. From the standpoint of archaeological methodology, this practice is unfounded, especially since positive evidence for the link between the Middle Paleolithic and the Neandertal is lacking. The simple formula Middle Paleolithic = Neandertal and Upper Paleolithic = *H. s. sapiens* cannot be transposed in any way. Even for France this idea has become hardly defensible.

In looking at the sites along the Upper Danube, which are surprisingly dense notwithstanding the limited area of approximately 4000 sq. km, we can make the following observations:

1. The morphologically definable late Middle Paleolithic is chronostratigraphically only slightly distant from the Aurignacian of the Upper Danube.

2. On the Upper Danube, the late Middle Paleolithic has adjusted to the same environment as the Aurignacian: a *Mammuthus-Rangifer-Equus* fauna with remains of *Cervus*. Copses of a certain size increased in number. The somewhat earlier Middle Paleolithic was marked by colder and more extreme conditions.

3. The late Middle Paleolithic population on the Upper Danube may have reached a density of 0.01 individual per sq. km, that is to say, the optimal value for the subarctic hunting populations.

4. Between the end of the morphologically defined Middle Paleolithic and the analogously defined Aurignacian, no dramatic deteriorations in climate took place. The changes that did occur were less important than the climatic decline during the course of the Middle Paleolithic.

5. The differences in technology between the Middle and the Upper Paleolithic can mainly be followed back to the changes in the preparation of the cores, passing from a flat prepared nucleus with a broad working face (at the maximum five blades out of one reduction platform) to a prepared disc-platform core (more than ten blades out of one reduction platform) (Fig. 14.12).

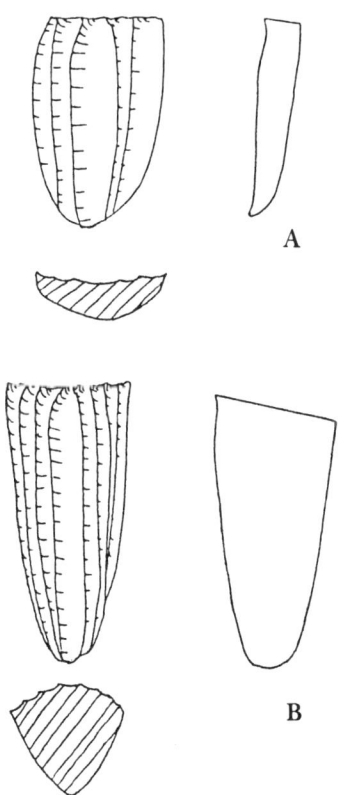

Figure 14.12 A) Blade core of the late "Middle Paleolithic" technique; B) blade core of the early Upper Paleolithic (Aurignacian core).

So it can be proposed that the Upper Danube region belonged to those areas where the transition from the Middle Paleolithic (or "late Lower Paleolithic") to the Upper Paleolithic was taking place. The findings in Haldenstein Cave demonstrate the probability of this continuity. But they attest at the same time to the incompleteness of the findings. Moreover, the distinction between Middle Paleolithic and Upper Paleolithic inventories can be interpreted fundamentally as internal modifications within a continuous movement. This seems in any case more likely than the indemonstrable theories which pretend to explain these differences in terms of diffusions, migrations, or exchanges of populations. It is much more realistic to consider southern Germany as part of a large area where the flake technique was constantly improved in situ up to the grade of perfection it reached in the Upper Paleolithic. Such an understanding of the contact with the Middle Paleolithic will be much less dramatic and closer to historical truth. In any case the Upper Paleolithic must have originated out of previous foundations. Even adherents of the migration theory have been obliged to acknowledge this fact on other occasions. Besides, the morphological differences between leaf-shaped-point inventories of the late Middle Paleolithic and those of the Aurignacian, which form the basis of the Upper Paleolithic in southern Germany, are relatively small. Only in the mature Gravettian/Pavlovian do the distinctions become important. The same observation is true for the difference between the Aurignacian and the Middle Paleolithic below the level of the leaf-shaped point. To classify the leaf-shaped-point Paleolithic as part of the Upper Paleolithic, or even the Aurignacian as part of the Middle Paleolithic, does not advance our understanding of the problem.

On the basis of the technohistorical and ecoarchaeological elements which guided our investigation, there is no decisive reason to postulate significant differences in the competence of the Neandertal and post-Neandertal populations. Once again, the thesis of the existence of continuity within this transition area seems to be most probable. Without the experiences of the Neandertal, *H. s. sapiens* could not have originated.

COMMENTS

OTTE: La définition du Paléolithique moyen, lié à l'interglaciaire et à la première moitié du Würm, s'oppose à deux arguments l'un théorique, l'autre documentaire. On ne peut fonder une distinction culturelle sur des bases chronologiques (nous serions tous des Iroquois autant que des paysans du Danube!) et de nombreux sites typiquement moustériens sont connus bien avant l'interglaciaire (par exemple: Biache, Vaufrey, Liège Sainte Walburge).

Dans les études chrono-stratigraphiques récentes (cf. G. Woillard et le Colloque de Rennes, AFEQ) le complexe du dernier interglaciaire est divisé en trois épisodes climatiques tempérés séparés par des oscillations rigoureuses. C'est ce cycle complet que l'on a récemment mis en évidence au site de la grotte de Sclayn, Belgique.

Ne faudrait-il pas aussi envisager l'idée de variations fauniques davantage dues aux méthodes de chasse et d'exploitation qu'à des changements dans les conditions environnementales?

Sur quelles bases peut-on se fonder pour aboutir aux reconstitutions paléo-démographiques que vous avez présentées?

Quels sont les arguments qui permettent de supposer un comportement axé sur la saisonabilité dès le Paléolithique moyen? Par exemple, disposez-vous dans votre région d'indices de migrations, de déplacements partiels ou de modifications du mode d'approvisionnement?

XV
Core Reduction, Flake Production, and the Middle Paleolithic Industry of Zobište (Yugoslavia)

Mark F. Baumler

INTRODUCTION

Much of Paleolithic archaeology is concerned with chipped stone assemblages and what these can tell us about the behavior, capabilities, and ethnic identity of prehistoric populations over space and time. Traditionally the focus of this attention has been upon the description and interpretation of retouched or secondarily modified pieces of stone, to the extent that until relatively recently only these artifacts were systematically retained from archaeological excavations. As our knowledge of the factors responsible for the variability in retouched stone tools and tool assemblages has matured over the years, it has become increasingly clear that these retouched pieces must now be examined and interpreted within the larger framework of the exploitation and utilization of lithic resources. Many of the views expressed in this volume (see in particular the chapters by Dibble, Jelinek, Marks, Montet-White, Rolland) call for an appreciation of stone tool manufacture, use, and discard that can no longer be acquired solely through the analysis of retouched pieces.

One aspect of lithic exploitation that seemingly must underlie the study of stone tools is the nature of prehistoric core reduction, or how lithic raw material was initially transformed into the flakes that were used as or made into most of the tools found in Paleolithic assemblages. The method used for the production of tool blanks from the reduction of nuclei is fundamental to the composition of lithic assemblages and arguably determines much of the morphology of the retouched pieces recovered from a given site. Yet our ability to actually study this behavior in any detail is in fact quite limited, generally being reserved to the context of narrowly patterned core reduction methods, such as blade production (see Ferring, ch. 21) or Levallois flake production (Boëda 1986).

Many archaeologists will immediately counter that a considerable body of literature relating to the mechanics involved in the detachment of flakes from cores is readily available. It is important in this regard to make the distinction between the "manner" and the "method" of core reduction. Crabtree (1972: 2), in describing these two aspects of lithic reduction, defined manner as the "determined angle and application of force" used in the removal of a flake. Method, on the other hand, he referred to as the "systematic and orderly flaking process, or the preconceived plan of chipping based on rules, mechanics, order and procedure" (1972: 2). More recently, this latter aspect, with its focus upon the sequence of events, has also been called the "production code" of lithic manufacture (Young and Bonnichsen 1984, 1985).

Most past and current studies emphasize the manner rather than the method of removing flakes and producing tool blanks, building upon principles of fracture mechanics and the evidence of control that could be placed over these by prehistoric flintknappers (e.g., Faulkner 1972; Speth 1972, 1975, 1981; Dibble and Whittaker 1981; Cotterell and Kamminga 1979). Evidence for the method of flaking cores, or the ways in which raw material was systematically and sequentially reduced to produce flakes, has not been as widely addressed. Frequently, one encounters only the analytical terms of "primary," "secondary," and "tertiary" flake removals or the subjective labels of "opportunistic" and "prepared" to describe the sequence of core reduction. At the same time, platform attributes, angles, and variable force applications are discussed in detail with the implicit assumption that in these resides the essence of technological behavior. In truth, both aspects of the flintknapping process are capable of informing upon the technological strategy expressed in a lithic assemblage. But, inasmuch as the manner of removing a flake is largely determined by the role of that removal in the method of reduction, and because the method may itself be more narrowly culturally defined (Crew 1975; Young and Bonnichsen 1985; Flenniken 1985), it seems that this latter aspect is worthy of greater attention than it has previously received.

This paper will attempt to provide some new perspectives on the analysis of flake assemblages at Paleolithic sites, and particularly in regard to the study of the method or sequence of core reduction.

THE STUDY OF CORE REDUCTION SEQUENCES

We currently derive much of our information on the sequences of prehistoric core reduction from two sources: replications and backfitting. Replicative studies in particular have had a long history in the analysis of prehistoric lithic technology (e.g., Bordes 1947; Semenov 1964; Bordes and Crabtree 1969; Newcomer 1975; for additional references see Honea 1983 and Flenniken 1984). The efforts of skilled modern flintknappers to reproduce stone tools have provided invaluable insights into the lithic manufacturing process and the techniques potentially used by prehistoric craftsmen. The problem with the application of much of this work to the study of actual lithic assemblages recovered in archaeological contexts, however, lies in the degree to which the experimenters replicate particular products rather than emulate the processes or method involved in their production. Most replications, especially those involving core reduction, focus upon only restricted aspects of the sequence, for example the production of a single type of flake. Rarely do they attempt to simulate the approach or steps leading up to and beyond the removal of these flakes. It is one thing to be able to prepare and detach a particular kind of flake; it is quite another to determine how a nodule was "decortified," whether one or more of these flakes were produced in a sequence, and whether other types of tool blanks were also produced. One is often struck by the close correspondence of a modern craftsman's Levallois flake and core with those which served as the basis for the replication, in contrast to the wide divergence in the byproducts or other flakes and debris produced by the knapper and those recovered at an archaeological site.

Ultimately, because the intent of prehistoric core reduction is less obvious and the methods appear also to have been more flexible, replications continue to serve primarily to demonstrate possible or feasible methods used by prehistoric knappers. We are still left in a position of having then to judge how closely the modern flintknapper behaves like prehistoric man, and this becomes increasingly less clear in evaluating the simulation of pre-modern *Homo sapiens* behavior (see Jelinek 1984b regarding Toth 1982). Thus, Flenniken's (1984: 200) dogmatic statement that flintknapping experiments are "the only methodology to establish and document prehistoric lithic technological behavior" would seem debatable.

Recent studies of core reduction involving extensive backfitting of pieces (Volkman 1983; Marks and Volkman 1983; Leroi-Gourhan and Brézillon 1983) have served to illustrate both the potential and the problems of undertaking an analysis of prehistoric core reduction sequences on the basis of replications alone. In these studies individual prehistoric knapping events have been partially or almost entirely reconstructed, allowing for little debate over the sequence of preparations and removals executed in the reduction of a piece of lithic raw material. Perhaps predictably, these reconstructions have not always agreed with previous notions or replications for the production of certain flake forms. On the basis of his reconstructions, for example, Volkman (1983) discovered previously unknown and quite different methods for producing Levallois points at Boker Tachtit in the central Negev. He was also able to demonstrate considerable variability in the reduction of individual cores as well as in the methods for producing similar flake forms (Marks and Volkman 1983). At the same time, these multiple core refittings, when observed more generally, showed clear evidence of patterned reduction "strategies," or characteristic and repeated methods for producing flake forms. At Boker Tachtit, the documentation of the change in these strategies over time has yielded what is at present our most complete view of technological change during the important transition from the Middle to Upper Paleolithic, serving as a classic demonstration of the value of studying methods of prehistoric core reduction. These kinds of refittings also served here and elsewhere to address questions of contemporaneity and intra- and intersite behavior to an extent previously unknown in Paleolithic archaeology (Marks, ch. 16; Hietala 1983; Leroi-Gourhan and Brézillon 1983; Cahen, Keeley, and Van Noten 1979; see also Hofman 1981). Unquestionably, therefore, backfitting provides the clearest way of documenting prehistoric reduction sequences and applying this knowledge to the study of prehistoric behavior.

Not all researchers, however, are able to partake in the enthusiasm generated by the above studies. For many, the economic impracticality of undertaking backfitting to study core reduction will continue to limit its application. Whether the problem involves homogeneity in the raw material, the limited extent of the excavated sample, or the sheer quantity of pieces involved, the labor-intensive nature of refitting studies often abrogates their implementation. In these cases we simply will never have the opportunity to actually reconstruct individual knapping sequences. While this will necessarily limit the verification of a given model of core reduction, it need not exclude altogether the possibility of studying core reduction sequences directly through archaeological materials. The existence of repeated patterns in a lithic reduction strategy (demonstrated in refitting studies), coupled with the information related to the process of manufacture preserved in chipped stone morphology, should provide a means by which a reconstruction of the typical core reduction sequence or sequences at a site can still be obtained at an assemblage level of analysis. The extent to which these generalized models approximate prehistoric reality depends less upon actual backfitting or replication and more upon the level of our understanding of the principles of core reduction and how these are expressed in lithic artifacts.

Elsewhere (Baumler 1987), I have attempted to make explicit and bring together the principles and properties of lithic reduction as they apply to core reduction, and to show how these can be used in the development of a methodology for studying core reduction sequences in archaeological core and flake assemblages. While beyond the scope of the present paper, it is important to recognize that core reduction is structured by some very absolute limitations and inherent predilections in the forms it will take. Certain of these limitations are shared with all types of lithic reduction owing to the characteristics of lithic material, the subtractive and directional nature of the reductive process (Collins 1975), and the manner and method in which the latter can be successfully applied to the former. It would be a mistake, however, to think that models for the manufacture of bifaces or the retouching of flake tools can be directly applied to the study of core reduction. As a distinct class, core reduction must also be studied from the perspective of how it differs from other lithic reduction efforts. In particular, properties arising from the production of flakes rather than flake scars and the dynamic nature of relationships between cores, tool blanks, and preparatory flakes are specific to core reduction and important to its interpretation (Baumler 1987: 18-31).

In effect, the task of reconstructing the core reduction sequence, much as the act of creating it, must rely upon a continuous reevaluation of the state of the core from the first to the last removal. The majority of cores found in archaeological contexts manifest this state only in their final and generally "exhausted" form. While providing important landmarks for late reduction, most cores cannot be expected to retain evidence of earlier efforts. Consequently the analyst must rely heavily upon the flake and flake-tool assemblages to be a source of knowledge about the cores, or more appropriately, the core states, which no longer exist. Short of refitting, the key to understanding a core reduction sequence after it is completed lies in understanding the relationships among the flakes and between the flakes and cores in a lithic assemblage.

In the remainder of this paper, I will summarize one such attempt to analyze an archaeological flake assemblage in terms of the cores that produced it. While this exercise is taken from a larger study (Baumler 1987), and necessarily abbreviated, it is hoped that it will serve to raise the considerations necessary for the analysis of prehistoric core reduction sequences, and to describe the means by which they may begin to be addressed. The Middle Paleolithic site of Zobište in Yugoslavia provides the setting for the study.

THE ZOBIŠTE ASSEMBLAGE

The site of Zobište is located in northern Bosnia in the north-central part of Yugoslavia (Fig. 15.1). This is hilly, dissected country forming the juncture of the Pannonian Basin to the north with the mountains of central Yugoslavia rising to the south.

Zobište is one of numerous Middle and Upper Paleolithic open-air stations in this area recorded by Djuro Basler of the Zemaljski Muzej in Sarajevo during surveys and excavations begun in 1949 (Basler 1976, 1979). The site is situated on a high limestone butte overlooking a bend in the Ukrina River, a small northwest-trending tributary of the major eastward-flowing Sava River (Fig. 15.2). This location commands a panoramic view of the Ukrina Valley, a factor which undoubtedly contributed to its use by Paleolithic hunters and gatherers.

Excavations at Zobište were conducted in the summer of 1980 under the direction of Anta Montet-White of the University of Kansas. This fieldwork was part of a larger joint American-Yugoslavian Paleolithic research project involving excavations at several localities, the results of which have been recently summarized (Montet-White, Laville, and Lézine 1986). The initial stratigraphic interpretation suggests that several occupation horizons are represented at Zobište in the uppermost meter of predominantly clayey deposits attributable to the Upper Pleistocene. Thermoluminescence dates of 97,500 B.P. ± 7000 and 85,500 B.P. ± 8500 are available for the lowest level of the site (Montet-White, Laville, and Lézine 1986: 86).

The artifacts recovered from Zobište are limited to stone, with organic materials typically only rarely preserved in the northern Bosnian open-air stations. The chipped stone tools from all major levels of the site are typologically Middle Paleolithic in form, although a few readily distinctive Late Gravettian blades and blade tools (including backed bladelets) were found at the top of two of the excavated squares. In all, some 4900 pieces of chipped stone were collected that can be attributed with some certainty to the Middle Paleolithic occupations (Table 15.1). A full range of reduction products appears to be represented by these, including tested and rejected cobbles, cores, fully cortical flakes, partially cortical and noncortical flakes (both large and small), and quantities of formless debris or shatter. Retouched tools (both complete and broken pieces) are relatively rare, with a total number of 176 or 3.6% of the lithic sample. A number of flakes also show evidence of regular microflaking, however, which can likely be attributed to use-damage. Most of the retouch proper is limited in extent and invasiveness. Various forms of sidescrapers and marginally retouched pieces dominate the identifiable tool assemblage (Fig. 15.3). Naturally backed knives are common and frequently retouched. Typological Levallois flakes and flake-blades are also present in limited quantity (total complete = 82), constituting approximately 11% of all complete unretouched and retouched flakes larger than 2 cm.

In all respects the assemblage can be discussed as a whole and compares favorably with other Middle Paleolithic assemblages recovered from nearby sites

TABLE 15.1
ZOBIŠTE CHIPPED STONE ASSEMBLAGE

	Frequency		Weight	
	n	%	grams	%
Complete flakes <2 cm	716	14.6	8176.1	24.0
Complete flakes >2 cm	804	16.4	461.4	1.3
Flake fragments	2343	47.8	6131.3	18.0
Shatter	962	19.7	9234.0	27.1
Complete cores	31	.6	5083.0	15.0
Core fragments	34	.7	1699.0	5.0
Other (tested cobbles)	7	.1	3269.0	9.6
Totals	4897	100.0	33,953.8	100.0

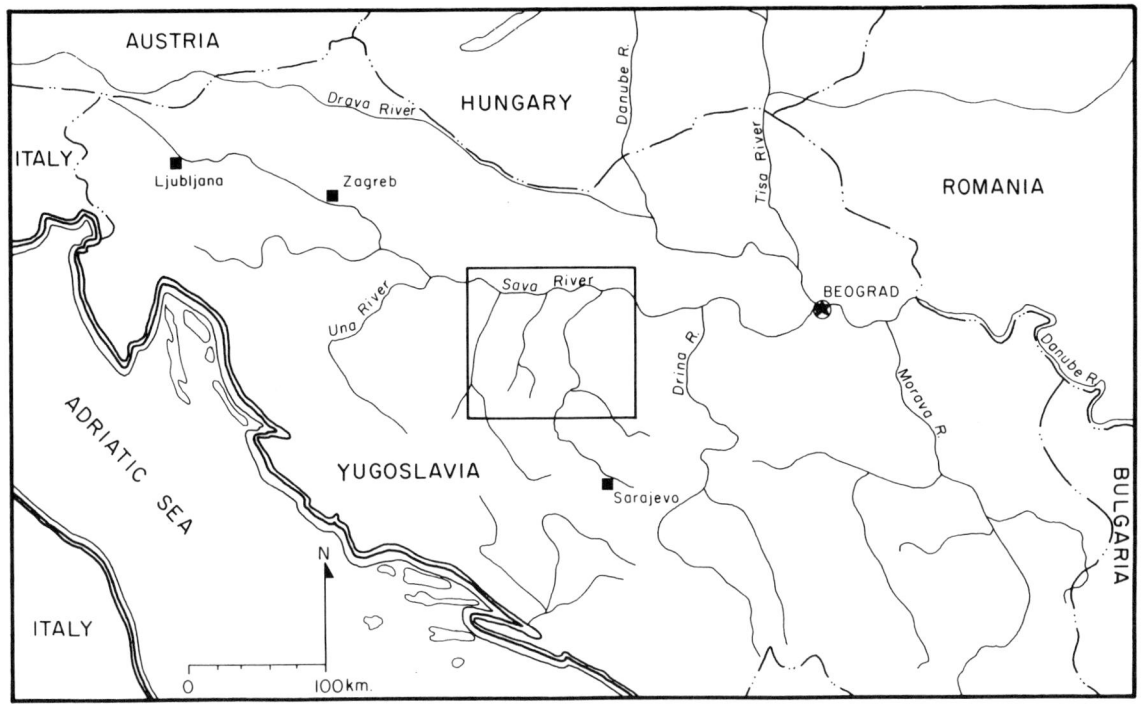

Figure 15.1 Map of Yugoslavia and surrounding countries (see Fig. 15.2 for inset).

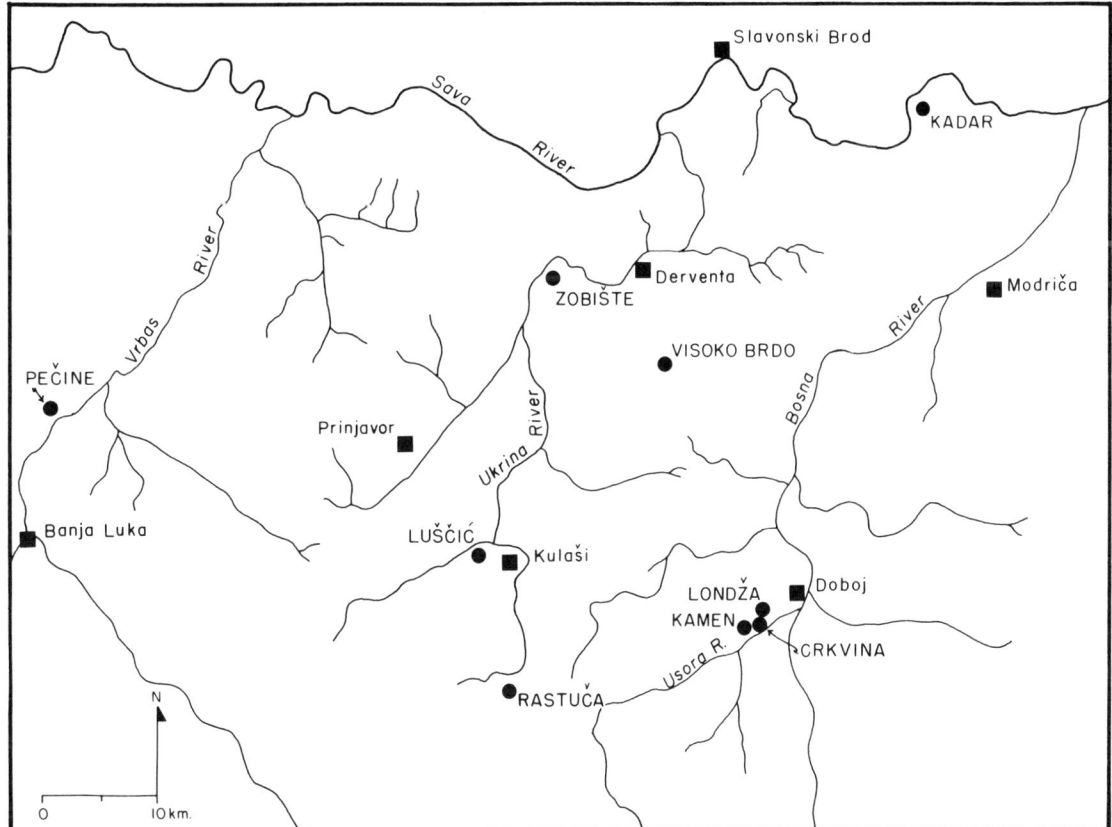

Figure 15.2 Map of northern Bosnia depicting location of towns (squares) and major Paleolithic localities (circles).

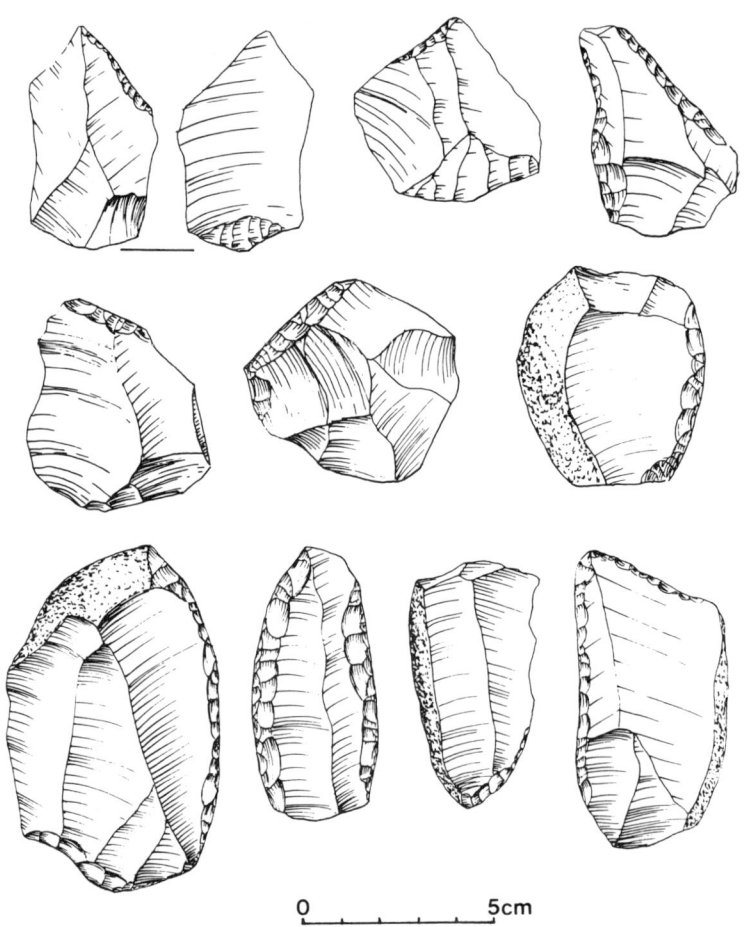

Figure 15.3 Zobište: miscellaneous retouched flakes (taken from Montet-White, Laville, and Lézine 1986: fig. 27).

(see Fig. 15.2), specifically those described from Visoko Brdo (Basler 1962; Wobst 1979), Londža (Basler 1961, 1971), and Pećine (Gralyuk 1979). In regional surveys, most authors have pointed to the internal homogeneity of the Bosnian Middle Paleolithic while commenting upon its apparent uniqueness among surrounding traditions (Gábori 1976a; Ivanova 1979; Montet-White, Laville, and Lézine 1986).

RAW MATERIAL

One of the first considerations involved in the study of core reduction sequences is the nature of the available raw material. The raw material utilized at Zobište was exclusively radiolarite, a fine- to medium-grained, deep-sea-deposited chert that outcrops in the central Bosnian mountains as well as other ranges in southeastern Europe and the Near East (Kozlowski et al. 1981). This material is locally available in the form of redeposited stream cobbles forming gravel bars along the Ukrina River. A study of the relative quantity and size of cobbles at one of these gravel bars just below the Zobište butte was undertaken in 1980 (Montet-White, in press). This study revealed an 80% frequency of radiolarite among all cobbles, with the sizes of these ranging from 40 to 120 mm in maximum dimension. The majority of the cobbles, however, fell between 40 and 75 mm; only 18% of the cobbles were larger than 75 mm and considered most acceptable for knapping. The cobbles vary somewhat in shape but most are subspherical to subcubical. Weight was not quantified in Montet-White's study, but can be expected to range from 0.5 to 2 kg for the larger nodules. The largest core recovered at the site, which represents most of a very large and only slightly reduced nodule, weighs 1.5 kg. The cortex is predominantly black or brown and does not extend far into the nodules. The color of the radiolarite itself is highly variable, including yellows, greens, browns, reds, and blacks with various banded and mottled variations of the same.

The quality of the material overall is very good, despite the propensity for smaller nodules to break along frost fractures (Montet-White, in press). Cleavage along frost-crack planes may be responsible for elevating the percentage of shatter (nonflake) and amorphous chunks in the collection, representing ca. 20% in frequency and 27% in weight of the total chipped stone. This did not, however, prevent the detachment of large flakes: some with lengths as great as 80 mm are known in the collection. It is probable that in selecting for greater size, there was also a selection for more frost-free nodules.

With regard to core reduction, the focus on a single raw material with a limited range of size and shape variability provides some control for the initial set of lithic parameters.

CORES

The cores recovered from Zobište number 65, of which 31 are complete. For the most part these discarded cores are remarkably similar, suggesting a strong pattern to the method and point at which the reduction sequence was concluded. Specifically, at the time of their discard, 25 (80%) of the complete cores have a single, radially or subradially flaked, circular face which in all but two cases is opposite a flat or slightly rounded cortical base (Fig. 15.4). The sides of these cores (representing the platform) are perpendicular or slightly inverted towards the base and in most cases (16 out of 25) are only partially flaked. About half of the cores have edges with evidence of platform faceting.

This type of core might be classified as a classic Levallois core, although only some of them in fact retain the scar of a removed central flake (e.g., Fig. 15.4: 1), leaving the remainder to be classified after Bordes (1961b: 87, pl. 99) as "nucléus Levallois inachevé" (e.g., Fig. 15.4:2). Some of these latter "unstruck" Levallois cores, however, also resemble disc cores except for the fact that the core face is typically flat or only slightly domed and the cores themselves are generally quite small, some less than 30 mm in maximum dimension and under 20 mm thick (Table 15.2). Exceptions include three relatively large cores (over 90 mm in maximum dimension) whose function as either disc cores or Levallois cores seems equally probable (e.g., Fig. 15.4:3).

The remaining six complete cores include three single-platform and three double-platform cores.

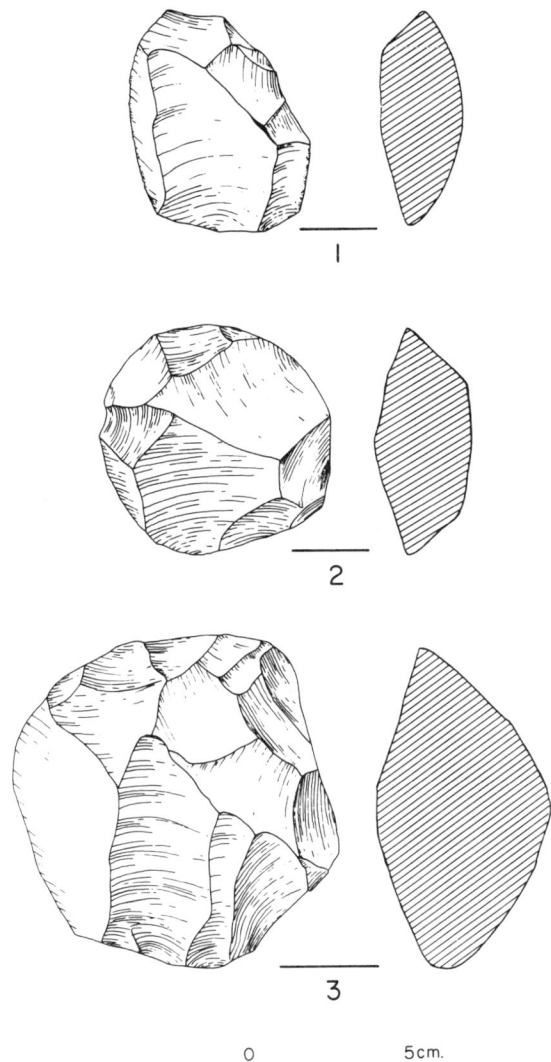

Figure 15.4 Zobište: radially flaked cores (adapted from Montet-White, Laville, and Lézine 1986: fig. 26).

Two of the latter have opposing platforms. Although individually quite variable, taken together these cores are characterized by their greater extent of remaining cortical surface and larger size relative to most of the cores described above (mean dimensions: length 67 mm; width 65 mm; thickness 36 mm; weight 368 g). Given their size and appearance, it is apparent that some of these cores clearly represent less-reduced nodules than the majority of the radial cores. At least half of them also appear to represent the reduction of atypically shaped nodules.

The discard of predominantly radially and subradially flaked cores is further emphasized by the

TABLE 15.2
RADIALLY FLAKED COMPLETE CORES (n = 25)

	Median	Mean	S.D.	Range
Length (mm)	53.9	59.5	18.7	40–118
Width (mm)	49.7	51.6	14.9	36–91
Thickness (mm)	19.4	21.8	9.5	9–49
Weight (g)	73.0	114.9	147.7	26–601

broken cores. Thirty of the 34 recognizable core fragments can be identified as pieces of this type of core. Most represent very thin, small pieces of raw material broken in the attempt, largely futile, to remove a central flake from an exhausted radial core. In this respect these fragments support the interpretation of the small complete radial cores as prepared "Levallois" cores which may have been too thin to successfully strike, or from which the final attempt at a central flake removal was only partially successful, leaving no evidence of a major scar.

In sum, the cores at Zobište clearly suggest that reduction was intensive and largely oriented towards radially prepared, "Levallois flake" production. The overall homogeneity of the core assemblage further argues for a well-developed and repetitive core reduction strategy. Given the intensive nature of the reduction at Zobište, however, it is also clear that the reduction sequence or method of core reduction is unlikely to be fully reflected in these cores themselves. It is necessary, therefore, to look to that part of the lithic assemblage that actually represents the course of the sequence itself, that is, the flake assemblage.

FLAKES

If we are interested in the method and not simply the manner of flake production, the analysis of the flake assemblage must proceed from the perspective of the reduction of cores. As a piece of a previous core, each flake is a partial record of the core from which it was detached. A description of the flake's exterior surface, therefore, is effectively a description of part of the core at the time the flake was removed. For tool blanks this is tantamount to a representation of what was once a prepared, or at least acceptable, core face and platform, while for most preparatory flakes it reflects an effort to achieve the same. Important aspects of these exterior surfaces to be considered here for reconstructing the reduction sequence include the number and orientation of flake scars as well as the quantity and position of cortex.

Exterior flake scars represent previous removals from a core and, relative to the axis of percussion of the flake, indicate in what direction(s) flakes were being detached prior to the moment of a flake's removal. This in turn reflects the orientation of platforms on the core and the method of its reduction at a particular point in time. The number of these flake scars can be further indicative of the amount of previous reduction (Munday 1976), inasmuch as early removals from a core will generally have fewer previous flake scars than later ones. The number of scars will also be affected, however, by the type and extent of preparation and the nature of the prior removals. A large flake removal, for example, may yield a single large scar on subsequent removals regardless of their place in the reduction sequence. Taken alone, the number of flake scars as an indicator of the place of a flake in the reduction sequence must therefore be interpreted with caution.

The presence of cortex on the exterior surface of flakes, especially with nodular raw material such as that used at Zobište, is generally recognized as being associated with early reduction efforts. While some cortex may still be removed very late in the reduction of cores, the majority of cortical flakes (and particularly the larger flakes) will be detached at the outset of the sequence. Less appreciated perhaps is the fact that the position of cortex on the flake surface may also be very useful in determining how cortex is being removed from the nodule. In preparing different types of cores, the removal of cortex may proceed by quite different methods; these can be expected to be reflected by the position of the cortex on the exterior surface of the decortication flakes.

Further information about the core can also be derived from the platform of the removed flakes, although, as argued earlier, this more directly relates to the manner of individual detachments than to the method of core reduction. The size and shape of the removed flakes are also directly related to core morphology, both before and after the removal. Because we are dealing with a reductive technology, each flake provides minimum dimensions of the prior core face and, in the case of tool blanks, will frequently approximate its maximum size in at least one dimension. As the core is reduced we may expect these dimensional parameters to change, affecting not only the potential dimensions of the removed blanks but perhaps the method of their production as well. The flake's size and shape also reflect what kind of scar and ridges will be left on the core after its removal. The necessity and type of core repreparation following the detachment of a blank can be partially predicted by the nature of this remnant scar. In this regard, blade production is frequently a "self-perpetuating" method, while other types of tool-blank production may involve considerable repreparation, contributing to the idea of blade technology as a more efficient use of raw material.

The analysis of the flake assemblage recovered from Zobište was structured by the above considerations. The results presented here are limited to complete flakes (both retouched and unretouched) greater than 2 cm in maximum dimension, or a total of 716 flakes. For each flake the percentage of cortex on the exterior surface was estimated in eight categories ranging from noncortical, or 0%, to completely cortical, or 100%. In addition to amount, the placement of cortex on flakes was recorded as present or absent in each of four quadrants partitioning the exterior surface of the flake, i.e., left proximal, left distal, right proximal, and right distal (Fig. 15.5b). The presence or absence of natural (cortical) backing was also noted. The number of flake scars (exclusive of small platform-preparation scars) and their pattern on the exterior surface of the flake were also recorded. The latter was accomplished by determining the angle of origin of previous flake scars relative to the axis of percussion of the flake under study. To facilitate this determination, originations were limited to four possible quadrants or directions (Fig. 15.5a). Specifically, the quadrant 1 count is a tally of scars originating from the same general platform direction as the flake removed, quadrants 2 and 4 quantify the scars from the right and left lateral edges respectively, and the number of scars from quadrant 3 represents flakes removed from a platform opposite the present flake platform. This technique of describing flake-scar pattern was previously applied by

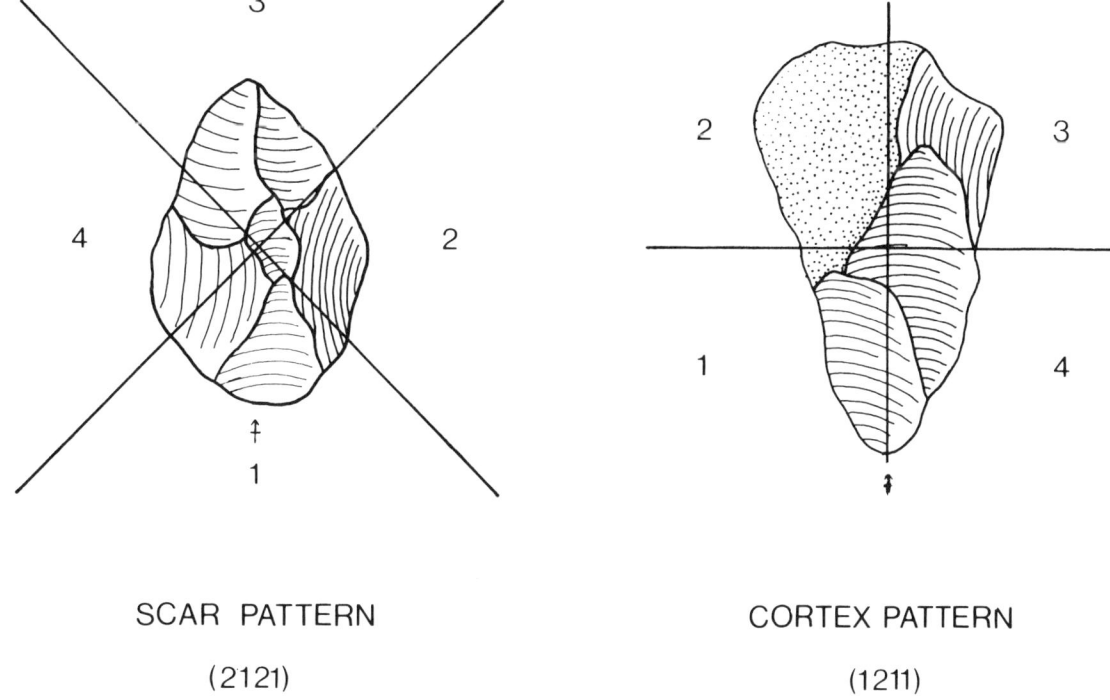

Figure 15.5 Method for the recording of the exterior surfaces of complete flakes: (a) scar angles; (b) cortex placement.

Crew in a technological study of Levallois flakes from the Eastern Mediterranean Middle Paleolithic (1975) and in the description of a sample of flakes from the Mousterian site of Rosh Ein Mor in the Negev (1976). It is also similar to the technique more recently applied by Sirakov (1983) at the Samuilitsa II Cave in northern Bulgaria. In addition to the counting of scars from each of the above directions, flakes with three or more scars were subjectively classified into one of three aggregate scar-pattern categories: unidirectional, radial/subradial, and irregular or other. Finally, size and shape of the flakes studied are represented by measurements of length, width, thickness (after Jelinek 1975: 304), as well as weight.

TOOL BLANKS

Determining the goal of core reduction through the examination of the flakes used as tools can be of great assistance in delimiting the general parameters involved in the method of reduction (Baumler 1987: 35-44). For the purposes of this study, intended tool blanks are identified by their evidence of use, with use defined by the presence of retouch or macroscopic, continuous edge damage. While not all intentionally produced blanks may exhibit such evidence, the majority should and this objective criterion is to be favored over subjective feelings regarding the intent of the knapper.

Table 15.3 presents summary descriptive statistics for the extent of cortical cover, size, and shape of the samples of complete flakes and flake tools greater than 2 cm at Zobište. It is clear that the assemblage of tools (reflecting "blanks") exhibits a greater average size (except thickness) and elongation, as well as a lower percentage of cortex, than does the assemblage of flakes without evidence of use (taken here to represent primarily "preparatory flakes"). Such overall size differences are not uncommon and may even be expected given the different functions of the two types of flakes. Minimizing waste is equivalent to limiting the amount of unuseful preparatory removals and hence limiting the size of the majority of the preparatory flakes. Tool blanks, on the other hand, usually must exceed a minimum size, below which they will not properly function as tools. The production of flakes for use with little or no cortex is also a common practice and probably relates to a general (but not necessarily universal) desire for noncortical working edges.

Less predictable, perhaps, is the lack of standardization in the morphology of the flakes used as tools, reflected here by the large standard deviations for all the recorded continuous attributes. This does not appear, moreover, to be a case of different blanks produced for different tool types, as there is no evidence for this at Zobište in the kinds of retouch or microflaking observed in the assemblage. Apparently, a consistent single shape or size was not a major criterion in the production of blanks at Zobište, contrary to many other models of blank production. In fact, I have argued elsewhere (Baumler 1987) that on the basis of the lognormal size distributions of the

TABLE 15.3
COMPARISONS BETWEEN COMPLETE FLAKES AND FLAKE TOOLS ≥2 CM

	Flakes (n = 565)		Flake Tools (n = 151)		
Cortex					
noncortical	246	(43.5)	87	(57.6)	
partially cortical	259	(45.9)	60	(39.8)	X2 = 14.5, df = 2, p >.001
cortical	60	(10.6)	4	(2.6)	
Size					
mean length (mm)	32.6	(11.9)	44.1	(13.8)	t = 10, df = 714, p >.001
mean width (mm)	26.7	(9.1)	31.3	(9.2)	t = 5.51, df = 714, p >.001
mean thickness (mm)	6.7	(4.2)	6.9	(2.9)	t = 0.54, df = 714, p <.500
mean weight (g)	10.1	(13.4)	16.2	(12.9)	t = 4.98, df = 714, p >.001
Shape					
mean length/width	1.3	(0.47)	1.5	(0.55)	t = 54, df = 714, p >.001
mean width/thickness	4.8	(2.10)	5.0	(1.70)	t = 1, df = 714, p <.100

flake tools alone, a major aspect of the method of core reduction at Zobište appears to have been an attempt to maximize the size of tool blanks while working within the limitations imposed by the continuous reduction in the mass of the core.

While the relatively simple criteria of size, shape, and percentage of cortex are sufficient to distinguish the majority of used from unused flakes, these criteria can be met in a variety of ways and do not themselves characterize the method of producing the blanks or the strategy for reducing the core. In this respect many studies of the flakes "selected" for use as tools at Paleolithic sites fall short of actually analyzing the attributes that can depict how these blanks were produced. Data on the scar pattern and placement of cortex on the 151 complete tools from Zobište, in fact, suggest that these blanks were not simply produced with size and shape characteristics in mind.

Of the 64 tools with remnant cortex, for example, 41 (64%) are naturally backed, with most, if not all, of the cortex limited to one or the other lateral edge, forming an abrupt angle with the remainder of the exterior surface. Among the unused flakes, natural backing occurs on only 23% of the sample of cortical or partially cortical flakes. Moreover, of 39 flakes in the entire complete-flake sample classifiable in the more restricted category of "naturally backed knife" blanks, 23 (59%) show macroscopic evidence of use (edge damage or retouch). Thus, whereas cortex was generally removed prior to blank production (58% of the tools are noncortical), natural backing appears to have been a desired feature of many tool blanks, accounting for most of the blanks with remnant cortex. The production of such flakes is indicative of the striking of a core face near its edge adjacent to an unflaked surface. Their frequency, intentional or not, can be expected to be higher in industries employing nodular raw material (Jelinek 1975: 303-304). At Zobište, the frequency of natural backing in the tool assemblage, however, suggests that this aspect of nodule reduction was both encouraged and intentionally exploited (e.g., Fig. 15.3:9,10).

With regard to scar pattern (Table 15.4), the tools are characterized by a higher-than-expected percentage of unidirectional and radial/subradial scar patterns, both generally indicative of separate and prepared core reduction strategies. If tool blanks were being removed simply as the opportunity for the detachment of a sufficiently sized, noncortical or naturally backed blank presented itself, we would not expect to see such consistent scar patterns in the blank assemblage. In the Zobište collection, 57% of the tools with three or more scars (n = 108) have either unidirectional or radial/subradial exterior scar patterns. Moreover, while only 18% (47 out of 266) of all the flakes (with three or more scars) classified as having irregular scar patterns show evidence of use, 41% of the unidirectional and 40% of the radial/subradial flakes exhibit such evidence. These two types of flakes include the majority but not all of the typological Levallois blades and flakes (56 of the 82), which traditionally would be considered as inten-

TABLE 15.4
EXTERIOR FLAKE-SCAR PATTERN
FOR COMPLETE FLAKES AND FLAKE TOOLS >2 CM*

	Flake Tools		Flakes	
	n	%	n	%
Unidirectional	29	26.9	42	14.0
Radial	32	29.6	49	16.3
Irregular/Other	47	43.5	219	69.7
Totals	108	100.0	300	100.0

* flakes with three or more scars

Scar Patterns (All) by Flake Use:
  $X2 = 25.505$, df = 2, $p > .001$

Scar Patterns (Unid./Radial vs. Irregular) by Flake Use:
  $X2 = 25.470$, df = 1, $p > .001$

tionally produced blanks. Seven of the 25 naturally backed knives with three or more scars also have unidirectional scar patterns. From the perspective of core reduction, therefore, the production of the majority of blanks at Zobište would appear to have proceeded from either a single-platform, unidirectional, "blade" approach or a multiplatform, radially prepared, "classic Levallois" approach. The fact that not all of the flakes attributable to these two approaches show evidence of use might be due in part to factors of their size and cortex as well as to problems in identifying use.

Why then do many of the flakes used as tools fail to exemplify fully either of these two approaches? In other words, why do 43% of the tools on blanks with three or more scars have irregular/other scar patterns? In part this may reflect the operation of other desired criteria, such as natural backing. Twelve of the 25 naturally backed knives with three or more flake scars have irregular/other scar patterns. Undoubtedly some of these blanks with irregular/other scar patterns are also the product of a unidirectional or radial approach but fail to clearly document this fact. The removal of a flake from a radially prepared core, for example, will often not cover the entire core surface and consequently not preserve the complete evidence of its preparation. The fact remains, however, that flakes with irregular scar patterns make up a larger percentage of the blank assemblage than expected if core reduction strategies involving predominantly radial or unidirectional preparation were being employed.

Another question concerns the relationship between the tool blanks and the cores recovered from Zobište. While the radial/subradial blanks find a clear correlate in the types of cores discarded at the site, there is no such association for the remainder of the blanks. The cores responsible for the production of blanks with unidirectional or even irregular scar patterns are simply not present in the numbers one would expect given the tool-blank assemblage.

The explanation for these discrepancies requires that we no longer limit ourselves, as many studies do, to a discussion of blanks and cores alone but rather attempt to integrate these within a more dynamic analysis of their production and reduction respectively. For this, all the flakes can profitably be considered together and examined for evidence of the configuration of the cores from which they were removed.

THE DYNAMICS OF CORE REDUCTION

INITIAL REDUCTION

The initial method by which nodules such as those used at Zobište were reduced can best be monitored through the examination of flakes exhibiting remnants of the exterior surface of the nodule. Particularly relevant are the placement of cortex and direction of scars on the exterior surface of partially cortical flakes, as these features are related to the method of removing cortex and preparing the core face for initial blank production. Completely cortical flakes are themselves less informative than partially cortical flakes in that they cannot be oriented in any clear fashion with previous or later removals from the core.

Figure 15.6 graphically presents some "types" of partially cortical flakes and their relative representation in the Zobište collection. Only flakes with cortex on the exterior surface proper are depicted (n =220), disregarding for the moment those with cortex only on the platform or as natural backing, in order best to represent the nature of the core's face. The types are defined here by the position of the remnant cortex and are arranged from top to bottom (except for the last) to reflect the decreasing percentage of cortex. Within this arrangement the types are further grouped, with flakes representing the prior removal of cortex from a quadrant or quadrants adjacent to the platform above, and those types with cortex removed opposite the platform below. What is shown in this typology and organization of the partially cortical flakes is the high frequency of flakes in each paired group with cortex previously removed adjacent to the platform (depicted here by hatch marks slanting up to the right in the frequency bars of these types). Conversely, there is a very low percentage (less than 10%) of flakes with cortex removed away from, but not near, the platform. Alone, this simple sorting strongly suggests that the removal of cortex proceeded from a single orientation and platform. If several juxtaposed core platforms were in use at this early stage of reduction (as in the preparation of a bidirectional or radial core face), one would expect to find a much higher incidence of partially cortical flakes with cortex on the proximal but not the distal end, owing to the higher probability that flake

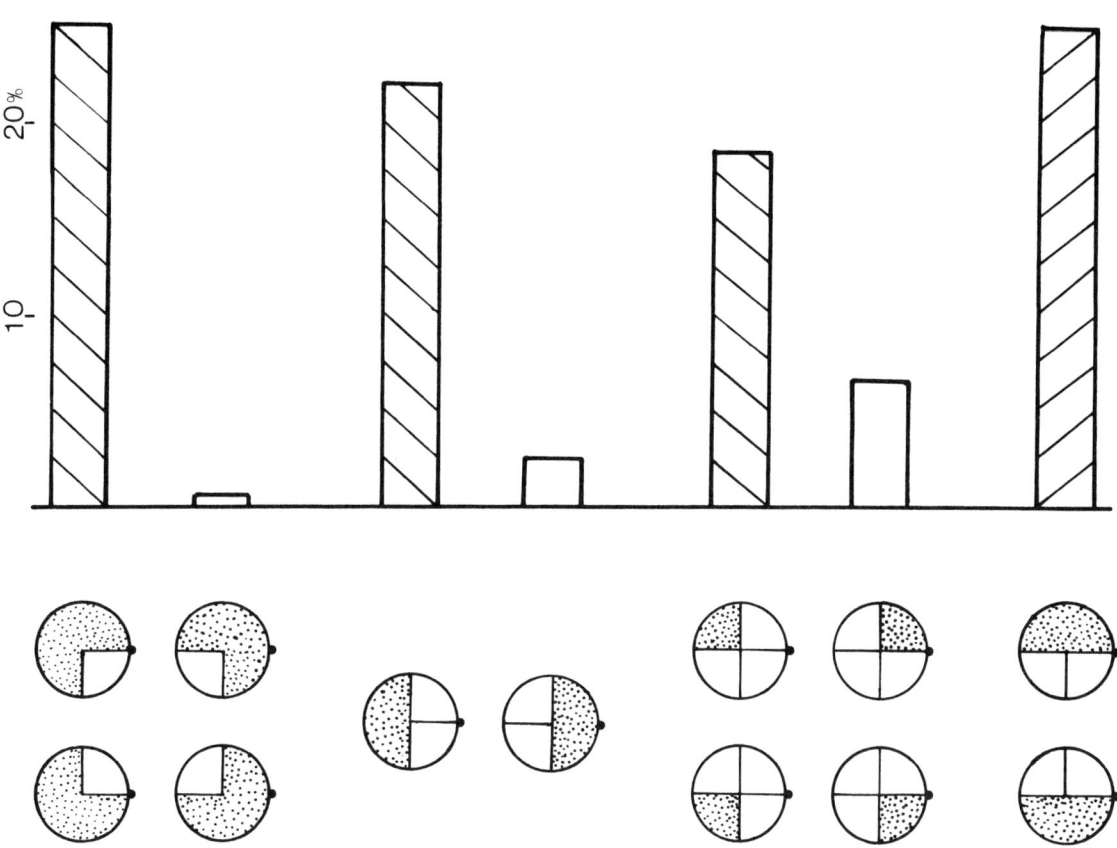

Figure 15.6 Zobište: types and relative frequencies of complete partially cortical flakes and flake tools >2 cm.

removals would intersect scars on the core face produced from an adjacent or opposite platform (see Baumler 1987: 54-56).

This interpretation is supported by data on the origin of prior scars on the partially cortical flakes. The cortex pattern illustrated at the bottom of Figure 15.6 is, for example, more ambiguous than the others as to the probable manner in which the cortex had previously been removed. Yet when we add the information, collected on scar directions, that over 75% of the total recorded scars on this type of flake originate from the same direction as the flake itself, it is quite clear that they reflect a predominantly single-platform initial reduction strategy. Indeed, when we combine, as in Figure 15.7, the data of flake-scar origin with those of cortex, the unidirectional approach taken in the initial reduction of the Zobište nodules is readily apparent. The wedge diagrams in Figure 15.7 reflect the relative contributions (expressed as percentages) from each of the four recorded directions, with those from quadrant 1 (the same direction as the removed flake) shown at the top,

quadrant 2 on the right, quadrant 3 at the bottom, and quadrant 4 on the left. Clearly illustrated by these diagrams is the dominance of previous flake scars from the same platform direction as the removed flake for all the partially cortical flakes, particularly those with more than 50% cortex.

The data on both placement of cortex and flake scars on partially cortical flakes, therefore, support the view of an initial reduction strategy favoring the preparation of a unidirectionally flaked core face. Although only a few discarded cores exist to illustrate this strategy, it is nonetheless evident in the flake assemblage representing this initial stage of core reduction. From Figure 15.7 it is also evident that as cortex decreases in amount (i.e., is further removed), the relative percentage of flake scars from other directions increases until the noncortical flakes exhibit less than 50% of the exterior scars originating from the same direction as their own removal. Thus, while initial reduction appears to reflect a single-platform or unidirectional approach, later reduction, as represented by noncortical flakes, appears to be consid-

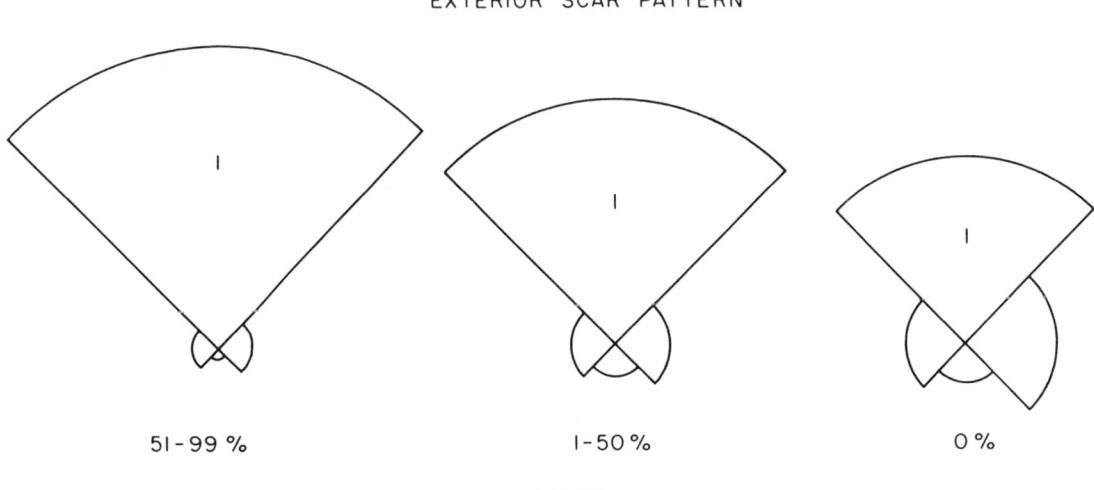

Figure 15.7 Zobište: relative percentage of exterior flake-scar angles on partially cortical (<50% cortex and >50% cortex) and noncortical (0%) flakes and flake tools <2 cm.

erably more variable and not entirely consistent with this strategy.

LATER REDUCTION

Later core reduction at Zobište is reflected primarily in the sample of noncortical flakes and presumably by the majority of the discarded cores. The sample of complete noncortical flakes larger than 2 cm includes 333 pieces. By limiting this discussion to only those flakes larger than 2 cm, I have necessarily excluded a large number of noncortical preparatory flakes. Nonetheless, the present sample is adequate for detecting major trends in later core reduction at Zobište and, in some respects, avoids problems encountered in determining the place of smaller flake removals in the sequence.

As discussed earlier, tool-blank production at Zobište, for the most part, commenced after the removal of cortex. The major exception is the production of naturally backed knives, which appear to have been a preferred form of tool blank. These special kinds of partially cortical flakes are in reality noncortical (or mostly noncortical) on their exterior surface proper, with the cortex limited to one edge of the flake. Figure 15.8 shows the exterior scar data collected for the 39 complete naturally backed knives recovered at Zobište in the same manner as earlier depicted for the flake assemblage as a whole. If the scar pattern on the exterior surface of the naturally backed knives is effectively a representation of the core faces from which they were derived, it is clear from Figure 15.8

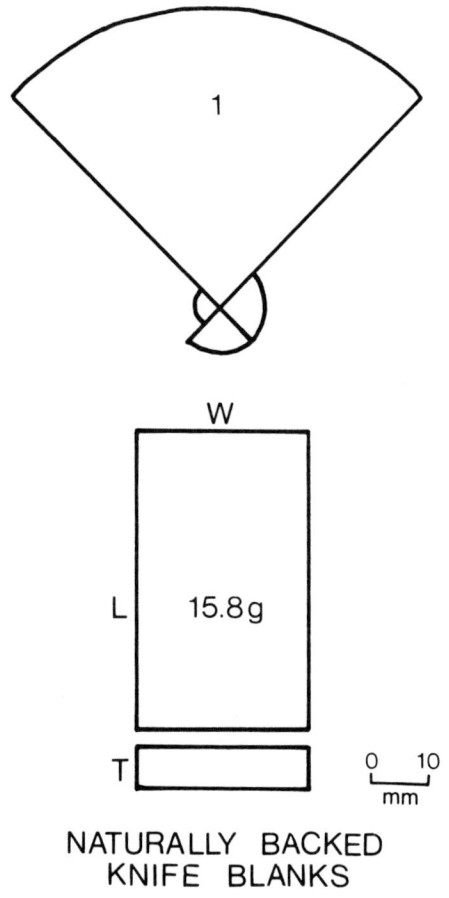

Figure 15.8 Zobište: mean dimensional data and exterior flake-scar angles on complete naturally backed knife blanks <2 cm.

that these faces are markedly dominated by scars derived from the same or a similar platform as the "knives" themselves. Despite the fact that the majority of these flakes with more than two scars have been classified as having irregular scar patterns, the predominantly unidirectional focus of the core reduction method immediately prior to their removal is revealed by the individual scar directions. The reason more of the naturally backed pieces do not fall into the unidirectional category of scar pattern is in many cases the result of a single scar originating from another direction (perhaps a preparatory flake removed to ensure the successful detachment of the core edge). Moreover, 13 (or one-third) of the naturally backed knives have only one or two flake scars and hence were not coded as to scar pattern. This low number of scars is typical of the naturally backed knives (mean scar number = 3.5) and, together with their relatively large size (mean weight = 15.8 g; see Fig. 15.8), prevailing unidirectional scars, and presence of cortex, is strongly suggestive of their removal early in the reduction of the core. It is not difficult, given the type of initial cortex removal seen above, to imagine the production of naturally backed knives as some of the first blanks produced from the cores at Zobište.

The scar data for the completely noncortical flakes, as previously depicted in Figure 15.7, have already been remarked upon for the apparent contrast with the scar data for the partially cortical flakes. Whereas the initial reduction of the nodules and the production of naturally backed knives show a clear emphasis upon unidirectional, single-platform flaking, the noncortical flakes appear (as an assemblage) to be the result of the use of multiple platforms on a single core face. But we have also previously observed that the scar patterns on noncortical flakes, both used and unused, are not homogeneous but rather range from unidirectional to radial. Clearly, the noncortical-flake assemblage's scar pattern depicted in Figure 15.7 is composite.

Figure 15.9 and Table 15.5 break down the sample of noncortical flakes with three or more scars (n = 258)

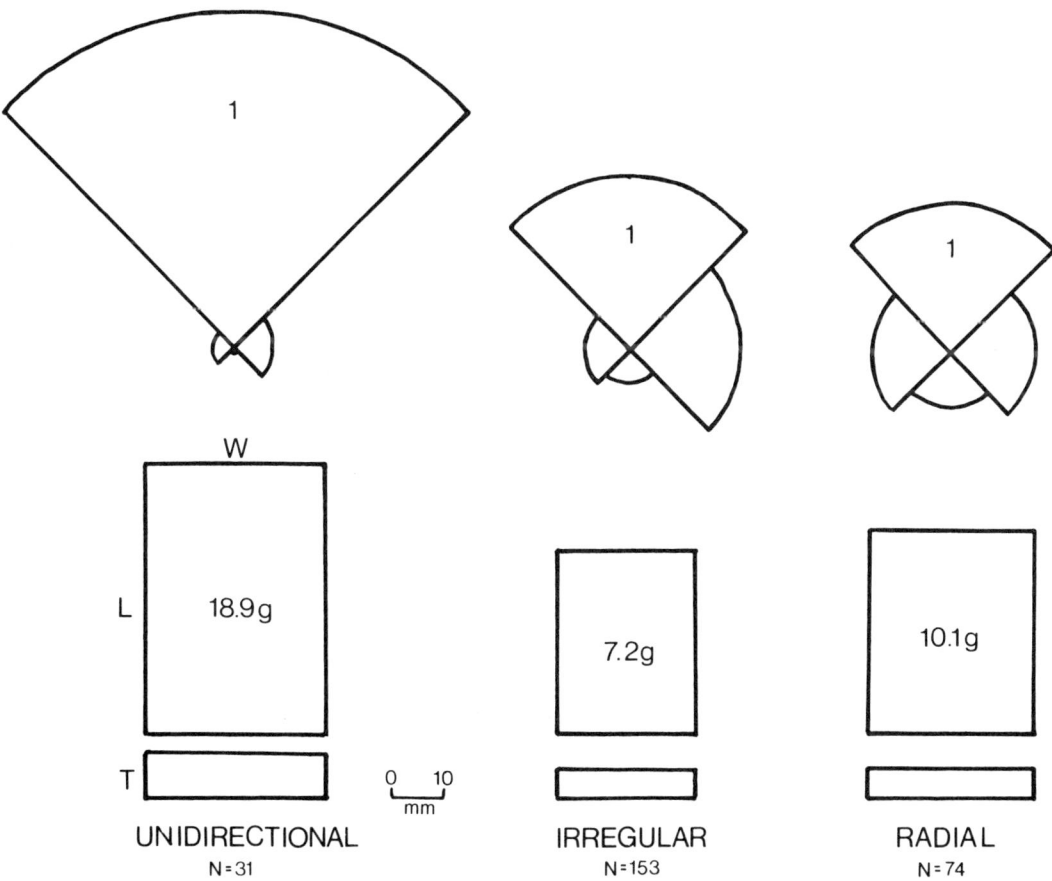

Figure 15.9 Zobište: mean dimensional data and exterior flake-scar angles on complete noncortical flakes and flake tools <2 cm (with three or more flake scars).

TABLE 15.5
SIZE BY SCAR PATTERN FOR COMPLETE FLAKES AND FLAKE TOOLS <2 CM**

	Unidirectional (n = 31)		Irregular (n = 153)		Radial (n = 74)	
	mean	s.d.	mean	s.d.	mean	s.d.
length (mm)	46.8	13.7	31.9	10.4	36.2	12.0
width (mm)	31.8*	8.9	24.7	7.7	30.0*	10.1
thickness (mm)	7.7	3.3	5.4*	2.7	5.3*	2.3
weight (g)	18.9	14.6	7.2	7.1	10.1	10.1

** flakes with three or more scars
T-tests: unidirectional vs. irregular vs. radial
* = no significant difference (p <.05)

into their assigned scar-pattern categories. Of particular interest are the mean dimensional data indicating that the noncortical flakes detached from single-platform cores (i.e., with unidirectional scar patterns) are on the whole significantly larger than those struck from radially prepared cores. It is also evident that flakes with irregular scar patterns are generally smaller than those with either of these two patterns.

In interpreting later core reduction from these differences, it is necessary to consider the relationship of each scar pattern to the type of cores discarded and the method of initial reduction described above. In this regard, the flakes with unidirectional scar patterns clearly reflect a continuation of the reduction method begun by the initial removal of cortex and preparation of the core faces. Their greater length and overall greater size, moreover, are consistent with their early removal. In fact, several of these flakes are over 70 mm in length and could have been produced only from relatively fresh nodules. Unidirectional core reduction, on the other hand, is not well represented by the cores, only three of which show the use of a single platform. These cores alone cannot be responsible for the number of noncortical flakes with unidirectional scar patterns, much less for the quantity of naturally backed knives and other partially cortical flakes derived from single-platform cores. We must conclude, therefore, that unless the cores that produced these flakes were systematically abandoned elsewhere, on or off site, the morphology of the cores was sufficiently altered by further reduction as to make them unrecognizable.

The situation with the flakes with radial scar patterns is quite different. This scar pattern is in agreement with the type of core most frequently represented in the assemblage, and the average size of the radial flakes is consistent in particular with the smaller radially prepared cores discarded at the site, as illustrated in Figure 15.10. Interestingly, none of

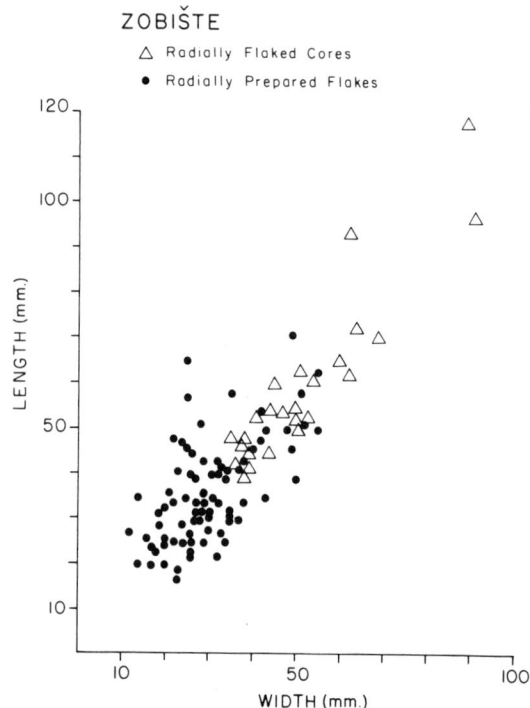

Figure 15.10 Zobište: scattergram of length and width for complete radially prepared flakes and cores.

these flakes appear to derive from very large cores, such as the three largest radially flaked cores in the sample. This suggests that these large radial cores, which are indeed "unstruck," were not intended to produce "Levallois" flakes from the center of the core face. Instead, radial blank production appears not to have occurred until the mass of the core had been considerably reduced. Additional evidence for this very late removal is reflected in the complete absence of cortex on the exterior surface proper of the 81 flakes recorded with radial scar patterns. If flakes with radial scar patterns were being removed at the beginning of the reduction sequence as well as at the end, we would not expect to see such a complete absence of exterior surface cortex. The flakes with radial scar patterns, therefore, appear to have been consistently produced as a last stage in the reduction sequence, when the need to maximize the area of removal of the core face was greatest.

The place of the noncortical flakes with irregular scar patterns in later core reduction is perhaps the most difficult to establish. Considering their relatively small average size, it is likely that many represent the preparation of cores for the other two scar patterns, particularly those with radial scar patterns. This is supported by their greater representation among the unused flakes. That they also make up a significant portion of the flakes used as tools, however, suggests that they are not entirely preparatory waste flakes selected for use or accidents in the production of other blanks. Rather it would appear that some of these flakes are tool blanks produced from the reduction of a multiplatform core not unlike the few large radially flaked cores in the assemblage. The low frequency of these large cores at the site, coupled with the evidence for the initial preparation of single-platform cores, further suggests that this method of "disc-core" reduction represents a technological transition between the production of blanks with unidirectional and radial scar patterns. Despite the rather restricted opportunity this stage would have offered for the production of large blanks, this intermediate technology was capable of producing flakes for use as tools while it also prepared the cores for final reduction by the classic Levallois method.

DISCUSSION

A model of the flake core reduction sequence at Zobište based upon the previous analysis is presented in Figure 15.11. This model represents an assemblage view of core reduction at the site and does not exclude the possibility that some nodules were reduced by an alternate method or, more likely, by only a part of the method depicted here (i.e., small nodules may have been reduced by means of only the later steps of the proposed reduction sequence).

The reconstruction begins with the observation, made on partially cortical flakes, that the initial reduction of nodules proceeded predominantly from a single platform. This unidirectional reduction continued on the initial noncortical face of the core, perhaps only for a short time, and produced two types of blanks preferred for use as tools: naturally backed knives and elongated flake-blades (including typological Levallois blades). As the configuration and size of the core rapidly changed during this early reduction, it soon became necessary, desirable, or more efficient to alter the method of production to one based upon radial preparation, by which flakes could be removed that would carry off more of the surface of the core face. If the core was sufficiently large, this technological shift might initially result in the production of tool blanks with irregular scar patterns from a "disc"-like core, and culminate with the production of blanks generated from the faces of radially prepared cores. Finally, when the cores could no longer yield a central flake removal or were broken in the attempt, they were discarded.

This model of continuous, yet shifting, reduction accounts for both the presence and the dimensions of unidirectionally prepared partially cortical and noncortical tool blanks in an industry otherwise characterized by the production of flakes with radial scar patterns and the discard of exhausted radially prepared cores. The frequency and dimensions of the various blank types also correspond with those predicted by this reduction sequence, with fewer large blanks produced by early, single-platform core reduction, followed by more numerous but smaller flakes generated by a radially prepared core.

Some independent support for the model is also provided by the raw material. While it was not possible to backfit or conjoin many artifacts in the course of the analysis, the distinctive and variable colors of radiolarite in the assemblage did allow for the definition of a number of raw-material groups that very probably represent pieces derived from the same nodule. While most of these concern primarily small and/or broken flakes and shatter, four of the groups are noteworthy. Two involve the association of naturally backed knives with, in one case, a radially prepared core and, in the other, two flakes with radial scar patterns. Another group includes a radially prepared core and flake which appear to have come from the same nodule as a flake-blade with unidirectional flake scars. The last group includes, among other pieces, both a radially and a unidirectionally prepared flake. These independent associations serve to demonstrate that different stages with different resultant blank types were indeed involved in the reduction sequence of individual nodules at Zobište.

One of the more interesting issues raised by this reconstruction of core reduction at Zobište is how it would be interpreted through a traditional classificatory approach. Individually, each of the products and byproducts of reduction at the site can and has been previously categorized, i.e., Levallois core, disc core, Levallois flake, "Levallois" flake-blade, naturally backed knife, "normal flake," etc. Behind each of these labels is a large body of thought and preconception regarding the role that each played in the manufacture of prehistoric stone tools. Is Zobište's a Levallois industry or not? Is it more or is it less; or is it simply another variant on the theme? When considered altogether, the picture painted here for Zobište is likely to be quite different than that envisioned through examination of any given component. We must ask ourselves if the parts of a lithic industry can indeed be understood separately from the whole, and whether the whole itself is merely the sum of its parts. I think the answers we choose to these kinds of questions will have a considerable effect upon the course that the analysis and comparison of lithic assemblages is to take in the future.

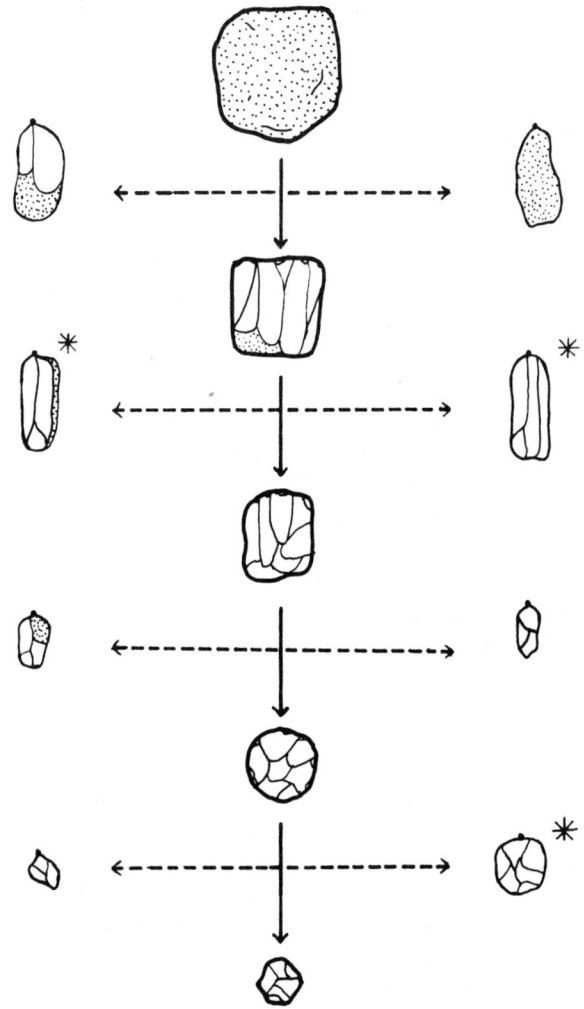

Figure 15.11   Reconstructed model of core reduction sequence at Zobište.

CONCLUSIONS

Potentially no less important as a cultural/behavioral indicator than the form and manufacture of bifaces and other retouched pieces, the detailed study of prehistoric core reduction sequences nonetheless has not received the same degree of attention or has been reserved for special circumstances where it is possible to backfit flakes onto cores. As a result, a comprehensive theory and methodology treating this essential aspect of lithic reduction is currently lacking.

This is not to say, however, that archaeologists have not long been interested in the technological aspects of core reduction. Any cursory review of the Paleolithic literature over the past 25 years will serve to show that this is not the case. The majority of these studies do focus, though, upon the *manner* in which individual flakes were removed and less upon the actual *method* of core reduction. This emphasis continues today albeit on a more sophisticated level, enhanced by experimental studies in fracture mechanics and carefully recorded replications. Because of this work, we now have a very good understanding of the importance of platform attributes and force applications in determining how flakes are detached and how these variables were manipulated by prehistoric knappers. Consequently, very few lithic reports are considered complete today without a section relating to technology as it is expressed in flake-platform variables.

Discussions of the method by which nodules were transformed into flake tools have, in contrast, been less well focused, often relying primarily upon subjective considerations and what Marks and Volkman (1983: 15) have referred to as "traditional wisdom" regarding the production of tool blanks. Quite naturally, perhaps, the study of this aspect of reduction has also concentrated upon the discarded cores or a particular flake type recovered at a site. This has resulted in an unnecessarily static view of core reduction, reflected in the nature of both our flake and core typologies, as well as the classifications of whole industries. Bordes, who can be credited with a major influence on the way we study Paleolithic chipped stone today, recognized early on that cores were dynamic objects which could undergo considerable transformation, as, say, from a Levallois core to a discoid core (Bordes 1961b: 89). Neither he nor others who have addressed core reduction from an essentially typological standpoint (e.g., Wendorf and Schild 1974), however, have been entirely successful at recreating the continuous nature of core reduction and flake production.

In this paper as well as others in this volume (see Ferring, ch. 21, and Montet-White, ch. 23), the framework for a systematic analytical approach to the reduction of lithic raw material has been introduced and applied to actual data from various parts and time periods of the Old World. While pursuing different avenues of inquiry, each of these represents an attempt to deal objectively with the issues surrounding the production of tool blanks as these are reflected in the structure and composition of lithic assemblages. It is to be hoped that continued research along these lines will ultimately yield an understanding of prehistoric core reduction that is at once more dynamic and also more realistic.

ACKNOWLEDGMENTS

Funding for the 1980 excavations at Zobište was provided by grants from the National Geographic Society and the University of Kansas General Research Fund. The author's participation was further supported by a grant from the University of Arizona Graduate Student Program Development Fund. I wish to thank Dr. Djuro Basler for loaning the Zobište collection for analysis and the following for their comments upon various aspects of this paper: Arthur J. Jelinek, Anta Montet-White, John W. Olsen, Deborah I. Olszewski, and Hansjürgen Müller-Beck. Understandably, the viewpoints taken and expressed in the paper are solely my responsibility.

DISCUSSION

MÜLLER-BECK: Bordes defined the Levallois method as a dynamic process, and that it is a dynamic process was quite clearly shown in this paper. And, of course, blades are a byproduct of the Levallois technique. But which comes first: the blades or the Levallois flakes? Here it seems that blade-like flakes are coming first. This should be checked in different assemblages.

STRAUS: Why do you think they are going to these lengths of economy if they have an abundance of raw material available in the riverbed right nearby?

BAUMLER: While the raw-material source is close, it is a long walk up and down that hill. However, I do not know whether or not this reduction sequence is directly related to any such economic concerns.

MARKS: It seems to me that this has really nothing to do with any kind of economizing behavior, but with a desire to have at least three different kinds of flakes. There would not be any reason to change shape if one were merely willing to put up with shorter or smaller elongated pieces. Perhaps this is a single reduction sequence which produces a series of predictably different objects.

KOZLOWSKI: This operational chain starts with the unprepared core, to a single-platform core for blades and flakes, which is transformed in the final stage of reduction into a discoidal core. I have made a reconstruction of the same method for the Early Neolithic, for the Linear Pottery Culture, which also starts with a single-platform core and finishes with a discoidal core. And they use all three types of blanks, even the naturally backed knives. But I think that this technique is the opposite of the Levallois technique, because in the latter the preparation is distinct and separate from the reduction of the core.

BAUMLER: But the later stages of this do involve a degree of preparation.

KOZLOWSKI: Nonetheless, in my opinion, I would not call this Levallois. I think that the essential feature for the distinction between Levallois and the discoidal core is the presence of the prepared platform. Also, in the Levallois core, the flaking surface is limited by the core edge, while in the case of the discoidal core, there is no such limit because one can produce several different kinds of flakes.

BAUMLER: I think the currently accepted definition of Levallois does not depend on a prepared striking platform—it can also be cortical. I would not call these cores discoidal because they are not peaked, but flat. That's why I wanted to raise these questions, because we should stop using such ambiguous terms and begin to think of these techniques as dynamic processes which may not involve discrete stages.

FERRING: The critical point is that if you must go through certain transformations, then we do not know if the flintknapper produced those transformation flakes for any purpose other than as part of the transformation. An example of this is the *lames à crêtes*. These are necessary byproducts of certain kinds of blade techniques and they are often highly selected as tool blanks. Are they products or byproducts?

XVI

The Curation of Stone Tools during the Upper Pleistocene

A View from the Central Negev, Israel

Anthony E. Marks

INTRODUCTION

It has often been stated that there were profound behavioral differences between the peoples of the Middle and Upper Paleolithic. On the most general level, there have always been claims that the Middle and Upper Paleolithic represent different "culture types" (Binford 1968a) and that "paleoculture" characterized the activities of the Middle Paleolithic folk, while "fully cultural behavior" was the norm during the Upper Paleolithic (Jelinek 1977). These general conclusions have been based, in part, on specific comparisons between the archaeological records of the Middle and Upper Paleolithic (e.g., Mellars 1973; White 1982; Straus 1983a). It must be pointed out, however, that virtually all comparisons have used data from Europe with little, if any, consideration given to other parts of the world. The European information does, indeed, provide a solid basis for inferring significant behavioral differences between the European Neandertals and the modern humans of the early Upper Paleolithic. Whether these are ones of kind rather than degree, however, is still controversial (Wynn 1986).

The richness of the European archaeological record for the Upper Paleolithic is striking—its art, its elaborate bone industry, the presence of personal ornaments and, in some cases, its economic specialization all stand in marked contrast to what is known or inferred about the European Middle Paleolithic (Mellars 1973; White 1982). As importantly, the dichotomy in fossil types from the European Middle and Upper Paleolithic adds yet another difference and, perhaps, an evolutionary explanation for the inferred behavioral differences (Trinkaus 1983).

In spite of the obviously geographically limited data base, recent discussions (e.g., White 1982 with comments) tend to exhibit a certain global tone, as if what has been seen in only parts of Europe accurately represents what was happening in the rest of the world as well.

For the Near Eastern Levant, at least, the European data have little relevance. The marked differences seen in Europe between the material cultures of the Middle and Upper Paleolithic are not, for the most part, paralleled in the Levant (Belfer-Cohen 1986) or become tenable only when the late Upper Paleolithic Levantine Aurignacian (the Levantine Aurignacian C of Lebanon) is compared with the Middle Paleolithic Levantine Mousterian. There are some similarities to the European situation, however, the closest of which lies in the differences between the Levantine Middle and Upper Paleolithic lithic technology and typology. There, at least, a dichotomy between the Middle Paleolithic Mousterian and the Upper Paleolithic Ahmarian (Gilead 1981; Marks 1981a) and Levantine Aurignacian (Garrod 1954) seems to place them in different technocomplexes (although even this may not stand unchallenged, since some of the Levantine Mousterian has many more Upper Paleolithic traits than does any European Mousterian). In addition, the clear in-situ evolution from Middle to Upper Paleolithic (Marks 1983a, b, 1985) adds considerably to the problem of just when one technocomplex ends and the other begins. Thus, although lithic technology and typology are among the clearest parallels between Europe and the Levant, even they are not as tightly drawn as some might wish (Copeland 1983).

In other more or less permanent manifestations of behavior, such as art and personal ornamentation, the Levantine Upper Paleolithic is sorely lacking. Aside from two questionable engraved slabs dated to the

Levantine Aurignacian (Belfer-Cohen and Bar-Yosef 1981), there is no mobile art until the Epipaleolithic Natufian, after 10,000 B.C., and no cave art at all. Personal ornaments are extremely rare until the Natufian (Belfer-Cohen 1986), although a few perforated shell, tooth, and bone items have been reported from Hayonim (Belfer-Cohen and Bar-Yosef 1981), Jabrud (Rust 1950), and Ksar Akil. In all cases, however, they are associated with the later Levantine Aurignacian, rather than with the earlier Ahmarian or its temporal equivalents in Lebanon, the Levantine Aurignacian A and B (Copeland 1975). The same situation pertains to bone tools: they are found only sporadically in early Upper Paleolithic contexts (Rust 1950; Newcomer and Watson 1984), coming into their own only in the late Levantine Aurignacian (the Levantine Aurignacian C of Lebanon) (Belfer-Cohen and Bar-Yosef 1981; Newcomer 1974). Even then, their unimpressive numbers and limited variety led Garrod (1953, 1954) to note this as one of the significant differences between the European and the Levantine Aurignacian.

It is possible but not necessary to continue this recitation of the differences between Europe and the Levant; the point should have been made by now. Only one last contrast must be made. In the Levant, unlike in Europe, there is no clear dichotomy between the late Middle Paleolithic and Upper Paleolithic fossil types. Neandertals and anatomically modern humans are both associated with the late Levantine Mousterian (Vandermeersch 1981; Bar-Yosef et al. 1986), although only modern humans are posited to be associated with the Upper Paleolithic. This situation truly confounds the issue because in the Levant both the Middle and early Upper Paleolithic lack the traditional evidence for "fully cultural behavior," in spite of anatomically modern humans' being the probable makers of both. Seemingly, in the Levant, at least, *Homo sapiens sapiens* and "fully cultural behavior" do not fully correlate, throwing some doubt on bioevolutionary explanations in this particular case.

What should our expectations be? If much of the traditional evidence for profound behavioral differences between the Middle and Upper Paleolithic in Europe cannot be validated in the Levant, does this mean that there were no significant differences other than the way people chipped stone? In fact, there do appear to be some marked differences between the Levantine Middle and Upper Paleolithic cultures but, it seems, they do not always follow expectations based on the European data. This paper will examine one major area of potential difference, using data from the central Negev, Israel: the curation of artifacts as seen through both the artifacts themselves and settlement patterns as they relate to raw-material acquisition.

THE QUESTION OF CURATION

One of the more recently postulated differences between the Middle and Upper Paleolithic peoples was in their manufacture, use, and discard of tools (e.g., Binford 1973, 1977, 1983b). This does not relate to traditional technological observations (Levallois vs. blade methods of core reduction, or different kinds of retouch), but rather to the way people of each period approached tool manufacture as part of their technological system. Basically, it has been asserted that during the Middle Paleolithic tools were expediently produced, used, and discarded, while during the Upper Paleolithic, for the most part, tools were produced in advance of any specific activity requirement and, after use, were curated for future needs. This type of behavior has been called a "curated technology" (Binford 1973: 242) and, one expects, should be taken to represent an example of "fully cultural behavior." In this framework, those tools with the greatest importance in the system are least likely to be found at archaeological sites; they will have the longest lives, since they are most likely to be curated and fixed when broken or dull (Binford 1973: 243). A logical part of such curational technology is what has been called "caching" strategy, where unfinished tools or unexhausted ones were left in caches around the landscape "which insures the dispersion in the habitat of goods and materials which might be needed later" (Binford 1979: 270).

These predictions come mainly from ethnoarchaeological observations of the Nunamiut Eskimo, with brief reference to observations of some Australian Aborigines (Binford 1973, 1979), and really have yet to be tested in Pleistocene archaeological contexts. In fact, the idea of curation of cultural items during the Upper Paleolithic is appealing and certainly probable, given the presence of such labor-intensive bone tools as *bâtons de commandement*, barbed harpoons, and eyed needles, not to mention fully carved mobile art and personal ornaments. Although it is extremely difficult to prove that any class of these items, or even single examples, were actually curated and not merely produced when needed and then discarded, it is unreasonable to think otherwise because of the time involved in making them. On a more mundane level, curation might be inferred in some cases where chipped stone tools are made on locally exotic rocks, although it is not always certain whether rocks are local or not (Masson 1982; Demars 1982). Only in a very few cases has long-distance movement of flint been documented for the Pleistocene (Schild 1976), and then it is not clear whether it is the tool per se that is being curated or the raw material (Geneste 1986).

There have even been some claims for caches during the Upper Paleolithic (Smith 1966), although often it is difficult to know whether they should be thought of as purely profane (Bégouën and Clottes 1982). On the other hand, to my knowledge, there is no direct evidence for the absence of generally similar behavior during the Middle Paleolithic. In fact, where diachronic studies have been done, there is little difference in the distances gone to acquire raw material during the Middle Paleolithic and the Upper Paleolithic (Torti-Zannoli 1983). It would seem that the absence of obviously labor-intensive items in the Middle Paleolithic has been taken as proof of the general absence of curation. Surely, the very claims for the Upper Paleolithic caches and other forms of chipped stone curation are not sufficient in number or in certainty, relative to all Upper Paleolithic data, to make their absence in the Middle Paleolithic significant.

Evidence of any sort is difficult to come by, and archaeologists are just beginning to confront this issue for the Middle Paleolithic (Tavoso 1984; Geneste 1986). Part of the problem lies with the traditional Middle Paleolithic systematics, since they are almost exclusively oriented toward descriptive typology and technology of discarded artifacts, especially abandoned tools. As has been noted already, even the typological system used for the Middle Paleolithic is not comparable in what it measures to that used for the European Upper Paleolithic (Binford 1973; White 1982: 169). In fact, until recently the almost single-minded emphasis on tools and their morphology in both traditional Middle and Upper Paleolithic studies has made it nearly impossible to judge whether curation was or was not present at most published sites and, if so, to what degree and of what kind.

To understand when tools were produced, used, and discarded, it is necessary to begin with the patterns of raw-material availability and acquisition, as well as the location and timing of blank production, because no tool can be produced, expediently or otherwise, without the immediate availability of a blank on which to make it. It is also useful to be able to reconstruct the life history of specific artifacts, as well as the more general life expectancies of classes of tools, in both form and space from their manufacture to their abandonment. Without question, this is asking a great deal from archaeology and it is unlikely that any specific study will be able to acquire all this information. Yet without at least some of it, nothing significant can be said about the general presence or absence of curation.

If there were profound behavioral differences in the degree or kind of foresight applied to tool production and conservation between the Middle and Upper Paleolithic, then these should be reflected in the assemblages from each period, not only in terms of artifact content but also in relation to resource availability. If Middle Paleolithic artifacts were only produced and used expediently and then immediately abandoned, they should occur—in fact *must* occur— close to where raw material was naturally available, while in the "curated" technology of the Upper Paleolithic there should be no necessary spatial association between sites and raw-material sources. In addition, Middle Paleolithic tools should show little evidence for movement away from the materials involved in their manufacture—cores, preparatory flakes, etc.—while Upper Paleolithic tools might be found far from their production areas. Granted, these expectations are much more general than is optimal for testing the presence or absence of stone-tool curation as cultural behavior, but they are also more likely to be testable given most archaeological studies. In particular, recent studies in the Levant have provided some of the needed information, although certainly not all.

DATA FROM THE CENTRAL NEGEV, ISRAEL

These studies took place between 1969 and 1980[1] (Marks 1976b, 1977, 1983b). Their main focus was on the relationships between environmental change and culture change throughout the Upper Pleistocene, and the question of artifact curation per se was not part of the research design. The work called for a systematic, complete survey of 55 sq. km, including flint and water resources, and the sampling of most sites, whether in situ or not. Thus, many small surface sites were studied which traditionally would have been ignored and they, together with the more impressive sites, provided a corpus of data rarely seen in the Levant. These data establish a basis for comparisons between Middle and Upper Paleolithic settlement patterns as they relate to sources of raw material.

A total of 21 Middle Paleolithic sites and 18 Upper Paleolithic occurrences were mapped, of which 11 Middle Paleolithic and 16 Upper Paleolithic sites were tested (Marks 1981a, b). Thus, within a single completely surveyed area, there is a good sample for comparisons between the two periods. These comparisons have taken two tracks, each initially period-specific. The first involved defining intersite variability of whole artifact assemblages dating to the Middle Paleolithic (Crew 1976; Munday 1976, 1979). Upper Paleolithic studies, because of greater intersite typological variability, tended to emphasize traditional typological descriptions but with the addition of detailed data on other, non-tool artifact classes (Ferring 1976, 1977; Marks 1976a; Marks and Ferring 1976; Larson and Marks 1977; Jones, Marks, and Kaufman 1983).

The second track took on importance somewhat later because of its clear potential at those sites excavated late in the long history of the Central Negev Project: the study of intrasite variability through a combination of traditional mapping of individual artifacts (Hietala and Stevens 1977; Hietala 1983) with the reconstruction of discarded cores and tools back to their earlier states (Volkman 1983; Marks and Volkman 1983, 1987). This approach has been used with great effect to test for artifact movement through stratified deposits (Cahen and Moeyersons 1977; Villa 1982); to link artifact concentrations at a single site (Cahen, Keeley, and Van Noten 1979), although not necessarily proving exact contemporaneity while doing so (Bordes 1981a); and, in the Negev case in particular, to define core-reduction strategies well beyond the limits of morphological inference and replication (Volkman 1983). Its application to testing for the presence or absence of curated lithic artifacts is somewhat indirect, but nevertheless informative.

A comparison of the Middle and Upper Paleolithic sites in the survey zone shows that there are striking differences between them. These differences may be seen weakly expressed in the location of sites relative to two major, spatially fixed resources: water and flint (Marks and Freidel 1977). More strongly, they may be seen in the degree of intersite variability within each period and, finally, in marked differences in the acquisition and movement of lithic materials between and within sites.

The location of Middle Paleolithic sites can be tied directly to two different resources and, by inference, to a third. Two sites, D15 (Crew 1976) and D35 (Munday 1977), occurred almost directly adjacent to then-functioning perennial springs in places without immediately available flint sources. A number of sites were located on or directly adjacent to outcrops of Eocene flint in locations far removed from predictable surface water (Munday 1976). Another group of sites was well away from both flint and water sources in locations on or overlooking favorable ungulate habitats. Presumably, these latter were in close proximity to areas favorable for the collection of plant resources, as well. A fourth location, on the terraces along the major drainages, is probable but could not be confirmed securely because of massive post-Middle Paleolithic erosion. A few scattered remnants of Middle Paleolithic sites, however, were found in positions derived from originally higher terrace formations (Goldberg and Brimer 1983), and it is likely that during the Middle Paleolithic such sites were common.

The location of Upper Paleolithic sites may be linked with surface water, in the form of perennial springs as at Ein Aqev (Marks 1976b) and Ein Aqev East (Ferring 1977), or that of ponds or flowing streams as at Boker Tachtit and Boker (Goldberg 1983; Horowitz 1983; Marks 1983a). The other typical location is on high ground overlooking the grass plains, as in the Avdat area (Ferring 1976; Marks and Ferring 1976), or overlooking the broader expanse of western Sinai, as do the Upper Paleolithic sites on the Har Harif (Larson and Marks 1977). There is only a single Upper Paleolithic site (Akov) located on or directly adjacent to a flint outcrop. In most cases, however, such outcrops are reasonably close, although in the Har Harif the sites appear to be far from their flint source. Those sites in the Nahal Zin (Boker Tachtit and Boker) certainly had considerable flint in the immediate area; they might be considered the only sites of either period where flint and surface water were both available and abundant.

In most cases, the positioning of Upper Paleolithic sites represented a spatial compromise between the location of major resources: water, flint, and game. During the Middle Paleolithic most sites seem to have been focused on a single resource. This difference in the location of sites relative to static resources carries further into intersite assemblage variability during both the Middle and Upper Paleolithic.

On the basis of assemblage characteristics, it has been possible to define three site types for the Middle Paleolithic occupations and, because of their usually clear spatial associations with different resources, to attribute general functions to them: workshop/quarries, ephemeral hunting and gathering (?) camps, and base camps. Not surprisingly, the workshop/quarries are on or adjacent to flint outcrops. The base camps are adjacent to large perennial springs, while the hunting and gathering sites are mostly segregated spatially from permanent water sources, although they may be near flint outcrops. The ephemeral sites show the greatest spatial and assemblage variabilities and thus, as a type, may represent a number of unrelated activities or combinations of activities.

Each site type and its associated assemblages may be described as follows:

1) Workshop/Quarries—Site area is directly related to the size of the associated outcrop. Artifact densities per square meter are moderate and generally uniform over the major portions of each site. The percentage of cores tends to be high and cores are generally large. The ratio of Levallois pieces, broken and complete, to struck Levallois cores is generally less than 1:1. On average, there are almost five struck Levallois point cores for every complete or broken Levallois point (Table 16.1).

2) Base Camps—Both base camps are large with significant in-situ cultural deposits. Artifact densities are high in all areas of the sites, although core percentages are low and the cores tend to be quite small. The ratio of Levallois pieces to Levallois cores is high and there are, on average, over 17 Levallois points for every Levallois point core. Retouched tools are no more common than at other kinds of sites, but they tend to be more complete and more typical than those at the workshop/quarries. The percentage of retouched tools at the base camps, however, is well below that found at early Levantine Mousterian cave occupations further north, while the percentage of cores is about the same (Jelinek 1982a: 75; Marks and Volkman 1986).

3) Hunting and Gathering Camps—These are comparable in size to the workshop/quarries, although the location of two, D51 and D52, on deflated eolian silts, has artificially increased their size and, by scattering the artifacts, has made both their present size and their artifact densities meaningless (Table 16.1). Artifact densities at the other sites are very low. There are proportionately a good number of large cores, particularly at sites near flint outcrops, and the ratios of Levallois pieces to struck Levallois cores range from about 2:1 to just over 4:1.

When compared (Table 16.1), a number of the attributes do not overlap, and for the most part these site types can be justified by the differences in their assemblages *combined* with their spatial associations with differing resources. The rather consistent overall proportional occurrence of retouched tools in the assemblages, however, suggests that the workshop/quarries also served, at times, as hunting stations. Every site is typologically and technologically within the Early Levantine Mousterian of Tabun D type (Jelinek 1981; Marks 1981a), so the differences between them cannot be readily accounted for by evolutionary change, adjustment to environmental shift, or developmentally unrelated Mousterian populations.

In addition to the differences already noted, there are others in artifact size and scar-pattern complexity which reflect economizing behavior as linked with site distance from raw material and intensity of occupation (Munday 1976, 1979). Cores and flakes at workshop/quarries are larger than those at the base camps, while the size of artifacts at the ephemerally occupied sites relates directly to their distance from the nearest source of raw material (Table 16.1).

Upper Paleolithic sites in the Avdat/Aqev area are in many ways quite different from those of the Middle Paleolithic. Each site consists of several small artifact concentrations. Site size was thus determined more by the stability of the landsurface than by group size. For instance, the site Ein Aqev, situated in an aggrading terrace, is only ca. 50 sq. m in area but consists of a series of stratigraphically positioned, mostly overlapping concentrations of less than 25 sq. m each (Marks 1976a). Where surfaces were more stable, as at Ein Aqev East (Ferring 1977), the surface area may be in the hundreds of square meters but, when examined closely, the site consists of a series of isolated or partly overlapping artifact concentrations, each one no larger than about 25 sq. m. Within each site, each concentration is very much like every other. There is little to no variability in core percentages. At Boker BE, for example, where the occupations were stratified, the total range in core percentages for six occupations of the same industry was only from 1.3 to 3.7% (Jones, Marks, and Kaufman 1983: 302). Even intersite variability in core percentages is minimal,

TABLE 16.1

ATTRIBUTES OF LEVANTINE MIDDLE PALEOLITHIC SITES IN THE CENTRAL NEGEV, ISRAEL

	Size (sq. m)	Artifact density (sq. m)	% Cores	Lev. bnk: Lev. core	Lev. pt: Lev. pt. c.	% Ret. Tools	Mean Core Wt. (g)
A. Base camps							
D15 (600)	1200	68.9	6.5	16:1	17.5:1	8.4	46.9
D35s (600)	>2000	17.6	5.3	19:1	18.7:1	5.5	78.4
D35,1 (600)	>2000	41.5	6.4	11:1	6.9:1	4.5	77.6
D35,c (600)	>2000	97.0	3.2	96:0	46:0	3.9	49.8
B. Workshops							
D2 (0)	1	11.7	26.9	1:1.8	1:7	7.9	154.9
D42 (0)	270	25.6	13.7	1:1.2	1:2.5	5.3	124.7
D44 (75)	750	36.3	13.2	1.3:1	1:5	6.1	159.6
C. Ephemeral							
D45	24	25.7	8.4	3:1	0:2	4.2	87.5
D51	*	*	9.3	2.4:1	3.5:1	6.8	108.9
D52 (1200)	*	*	12.7	4.2:1	1:1	5.6	43.7
D33 (0)	600	2.2	13.5	2.6:1	1.2:1	1.8	253.4
D46 (0)	450	2.8	17.3	2.9:1	2.3:1	4.6	156.0
D40 (10)	650	5.0	23.9	1.9:1	1.6:1	3.2	190.0

* indicates the site was heavily deflated, making site size and artifact density meaningless. Numbers in parentheses indicate distance from raw-material source, not considering changes in elevation which, at times, are sizable. Distance is given in meters. (After Munday 1976, 1977, 1979)

regardless of any one site's distance from raw material.

In spite of the structural differences in Middle and Upper Paleolithic assemblage variability, sites from both periods provide evidence for considerable importation of flint. The absence of workshop/quarries during the Upper Paleolithic and the extremely stable percentages of cores among their assemblages indicate that blocks of raw material usually were collected and carried back to the sites for reduction into cores. Distances may not have been great, perhaps no more than a few hundred meters, but the very similar proportions of various types of core-reduction products (primary elements, core-trimming flakes, core tablets, etc.) at sites with the same basic technology (Ahmarian vs. Levantine Aurignacian) indicate that there was a standard procedure for raw-material importation and reduction.

A quite different pattern seems to have obtained during the Middle Paleolithic. While some unmodified blocks of flint undoubtedly were carried into the base camps and the hunting stations away from flint outcrops, the workshop/quarries indicate that it was either blanks or shaped cores, quite probably both, that were most often imported into the other sites. The extreme difference in the ratios of Levallois pieces to Levallois cores between the base camps and the workshop/quarries strongly suggests that many of the Levallois blanks produced at the workshop/quarries were exported from them and imported into the base camps.

On a more basic level, however, the tons of chipped flint at the base camps are unlikely to have come from the workshop/quarry sites a flake at a time. The numerous small, exhausted cores at the base camps are clear evidence for intensive raw-material reduction. The extremely small size of the cores at the ephemeral hunting station D52 (Table 16.1) also reflects such behavior, which is not surprising, considering it would have been a round trip of over 2 km to get additional raw material.

It is more likely that shaped cores were more often imported into sites than were flakes and points. This can be seen most clearly at the ephemeral sites away from flint outcrops, such as D51 and D52, where a rather high percentage of cores is associated with a relatively low percentage of primary elements (Munday 1976).

Yet from all these data, it is not possible to point to a single specific core at a base camp or an ephemeral camp and demonstrate that it was produced at a specific workshop/quarry. On the other hand, it is clear—in fact, obvious—that virtually all the lithic artifacts from sites such as D51, D52, D15, and D35 were imported from some distance, since there was *no* raw material naturally available at those localities.

Lewis Binford (1983b: 235), ignoring all the other variables, has suggested that the differences in size between artifacts at the base camps and those at the workshop/quarries were

> the consequences of the behavior of occupants who arrived at a site unequipped with an adequate tool kit (an essentially 'non-curated' technology). They then searched around the site for raw materials and finding artifacts which had been introduced by previous occupants, they reduced them into tools.

This scenario cannot work, since *every* occupant who arrived at the site, by the definition of having a non-curated technology, would have arrived empty-handed! There never would have been any artifacts introduced into such a site at all and, as a result, there would not be a site there today. Also, the percentages of retouched tools at the base camps are not higher than at the other sites, so that differential retouched tool manufacture from already-existing blanks must have been, at best, a minor component of traditional tool production. Rather, there appears to have been a general pattern in core reduction and tool production, but with the acceptance of smaller products at the base camps and the ephemeral sites away from flint outcrops as a necessary price for not having to go some distance to collect additional flint. It appears that during the Middle Paleolithic preferred occupation was adjacent to permanent surface water. Since water could not be moved as efficiently as flint, flint was brought as cores and blanks to the water's edge.

In order to tie down the evidence for habitual movement of cores during the Middle Paleolithic and the possible absence of such habitual movement during the Upper Paleolithic, it is necessary to look at another data set from the central Negev. Rather than from a series of sites across the landscape, these data come from the stratified site of Boker Tachtit, which documents the technological transition from the local terminal Mousterian to the earliest Upper Paleolithic (Marks 1983a, b, 1985).

The site of Boker Tachtit was situated at the edge of a partly spring-fed pond in the bottom of the Nahal Zin, just upstream from its juncture with the Nahal Havarim (Goldberg and Brimer 1983). The Nahal Zin is a canyon with steep walls some 130 m high behind Boker Tachtit. Along the top of the canyon are outcrops of Eocene flint conglomerates; considerable amounts of flint weather out of the cliff edge and are brought down to the canyon floor as scree. The area of Boker Tachtit thus had predictable supplies of both water and flint immediately available to those who camped there.

The site consists of four stratigraphically isolated, primary-context living floors in fine overbank pond sediment (Goldberg 1983). Each occupation was partly eroded, but sufficient remained intact of three of the four levels that both reasonable assemblages and excellent intrafloor spatial data were recovered. Since the focus of this paper is the potential differences in curational habits between the Middle and Upper Paleolithic, only data pertaining to that issue will be examined, and then only those from the lowest floor (Level 1), which is considered terminal Mousterian, and the uppermost floor (Level 4), which is considered earliest Upper Paleolithic (Marks 1983a: 83–84). Since these two floors represent part of a rather short developmental sequence, major differences might not be expected, but some differences should be present. Since the designation of Boker Tachtit Level 4 as earliest Upper Paleolithic has been questioned (Copeland 1986), it is important to note in this context that the basis for calling it Upper Paleolithic does not relate to observed or inferred curational behavior. Rather, it has to do with differences in basic core-reduction strategies (Marks 1983b, 1985; Marks and Volkman 1983).

One of the advantages of this comparison is that both assemblages, Level 1 and Level 4, come from the same locality, existed under the same regional and local environmental conditions (Horowitz 1983), and were incorporated into the sediments under the same specific geomorphological processes (Goldberg 1983). The people who made each assemblage had access to the same resources, over the same distances. In addition, both assemblages are typologically very similar (Jones, Marks, and Kaufman 1983), so that just about every other thing is equal—a very rare, if not unique, situation.

The Boker Tachtit artifact samples have undergone extensive conjoining (Volkman 1983), as well as intensive intralevel and interlevel technological and spatial analyses (Hietala 1983, 1984). The reconstructions permit us, for the first time in the Negev, at least, to refer to specific blocks of raw material, the cores produced from them, the blanks struck from the cores, the tools produced on those blanks, and ultimately the places where those tools were discarded.

The two elements which directly concern curatorial habits are the spatial aspects of core reduction and final core location, and the distance between discarded retouched tools and the blocks of raw material from which their blanks came. While distances here are small, and the scale is intrasite rather than intersite, the principle governing the presence or absence of curation remains valid.

A total of 58 cores were recovered from Level 1 and 52 from Level 4. Of those from the Mousterian Level 1, 32.8% were wholly or extensively reconstructed and 13.8% had at least a few pieces conjoined with them, while a full 53% went without a single conjoined artifact. In fact, of those latter 31 cores, the excavated area of Level 1 contained no blanks or tools with their specific textures and color configurations. It would thus appear that these 31 cores had been brought into the site *after* shaping but were not further reduced, and that at least 17 others had been produced onsite from blocks of raw material, while the remaining seven might fit into either category. This apparent dichotomy in core-production location was confirmed and clarified by the reconstruction of five blocks of raw material from Level 1, where all pieces were present except for the cores themselves. These cores, all unstruck Levallois point cores, had been removed from the site, leaving only their "shells." The general inferences regarding differential core production and core movement between Middle Paleolithic sites were thus confirmed by specific examples from this terminal Mousterian level at Boker Tachtit.

The pattern for cores in the Upper Paleolithic Level 4 is quite different. Of a total of 52 cores recovered, 67% underwent extensive reconstruction, while another 5.8% had a few pieces conjoined with them. Only 14 cores, 26.9%, went without any refitting, but in all cases blanks appropriate in texture and color were present in the sample. There were no cases of reconstructed blocks of material without their associated cores.

Unfortunately, lack of additional data from even later Upper Paleolithic sites in the area precludes the assertion that during the Upper Paleolithic shaped cores were never moved from site to site. Even in Boker Tachtit Level 4, those 14 cores without conjoins may have been carried into the site already shaped, with the similar blanks representing on-site reduction. In fact, one highly reconstructed core (Volkman 1983: 182-183) still lacked cortex on the flaking surface and on the striking platform. Hence this core, too, might well have been imported into the site in its reconstructed state. It appears, in this light, that the difference in treatment between the cores of Levels 1 and 4, in spite of being marked, may be one of degree rather than kind.

Curation in relation to tools and tool production is a more complex problem. Of the 89 tools recovered from Level 1, only 28 (31.5%) were fitted back onto cores, while another five (5.6%) were conjoined with other pieces but, so combined, still failed to fit back onto the reconstructed cores. Therefore, just under 40% of the terminal Mousterian tools can be securely placed as having been produced at the site.

For the Upper Paleolithic Level 4, the percentages are considerably lower. Only 32 out of 183 tools (17.5%) were fitted back onto cores, while another 22 (12.0%) conjoined with pieces of debitage but not with cores. In Level 4, therefore, only somewhat under 30% of the tools can be confirmed as produced on-site. This difference between the terminal Mousterian level and that of the Upper Paleolithic is weakly suggestive of some possible behavioral differences. Given the data, it is more likely that some of the tools from Level 4 were produced elsewhere and carried into the site than that any of the tools found in Level 1 were brought in. In at least four cases, movement of tools into the site during the Level 4 occupation can be confirmed. A group of four endscrapers, all conjoinable with one another, were produced on a very unusual reddish speckled flint of which there was only one other piece, an unretouched blade, in the excavated portion of the floor. These four, at least, as well as the blade, were imported; from how far, however, is unknowable—it could be a matter of meters or kilometers. Still, this is the earliest clear example from the Negev for the presence of tools made on flint exotic relative to the rest of an assemblage.

A somewhat different approach more strongly suggests some possible behavioral differences regarding tool use and discard between the terminal Middle Paleolithic and the earliest Upper Paleolithic. This centers on the spatial relationships between locally produced tools and the cores or debitage clusters from which their blanks came. In Level 1 there were one amorphous and two clear artifact clusters, consisting of cores, tools, and debitage. In spite of a high percentage of conjoins for the floor as a whole, there were only five instances where an artifact in one cluster fit together with an artifact in another: 1.9% of all conjoins for that level (Hietala 1983: 220). If we consider only the two clear clusters, where over 35% of the tools were conjoined with cores, the distances between the tools and their conjoins were minimal (Table 16.2). With the exception of a conjoin cluster of three tools, debitage, and a core where the *core* had been moved some 2.5 m from the tools and associated debitage, all tools were within 2 m of their cores and well over half were discarded within 1 m.

TABLE 16.2
DISTANCE OF TOOLS TO THEIR CONJOINS

Distance	Level 1 no.	Level 1 %	Level 4 no.	Level 4 %
<1 m	18	64.3	13	43.3
1-2 m	9	32.1	7	23.3
>2 m	1	3.6	10	33.3

Level 4 contained two clear concentrations, and the percentage of artifacts in one cluster that conjoined with those of the other was fairly high, 5.9% (Hietala 1983: 235). When only tools are considered, this figure increases to 14.8%, indicating that tools were somewhat more than three times as likely as any other artifact class to be found in the cluster different from where their associated cores and debitage were. Not surprisingly, this statistic is correlated with increased distance between the tools and their associated cores. In this case, one-third of all conjoined tools in this level were more than 2 m from their cores, while fewer than half were within 1 m (Table 16.2). In a few cases, the distance between discarded tools and their associated cores exceeded 3 m, a situation not present in Level 1 (Hietala 1983: figs. 8-20, 8-24).

There are thus considerable differences between the two levels in the spatial distribution of tools and their associated cores. Although the distances involved are not great, it is certainly clear that tools in the Upper Paleolithic level tend to be farther from their cores than do tools in the terminal Mousterian level. Yet, aside from the four endscrapers of exotic flint in Level 4, there is little evidence for the actual importation of tools into the site. In fact, it may be argued that the increased distances between retouched tools and their associated cores might be the result of two different occupations; the tools from the first occupation could have been scavenged during the second and brought to the second, later area of activity. While this is a tempting explanation, it cannot hold because tools originating in each concentration are found discarded in the other. It may well be, however, that this situation reflects tool sharing rather than even nascent curation. Whichever the case, it suggests a change in behavior on the part of the people who occupied Boker Tachtit.

Finally, no evidence for "caching" behavior was recognized at either Middle Paleolithic or Upper Paleolithic sites. The clear multiple reoccupations of the Upper Paleolithic sites, though, suggest that the site itself—the cores, blanks, and tools left behind—constituted a cache to be returned to at a later date. The rather high percentage of cores still structurally sound and unexhausted at most Upper Paleolithic sites, as well as the complete but unmodified blades, flakes, and other debitage were surely as usable as any buried cache. This would apply equally well to many of the Middle Paleolithic sites, making "caching strategy" non-discriminating between the Middle and Upper Paleolithic.

CONCLUSIONS

Given these data, what can be said about behavioral differences between the late Middle and early Upper Paleolithic of the central Negev, regarding expedient versus farsighted (curational) approaches to the manufacture and use of chipped stone tools? Without question, there were marked differences between the Middle and Upper Paleolithic approaches to raw-material acquisition and the location of some core reduction, relative to the location of some other activities. It is also probable, but certainly less clear, that there were differences in the locations of tool manufacture, use, and discard. Yet can it be said that during the Middle Paleolithic tool-producing behavior was expedient, while during the Upper Paleolithic it was not? The data, fragmentary though they may be, do not permit such a simple dichotomy to be made. If pressed, however, one would have to answer no!

During the Middle Paleolithic, flint outcrops were usually exploited as sources for raw material for the immediate production of shaped cores, which were then exported to either base camps or hunting stations for further reduction. Even at such an ephemeral camp (albeit near raw material) as that of Boker Tachtit Level 1, there is proof for both importation and exportation of shaped cores. This is certainly a form of curation. Also, there is good inferential evidence for curation in the markedly different ratios of Levallois pieces to Levallois cores at base camps compared to those at workshop/quarries; these can be explained most easily by the exportation of Levallois blanks out of the workshop/quarries and into the base camps. The latter behavior may relate to tool curation, depending upon how one views unretouched Levallois pieces. If the most conservative view is taken, that they are no more than specialized blanks, then it still may be said that during the Middle Paleolithic curation existed, centering around cores and blanks for tools rather than around tools themselves.

Evidence for curation of any sort during the early Upper Paleolithic is not nearly so strong. For the most part, nearby blocks of unmodified raw material were brought onto the site for reduction, although some shaped cores might have been introduced as well. There is no evidence for specific workshop/quarries or for core export, and it is likely that the Middle Paleolithic pattern of core curation was no longer habitual. Curation of tools might be implied by the data from Boker Tachtit Level 4, but only on a minor scale. Certainly, tools were moved around the site more than had been the case during the terminal Mousterian occupation, but whether this can be called tool curation is problematic. Only the presence of the four tools of exotic flint points clearly to the importation of tools into the site. It looks as if the differences in tool discard that can be documented are probably ones of degree rather than kind. For the tools, at least, in both the terminal Mousterian and the early Upper Paleolithic occupation at Boker Tachtit, the data available indicate that the majority of tools were made, used, and discarded within an arm's length of the cores from which they came!

These data suggest that in the Negev the curation of chipped stone tools was not an important part of either period's technological system; the tools found there on floors of both periods will probably reflect the activities carried out on those floors. Beyond the details presented above, there are two additional arguments for accepting these conclusions. First, the Negev has abundant sources of flint, although their distribution does not coincide spatially with permanent water and grazing areas. No occupant, whether Middle or Upper Paleolithic, needed to travel very far to acquire good-quality flint. It must be assumed by the spatial redundancy of Upper Paleolithic ephemeral site reoccupations (Marks and Freidel 1977) that during all but the first occupation of each group, the occupants knew full well that flint was readily available in the area and that, therefore, few if any chipped stone tools needed to be carried in.

Second, it is probably inappropriate to consider chipped stone tools a focus of curational habits even in technological systems that otherwise might emphasize curation. It is most likely that in curated technologies in flint-rich areas it was the bone tools, the wooden hafts, the arrow and spear shafts that were curated, not the chipped stone tools. Simply put, virtually any chipped stone tool known from the Upper Paleolithic of the Levant, given an appropriate blank, takes only a matter of seconds to make—a minute or two at most. In addition, the probable life expectancy of any of these tools can be measured in minutes. Scrapers need almost continuous resharpening, burins must be modified often by the removal of burin spalls, while tools useful for cutting are produced with almost every blank removal. Why curate such tools? They might be curated, or at least sharpened and resharpened (Dibble 1984a), if there were a paucity of potential blanks on hand, as might have happened in a cave in the northern Levant during a cold week or if there was planned movement into an area where resources were unknown or where they were known to be absent.

Certainly some tools or cores must have been carried around during both the Middle and Upper Paleolithic to deal with unexpected or even planned exploitation of ephemeral resources: the butchering of an unexpected kill, the scavenging of a large herbivore, the cutting of a branch perfectly shaped for a spear shaft, etc. Yet curated tools in areas such as the Negev will represent a trivial proportion of the chipped stone tools made, used, and discarded. Such curated tools are more apt to be important in the technological system and more identifiable, as well, in areas where flint sources are lacking or widely separated. The information from the Negev leads to an interpretation of curational flexibility and selectivity during both the Middle and Upper Paleolithic, rather than to a dichotomous presence or absence of such behavior.

NOTE

1. This work was carried out with the support of National Science Foundation grants GS-42680, BNS 76-81646, and BNS 79-04931.

DISCUSSION

DIBBLE: It appears that according to several different variables, such as core size, the number of cores, flake size and so forth, there is a fairly predictable relationship between these and the distance from raw material during the Middle Paleolithic. It certainly represents an "intelligent" use of raw materials, perhaps a conservation of materials. But in other ways it bothers me that so much of this kind of variability is so predictable. That is, once we control for the effects of raw-material availability, technological and function constraints, then there is not much left. I wonder if, during the Upper Paleolithic, we see more arbitrary rules or arbitrary styles that more often override these effects of raw-material availability.

MARKS: But this pattern relating to raw material is equally valid for the Upper Paleolithic in the lower Negev.

DIBBLE: It is undoubtedly true that later hominids also exhibit an intelligent use of materials. But it is a question of how much more lithic assemblage variability is unexplainable by such factors, and thus may be related to arbitrary styles which, by definition, may not be explainable. So, do we see more or less unexplained or residual variability in the Middle Paleolithic?

FERRING: Do you think that this movement of cores before the transition is more or less efficient?

MARKS: First of all, I don't believe that all the Levallois points and flakes at the base camps were produced on those cores that were imported in. In the early Middle Paleolithic one can easily classify probably nine different flake types, and it is clear that they are not simply from one series of reduction. Some can be. But in other cases, you simply can't get from one type of core to another by reducing it further. One would have to, at least in some cases, work the core differently to obtain different kinds of results. So I think in a sense they were not very efficient. They have different reduction strategies with different morphological items. For the Upper Paleolithic, my interpretation is that a single reduction strategy becomes much more efficient because one can produce a series of radically different blanks in one reduction strategy. And, furthermore, tools are made on all of them. So, in a sense the Quina Mousterian was less efficient in that it took more flint to produce what they wanted. By the Upper Paleolithic they were infinitely more efficient and producing a much greater range of material with a single system.

ROLLAND: For your study it is important to have a good knowledge of water and flint resources. The Negev is a marginal area, so a small change in the precipitation can dramatically change the situation. Complicating it further is the considerable amount of erosion that has taken place. How well can you control these variables?

MARKS: Better than in most areas. Because we are in a desert, all of the geological surfaces can be seen very easily and there is almost no historic disturbance.

XVII
Nouvelles découvertes dans le Paléolithique d'Asie centrale soviétique

Miklós Gábori

En Asie centrale soviétique, le Paléolithique inférieur était pratiquement inconnu il y a huit ans. Sur ce vaste territoire—en Kazakhstan, en Turkménie, en Uzbéghistan et en Kirghizie—il n'y avait que quelques gisements de surface et quelques outillages qui étaient rangés dans le Paléolithique inférieur exclusivement par des critères typologiques, comme p. ex. Koukhipios (dans la partie méridionale de Tadjikistan) et quelques industries avec des choppers, des chopping-tools dans le bassin de Fergana (Ouch-Kourgane, Hodjaba-Kourgane, On-Artcha, etc.).

Cette situation changea par les fouilles de Honako II, Karataou I et Lakhouti I. Tous les trois gisements se trouvent dans le territoire central de Tadjikistan—le dernier déjà sur la bordure du Pamir—dans un loess épais ou dans un sol fossile faible (dans une profondeur de 80-65-45 m). La datation de ces industries est connue par les publications récentes (Honako: 500,000 ans??; Karataou: 200,000; Lakhouti: 150,000), mais elle est encore aujourd'hui assez problématique. La cause de l'incertitude remonte aux circonstances climatiques du territoire, à la difficulté de leur détermination chronologique, c'est-à-dire au milieu naturel spécifique du Pléistocène moyen et supérieur. Je voudrais retourner plus tard sur ces problèmes.

L'industrie de cette civilisation dite "Karataou" se caractérise par des outils de galets, souvent d'une très grande dimension, par des choppers et des chopping-tools massifs, mais les racloirs et les éclats levallois sont aussi fréquents. Ces derniers se trouvent à Karataou (Fig. 17.1) et à Lakhouti (Fig. 17.2). Nous devons laisser de côté les relations stratigraphiques intéressantes et leur évaluation climatologique.

C'est ici qu'on doit mentionner encore les bifaces acheuléoïdes trouvés sporadiquement. Ils sont connus surtout aux environs du lac Issik-Koul, du lac Balkhas, et en outre loin, à l'ouest, sur la péninsule Krasnovodsk, mais, malheureusement, toujours sans stratigraphie, en surface. L'existence d'une civilisation acheuléoïde n'est donc pas prouvée. Quant à leur origine, ce sont Iran ou Pakistan qui peuvent entrer en ligne de compte, mais d'après leur caractère, il n'est pas exclu qu'ils appartiennent à une industrie mésolithique quelconque(?). Par contre, il est établi que les outillages mésolithiques de l'Asie centrale (la civilisation Hissar, dans les vallées de fleuves méridionales du Tadjikistan; et la civilisation Djeitoun à l'ouest, en Turkménie) diffèrent nettement de ces bifaces.

En tout cas, ces trois gisements nouveaux n'expliquent pas la richesse relative du Paléolithique moyen, ni son origine. Il y a un hiatus incontestable entre le Paléolithique inférieur et le Paléolithique moyen; une lacune qui, d'après mon opinion, au sens géochronologique, dure à partir du Riss jusqu'au commencement du Würm ancien.

Les industries du Pléistocène supérieur commencent donc dans le Würm ancien. Leur date supérieure ne peut pas donc être déterminée assez précisément, étant donné qu'on peut constater parfois des survivances intéressantes.

Le nombre des sites du Paléolithique moyen monte à peu près à 80, dont la plupart en Uzbéghistan et en Tadjikistan. La cause de la densité n'est pas seulement la recherche intense, mais la morphologie et paléographie variées de ces territoires. Il y a parmi eux des cavernes, des stations de loess, situées dans les terrasses, ou dans le désert et quelques gisements situées à côté des fontaines d'autrefois ou des petits lacs. Ils peuvent être classifiés d'après leur situation—une telle classification existe effectivement—et il y a des différences typologiques, faciologiques entre leurs industries. Aujourd'hui, il semble être plus convenable encore de les grouper d'après les types d'industrie, qui donnent peut être une chronologie relative aussi.

Figure 17.1   Karataou en Tadjikistan.

La première est le *Moustérien ancien* ou *Moustérien levallois* de type d'Asie centrale—étant donné que cette industrie diffère vivement de toutes celles qu'on connaît à l'est de l'Oural. Mais cette constatation est valable dans le cas des autres groupes aussi.

Ce groupe se caractérise par des outils de grande dimension, les lames épaisses sans retouche et travaillées très faiblement. Les pointes moustériennes, les racloirs sont rares et le débitage est levallois. Les outils discoïdes sont frappants, de même que les hachoirs de galets roulés de grande dimension, dont l'une des bordures est seulement retouchée (on trouve souvent des retouches scalariformes, ce qui est la conséquence de la matière première)—qui sont des types archaïques.

Nous ne mentionnons que quelques gisements importants.

Kaira-Koumi est un gisement de grande dimension dans le désert, le long de la rivière Sir-Daria (en Tadjikistan du Nord; Fig. 17.3). Les outils se trouvent dans une quantité extraordinaire sur la surface et sous les couches d'argile sablonneux, creusés par le vent. La plupart d'eux sont des lames simples, parfois des racloirs sur lame, racloirs simples de débitage levallois. Il n'y a pas de faune, mais d'après le caractère de l'industrie et les observations morphologiques, le matériel peut être rangé dans cette phase ancienne. (C'est un territoire de dépression, avec les restes des montagnes enfoncées.)

L'industrie d'Amir-Temir et celle de la grotte de Hodjakent sont d'un caractère analogue (ce dernier est située dans le prolongement occidental du Tien-Chan), et puis l'outillage des couches inférieures de la grotte Abi-Rakhmat (Fig. 17.4-5). Mais ce dernier est important plutôt du point de vue du groupe suivant et de l'évolution ultérieure.

Nous mentionnons encore deux sites moins connus, en signalant les différences locales. L'un est Amankoutan, au sud de Samarkande, non loin de la caverne Techik-Tach. Son industrie se compose de petits éclats quartzites. Ils sont courts, triangulaires, à peine retouchés, avec une base clactonienne. Une autre partie de l'outillage est en diorite noir: des lames courtes, avec une base semblable. Cette matière est assez archaïque et "étrangère" parmi les autres. En se servant d'une analogie lointaine, elle est semblable aux

Figure 17.2   Lakhouti en Tadjikistan.

industries d'éclats de l'interstade Riss-Würm en Europe centrale. La faune est analogue à celle de Techik-Tach, elle est indifférente; mais, cette petite grotte était en vérité une station de travertin. On retrouve les mêmes types à 20 km d'ici, dans la grotte Tokalik aussi.

L'autre station est Djarkoutan, à proximité de Chakhristan, petite ville aux VIe-VIIe siècles. C'est qu'on appelle la "terrasse de Tachkente" qui est bien datée et qui contient, sur beaucoup d'autres lieux aussi, du Paléolithique moyen. Là, ce sont les lames de grande dimension qui dominent, les pointes moustériennes sont de nouveau rares, et il faut souligner les hachoirs typiques, pour lesquels il faudrait trouver un terme à part. Ce sont des galets de grande dimension, ronds, plats, roulés, travaillés sur l'un des bords. Leur sélection est claire d'après la forme et la dimension. Ils sont presque analogues aux pièces de Tchoukoutien, et il ne serait pas difficile de voir en eux une transition de la "civilisation Karataou."

Houdji est une nouvelle station en plein air, non loin de Douchanbé, la capitale du Tadjikistan. La couche archéologique est une épaisse masse contenant du charbon et de la cendre, dans laquelle, sur un terrain de 40 m^2, V. A. Ranov a trouvé plusieurs milliers de pièces. Il détermine l'industrie comme levalloiso-moustérienne; la datation C-14 donne 38,000 ans.

Comme on peut voir, ce groupe et les autres aussi sont assez vagues.

Il y a plusieurs gisements importants qui appartiennent au *Moustérien évolué*, mais il y a des différences marquées parmi leurs industries. Les outillages sont en général d'un débitage levallois, les talons sont facettés; les types caractéristiques sont: les racloirs bien retouchés; les lames; les pointes minces, allongées; les nucléus discoïdes. Ce type d'industrie est très évolué sur quelques sites. Il est à souligner qu'il y a parfois une différence vive entre le matériel de deux cavernes aussi. Techik-Tach et Abi-Rakhmat sont des exemples excellents à cet égard.

L'industrie de Techik-Tach ne fut jamais publiée dans sa totalité. En étudiant le matériel, on peut constater qu'ici on accentuait toujours le "Moustérien," et on publiait quelques outils typiques. En réalité l'outil parfait est très rare; l'industrie est, on

Figure 17.3 Kaira-Koumi: gisement moustérien de type d'Asie centrale en surface.

Figure 17.4 La grotte Abi-Rakhmat (Tien-Chan): sur le mur la ligne montre l'hauteur du remplissage.

pourrait dire, pauvre en pièces typiques, et ce sont en premier lieu les grandes lames grossières, les éclats, les grands disques qui dominent. La plupart d'eux sont à peine retouchés. Il faut accentuer de nouveau le caractère d'Asie centrale—la matière première, le débitage lourd, la patine caractéristique, c'est-à-dire les caractéristiques qui sont générales jusqu'à l'Extrême-Orient (p. ex. Hodjakente, quelques outillages à Sin-Kiang, Bian Obo en Mongolie, Tin-Tsoun en Chine).

Le fait que la squelette de *Homo sapiens neanderthalensis* était entourée de cornes de *Capra sibirica*, fut toujours un peu obscur. C'est cette dernière espèce qui domine dans les couches aussi (à peu près 38 individus), ce qui montre avant tout la spécialisation de la chasse. Cette direction de la chasse est en tout cas assez rare (la caverne Subalyuk en Hongrie, la caverne Repolust en Autriche). Une note à part: on trouve, chez les Kirghizs, aujourd'hui aussi et très rarement, des sites mortuaires avec des cornes de *C. sibirica*(!).

L'autre gisement très important est Abi-Rakhmat, dans la montagne Tchimgan, en Uzbéghistan. Cette grotte n'est pas d'origine karstique, jamais de l'eau ne

Figure 17.5 L'entrée de la grotte Abi-Rakhmat: à droit, une petite chute d'eau.

coulait pas en elle. Son remplissage est un loess éolique, sédimenté du dehors. Elle n'est pas profonde, sa grande ouverture donne au sud, sur le fleuve Tchatkal; un ruisseau coule audessus de la grotte, qui tombe en cascade à côté de l'entrée. D'après la morphologie de la vallée, il devait fonctionner dans le Pléistocène supérieur aussi. C'est à cause des circonstances naturelles optimales qu'on y trouve neuf couches archéologiques avec 21 horizons. Aux niveaux inférieurs il y a une phase ancienne du Paléolithique moyen, puis une phase évoluée, et au niveau supérieur des industries de type paléolithique supérieur.

Les types dominants sont les suivants: éclats levalloisiens, lames retouchées, pointes moustériennes minces, et les variantes de ceux-là, très fins, comme une lame, et légers. Ce sont les pièces massives antérieures qui manquent, les outils sur galet, et on peut constater une évolution dans les niveaux supérieurs, mais qui ne mène à nulle part. La faune est homogène, identique à l'actuelle, parmi eux l'*Hystrix* (porc-épic) aussi qui vit, aujourd'hui encore, sur ce territoire.

Toutkaoul est une station au méandre du fleuve Vakhs, dans les couches de la terrasse qui donne cette même industrie évoluée (Figs. 17.6-8).

A l'est d'ici, on trouve la caverne Ogzi-Kitchik (Figs. 17.9-10). Les couches de civilisation se retrouvent devant la caverne, au pied d'un mur de roc vertical, épaisses de 6 à 10 m. Leur industrie est un Moustérien évolué qui montre une évolution intérieure. Quant à la faune, outre les espèces générales, on trouve le rhinocéros laineux, l'âne Pléistocène aussi. Comme une spécialité de ce gisement, on peut mentionner qu'on a trouvé les débris de carapaces de 1200 tortues, et cela exclusivement dans les couches d'habitation. L'analyse palynologique montre un climat frais et humide, et la datation de C-14 de la couche moyenne est 38,000 ans. (C'est à peu près la période du Würm I.)

Dans cette période(?) on connaît encore quelques industries variantes ou locales. Dans les stations Koutourboulak et Koulboulak qui se trouvent à côté des lacs d'autrefois, avec plusieurs couches, sont surprenants les racloirs simples et doubles très concaves, biconcaves, qui donnent des formes singulières, variées.

Enfin, voici de nouveau une station de plein air, Chougnou, au Pamir, à une hauteur de 2000 m, dans les couches inférieures avec un Moustérien tardif (35,000-30,000 ans), aux niveaux supérieurs avec du Paléolithique supérieur (10,700 ans).

Le troisième type d'industrie est le *Moustéro-Soanien*.

Figure 17.6   Le méandre du fleuve Vakhs: au milieu et en notre côté, le gisement Toutkaoul I.

Figure 17.7   Le méandre du fleuve Vakhs: aujourd'hui le lac de la centrale électrique de Nurek.

Figure 17.8 Toutkaoul I pendant les premières fouilles. Dans le profil, Moustérien et civilisation Hissar I.

Ses types caractéristiques sont: d'une part les choppers, les chopping-tools—non seulement avec des enlèvements, mais très bien retouchés aussi—leurs variantes, les galets aménagés; d'autre part, les types moustériens pris au sens large. Les outils du Soanien évolué peuvent être distingués nettement des industries de choppers anciens, et dans ces outillages les lames sont très rares.

La station la plus importante est Karaboura (Fig. 17.11), dans la terrasse méridionale du fleuve Vakhs, immédiatement à la frontière d'Afghanistan. Ces industries sont relativement tardives sur d'autres territoires aussi et sont en connexion avec les industries des Indes, du Pakistan. Leur existence dénote ici non pas une influence, une pénétration culturelle, mais l'immigration d'une population.

Il est très facile de résumer le *Paléolithique supérieur*. D'une part, il est très intéressant que la phase initiale du Paléolithique supérieur est tout à fait inconnue. A partir de 30,000 à 14,000 ans, ce territoire est pour ainsi dire vide. D'autre part, dans la période suivante, on trouve au surplus dix sites plus ou moins importants.

Parmi les fouilles anciennes, on peut mentionner Samarkande—dans la ville, dans une colline de loess, au lieu du parc actuel du Komsomol. Son industrie est très évoluée (grattoirs, grattoirs doubles, lames); il est possible qu'elle appartient déjà à l'Epipaléolithique. Il est à noter qu'au dessous des couches archéologiques il y avait des outils moustériens, et ils se rencontrent dans le Paléolithique supérieur aussi.

Parmi les sites récents, on peut mentionner de nouveau les couches supérieures de Chougnou. Nous sommes d'avis qu'on peut établir ici un rapport d'évolution véritable entre le Paléolithique moyen et supérieur, ou une survivance, ce qui n'est pas absolument rare en Asie centrale.

Un tel rapport peut être établi entre le Paléolithique supérieur et le Mésolithique qui est beaucoup plus riche. Nous pourrions parler p. ex. sur les industries du Pamir, mais ce sujet intéressant a été déjà élaboré par V. A. Ranov. L'un des gisements importants est Ochkona, dans le Pamir d'Est. Ses quatre couches d'habitat sont connues par une industrie locale qui est analogue aux matériels de Sibérie et de Tibet. (La datation de C-14 de la deuxième couche est 9550 ans.)

Figure 17.9   La grotte Ogzi-Kitchik: fouilles 1972.

Figure 17.10   La grotte Ogzi-Kitchik: fouilles 1977.

Du point de vue climatologique et oecologique, il est intéressant qu'à cette époque-là l'homme montait dans la région des plus hautes montagnes.

Notre tâche ne consiste pas à énumérer les gisements. Dans la littérature on peut trouver chaque donnée, chaque détail. C'est pourquoi nous nous bornerons à résumer quelques observations générales.

1) La première: c'est la difficulté de la datation géochronologique. La cause en est, comme je l'ai mentionné, que l'Asie centrale est géographiquement extrêmement morcelée. Ce territoire se compose des régions tout à fait divergeantes les unes des autres. Le caractère des sédiments du Pléistocène ou leur érosion, leur stratigraphie varient d'une région à l'autre.

Dans la plupart des gisements il n'y a pas de faune et de flore. Si l'on trouve une faune, elle se compose généralement d'espèces homogènes, indifférentes, elle est pour la plupart identique à celle d'aujourd'hui. C'est cette difficulté qu'on constate parfois dans les cavernes aussi. Les indicateurs de "froid" et de "chaud" sont tout simplement les conséquences de l'altitude du même petit secteur géographique.

Les terrasses de fleuve sont bien datées, mais les loess causent de nouveau des problèmes. Les loess sont ici extrêmement épais, en même temps la sédimentation éolienne est très rapide, d'ailleurs elle est visible aujourd'hui aussi. Les sols fossiles sont minces, faibles.

Il est possible que sur ce territoire toujours sec on n'indique qu'une forêt de buisson. (Un climat forestier peut être constaté dans la couche V de Lakhouti, un climat frais et humide dans la couche inférieure d'Ogzi-Kitchik.)

2) Les industries sont beaucoup plus simples, plus homogènes qu'en Europe. En même temps, on ne connaît pas un seul gisement où deux industries différentes se suivraient stratigraphiquement. Il semble que l'époque du Paléolithique inférieur correspond à l'avant dernier glaciaire; il est suivi d'un hiatus. Le Paléolithique moyen correspond au début du dernier glaciaire; on ne trouve le Paléolithique supérieur qu'à la fin du Pléistocène.

3) L'origine du Paléolithique inférieur est incertaine. Le Paléolithique moyen est une pénétration étrangère venant du Proche-Orient (Iran, Irak), mais on doit tenir compte des rapports d'Asie intérieure aussi. Nous avons déjà vu l'origine du Moustéro-Soanien, et le Paléolithique supérieur a évolué à partir de bases locales.

4) Les types d'industrie peuvent être contemporains aussi, mais il y a des divergences entre les gisements d'une situation différente. L'industrie d'Amankoutan, en travertin, ne peut être trouvée p. ex. sur un autre site. Les stations des terrasses se caractérisent par les

Figure 17.11 Karaboura: le gisement est sur la tête de colline.

outils de galet de grande dimension, mais ceux-là et les instruments à trancher en galet sont tout à fait rares. Par contre, dans les cavernes, les outils bien retouchés sont rares; dans une autre caverne par contre le spectre de type est large—il y a beaucoup de types bien travaillés. Dans les déserts, ce sont les lames qui se rencontrent en grande quantité. Enfin, le Moustéro-Soanien n'est pas encore apparu dans les cavernes. Selon mon hypothèse: il n'apparaîtra même pas.

5) La cause des différences, c'est la diffusion, la direction de l'origine des civilisations. Mais, de mon avis, ce qui joue ici un grand rôle, ce sont les grandes distances, les divergences du milieu naturel, l'oecologie, la saisonnalité, et enfin l'isolation qui crée les petites faciès locales.

6) C'est la distance des groupes, des groupes humains entre eux, et l'isolation extrême qui est la cause de ce que les types d'outils survivent extrêmement longtemps. Les lames épaisses ou les outils de galet continuent à survivre dans le Paléolithique entier, ils le "colorisent" pour ainsi dire. Les types du Moustérien surgissent de nouveau dans le Paléolithique supérieur, dans le Mésolithique, et les choppers "retournent" dans la civilisation Hissar. La situation est donc analogue à celle de Sibérie, où les types "moustériens" survivent pour ainsi dire jusqu'au Néolithique; ou en Transbaikalie, où on trouve dans le Mésolithique de nouveau des industries de chopper. Il est donc probable qu'on doit compter ici avec une "retardation continuelle." Et il y a encore une question que j'ai déjà écrite à propos de la Sibérie du Sud: jusqu'à quand cette civilisation tardive pouvait-elle survivre dans le "Néolithique récent" de quelques groupes d'hommes du Taïga.

XVIII

The Implications of Improved Chronological Determinations for the Soviet Central Asian Paleolithic

Richard S. Davis

INTRODUCTION

The establishment of regional chronologies is fundamental to archaeological interpretation. Whatever the prevailing theoretical orientation or the stated goals of research, control of time inevitably plays an important role. Over the past several decades in Soviet Central Asia, revisions in the regional chronology for the Paleolithic have led to reinterpretations of the dynamics of that area's cultural history.

This paper will review some of the major aspects of the dynamic interplay between Paleolithic calibration and Central Asian Paleolithic interpretation. In agreement with the goals of this symposium, I will try to show how methodological developments have made an impact on Paleolithic research and also attempt to prognosticate a bit on how this relationship may continue in the future.

THE PALEOLITHIC ARCHAEOLOGICAL RECORD OF SOVIET CENTRAL ASIA

As noted in the paper in this volume by Gábori (see ch. 17), the regional record of the Soviet Central Asian Paleolithic now extends back into the Middle Pleistocene and perhaps earlier. There are Lower Paleolithic sites found stratified in thick loess deposits in southern Tadzhikistan (Davis, Ranov, and Dodonov 1980); and surface localities in central and southern Kazakhstan (Klapchuk 1976; Alpysbaev 1979), near the eastern Caspian shore (Medoev 1982); and also recently reported finds in Turkmeniya (Liubin 1984). Middle Paleolithic localities are well known in rockshelters, on major river terraces, and in interfluvial contexts (see Ranov and Nesmeyanov 1973 for a review). In fact, Middle Paleolithic occurrences are the best known and most widely documented in Central Asia. Upper Paleolithic sites, however, are extremely rare (Samarkand site and Shugnou are the only ones yet identified) and seem only to be known from the time after the last glacial maximum.

Soviet and Western archaeologists have long sought ways to relate and compare Central Asian industries to other regions in Asia, Europe, and Africa. It is within this context that chronological reckoning has played the most important role. In advance I will conclude that there has been a long-standing tendency among Soviet archaeologists to place the Central Asian record within the same general chronological and developmental sequences known from other areas of Eurasia, and currently there is a strongly developing tendency to push back chronologies into the Lower Pleistocene. The impetus for this situation is based on new chronological determinations as well as perhaps a theoretical predisposition to make that the case.

CENTRAL ASIAN PALEOLITHIC CALIBRATION IN THE 1940s—1970s

The most famous Central Asian Paleolithic site is also one of the first found: Teshik Tash. It is particularly well known for the burial of a young child, reportedly surrounded by a ring of goat horns. The academician A. P. Okladnikov excavated this site in 1938-39, and the results were published in full after the war. The age of the Middle Paleolithic deposits was given by Okladnikov and paleontologist V. I. Gromova as Mindel-Riss or immediately post-Riss. As Movius noted in his 1953 review of Central Asian archaeology, such an early date was extremely unlikely because the fauna (mainly *Capra siberica*) was clearly Upper Pleistocene and very modern.

Tacitly Movius attributed this early dating by Okladnikov to a theoretical predisposition—namely, that the Soviet archaeologists held to a firm stadial evolutionary approach to prehistory in which there was a Neandertal-Mousterian phase antecedent to the *Homo sapiens sapiens*—Upper Paleolithic phase. According to Soviet thought at the time (and to a certain extent even today), Western archaeologists relied too much on the interpretation of Cro Magnon and associated Aurignacian culture as expressions of a superior race which overwhelmed the inferior Neandertals. I agree with Movius that Okladnikov may have been disposed, therefore, to date Teshik Tash definitely early enough to be in agreement with the stadial theory of succession of Neandertal to modern *H. sapiens*. To underscore the pervasiveness of stadial thinking in Soviet archaeological thinking at that time, it is necessary only to point out that not until the mid-1950s was synchronic cultural variability widely recognized in Soviet archaeological circles. This recognition came as a result of A. N. Rogachev's Upper Paleolithic excavations in the Kostenki-Borshevo region of the Ukraine (Rogachev 1962). Through fairly detailed typological and stratigraphical comparisons of several sites, Rogachev demonstrated the coexistence of culturally variant groups.

Following the publication of Teshik Tash, numerous Paleolithic localities were discovered in Central Asia and published in the 1950s and 1960s. Okladnikov continued his work and many others became active, including V. A. Ranov, D. H. Lev, A. G. Medoev, X. A. Alpysbaev, R. X. Suleymanov, A. V. Vinogradov, and U. I. Islamov. Summary works by Okladnikov (1966) and Ranov (1965) appeared in due course. The basic culture-historical picture drawn by both Okladnikov and Ranov was that Central Asia could be seen as a junction of cultural traditions emanating from both east and west.

> It seems possible to us to concur that the route of development of the cultures of ancient man was not singular; that already in the Lower Paleolithic more than 300,000 to 500,000 years ago, two basic regions took shape in which the evolution of culture went by separate paths: East Asian and Mediterranean-African. From this it is natural to conclude not only about the known similarity in the development of ancient cultures in Middle and East Asia, but also that there were definite contacts, concrete cultural-historical ties between the primitive populations of these countries in the Lower and Middle Pleistocene. (Okladnikov 1966: 22)

It is not difficult to see the similarity between this model and Movius's two-culture concept, which featured an eastern Chopper-Chopping Tool tradition and a western Core and Biface tradition. Indeed, Okladnikov acknowledged Movius's work and was careful to point out that there were no handaxes in Central Asia (with the exception of one or two stray surface finds in the *western* part of the territory!).

Ranov subsequently elaborated on this theme, but developed a picture of Central Asia as a meeting ground of cultural traditions from the Near East, Siberia-Mongolia, and South Asia. He formalized a characterization of the Central Asian Paleolithic into two groups:

> The first group (A) we tie to sites located to the west and southwest of Middle Asia and provisionally call them "cultures of Near Eastern type," and the second (B) with sites of eastern tendencies and we call them "cultures of eastern Asiatic type. . . ." (1965: 4)

Ranov included sites of the Siberian-Mongolian type in group B. It should be pointed out that Ranov has repeatedly held that this division extended throughout all Paleolithic time in Central Asia; that these two parallel phyla coexisted into the Holocene.

Ranov solidified the South Asian connection on the basis of discoveries at Kara Bura in 1957. Kara Bura is a large open-air site found in alluvial context on the left bank of the Vaksh River in southern Tadzhikistan. The site yielded more than 8000 artifacts, but all of them are from redeposited contexts. The salient feature of this industry is that a large fraction of it consisted of pebble tools: core scrapers, choppers, and chopping tools. These were fabricated from cobbles occurring locally in the alluvial gravels. There were also many flake tools, including Mousterian points and scrapers which Ranov described as Mousterian (Ranov and Nesmeyanov 1973: 16). On the basis of the sizable pebble-tool component, Ranov named the industry "Mousterian of Soan Tradition," thus linking it with the well-known pebble-tool and flake industries of the Punjab. South Asian archaeologists such as S. P. Gupta have supported this analysis:

> It is probable that the Soan Culture, originating in the Beas-Sutlej basin moved westward in the Soan region, crossed the Himalayas and then reached the Pamir-Altai system of mountains at a very early stage, somewhere during the uppermost Middle Pleistocene period. (Gupta 1979: 123)

Both Okladnikov's and Ranov's culture-historical reconstructions were worked out in the absence of developed relative or absolute chronologies. Generalized technological and typological comparisons of chipped stone industries over broad areas of the Old World were the underlying method and basis of their syntheses. In sum, in the 1950s and 1960s Soviet Central Asian archaeologists looked to South and Southeast Asia for the genesis of their pebble-tool industries. Chronological priority was assumed to be held by the South Asian Soan. In the 1950s and 1960s no C-14 determinations of Pleistocene age associated with Paleolithic materials had been made in Central Asia. Relative dating of alluvial terrace sites was based on a four-phase Quaternary model plagued with correlation problems in the tectonically active highlands of Central Asia.

NEW PALEOLITHIC CALIBRATIONS IN THE 1970s

The picture of Central Asian Paleolithic archaeology began to change dramatically in 1972, following the discovery by the geologist Lazarenko of a pebble tool in the 6th buried soil (pedocomplex) in a deep loess deposit near the village of Karatau in southern Tadzhikistan. Nearly 1000 m above the Vaksh River, thick loess deposits mantled the ridgetops and numerous exposures revealed buried soil horizons within the loess. Subsequent investigation by a number of other geologists and excavations by Ranov led to the discovery of approximately 12 loess sites which had pebble and flake tools in the 5th or 6th buried pedocomplexes (counting from the top). Two loess localities, Karatau and Lakhuti, were excavated over relatively large areas. Karatau had over 200 chipped-stone artifacts exposed in an excavation that opened 124 sq. m. At Lakhuti in the 5th buried pedocomplex more than 200 sq. m were opened and more than 1000 artifacts were found.

These loess sites are very significant primarily because for the first time in all of Soviet Central Asia, Lower Paleolithic materials were found in deposits which could be dated and studied for paleoenvironmental information. The geologist Dodonov (Dodonov and Ranov 1984) identified the buried soils as consequences of interglacial or interstadial climates and assigned the intervening loess to stadial periods. The Brunhes-Matuyama paleomagnetic horizon was identified at several separate loess sections, and above that boundary Dodonov consistently counted ten buried pedocomplexes. He went on to correlate them to stratified loess deposits in the Ukraine, Eastern Europe, and China. Thermoluminescence dating was carried out by Shelkoplyas. A range of determinations bracketed the 5th pedocomplex of Lakhuti at approximately 130,000 years B.P. and the 6th buried pedocomplex at Karatau at 200,000 years. Dodonov correlated these pedocomplexes with the Riss-Würm Interglacial and a Riss interstadial respectively. Assuming the interpretation to be correct (and if anything the TL dates are probably too young), we may take these loess sections as good evidence of hunter-gatherer occupation in Central Asia in the late Middle Pleistocene.

With this much firmer set of data in hand, Ranov kept to the culture-historical model he had developed in the 1960s but hinted at another possibility:

> Thus the cultural ties of Middle Asia with India begin from time immemorial. Of course, it is difficult for the time being to say whether there was a direct migration or whether there was the growth of Paleolithic cultures along similar lines due to the similarity of ecological conditions and raw materials. (Dodonov and Ranov 1977: 23)

In any case South Asia was the basis for comparison.

In 1981 at the southern Tadzhik loess locality of Kuldara, a "small collection of undoubted artifacts from the 11th and 12th paleosols (the XIth pedocomplex)" were discovered (Dodonov and Ranov 1984: 77). In all, 52 pieces of chipped stone were excavated in good stratigraphic context. Because the XIth pedocomplex is below the Brunhes-Matuyama boundary, it must be more than 700,000 years old. Dodonov and Ranov in fact estimate it to be on the order of 800,000 years (1984: 77). Leaving aside the fact that no stratigraphic section or detailed description of the site's contents has been published as far as I am aware, it is instructive to see how it has been interpreted. (Ranov did, however, present the site at an All-Union Archaeological Conference in 1985.) In essence, the find at Kuldara quadrupled the scope of time for the occupation of Central Asia. The question to be discussed now is how this dramatic expansion of the chronology effected a re-analysis of the cultural history.

In the beginning of 1986, Ranov and his colleague Gladilin of the Archaeological Museum of Kiev published a new theory concerning the initial populating of the territory of the USSR. Gladilin had for several years been excavating the site of Korolevo in the Carpathians. Korolevo is also a loess locality where the Brunhes-Matuyama boundary has been identified. In the 7th and 8th "cultural horizons," which both lie below the Brunhes-Matuyama boundary, large collections of chipped-stone tools were found: more than 3500 in the 7th and more than 300 in the 8th. In summary fashion Gladilin describes these industries as follows:

> According to their type and technique of preparation they can be attributed to the group of so-called late Olduvai or early Acheulean Industries of East Africa, the Near East and the south of Western and Central Europe, the time of which is approximately one million years. (Gladilin and Ranov 1986: 30)

Based on the interpretation of the great antiquity of Korolevo and Kuldara, Gladilin and Ranov suggest the following for the derivation of the earliest inhabitants on the territory of the USSR. Beginning approximately 1.5 million years ago, *H. erectus* or possibly even *H. habilis* began to settle areas outside of East Africa. (Ranov and Gladilin hold that East Africa was the place where the development of early humanity first occurred; they refer to this as the theory of narrow monocentrism.) They postulate these early populations passed through the Near East and continued both northwest and northeast, to European Russia and Central Asia respectively. The authors are clear that they offer the above reconstruction only as a possibility based on some general resemblances (unspecified) between Korolevo, Kuldara, and the "late Oldowan," and also, of course, on the expanded chronology.

What a difference the expansion of the scope of time makes! Instead of looking to South Asia and the Chopper-Chopping Tool tradition, the discovery at Kuldara allows Soviet Central Asian archaeologists to look to the original source: East Africa. And with Korolevo to the west, it is now possible to think of wide areas of Soviet territory populated at a very early time. In this vein mention should also be made of Okladnikov's suggestion that the site of Ulalinka Creek in the Altai region was considerably older than the Brunhes-Matuyama; and Y. Mochanov's newly discovered site of Dering-Tyuryakh above Yakutsk on the Lena River, on a 120-m terrace whose excavator estimates its age at more than a million years.

For some time the tendency in Central Asia has been to find great antiquity for human settlement. For example, Medoev, reflecting on the primitive pebble tools found on the Mangyshlak Peninsula of the eastern Caspian, concluded:

> These most ancient traces of fossil hominids certainly open new routes for the search for still more ancient stone industries in the southern territories of the USSR, and move the area of the origin of man from east Africa to inner Asia. (1982: 44-45)

While few Soviet archaeologists would take such an extreme position, the emerging school of thought would favor early and widespread settlement of the territory of the USSR. On the basis of such an early beachhead, local regional cultures evolved in relatively parallel fashion. There would be no need, in the case of Central Asia, to look to South and Southeast Asia for early contacts or influences. Local traditions could generate their own technological progress. For example, Ranov and others have referred to the local development of Levallois technique between the times of Karatau and Lakhuti (Ranov and Zhukov 1982).

In conclusion, I would observe that the expanded time scale of Central Asian Paleolithic archaeology is indeed valid and should be recognized as a major accomplishment. The route of population movement out of Africa proposed by Gladilin and Ranov is not yet well supported, however, and of course that kind of culture-historical analysis is particularly difficult to sustain. Among other things, the expansion of the scope of time means Soviet Central Asian Paleolithic archaeology no longer requires a more recent diffusion model to interpret its prehistory. The more complex task now is to build common typological and technological systems of classification, develop ecological models based on hunting and gathering behavior, and turn away from the elements of stadial and progressive thinking which have dominated Soviet archaeological thinking in the past.

DISCUSSION

KOZLOWSKI: I agree with the evaluation of the significance of this stadial approach in Soviet archaeology. We must keep in mind that the development of the pebble-tool tradition continued in Central Asia late into late glacial times, perhaps into the Early Holocene times.

I have some remarks concerning the northern sites where these pebble tools have been found, sites such as Oulalinka. The site stratigraphy was very well studied and well dated at about 200,000 years. But the pebble tools from this site are very questionable. I have studied this collection and also that from Piblimoski and, in my opinion, they do not contain true tools. They are simple, fragmented pebbles without any human interference. I think this is especially important here in North America because these sites are considered by some American scholars as relevant to the question of the early peopling of the Americas.

It is important to point out problems concerning the development of lithic industries in Soviet Central Asia, especially the fact that we have many gaps. We have an important gap between pebble industries and typical Levallois Mousterian industries and one between the pebble industries and Mousterian industries with high ratio of sidescrapers. In my opinion there must be a parallel development of the Levalloisian and of the Mousterian rich in sidescrapers. My view is different from that of Miklós Gábori, who separates the early Levalloisian from the later Mousterian. I see no argument in support of this chronological interpretation.

The other interesting problem in Soviet Central Asia is the problem of the industries with bifacial points, especially those from the Baikash region in the eastern part of Soviet Central Asia. And this problem is extremely important also for American archaeologists who are looking for the origins of the bifacially worked implements of North America in Eastern Asia and especially in northeastern Asia. We must find the roots of this bifacial technology somewhere else, to the south, because in Eastern Asia there are no bifacially worked implements in the Middle Paleolithic. Another very interesting question is the possibility of continuity of the Levalloisian in Soviet Central Asia during the Late Interpleniglacial. There are some carbon-14 dates from South-Central Asia of about 30,000.

ROLLAND: Regarding the Oulalinka industry, Annette Laming visited those sites and came to exactly the same conclusion. I had the same feeling based on the illustrations.

DAVIS: In 1973, Romanoff and Gregorief advanced the concept of a post-Mousterian or a persistent Mousterian. In other words, in Soviet Central Asia there are only basically two Upper Paleolithic sites; they are dated by carbon-14 and geologically to the end of the last pleniglacial. According to Romanoff and Gregorief, it may be that Middle Paleolithic-type industries are lasting much longer in this region, thus making Central Asia a zone where transition to blade industries occurs late.

PART 3

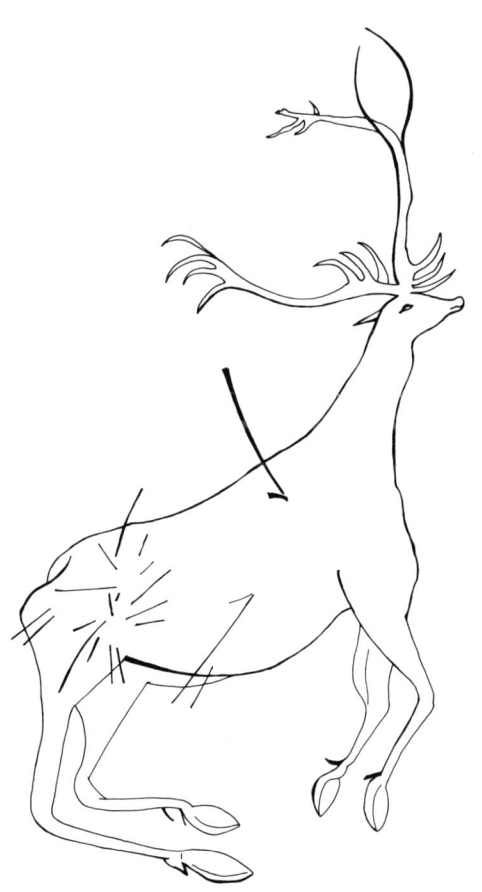

XIX

Integration of Late Quaternary Climatic Records From France and Greece

Cave Sediments, Pollen, and Marine Events

William R. Farrand

INTRODUCTION

Stratigraphic sequences in prehistoric caves can lead to detailed interpretations of past climatic events based on sediment types, fossils, and radiometric dating. On one hand, fine-scale events can be discerned owing to high sedimentation rates measured in tens or hundreds of centimeters per century. On the other hand, these climatic sequences must be filtered for local influences, natural and anthropogenic, not related to the regional climate. Moreover, the relative weighting of the climatic signal from one cave site to another, or even from one bed to another within a given site, is commonly very subjective. Therefore the information from a single site, no matter how carefully studied, cannot be considered *a priori* to be necessarily representative of a region.

In contrast, paleoclimatic records from pollen studies and from deep-sea cores integrate regional or even hemispheric climatic information, but temporal resolution within these records is much poorer, especially in the case of deep-sea core stratigraphy, where sedimentation rates of 1 cm (or much less) per 1000 years are common. On the other hand, pollen and deep-sea records span much longer periods of uninterrupted sedimentation, providing internally comparable data over a much longer time span than can be obtained from an individual archaeological site.

The purpose of this paper, therefore, is to compare detailed cave-sediment records and broad-scale pollen and marine records in terms of both the timing and the amplitude of their climatic signals. We shall begin with the cave and rockshelter stratigraphy of the middle part of the last glacial cycle in the Dordogne region of southwestern France, where numerous sites have been studied by Laville (1975) in addition to my own studies in Abri Pataud (Farrand 1975a, b). Comparisons will be made with the long pollen record of Grande Pile (Vosges, France) and ultimately with the deep-sea oxygen-isotope stratigraphy. Secondly, Franchthi Cave (Peloponnese, Greece) will be examined. It is, unfortunately, the only site known in detail from the Greek peninsula, and caution must be used in extrapolating regional conditions, as was mentioned above. Still, the concurrence of a number of lines of evidence—cave sediments, fossils, local geomorphology, and sea-level history—helps to sort out regional from local influences. The Franchthi sequence will then be compared to the regional pollen record of the Eastern Mediterranean (van Zeist and Bottema 1982) and the Mediterranean deep-sea stratigraphy.

By way of background, it can be pointed out that an initial attempt at integration of cave sites, sea levels, and isotopes was done for several Levantine sites (Farrand 1982), primarily et-Tabun (Israel) and the Adlun caves (Lebanon). (See also Jelinek 1982b.)

DORDOGNE ROCKSHELTERS

REVIEW OF PREVIOUS STUDIES

This classic region of Middle and Upper Paleolithic sites is one of the few where a multiplicity of sites have been studied in detail for their sedimentary records. Other areas of relatively intense study are Provence (Bonifay 1962; Miskovsky 1974) and northern Spain (Butzer 1981). Laville's (1964, 1975) study of some 21 Dordogne sites is a landmark for paleoclimatic reconstruction based on sediment analysis. A few other studies in the same area have added important details for several more sites (Farrand

1975a, b; Le Tensorer 1981; Texier 1973b; Kervazo 1973). These studies cover "Riss," "Würm," and Holocene sites, and they furnish a much finer-scale subdivision of past climatic fluctuations than the usual stade-interstade partitions.

We are concerned here with the *Würm récent* (formerly "Würm III") stade of the French chronology, and in particular with the first ten climatic phases recognized by Laville. They are characterized as "very cold and dry," "mild and humid," "cold and dry," "moderate and humid," etc. (Fig. 19.1A). The basis for these epithets is his interpretation of the abundance and size of rock debris (freeze/thaw *éboulis*), carbonate concretions (illuvial vs. travertine), leaching of $CaCO_3$, porosity and roundness of the rock fragments, frost flakes (*plaquettes de gel*), etc. The variations in these parameters vertically through the stratigraphic sequence at a given site lead to a climatic pattern that can be correlated with patterns derived from other sites in a qualitative way. But the idiosyncratic nature of rockshelter sites, as a function of differences in bedrock type, exposure, size, intensity of habitation, etc., militates against quantitative correlations. Moreover, the overprinting of weathering phenomena on the primary sediments obscures some characteristics of the latter while, at the same time, providing information on paleoclimate during periods of nonsedimentation.

As in any correlation, the integrity of a given pattern or sequence, as measured against other patterns in the set being correlated, leads to reinforcement of one's interpretation, or to the recognition of hiatuses or spurious signals in one or more of the sequences. Such cross-checking is very important in dealing with cave and rockshelter sediments, where paleoclimatic interpretations are necessarily subjective, and this is certainly one of the great strengths of Laville's studies. Nevertheless, the same subjectivity opens the door to alternative interpretations, especially in the case of different researchers, who are perhaps using different techniques or have different points of departure.

It is in this light that I have reviewed the interpretations, both mine and Laville's, of the Abri Pataud sequence within the framework of Laville's "standard" sequence for southwestern France. My archaeological colleagues pointed out that Laville's correlation of the Pataud and some other sequences did not seem logical in view of their interpretation of the cultural sequence for the region. I would be the first to argue, however, for independence of sedimentological and archaeological interpretations. Indeed, one important goal of sedimentological studies in archaeological sites is the establishment of a stratigraphic sequence that is independent of archaeological interpretations. Only in this way can the question of contemporaneity of certain typological entities (artifacts or features) in different parts of a site or in different sites be evaluated. On the other hand, if the results of sedimentological correlations show an offset in time (or environment) of certain cultural manifestations, then there is reason to go back to the data and reevaluate, that is, to verify, reconfirm, or reject the previous interpretations.

The following discussion consists of two parts. First, there is a quick review of the Pataud stratigraphy and my arguments for some revisions in the correlation of part of the Pataud sequence with the "standard" classification of Laville. Second, this revised classification will be compared to the paleoclimatic signal derived from the Grande Pile pollen diagram, which presumably represents the regional climate of West-Central Europe.

THE ABRI PATAUD

The sedimentology of the Pataud rockshelter has been published previously in detail (Farrand 1975a, b) and need not be repeated here. Moreover, an updated summary of the Pataud sediments will appear soon along with a detailed discussion of regional correlations (Farrand, in prep.). This paper will therefore deal with only the main outlines of the sequence, concentrating on those parts that are central to the present discussion.

The Pataud sequence is about 8.25 m thick and can be subdivided into six lithostratigraphic units, each of which may consist of one or more archaeological horizons ("levels") and one or more sterile horizons ("*éboulis*"). These are summarized as follows, and are depicted graphically in Figure 19.1A:

Geological Strata	*Levels & Eboulis*
a1 Pale brown to pale yellow *éboulis*	Eboulis 0-1
	Level 1
	(Protosolutrean)
	Eboulis 1-2: upper
a2 Brown *éboulis*	Eboulis 1-2: middle
a3 Pale yellow *éboulis*	Eboulis 1-2: lower
	Level 2
	(Protomagdalenian)
	Eboulis 2-3: upper
a4 Light reddish brown	Eboulis 2-3: basal

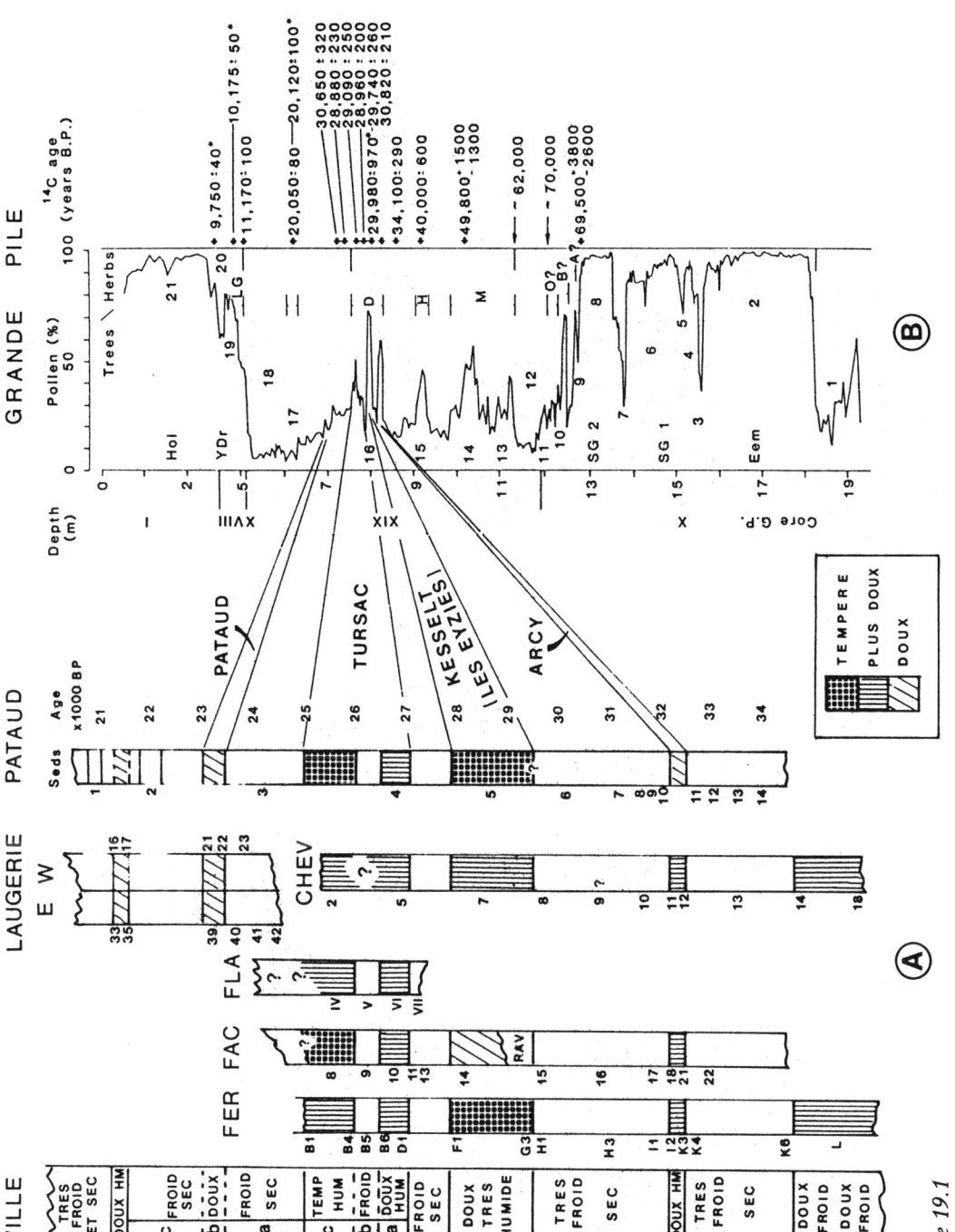

Figure 19.1

A. Stratigraphic columns for six sites in southwestern France plotted against a portion of Laville's (1975) "standard" sequence of climatic phases (at left). The chronology for all six sites is based on correlation with radiocarbon dates from Abri Pataud. The intensity of the milder phases shown by the patterns is based on my interpretation of the laboratory data in published reports. FER=La Ferrassie, FAC=Abri du Facteur, FLA=Le Flageolet I; the other sites are Laugerie Haute Est (E) and Ouest (W), La Grotte de la Chèvre (CHEV), and Abri Pataud. [Note: Taking into account new radiocarbon dates for Le Flageolet I presented during this conference (Rigaud, ch. 25), the age of Couche IV may be much younger—ca. 23 Kyr B.P.—than shown here.]

B. Generalized interpretation of the pollen diagram from Grande Pile (Vosges, France) showing variations in the total arboreal pollen and radiocarbon dates (from Woillard and Mook 1982). The interpreted positions of French interstades or oscillations are based on chronological position. D, H, and M are the northwestern European interstades Denekamp, Hengelo, and Moershoofd, respectively, as placed by Woillard and Mook.

a5	Pale yellow *éboulis*	Level 3 Perigordian VI and *Eboulis* 3-4: Yellow (laterally equivalent facies)
b	Strong brown sandy loam with rare rocks	*Eboulis* 3-4: Red *Eboulis* 3-4: Tan & Pebbly Red
c	Dark reddish brown *éboulis* with abundant artifacts	Level 4 (Noaillian)
d	Strong brown coarse *éboulis*	*Eboulis* 4-0
e	Dark (reddish) brown *éboulis* and midden with abundant artifacts	Level 5 (Middle Perigordian)
f1	Pale yellow, sandy	*Eboulis* 5-6, Level 6, *Eboulis* 6-7, Level 7, *Eboulis* 7-8, Level 8, *Eboulis* 8-9, Level 9, *Eboulis* 9-10, Level 10, *Eboulis* 10-11: Yellow
f2	Strong brown, sandy *éboulis*	*Eboulis* 10-11: Wash
f3	Very pale yellow	Level 11, *Eboulis* 11-12, Level 12, *Eboulis* 12-13, Level 13, *Eboulis* 13-14, Basal *Eboulis*

An important difference of opinion exists with respect to the placement of *Eboulis* 3-4: Red and Level 4 within Laville's sequence. *Eboulis* 3-4: Red is by far the most heavily weathered horizon at Abri Pataud, showing many characteristics of a fully recognizable soil—oxidation, leaching of carbonate, clay enrichment, etc. (Farrand 1975a, b). On this basis, I believe that it should be correlated with horizons showing comparable degrees of weathering in the same general time range at other sites, namely Couches B1 through B4 at La Ferrassie, Couche 8 at Le Facteur, and probably Couches 1 through 4 at Le Flageolet I, all of which Laville (1975) has placed into his Phase VIIc, an interval of temperate, humid climate. Laville, to the contrary, correlated Pataud *Eboulis* 3-4: Red with somewhat less weathered horizons in those other sites, namely Ferrassie B6-D1, Facteur 10-11, and Flageolet 6, while equating a very weakly weathered horizon, Stratum *a4* at Pataud, with those strongly weathered horizons listed above in the other sites. The weathering of Stratum *a4* is barely perceptible in the field, being recognized primarily by its slightly darker color. Lab analyses show only slight decreases in rock fragments and in $CaCO_3$, and some increase in silt and clay, but no dramatic changes on the order of those documented for the Phase VIIc interval in the other sites named above. If sedimentoclimatic correlation has any validity at all, this arrangement seems clearly out of line.

I therefore suggest a new correlation, as shown in Figures 19.1A and 19.2, wherein Pataud *Eboulis* 3-4: Red is placed into Laville's Phase VIIc. This shift calls for other adjustments of the Pataud stratigraphy. Level 4, which shows a moderate degree of weathering (reduced number of rock fragments, which exhibit increased rounding and porosity, abundant illuvial concretions, and abundant eolian sand), seems to be a reasonable correlate of Laville's Phase VIIa. On the other hand, Stratum *a4* of Pataud appears to be more comparable to a minor, mild subphase within the Perigordian VI at Laugerie Haute (Couches Ouest 21, 22, and Est 39). I have inserted this episode as Phase VIIIb in Laville's scheme; Laville did not designate it as a separate subphase in his work, although his data support such a step.

CLIMATIC PATTERNS IN THE ROCKSHELTER SEQUENCE

Having made the adjustments discussed above in the placement of the Abri Pataud sequence, we can now look at the general character of the paleoclimatic record in southwestern France as interpreted from the rockshelter sediments. (This will be only a summary of a discussion that I have elaborated elsewhere in Farrand, in prep.) The point of departure is a comparison of the interpretations of some individual rockshelters that provide good records for the mid-Würm III, namely La Ferrassie, Le Facteur, Le Flageolet I, La Chèvre, and Abri Pataud. The relative strengths of the milder intervals, Laville's Phases III, V, and VII, are shown schematically in Figure 19.1A against a uniform time scale based on the radiocarbon dating at Abri Pataud. In this figure it can be seen that the relative strengths of successive mild intervals are different in the different sites. These interpretations are my own, based on close examination of the original data presented by Laville (1964, 1975). The following are examples of the differences, for Phases V, VIIa, and VIIb, respectively:

Ferrassie: strong-intermediate-intermediate
Facteur: weak-intermediate-intermediate
Flageolet: [?]-intermediate-intermediate
Chèvre: intermediate-intermediate-intermediate
Pataud: strong-intermediate-strong

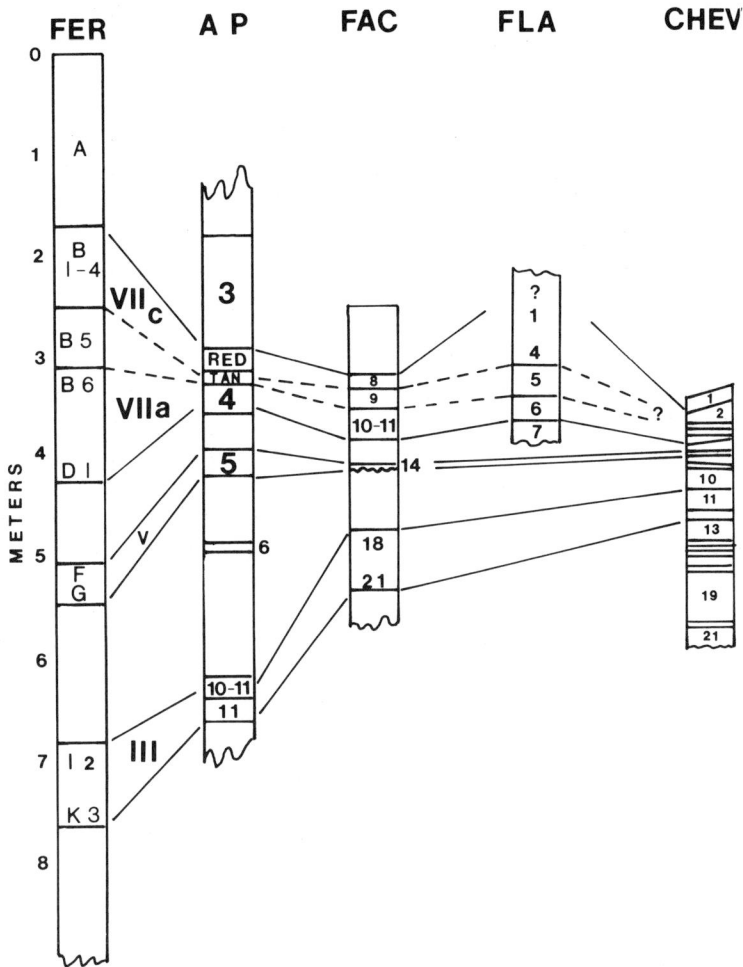

Figure 19.2 Stratigraphic columns for five of the sites shown in Figure 19.1A, showing the true thickness of the various strata attributed to a given climatic phase, all plotted on the same thickness scale. The correlations are the same as in Figure 19.1A. AP=Abri Pataud.

The point of this comparison is that, while the correlations of climatic patterns among the sites is reasonable, the climatic characterization of any given climatic phase is equivocal across the region.

Moreover, the inferred relative duration of each mild phase appears to be different in different sites. In the absence of a sufficient number of absolute dates, one can consider the thicknesses of the sediments representing the mild phases as indexes of relative duration. In Figure 19.2 I have plotted the absolute thicknesses of the strata attributed to Phases III, V, VIIa, and VIIc for these five sites. It is immediately obvious that the total thickness of Phase VII sediments in La Ferrassie is much greater than that of Phase VII deposits in any other of these sites. On the other hand, Phase V deposits in La Ferrassie and Abri Pataud are of comparable thickness, and Phase III deposits are of approximately the same thickness in all five sites. Therefore, the relative durations of these episodes cannot be estimated unequivocally from sediment thicknesses in a single site. Unfortunately, there are too few absolute dates from these sites to allow a similar comparison among the sites in absolute time.

Thus, just as the strength of the climatic signal is not uniformly recorded from site to site, the apparent (relative) duration of the climatic episodes is not uniform among the sites. The idiosyncratic nature of rockshelter sites, undoubtedly combined with a variable human presence, clearly modulates both the intensity and duration of the paleoclimatic signal. This conclusion in no way precludes the possibility of paleoclimatic interpretation of rockshelter sediments.

Nor does it negate the intersite correlations that have been made by Laville, myself, or others. Nevertheless, it argues strongly for caution in both intersite and interregional correlations.

COMPARISON OF THE DORDOGNE SEQUENCE WITH OTHER PALEOCLIMATIC RECORDS

On the basis of absolute dating, the detailed sedimentoclimatic record of rockshelters in southwestern France can be directly compared with other kinds of proxy climatic records. The most obvious candidate for comparison is the Grande Pile pollen record, because it was derived from an area not far distant from the Dordogne and because it presents a long, continuous record with a strong regional climatic signal. The Grande Pile record has, in turn, been correlated with the deep-sea oxygen isotope record, which conceivably opens the door to the possibility of global correlations.

The Grande Pile peat bog is situated on the southwestern slope of the Vosges mountains in northeastern France, some 500-600 km north-northeast of the Dordogne sites. Continuous cores 13 and 15 m long have been recovered. The pollen-bearing sediments rest on till of a glaciation older than the last (or Weichselian) one, and the bog was not covered by moraines of the last glaciation. The vegetation history has been studied in great detail by Woillard (1978, 1980) and dated by radiocarbon (Woillard and Mook 1982), and the magnetostratigraphy has been interpreted by Mörner (1979), who has also made paleoclimatic interpretations based on his reading of the sediments.

A generalized curve of the Grande Pile pollen diagram is reproduced here (Fig. 19.1B). It is taken directly from Woillard and Mook (1982) and shows simply the proportions of arboreal (AP) and non-arboreal (NAP) pollen. The main features of the curve are obvious: high AP percentages in the Holocene and in the lower part of the curve, prior to about 70,000 B.P., and low to very low percentages of AP in the intervening portion. The tree taxa included in the high AP portions of the curve are largely those of a mixed-oak forest with some *Corylus* (hazel), whereas the tree genera in the middle part of the curve are boreal forest (conifer) types.

My purpose here is to examine only the central portion of the Grande Pile curve, that which is chronologically equivalent to the "Würm III" sites of southwestern France, in order to compare the timing and relative intensity of "interstadial" events. There are many radiocarbon dates for the Grande Pile core, but unfortunately there is considerable confusion (due to overlaps and inversions) in the range from 28,000 to 31,000 B.P., which is of critical importance for our purposes. This means that the three prominent AP peaks in that range have not been individually dated. Moreover, it is clear from the radiocarbon dates that the vertical axis of the Grande Pile diagram is not a uniform time scale. Nevertheless, one can be readily persuaded that those three peaks must correlate with the Dordogne mild Phases III, V, and VII of Laville, or in the terms of palynologists, the Arcy, Kesselt (or Les Eyzies), and Tursac Interstades or Oscillations. The Würm Interstade (formerly WII/WIII) of the French chronology, occurring about 40,000 B.P., appears to correspond to a strong AP peak at Grande Pile. It is recognized only at La Ferrassie and La Chèvre, of the sites under consideration here (Fig. 19.1A).

The Laugerie (WIII/WIV) and Lascaux Interstades, recognized by palynologists (Leroi-Gourhan and Renault-Miskovsky 1977), are essentially imperceptible in the Grande Pile diagram, as Woillard has previously noted (Woillard and Mook 1982). This is no longer surprising in view of the downgrading of the WIII/WIV fluctuation within the French chronology (Laville, Raynal, and Texier 1986). This anomaly serves to emphasize the conclusion that local pollen records, especially in rockshelter settings, may not be true reflections of regional climatic events. In any case, if the Laugerie "Interstade" is poorly represented at Grande Pile, it should not be surprising that the weak mild episodes of Laville's Phases VIIIb and IX cannot be seen there either.

One can, therefore, draw the conclusion that certain sedimentoclimatic intervals in rockshelters can be useful in regional correlation, while others have only local significance. Specifically, for the *Würm récent* Laville's Phases I, III, V, and VII appear to reflect regional paleoclimate, while Phases VIIIb and IX do not. Moreover, when it comes to a comparison of the relative importance of these episodes in the different kinds of records, one finds some ambiguities. For example, Laville's Phase III appears to be relatively short-lived and not very strong, while its apparent correlative at Grande Pile is a major peak, both in the AP curve and in Mörner's sediment analysis. Another discrepancy concerns the tripartite Tursac Oscillation, which is quite pronounced at Abri Pataud and Le Facteur. It is neither tripartite nor as intense in the Grande Pile diagram.

Going still further and considering global correlations, we find little reassurance that the detailed climatic phases in rockshelter sequences can be recognized in hemispheric or global records. This is a consequence of the nature of the proxy data records that one is forced to depend on, namely deep-sea core stratigraphy. Slow rates of sedimentation combined with bioturbation at the sediment-water interface effectively obscure details of the climatic signal that have durations of 1000-2000 years or less. Nevertheless, it is tempting to correlate the fine-scale wiggles on oxygen-isotope curves with terrestrial events. Woillard (1980) herself has suggested such correlations in the case of two deep-sea cores, one from the northeast Atlantic and one from the equatorial Pacific, where relatively high sedimentation rates preserve a fair amount of detail (Fig. 19.3). I leave it to the reader, however, to be convinced that the small-amplitude variations in oxygen-isotope values can be correlated with confidence even between these two deep-sea cores, let alone with the Grande Pile pollen core.

FRANCHTHI CAVE, GREECE

INTRODUCTION

Franchthi Cave is located in the Argolid Peninsula of the Peloponnese in southern Greece. The entrance to the cave is about 11 m above present sea level and some 50 m inland from the present marine shoreline. This karstic cavity is about 150 m long and is partly filled with a variety of sediments, some of which extend well below sea level. Excavations under the direction of T. W. Jacobsen of Indiana University during the years 1967-76 revealed that the upper 10-11 m of the sedimentary fill are rich in Neolithic and Mesolithic remains and enclose a sparse Upper Paleolithic occupation dating to at least 30,000 or 35,000 B.P.

Preliminary reports on the Franchthi excavations (Jacobsen 1973a, b, 1976) are available, but definitive descriptions are just now going to press, and the final interpretations are not yet made. In addition to the study of the excavations proper, ancillary research in the surrounding area has shed much light on environmental and climatic change during the period of prehistoric habitation. Especially important are the studies of Pope and van Andel (1984) on geomorphic evolution of the Franchthi landscape, and of Shackleton and van Andel (1986) on changing environments and marine resources as a function of sea-level rise during late-glacial time. In this paper I shall draw upon the studies of my colleagues and integrate them with my own sedimentological research at Franchthi in order to sketch a paleoenvironmental sequence that can be compared with regional paleoclimatic records. At this point it should be made clear that the interpretations that follow are my own and not necessarily those of my Franchthi colleagues.

FRANCHTHI STRATIGRAPHY

The stratigraphic succession in Franchthi Cave is shown in Figure 19.4, where correlations between the two major trenches are indicated. Briefly summarized, the sedimentary sequence is as follows, from bottom to top:

Stratum P: The lowest sediments exposed in the excavations are reddish brown clay loams with many very large limestone blocks indicating repeated rockfalls from the cave ceiling. Sparse Upper Paleolithic flints and large mammal bones, mainly equids, occur throughout.

Stratum Q: Pale gray tephra (volcanic ash), very pure and up to 5-6 cm thick in Trench FA; very sharp lower contact. Chemical and mineralogical analyses indicate that the tephra was wind-transported from the Naples area in Italy. It is apparently the same as the Gray Campanian Ash of that region, which is also found widely on the ocean floor around southern Greece (Vitaliano et al. 1981).

Stratum R: More reddish brown clay loams and loams, similar to Stratum P.

Strata S and T: A series of rockfalls with reddish brown loam matrix. Two successive rockfalls can be distinguished in Trench H1. Stratum T appears absent in Trench FA, where there is a rather major hiatus (unconformity), perhaps some 5000-6000 years long.

Stratum U: This unit marks the beginning of less bouldery sedimentation and is accompanied by more

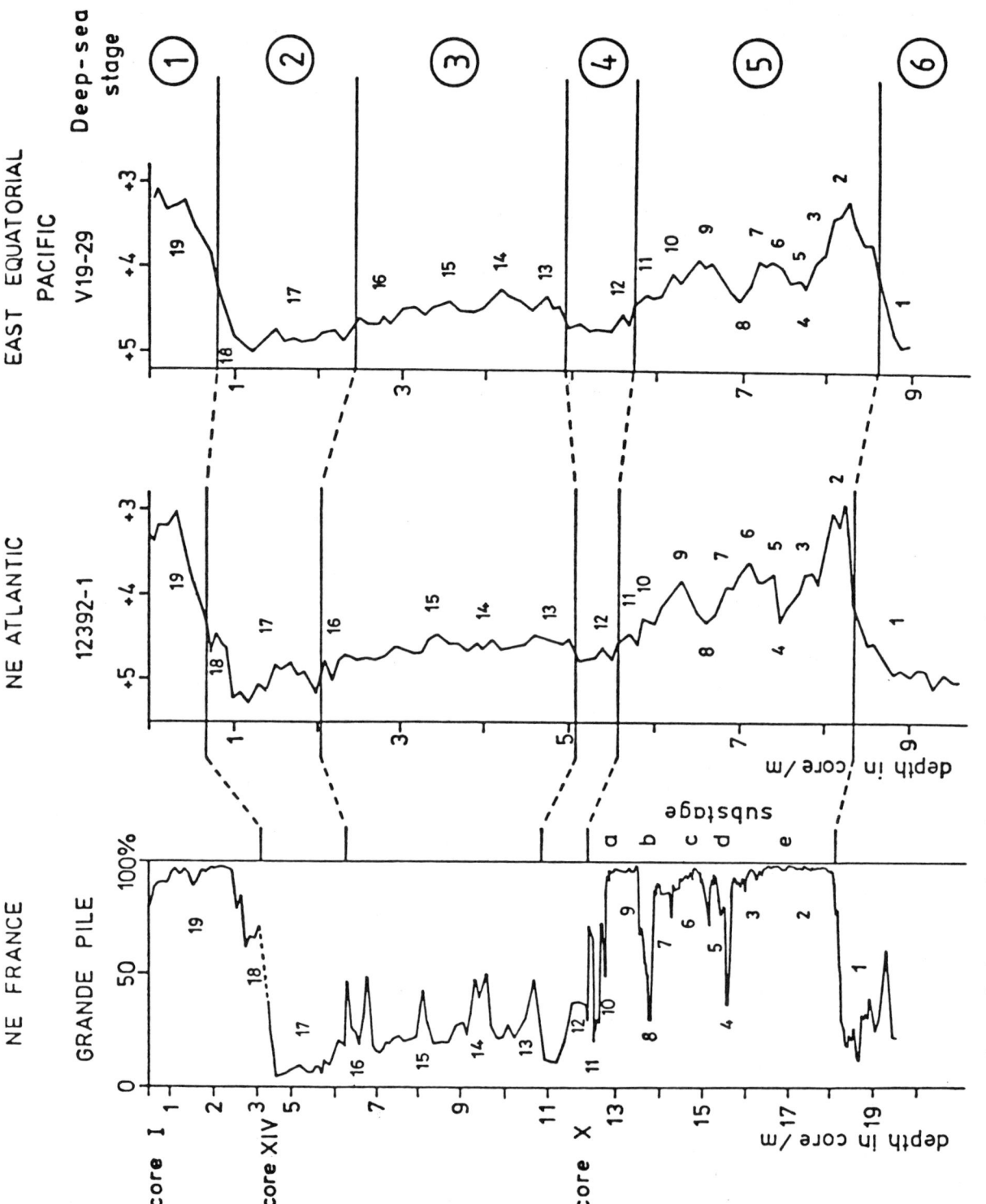

Figure 19.3 Correlations of the Grande Pile pollen curve with deep-sea cores (from Woillard 1980).

INTEGRATION OF LATE QUATERNARY CLIMATIC RECORDS FROM FRANCE & GREECE 313

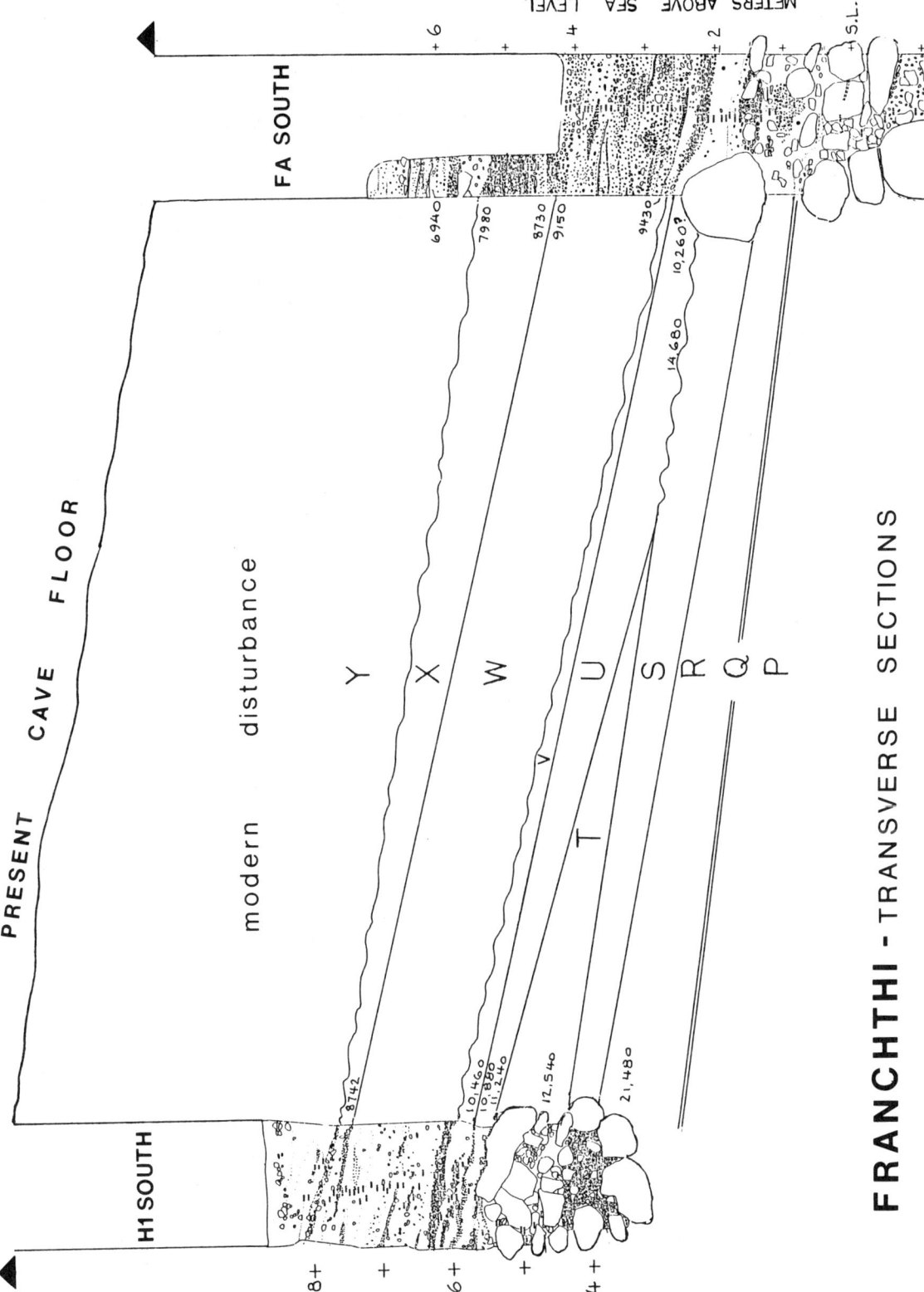

Figure 19.4 Correlation of strata exposed in Franchthi Cave, Greece, along with key radiocarbon dates. The south faces of trenches FA and H1 are shown as one would see them in looking toward the interior of the cave. The horizontal distance between the trenches is 14 m. Wavy lines indicate unconformities.

intense habitation of the cave, a microlithic final Upper Paleolithic industry. In Trench H1 this stratum encloses several very rich snail middens, composed very largely of *Helix figulina,* a large land snail similar to *H. pomatia,* and also some marine shells and animal bones. In Trench FA no extensive middens were found, but snails, bones, and artifacts are present throughout in a reddish brown loam with abundant rock fragments.

Stratum V: A very rocky stratum in which many limestone fragments are relatively well rounded and have heavy weathering rinds; reductions in matrix $CaCO_3$ and pH also indicate a weathered horizon. Radiocarbon dates suggest a hiatus of several hundred years at the top of this layer. This horizon contains the last clear indications of Upper Paleolithic industries (Perlès, in press).

Stratum W: This is a thick stratum, but it accumulated rapidly, as much as 150-200 cm per century. It is characterized by grayish brown loams and sandy loams with abundant small rock fragments (mostly 8 to 64 mm) and much cultural debris. Much of the fine matrix must have been brought in by the inhabitants, intentionally or unintentionally, because it cannot be derived autochthonously from the cave bedrock. The base of this stratum corresponds to the beginning of Mesolithic industries, as recognized by C. Perlès.

Stratum X: An even more rocky layer, with rock fragments mainly in the 32- to 128-mm range and rather little matrix between them. As in the case of Stratum V, many rocks in the upper part of this unit in Trench FA are somewhat rounded and have white weathering rinds, and reduced $CaCO_3$ and pH also indicate weathering. The upper surface of Stratum X appears to be another unconformity of a few hundred years, based on these sedimentary criteria and radiocarbon dates. The hiatus may be longer in Trench H1, where Stratum X is considerably thinner than in FA and where the weathering indicators are absent. These observations suggest that the original top of Stratum X may have been removed by erosion in the area of Trench H1. The upper limit marks the end of the Mesolithic in Franchthi.

Stratum Y: Light brown silty or sandy loam with rock fragments fewer and smaller than in underlying strata, and abundant artifacts and cultural debris, especially potsherds and sheep/goat bones. The sedimentation rate was rapid, up to 40 cm per century. The lowest levels of this stratum enclose an aceramic Neolithic with sheep/goat and domestic wheat and barley, followed by a fully ceramic Neolithic industry.

At or during the final phases of the Neolithic a major collapse of the cave ceiling occurred, producing an enormous pile of breakdown debris, with many limestone blocks measuring several meters in thickness and length. This breakdown resulted in the opening of a "window" to the sky, some 20 m across, in the middle of the cave. Another, smaller breakdown window at the innermost end of the cave and breakdown of the cave brow also occurred in late to final Neolithic times. These breakdowns were not necessarily simultaneous, but they all may have been the results of earthquakes.

Stratum Z (not shown on Fig. 19.4): Light gray, homogeneous rocky rubble of very recent age, up to several meters thick, with a mixture of prehistoric and modern artifacts and ash lenses dating to the past century.

ENVIRONMENTAL CHANGE AT FRANCHTHI

Interpreting the paleoclimatic signal in the Franchthi sequence is not straightforward, and unfortunately Franchthi stands alone in this part of the world in terms of detailed sedimentological analysis, eliminating the possibility of cross-checking one's interpretations by correlation with other sites. The cave sediments give no indication of freeze-thaw activity, thus obviating many sorts of interpretations made in French caves, and the sediments of the Mesolithic and Neolithic phases in Franchthi are strongly influenced by human activity that obscures any climatic signal.

Nevertheless, the primary sediments and weathering indicators, along with the radiocarbon chronology, do reveal a depositional history that, either alone or in combination with other types of data, must bear some relation to the environment that prevailed outside the cave. It is clear that deposition was not continuous in the cave, nor was it uniform from one part of the cave to another at all times. Gaps within the series of radiocarbon dates and evidence of weathering (chalky weathering rinds, leaching of $CaCO_3$, and secondary carbonate crusts on snail shells) indicate hiatuses at the end of the Paleolithic (ca. 9800-9500 B.P.) and again between the Mesolithic and Neolithic (ca. 8000-7500 B.P.) in both major trenches. Sedimentation appears to have ceased for several thousand years, however, in the area of Trench FA, from ca. 15,000 B.P. to ca. 11,300 B.P., while it continued—perhaps sporadically—in the vicinity of Trench H1 (Stratum T). The latter conclusion was first suggested by studies of the artifacts (Perlès, in press) and the fauna (S. Payne, pers. comm.), although it was not immediately obvious in the sedimentary record. Closer evaluation reveals that the top of Stratum S in Trench FA does show signs of leaching of carbonate, rounding of rock fragments, and chalky snail shells, consistent with a pause in sedimentation at that horizon.

The sedimentary history from 15,000 to 5000 B.P. in the Franchthi Cave is summarized in Figure 19.5, along with other information derived from my colleagues' results. The rate of sedimentation and the positions of hiatuses are shown for Trench FA. Prior to 15,000 B.P. the character of sedimentation within the cave was slow accumulation (1-2 cm per 100 years) of sporadic rockfalls from the cave ceiling accompanied by the inwashing of reddish brown clay loam. The latter presumably was derived from surface soil (terra rossa) above the cave that washed in through fissures through the cave roof. Although humans used the cave during this time, their impact on sedimentation was minimal. This kind of sedimentation continued in the central, forward part of the cave (Trench H1 area) until ca. 11,500 B.P., but ceased in the area of Trench FA, which is located much closer to the side wall of the cave.

After ca. 11,500 B.P. the sedimentation rate increased, apparently as a direct consequence of human activity, which brought various materials into the cave, either intentionally or unintentionally. This would have included foodstuffs, wood or brush for fires and constructions, and "dirt" (sand and mud) on people's feet or attached to these other materials. In any case, the sedimentation rate tripled in the phase between 11,500 and 9500 B.P., which includes several thick land-snail middens.

After a gap of a few centuries sedimentation resumed at an even greater rate, up to 150-200 cm per 100 years during the Mesolithic occupation. Sedimentation slowed toward the end of the Mesolithic, and then another hiatus of several hundred years intervened before Neolithic inhabitants came to leave their traces in the cave. Rapid sedimentation again occurred during the earlier part of the Neolithic occupation, up to 40 cm per 100 years. The interpretation of the latest part of the Trench FA curve, younger than 5500 B.P., is problematical because considerable postdepositional disturbance is indicated in some places by finds of modern potsherds.

It is interesting to note that the unconformities that separate the Paleolithic from the Mesolithic and the Mesolithic from the Neolithic occur at the top of particularly rocky layers (Strata V and X), which have rather little fine matrix between the rock fragments. If the matrix is largely anthropogenic, as suggested in the preceding paragraph, then one might draw the conclusion that human use of the cave declined in the intervals just preceding the hiatuses. In this scenario, the rate of accumulation of rock fragments may have been more or less constant with time. Alternatively, the rate of detachment of rock fragments from the cave ceiling and walls may have increased for some reason, discouraging occupation of the cave for some length of time, followed by cessation of all sedimentation for a few centuries during which solution weathering attacked the sediments exposed on the cave floor. Clearly we need corroborative evidence from other sites in Greece in order to choose between these alternatives.

In an attempt to evaluate these alternative hypotheses, let us first assume that the intensified rock accumulations and the succeeding periods of quiescence were controlled by environmental, perhaps climatic, variations. The cave limestone dips very steeply, nearly vertically in places, and individual beds are highly fractured, so that the rock fragments that ultimately will be detached are more or less preconditioned in shape and size before they fall to the cave floor. One can hypothesize that an unusually moist period would increase the infiltration of soil- or groundwater through the overlying bedrock, detaching rock fragments. Once all the readily detachable fragments fall, sedimentation would decrease strongly or stop altogether, although the ambient soil moisture would still be sufficient to attack the rock fragments on the cave floor, leaching them and translocating the $CaCO_3$.

If this hypothesis is correct, one should expect to find corroboration in other paleoenvironmental indicators in this region. Looking first at biological remains preserved in Franchthi sediments, one finds suggestions of environmental change in the large and small mammals (Payne 1982) and in marine shellfish (Shackleton and van Andel 1986). The latter reflect changing coastal environments as the sea level rose during deglaciation, and thus the changing availability of marine resources, but they tell us little if anything about local or regional climate. Nevertheless, it is conceivable that periods of rapidly changing sea level alternating with periods of stabilized sea level might induce local environmental change. Submerged benches on the sea floor around the Argolid Peninsula

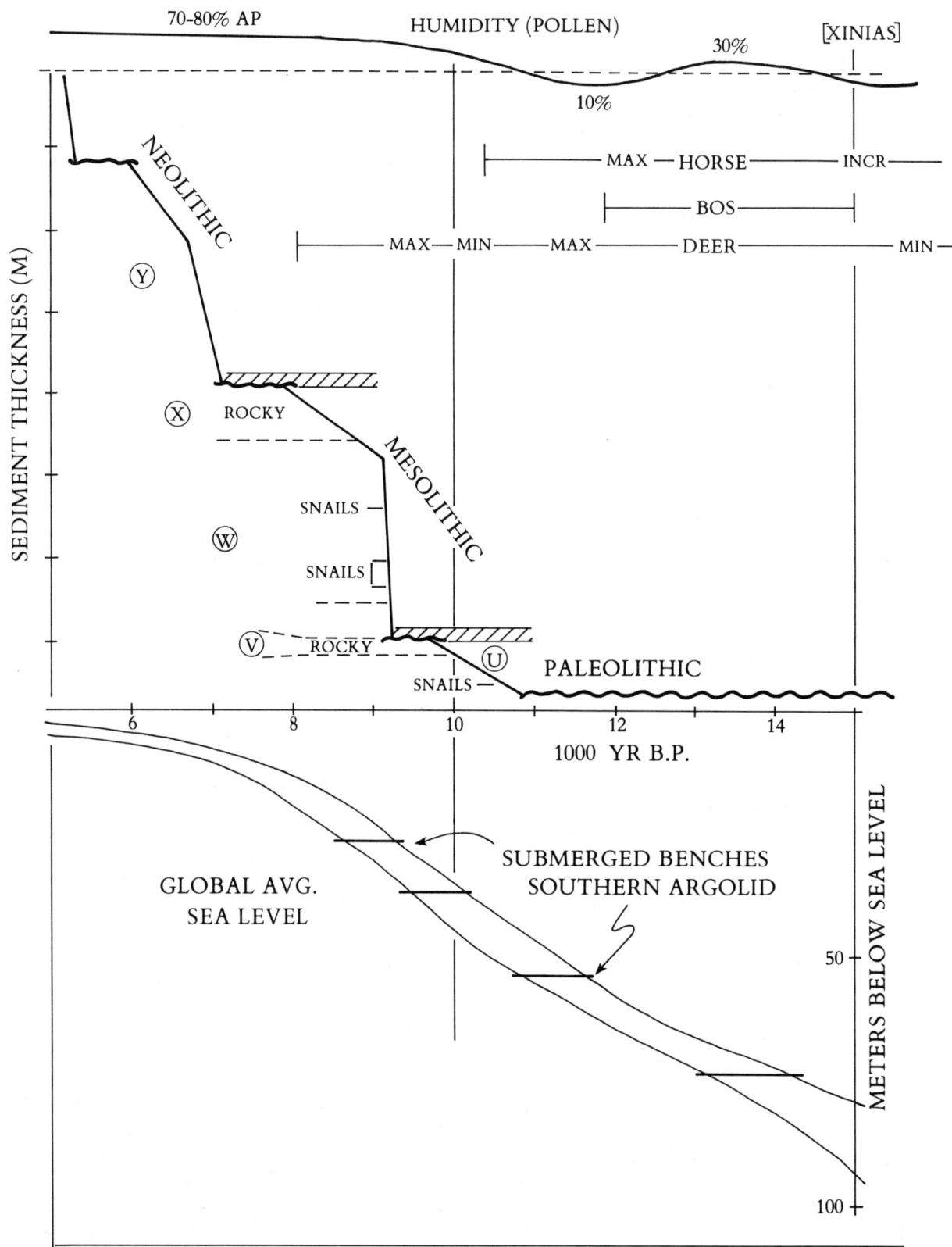

Figure 19.5 Schematic summary of Franchthi sedimentation and contemporaneous variations in environmental conditions for the period from 15,000 to 5000 B.P. Sedimentation rate is shown by the steepness of the heavy solid lines, and unconformities are indicated by wavy lines. Strata U, V, W, X, and Y are the same as in Figure 19.4. Variations in the large mammal fauna are after Payne (1982). Sea-level information follows the interpretation of van Andel and Lianos (1984), and the humidity curve is based on the percentage of arboreal pollen (AP) from the site of Xinias as interpreted by van Zeist and Bottema (1982).

have been mapped by van Andel and Lianos (1984). The four most prominent ones can be dated indirectly by comparing their depths to an average global sea-level curve (Fig. 19.5), yielding approximate ages of 13,000-14,000, 11,500-11,000, 10,000-9500, and 9000-8500 B.P. As seen in Figure 19.5, these sea-level events do not bear any apparent relationship to sedimentation events on the Trench FA curve.

The mammals, on the other hand, may provide climatic information, if one can filter out human selectivity in hunting activities, since herbivores depend on climatically determined vegetation for their food and shelter. On this basis, Payne (1982) suggests a local climatic scenario of an open, dry landscape prior to about 15,000 B.P., changing to damper woodlands based on the abundance of *Bos/Bison* from 15,000 to ca. 12,000 B.P., followed by an increasing tree and brush cover with deer until ca. 8000 B.P. With the onset of Neolithic habitation, the fauna is 90% domesticated sheep and goat, thus obscuring any climatic signal.

Pollen was too poorly preserved in the cave sediments to be useful in paleoclimatic reconstruction. However, a generalized curve of arboreal pollen (AP) abundance at the site of Xinias in central Greece is shown at the top of Figure 19.5. This is one of the few pollen sites in Greece on which regional climate may be reconstructed (van Zeist and Bottema 1982). This curve is supported by three radiocarbon dates, including one at 10,580 B.P. that marks the transition from pine-dominated woodlands to oak-dominated forests. The AP peak (30%) at 14,000-13,000 B.P., which is mostly pine, is coincident with the *Bos* peak of the Franchthi fauna in suggesting an episode of increased humidity. After this, around 11,500 B.P., the pine woodlands appear to thin out to the benefit of nonarboreal vegetation types, suggesting drier conditions, and then ca. 10,600 B.P. the mixed oak forest begins its dominance.

Another pollen diagram, from Lake Kopaïs just north of the Isthmus of Corinth, supports the Xinias core, but it is not as well dated (Turner and Greig 1975). Van Zeist and Bottema (1982) insist that the pollen record indicates only changes in "humidity" or available moisture, not fluctuations in absolute amounts of precipitation. "Humidity" integrates changes in precipitation and changes in temperature and evaporation rate, which may reinforce or cancel each other at different times.

Another approach to information on environmental change in the region around Franchthi Cave is to compare the history of alluviation and colluviation as interpreted by Pope and van Andel (1984). These researchers have examined the sedimentary fills in the lowlands of the southern Argolid Peninsula, identifying debris flows, braided stream-channel and flood deposits, overbank and distal fan sediments, and periglacial *grèzes litées*. (The latter facies is found only in deposits older than 250,000 years.) Intercalated among these sediments are a number of buried soils that have been dated by artifacts and by uranium-thorium dating of pedogenic carbonate Cca horizons. For our purposes, the results of Pope and van Andel's study indicate a long period of geomorphic stability and soil formation from about 32,000 to 4500 B.P. None of the variations seen in the cave sediments, in the fauna, or in the regional pollen studies appear to have been strong enough to have disrupted this stable land surface, in spite of the fact that the period in question encompasses the last major advance and retreat of northern ice sheets.

In summary, we have seen that, in spite of some agreement between the regional pollen record and the Franchthi fauna, there is no apparent relation between either of them and the sedimentary and weathering history in the cave. In a general way, the increase in humidity marked by the onset of the oak forest is contemporaneous with the rocky Strata V and X and the subsequent hiatuses, but the pollen record does not include oscillations to which the sediments between the rocky horizons could be attributed. This lack of success in finding regional climatic patterns that match those implied by the cave sediments is disappointing from the point of view of a climatic sedimentologist. The explanation may lie in one of the following, or some combination thereof:

(1) the idiosyncratic nature of cave sedimentation;

(2) insufficient knowledge of regional paleoclimate; or

(3) an overriding influence on cave sedimentation by human activity.

There is very little in the way of variation in the local bedrock to which one might attribute variations in the accumulating sediments. On the basis of our present knowledge there were no changes in the configuration of the cave during the time interval in question. It is not known, however, when the breakdown window in the center of the cave first opened. It is conceivable that a smaller window opened during Paleolithic or Mesolithic occupation, but, if so, the evidence is now deeply buried under the great mass of post-Neolithic breakdown. Another unknown is the role of earthquakes. Earthquakes are frequent occurrences in this tectonically active circum-Aegean area. The abundance of rock fragments without a significant amount of fine matrix in Strata V and X might be attributed to earthquakes that shook loose all the unstable rock of the cave ceiling and walls, such that no further sedimentation would occur until weathering loosened the bedrock surface once again.

The regional paleoclimate is known mainly from pollen studies, but long pollen diagrams are still not abundant in the Eastern Mediterranean sector. Van Zeist and Bottema (1982) have summarized data from northern and central Greece, western Anatolia, and the Levant, and Farrand (1981) has assembled data from the latter two areas as well. These summaries show a reasonable degree of similarity across the region, and some of the minor differences between diagrams may be the result of inadequate chronological control. Nevertheless, none of them show fluctuations in the 10,000 to 7000 B.P. range that are similar in magnitude to variations in the cave sediments; on the other hand, rather marked oscillations recorded by pollen in the 20,000 to 15,000 B.P. range and again between 30,000 and 20,000 B.P. do not appear to find their parallels in the Franchthi sedimentary record.

The last alternative, namely a very strong anthropogenic overprint on the natural sediments, is not very satisfactory either, at least not as the only cause. Certainly human importation of sediments, in the broadest sense and in ample quantity, did occur during Mesolithic and Neolithic times. Unfortunately, we do not have information on the intensity of human occupation at Franchthi Cave independent of suggestions based on sedimentation rate. But the repeated coupling of rock-fragment layers and unconformities, during which times the cave appears not to have been occupied, suggests a process or processes over and above human control. Moreover, sparse occupation of the cave during Paleolithic time did not result in the deposition of rock-fragment layers like Strata V and X and ensuing hiatuses. Thus, human agency is not an adequate answer.

CONCLUSIONS ON FRANCHTHI

Sedimentological and stratigraphic analysis has revealed many important details of the history of the filling of Franchthi Cave, and these details will be important in deciphering the history of human activities in the cave and the surrounding area. Still at this point the sedimentary history cannot be integrated with the regional paleoclimate except on the broadest level. From 30,000 B.P. (or earlier) until ca. 11,500 B.P. sporadic rockfalls and the inwashing of red soil sediment dominated the infilling. After 11,500 B.P. the human presence made a large impact on the sedimentation processes and rate. This shift in style of sedimentation more or less corresponds to the end of the last glaciation in more northerly latitudes and the beginning of the Holocene. That relationship may be merely coincidental, though, given that detailed comparison of regional paleoclimates based on pollen studies does not reveal a close correlation between vegetation types and the beginning of the Holocene epoch.

GENERAL CONCLUSIONS

Two examples of cave-sediment studies have been discussed, one based on a group of cave and rockshelter sites in southwestern France, and the other on a single cave site in Greece. In both examples the sedimentary histories were compared to regional paleoclimates based largely on pollen analysis. In the French case quite reasonable correlations can be made between cave-sediment "climate" and pollen "climate." It was pointed out, however, that neither the apparent amplitude nor the duration of the climatic signal is precisely the same in the two different kinds of records. Moreover, some "climatic events" read from the rockshelter record seem to have been too weak or too local to have left an impact on regional vegetation that gave rise to the pollen record. In addition, the rockshelter and pollen records were compared to global (or hemispheric) proxy climatic records interpreted from deep-sea sediments, but the much poorer time resolution stemming from very slow sedimentation rates and bioturbation prevents unambiguous recognition of short-lived events recognized in the rockshelter sediments.

For the second example, that of Franchthi Cave in southern Greece, it is difficult at this stage in the development of our knowledge to correlate sedimentary events with regional paleoclimatic fluctuations. Part of the difficulty may be a result of the fact that these fluctuations are still not abundantly documented in this area. Alternatively, as was the case in France, some of these events may have been too insignificant to have been registered in regional vegetation history. Still another alternative lies in the importance of human activity within the cave. Anthropogenic sediment input and rearrangement of the accumulating natural deposits can produce sedimentary "events" totally unrelated to the external environment. As I emphasized in the discussion of the French rockshelters, a single site may not yield a representative picture of external environmental changes. Until more Greek cave sediments are studied in this kind of detail, it will not be possible to understand the reasons for this lack of agreement in the different kinds of proxy climatic records.

DISCUSSION

KOZLOWSKI: What is the basis for the age determination of the ash levels? We have recently identified ash layers at several sites in the Balkan Peninsula, especially at Temnata, a cave site in Bulgaria we are in the process of excavating. It could become a very important stratigraphic marker for this period.

FARRAND: In the last 50,000 years there must have been at least eight or ten different tephra in the Aegean area. Several of them came from the Italian area, some from Santorini. The first question, if you have a tephra, is to know which one is it? There are chemical and mineralogical ways of fingerprinting it to be quite sure that it the same as what has been called Piscia ash in the deep-sea cores, although we do not think anymore that it comes from Piscia, but from Campania, which is just close by.

The indirect dating comes from several different ways. I did not get to the radiocarbon dates from Franchthi but we have about sixty radiocarbon dates. The lowest one is about 23,000 years and it is 20 or 30 cm above the ash. Knowing the approximate sedimentation rate we can extrapolate down to the ash layer. The date comes out to 27,000 or 28,000 and perhaps more. The ash can also be bracketed in the deep-sea cores by recognition of the foram zones, which are at least indirectly dated too. It not extremely satisfactory, but it is in the 30,000 to 35,000-year range. There are some occurrences of the Campanian ash, which is what we have on land in the western Italy area, which have some radiocarbon dates on wood associated with them. Again they are not specifically on the ash but closely associated with it, and it puts it in the upper 20,000–30,000 range. I would like to think, on the basis of the sedimentation rate as I would reconstruct it at Franchthi, that the date is closer to 30,000 than it is to 35,000.

KOZLOWSKI: But this corresponds well with Temnata Cave. There we have dates of 32,000 years for Layer 3 and 28,900 for Layer 2, which would place the ash between 32,000 and 29,000.

FARRAND: In terms of age that sounds good; I worry about the distribution of the ash. The distribution of this ash is well documented: in northern Bulgaria, the ash would be very thin.

JELINEK: On the other hand, you are assuming all kinds of wind patterns and other things in looking at this.

FARRAND: That point is well taken. There are winds that blow from the south across and toward northern Greece, but, with respect to this particular volcanic ash, the source is in Italy, not in Greece.

XX
Changing Assemblage Diversity in Perigord Archaeofaunas

Jan F. Simek
Lynn M. Snyder

INTRODUCTION

In recent years, Paleolithic archaeologists and paleoanthropologists have shown a revived and intensified interest in a series of apparent biocultural changes that occurred among human groups in Western Europe some 35,000–40,000 years ago. This time period witnessed the evolution or replacement of the archaic, Neandertal form of *Homo sapiens* by anatomically modern forms of that species. At approximately the same time, the Middle Paleolithic Mousterian stone-tool assemblages found over much of Europe in Pleistocene deposits also evolved into or were replaced by technologically distinct assemblages referred to as "Upper Paleolithic." Most recent discussions of this period emphasize differences between the Middle and Upper Paleolithic (e.g., Mellars 1973; Trinkaus 1983; White 1982) and attempt to link these differences to biologically based causes.

A variety of data has been examined to support arguments for dramatic change at the Middle-Upper Paleolithic boundary. For example, stone-tool technology has long been emphasized (e.g., Bordes 1968a; Mellars 1973), and stone-tool function has been discussed (e.g., Binford 1982; White 1982). Symbolic materials (i.e., durable artwork, crafts, and mortuary data) have also been considered (Harrold 1980; White 1982). Finally, changing patterns of resource utilization, and especially of faunal subsistence choices, have been cited as evidence for important behavioral changes at this time (Mellars 1973; White 1983). For all of these dimensions, it is argued that the Upper Paleolithic sees an increase in overall complexity relative to the Middle Paleolithic, and this heightened variability is often characterized in terms of increasing assemblage diversity.

In this paper, we will investigate this asserted change pattern in one of the above-mentioned data sets—faunal assemblages recovered in association with Late Pleistocene archaeological materials in the Perigord region of southwestern France. In performing this assessment, we demonstrate a shift to less diverse resource bases, but it happens later in time than the "transition." We also argue that changing patterns of animal resource use may actually represent evolutionary responses to global climatic changes and are not related to increased intellectual capability, better locomotive skills, or other vitalistic causes.

BACKGROUND

Most recent discussions of Late Pleistocene archaeofaunas from Europe have stressed the "specialized" or "less diverse" assemblages associated with Upper Paleolithic archaeological traditions. Of course, this notion has some antiquity, dating back to Breuil's (1912) initial observations concerning Paleolithic systematics. In recent literature, however, this supposed pattern is part of a larger set of changing technological behaviors (Dennell 1983; Binford 1968b; Mellars 1973; White 1982: 171). Mellars, for example, argues that reindeer (*Rangifer tarandus*) dominate faunal assemblages from Chatelperronian, Aurignacian, and later Upper Paleolithic sites, while Mousterian assemblages are as often associated with bovids or red deer (*Cervus elaphus*) as with caribou (1973: 260-264). White, taking issue with Mellars, computed live-weight estimates for the same faunas and concluded that, while Upper Paleolithic diets may have been more general than

Mellars believes, hunting patterns still emphasized reindeer in the Upper Paleolithic in order to generate other, nonfood resources like antler and sinew (1982: 170-171). For different reasons, then, both Mellars and White agree that in the Upper Paleolithic, "there is much greater emphasis on a single species of animal (almost always reindeer in southwestern France) as the major food resource" (White 1982: 170). An obvious implication of this argument is that Upper Paleolithic archaeofaunas are less diverse than those produced by the comparatively more generalized Mousterian peoples.

We do not think that any Paleolithic archaeologist would dispute the statement that Late Pleistocene change in resource use was an evolutionary phenomenon. If specialized procurement patterns (and the complex technologies that may have supported them) evolved, then only the interplay between phenotypic (i.e., economic) variation and selective forces can adequately explain the shift to specialized economies. Evolutionary theory, in turn, implies that change occurred over time in response to selection. In other words, evolutionary explanation is predicated on chronological control (Dunnell 1980). Yet recent studies of the Middle-Upper Paleolithic transition in France have employed a decidedly typological, non-historical approach. By definition, typological analysis focuses interest on differences between types rather than on evolutionary process (Dunnell 1980; Rindos 1986). This is because recent studies of the transition have left out time and have found differences by emphasizing them; they are therefore non-evolutionary despite explicit or implicit intent.

THE DATA

THE SAMPLE

Data utilized in this study were taken from published faunal lists provided in Delpech 1983, Movius 1975, and Montet-White 1982a. Numbers of identifiable specimens were tabulated for 142 animal species or groups. Thirty-eight large-mammal species and 104 small-animal species, including rodents, insectivores, birds, fish, reptiles, and amphibians, are represented. A total of 96,372 identified specimens (NISP) compose the sample; the distribution of these bones among general species groups is given in Table 20.1.

Ninety-seven faunal assemblages come from 13 archaeological sites. The entire range of Upper Paleolithic cultural traditions is represented. All 97 assemblages were analyzed recently. Thus, we can assume that identifications were attempted for all bones collected by the original site excavators. The collections were made at different times and by different prehistorians, however, and this variability may have affected the faunal assemblages recovered from different sites (Delpech 1983; Rigaud and Simek 1987). As will be seen, this potential source of variability can be easily assessed. Table 20.2 presents the 13 sites considered, the number of assemblages recovered from each, the cultural traditions represented, the excavator, and the year that collections were begun.

In selecting the 13 sites employed here, we have attempted to incorporate all materials available in the published literature from a relatively small region in southwestern France: the Périgord of Aquitaine. It is unfortunate that so few sites have been accorded the kind of detailed study that is required for this kind of work. Indeed, Bouchud's analysis of the Abri Pataud faunas (1975), Rogers's studies of data from Le Malpas (1973), and Delpech's regional study of Upper Paleolithic faunas (1983) provide the only reliable and sufficiently detailed accounts (treating both macro and micro remains) of Périgord Late Paleolithic faunas. Thus we have used all three of these data sets.

TABLE 20.1
NUMBERS OF IDENTIFIABLE SPECIMENS (NISP) FOR PERIGORD UPPER PALEOLITHIC ANIMAL BONES

Group	NISP
large herbivores	73,436
carnivores and mustelids	1,223
hares and rabbits	6,871
rodents	7,151
insectivores	530
reptiles and amphibians	2,968
fishes	3,123
bats	8
birds	1,062
Total:	96,372

TABLE 20.2
SITES, NUMBER OF LEVELS CONTRIBUTED BY SITE, EXCAVATOR, YEAR OF EXCAVATION,
AND ARCHAEOLOGICAL TRADITIONS REPRESENTED

Site	Levels	Excavator	Year	Trad.
Roc de Combe	15	Bordes	1966	a,b
La Ferrassie	7	Delporte	1968	a,b,c
Caminade Est	2	Sonneville-Bordes	1954	b
Maldidier	3	Rigaud	1966	b,c
Le Flageolet I	5	Rigaud	1967	b,c
Laugerie-Haute Est	7	Bordes	1957	e
Laugerie-Haute Ouest	10	Peyrony	1921	d,e
Le Madeleine	17	Bouvier	1973	f
Le Flageolet II	4	Rigaud	1967	f
Pont d'Ambon	5	Celerier	1971	f,g
Gare de Couze	2	Bordes	1960	f
Abri Pataud	13	Movius	1958	b,c,d
Le Malpas	7	Montet-White	1967	e

As in Figure 20.3: a = Chatelperronian, b = Aurignacian, c = Upper Perigordian, d = Würm III/IV industries (Protomagdalenian and Aurignacian V), e = Solutrean, f = Magdalenian, g = Azilian.

THE VARIABLES

Given conventional expectations for characteristic patterns of change in faunal composition during the Upper Paleolithic, variables and techniques appropriate to evaluating such changes can be proposed.

The variable most relevant to examining evolutionary change is rather self-evident. Evolution is a historical process (Dunnell 1980), and its measurement requires a reasonably precise and continuous characterization of time. As was discussed earlier, prehistorians interested in the Middle-Upper Paleolithic transition have rarely employed continuous chronological measures, preferring instead to compare generalized "Middle" Paleolithic attributes to either an "early Upper" or an even more general "Upper" Paleolithic tradition. More refined chronological distinctions either concentrate on single sites (Chase 1986) or look at change between but not within traditional culture classes (e.g., Freeman 1973; Straus 1977).

The lack of rigorous chronological measurement in examining change in faunal assemblages is surprising when one considers that, for many areas of the world and especially for the pivotal Perigord region of southern France, a more than adequate temporal sequence for key sites has been available for some time (Laville, Rigaud, and Sackett 1980). Laville's "chronostratigraphy" for the Perigord provides relative, or ordinal, sequencing of various sites from all Late Pleistocene time periods. And although ordinal sequences do not provide the same precision as absolute dates (rates of change cannot be estimated), they are far preferable to typological units ("Middle" vs. "Upper" Paleolithic), which are theoretically incompatible with evolutionary process (Lewontin 1974; Rindos 1986).

All of the 13 sites composing our sample have been placed within Laville's regional scheme; thus, each level within a site is ordered in reference to every other level in the sample. Given the resolution attained by Laville's Perigord chronostratigraphy, several archaeological levels may be grouped into any one of the identifiable climatic oscillations. Thus, the 97 sample levels are organized into 40 different chronological phases spanning the Recent Würm.

Using Laville's chronostratigraphy, we have a sequential measure of time that approximates a continuous variable (Neter, Wasserman, and Kutner 1985; Zar 1984). The second variable of concern here measures assemblage diversity in continuous fashion. A number of diversity indices are available, primarily generated by quantitative work in two areas: plant ecology (e.g., Pielou 1975) and information theory. Perhaps the best-known diversity measure is Shannon's H' statistic, also called the "Shannon-Weaver Index" (Shannon 1948). This measure characterizes the diversity of an assemblage (of plants, animals, artifacts, etc.) in reference to data expressed as frequency counts of cases classified according to nominal categories. It is precisely for this reason—utility in examining nominal data—that diversity measures of many kinds have seen wide usage in archaeology (e.g., Conkey 1980; Grayson 1984; Kintigh 1984). While it has been the most widely employed statistic, H' is rather dependent on the number of classes composing the classification scheme (Pielou 1975: 15). Because of this problem, Pielou (1975) argued that diversity, as conventionally conceived, comprises two separate components reflecting different dimensions of frequency data; she called these Taxonomic Richness and Evenness.

Simply expressed, assemblage richness can be measured by counting the number of classes (or species) in an assemblage. An assemblage that has many different kinds of artifacts or many different species would be labeled "diverse." Many treatments of the Middle-Upper Paleolithic transition seem to refer to this aspect of the concept (e.g., White 1982), so that Upper Paleolithic assemblages allegedly have more kinds of artifacts or animals present than do Middle Paleolithic ones. There are difficulties, however, with using richness as a measure of diversity. For example, an assemblage of five artifacts can have a maximum richness of five; is this assemblage less diverse given its sample size than an assemblage of 500 artifacts containing only six classes? Obviously, assemblage richness is meaningful only in relation to the size

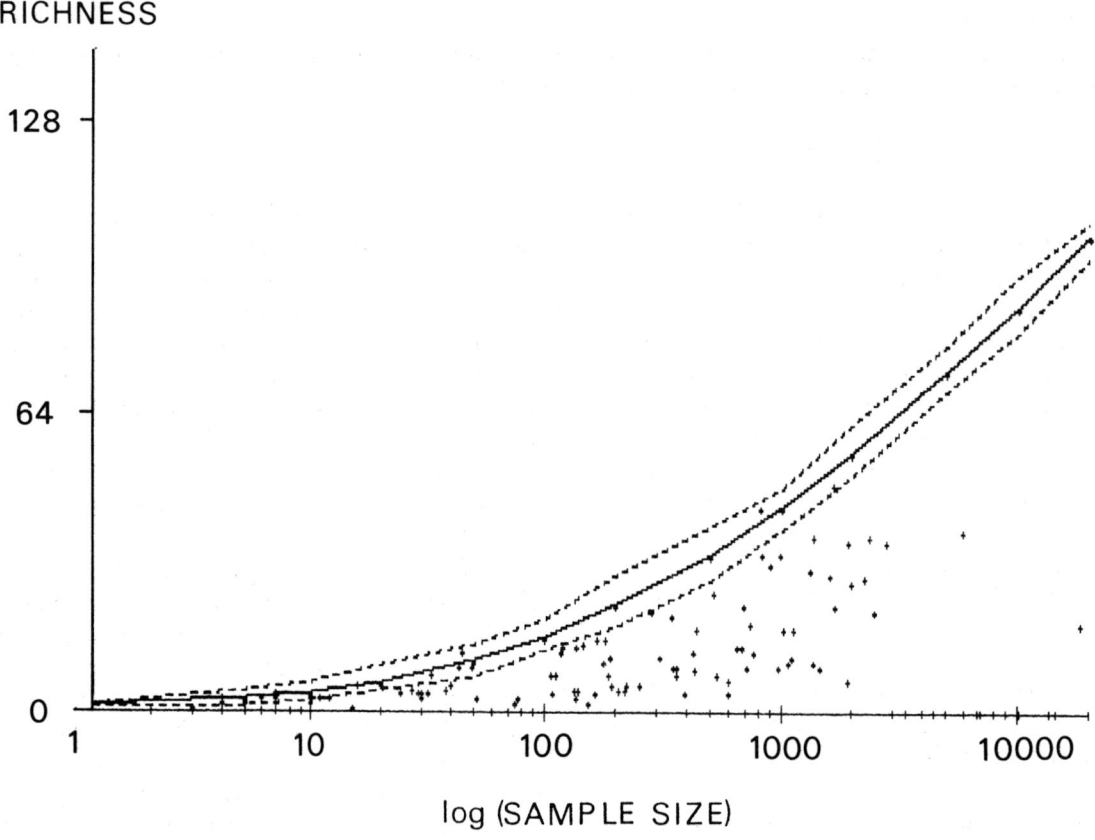

Figure 20.1 Simulated random relations between faunal-assemblage richness and sample size. Solid line shows simulated mean values at various sample sizes. Broken lines show 95% confidence interval around simulated mean values. Points indicate observed taxonomic richness values for Perigord Upper Paleolithic sites.

of the sample being considered. Grayson (1984) has discussed and illustrated these effects in detail and concludes that, to use richness as a useful measure of diversity, sample-dependent richness values must be rejected as random effects.

The second component of diversity identified by Pielou is evenness (J'), a measure of how nominal categories are filled by the assemblage sample. Independent of the number of classes composing the classification scheme, evenness represents the diversity of an assemblage standardized by the maximum possible diversity for a classification scheme. Thus, a high evenness value indicates a "diverse" assemblage. As with richness, there is reason to believe that sample effects may be important for evenness and should be assessed before individual assemblages are called diverse (Kintigh 1984).

Two approaches to assessing sample-size effects on diversity indices have been proposed by archaeologists in recent years. Grayson (1984) has advocated a regression-based technique, but this technique has proved useful only for frequency distributions analogous to allometric functions. A second approach, the one used here, was developed and proposed by Kintigh (1984). This technique employs Monte Carlo simulation methods to establish expected richness and evenness values for any sample size based on a theoretical or empirical model for randomness.

Figure 20.1 shows the results of simulation analysis for Upper Paleolithic faunal assemblage taxonomic richness. Nearly all of the Upper Paleolithic faunas considered have significantly fewer species than predicted by random sampling. In other words, richness values are not determined by sample-size variation. That all assemblages are less rich than expected is curious, implying that each faunal assemblage is a limited sample of a much more diverse regional fauna. Low taxonomic richness among Upper Paleolithic

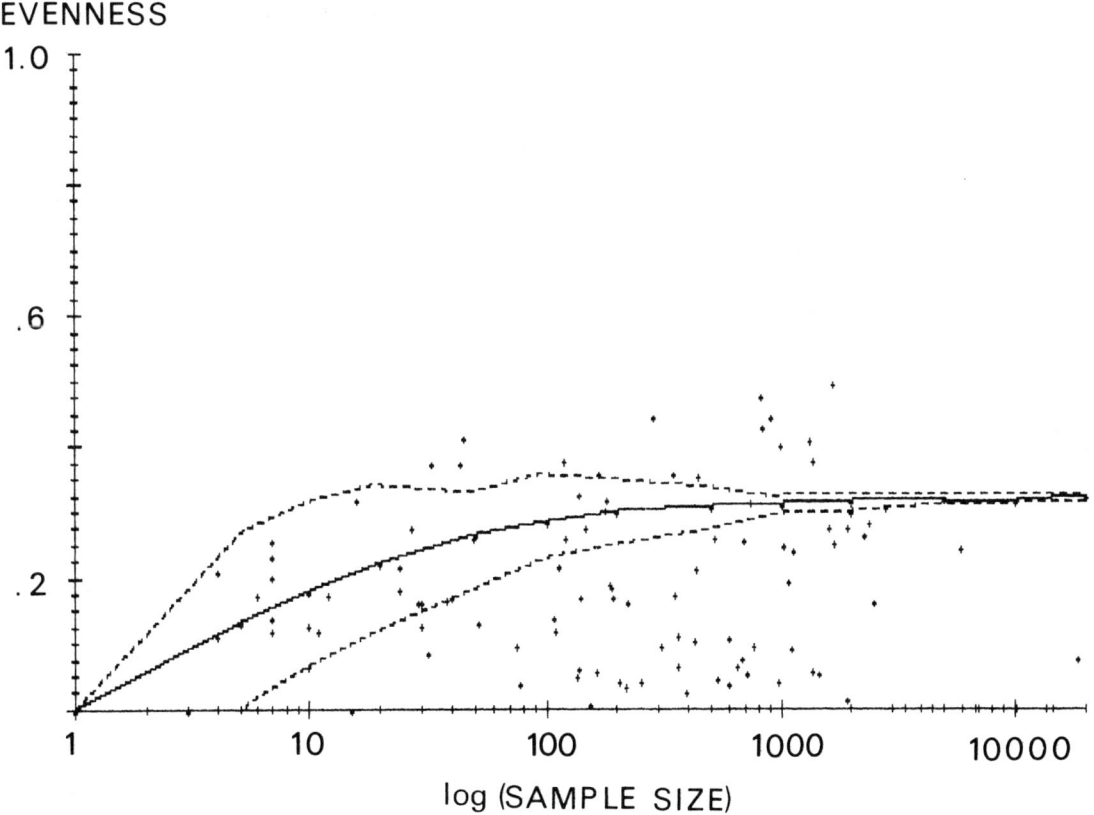

Figure 20.2 Simulated random relations between faunal-assemblage evenness and sample size. Solid line shows simulated mean values at various sample sizes. Broken lines show 95% confidence interval around simulated mean values. Points indicate observed distribution evenness values for Perigord Upper Paleolithic sites.

archaeofaunas certainly warrants examination, but because none of the assemblages are diverse on the basis of richness, sources of this variability will be discussed in another paper. For the remainder of this study, only assemblage evenness, which exhibits more variation, will be considered.

Figure 20.2 depicts the result of simulation analysis for assemblage evenness. Here the pattern is quite distinct from that encountered with richness. While many assemblages still show evenness values significantly smaller than the random model predicts, a reasonable number have random values and some are more even than expected. Here, there is variation to be explained—variability that may, of course, have been generated by numerous causes. While we are most interested in variability produced by changing patterns of resource use by humans over time, other potential causes must be considered.

CHANGE OVER TIME

Chronostratigraphic ordering and calculation of assemblage evenness yield two variables that will allow the process of change in faunal diversity to be assessed over time. The nature of these variables indicates regression as an appropriate means for examining variable relations. Because it is the effect of time on faunal diversity that is of interest here, sequence position was defined as the predicator (independent) variable and evenness as the response (dependent) variable, and the data were analyzed using the SAS General Linear Models procedure. The regression equation with the best fit for these data (Fig. 20.3) is a cubic (i.e., third-order) power function (Neter, Wassermann, and Kutner 1985). This regression model has the following form: *Evenness* = -8.13 + .49(Seq) -.01(Seq^2) + .0001(Seq^3). Associated significance tests show an F value of 25.03 ($p > .0001$) and an R-square value of .4467, indicating that nearly 45% of the variance in faunal evenness can be accounted for by chronological position of the

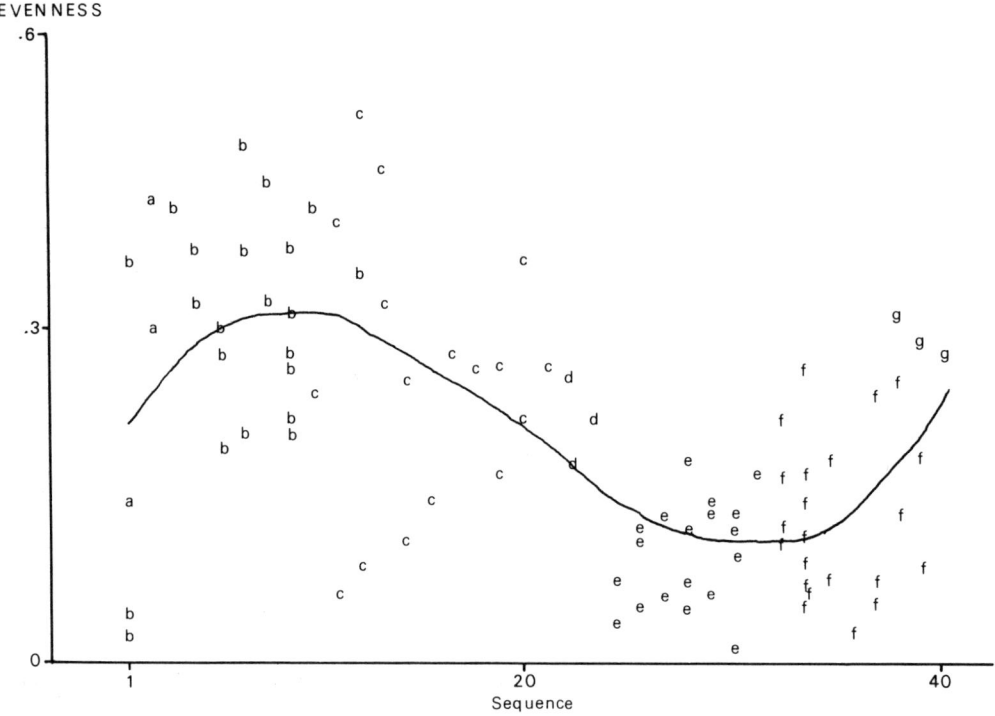

Figure 20.3 Cubic polynomial regression model for Upper Paleolithic faunal-assemblage diversity over time. Solid line shows model curve. Letters indicate observed assemblage values according to traditional cultural units: a = Chatelperronian, b = Aurignacian, c = Upper Perigordian, d = Protomagdalenian and Aurignacian V, e = Solutrean, f = Magdalenian, and g = Azilian. Model is significant ($p > .0001$).

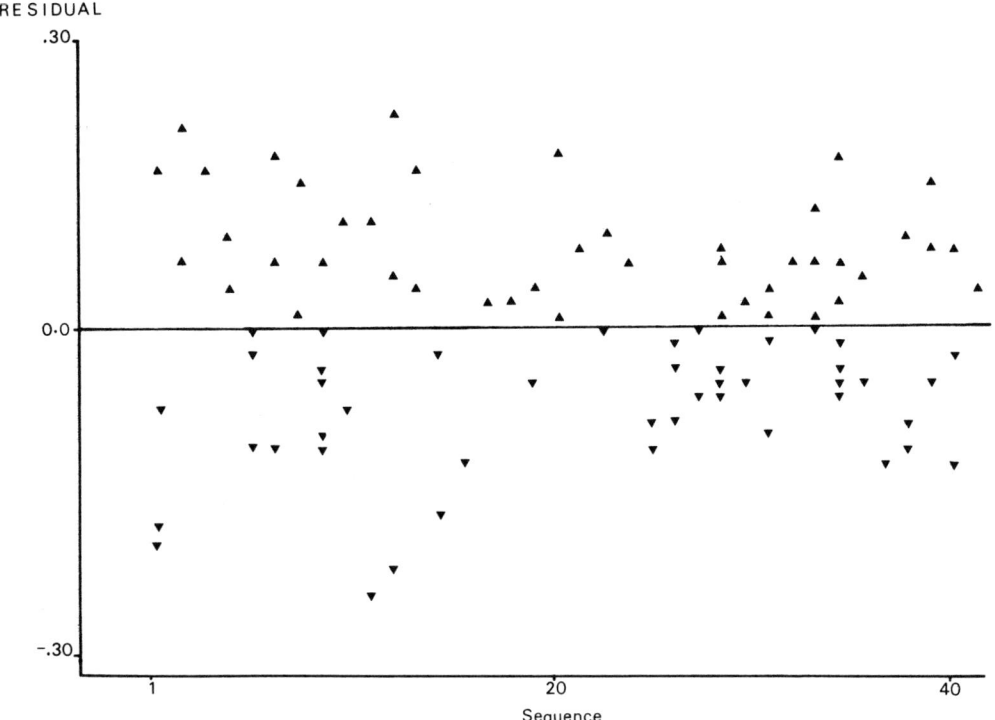

Figure 20.4   Residual plot for function shown in Figure 20.3. Note homoscedasticity of values over time.

assemblages. Regression residuals (Fig. 20.4) are evenly distributed and show homoscedasticity, supporting indications of an appropriate and successful use of regression.

This polynomial regression points to several important aspects of change in faunal diversity during the Upper Paleolithic in the Perigord. Change is evident within the time period, but its chronological position points to the Upper Perigordian as a pivotal time in the shift from diverse, generalized faunal assemblages to less diverse, specialized assemblages. If anything, assemblages from the earliest Upper Paleolithic (Chatelperronian and Early Aurignacian) are less diverse than those dating to the middle part of the Aurignacian sequence; maximum assemblage diversity occurs between the third and fourth phases of Laville's Recent Würm stage. Beginning with the Upper Perigordian, assemblage diversity begins a long decrease, spanning the 10,000 radiocarbon years from the end of the Upper Perigordian to the Early Magdalenian (Laville's Recent Würm phase 17). Solutrean sites in the Perigord, and especially Late and Final Solutrean, show the least diverse, most specialized assemblage profiles. The Magdalenian sees the beginning of another upward trend in faunal assemblage diversity, with an increase in evenness continuing into the Azilian.

Of course, the observed variability over time might be due to a number of factors. Regression analysis indicates that processual change in faunal diversity characterized the period from ca. 35,000 to ca. 10,000 B.P. in the Perigord region. What caused the change has not been identified. To address the causes of temporal change in diversity, a second set of analyses were performed. Because some categorical or factor variables are analyzed here, this second set of tests employs unbalanced analysis of variance in addition to linear regression.

CAUSES AND EFFECTS

Several potential sources of variability in archaeofaunas have been identified by archaeologists in both Europe and North America. These include environmental selective pressure for change and other, more recent sources of sample bias. In the case of Perigord faunas, one of the most important of the latter involves changing research goals over the past 200 years of work in the region (Rigaud and Simek 1987; Sackett 1981: 94; Straus 1977: 59).

TABLE 20.3

RESULTS OF ANALYSIS OF VARIANCE ASSESSING EFFECTS OF HISTORIC FACTORS ON FAUNAL ASSEMBLAGE EVENNESS FOR PERIGORD UPPER PALEOLITHIC SITES

Factor Variable	F	$p > F$	R-Square
Excavator	7.86	0.0001	0.42
Year	12.40	0.0001	0.56
Excavator/Year	9.98	0.0001	0.59

EXCAVATION HISTORY

To evaluate the effects of excavation history on assemblage evenness, we defined two categorical variables, one the site excavator and the other the year the excavation of an assemblage began. In both cases, unbalanced ANOVA was performed using SAS General Linear Models procedure to test the effects of these factors on faunal diversity. These designs were mandated by the unequal sample sizes within different categories for all factors.

Analyses of the two historical factors show significant effects on faunal evenness, suggesting that there may be several opposing sources of variability in the Perigord sample (Table 20.3). The amount of variation in evenness attributable to the chronological process defined by regression and the variance that must be attributed to changing recovery techniques can also be determined through analysis of variance. To accomplish this test, a chronological factor variable, assemblage tradition, is introduced and the effects of excavator and year are determined after gross chronological variation is accounted for (Table 20.4). While 63% of the variance in evenness can be attributed to time and the archaeologist, 75% of that variance is chronological (Type I F = 16.64 for tradition and only 5.17 for excavator). A similar pattern obtains for year of excavation: of the 65% variance accounted for, nearly 77% is due to variance by archaeological tradition. Thus, while excavation strategy certainly affects assemblage diversity significantly, by far the most important cause of variability is change over time.

ENVIRONMENTAL EFFECTS

In addition to excavation history, another potentially important influence on changing faunal diversity is fluctuating climate such as characterized Late Pleistocene Europe. Comparison of the regression function derived here with the Grande Pile pollen profile (Woillard 1978; Woillard and Mook 1982) shows a remarkable coincidence between changing global climates and faunal diversity in the Perigord (Fig. 20.5). When radiocarbon dates are used to tie the faunas to the pollen profile, maximum assemblage diversity corresponds to the warm maximum of the Denekamp phase (ca. 29,000 B.P.). From the Denekamp maximum, the Grande Pile indicates a long

TABLE 20.4

RESULTS OF ANALYSIS OF VARIANCE ASSESSING THE EFFECTS OF HISTORIC FACTORS ON FAUNAL ASSEMBLAGE EVENNESS AFTER CHRONOLOGICAL EFFECTS ARE REMOVED

Factor Variable	SS	F	$p > F$	R-Square
Tradition/Excavator				
source	0.95	10.08	0.0001	0.63
tradition	0.68	16.64	0.0001	
excavator	0.27	5.17	0.0001	
Tradition/Year				
source	0.98	10.03	0.0001	0.65
tradition	0.67	17.25	0.0001	
year	0.31	5.21	0.0001	

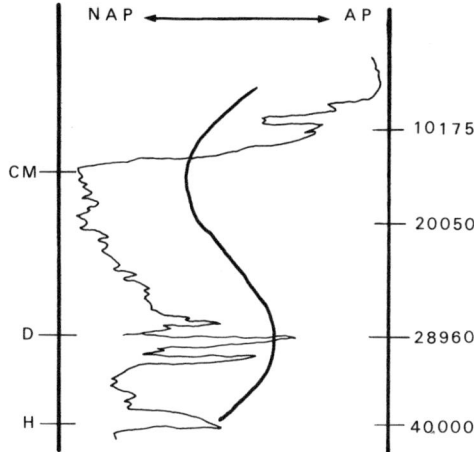

Figure 20.5 Regression line derived for Upper Paleolithic faunal diversity (heavy curve) plotted with Grande Pile pollen profile (light curve). Dates (right) are in C-14 years before present. Climatic phases (left) are: H = Hengelo, D = Denekamp, CM = Late Glacial Cold Maximum. Grande Pile profile after Woillard and Mook 1982.

deterioration in climate leading to the Last Glacial Maximum cold phase (ca. 17,000 B.P.). Faunal diversity in the Perigord records this deterioration with a coincident long decrease, and minimum assemblage evenness values (i.e., faunas dominated by one or few species) occur when the Grande Pile profile indicates coldest conditions.

Support for the interpretation of faunal diversity in terms of changing climates is provided by a second regression analysis of the Perigord faunas. Here, the effects of sequence position on small-animal species were assessed. Small animals (rodents, birds, bats, reptiles, and amphibians) may well have been introduced into the samples by nonhuman agents. Thus, if a pattern similar to that observed for all animals is detected here, changes were probably linked to causes other than human selection. Again, a cubic function proved the most effective model for evenness change: *Evenness* $= -12.44 + .73(Seq) - .01(Seq^2) + .0001(Seq^3)$. Figure 20.6 shows the regression plot for these data. Significance tests associated with this regression show an F value of 10.18 ($p > .0001$) and an R-square value of .2493. Homoscedasticity characterizes the residuals. Except for a greater increase in small-animal assemblage evenness at the end of the sequence, this pattern is identical to that defined for complete faunas.

These results strongly suggest that patterned change in Perigord faunal-assemblage diversity reflects climatically induced changes in the animal-resource mosaic. As Margalef (1968) has noted, warm forest biomes tend to be low-biomass, high-diversity environments with many species but low population numbers for each. Arctic biomes are the opposite, with low species diversity but high biomass. A random-encounter predation pattern in the first habitat would produce diverse faunal assemblages. The same strategy in the second habitat would produce low-diversity assemblages. In short, given changing Late Pleistocene climatic regimes, no change in subsistence strategy is required to account for changing faunal-assemblage diversity.

CONCLUDING REMARKS

In sum, analysis of faunal diversity from Upper Paleolithic sites in the Perigord has shown that strong, statistically significant patterns of change can be defined. Faunal assemblages from early Upper Paleolithic contexts are diverse, with maximum evenness values occurring at the Recent Würm Phase 3-4 chronostratigraphic boundary. Deteriorating conditions beginning at the end of the Denekamp warm oscillation saw the appearance of Upper Perigordian artifacts in the Perigord; slightly later, a long trend toward specialized, nondiverse faunal assemblages began. This trend culminated at the end of the Solutrean under maximum cold conditions. With the appearance of the Magdalenian, a reversed trend towards more generalized faunas began as the end of the Würm approached. This change pattern mirrors global climatic changes, as read from the Grande Pile pollen core, and this suggests that human subsistence choices might have been influenced to a great degree by the nature of the local biome. In fact, there is no need to posit change in human organizational structures (social, economic, or technical) to account for observed changes in faunal diversity.

In addition to implicating climatic change as a major cause of variation in evenness, we have also shown that assemblage diversity is determined in part by excavation history. We strongly suspect that history has affected differential recovery of animal species, probably favoring larger animals. Still, most of the evenness variation in the Perigord sample can

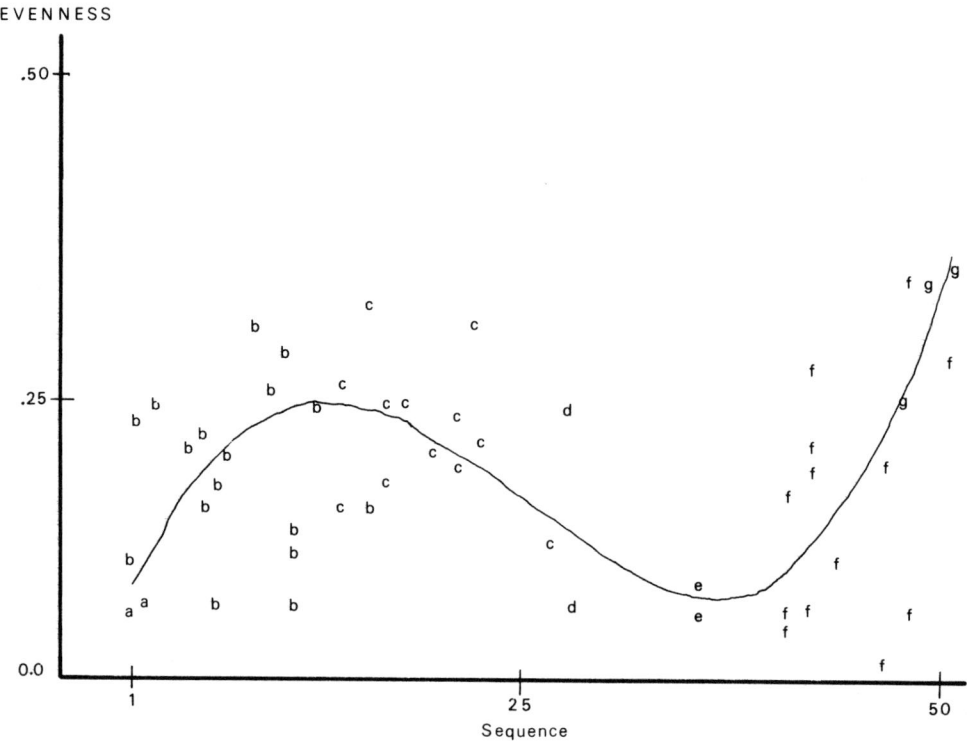

Figure 20.6 Cubic polynomial regression model for Upper Paleolithic small-animal assemblage diversity over time. Solid line shows model curve. Letters indicate observed assemblage values as in Figure 20.3. Model is significant ($p > .0001$).

be attributed to chronological processes directly related to global climate changes with secondary influences from excavation histories.

In the absence of compelling data indicating changing human procurement strategies, we prefer to ascribe the process defined by regression to environmental change and human sampling of the available resource mosaic. Moreover, these data indicate that adaptations to changing resource availability occurred entirely during the Upper Paleolithic. If what appeared to be a transition from generalized to specialized resource exploitation happened within the Upper Paleolithic, then vitalistic explanations invoking biological changes from Neandertals to modern humans are obviously precluded. By the Late Aurignacian, modern humans had occupied Western Europe and Neandertals were gone. Thus, change in faunal diversity involved only a single hominid form.

Evolutionary theory predicts that observed behavioral responses are the first applied by organisms under selective pressure, and biological change is induced only after behavioral changes fail to achieve fitness (Lewontin 1974). Thus, had specialized procurement failed to answer humanity's Late Pleistocene selective dilemmas (those reducing the fitness of earlier, less diversified subsistence strategies), then our results indicate that biological change should have been the next response, occurring after ca. 16,000 B.P. We have no evidence for biological change after this time. Both theoretically and empirically, then, specialized resource use had no developmental links to the origins of modern humans in Western Europe.

In conclusion, we believe that we have shown how an evolutionary approach, one that emphasizes fine-scale chronological control, yields far more precise, processual information than typological comparisons. In particular, recent assertions that the Middle Paleolithic differs significantly from the Upper Paleolithic in terms of resource utilization is a gross oversimplification of a complex process. This, in fact, was observed in Cantabria by both Freeman (1973) and Straus (1977). Indeed, exploitation strategies changed from general to specialized, but those changes occurred entirely within the Upper Paleolithic and were caused by changing Pleistocene climates. Thus, specialized predation patterns have little or nothing to do with biological changes from Neandertal to modern humans. We suspect that many of the other dimensions often used to differentiate Middle from Upper Paleolithic cultures (stone-tool assemblage diversity, art objects, etc.) may also exhibit complex developmental trajectories that may or may not be related to biological change. We do not mean to argue that no changes occurred between Middle and Upper Paleolithic; however, we believe that typological comparisons have made complex processes appear simple and have emphasized differences over process. An evolutionary approach to Paleolithic culture change requires a different outlook on method.

ACKNOWLEDGMENTS

The authors wish to thank F. Delpech and J.-P. Rigaud, who provided data for this study. Rigaud, M. Conkey, W. Farrand, D. Grayson, H. Laville, A. Marks, M. Otte, and F. Smith made useful comments on earlier drafts of the paper. Computing facilities were provided by the University of Tennessee and the UTK Department of Anthropology.

DISCUSSION

CHASE: I think that there is another trend in addition to the change through time. If you look at the variability in diversity between assemblages (see Fig. 20.3), in the early UP, when there is a central tendency toward moderate diversity, there is a range all the way from extreme diversity down to extreme specialization. In the Solutrean, everything is specialized. Later, there is again more variability in diversity. In other words, along with the temporal trend in the average diversity values, there is another trend of narrowing and broadening in the variability among assemblages. This indicates to me that there may be other factors operating here. It would be nice to know, on a site-by-site basis, whether it is the ungulates, for example, that make one assemblage look specialized, while another "generalized" assemblage has in addition substantial quantities of lagomorphs. Another thing that would be nice to know is the seasonality of these occupations: Are generalized occupations covering a larger range of seasons, for example? And finally, are we seeing differences in the range of economic activities being undertaken at these sites? In other words, are we sometimes looking just at exploitation sites—i.e., kill sites or procurement sites—and other times at consumption sites? Perhaps this could be examined by looking at the relative frequencies of various skeletal elements.

SIMEK: This is basically a question of homoscedasticity, that is, whether the variances are equal from one end of the line to the other. While there is some increased variability earlier on in the sequence, I think that it involves relatively few sites and that the overall pattern exhibits equal variance.

STRAUS: We confuse the terms specialized and diversified. I know that in northern Spain, one can have specialized sites that are part of a highly diversified system. So, when we use these terms their meaning depends on the level at which one is talking. Further, while I do agree that climate is not the sole determiner of faunal exploitation, we also should not go too far in one direction or the other about excluding environmental effects, since the fauna available for exploitation will depend on local environmental conditions.

SACKETT: Why do you imply that a cold period is a time of crisis and stress? I would think that it would promote big, gregarious herbivores.

SIMEK: I would argue that it is not so much the cold itself that causes stress, but rather the change. The two inflections in this curve correspond to a deterioration of the climate. It seems that the behavioral changes are occurring in response to some environmental stress.

FARRAND: I have reservations about climatic interpretations based on sediments. Based on the sedimentology, Laville's phases 5 and 7 are the warmest during the late Upper Pleistocene. When we correlate this with the Grande Pile record, there are three peaks exactly at phases 5 and 7, which is the time of the middle inflection point of your curve. Thus, there is a big, or even the biggest, climatic change right at this time.

LAVILLE: I would predict that the same results would be found for the Early Würm assemblages.

There are clear associations between climate and faunal assemblages in that faunal assemblages are more varied during periods of temperate climate. What is presented here follows the long-term general trends I have identified for the Recent Würm, with faunal assemblages being more impoverished during the pleniglacial.

KOZLOWSKI: In the Middle Paleolithic too there are sites that are not very diversified and others that are very generalized. I think that in this case there is a relation between the geographic position of sites and the diversity of the remains. In fact, in Eastern Europe faunal assemblages are more specialized than in the west because of climatic circumstances. In the early Upper Paleolithic of Central Europe, the faunal material is also very diversified, with high numbers of species. In the Late Paleolithic, there is a more specialized mode of hunting. But in the middle part of the Upper Paleolithic, the geographic factor is important. In the northernmost part of Europe, for example, the faunal assemblage consists of 99% mammoth. So, we must always consider both time and space factors. In order to see geographic and climatic effects on faunal assemblages most clearly, we should pay more attention to natural accumulations of bones in paleontological sites.

MÜLLER-BECK: Even in the archaeological sites, not all of the species reported are definitely hunted. This is especially true for the smaller animals.

BOSINSKI: Major changes in faunal exploitation noted in the middle part of the Upper Paleolithic correspond to other changes as well, at least in Central and Eastern Europe. There are arguments that this was the time when the spear thrower was invented as a new weapon and it coincides with the occurrence of Venus figurines. This is the time also that the social system changed, with big houses where large groups lived under one roof.

SIMEK: There are also indications from the Perigord region that there was a shift, from the Aurignacian to the Upper Perigordian, in the utilization of local versus exotic raw materials.

COMMENTS

OTTE: La valeur du gradient observé au cours du Paléolithique supérieur (évoluant vers une faune plus spécialisée) devrait être confirmée par l'introduction d'un paramètre supplémentaire. En effet, avec l'évolution des cultures du Paléolithique, on observe une extension des aires occupées et une spécialisation de chaque installation située à leurs confins. De telle sorte qu'une apparente "spécialisation" de la faune pourrait n'être due qu'à un éclatement plus marqué des activités dans des sites désormais séparés mais, si l'on en fait le total, la gamme de la faune prélevée est tout aussi large. Il s'agirait donc d'introduire un paramètre correspondant à l'extension du territoire occupé (définie par exemple à partir de l'étude des matériaux lithiques exploités) afin de vérifier si la diversité introduite avec le temps correspond à une spécialisation localisée ou a une spécialisation générale, propre à un groupe culturel. L'échelle de la région (ici le Périgord) devrait donc varier selon la période considérée. Ce fait est particulièrement net lorsque l'on considère la fin du processus et que, avec l'Azilien, on observe de nouveau une gamme de faune apparemment moins "spécialisée". Ne s'agit-il pas là du simple reflet de la contraction du territoire occupé durant l'Alleröd par le même groupe et, par conséquent, le téléscopage d'activités jadis séparées dans l'espace?

Si ce phénomène de transformation du comportement vis-à-vis de la faune semble se dérouler *durant* le Paléolithique supérieur, de quelle manière s'est manifesté le passage précédent: du Paléolithique moyen au supérieur? La recherche fut-elle appliquée à cette transition et quels en furent les résultats?

XXI
Technological Change in the Upper Paleolithic of the Negev

C. Reid Ferring

INTRODUCTION

This paper focuses on technological variability among Upper Paleolithic assemblages from the Negev. In particular, I will discuss methods that explicate blade reduction strategies via analysis of metric and nonmetric attributes in lieu of *a priori* categories of debitage. Application of these methods to post-transitional Upper Paleolithic assemblages from the Negev (Ferring 1980) is discussed in terms of technological variability and change.

The assemblages discussed here are from sites in the central Negev Desert of Israel (Fig. 21.1). These were discovered and studied as part of the Central Negev Project (see Marks 1983b). In this area, Upper Paleolithic sites were concentrated around major perennial springs in the Nahal Zin drainage basin (Marks and Ferring 1976); a few Upper Paleolithic sites were discovered farther to the west, near the Sinai border (Larson and Marks 1977). In situ sites were located in

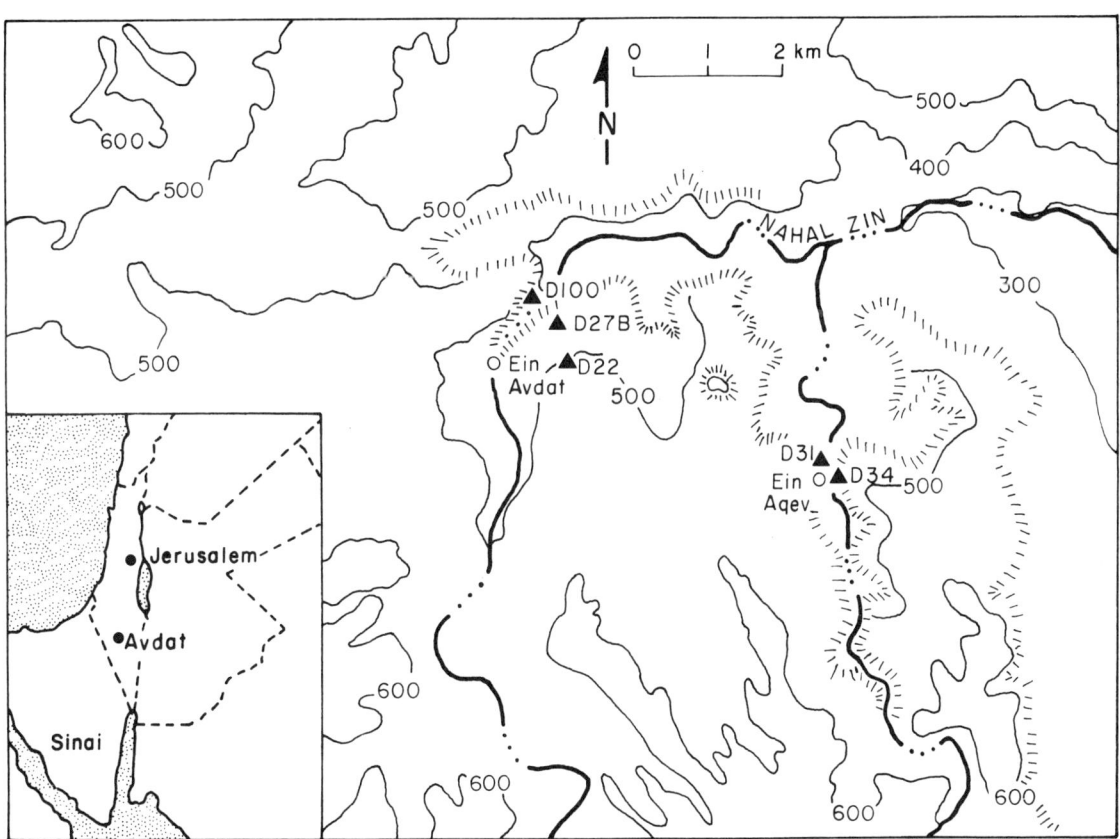

Figure 21.1 Map of the Avdat area, central Negev, Israel, showing locations of Upper Paleolithic sites. Contour intervals are meters MSL.

alluvium or colluvium along Nahal Zin and Nahal Aqev. Surficial sites occurred on the plateaus overlooking these drainages, often near sources of flint. Today, the central Negev receives an average of 75 mm of rain annually. During the Upper Paleolithic, this area was inhabited by mobile groups, probably during periods of relative moisture. Given the duration of the Upper Paleolithic in this region, the number of sites is extremely small, and at no time were occupations intensive.

Each of the assemblages considered below has been described in monographs and articles generated in the course of the Central Negev Project. The discussions and most of the data presented here are derived from a subsequent study that focused on the technology of blade manufacture in the Upper Paleolithic and Epipaleolithic (Ferring 1980). The objective of that study was to evaluate in more detail the nature of changes in blade-production technologies between ca. 37,000 and 10,000 B.P. Here, only the Upper Paleolithic data are considered. Following discussion of the methods employed, a summary of the results is presented.

LITHIC REDUCTION STRATEGIES

Lithic reduction strategies are assemblage-specific patterns of core reduction (Sheets 1975; Bradley 1975). Two major categories of reduction strategies are: 1) debitage-production strategies, having retouched tool blanks or Levallois tools as specific products; and 2) biface-core strategies, having bifaces or core tools as specific products (Ferring 1980). This paper is concerned with debitage-production strategies, and in particular, blade reduction strategies.

All lithic reduction strategies have certain components in common. Included are selection of core blanks, decortication and preforming of cores, core-shape maintenance, and, most importantly, production of specific tools and/or tool blanks. To study a lithic reduction strategy, it is advantageous to describe each of these components via artifact analysis; subsequently, these analyses serve as a basis for assemblage comparisons.

TOOL BLANKS: SPECIFIC AND EXPEDIENT

Perhaps the most problematic aspect of reduction strategy analysis is tool-blank manufacture. The problem comes down to whether blanks for retouched tools were produced as a focus of the core-reduction process, or whether debitage was generated in quantity and then certain pieces were selected and used as tool blanks because they exhibited suitable morphology. In the Upper Paleolithic assemblages from the Negev, at least, both modes of blank generation are evident: certain tool types (particularly armature) are made on interior blades with very specific morphology, while other tool classes (e.g., retouched pieces and denticulates) are made on blanks that vary markedly in form. More importantly, the specific tool blanks rarely exhibit attributes indicative of core preparation, core maintenance, or errors. In other words, as a first level of analysis, one can segregate the debitage into two categories: those with attributes indicative of core preparation, maintenance, or errors; and those without such attributes. I consider the latter the specific "interior products" of the given reduction strategy.

KINDS OF REDUCTION STRATEGIES

There is abundant evidence supporting the conclusion that Paleolithic flintknappers expanded their repertoire of reduction strategies to meet varying tool-blank production needs. Certain Upper Paleolithic industries from Europe, for example, exhibit both blade and biface reduction strategies in the same assemblages; these situations signify different reduction strategies employed for producing different tools and tool blanks. In other cases (examples from the Negev are discussed below), a single reduction strategy clearly sufficed to generate all of the necessary tool blanks in the assemblage.

The number and relationships of reduction strategies represented in an assemblage reflect the different tool-blank requirements of the flintknappers. A single reduction strategy has only one specific interior product—for example, blade blanks for El Wad points. Other tool blanks in such an assemblage would be selected from the cortical debitage, core-maintenance debitage, etc.

A serial reduction strategy entails production of multiple interior products, but from the same core. This situation has been well demonstrated by core reconstructions at Boker Tachtit (Volkman 1983), which showed shifts from Levallois point production to blade-blank production in the course of reducing a single core. For assemblages that have not been refitted, serial reduction strategies could be very difficult to detect, particularly if samples of one of the specific products are small.

Multiple reduction strategies entail separate core-reduction sequences for each specific product (Ferring 1977, 1980). I would not consider minor accommodations for raw-material size/shape (Volkman 1983) as evidence for multiple reduction strategies. The criterion is multiple interior products, generated through separate reduction sequences.

METHODS OF TECHNOLOGICAL ANALYSIS

Virtually all of the assemblages from the Negev had been described previously (see Marks 1976b, 1977, 1983b). The methods used to further study technological variation were modified and expanded from those used in the Central Negev Project. While reconstruction of the reduction strategies for each assemblage was an immediate goal, it became clear that fuller understanding of basic attribute relationships was needed. Thus, the restudy of these assemblages focused on patterns of metric variability among the debitage based on nonmetric technological attributes (Ferring 1980).

Independent variables for the analyses included dorsal cortex percent, dorsal scar patterns, terminations, platform preparation, and lipping. The dependent variables were debitage size ([length × width × thickness]/1000) and shape (length/width ratio). One-way ANOVA and t-tests were used to evaluate the size/shape variation given the independent variable states. Since blade technologies were being investigated, debitage elongation, or the tendency for "blade-like" shapes, was a principal criterion for evaluating the relation of specific attribute states with blade-removal components of the reduction strategy. In all of the analyses debitage size and shape were treated as continuous variables. No *a priori* "types" of debitage were employed. The sequence of technological-metric analyses was determined by the components of reduction strategies: decortication, preforming, core maintenance, errors, and internal core reduction.

In the following discussions, data from the Negev Upper Paleolithic assemblages are used to illustrate the results of specific parts of the analysis (Ferring 1980). In the last part of the paper, the overall results of the study are summarized.

DECORTICATION AND PREFORMING

Rather than use the usual definition of primary elements (pieces having more than 50% dorsal cortex), cortex presence was used as an ordinal variable, ranging from 1-20% to 81-100%. Both the metric and nonmetric attribute associations with the ordinal classes of cortex were revealing in terms of assemblage-specific patterns of decortication. For example, the sample from Sde Divshon (D27B) shows that scar pattern and platform preparation were more complex on pieces having intermediate amounts of dorsal cortex (Table 21.1). Debitage having between 1 and 50% cortex is clearly different from the interior debitage, which is dominated by unidirectional scar patterns and unfaceted platforms.

Metric analyses showed that debitage size decreased with lesser amounts of cortex, and that debitage length/width ratios increased inversely with dorsal cortex. In almost every case, t-test comparisons of debitage size and shape showed significant differences between the interior debitage and any of the cortical debitage classes. Clearly the *a priori* classification of debitage with less than 50% cortex as "blades" or "flakes" results in grouping debitage associated with significantly different aspects of core reduction. As a result, I placed all cortical debitage in the decortication-preforming category, and focused subsequent analyses on the interior debitage. By using cortical groups as a basis for description and comparison, however, I was able to observe different patterns of core preparation and maintenance among the study samples.

ERRORS

Debitage with hinged or overpassed terminations occurred with an average frequency of about 12% in the study samples (Table 21.2). Since these pieces terminated abnormally, their size and shape contribution to the debitage sample variation should obviously be controlled for. This was accomplished by placing all these pieces in an "error" group.

CORE MAINTENANCE

Interior *lame à crête* and interior core tablets were placed in the maintenance category automatically.

TABLE 21.1

ATTRIBUTE FREQUENCIES FOR CORTICAL DEBITAGE FROM SITE D27B

Percentage of Dorsal Cortex Attributes	100-81	80-61	60-41	40-21	20-1	none	n
n	17	30	44	81	50	171	
Cortex Location							
lateral	23.5	33.3	40.9	58.0	36.0	—	97
lat.-dist.	5.9	20.0	22.7	9.9	—	—	25
distal	—	20.0	22.7	23.5	46.0	—	58
peripheral	—	10.0	4.5	3.7	—	—	8
proximal	—	6.7	6.8	4.9	10.0	—	14
central	70.6	10.0	2.3	—	8.0	—	20
Scar Pattern							
cortex	64.7	—	—	—	—	—	11
unidirectional	5.9	73.3	61.0	35.8	42.0	66.7	208
bidirectional	—	6.7	14.6	17.3	28.0	13.3	58
transverse	17.6	6.7	4.9	7.4	8.0	2.4	21
opposed	5.9	6.7	14.6	16.0	16.0	9.7	46
lame à crête	5.9	6.7	4.9	23.5	6.0	7.9	40
Platform							
crushed	11.1	10.0	9.8	6.9	7.3	7.9	35
unfaceted	55.6	63.3	54.9	58.4	60.0	78.1	288
faceted	5.6	10.0	23.5	30.6	23.6	11.2	80
cortex	27.8	16.7	11.8	4.0	9.1	2.8	31
Percent Lipped	12.5	59.3	56.5	40.4	54.9	65.9	218

TABLE 21.2

REDUCTION-COMPONENT FREQUENCIES AND TOOL-BLANK USE FOR NEGEV UPPER PALEOLITHIC ASSEMBLAGES

Reduction Component	Sites						
	100A	27B	100BE4	100BE3	D22	D31	D34
decort.-preforming	55.4	58.9	54.6	45.7	69.2	53.5	60.2
interior maintenance	12.5	15.7	15.8	19.8	12.4	22.6	12.5
interior errors	12.5	12.5	12.3	14.9	10.6	8.8	13.1
interior products	19.3	12.9	17.2	19.4	7.6	15.1	13.9
n	487	433	430	448	433	441	503
Percent Blank Use*							
blade	12.5	15.1	5.4	8.7	8.7	14.6	10.4
bladelet	-	-	-	-	-	11.1	15.3
flake	5.7	6.6	3.0	6.2	11.8	11.9	3.9
primary element	4.4	5.9	3.6	7.3	7.6	13.7	4.8

* Blank-use data from: Ferring 1976, 1977; Jones, Marks and Kaufman 1983; Marks 1976a; Marks and Ferring 1976. Other data from Ferring 1980.

Since parallel *arêtes* on the core's working face are required for consistent blade production, it was predicted that debitage with nonparallel scar patterns was also associated with core maintenance (and/or late stages of preforming). Comparisons of interior debitage size and shape variation for parallel versus nonparallel scar patterns supported this prediction (Table 21.3). Bidirectional (unopposed) scar patterns were, with one exception (site D22), associated with debitage that was significantly larger and less elongated than unidirectional scar patterns.

Opposed-platform cores are relatively common in these assemblages, yet debitage with opposed scar patterns was consistently larger than pieces with unidirectional scar patterns (Table 21.3; Figs. 21.2, 21.3). In most cases opposed scar patterns were also associated with significantly less elongated debitage as well. These results suggest that opposed detachments were often part of core maintenance, not normal blade production. Using opposed platforms to recover from hinging is efficient for blade core reduction, since the maintenance scars are parallel with the core's working face. In certain of the study assemblages, interior debitage with opposed scar patterns was much larger than the other interior debitage (compare scar-pattern data in Figs. 21.2 and 21.3). The significance of these assemblages is discussed below.

INTERIOR-PRODUCT DEFINITION

Interior products of reduction were defined in two steps. The first was by exclusion of the interior debitage that had previously been assigned to core maintenance or errors. For the remaining debitage, attribute comparisons were made between metric attributes (size and length/width ratios) and platform modes. The different attribute modes were used as described below, to partition the interior debitage into subsamples for comparison of metric attributes. Attribute modes associated with elongated debitage

TABLE 21.3
T-PROBABILITIES FOR INTERIOR DEBITAGE SIZE AND SHAPE,
BY SCAR PATTERN AND PLATFORM TYPE

| | Scar Patterns | | | |
| | unidirectional-opposed | | unidirectional-bidirectional | |
Site	size	shape	size	shape
100A	.003	.000	.000	.043
D27B	.001	.651	.000	.000
100BE4	.005	.022	.001	.000
100BE3	.005	.099	.000	.006
D22	.007	.064	.863	.275
D31	.000	.001	.000	.001
D34	.000	.007	.005	.102

| | Platform Types | | | |
| | crushed-unfaceted | | crushed-unfac./faceted | |
Site	size	shape	size	shape
D100A	.065	.380	.002	.000
D27B	.895	.671	.190	.000
D100BE4	.323	.206	.003	.000
D100BE3	.656	.557	.009	.000
D22	.058	.624	.034	.001
D31	.000	.000	.000	.000
D34	.010	.008	.000	.000

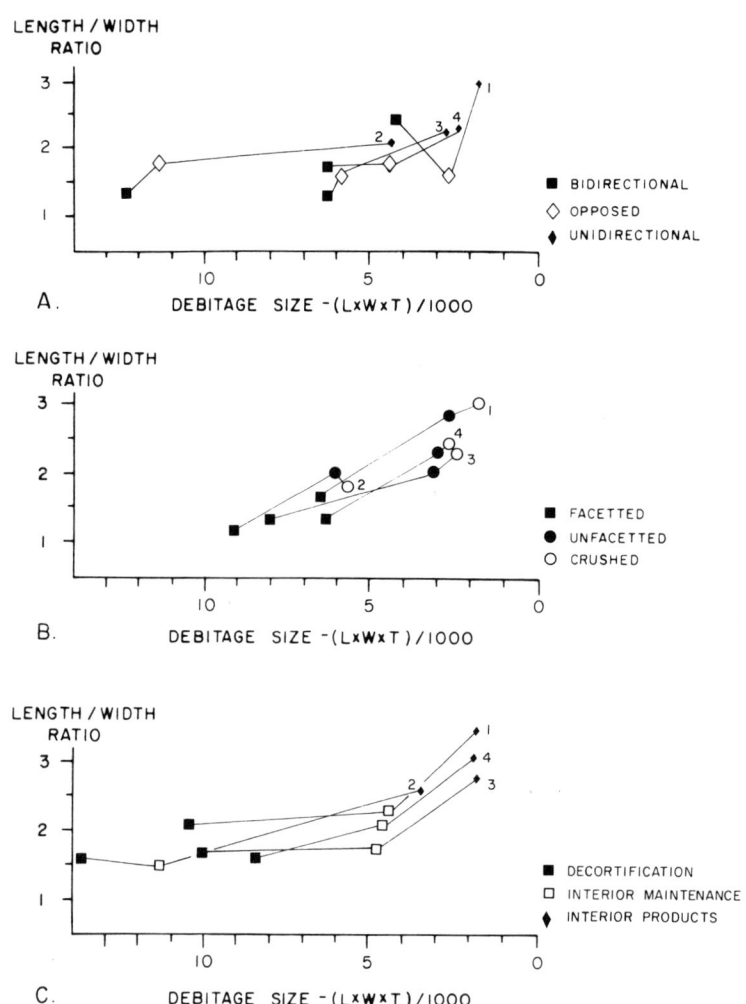

Figure 21.2 Metric variability for single-reduction-strategy Ahmarian assemblages. Shown are mean size and shape for: a) interior debitage by scar pattern; b) interior debitage by platform type; and c) reduction-strategy components. Sites are: 1) D100A; 2) D100BE Level 4; 3) D100BE Level 3; and 4) D27B.

(i.e., blades) were used to define the interior products. This was done separately for each assemblage, and different attribute relationships among the assemblages were clear.

Platform modes for interior debitage were also used to partition and compare size and shape variability. Since the frequency of unfaceted and crushed platforms was very high for interior debitage in all the assemblages, these platform modes were contrasted first. Five of the assemblages showed striking similarities in debitage size and shape when crushed and unfaceted platform groups were compared (Table 21.3). Two assemblages (D31 and D34) showed significant differences for the same comparison. In all the study samples, multifaceted and cortex platforms were associated with larger and usually less elongated debitage, again showing that these platform modes were related to different aspects of core reduction than the simple platform modes (unfaceted and crushed).

Platform lipping, characterized by a higher angle between the ventral surface of the debitage and the small ventral area between the platform and the bulb of percussion, is a manifestation of the core-platform

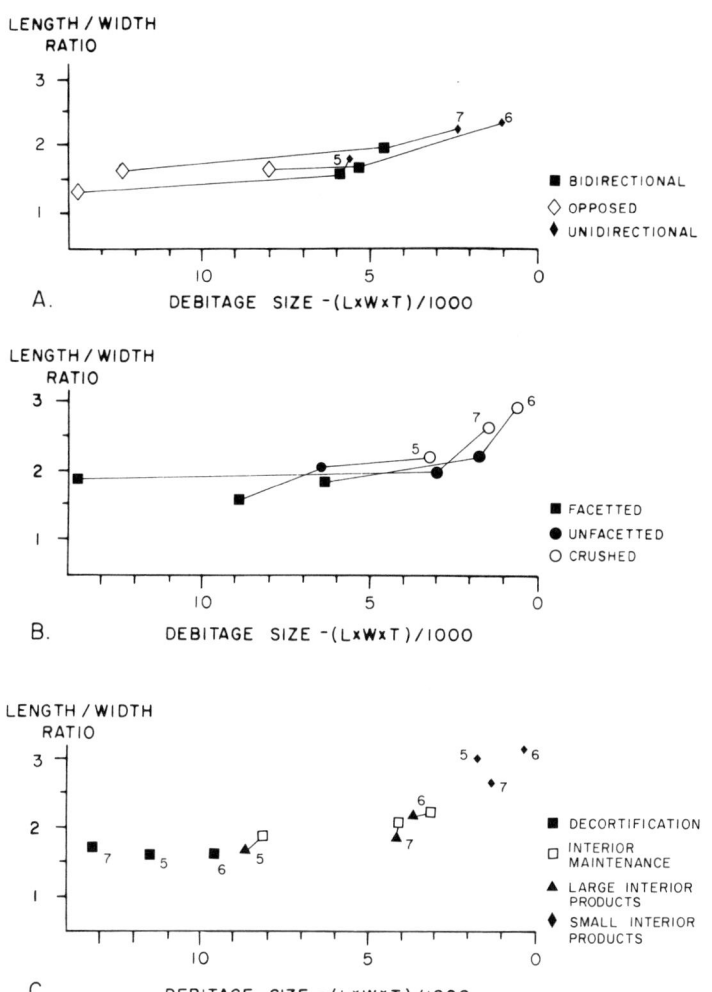

Figure 21.3 Metric variability for multiple-reduction-strategy Upper Paleolithic assemblages. Shown are mean size and shape for: a) interior debitage by scar pattern; b) interior debitage by platform type; and c) reduction-strategy components. Sites are: 5) D22; 6) D31; and 7) D34.

angle (see Ferring 1980). "Lipped" platforms are those associated with acute core-platform angles, unlipped are associated with higher angles. Lipping is mechanically controlled: it does not reflect mode of detachment, nor is it limited to pieces with unfaceted platforms. Its significance for blade-production technologies lies in the importance of acute core-platform angles (Figs. 21.4, 21.5); these require less force to initiate fracture (Faulkner 1972). Thus acute core-platform angles enable the flintknapper to detach blades more easily and presumably with fewer errors. Comparing lipped and unlipped platforms showed that lipped (and crushed) debitage was significantly smaller and more elongated than debitage with unlipped platforms.

SUMMARY

The technological analyses resulted in assemblage-specific classification of debitage into four groups (Table 21.2). For each of the assemblages, cortical and maintenance debitage is significantly larger and less elongated than the interior products (Figs. 21.2, 21.3). The latter are mainly small, very elongated blades—many if not most would be classified as bladelets; for some of the assemblages, multiple reduction strategies were recognized and will be discussed below.

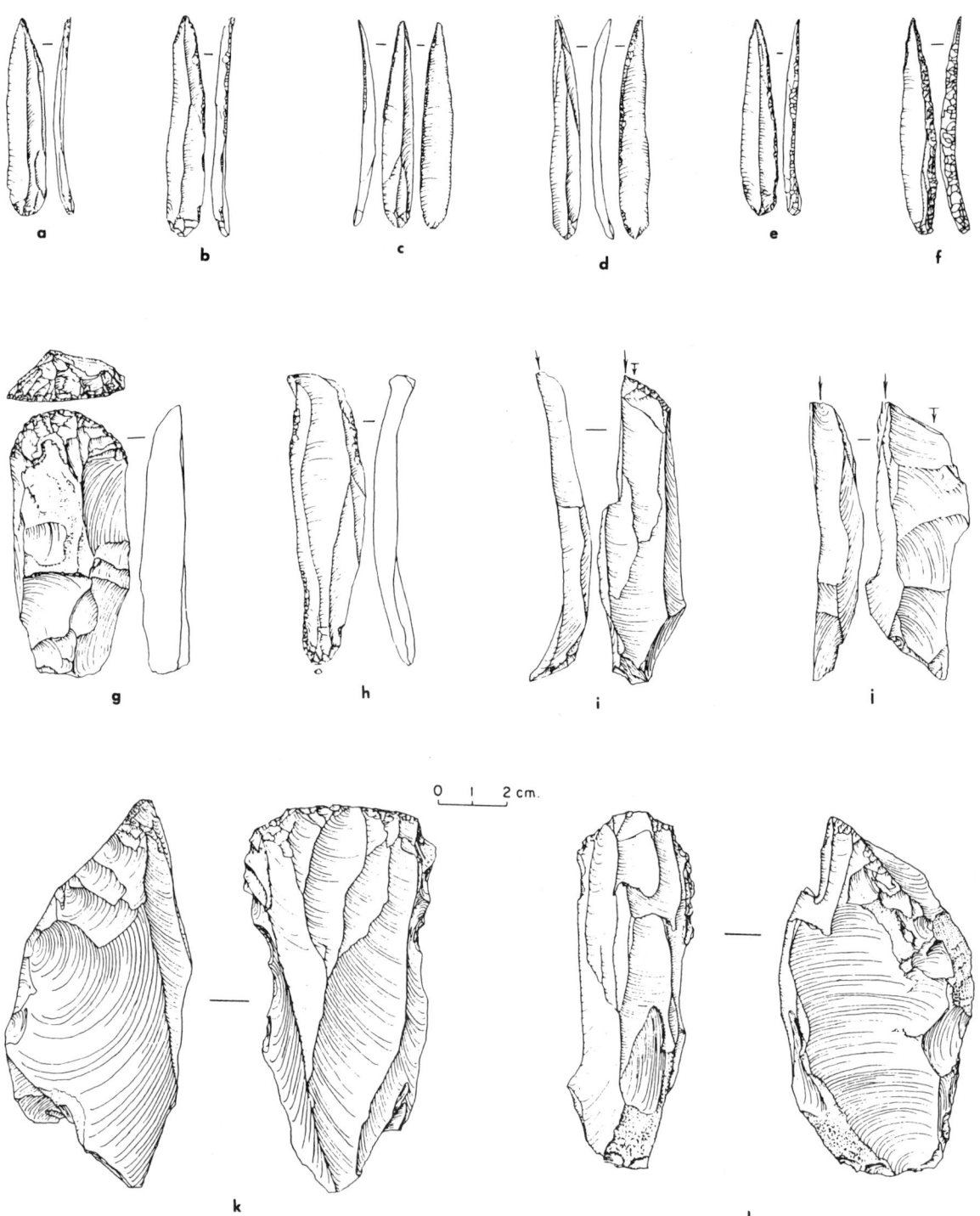

Figure 21.4 Lithic artifacts from D100A, an Early Ahmarian site in the central Negev: a-c) El Wad points; e-f) backed points; g) typical endscraper; h) retouched blade; i) burin on convex oblique truncation; j) burin on snap; k-l) single-platform blade cores. Note acute core-platform angles. (From Jones, Marks, and Kaufman 1983)

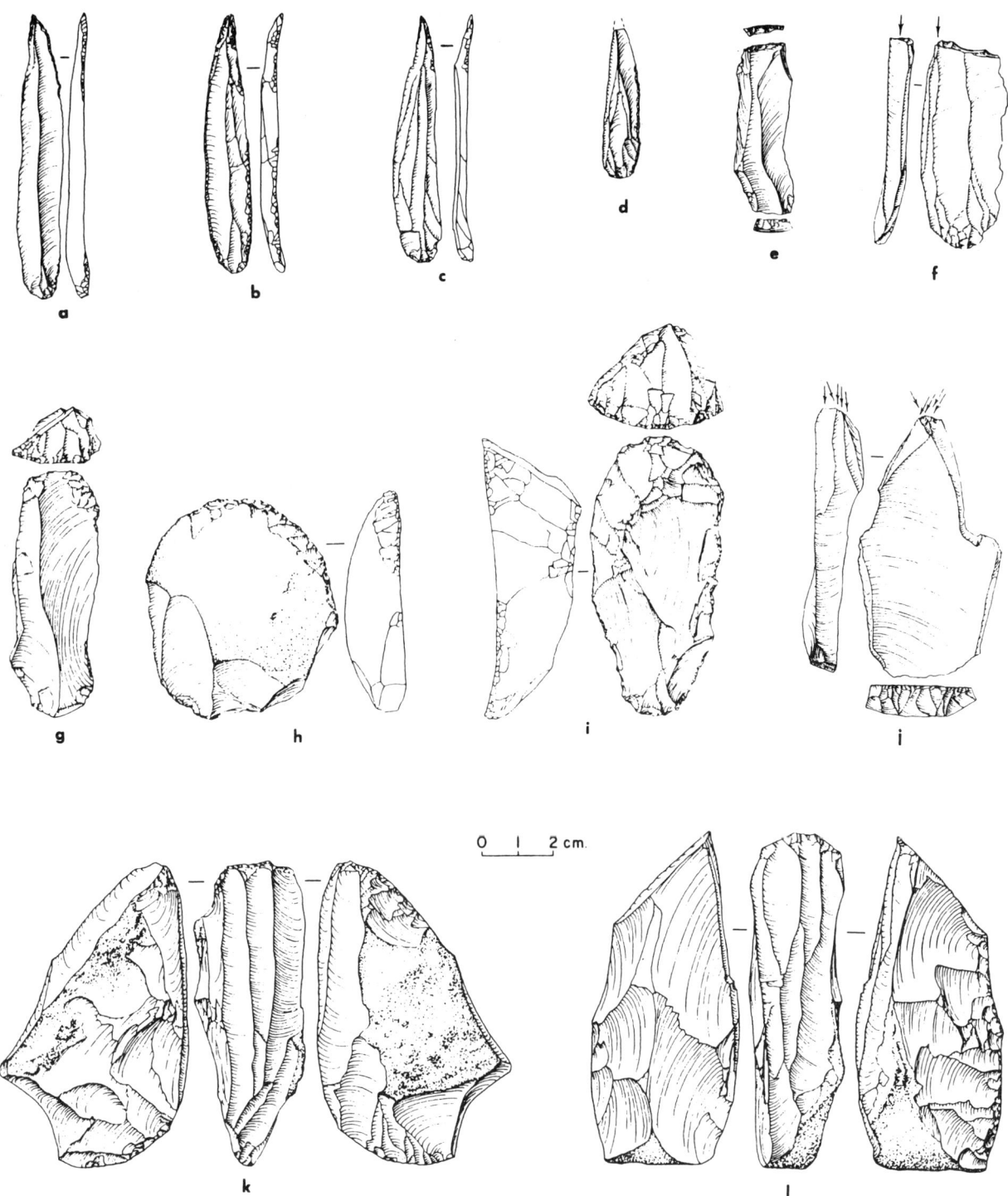

Figure 21.5 Lithic artifacts from Sde Divshon (D27B), an Early Ahmarian site in the central Negev: a-d) El Wad points; e) double truncated blade; f) burin on truncation; g-h) typical endscrapers; i) thick endscraper on lame à crête; j) dihedral burin on core tablet; k-l) blade cores. Note remnants of preforming on cores, especially "dorsal keel" on l. (From Ferring 1976)

TECHNOLOGICAL VARIABILITY IN THE UPPER PALEOLITHIC OF THE NEGEV

One striking aspect of the Upper Paleolithic sites in the Negev was the fact that no two sites were very similar in terms of tool typology (Marks and Ferring 1976; Marks 1981b). There were, however, technological similarities between a number of the assemblages, suggesting affinities at a coarser scale. Thus, continued analyses of these assemblages were pursued, in order to describe more fully this record of technological variability and change. Today, the patterns of technological variability and change can be discussed with benefit of continued research in the Negev and Sinai.

Two major groups of Upper Paleolithic blade-producing technologies were defined: those exhibiting single reduction strategies, and those with multiple reduction strategies. The former assemblages belong to what has since been named the Ahmarian tradition (Marks 1981b; Gilead 1981). Assemblages with multiple reduction strategies are younger, and belong to both the Ahmarian and Levantine Aurignacian traditions.

THE EARLY AHMARIAN TRADITION: SINGLE REDUCTION STRATEGIES

Following the Middle to Upper Paleolithic transition, blade technologies in the southern Levant shifted to soft-hammer, classic blade-bladelet manufacture. This technological focus was in place as early as ca. 37,000 B.P. in the Negev, and persisted until at least 26,500 B.P. in the Negev and Sinai (Marks 1983b; Bar-Yosef and Belfer 1977; Goring-Morris 1985). Four of the assemblages considered here belong to this group: Boker (D100) Area A; Boker BE Levels IV and III (Jones, Marks, and Kaufman 1983); and Sde Divshon (D27B) (Ferring 1976).

These Early Ahmarian assemblages exhibit minor variations in certain components of reduction—core-blank selection, decortication, and core maintenance. Overall, however, they share remarkably similar reduction strategies, focused on production of slender, elongated interior blades. Each of the assemblages is characterized by careful core preforming and shape maintenance. Core tablets were used quite extensively, and acute core-platform angles were characteristic (Figs. 21.4, 21.5).

The internal products of these assemblages are uniform: small, narrow blades that were undoubtedly produced for El Wad points and retouched blade-bladelet blanks. These tools all exhibit minor retouch; i.e., the debitage blank closely approximates the final morphology of the tool. In this sense, the Early Ahmarian technologies can be considered "specialized," in that blade blanks with specific morphology were the focus of the reduction strategies.

In Ahmarian assemblages from the Negev and Sinai, blade frequencies are highly correlated with point frequencies (Fig. 21.6). Tool-class frequencies vary markedly among these assemblages, reflecting intersite functional variability. The positive correlation between blade-production efficiency and point manufacture indicates that blank production was indeed focused to meet varying functional requirements. In other words, Ahmarian flintknappers did not simply make blades; they produced blades with specific shapes, and in numbers sufficient to meet their needs for manufacture of specific tools. In this case, then, frequencies of Ahmarian debitage "types" would be meaningless as indices of cultural affiliation.

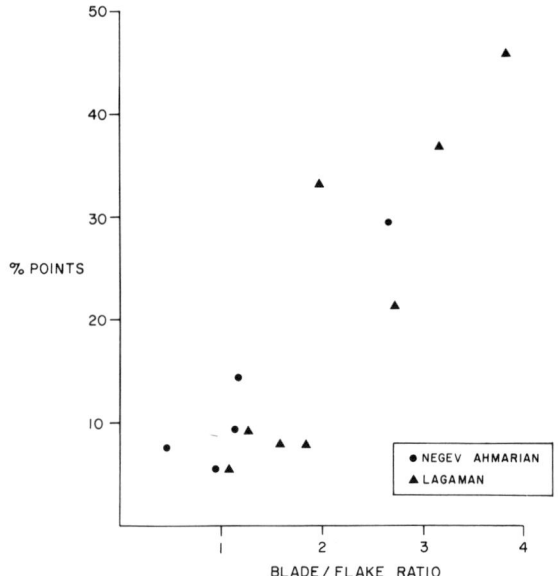

Figure 21.6 Plot of point frequencies and blade/flake ratios for Lagaman and Negev Ahmarian assemblages. Sites plotted here are Lagama V, VI, VII, VIII, XI, XII, XV, and XVI (data from Bar-Yosef and Belfer 1977); and D100A, D100BE (Levels 3, 4, and 6), and D27B (data from Jones, Marks, and Kaufman 1983; Ferring 1976).

Because of rather extensive Ahmarian core preforming and maintenance, numerous larger blades and flakes were generated as technological byproducts. These pieces were used (selected for) as blanks for large tools and are regarded as expedient tool blanks. Despite the numerical preponderance of debitage associated with decortication and core maintenance, the use of flakes and cortical pieces for tool blanks is almost always less than that of blades (Table 21.2). Different patterns are evident for multiple reduction strategies, as discussed below.

THE LATE AHMARIAN TRADITION: MULTIPLE REDUCTION STRATEGIES

The Late Ahmarian is poorly known at this time, yet its few manifestations are radically different from even the youngest Early Ahmarian assemblages. Both technological and typological changes are evident. The first Late Ahmarian site excavated in the southern Levant was Ein Aqev East (D34), located in the central Negev (Ferring 1977). Subsequently, a similar assemblage was recovered from the northern Sinai (Gilead 1977; Goring-Morris 1985). Although no radiometric dates are available, these sites probably date to ca. 20,000 B.P., based on stratigraphic evidence (Goldberg 1976).

Typologically, these assemblages are characterized by abundant microliths (Fig. 21.7). Most are Ouchtata bladelets or bladelets with fine, continuous retouch. Backed bladelets and points are rare. Large tools include endscrapers, burins, and truncated blades.

Late Ahmarian lithic technology is characterized by multiple reduction strategies (Ferring 1977, 1980). Large blades were produced through reduction of large blade cores, many of which employed opposed platforms. Large cores were also used to generate secondary core blanks (Bradley 1975; Ferring 1980). These thick blades and flakes served as blanks for most of the bladelet cores.

Production of bladelets was the focus of a separate reduction strategy. Bladelet cores are predominately simple, single-platform varieties (Fig. 21.7). Pyramidal bladelet cores, characteristic of Epipaleolithic technologies, are very rare. The bladelets in the Ein Aqev East assemblage are very small, flat or incurvate, and quite thin; they differ from most Epipaleolithic bladelets, which are thicker blanks for backed microliths.

The Late Ahmarian multiple reduction strategies reflect divergent tool-blank requirements that could not be met efficiently by single reduction strategies. While serial reduction strategies might have been employed (first generating large blades, then bladelets from the same core), the substantial size difference between the microliths and larger tools suggests that the distinction between blade and bladelet production was clear.

The Late Ahmarian assemblages signify a potentially important phase of technological and typological change, separating the Early Ahmarian from the Epipaleolithic. Of particular technological interest is the introduction of a well-defined bladelet technology, distinct from blade production. In the Early Ahmarian, bladelets (*sensu stricto*) overlap morphologically and metrically with blades, and both were generated as part of single reduction strategies. Late Ahmarian bladelet production was clearly associated with a new emphasis on true microlithic tools—a trend that continued, albeit with further technological change, in the Epipaleolithic. Gilead (1986) has criticized the use of the term "Epipaleolithic" in Levantine prehistory. One of his arguments for this position is that "bladelets" occur in Upper Paleolithic assemblages, even quite early ones. While this statement is true, it is only true when *a priori* metric definitions for debitage types are employed, and when the full technological context of these artifacts is ignored. "Bladelet" production in the Early Ahmarian, Late Ahmarian, and Epipaleolithic was accomplished by radically different, changing reduction strategies. To isolate by prior definition this artifact "type," and through its temporal distribution infer technological-cultural affinities, slights the behavioral significance of lithic reduction, and the significance of homologous versus analogous artifact form.

THE LEVANTINE AURIGNACIAN TRADITION

The Levantine Aurignacian is technologically and typologically distinct from the Ahmarian (Marks 1981b; Gilead 1981). While a number of assemblages were recovered from the central Negev, most were from surface sites and their temporal range is poorly known. At Boker BE a small, probably Levantine Aurignacian assemblage was stratigraphically superimposed over Ahmarian assemblages, and was dated to ca. 25,500 B.P. (Jones, Marks, and Kaufman 1983). The only other radiometrically dated Levantine Aurignacian site in the Negev is Ein Aqev (D31), which was occupied ca. 17,500 B.P. (Marks 1976a).

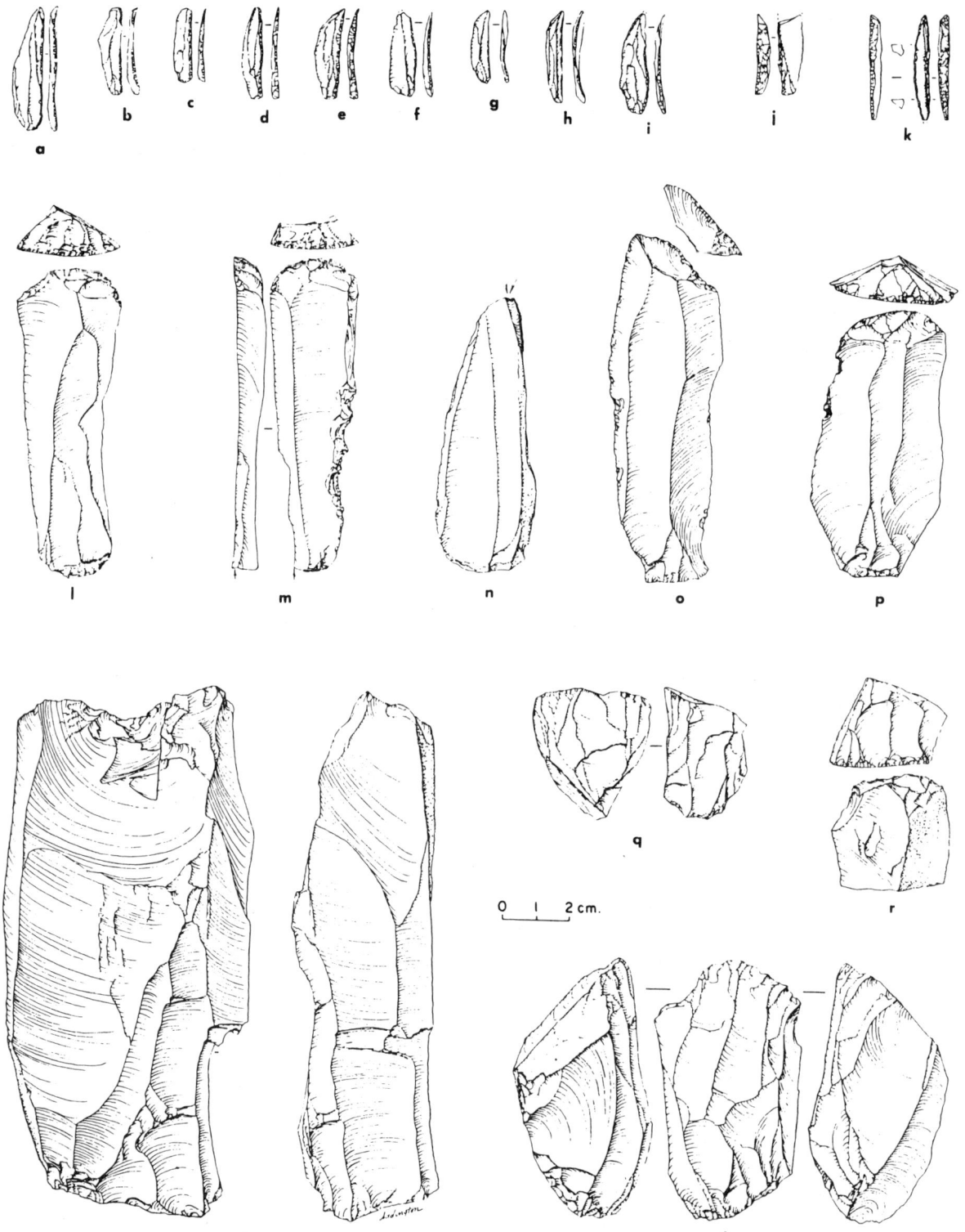

Figure 21.7 Lithic artifacts from Ein Aqev East, a Late Ahmarian site in the central Negev: a,b,f-i) Ouchtata bladelets; u) backed bladelet fragment; k) microgravette; l,p) typical endscrapers; m) composite tool; n) dihedral burin; o) obliquely truncated blade; q,r,t) bladelet cores; s) opposed-platform blade core. (From Ferring 1977)

Two Levantine Aurignacian assemblages from the Negev, Ein Aqev and Arkov (D22), exhibited clear evidence of multiple reduction strategies. The small sample of interior debitage from Arkov, coupled with use of tabular flint at this site, made comparison of this assemblage with others difficult. Nonetheless, two reduction strategies—one for large blades, and the other for production of small, twisted bladelets—were evident.

The Late Levantine Aurignacian assemblage from Ein Aqev also exhibited multiple reduction strategies. Here large blades and flakes were detached from large blade and flake cores, many of which exhibited opposed platforms (Fig. 21.8). The large debitage from this reduction strategy was used for large tool blanks, and also as secondary blanks for small, carinated core-tools. These cores were used to produce small, twisted bladelets that served as blanks for the numerous *lamelles Dufour* in the tool assemblage. The apparently frequent use of flakes and primary elements as tool blanks here, and for D22, contrasts with the single-reduction-strategy assemblages (Table 21.2). Many of the tools made on these blanks are carinated "core-tools," which served as cores for bladelet tool-blank production, regardless of any other functions they may have had. At D34 these secondary cores were larger and did not pose the typological problems of the burin/scraper-type artifacts from Ein Aqev and D22.

While both the Late Ahmarian and the Late Levantine Aurignacian exhibit multiple reduction strategies, the assemblages of these two traditions are technologically distinct. As suggested earlier (Ferring 1980), the strategies for producing large blades are quite similar for the assemblages from Ein Aqev and Ein Aqev East. Bladelet-producing strategies, however, are very different. In their late stages, these traditions contributed to a phase of industrial and probably adaptive diversity that separates the early Upper Paleolithic from the Epipaleolithic.

DISCUSSION AND CONCLUSIONS

Upper Paleolithic assemblages from the Negev provide a record of technological variability and change that is significant with regard to both synchronic and diachronic variability among the Ahmarian and Levantine Aurignacian traditions. Indeed, it is at the technological level that these traditions appear most clearly (Ferring 1980; Marks 1981b). While typological differences between Ahmarian and Levantine Aurignacian assemblages may be sufficient to identify the tradition of an assemblage, technological differences are also sufficient. More importantly, assemblages within each tradition exhibit functional variability that is reflected in the proportions of tool types (Marks 1981b), and, as shown here, in the site-specific patterns of tool-blank production. In technological terms, these traditions are evident in how blades were produced, not in the frequency of any *a priori* class of debitage. Functional variability and differences in the proximity and form of raw materials should impose specific kinds of technological variability on assemblages within and between traditions. These factors argue strongly for analytical methods that explicate intra-assemblage variability as a prelude to assemblage comparisons.

The methods used here are obviously premised on attribute analyses of debitage assemblages. The most accurate means to define reduction strategies is core refitting (e.g., Volkman 1983). A number of factors will prohibit core refitting: high artifact densities, budgetary constraints, and even the archaeologist's lack of experience or of adeptness at this difficult task. It is important that those refitting studies provide feedback for those who continue to use assemblage-based methods of analysis; our interpretation of specific attributes, metric and nonmetric, can be greatly improved by reporting the refitting data in traditional format.

UPPER PALEOLITHIC TECHNOLOGICAL CHANGE

In the Negev, Early Ahmarian single reduction strategies appear to have prevailed for 12-15,000 years with little significant change. These reduction strategies focused on production of small interior blades that served as blanks for armature and a few other tool classes. Because of careful core preparation and maintenance, larger blanks for other tools were generated as technological byproducts; serial reduction strategies may have been practiced, but core refitting would be necessary to confirm this.

Following the period of Early Ahmarian prevalence in the Negev, Levantine Aurignacian technologies appear, possibly as early as 30,000 B.P., and

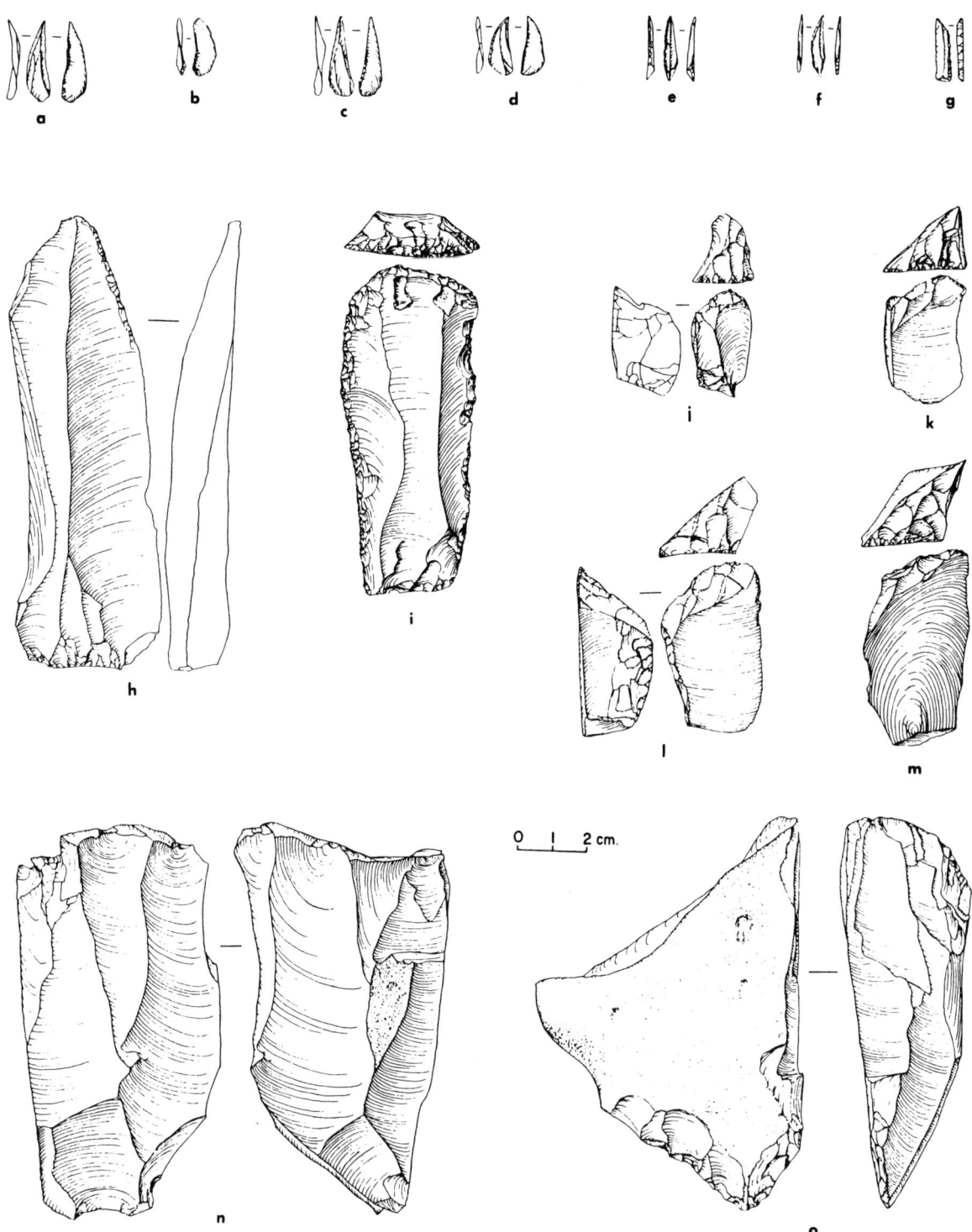

Figure 21.8 Lithic artifacts from Ein Aqev, a Late Levantine Aurignacian site in the central Negev: *a-d*) lamelles Dufour; *e*) retouched bladelet; *f*) microgravette; *g*) backed and truncated bladelet; *h*) retouched blade; *i*) endscraper on retouched blade; *j-m*) carinated core-tools; *n*) opposed-platform blade core; *o*) single-platform blade core. (From Marks 1976a)

persist alongside Ahmarian ones. Characterized by multiple reduction strategies, the Levantine Aurignacian technologies contrast markedly with the Ahmarian. The strong typological differences between these traditions strengthen the conclusion that these were discrete yet sympatric industrial traditions.

After 20,000 B.P., the Late Ahmarian and Late Levantine Aurignacian are present. Both exhibit multiple reduction strategies, with separate reduction sequences for blade and bladelet production. Their respective strategies for bladelet production are quite different, and different microlithic tools were made on the bladelet blanks. The Negev assemblages represent a period of cultural and adaptive complexity, separating the early Upper Paleolithic from the Epipaleolithic (Goring-Morris 1985). This period of apparently rapid technological change is critical with respect to more fundamental changes in economy and social organization that surrounded domestication of plants and animals in succeeding millennia.

Technological analysis can provide critical insight into the affinities of Upper Paleolithic assemblages. In the course of reconstructing lithic reduction strategies, data complementary to the study of raw-material procurement and functional variation between assemblages can also be gained. While classifications of debitage and the use of certain technological indices are helpful for descriptive purposes, analysis of assemblages as reduction systems has the potential to enhance our interpretations of metric and nonmetric variability within and between assemblages. Since blade production is characteristic of many Old World industries, improved methods of studying those technologies should be continually sought.

DISCUSSION

MONTET-WHITE: Perhaps the most interesting point that was brought out in Ferring's paper is the fact that what he calls reduction strategy can be used not only to describe a particular assemblage, but to characterize a particular phase and a particular area. Obviously what you demonstrated in your paper is that they are strategy changes through time, and I can add to this that the kind of reduction strategy that I have studied in Yugoslavia is significantly different from what you describe, even though the end product, the tools if you want, are probably quite similar. So there is here a dimension of variability that can be quantified and can be used to characterize groups or sets of assemblages both in a chronological and in a spatial dimension. I also wanted to emphasize the fact that blade technologies tended to produce predictable results. The degree of control achieved in the Upper Paleolithic, at least in the blade industries, is quite remarkable, where you can almost predict the width and the thickness of a blade by taking the platform measurements or vice versa. To what degree is the blank size related to the size, shape, and quality of raw-material blocks?

FERRING: In general in the central Negev the raw material was abundant and of very good quality.

MONTET-WHITE: But what shape?

FERRING: There is some tabular, some nodular. But I agree, that's why I emphasized analysis of the decortication process. Frankly, I think that when comparing blade assemblages the biggest mistake we're making is not recognizing pieces that have no cortex at all. That is where most of the final blade production is going on.

MONTET-WHITE: I guess the point I'm trying to make is that it would interesting to see to what extent reduction strategies are related to raw material. My other question concerns the differentiation you establish between blade and bladelet. In the Central European industries, I can show you both large blades and very small blades, we call them microblades, but they are part of the same sequence. In most cases bladelets are really the end product of the blade core reduction. Whereas in the Negev, you have the same products, blades and bladelets, but a very different reduction strategy. In the northern Bosnia series, I could not really set a quantitative limit between blade and bladelet because if you plot the maximum dimensions, you obtain a skewed but still single distribution. This is not the case in the Negev, and it illustrates an interesting difference in reduction strategy. Processes of blank selection are another dimension of variability that you refer to.

MARKS: I do not agree with the dichotomy between the intentional product, i.e., a blade with certain characteristics, and the non-intentional pieces that were necessary products of core maintenance. In the Negev Upper Paleolithic only about half of the tools are made on blades. The rest are made on core tablets, core-trimming flakes, *lames à crêtes*, primary flakes, and often on blades with very complicated scar patterns.

It seems to me that the small bladelet for the El Wad point is a final desired product and it seems that every core in the early Upper Paleolithic is working toward that. There are no flake cores, nor any big blade cores in these early Upper Paleolithic sites. All the blanks, which cover the full range of blanks used for the production of the total range of tools in the assemblage, are produced in this one reduction strategy. So it seems to me that one should look at a reduction strategy more in the sense suggested by Baumler, in that you look at what was produced and you also look at what is used along the way.

FERRING: We have two different types of blank used. First, those that are produced as intentional products whose narrow range of morphology is the primary objective of the flintknapper. Second, we have a lot of byproducts, core tablets, *lames à crêtes*, etc., that were *selected* for retouching. This selection results in a limited morphological range.

MARKS: But in the example of the small bladelets for El Wad points, if that is all they wanted, they could have started with narrower cores. Why produce such large blades if, in fact, you don't really want them? By the Epipaleolithic they do not seem to want them anymore and so they are no longer there.

FERRING: There is still intentional preforming that must be done and which will produce these byproducts. I would predict that to replicate this small-bladelet morphology without much preforming would require a very careful selection of nodules with a particular morphology.

XXII

Problems of Continuity and Discontinuity between the Middle and Upper Paleolithic of Central Europe

Janusz Kozlowski

The distinction between the industries of the Middle and Upper Paleolithic is generally thought to be an important example of continuity or discontinuity in the evolution of stone industries. Differences between them in certain characteristics are clear, especially when each complex as a unit is compared with the other. But these comparisons are usually limited to single aspects of material culture, subsistence patterns, or symbolic behavior. It would be much more interesting to examine these several aspects of material culture, technology, and morphology simultaneously in a dynamic and stylistic approach, with stone tool function reconstructed on the basis of use-wear analysis and correlated with bone industry; and settlement structures and symbolic manifestations interpreted in terms of contextual factors such as paleogeography, faunal remains, and raw-material economy. Each aspect of material culture and subsistence economy corresponds to different behaviors of prehistoric man and implies different explanations in anthropological terms. Only such an integrated, "multidimensional" picture of Middle-Upper Paleolithic transition can be compared with the occurrence of physical remains of Neandertal and modern man in different cultural units.

There are three primary hypotheses to account for continuity and/or discontinuity in aspects of the material culture and subsistence economy that might be related to a biological transition from Neandertals to modern man. These are:

1. That there was a *local evolution* or transformation of an indigenous sociocultural system due mainly to the adaptation to local environmental conditions. These behavioral changes would be accompanied either by a corresponding biological change of the local population or by the persistence of a biologically unchanged local population.

2. That there was a *population change* due to migration, manifested by population shift from one territory to another. New, intrusive people, presumably of a different biological type, appear with their own sociocultural system, frequently representing a different cultural tradition. Population shifts in the early periods would be due mainly to alternations or changes in the ecological subsystem that were beyond the adaptative possibilities of a given population, thus forcing these groups to move in search of new environments similar to their traditional ecosystems.

3. That local population was exposed to new lifeways and different cultural aspects, which induced *indirect diffusion* of new cultural elements and subsequent acculturation of local populations.

In Europe, the transition between the Middle and Upper Paleolithic was preceded by the peak of Pleniglacial A, accompanied by an ice-sheet advance (the Leningrad and Torun stages). Important cultural events in the Central European Middle Paleolithic are closely related to these climatic events of the period. The glacial peak which ended the Early Vistulian was a relatively late and short climatic event corresponding to the isotopic stage 4, preceded by the long evolution of the Early Vistulian with relatively mild conditions. The colder oscillation contributed to the gradual extermination of thermophilous species in the northern part of Central Europe, but this process was not a simple reverse picture of remigration in the Late Glacial (Welten 1981). The first period after the Odderade Interstadial was characterized by a cold steppe vegetation in the northern part of Central

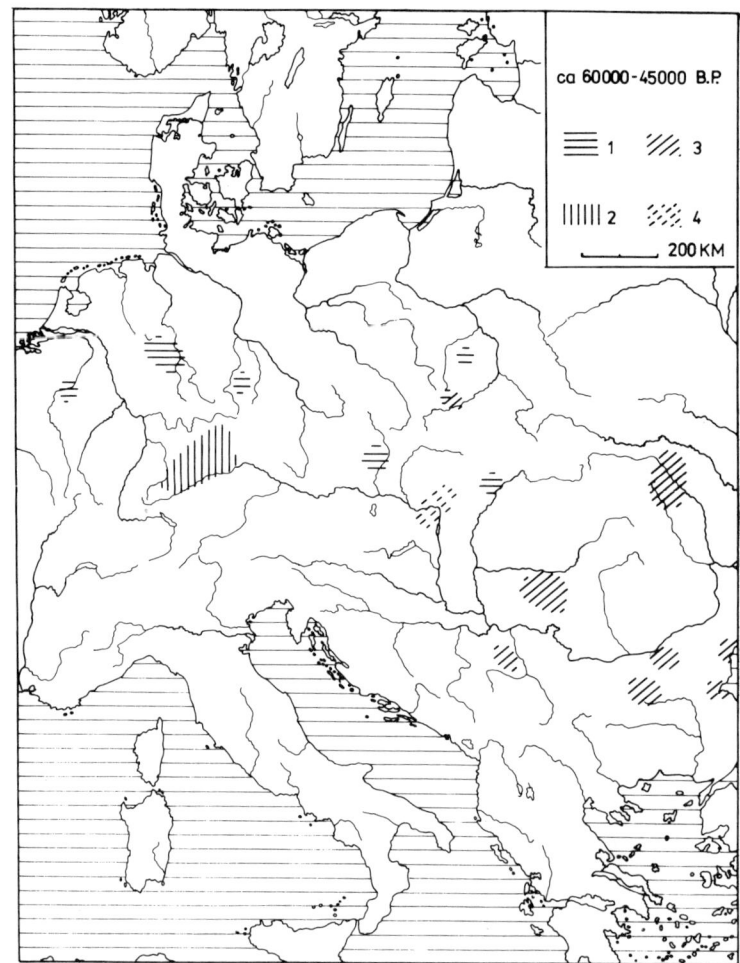

Figure 22.1 Map of Central Europe at the end of the Early Würm, 60,000-45,000 years B.P. 1—Post-Acheulian industries; 2—Altmühlian Mauern group; 3—Moustero-Levalloisian or Typical Mousterian with/without leaf points; 4—Jankovichian.

Europe and by an actual southward shift of the forest. But the glacial peak, with an ice-sheet transgression slightly south of the Baltic Sea basin, was a later event, separated from the previous stage by a warmer phase called Durnten or Ognon III Interstadial in classical West European pollen sections (Woillard 1979; Welten 1981). The date of the beginning of the glacial peak is not easily established. Many authors have suggested 60 Kyr (Haesaerts 1984) or 70 Kyr (Madeyska 1982). The latter suggestion is based on thermoluminescence (TL) dates from Pleniglacial A loess from the site of Krakow-Zwierzyniec (71,700-67,600 years B.P.), but recently obtained TL dates from Zwolen (77 Kyr) fall in the middle of the period between the first and the maximum cooling of the Early Vistulian (Schild and Sulgostowska 1986). For this reason the former evaluation of 60 Kyr seems more plausible. The end of the Pleniglacial maximum is relatively well dated to 51-43 Kyr by TL determinations from the sediments directly overlying the glacial till in the Lower Vistula region (Drozdowski 1980).

During this 10-Kyr period of the Pleniglacial maximum we can trace the following cultural transformations (Fig. 22.1):

1. In the period immediately preceding the glacial peak, two different zones are distinguished: the Moustero-Levalloisian in the Balkan-Middle Danube area and the Post-Acheulian (also called the Micoquian) in the zone situated north of the Danube. Other Mousterian facies, Eastern Charentian and Denticulated Mousterian, are widely spread over this area.

2. Both the Moustero-Levalloisian of the Balkan

type and the Post-Acheulian developed leaf points almost simultaneously during the periods of climatic deterioration and development of steppe environments. This technological transformation is partially due to the development of the bifacial technique of handaxes and asymmetrical bifacial knives (mainly in the northern zone). To some extent it may also be traced to an independent innovation: using special flat nodules for manufacturing leaf points (especially in the southern zone). Because spearpoints were used for big-game hunting in steppe environments, this innovation may be interpreted as functional.

3. In the northern zone the transformation of Middle Paleolithic bifacial assemblages was also territorially divergent. The eastern subzone has evidence for the latest Post-Acheulian assemblages in the stratigraphic position immediately preceding the glacial maximum: without leaf points (e.g., Ciemna Layer 5) and with them (Kulna Layer 7a; the radiocarbon date from this layer is only the indication of minimum age). After the glacial maximum the Szeletian seems to be the unique continuation of this phylum.

4. In the southern zone the Moustero-Levalloisian with leaf points developed from the end of the Early Vistulian until the beginning of the Interpleniglacial. This situation has been confirmed in the eastern Balkans (Muselievo, prior to the glacial maximum [Haesaerts and Sirakova 1979]; Samuilitsa II [Sirakov 1983]; and Temnata Layer V, dated to the beginning of the Interpleniglacial [Kozlowski, Laville, and Sirakov, in press]) and in the eastern Carpathians and Moldavia (which has a long sequence with leaf points from Ripiceni-Izvor, ending with Layer IV, dated at more than 42 Kyr [Păunescu 1965]). In the latter region longer persistence of the Mousterian until 28 Kyr seems doubtful, as it is based on incorrect dates from the Berlin Laboratory (Honea 1986).

5. The first northward shift of the Moustero-Levalloisian with leaf points falls in the period immediately preceding the glacial maximum. This event contributed to the origin of the Jankovichian, formerly known as the Transdanubian Szeletian. This proposition has been confirmed by Gábori-Csánk's (1983) excavation in the Remete Cave near Budapest, showing strongly marked Levallois characteristics and leaf points associated with Neandertals in the layer dated to the end of the Early Vistulian. The industry of Remete Cave, as is true of several Transdanubian sites with leaf points, shows close analogies to the eastern Balkan zone and cannot be seen (as is claimed by Gábori-Csánk) as a "modified form of the Micoquian." It is possible that this northern expansion of the Mousterо-Levalloisian with leaf points reached the Upper Vistula basin, where a similar assemblage (unfortunately relatively poor) is known from Krakow-Zwierzyniec, in the Lower Upper Loess from the Older Pleni-Vistulian.

The Mousterо-Levalloisian with leaf points practically vanished in the Interpleniglacial without consequences for the Middle-Upper Paleolithic transition. The unique exception is the Bohunician, an industry technologically and morphologically related to the Mousterо-Levalloisian with leaf points, but characterized by the presence of an Upper Paleolithic component (Oliva 1984; Svoboda 1985). At the eponymous site (where the Bohunician is stratified directly under the buried soil [Valoch 1982]) it is dated at 42,900 + 1700/−1400 years B.P. (GrN-12606), and at Stránská Skála III (in the buried soil) at 38,500 ± 1100 (GrN-12297) and 38,500 + 1400/−1200 years B.P. (GrN-12298).

The technological tradition of the Bohunician is distinctly Levalloisian, which is reflected not so much by the high Levallois index (5.80-20.14) as by the Levalloisian character of cores, both single- and double-platform (33.1 and 21.7% respectively), as well as Levallois point cores (7.5-15.9%). The high proportion of the latter results in an increase in the Levallois typological index (ILty) from 36.0 to 50.34.

Besides Levalloisian features, another distinctive trait of the Bohunician is the high proportion of blade blanks. This is reflected in the high blade index (ILam) of from 31.4 to 44.9 and the bladey character of most of the cores (on average 84.2% of cores display blade scars). In view of this decidedly blade-oriented technology there is a surprisingly small percentage of blade cores with the characteristic Upper Paleolithic crests situated in the central part of the flaking surface. Cores with this feature amount to only 1.1% in the group of single-platform cores, and 2.3% in the double-platform group, despite the fact that materials from Bohunice contain trimming blades.

The same tendencies are observed in the surface finds from Ondratice, where undoubtedly the main bulk of materials belong to the Bohunician (Svoboda 1980). Core preparation at this site is also Levalloisian represented by 52.4% of the single-platform cores and 5.9% of the double-platform specimens. Upper Paleolithic examples amount to 7.8%, but these may be additions from other cultures (e.g., the Szeletian or Aurignacian). Svoboda's (1980) interpretation of the

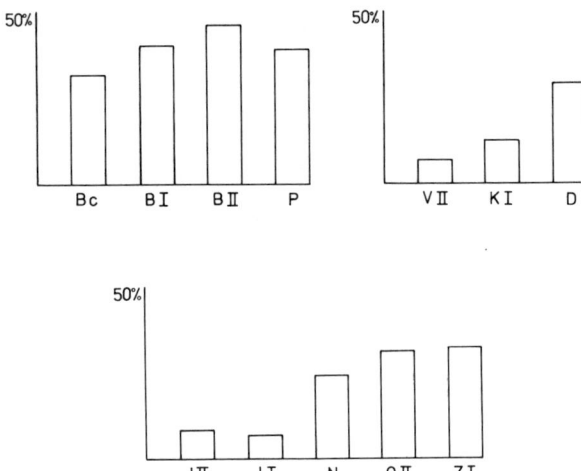

Figure 22.2   Blade index in several early Upper Paleolithic industries in Central Europe—Bohunician: Bc - Bohunice quarry, BI - Bohunice I, BII - Bohunice II, P - Podolie; Aurignacian: VII - Vedrovice II, KI - Kuparovice I, D - Divaky; Szeletian: JI - Jezerany I, JII - Jezerany II, N - Neslovice, O - Orechov, ZI - Zelesice I.

core technology at Ondratice is questionable. He suggests that this technology was a transitional phase between the Levalloisian and the Upper Paleolithic core technologies, and distinguishes a special group of "cores with upright preparation" that he considers transitional between Levalloisian and Upper Paleolithic cores with "frontal crests." I believe that these cores are an intermediate form not so much between Levalloisian and Upper Paleolithic cores, as between Levalloisian and discoidal cores. Consequently, I see the Bohunician assemblages as an advanced phase in the development of Levalloisian technology and not as part of a development from the Levalloisian to the Upper Paleolithic technology.

As has already been mentioned, the Bohunician displays a very high Levallois typological index. Among the retouched tools, on the other hand, are found endscrapers and burins on flakes and blades. The quantity of these Upper Paleolithic tools ranges, on the average, from 11% (endscrapers) to 1% (burins). They represent common components of the Upper Paleolithic typological substratum and are not distinctive for any particular unit.

Another controversial point is the significance of the Bohunice industry for the origins of the Upper Paleolithic. For Svoboda the Bohunice industry is a kind of "synthetotype" with an unspecialized, flexible toolkit and technology, which could have formed the basis for different Upper Paleolithic technocomplexes (i.e., the Szeletian, Jerzmanowician, Aurignacian). Thus, for him, the Bohunician is a "transitional stage" between the Middle and Upper Paleolithic, in the same way as are those "transitional industries" with Levallois technology known from the Negev. I am inclined, however, to ascribe the Bohunician to developed complexes with Levalloisian technology comprising an Upper Paleolithic typological component. This evolution, in my view, did not lead to the Upper Paleolithic technology proper or to any specific Upper Paleolithic cultures, and changes in the values of laminar index are not progressive (unidirectional) in the Early Paleolithic sequence (Fig. 22.2). The Bohunician constitutes, then, a kind of dead end which did not bring about the formation of Upper Paleolithic complexes: the Bohunician vanished in the middle of the Interpleniglacial.

A separate problem is the occasional occurrence of leaf points in the Bohunician. Oliva (1984) reports that leaf points at Bohunice (3-5%) and Podoli (4%) are made in quartzite imported from the Moravsky Krumlov region, whereas the remaining Bohunician artifacts are made in hornstone from Stránská Skála. Leaf points can be interpreted either as proof of contacts with the Szeletian, or as Bohunician artifacts produced in specialized workshops (similar to leaf points of the Moustero-Levalloisian in the Balkans).

The second type of transformation undertaken by Middle Paleolithic assemblages led to the emergence of cultures with leaf points proper. In the uplands of Central Europe these include first of all the Szeletian, formed on the base of Middle Paleolithic assemblages with bifaces and asymmetrical knives of the Bustein-Konigsaue-Pradnik type. This hypothesis has been put forward by Valoch (1966, 1986) on the basis of the transitional nature of finds from Jezerany in Moravia. Subsequently Ringer (1982) published similar materials from a site near Sajobabony in northeastern Hungary. The finds from Jezerany and Sajobabony confirm the presence of asymmetrical knives in Moravia and northeastern Hungary, but since they are surface finds whose homogeneity has not been established beyond doubt, they are not decisive evidence in the question of the transformation of this facies of the Middle Paleolithic into the Szeletian.

At Jezerany I and II the Upper Paleolithic component is insignificant. It does not exceed the values known for the Mousterian complex (16.3-23.8%). Middle Paleolithic tools amount to 64.2 and 73.4%,

TABLE 22.1
EARLY UPPER PALEOLITHIC LEAF-POINT INDUSTRIES

	ILam	IG	IB	IPf	Mid. Pal.	Up. Pal.
Jezerany I	8.30	10.31	1.42	11.52	73.40	16.31
Jezerany II	10.31	12.84	3.67	11.24	64.22	23.85
Neslovice	24.50	21.80	6.90	13.60	41.80	38.10
Orechov I	33.80	21.90	6.30	4.70	38.20	43.70
Orechov II	32.00	29.20	4.50	7.40	44.40	39.40
Zelesice	32.20	34.60	10.50	5.80	28.10	53.80
Dzierzyslaw I	24.90	21.70	10.20	15.40	35.80	48.00

TABLE 22.2
CORES

	Middle Paleolithic Cores			Upper Paleolithic Cores			
	irregular	discoidal	Levallois	1-pl.	2-pl.	90	carinate
Jezerany I	34.45	24.32	0.67	14.86	5.40	5.40	—
Jezerany II	33.00	21.35	—	15.53	4.85	4.85	—
Neslovice	19.10	11.10	0.60	50.00	19.10	—	—
Orechov I	14.60	8.30	11.10	36.80	29.20	—	—
Zelesice	6.00	12.00	2.00	56.00	24.00	—	—
Dzierzyslaw	23.30	5.00	1.70	46.60	20.00	—	3.20

including typical bifaces as well as asymmetrical knives (19 and 16 specimens from Jezerany I and II, respectively). In respect of technology these inventories cannot be assigned to blade ones (ILam is 8.3 and 10.3 respectively). Single- and double-platform cores, specimens with changed orientation—both flakes and blade-flakes—amount to 25.6 and 26.2%, whereas all the Middle Paleolithic forms (discoidal, multiplatform) make up 58.7 and 53.4%, respectively. Therefore, the technological inventories at Jezerany are distinctly Middle Paleolithic (Tables 22.1-2).

Technological changes take place only in later Szeletian assemblages of Moravia, probably from the second half of the Interpleniglacial. Except for a few Szeletian artifacts from the cave of Pod Hradem, no radiometric data are available for this phase of the Szeletian. The stratigraphic position of the assemblage from Dzierzyslaw in Upper Silesia, however, points fairly clearly to the later part of the Interpleniglacial following the formation of the Interpleniglacial soil. The later phase of the Moravian Szeletian (Neslovice, Orechov, Zelesice, Dzierzyslaw) is characterized by a distinct increase in the Upper Paleolithic typological component (ranging from 38.1 to 53.8%), represented by endscrapers, burins, retouched blades, and perforators. Technology as well evolves towards blade technique (ILam 24.5 to 32.2), with the number of Upper Paleolithic cores markedly increasing (single-platform cores—36.8-50.0%; double-platform—19.1-29.2%). The proportion of multiplatform and discoidal cores drops. It is noteworthy that some Aurignacian elements, such as endscrapers and carinate cores, appear in this phase of the Moravian Szeletian.

The evolution of the Moravian Szeletian is an example of the transformation of a Mousterian with bifacial tradition into assemblages with leaf points lacking the Levallois technique, and subsequently, during the Interpleniglacial, of the leptolithization of these assemblages under a foreign influence, this influence being the Aurignacian.

The evolution of the Szeletian in the Bukk Mountains must have had a similar nature. The specific

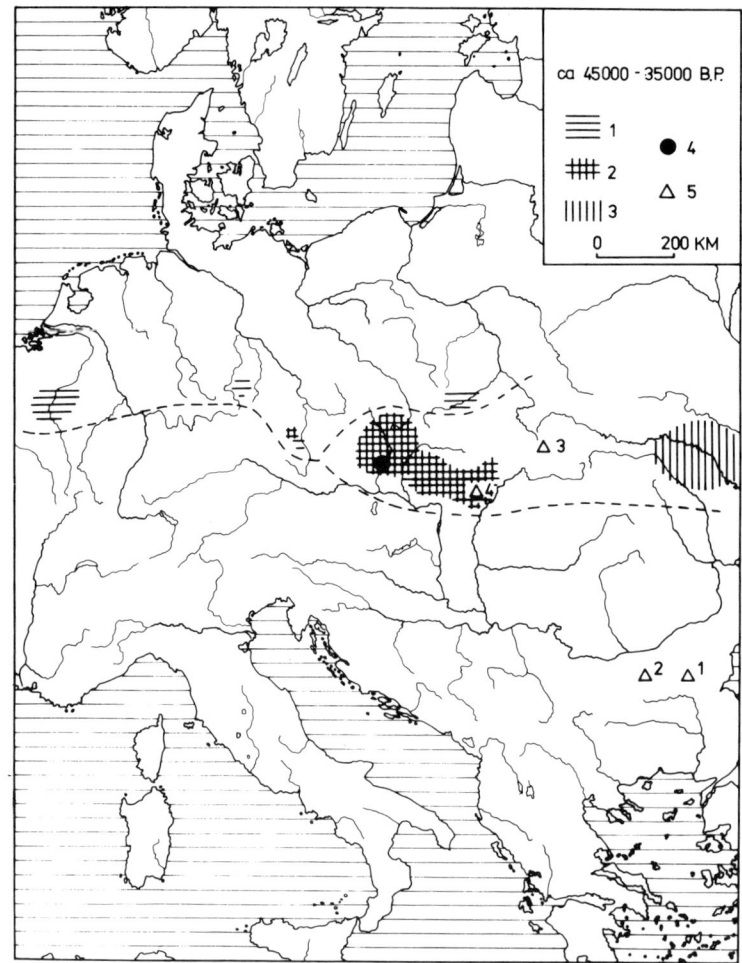

Figure 22.3 Map of Central Europe in the early Interpleniglacial. 1—Lincombian-Ranisian-Jerzmanowician; 2—Szeletian: Bukk and Moravian groups; 3—Szeletian: Moldavian group; 4—Bohunician; 5—Early Aurignacian: Bachokirian 1 - Bacho Kiro, 2 - Temnata Cave, 3 - Korolevo, 4 - Istallosko.

character of cave assemblages, stripped of most cores and debitage, makes it difficult to describe technological processes. But in the area occupied by the Bukk Mountains group an early phase is recorded, possibly derived from the Babonyian and dated in the lower layer at the Szeleta Cave to more than 41,700 years B.P. (GXO-197). This phase has a small Upper Paleolithic component, the blade aspect is only weakly marked, and tools (endscrapers, retouched blades) are represented entirely by the Upper Paleolithic typological substratum (i.e., without diagnostic forms). The later phase, known so far only from the upper level at the Szeleta Cave, has not been documented beyond all doubt. It is questionable whether the distinctly Upper Paleolithic elements from the upper layer at the Szeleta Cave are indeed an integral part of the Szeletian assemblage. The leaf points from the upper layer, though, are undoubtedly more advanced than the points in the lower layer. If the inventory of the upper layer is homogeneous, then the Szeleta Cave would represent the later phase of the Szeletian enriched by the leptolithic component, probably of allochthonous derivation.

The development of the second (lowland) zone of Interpleniglacial industries with leaf points offers more problems (Fig. 22.3). Here these points are only partly bifacial and are made on blades (in contrast to true Szeletian points). The range of these industries is decidedly more northwestern, extending over the uplands of the western part of Central Europe and the lowland part of Northwestern Europe. They make up a large complex distributed from Great Britain to

Poland called the Lincombian-Ranisian-Jerzmanowician (Kozlowski and Kozlowski 1981; Campbell 1986).

In the western subzone the Post-Acheulian ("Micoquian") industries developed in a different direction, what I have termed the Mauern-Ranis phylum. The direct comparison between Weinberghöhle (Mauern) Layer F and Ilsenhöhle near Ranis (Layer 2 or X) gives an impression of discontinuity (Allsworth-Jones 1986). These two assemblages are considered contemporaneous. Ranis 2 falls probably in the colder phase after the Hengelo Interstadial, if we take into account the very low ratio of AP and presence of tundra species with *Selaginella*. The attribution of Layer F in Weinberghöhle to the Hengelo Interstadial now seems very unsure; the very sharp boundary between this layer and overlying Layer E (with some Aurignacian finds) seems to indicate a strong erosional phase, which covers probably the first half of the Early Interpleniglacial. Typical thermophilous and forest species in Layer F (*Castor, Felis silvestris*) are compatible rather with one of the earlier Vistulian interstadials than with the Hengelo one. If we accept this re-evaluation of the age of Mauern, its industry and that of Ranis 2 are then separated by a relatively long timespan.

Recently some new sites have been excavated which cover this period. One worth mentioning is the Couvin Cave (Belgium), which furnished an interesting industry characterized by leaf points closely resembling specimens from Mauern, but bearing some technical features indicative of progressive tendencies. Blank-production techniques are principally Mousterian, but many scars show a tendency towards short and thin bladelike flakes. Among the tools sidescrapers are dominant, but certain new types appear, especially blades with distal or proximal part thinned by Kostenki technique. This industry is certainly older than 40,000 years (Ulrix-Closset, Otte, and Cattelain 1986). Zeitlarn, a surface site on the Upper Danube, has the same transitional position between the Mauern-type and Ranis-type industries (Schönweiss and Werner 1986). The material from this site has been considered Szeletian by Valoch. In my opinion, however, the leaf points' morphological features (e.g., pointed bases) and technical attributes (subsequent chipping of both sides and faces instead of alternate bifacial working of each side), as well as the blade technology and the presence of implements thinned distally by Kostenki technique, preclude the attribution of this collection to the Szeletian. The presence of discoidal endscrapers is considered a typical "Szeletian" feature in this collection. But in fact this type of tool is well known from the Central European Post-Acheulian ("Micoquian"), especially of the Schambach and Ciemna type. The same transitional position is occupied probably by Layer II of Grossen Grotte near Blaubeuren in West Germany, which furnished not only leaf points but also a bone spearpoint with unsplit base (Wagner 1983).

The difficulties encountered in the description of this complex result primarily from the fact that the sites known so far are mostly hunting camps with a high proportion of leaf points and low frequency of debitage, cores, or even retouched tools other than points. The lack of residential camps and workshops makes it difficult to characterize this unit, notably its technology and complete toolkit. Our knowledge about this complex is very incomplete because it has been possible to uncover only the traces of peripheral settlement in the northernmost part of the upland zone, represented by short-term hunting camps; the main area of this settlement remains inaccessible because of the erosional and depositional effects of the Pleniglacial B ice-sheet advance.

The origins of the northern cultures with leaf points, as we said, are found in the south German Altmuhlian—recorded in the Weinberghöhle at Mauern—which developed in the territory previously occupied by the Bockstein culture. The blade component at this site is not well developed, however. These are blades obtained (probably accidentally) from single-platform cores without initial preparation, or possibly from cores with multiple orientation. This is evidenced by a few cores from the investigations of L. F. Zotz and A. Bohmers, and by blades with cortical surfaces located even in the center of the dorsal side. Moreover, when traces of transversal scars occur on blades they are oriented from lateral edges and not from the frontal crest. We can conclude, therefore, that the Upper Paleolithic blade technique does not occur at the Weinberghöhle. Yet this site did yield single leaf points on blades (Bohmers 1951: pl. 27:2-3) or blade-flakes (Zotz 1955: pl. 66). Retouched tools are predominantly Middle Paleolithic sidescrapers.

Further evolution of the Interpleniglacial assemblages with leaf points, for example at the Ilsenhöhle at Ranis, shows an increase in the production of blades used in the manufacture of leaf points, and the emergence of Upper Paleolithic tools such as retouched blades, burins, and (to a lesser extent) endscrapers (Fig. 22.4). Because of the lack of cores and debitage the exact nature of blade technique or its

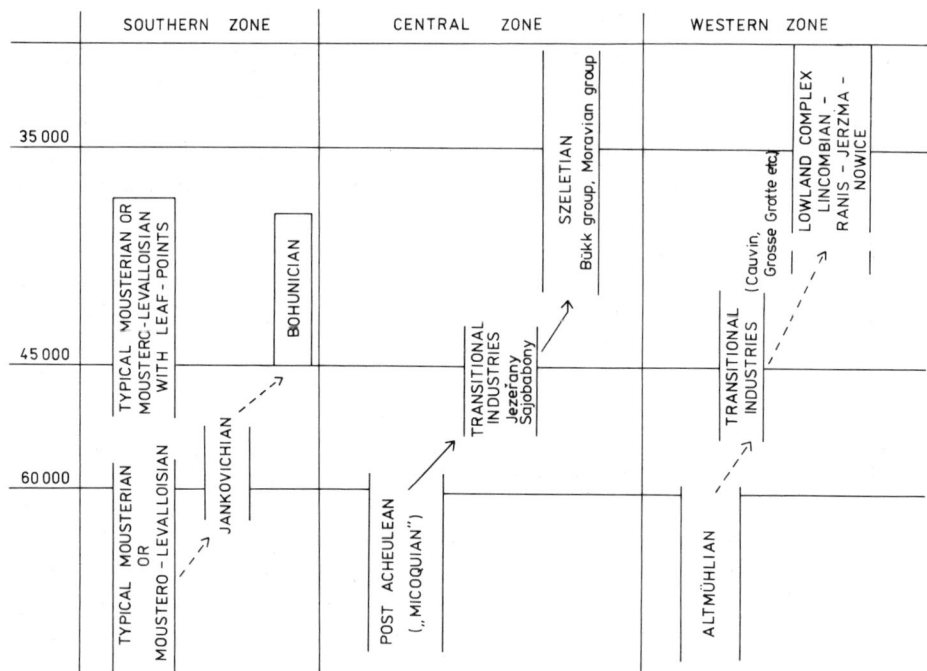

Figure 22.4 Evolution of the late Middle Paleolithic and early Upper Paleolithic leaf-point industries in Central Europe.

origin in these assemblages cannot be easily determined: Was it the outcome of a local evolution parallel to the evolution of leaf points, or was it adopted from other culture units? The problem is further complicated by tools affiliated with the Upper Paleolithic substratum that are found in the Ranisian and the Jerzmanowician. Also, the occurrence at some British sites (e.g., Phynnon Beuno) of Aurignacian endscrapers in association with leaf points cannot be treated as evidence of Aurignacian influence, since the homogeneity of British cave finds from old investigations has not been confirmed.

In the northern part of the loess uplands, abundant evidence suggests very old roots for the true Upper Paleolithic technologies; thus they may be independent of the leaf-point industries in other parts of Europe. In the Late Rissian layers in Piekary IIa near Krakow are found blade cores with a central crest, producing typical Upper Paleolithic blades retouched in backed implements and endscrapers. In the Early Vistulian layer of the Rocourt quarry near Liège is found a small concentration with typical single-platform blade cores with prepared flaking face, and Upper Paleolithic tools (burins, truncations). This industry has parallels in the upper layer of Rheindalen in West Germany and at Seclin in northern France, both dated to the Early Vistulian before Pleniglacial A. We have no evidence for the continuity of such industries during the Pleniglacial A, less so far in the beginning of the Interpleniglacial, but we cannot exclude the influence of local blade technologies on the emergence of the blade/leaf-point complex of the lowland early Upper Paleolithic.

Increasing data bear witness to the persistence of both the Szeletian and the Lincombian-Ranisian-Jerzmanowician complex until the industries with backed points (Gravettian) emerged.

An analogous developmental sequence, although delayed, took place in Eastern Europe. In this area some of the industries with bifaces and asymmetrical bifacial knives (type of Zaskalnaya V [Kolosov 1978]) form the nucleus of the Sungirian, with very fine triangular leaf points with concave bases (Boriskovski 1984). The onset of the evolution of the Sungirian is placed at ca. 32,000 years B.P. at the earliest, continuing until the emergence of advanced eastern Gravettian assemblages. In this situation it is plausible that the Upper Paleolithic component in these Sungirian assemblages may derive from different Upper Paleolithic units developing in parallel, perhaps from early cultures with backed points. A more serious hindrance in the investigation into the origin of the Sungirian is the large chronological hiatus between pre-Interpleniglacial Middle Paleolithic assemblages with triangular leaf points and the Sungirian proper, whose earliest traces in the region of the middle Don are not earlier than 32,000 years B.P.

We have no explanation so far of the origin of another group of industries with leaf points referred to as the Moldavian Szeletian. In this group the *fossiles directeurs* are morphologically more similar to the Szeletian of the western Carpathian zone. This group is distributed in the area previously (i.e., in the pre-Interpleniglacial) occupied by the typical Mousterian or Moustero-Levalloisian with a leaf component (Ripiceni type) and by the denticulated Mousterian (Stinka type) with occasional leaf points. Their presence does not account for the origin of tools accompanying the "Moldavian Szeletian" leaf points (Borziak, Grigorieva, and Ketraru 1982; Ketraru 1973).

Our knowledge of cultures at the beginning of the Interpleniglacial is limited by the fact that sediments and paleoclimatic sequences from that period are rare and poorly recognized. Soils directly on the Lower Upper Loess, i.e., prior to the sedimentation of the Middle Upper Loess, are rare and are frequently eroded. Soils dated to the second half of the Interpleniglacial developed directly on the erosional surface of the Lower Upper Loess. In the northern part of Central Europe the first half of the Interpleniglacial saw the formation of pseudogley soils grading to arctic brown soils. These soils, however, like the contemporaneous cave sediments, were frequently removed by erosion.

The continuity of cultural development in the first half of the Interpleniglacial was thus disturbed by postdepositional factors causing poor preservation of sediments from this period. Those archaeological remains that did survive show the adaptation to the ecological conditions of the Interpleniglacial. This does not mean a transition to the Upper Paleolithic in all aspects of material culture. The development of Levallois technique does not lead to the Upper Paleolithic blade technology, since the method of core preparation and processing was different. The processing of the Upper Paleolithic blade core started from the removal of the lateral trimming edges and cannot be the result of the development of the Levallois core, whose exploitation started from the large surface previously prepared from lateral edges. Only the Upper Paleolithic core was able to produce a large number of highly standardized blades.

The occurrence of typical Upper Paleolithic cores and retouched tools (endscrapers, retouched blades, truncations, burins) in industries with leaf points cannot be explained as a process of local evolution. It is striking that the Middle Paleolithic industries in the period prior to the Interpleniglacial contain an insignificant Upper Paleolithic component (both technological and typological), although these assemblages contain leaf points just as do those of the Interpleniglacial itself.

In terms of paleoanthropology we may reasonably assume that Szeletian populations had, at least to some extent, Neandertal features. The tooth (third lower right) found by Hillebrandt in the Szeleta Cave shows features distinctive of the classical Neandertal Man from Subalyuk and Krapina (Thoma 1972). Regrettably we do not know what the earliest populations from the northern complex of leaf points (Lincombian-Ranisian-Jerzmanowician) were like, although the late sections of this complex show the presence of modern man, and the same is true in the developed Sungirian.

The above-mentioned facts lead us to conclude that the "leptolithization" process, taking place in the first half of the Interpleniglacial and embracing leaf-point complexes in both the central (Szeletian) and eastern (Sungirian) zones, must have been prompted by some internal stimuli. Only in the case of the lowland complex (Lincombian-Ranisian-Jerzmanowician) can local evolution of blade technology not be excluded. The cause of internal stimuli may be sought in the Proto-Aurignacoidal assemblages in Central Europe, which occurred in the Balkans (e.g., at Bacho Kiro Cave, Bulgaria, Layer 11 [Kozlowski 1982]) and in southern Moravia at the open-air sites of Vedrovice II and Kuparovice I. They are characterized by a developed blade technique with single- and double-platform cores, punch technique, a very high ratio of Upper Paleolithic blade tools (burins, endscrapers, retouched blades, truncations), and a very low ratio of Middle Paleolithic tools (2.13% sidescrapers in Vedrovice II, and 1.04% in Layer 11 of Bacho Kiro Cave). These industries emerge at the beginning of the Interpleniglacial or even earlier, with no traces of local evolution. This can be clearly seen in Bacho Kiro Cave, where, during the same warmer paleoclimatic phase before 40,000 years B.P., the typical Mousterian gives way to the early Upper Paleolithic—the Aurignacoidal industry called the Bachokirian. This industry shows a total typological, technological, and raw-material hiatus in relation to the local Middle Paleolithic. A similar situation has recently been recorded in the Temnata Cave in Bulgaria, near Karlukovo. Layer V on the terrace of the cave, representing the same warmer oscillation, contains the Middle Paleolithic sequence with leaf points; this is followed abruptly by the Upper Paleolithic Aurignacoidal industry similar to the Bachokirian, and later (after 32,000 years B.P.) by the typical Aurignacian of Layer 4 inside the cave (Kozlowski, Laville, and Sirakov, in press).

The chronological position of Vedrovice II in Moravia is not quite clear, although recently published data seem to confirm its link with the fossil soil formed before the Interpleniglacial. The hypothesis about the local derivation of this Aurignacoidal industry from the Moravian Interglacial industries (type Marsovice I, viz., the so-called Krumlovian) calls for a separate review.

The discovery of a tooth in Layer 11 in the Bacho Kiro Cave that displays features approximating modern man, although not devoid of archaic characteristics, would suggest that Aurignacoidal industries were produced by *Homo sapiens*. Similarly, bone remains from the Velika Pecina Cave in Yugoslavia confirm the links between the Aurignacoidal cultures and modern man.

The presence of Aurignacoidal assemblages in Central Europe at the very beginning of the Interpleniglacial (or even earlier), which are earlier than the oldest Aurignacian assemblages in Western Europe (cf. dates from Abri Pataud and Cueva Morín), may account for the modification of leaf-point industries towards the Upper Paleolithic. In Central Europe the Aurignacian and leaf-point assemblages are not distinctly interstratified like the Aurignacian and the Chatelperronian in Western Europe. But geochronological data and imports of lithic artifacts in both directions (e.g., Szeletian points made from quartz-porphyry from the Bukk Mountains are present in Aurignacian assemblages) bear witness to synchronous development of the two cultural traditions in the Interpleniglacial. This can be seen most notably in the development of early Aurignacoidal industries and the later typical Aurignacian concurrently with the Moravian, Bukk Mountains, and partly Moldavian Szeletian. Parallel evolution is observed as well for the Aurignacian and the northwestern leaf-point industries (Lincombian-Ranisian-Jerzmanowician).

The process described above thus consists of a gradual transformation of Middle Paleolithic assemblages with leaf points into Upper Paleolithic assemblages which also contain a variety of leaf-point types as a result of the confrontation with the allochthonous Aurignacoidal tradition. This process is analogous to that in Western Europe, where some Mousterian assemblages transformed into Chatelperronian, the latter to some extent the creation of the Neandertals. This change was also induced by the influence of the typical Aurignacian produced by *H. sapiens* who were contemporaneous with the Chatelperronian, as evidenced by a long sequence in southwestern France where these two units are interstratified.

In fact, correspondences between Central and Western Europe can be seen in later cultural evolution—some of the Central European assemblages with leaf points persist to give rise to the eastern Gravettian (e.g., the Moravian and Moldavian Szeletian), in the same way that the Chatelperronian contributed to the emergence of the western Upper Perigordian. This process, however, needs further investigation. Some units with leaf points did not undergo conspicuous changes, notably the units from the northwestern complex. These were pushed from the lowlands by the Pleniglacial II and expanded to the southwest (the emergence of the Proto-Solutrean, probably of Font Robert facies of the Upper Perigordian), or to the southeast (the beginning of the Jerzmanowice-Telman culture).

The present study has tried to give particular attention to the analytic aspects of the evolution of technology in the Middle Paleolithic and in the Upper Paleolithic leaf-point industries, and to their comparison to Aurignacian technology. An attempt has been made to show the development of technology in its dynamic aspects, through the stages of core processing and blank production in synchronous assemblages, as well as evolutionary aspects and diachronic modifications.

DISCUSSION

JELINEK: Such a presentation of the character of the Central and Eastern European industries that underlies the appearance of the Upper Paleolithic adds considerably to our perspective on problems of the Middle Paleolithic that are central to interests in cultural development. Some of these Middle Paleolithic industries in Eastern Europe are clearly associated with Neandertals, and their contemporaneity with the Mousterian in Western Europe makes us all feel comfortable. But one of the interesting aspects in this regard is that by 40,000 years ago or so, we do see an Aurignacian or an Aurignacian-like culture clearly in evidence in Eastern Europe, and we see it appear at the beginning of a relatively favorable climatic interval which would have made access to Western Europe easier, either across the plain or further to the south. We now need to know a little more about what was going on in places like Belgium during that pleniglacial interval, if, in fact, this was a route for the spread of that culture.

There is considerable discussion of culture change and insight into development of various patterns that is interesting and challenging. But part of it seems to me to be questionable: what began and continued in one spot and what came in as influence from another place? The aspect of the material that strikes me as important has to do with the early appearance of blade industries and the relationship of those industries to Levallois industries. Kozlowski remarked that one of his reasons for feeling that there is an Early Aurignacian evolving in situ in the southeastern part of the region is the early presence of a blade industry with many Upper Paleolithic tool types, and that this goes back as far as the interglacial or the penultimate glaciation. We can see such industries in a number of places. In the Levant, for example, is the Amudian, which occurs during the early part of the last glacial cycle. This is a good blade industry, with endscrapers, backed points, and burins. The same kind of thing occurs a bit later on in the Layer D Mousterian. But the Upper Paleolithic aspect of the industries that so intrigued Dorothy Garrod, François Bordes, and others is simply the result of the manufacture of blades. Once people started making blades, industries began to look Upper Paleolithic, no matter when they appear. The question is, why did they start making blades?

KOZLOWSKI: We have in Europe typical "Upper Paleolithic" blade technology, with cores prepared first with a central crest, removal of this crest, and continued blade removal along the side of the core. This technology exists in some assemblages of the Middle Paleolithic from sites that are usually close to the lowlands. These sites form a kind of belt from northern France to southern Poland. But we cannot see true continuation or a relation between these industries and the Upper Paleolithic.

STRAUS: I am going to second what you said. Blades and some of the consequent results of having blades appear and disappear in Africa and the Near East and Europe at different times, and different places. On the other hand there are also non-lamellar Upper Paleolithic industries. I think we are dealing with technological convergences, with the invention and reinvention of certain techniques. The limits of lithic technology are such that there are only a number of possibilities that can be thought up and they keep getting thought up time and time again. The question that should be more important is, When is this mutation so useful as to catch on and push selection in a certain direction? So, I think that rather than seeking phylogenetic linkages of some mysterious sort, we need to think a great deal about the interrelationship between the technological inventions and their adaptive significance.

OTTE: Kozlowski has shown that in specific regional areas there are technological links which are supposed to be in relation to the environment.

JELINEK: The problem of the leaf-shaped points is an interesting one. Their prevalence through this whole period suggests a particular type of technological innovation that had high adaptive significance.

MÜLLER-BECK: There is of course a problem of dating, a problem that we are not able to resolve at least in the Upper Danube. Radiocarbon dates are not so reliable. The dating of the *blattspitzen* is not sure.

KOZLOWSKI: I would like to emphasize the importance of the sequence at Zwolen, excavated by Schild and still unpublished. The sequence at this site goes from 100,000 until 77,000, with at least seven occupational phases showing the evolution of the leaf point. The other thing that is very important is that this site is one of the very few from the lowlands—usually the lowland sites were destroyed by the second pleniglacial. The site also has many implications concerning scavenging or hunting. Schild has discovered very specialized butchering areas at this site which are important for the understanding of the hunting behavior of Middle Paleolithic man.

BOSINSKI: Just an observation concerning the interglacial: at about 115,000 there is a well-marked forest soil and then three humus zones with loess deposition in between. But the real cold is on top of the three humus zones and this is about 65,000. From this period, as from the second pleniglacial, we know of no sites. The real loess starts after the first pleniglacial and lasts until the second pleniglacial of 20,000. There we have still Middle Paleolithic industries. The transition towards Upper Paleolithic to me is to be placed within the Hengelo. In our region, the first pleniglacial is quite clear about 65,000 on top of the third humus zone.

COMMENTS

OTTE: Les industries à pointes foliacées de la fin du Paléolithique moyen se distinguent par la technique du support: sur bloc dans celles du type Mousselievo (Bulgarie) et du Bükk, et sur éclat en Bavière ou dans les sites occidentaux (Couvin, Belgique). Ce sont ces dernières (faites sur éclats) qui vont se maintenir au début du Paléolithique supérieur sous la forme de Ranis (D.D.R.), Spy (Belgique) et du "Lincombien" (Angleterre) en modificant le support vers des formes laminaires. Les autres types (pièces sur blocs) ne semblent pas avoir subi la même mutation.

A ce sujet, je dois faire remarquer que les récentes fouilles de Couvin ont permis de dater l'industrie à pointes foliacées d'environ 46,000 ans B.P. (sous presse dans les Actes des Néandertaliens).

En ce qui concerne l'industrie laminaire de Rocourt (près de Liège, Belgique), découverte à la base des loess du *premier* pléniglaciaire, je dois signaler que les processus techniques utilisés sont plus proches de ceux du débitage levallois que de ceux du Paléolithique supérieur. La mise en forme et la préparation du bloc, la forme des talons correspondent en effet à des lames levallois très systématiquement obtenues. J'ajoute qu'en outre, on y trouvait différents outils du type Paléolithique supérieur: pointes à dos et burins.

A l'issue des différentes présentations précédentes, j'aimerais faire remarquer qu'il est de plus en plus évident qu'une origine polycentrique du Paléolithique supérieur européen doit être envisagée: Chatelperronien à l'ouest, pointes foliacées au nord et Aurignacien dans les Balkans. Tenant compte des dates anciennes récemment obtenues en Bulgarie, antérieures à celles du Proche-Orient, ne pourrait-on pas envisager la possibilité d'une origine européenne de cette culture?

En ce qui concerne les cultures de Moravie, extérieures au Szélétien, peut-on réellement considérer que les processus de débitage levallois utilisés à Vedrovice vont conduire à la technologie aurignacienne? De si profondes différences m'empêchent d'en être convaincu et ces ensembles paraissent plus clairement appartenir encore au Paléolithique moyen.

XXIII
Raw-Material Economy among Medium-Sized Late Paleolithic Campsites of Central Europe

Anta Montet-White

The object of this chapter is to introduce a model of raw-material economy derived from the study of medium-sized, open-air campsites where river cobbles formed the primary source of raw materials used in toolmaking. The site from which most of the data were obtained, Kadar in northern Bosnia, Yugoslavia, exemplifies a type of settlement as well as forms of raw-material processing that were widely distributed in Central Europe during the Eastern Gravettian (Montet-White, Laville, and Lézine 1986). Comparative data taken from other sites within the region support the notion that the Kadar model may be generalized to similar types of settlements exploiting a similar range of raw materials, with a comparable repertory of knapping techniques at their disposal.

The procurement, redistribution, transformation, and use of raw-material resources during the Late Paleolithic are viewed here as a sequence of planned and integrated activities which fit at least some of the basic assumptions of economic models. Like the "chaîne opératoire" defined by A. Leroi-Gourhan (Leroi-Gourhan and Brézillon 1966), the sequence of production activities includes not only the materials and the artifacts derived from them but, more important, the motor habits, designs, and choices of the flintknappers. Another goal of the study is to generalize beyond the analysis of a single site or a single event to arrive at a more broadly applicable model. In specifying the conditions under which the sequence of activities operated, a definition of the system's parameters can be reached. This view is in general agreement with the concept of lithic production systems presented by Ericson (Ericson and Purdy 1984: 2), who stresses the importance of considering lithic production "in the context of procurement exchange, technology and social organization." Archaeological data lend themselves more easily to the reconstruction of technology and procurement strategies. Intensity of site use can be used as a basis for definition of the settlement type to which the artifact assemblage belonged, if not of the social organization of the groups.

Jochim's statement (1976: 7) that "an important goal guiding economic behavior of hunter-gatherers appears to be the minimization of effort—or at least the maintenance of its expenditure within a predictable range," although intended to apply to food production, applies to raw-material economy as well. There was a need for choices in allocation of time and energy spent in obtaining lithic raw material and making stone tools. Decisions were reached at every level of the toolmaking process, from material selection to the discard of broken or useless tools, with the expectation of predictable results. During the period of time that a Gravettian group occupied a site, members of the group introduced into the camp varying quantities of raw material. Only a portion of the material was eventually used or made into tools, whereas a great deal was wasted, rendered useless by frost or broken during the knapping process. The level of acceptable loss, the minimum results to be expected, the means to compensate for unavoidable loss in order to maximize results are some of the questions to be addressed in order to understand a very important aspect of the economic behavior of Late Paleolithic groups.

In summary, raw-material economy is seen as the interrelation of three elements—raw-material source(s), settlement types, and technology, as illustrated in the following diagram:

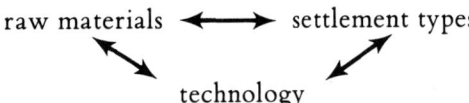

This attempt to model the raw-material economy of Late Paleolithic groups starts from, and works within the limits of, data recovered from Paleolithic sites by means of modern, systematic excavations. Traditional tool and debitage categories provide the means of sorting the sample of lithic debris into classes of artifacts which correspond to known stages of the lithic production sequence. Other kinds of information are needed to reconstruct the raw-material economy. The model is based on a series of indices that quantify losses and gains at every step of the reduction sequence as it took place at the campsite. A first series of indices provide quantitative estimates of raw-material reduction. These are:
—The rate of non-usable raw material, which measures the proportion of material shattered or lost at the campsite because of poor quality. This factor must have been taken into account by prehistoric flintknappers when they estimated the quantity of raw material to be brought into the site.
—The rate of material loss incurred during core preparation.
—The rate of blade production, which estimates the proportion of raw material transformed into desirable products.
—The rate of reduction, an estimate of the difference between blocks of raw materials and discarded cores which quantifies the degree of reduction of the original piece of raw material.

A second series of indices are designed as means of estimating the degree of blank use. They measure (a) the differential rates of blank use indicative of the selection of specific types of blanks, and (b) the degree of utilization and/or transformation of different kinds of tools.

The interplay of the different processes these rates measure defines an intrasite system of raw-material economy. The data must then be considered in view of other factors—origin and quality of the raw material, and perhaps more important, the type of settlement the campsite represents. Limited comparisons suggest that patterns will emerge within the variability of economic systems which will constitute the basis for a wider definition of the raw-material economy of Late Paleolithic groups.

MEDIUM-SIZED CAMPSITES

Eastern Gravettian sites vary in size from very ephemeral, specialized camps, where excavations have uncovered 10-30 tools in a total of 100-300 artifacts, to extensive and relatively permanent habitation sites, where artifact counts exceed 10,000 and retouched tools number in the thousands. The relative abundance of faunal remains and the presence of hearths mark the low-density sites as hunting stations. The majority of those recorded to date are located in the Pannonian Basin, along the Central Danube (Gábori and Gábori 1957; Dobosi 1987) and further south in Vojvodina (Basler 1979). Traces of brief occupations have been recovered in cave sites as well, particularly in the Slovenian Karst (Osole 1979). The large, intensively used campsites at the other end of the spectrum are considered more stable settlements. Dolni Vestonice, Willendorf II Level 9, and Pavlov fall within this category of settlements (Kozlowski 1986).

Between these two extremes are found several sites where retouched-tool counts fall between 200 and 1000 and total artifacts number in the thousands. Levels 5, 6, and 7 of Willendorf II, Petrkovice, Lubna, Puskari, Spadista (Kozlowski 1986), and Kadar fall within this middle range, to which the term "medium-sized campsite" is applied. Even when differences in excavation and recovery techniques are taken into account, the broad categories described above retain their validity, since artifact counts provide at least a gross estimate of site use. To arrive at a closer evaluation, however, other factors need to be considered, especially surface area and artifact density per units of surface area. Yellen (1977) has presented strong evidence in support of the contention that the surface area of artifact scatters and what he calls artifact richness, combining variety as well as abundance of tools, constitute effective measures of population size and/or length of occupation. As population size and length of occupation remain impossible to separate on the basis of archaeological data, at least for the present, it may be said that the variables defined by Yellen provide adequate measures of site-use intensity. Total numbers of tools and debitage, as well as estimates of variety in tool types, are the kinds of information generally available for Gravettian sites. In the case of Kadar a more complete definition of the settlement type can be set forth, since the block-excavations have uncovered a number of habitation features. A description of these features has been published elsewhere (Montet-White, Laville, and Lézine 1986), so a summary of the most significant features will suffice here.

The site of Kadar extends over a hilltop roughly rectangular in shape, about 110 m long and 25-30 m wide, with a surface area well in excess of 3000 m². Excavations uncovered a number of artifact concentrations. In one of the excavated areas (locality I-east) an oval-shaped zone of artifact scatter distributed around a posthole was interpreted as a dwelling (Montet-White and Johnson 1976). The interior space within the dwelling measured 7 by 4.5 m, with a surface area of about 28 m². The area of scatter surrounding the structure, the exterior domestic space, covered a surface area of about 113 m². The workshops identified nearby in locality I-west occupied areas ranging from 7 m² for structure A, a flintknapping workshop, to 3.2 m² for structure D, a cache of blades and flakes (Montet-White, Laville, and Lézine 1986). These figures fall well within the range of nuclear-unit scatters and special-activity scatters observed among K'ung Bushmen (Yellen 1977: 107). Furthermore, the tool assemblage included the complete range of tool types known for the Epigravettian of Central Europe. According to the Kadar example, the medium-sized campsite appears as a "base camp" marked by the presence of habitation features and a variety of well-defined activity areas, in contrast to specialized hunting or flintknapping camps. Group size and length of occupation remain within the range of relatively mobile hunting-gathering groups.

RAW MATERIALS: RADIOLARITE COBBLES

Radiolarite deposits are relatively abundant in Central Europe, where they occur mostly in Jurassic limestones. They are found in the Carpathians of southern Poland and northern Hungary, in the alpine piedmont of Austria and Hungary, in the mountains of central Bosnia, and their distribution extends eastwards to the Zagros Mountains. Their quality varies from coarse-grained with a texture somewhat analogous to quartzite, to very fine-grained and very similar to jasper. It is the latter that Late Paleolithic flintknappers preferred and exploited wherever they were present.

The Paleolithic people of northern Bosnia could have had access to mountain outcrops by following the river valleys upstream for distances of 30-50 km. The presence of quarries or workshops, however, has not been mentioned to date. Secondary sources, gravel bars and river terraces located within close range of the campsites, were more likely sources. In most instances, the nature of the cortex and the shape of the cortical surface indicate that river cobbles were indeed the most common source of raw material. The production system was local in character, with procurement and reduction activities taking place within a limited territory. The distance between the campsite and the nearest cobble beaches was 1 km or less in the cases of Luščić, Londža, and several other northern Bosnian sites. Exceptionally at Kadar, the distance was 5-10 km.

Two cobble samples were taken from the Ukrina River bed at points close to the prehistoric sites and analyzed in order to obtain the kind of information needed to understand the processes of raw-material reduction. The Ukrina is a southern tributary of the Sava; like the Vrbas and the Bosna Rivers, it springs from the mountains of central Bosnia, crossing the foothills in a generally southwest-to-northeast direction before reaching the Sava Valley. The valley widens as the river nears the Sava Valley. Notable differences distinguish the components of cobble beaches located in the valley's upper sections from those of the wider, lower sections where Zobište and Kadar are located. The sample of 500 cobbles

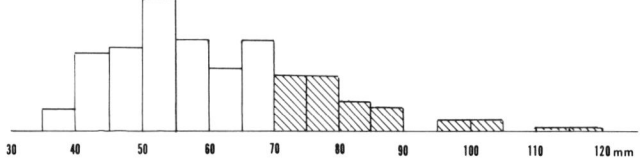

Figure 23.1 Histogram of maximum dimension for a sample of Ukrina River cobbles. Shading indicates size classes suitable for flintknapping.

immediately below the Mousterian site of Zobište may be considered representative of cobble assemblages found in lower valleys of the Sava River's southern tributaries. Therefore, it provides a useful set of information concerning the variety, size, and range of raw materials available to Late Paleolithic hunters (Fig. 23.1).

On the basis of measurements of the primary cortical flakes recovered from Kadar (Fig. 23.2), it may be inferred that cobbles selected for knapping ranged in size between 70 and 120 mm. Cobbles of this size range constitute 18% of the cobble sample; and fine-grained radiolarites, the preferred raw material of prehistoric northern Bosnian flintknappers, represent close to 80% of the sample. The odds of finding a cobble of good material and adequate size are thus on the order of 14%, but frost damage affected a large proportion of radiolarite cobbles. Experiments showed that, when frost damaged, the smaller cobbles tend to shatter into irregular, angular pieces which replicate the chunks and shatter recovered at the site. The larger pieces tend to split along transversal planes that flintknappers used as striking platforms. It is reasonable to assume that cobbles were tested before they were carried back to the campsite, especially since the number of primary cortical flakes is relatively low. Nonetheless, the high proportion of chunks and shatter indicates that the selection process was not entirely successful. The proportion of shatter to core is about 3 to 1; more significant, perhaps, is that the volume of shattered material has been estimated to represent about 24% of the total amount of raw material remaining at the site. The lack of comparative data makes it difficult to interpret such a figure and arrive at an evaluation of the effectiveness of the raw-material selection process at Kadar. It would appear that a loss of almost one-fourth of the raw materials remained within tolerable limits given the local conditions: easily accessible and transportable materials, but a distance of several kilometers between the campsite and the nearest gravel bar of the Bosna River.

The second stage in the production system in-

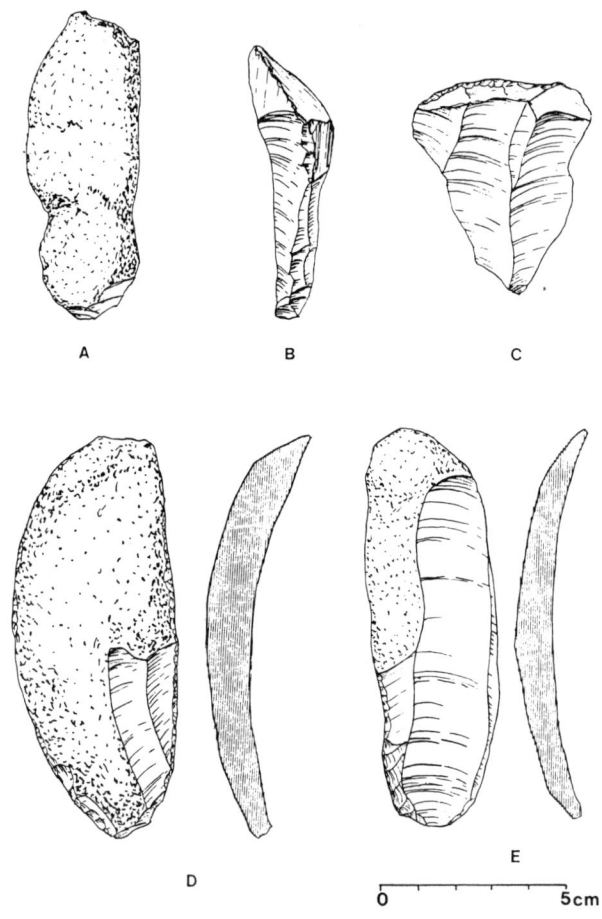

Figure 23.2   Cortical blades and byproducts of core preparation from Kadar.

cludes a series of integrated operations related to core preparation, blank production, and core reduction. With the exception of primary decortication flakes, all the byproducts of the production system are well represented in the assemblage, and well-defined workshops have been identified in one area of the site. Therefore, inasmuch as could be determined without extensive backfitting leading to the reconstruction of the original cobbles, it may be said that all the flintknapping operations took place at the site.

CORE PREPARATION

Partial trimming of both surfaces produced bifacial pre-cores with a well-characterized lateral crest and cortex preserved on one-half or one-third of the opposite side (Fig. 23.3e). Bifacial trimming accounts for the presence of a number of completely and partially crested blades (Fig. 23.2b). In other cases, blade removal started from one of the cobble's narrow edges after removal of a platform flake but without lateral preparation. A number of large cortical blades were the result of that process (Fig. 23.2a, d).

Because cortical flakes largely outnumber cortical blades, though, it would seem that pre-core preparation was a more common procedure than direct blade extraction. The proportion of cortical flakes and blades—including complete specimens and proximal fragments—to cores is about 3 to 1. The proportion of flakes—byproducts of continued core preparation—to cores is about 3.5 to 1. On the average, cortical and noncortical flakes account for 14%, a relatively small fraction, of the cobble's volume.

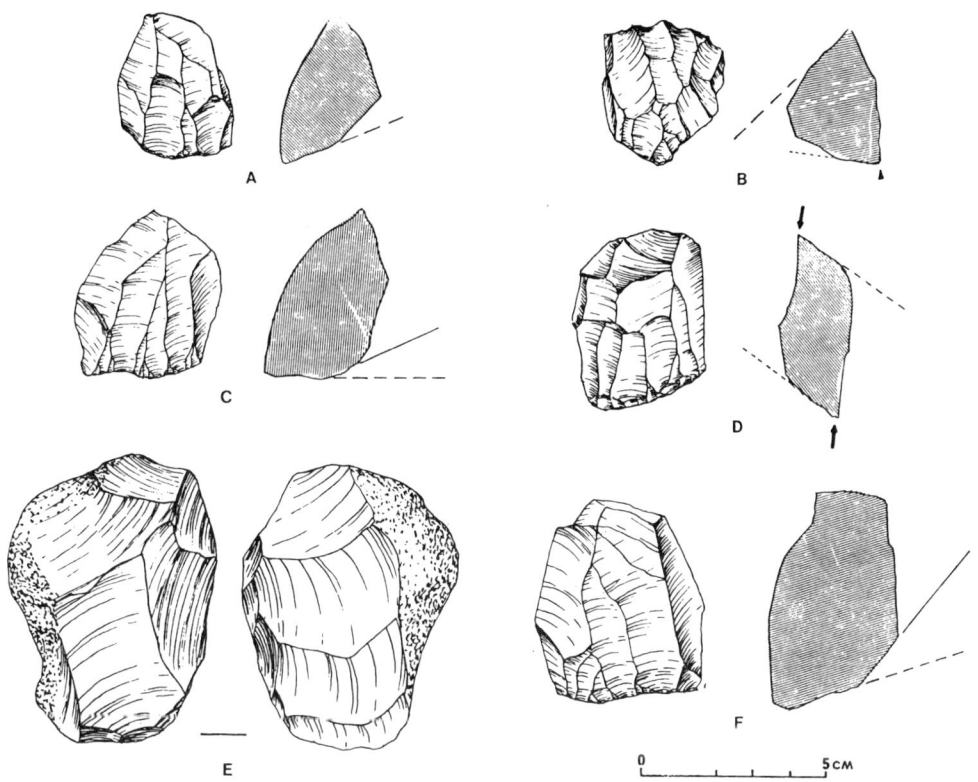

Figure 23.3   Radiolarite cores from Kadar.

BLADE PRODUCTION

It is generally accepted that, in Late Paleolithic times, the whole knapping process was aimed at maximizing the production of blades, and the techniques in use yielded predictable results. These points have been well documented by replication and backfitting. The evidence from Kadar corroborates these points. In addition, it provides an estimate in quantitative terms of the efficacy of the knapping process.

Platform remnants on blades are categorized as punctiform, lenticular, or flat; the latter were prepared by dorsal reduction and occasionally by grinding of the edge between platform and dorsal face. A number of studies (Fish 1979; Dibble 1985b; Dibble and Whittaker 1981) have demonstrated the direct relationship between platform preparation and blank morphology. In the case of blade assemblages, punctiform platforms tend to produce narrow and thin blades; this mode of platform preparation is predominant among bladelet samples. Wider platforms, either flat or lenticular, are associated with wider, thicker, and longer blades. The same kind of relationship between platform preparation and blank morphology was noted in a number of Central European Gravettian assemblages, not only at Kadar but at Willendorf II Levels 5, 6, and 7 (Austria); and Arka, Pillismarot, and Sagvar (Hungary). Indirect percussion was probably the predominant mode of blade detachment among Gravettian groups. It can be said that techniques of core preparation and motor behavior that controlled blade detachment were almost standardized within the region. The objective was not only to maximize the production of blades but also to control the chance of obtaining blades of a specified morphology.

The ratio of blades to cores is approximately 12 to 1 when complete blades, proximal fragments, and tools made on blades are included in the estimate. The value is probably too low in view of the high breakage rate noted within the habitation structure. In terms of volume, blades represent a relatively high percentage of the total raw material: the total blade assemblage, modified and unmodified blades included, represents about 27% of the average cobble's volume. More than one-fourth of the raw material was transformed into usable products—a figure that may be viewed as an acceptable return of the energy expended in transporting and transforming the blocks of raw materials.

Kadar cores share the morphological and technological characteristics of radiolarite cores from other Central European sites. The majority are single platformed, either subconical (43%) or prismatic (15%) in shape. Double-platformed cores represent 20% of the core sample and polyhedric specimens 15% (Fig. 23.3). They are small, as the mean dimensions presented in Table 23.1 indicate. The last pieces to have been removed were bladelets 3 to 4 cm long. Table 23.1 illustrates clearly the similarities between the Kadar specimens and the radiolarite cores from Willendorf I-North and Willendorf II Levels 5 and 6. The Willendorf series have similar technological attributes as well. Platforms are maintained by the removal of tabular flakes, and platform angles range between 55 and 65°. The close similarities among the four series are to be emphasized, as these constitute significant—if limited—evidence that the system of raw-material transformation developed here, largely from the Kadar industries, does have wider applications.

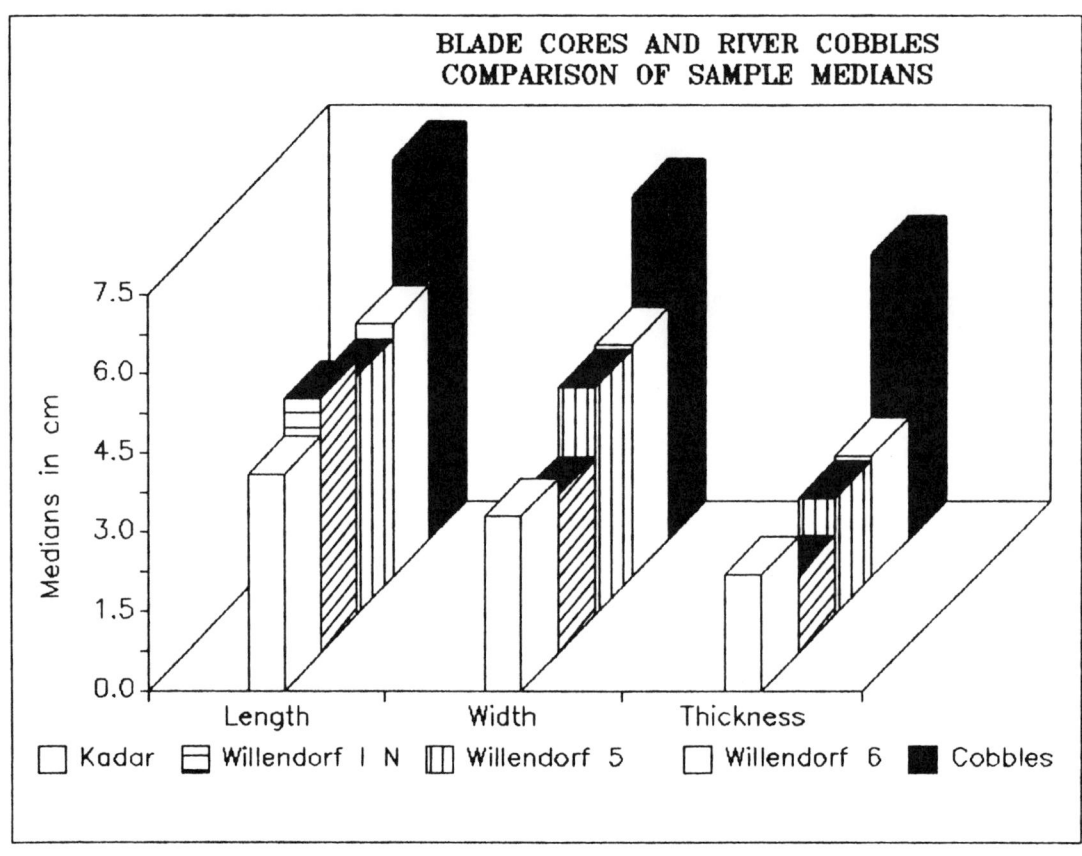

Figure 23.4   *Histograms displaying medians of length, width, and thickness for a sample of river cobbles and four core samples.*

TABLE 23.1
MEAN MEASUREMENTS OF
CORES AND RIVER COBBLES

	Ukrina cobbles	Kadar cores	Willendorf cores		
			I-N	II-5	II-6
Length	7.2	4.1	4.8	4.5	4.4
Width	6.5	3.3	3.0	4.3	4.4
Thickness	5.4	2.2	1.5	2.2	2.3

All dimensions are in cm. Group means for core samples: 4.5 × 3.8 × 2.1 cm. Distance from cobble sample measurements to group mean measurements: 49.8.

Comparisons drawn between core and cobble measurements provide a measure of material reduction achieved through the knapping process (Fig. 23.4 and Table 23.1). On the average, length and width are reduced by 2.7 cm and thickness by 3.1 cm. These figures may appear small, but in effect the reductions represent 43% of the cobble's maximum dimension, 49% of the width, and 59% of the thickness; the volume is reduced by almost 80%. It can be said that at these sites, flintknappers made very effective use of their raw materials. The effectiveness of the knapping process, possible when the material was of good quality, may have compensated for the loss due to frost damage.

A high incidence of breakage is one of the most striking features of the Kadar site. The rate is especially high within and immediately around the structure identified as a dwelling, which suggests that trampling may have contributed to the large quantity of broken pieces. In any case, the volume of splinters and small fragments represents about 16% of the average cobble's volume.

The pie diagram (Fig. 23.5) illustrates the manner in which the volume of an average cobble was divided among artifact categories. The major elements of the raw-material economy are clearly displayed: importance of material loss though shatter; minimal prepa-

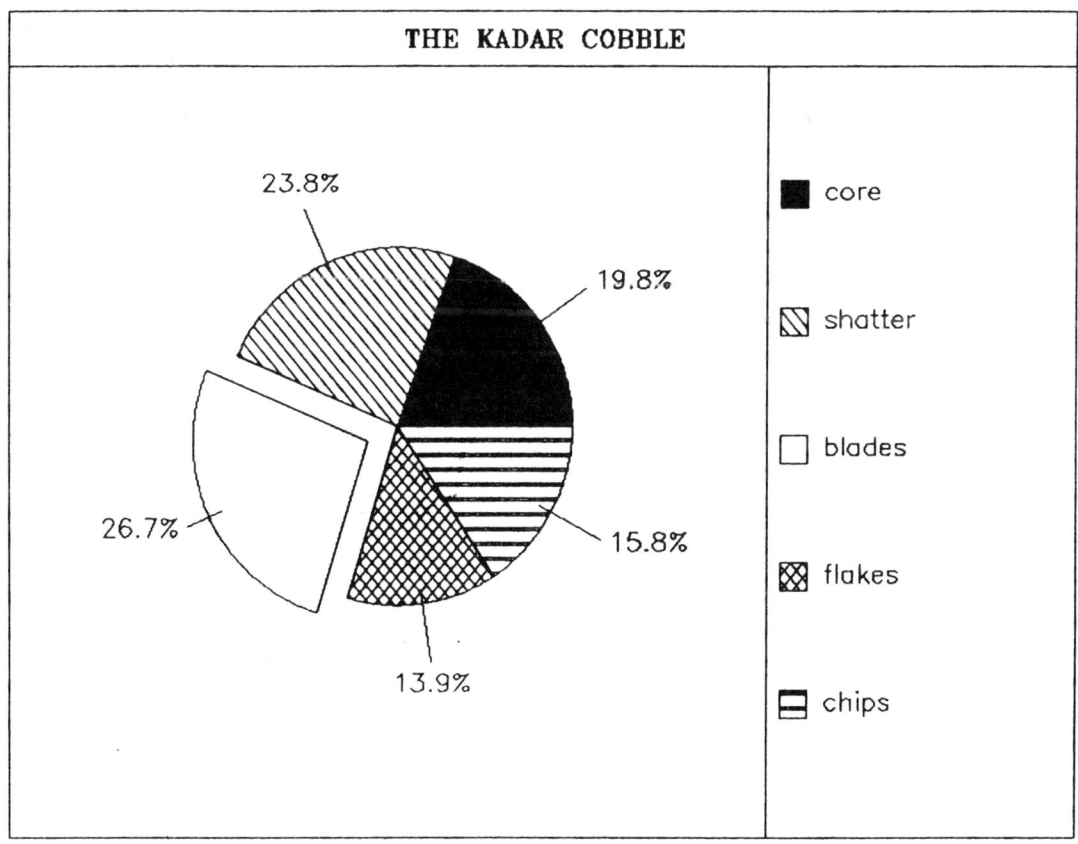

Figure 23.5 The Kadar cobble: pie graph illustrating the manner in which an average cobble was divided and the expected return (% of blades).

ration; well-controlled blade production; abandonment of cores after maximum reduction; and, lastly, importance of splinters and fragments. The latter are more an indication of intense use and therefore reinforce the notion of highly efficient use of raw material at the site. If the process of cobble selection was not successful in eliminating frost-damaged cobbles, the loss was maintained at about 24%. The exploitation of frostfree cobbles proceeded with a high degree of efficacy, with the careful preparation of striking platforms allowing for maximum core reduction.

Similarities in core morphology and core size noted between the Kadar and Willendorf samples support the contention that the Kadar model is representative of the modes of transformation and use of radiolarite cobbles by Gravettian groups. Assemblages from Willendorf 5, 6, and 7 are the most directly comparable to the Kadar assemblage. These were mentioned earlier as representative of medium-sized campsites, but accurate counts of cortical and noncortical flakes, of shatter, chips, and fragments are not available at this time for sites of the Central European Basin. For that reason, comparisons remain incomplete.

BLANK SELECTION

The second, and perhaps most important, aspect of raw-material economy relates to the processes of tool manufacture. As indicated above, the diversity of tool types is viewed as a manifestation of the variety of tasks performed at the site and is an indirect measure of the intensity of site use. Blank selection is the aspect of flint economy that is more directly related to raw-material economy. It is obvious enough that the need for certain types of blanks determined to a large extent technological choices. In most of the Eastern Gravettian assemblages, a large majority of tools were made from blade blanks, which shows maximum

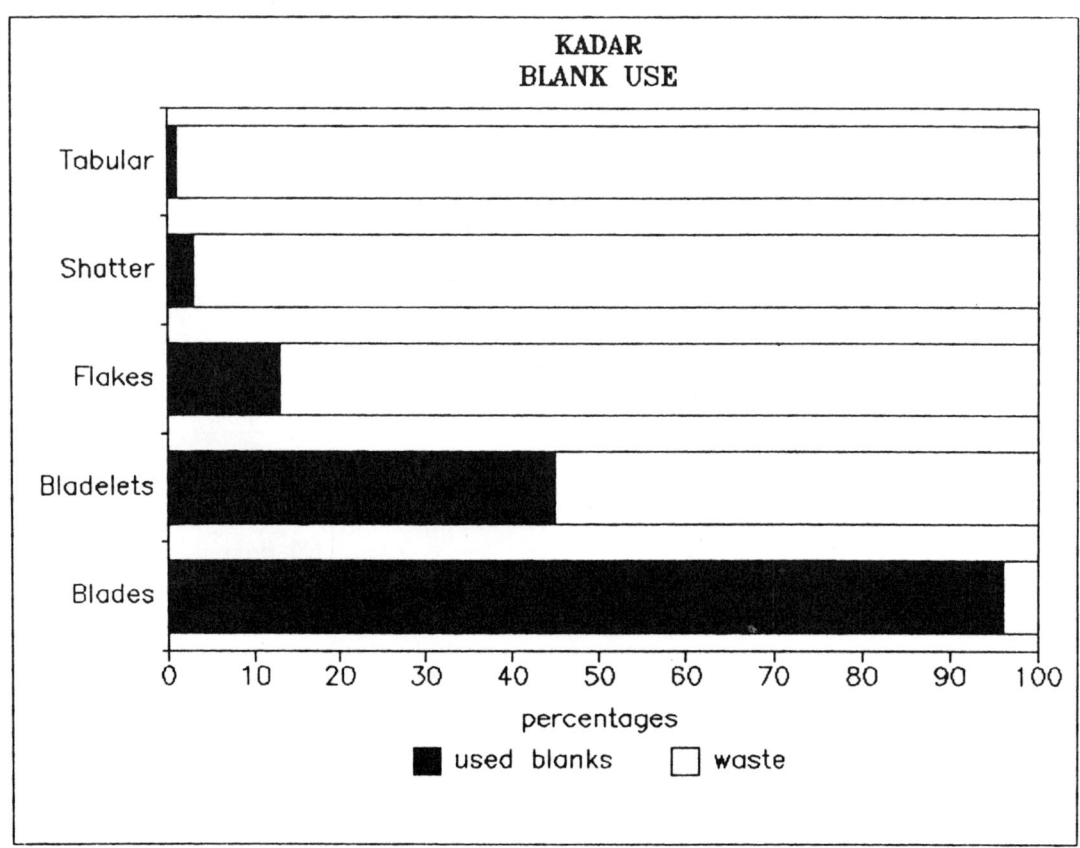

Figure 23.6   Histogram illustrating variability in use rate for different blank types.

use of blade blanks produced at the site and explains the very specialized character of the knapping technique. At Kadar, blank selection operated as follows (Fig. 23.6):

Blades wider than 20 mm, 95-99%

Blades 10-20 mm wide, 40-50%

Cortical and noncortical flakes, 10-15%

Chunks and shatter, 1-5%

Tabular pieces, <1%

A strong association exists between blade size and rate of selection. Almost all, if not all, of the largest blades were used as cutting tools—as indicated by the numerous lateral scars—and transformed into distal tools. The selection rate decreases significantly as width and thickness decrease. In the assemblages studied here, the decrease in selection rate occurs below 20 mm for the width measurement. A similar trend was noted in other assemblages as well. At Willendorf, the larger blades exhibit some degree of use and/or retouch. The rate of smaller-blade selection varies a great deal more, although it is difficult to quantify the differences given the conditions of most museum collections. Flakes, chunks, and tabular blanks were used in addition to, rather than as a substitute for, blades. The case of Kadar, where flake tools are at a minimum, does not appear to be unique. Very low percentages have been noted at other Gravettian sites. The question remains for collections resulting from older excavations where flake tools may not have been recognized or kept.

Patterns of blank selection become more obvious when one considers the differences in gross size between tool groups. A more detailed discussion of blank selection among Central European Gravettian industries has been presented elsewhere (Montet-White 1982b). For the purpose of that study, tools were separated into:

(a) armatures, which include all the backed pieces and shoulder points and were made on thin and narrow blades;

(b) the lateral tools, which include marginally retouched blades, a few sidescrapers made on often-cortical lamellar flakes, and notches and denticulates

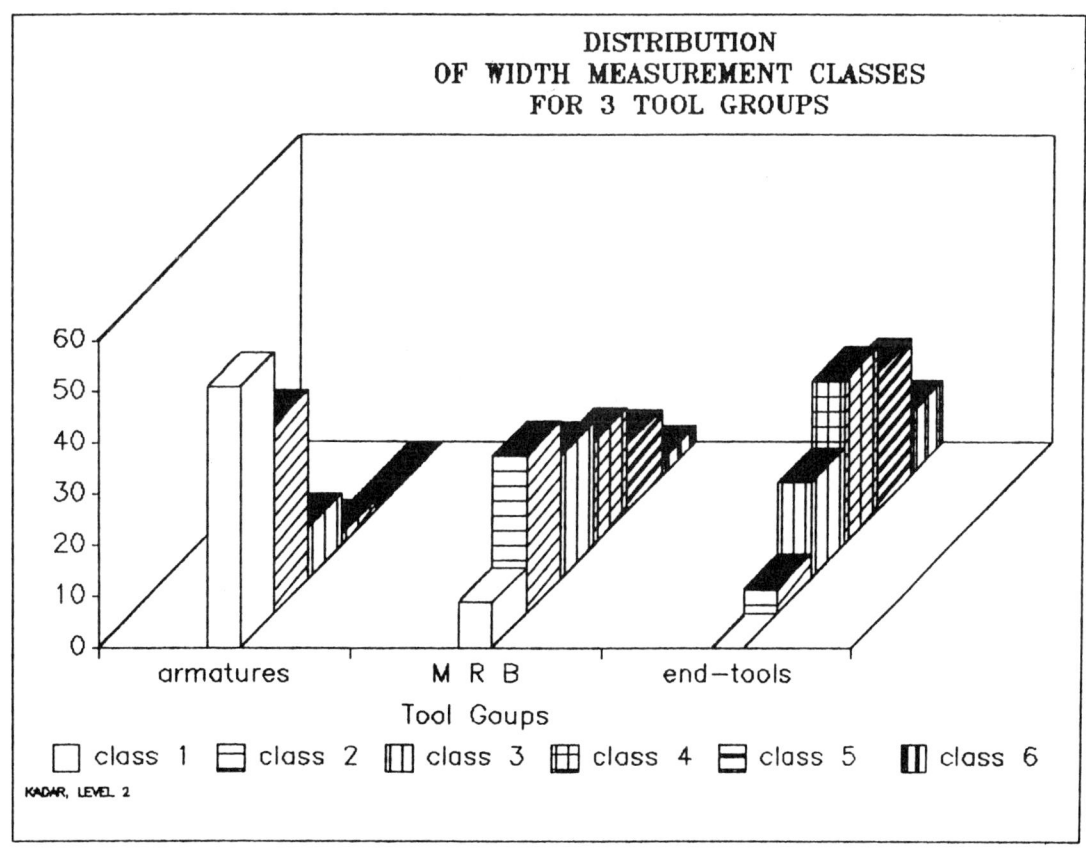

Figure 23.7 Histograms of width measurements illustrating the process of blank selection for different types of tools.

made on every kind of blank; and

(c) end tools, whose working edge is placed at one of the narrow extremities of a blade or lamellar flake. These include:

(c1) endscrapers, which are abundant and carefully made and form a homogeneous group, and perforators, which are few in number and atypical in morphology;

(c2) burins, which are abundant and extremely varied in shape and technique of manufacture, and truncations, which were made on all kinds of blanks.

Each of the groups is characterized by morphometric patterns that are almost standardized among Gravettian groups. Figure 23.7 illustrates the distribution of maximum width among the different tool groups. Width measurements range from 5 to 35 mm, with class intervals of 5 mm. End tools, endscrapers especially, occur on the widest blade blanks. Furthermore, the normal and leptokurtic distribution of width measurements for endscrapers is a strong indication of a high level of selection. In contrast, variability within the group of burins is reflected in the multimodal aspect of the distribution curve. Lateral tools are characterized by a normal, flat distribution curve indicative of the fact that a wider range of blades formed acceptable blanks for that group.

In summary, the blade assemblage was partitioned into at least three groups. The wider blades, which were also the longer and thicker, were selected primarily to make endscrapers but also burins. Other blanks including tabular pieces (platform flakes) were also used for burin manufacture. Before or after they were transformed into terminal tools, large blades were also used as knives, as indicated by wear scars along the lateral edges. Other blades too small for end-tool manufacture were used as cutting tools, whereas the smallest blades were transformed into armatures. At Kadar, a single group of complete, medium-sized blades was found within one of the artifact concentrations (I-west); it constituted the only "reserve" recovered at the site.

TOOL USE

The relative intensity of tool use and tool curation may be seen as one of the best indicators of raw-material economy at the site. Several variables are introduced in order to quantify estimates of tool use. The first set of variables measure the degree of reduction produced by retouching and sharpening of end tools. The second relate to the rate of tool breakage. Endscrapers (Fig. 23.8) provide the best sample on which these variables can be measured since, as mentioned above, they constitute a morphologically homogeneous group made from a selected segment of the blade assemblage. The metrical attributes that characterize blank selection are as follows:

median width is 24 mm;

the widths of 90% of the scrapers fall between 20 and 29 mm;

larger blades (>20 mm wide) form between 20 and 24% of the blade samples.

Figure 23.9 displays the means by which reduction due to retouching and sharpening was obtained. It illustrates a scattergram of length and width measurements for complete endscrapers—that is to say, specimens whose scraper edge is located at the distal end and whose bulb is still visible at the proximal end.

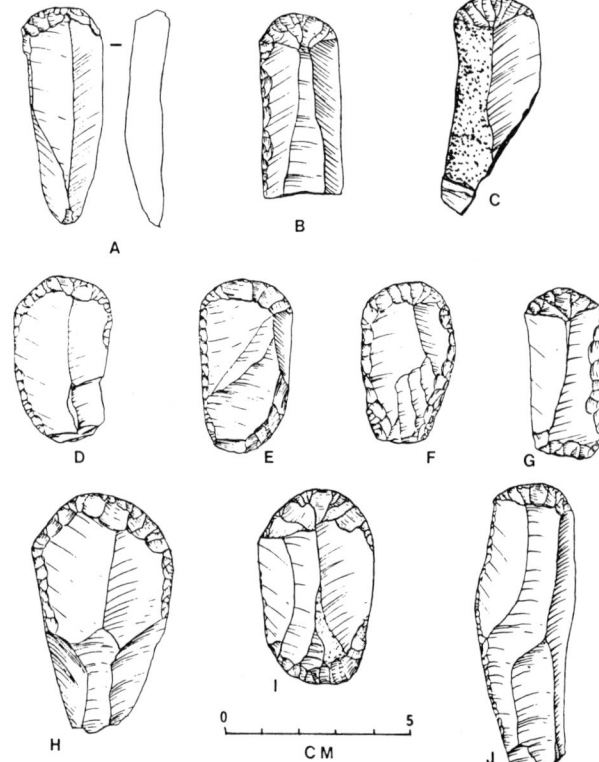

Figure 23.8   Endscrapers from Kadar.

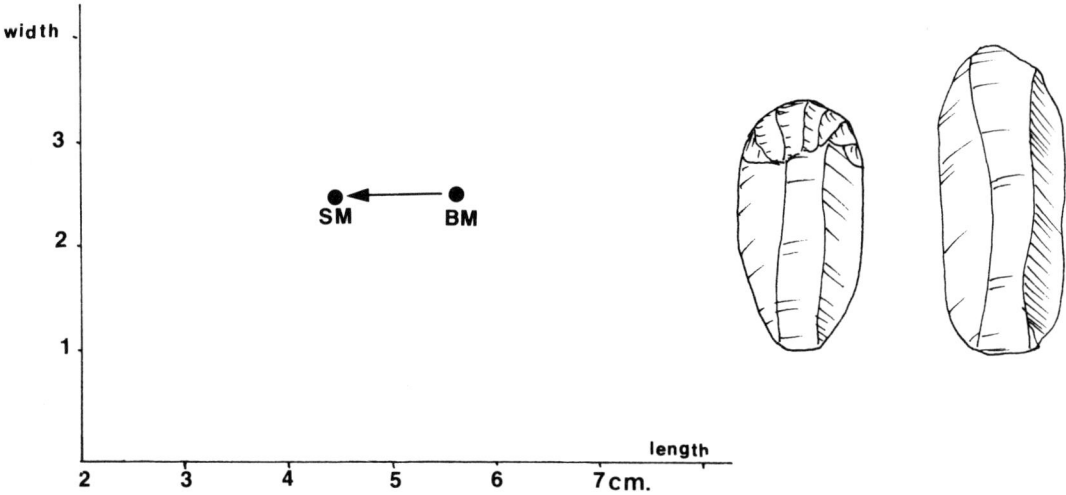

Figure 23.9 Graph illustrating the difference between median lengths of blade blanks and endscrapers as a means of estimating the degree of reduction resulting from making, and sharpening, endscrapers.

The median length of the scraper sample is shown in comparison to the median length of blades wider than 20 mm, since these are the blades from which the scrapers are made. The difference between the two medians was 12-14 mm. The reduction in length due to scraper end preparation was on the order of 20%.

Breakage affected a large number of specimens (Fig. 23.10). Thirty percent of the endscrapers were at the tip of a broken blade. In most cases, the break occurred at or near the blade midpoint or well above the bulbar area. Whether the scrapers were hafted or not, mid-length was probably the point where the greater pressure was applied. Breaks near the working edge are less common but still significant; the ratio of scraper tips to complete scrapers is 1 to 10.

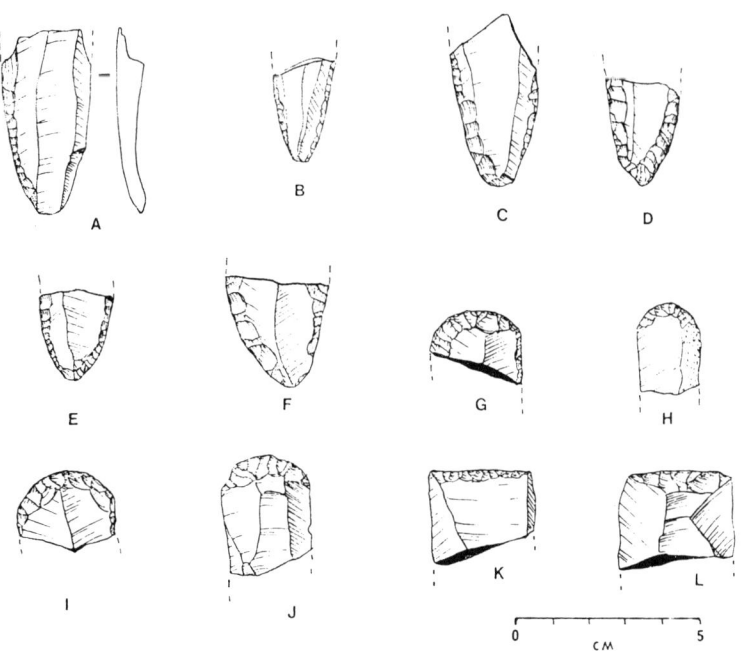

Figure 23.10 Scrapers and retouched blades illustrating breakage patterns.

SUMMARY

The model of raw-material economy derived from the study of Kadar is summarized in the form of a flow chart (Fig. 23.11). The model integrates patterns of blank selection, blank reduction due to retouching and sharpening (at least for endscrapers), and the breakage rates that characterize each of the major categories of tools. In spite of its apparent complexity, the flow chart is a very simplified and schematic representation of the very intricate and complex processes which constitute raw-material economy. The flow chart complements and continues the pie diagram (Fig. 23.5) which assembled the elements related to blank production.

While burins, retouched blades, and armatures abandoned at the site were for the most part broken and unusable, a much larger number of scrapers were left which still appeared usable. It may be that when people abandoned the campsite they took with them armatures (or more likely their weapons), large blades, and perhaps some burins—their hunting-butchering tools—but left behind the scrapers, perforators, and other processing tools.

The limited sets of comparisons presented in the course of the discussion indicate close relationship between the Kadar industries and the industries from Willendorf II Levels 5, 6, and 7. More extensive comparative analyses of blade blanks, retouched blades, and endscrapers have indicated strong similarities between Kadar and two sites located in Hungary, Sagvar and Arka (Montet-White and Basler 1977), in terms of blank selection and blank reduction.

The evidence supports the view that the Kadar model represents a pattern of raw-material economy which may be generalized to Gravettian industries made from the same, or at least a comparable kind of, raw material and associated with the same type of settlement.

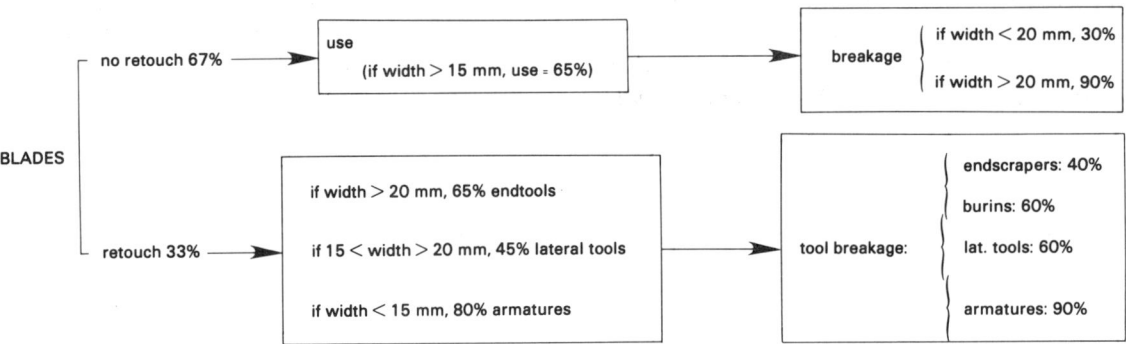

Figure 23.11   Processes of blade selection and tool use presented in the form of a flow chart stating conditions and observed probability.

DISCUSSION

ROLLAND: You raise the question of parsimonious use of lithic resources and I was wondering how this could be implemented in dealing with Middle Paleolithic assemblages. The first thing to think about is that in the Upper Paleolithic the techniques are already much more specialized and more easily identifiable because they are specific. The typology also appears much more specific, although perhaps we are deluding ourselves. This study is one of several examples we have now of very painstaking analysis of a particular site situation where we can follow the reduction sequence, or *chaîne opératoire*, from the quarrying stage right down to tool use and discard. You indicate that there are some multiple tools. I wonder whether these scraper-burins, scraper-pointed blades, etc., were not in fact successive stages in the long history of transformation of the tools. Another question: Can the same guidelines be applied to the study of other industries?

MONTET-WHITE: I think that there is no question that the model may be applied to other sites, Aurignacian or Gravettian. It is a matter of sample quality. To do this kind of study, you need the total assemblage and this implies recent, systematic excavations. Museum collections are not reliable.

ROLLAND: I think your goal was to find out how one can identify economizing behavior and define the parameters that measure economic behavior at this or any other site. This leads to questions that have wider dimensions; what are the circumstances or motivations which were present to produce that assemblage? I have tried to identify these to some degree in the Middle Paleolithic, but I imagine that one could do a better job with Upper Paleolithic assemblages, given the higher level of technological specialization.

MONTET-WHITE: I think that, given adequate samples, one could find similar patterns of core preparation and blade production at other Gravettian sites. I found very similar systems of cobble exploitation at other Gravettian sites. Processes of blank selection are very comparable with Willendorf. But there they used other blanks as well. I think it is more difficult to reconstruct breakage patterns.

ROLLAND: I agree that it is important to consider breakage patterns as an aspect of what happened at the site. You mentioned also the classification of sites.

MONTET-WHITE: One has to exercise a great deal of care because of differences in excavations and recovery techniques, and also of the problems of collection curation in museums which affect total artifact counts from different sites. Still, there appear to be recurring clusters that can be derived from total artifact counts, and tool counts available in the literature for sites that have been excavated. You have on the one hand very small sites with a handful of tools and artifact counts of 50 or 100. They occur in open sites of the Pannonian Basin as well as in some cave sites. There are, at the other end of the spectrum, sites like Willendorf Level 9 with thousands of tools. But in between is a cluster of—whatever the term used—campsites, where artifact counts are somewhere between 1500 and 3000, and tool counts in the hundreds. In the southern margin of the Pannonian Basin there are no large campsites; at least, they have not been found. But there are quite a number of the medium-size campsites.

KOZLOWSKI: I think that the major difficulty with the approach you propose is the diversity of raw materials, because you must do separate analysis for every kind of raw material.

MONTET-WHITE: Well, I think it can be done in cases where there are two, three, or perhaps even four types of raw materials.

KOZLOWSKI: And there is the question of how to calculate volume.

SACKETT: I don't understand what a *chaîne opératoire* is. Reduction sequence, as used in English by most of the Americans here, seems to be the series of steps that leads to the production of a pristine tool, while a *chaîne opératoire* seems to lead all the way to the point where the tool is discarded.

ROLLAND: Including use-breakage and resharpening.

STRAUS: So in English we should say reduction-use-discard sequence or something like that.

SACKETT: I have another question concerning the breakage of endscrapers. When a blade is snapped, the lift of the break can appear either on the dorsal or the ventral face, depending upon whether it is broken under pressure or flexion. Well, if this breakage is the result of usage we might be able to find whether we're dealing with pressure or flexion.

MONTET-WHITE: Most of the break surfaces are flat.

KOZLOWSKI: There is also a possibility that some blades were broken intentionally before they were made into endscrapers.

MONTET-WHITE: What varies from site to site is not so much the processes of endscraper production but the amount of reduction that occurs after manufacture.

OTTE: There are some Gravettian sites in Moravia where there are bone handles.

SACKETT: But these provided different breakage patterns.

XXIV
Upper and Final Paleolithic Settlement Patterns in the Rhineland, West Germany

Gerhard Bosinski

INTRODUCTION

The Rhineland of the western part of Germany is dominated by the Rhine Valley but includes the important tributaries of the Neckar, Main, Nahe, Lahn, and Mosel Rivers (Fig. 24.1). The southern part of the Rhineland is the Mainzer Basin, the central part is the Rhenish slate-massif including the Neuwieder Basin, and the northern part is formed by the Kölner Lowland-bay. The larger towns of this region are Mainz, Koblenz, Bonn, and Cologne (Köln). Upper Pleistocene deposits are mostly loess and volcanic material; therefore the chronology is based mainly on loess-stratigraphy and tephrochronology (Fig. 24.2; Löhr and Brunnacker 1974; Brunnacker 1978; Bosinski 1983a, b).

In this region, the late Middle Paleolithic continues after the first pleniglacial of the last glaciation. The transition to the Upper Paleolithic then takes place during the Hengelo period. The Aurignacian is placed in the cold period between Hengelo and Denekamp. The middle part of the Upper Paleolithic falls into the Denekamp period and the following cold stage (Bosinski et al. 1985). During the second pleniglacial human occupation seems to have been interrupted, since there are no archaeological sites of this period, but this stage is in the loess sections well defined by the Eltviller Tuff. The late Upper Paleolithic corresponds to the Bölling period and the Dryas II. During the Bölling there is Magdalenian material and later there are influences from the northwest (i.e., Hamburgian). The Final Paleolithic comprises the Alleröd and Dryas III (Younger Dryas) stages. The Alleröd material is represented by the Azilian (Federmessergruppen). During Dryas III the mountainous central and southern parts of the Rhineland seem to remain Azilian territory, but the lowland in the north is occupied by Ahrensburgian reindeer hunters. In the second part of Alleröd, about 9080 B.C., the eruption of the Laacher-See Volcano covered the central part of the Rhineland with pumice (Bogaard and Schmincke 1984).

UPPER PALEOLITHIC SETTLEMENT PATTERNS

ENVIRONMENT

The climate during the Upper Paleolithic was very dry. The ocean was cold and the predominating west wind brought no clouds. According to calculations by Frenzel for the second pleniglacial, the result of this pattern was a marked difference between warm summers (average July temperature +18° C.) and very cold winters (average January temperature -15° C.). The vegetation cover was the prairie-like grassland of the loess steppe; due to the lack of humidity, trees grew only in the river valleys.

The animal biomass, however, was high. The biotop was characterized by the combination of cold and dry, which brought together animals of the present subarctic (e.g., reindeer) and the present arid Central Asian region (e.g., saiga). The distinct seasonal difference caused herd migrations between the mountainous region in the summers and the sheltered valleys during the winters. Seasonal migrations of animal herds in the open grassland facilitated hunting activities. The spearthrower—an efficient weapon—

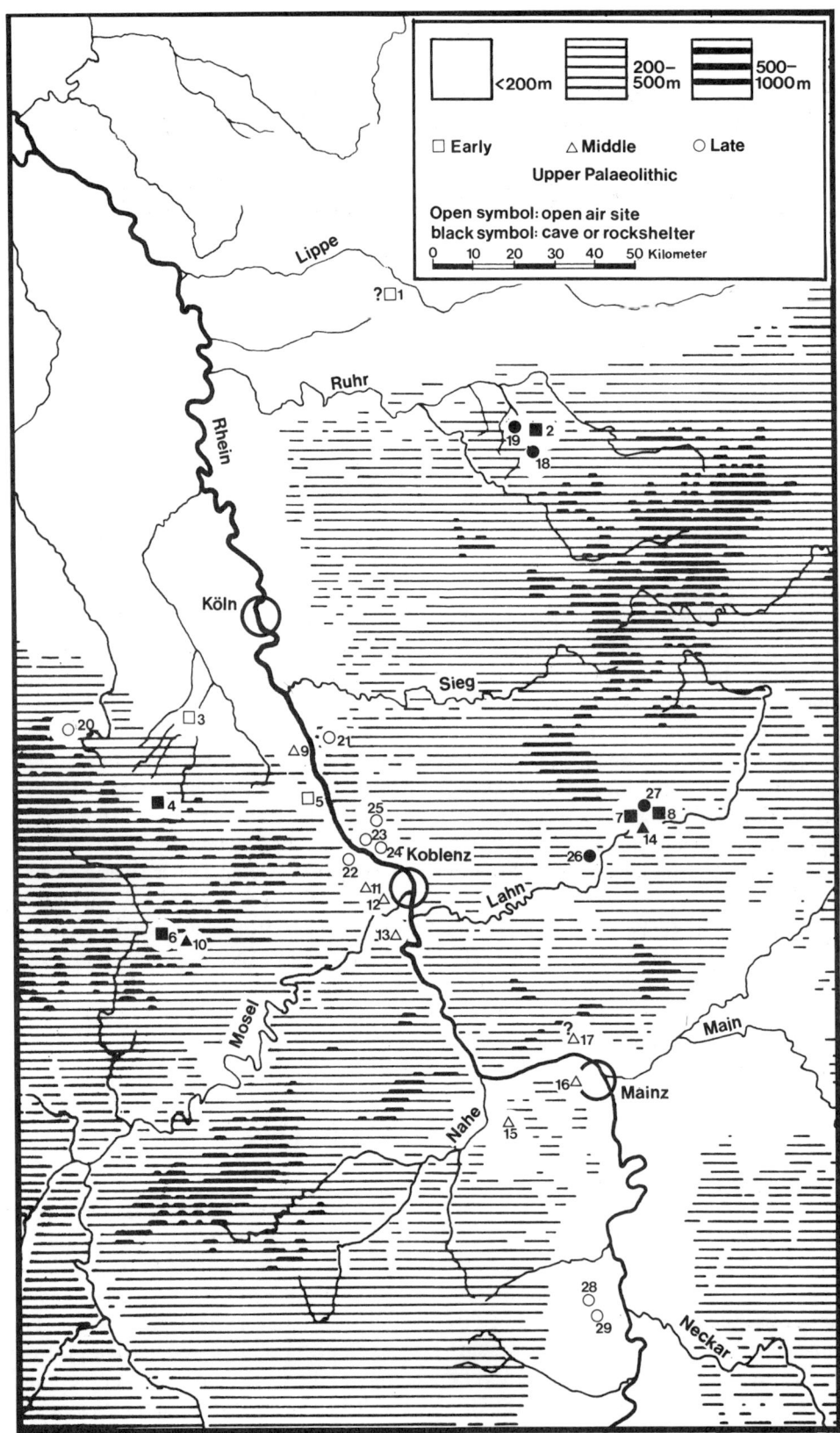

Figure 24.1

played an essential role as did the knowledge of meat conservation. This created a standardized organization of the hunter's life and led to a specialized settlement pattern (Fig. 24.1).

SETTLEMENTS (BASE CAMPS AND VILLAGES)

It seems clear that the locations of settlements were picked for comfort. As a general rule they were above the larger rivers on a slightly inclined step near a small watercourse, with a more or less extended plain on the opposite river bank. These areas receive ample sunshine, and to the north are sheltered by higher ground. This is called a seat position. Examples of such a choice of settlement place are Mainz-Linsenberg, Metternich, Andernach, and Gönnersdorf.

HOUSE CONSTRUCTION AND SEASONALITY

Houses of this period were always constructed on a slight slope. To gain a horizontal living surface the rearward part was excavated into the slope. The best-preserved and -studied house remains are from Gönnersdorf and can serve as examples (Bosinski 1979). Here the houses were round, with a diameter of 6-8 m, and the floor was paved with slate. The periphery may be marked by postholes; in other cases the builders may have used three-legged wall-posts. The middle post was placed in an especially deep pit or directly on the ground. The wooden frame was covered by animal hides. If horse hide was used, as it most likely was at Gönnersdorf, 40 hides would have been needed.

The fireplace was near the middle post. Fire was maintained in a pit that could be covered by stone slabs. In one instance a mammoth thighbone was placed beside the fireplace as a part of a grill construction. A lower grill was built of a reindeer's antler shovel, the tines forming a fork over the heat. The main entrance was to the southeast and opened downslope. This was an enclosed construction that stored the warmth. A second wall opening was on the weather side in the west, on the same level as the fireplace. Very likely it served to force out the smoke through the ridge hole (the main entrance being closed). Inside the house were cooking pits. Cooking was done with heated quartz pebbles in hide- or leather-covered containers. After use, objects tended to fall into these pits and so were favored for preservation. These houses themselves were thus clearly not transportable. The material needed to construct the wooden frame alone would fill a Volkswagen bus twice.

At Gönnersdorf there are three houses of this type and indications of a fourth dwelling. The seasons of occupation were different in that one house was used during the cold period (Poplin 1976), another during the summer. It must be emphasized that the size and construction of these houses are consistent. Russian archaeologists tend to argue that big houses were used in the winter and small tents in the summer. This

Figure 24.1 Upper Paleolithic sites in the Rhineland.

1. Datteln (Bosinski 1982b)
2. Balver Höhle (Hahn 1977)
3. Lommersum (Hahn 1977)
4. Kartstein-Höhle (Hahn 1977)
5. Remagen-Schwalbenberg (App et al. 1987)
6. Buchenloch (Hahn 1977)
7. Wildscheuer III (Hahn 1977; Terberger 1986)
8. Wildhaus (Hahn 1977; Terberger 1986)
9. Muffendorf (Veil 1978b)
10. Magdalena-Höhle (Weiss 1978)
11. Plaidter Hummerich (Bosinski et al. 1986)
12. Metternich (Hahn 1969)
13. Rhens (Hahn 1969)
14. Wildscheuer IV (Bosinski 1978c; Terberger 1986)
15. Sprendlingen (Bosinski et al. 1985)
16. Mainz-Linsenberg (Hahn 1969)
17. Wiesbaden-Adlerquelle (Bosinski 1978a)
18. Balver Höhle (Bosinski 1984)
19. Feldhofhöhle (Bosinski 1984)
20. Alsdorf (Löhr 1974, 1979)
21. Oberkassel (Verworn, Bonnet, and Steinmann 1919)
22. Andernach (Veil 1982a)
23. Gönnersdorf (Bosinski 1969)
24. Irlich (Bosinski 1979)
25. Segendorf (unpub.)
26. Wildweiberlei (Bosinski 1978b; Terberger 1986)
27. Wildscheuer V (Bosinski 1978d; Terberger 1986)
28. Fussgönheim I (Stodiek 1987)
29. Fussgönheim II (Stodiek 1987)

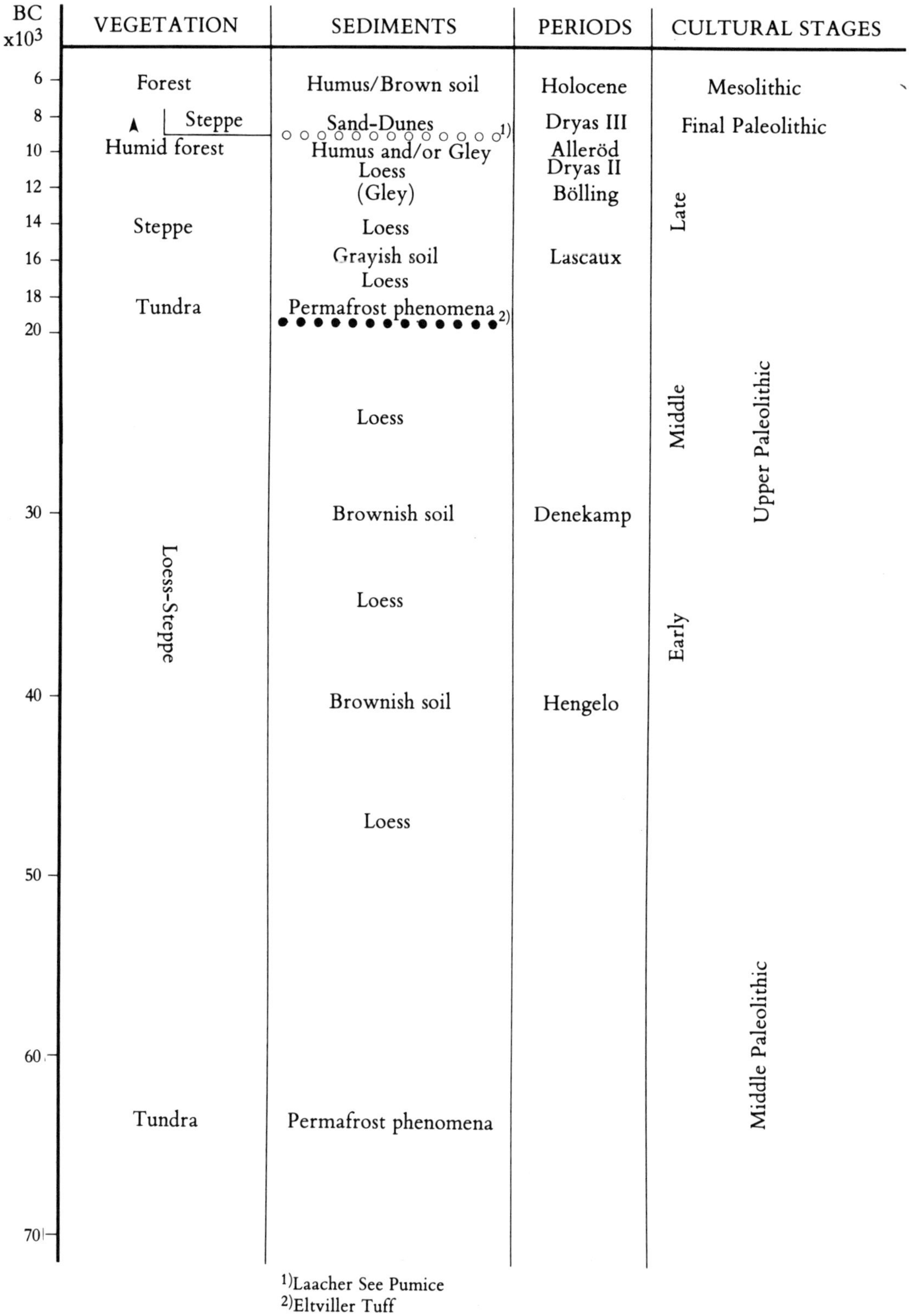

BC x10³	VEGETATION	SEDIMENTS	PERIODS	CULTURAL STAGES	
6	Forest	Humus/Brown soil	Holocene	Mesolithic	
8	Steppe	Sand-Dunes ⁰⁾¹⁾	Dryas III	Final Paleolithic	
10	Humid forest	Humus and/or Gley	Alleröd		
12		Loess (Gley)	Dryas II Bölling	Late	
14	Steppe	Loess			
16		Grayish soil Loess	Lascaux		
18	Tundra	Permafrost phenomena ²⁾			Upper Paleolithic
20		●●●●●●●●●●●			
		Loess		Middle	
30	Loess-Steppe	Brownish soil	Denekamp		
		Loess		Early	
40		Brownish soil	Hengelo		
50		Loess			
60	Tundra	Permafrost phenomena			Middle Paleolithic
70					

¹⁾Laacher See Pumice
²⁾Eltviller Tuff

Figure 24.2 Upper and Final Paleolithic chronology in the Rhineland.

interpretation, however, is based not on a seasonal analysis of the bone material but on ethnographic comparisons with modern hunter tribes of Siberia. The well-known settlement pattern of the present subarctic, with solid winter houses and transportable summer tents, is not a valid interpretation of Upper Paleolithic settlement pattern since the modern examples represent an adaptation to the climatic and environmental conditions of the subarctic region. Since during the Upper Paleolithic the sun was as high in winter as it is today, and the dry climate was almost without snow (which permitted hunting during the cold season), houses could be occupied in either season but each house seems to have been occupied for one season only.

In fact, these houses were used several times, always at the same season. At Gönnersdorf, the number of cooking pits, repaired and redone floor pavements, fireplace reconstructions, and very abundant artifacts are arguments for a repeated use of the houses (Bosinski 1979). So, we reconstruct the settlement as being inhabited the whole year, but by different groups who met only in the spring and fall. These groups used the same settlement but occupied different houses and came from different areas. In the winter habitation the raw material of the stone artifacts consists of Tertiary quartzite, chalcedony, and "baltic" flint (Franken and Veil 1983; Floss 1985). The nearest point where this flint occurs is towards the northeast at a distance of at least 100 km. This indicates a migration from that direction of the people who occupied the winter houses. On the other hand, the raw material used during summer habitations is Ardennes quartzite and flint from the Meuse region. This demonstrates a movement of about 120 km from the northwest.

At Andernach the lithic artifacts of one habitation are consistently made from Ardennes quartzite and Meuse flint. The residents worked this material outside the settlement, perhaps at the raw material's source, and brought only blades and bladelets to the site (Floss 1985; Floss and Terberger 1986). These preforms were specially selected for future tools—scrapers and burins on one hand, backed bladelets on the other—resulting in a thinned-out breadth distribution between blades and bladelets.

These different groups who met at the settlement came from different regions and, to a certain degree, had different traditions. If we take the art material as reflecting religious ideas, besides a basic conformity (representations of horses and women, for example) we find differences in the distribution of the representations. Mammoth, rhinoceros, and seal representations are associated with the winter habitations (the group from the northeast), while bird representations occur in the summer habitations and belong to the group from the northwest (Bosinski 1984a; Bosinski and Fischer 1980).

Several different species of animals are always represented. At Gönnersdorf the game of the summer habitation is different from that of the winter and clearly reflects the climatic difference between these two seasons. Horses predominate and were the most important game (Poplin 1976), but reindeer, red deer, bison, mammoth, rhinoceros, saiga, chamois, various species of birds, and fish are also present. Hunting of arctic fox and varying hare for furs took place only in winter; accordingly those animals occur only in the winter habitations and are quite numerous. None of these forms were captured at the site itself and probably none in close proximity. They were introduced from different hunting and fishing places.

ARTIFACTS

The artifacts from these sites are numerous and varied. At Gönnersdorf there are more than 50,000 lithic artifacts greater than 1 cm in dimension, including about 5000 retouched tools (Franken and Veil 1983). But such a comprehensive figure is only of statistical value, since the material from a single habitation is the relevant unit and should form the basis of any analytical study. The repeated use of the houses makes it difficult if not impossible to separate places of different activities, and the long use of these places by many people has led to thorough mixing. Nevertheless, there are recognizable areas that show persisting functions over the years. For example, the first Andernach concentration is characterized by a surprisingly high number of scrapers, which at this site are as numerous as the burins (Terberger 1985). Similarly, the second Gönnersdorf concentration shows a percentage of splintered pieces of about 20%. Other patterns can be seen in the distribution of borers, which are numerous in some areas and rare in others.

Working of bone, antler, and ivory also took place at the settlement. Shed male reindeer antler was collected and brought to the settlement to be worked, and there are many examples of groove-and-splinter technique (Tinnes 1984). Mammoth tusks were possibly also collected (and thus do not necessarily represent hunted animals). The ivory was worked

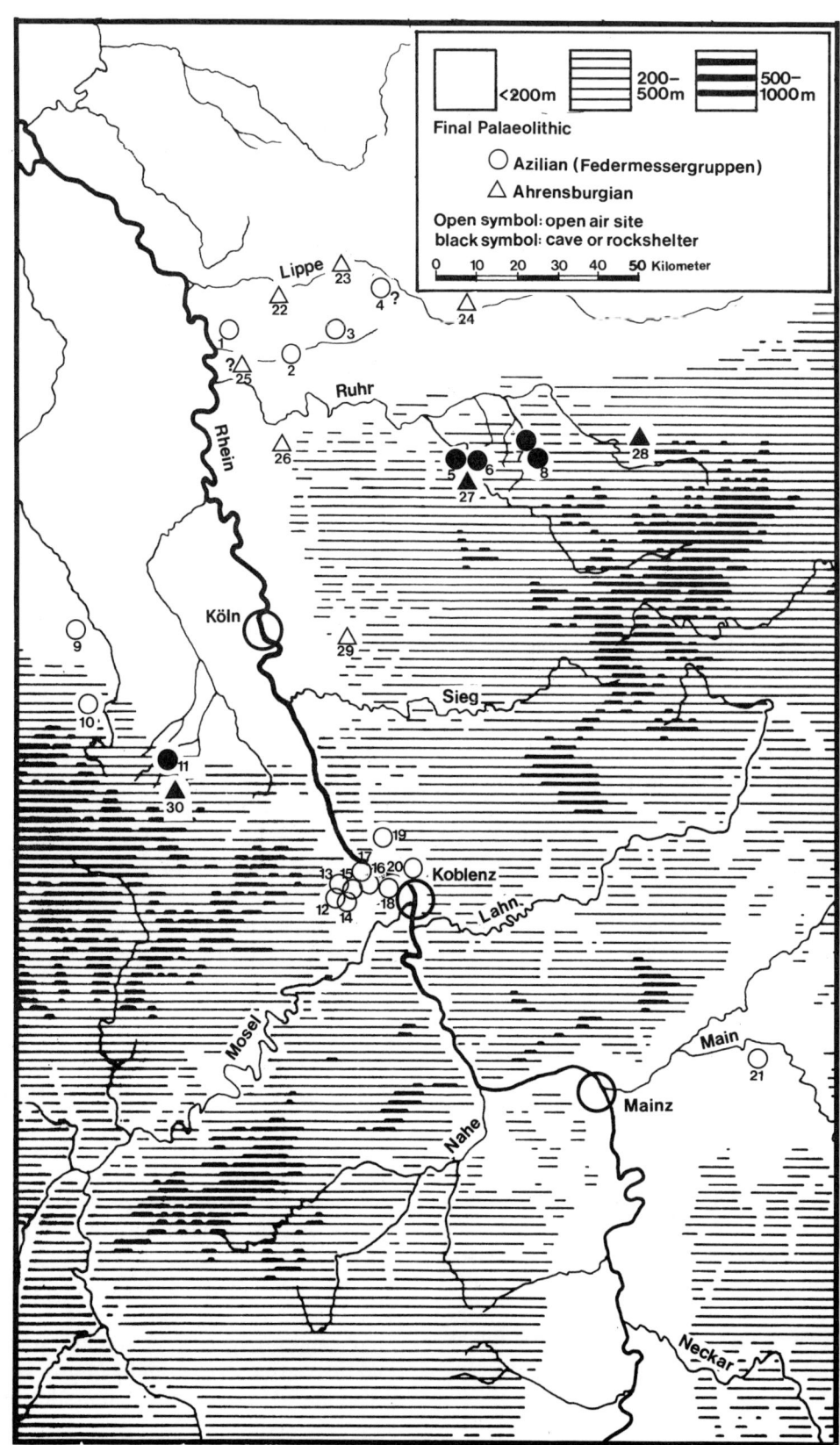

Figure 24.3

with a technique that resulted in straight splinters in spite of the curved tusk (Veil 1982a).

A common feature of Upper Paleolithic settlements is jewelry. Perforated teeth and snail shells from Tertiary deposits and from the Mediterranean occur at Mainz-Linsenberg, Gönnersdorf, and Andernach. At Andernach, a collection of 40 perforated Mediterranean snail shells was found in a small pit, perhaps originally stored in a bag representing a cache. Beads of fossil wood are known from Mainz-Linsenberg and Gönnersdorf. At Gönnersdorf the fabrication of such beads is shown by many half-finished pieces. A necklace with approximately 30 wooden beads and perforated fox and deer teeth was found in a pit (Bosinski 1969).

These settlements are further characterized by art objects. Venus statuettes are known from Mainz-Linsenberg, and many engraved slate plaquettes and antler and ivory statuettes have been found at Gönnersdorf and Andernach. The varied character of the material from Upper Paleolithic settlements, including jewelry and art, should be emphasized. This contrasts with the material that comes from auxiliary camps like hunters' camps.

TERRITORIAL AND AUXILIARY CAMPS

Most of the material found in the settlements was brought in from outside. This includes construction materials (wood and stone), fuel, raw materials for stone artifacts, antler and ivory, and, of course, captured animals, fish, and gathered foods (plants, eggs).

Some of those things are available in the immediate vicinity, others at a short distance or far away. Normally the material or animals would have been brought directly to the settlement; it is only occasionally that we find traces of such activities away from the habitation area. Isolated Aurignacian bone points in caves (Wildhaus, Buchenloch, and Kartstein; cf. Hahn 1977) are proof of visits by hunters. At the site of Segendorf, close to our research center at Monrepos, we found a few chips (including a burin spall) and some small bone fragments in the loess under the pumice as an indication of a short stay. On top of the Plaidter Hummerich Volcano, the loess of the crater depression yielded a fireplace with a scraper and a broken-off burin tip (Bosinski et al. 1986).

In the very small cave of Magdalena were found a fireplace, a few blades, flakes, and chips, a collection of shed antler from young reindeer, three perforated teeth from deer and wolf, and fragments of at least three decorated ivory bracelets (Weiss 1978). These finds reflect a brief human presence, perhaps one person, and it is not even sure that he or she stayed the night. Only exceptionally, for those activities of longer duration at greater distance from the settlement, was it necessary to stay overnight and to build a tent. The traces of such an auxiliary camp are rare. If we look through the publications on Upper Paleolithic settlement structures from Central and Eastern Europe, we learn much about settlements with solid houses and very little on temporary tents. Only if an auxiliary camp, e.g., a hunting camp, was used

Figure 24.3 Final Paleolithic sites in the Rhineland.

1. Dinslaken (Stampfuss and Schütrumpf 1970)
2. Bottrop (Bosinski 1982b)
3. Gelsenkirchen (Bosinski 1982b)
4. Petersberg bei Sinsen (Bosinski 1982b)
5. Martinshöhle (Bosinski 1984b)
6. Grürmannshöhle (Bosinski 1984b)
7. Feldhofhöhle (Bosinski 1984b)
8. Balver Höhle (Bosinski 1984b)
9. Barmen (Löhr 1978c)
10. Kinzweiler (Löhr 1978d)
11. Katzensteine (Löhr 1978b)
12. Thür (Brunnacker et al. 1982)
13. Rauschermühle bei Plaidt (Bosinski 1979)
14. Bassenheim (unpub.)
15. Miesenheim II (Street 1986)
16. Miesenheim III (unpub.)
17. Andernach (Bolus, in press; Street, in press)
18. Weissenthurm (Bosinski 1983a)
19. Niederbieber (Bosinski et al. 1982; Loftus 1984; Winter 1986)
20. Urbar (Löhr 1978e)
21. Dietesheim (Fruth 1979)
22. Gahlen (Richter 1981)
23. Marl (Bosinski 1982b)
24. Lünen (Bosinski 1982b)
25. Oberhausen (Bosinski 1982b)
26. Duisburg-Kaiserberg (Tromnau 1982)
27. Martinshöhle (Bosinski 1984b)
28. Hohler Stein bei Kallenhardt (Taute 1968)
29. Altenruth (Veil 1978c)
30. Kartstein-Felswand (Löhr 1978a)

repeatedly does the consequent accumulation of objects increase the chances of finding the site. An auxiliary camp has to be at the place of its purpose: where one can get raw material, collect snail shells, or capture animals. These are the only conditions of such a site and, contrary to the conditions for the location of primary settlements, there is no general rule in the choice of their location.

At Sprendlingen (Bosinski et al. 1985) the occupants placed their hunting camp on the highest point of the region, directly at the watershed between the Nahe and the Rhine, which afforded them a spendid view in any direction. The main purpose of this camp was reindeer hunting. In this case it is possible to determine that the herds had to come up from the west to traverse the plateau at its smallest part towards the Rhine Valley: the opposite direction makes no sense because the animals would smell the camps before the hunters could see them. Besides reindeer hunting, and the killing of at least two horses, another purpose of the camp was to collect Tertiary snail shells from the nearby Tertiary sand deposits. Obviously the gatherers took away the bigger, suitable pieces and left behind only small and broken shells.

The tent erected here was small and temporary. Near the fireplace was a working area with a concentration of flint inserts (backed bladelets, microgravettes), scrapers, and—somewhat surprisingly—burin spalls. Outside the tent was another activity zone for rougher work with burins and pointed blades. These tools are heavily used, resharpened, and often broken. The tools were brought into the site and there was very little blade production. Most of the stone working was in the form of resharpening (retouch and burin spalls).

The temporary use of the tent and the small number of artifacts (1259) and tools (176 before, 109 after conjoining) permitted a structural analysis and detailed reconstruction of activity zones. There are no indications of working bone, antler, or ivory. The jewelry consists of nine perforated Mediterranean snail shells, perhaps part of a necklace. There are no hints of art objects.

The close typological similarity and the corresponding stratigraphical position of Mainz-Linsenberg and Sprendlingen make it possible that the latter was an auxiliary camp of the former (they are separated by a distance of 28 km). It should also be mentioned that the perforated Tertiary snail shells of Mainz-Linsenberg are the same species as collected at Sprendlingen.

The site of Alsdorf (Löhr 1974, 1979), with its reduced set of stone tools, could also have served as an auxiliary camp for a special purpose.

BURIAL AREAS

Until now we have only one Magdalenian burial, from Oberkassel near Bonn (Verworn, Bonnet, and Steinmann 1919), and I mention it only to emphasize the lack of information. This grave, situated at the base of a basalt cliff overlooking the Rhine Valley, was of a man about 50 years old, a young woman, and a dog (Nobis 1979). It also contained some art objects. There were no traces of a settlement in the neighborhood and we have to consider the existence of specialized burial places as part of the settlement pattern.

SUMMARY OF THE UPPER PALEOLITHIC SETTLEMENT PATTERNS

To summarize, the Upper Paleolithic settlement patterns in the loess steppe are characterized by villagelike settlements with substantial houses. These settlements were inhabited repeatedly for a long period of time and by different groups. The settlement itself is at the center of a catchment area which was used for different purposes. If necessary, auxiliary camps with small, temporary tents were built at other locations.

The groups which met at the settlement came from different directions. The group territory was extensive, comprising a region more than 100 km in diameter. When they left the settlement it seems likely that they were heading for a similar settlement in another region, where perhaps they met other groups. Of course, the most troubling question of this interpretation is why did they leave? Admitting that one group was replaced by another necessarily implies that the resources to maintain life were not exhausted. We have seen, for example, that horses could be hunted in summer and in winter. The hypothetical answer could be that they left in correspondence with their social system. The length of the stay at a settlement being some months makes it probable that only one, at most two other settlements were used for the rest of the year. Thus we could call these groups relatively stationary.

SETTLEMENT PATTERNS IN THE FINAL PALEOLITHIC

Due to the availability of data, I will concentrate on the situation in the Alleröd period and not discuss the Younger Dryas at all.

ENVIRONMENT

During the Alleröd the ocean was warmer and the predominating west wind brought clouds and rain. The result was a cold and humid climate with moderate seasonal differences. The landscape was covered with forest, with birch and pine in drier areas and willow and poplar in wet depressions. There was much underwood and a rich herb vegetation (Street 1986).

The animal biomass was much lower than in the grassland. It was the biotop of a boreal forest with deer, moose, aurochs, and beaver, though occasionally chamois, ibex, badger, and—as a sign of open areas—horses occur (Street, in press). In general, these animals should have been nonmigratory. The organization of the hunter's life in this environment was more difficult than it was on the loess steppe. But by this time the bow and arrow had developed as a new and efficient weapon.

SETTLEMENTS

The choice of settlement location is similar, but less classic than in the Upper Paleolithic (see Fig. 24.3). At Andernach the Azilian used the same place as the Magdalenian. Niederbieber and Urbar are also in a seat position, but the "back" or upslope parts were not as efficient.

HABITATIONS

During the Final Paleolithic the habitations were smaller and less stable than in the Upper Paleolithic. At Urbar and Niederbieber they are round concentrations with distinctly concentric structures and diameters of 4-6 m (Loftus 1984; Winter 1986). The center is occupied by a fireplace in which wood and bone were burned. In contrast to the Upper Paleolithic, the fireplace and refuse areas are crowded with burnt flint; in fact, the occurrence of calcined bone and cracked flint is very characteristic of Alleröd sites.

Around the fireplace lies a zone with tools and retouching implements. Sometimes it is possible to define a special working place, e.g., one with scrapers. An outer circle is composed of bigger flakes and cores, and the periphery of the concentration is invariably characterized by unburnt bones. It is difficult to reconstruct the habitation and it is not even clear whether these concentrations are inside or outside a roofed area.

NUMBER OF HABITATIONS

At Niederbieber it looks like two or three such concentrations belong together and were used simultaneously. The distance between them is about 10 m. One argument for their contemporaneity is that they attest the same raw material in their stone artifacts and debris, but this is a preliminary observation.

The settlement area at Niederbieber was used over a period of time. The most recent find-concentrations and fireplaces were directly covered by pumice, but there are habitations deeper in the loess, and we hope to get a succession of Dryas II habitations and those of the Bölling period. In any case this area was inhabited repeatedly.

The single concentrations are characterized by a particular raw material used for the stone artifacts. There are chalcedony, Tertiary quartzite, and flint concentrations. It is obvious that each group used only one or at most two raw materials. This not only is true for Niederbieber but seems to be generally valid (Bolus, in press). The preferred raw material mostly comes from the middle Rhine region. But as in the Upper Paleolithic, there is also flint from the northeast and from the Meuse region.

The well-known difference between the excellent Magdalenian blade technique and the less careful flaking of the Azilian is reflected in the less careful choice of raw material by groups of the latter period. This could mask the spatial connections of Azilian people and the direction of their movements. Their habitations are smaller and were occupied for a shorter time than was true for the Upper Paleolithic houses. The seasonal indications at Niederbieber differ between the single concentrations, but always concern a restricted period of time, perhaps two months. Furthermore, these habitations were used only once and not repeatedly.

GAME

The Final Paleolithic habitations always yield bones of several animal species. Red deer and moose are normally present, often aurochs and beaver, and occasionally chamois, ibex, badger, or horse (Street, in press). It is a mixed game, but compared with Upper Paleolithic settlements, the number of individual animals represented is much smaller.

ARTIFACTS

Every concentration yielded a limited number of stone artifacts (about 2000 artifacts greater than 1 cm), including 150-200 retouched tools (Loftus 1984; Winter 1986). This is far fewer than in the Upper Paleolithic houses, but more than in Upper Paleolithic auxiliary camps. Sometimes it is possible to distinguish particular working areas, evidenced by a particular distribution of scrapers, burins, or Azilian points and backed bladelets. Working of bone and antler is uncommon in this period, and no jewelry has been found.

Art objects are very rare, but this is a common feature of the Final Paleolithic. Besides some retouching implements with linear decoration, there is a shaft smoother of reddish sandstone that bears an engraved ornament (Loftus 1982). Even if schematized, this engraving represents a final stylization of Magdalenian female representations. Thus, in spite of changed environment, toolkit, weapons, animals, and way of life, there are traditions linking the Upper Paleolithic in the loess steppe and Final Paleolithic in the Alleröd forest.

USE OF TERRITORY

The eruption of the Laacher-See Volcano and the pumice cover of the region gives us a chance to reconstruct the territory's use more completely than usual. The buried forest of Miesenheim II (Street 1986) and Thür (Brunnacker et al. 1982) preserved traces of human activities. Pebble tools and Clactonian flakes of quartz and quartzite were used to work wood, while flakes of flint could have served to bark trees. An isolated Azilian point in the ground indicates a hunter with bow and arrow. Perhaps it was he who killed the aurochs, young deer, horse, and the duck-sized bird whose bones were left in the Miesenheim II forest.

In a bog near Dinslaken were found three barbed bone points, traces of a hunting excursion (Stampfuss and Schütrumpf 1970). Below the Niederbieber site, we observed a working area with five retouching implements, many minuscule chips, and a few fragments of Azilian points and backed bladelets amid traces of fire (Bosinski et al. 1982). This seems to have been a place to retouch Azilian points and backed bladelets, and perhaps to shaft them with the help of heat. Twice (Miesenheim III, Bassenheim) we found isolated fireplaces under the pumice. Without doubt these were made by man, but there were not the slightest traces of stone artifacts or bones associated with them.

SUMMARY OF THE FINAL PALEOLITHIC SETTLEMENT PATTERNS

To summarize, the Final Paleolithic settlements consisted of smaller and probably transportable habitations. The human groups were smaller too and they stayed for a limited time, perhaps one or two months. There are no hints of auxiliary camps, e.g., hunting camps, in the Azilian. Such auxiliary camps were not necessary, because the whole group itself was less stationary than in the Upper Paleolithic and moved through its territory. Thus, it could be that the size of the group territory was smaller than in the Upper Paleolithic. Lithic raw material seems to have been less important, and thus its information with regard to distances and mobility could be arbitrary.

DISCUSSION

RIGAUD: Do you see Pincevent as a satellite site?
BOSINSKI: Yes, that is what it looks like to me, with small tents, only reindeer, no hearths, no bone tools, no traces of occupation besides reindeer hunting, no art, no traces of the kind of activities that concerned the whole group.

RIGAUD: Do you think that the high mobility we observe in the final Upper Paleolithic can be related to a different economic system, or do you think that the economic system in the Azilian was less efficient than in the Magdalenian?
BOSINSKI: The main point of my paper was to

define the differences between Upper Paleolithic and Azilian, and I tried to make clear that the landscape and climate were very different.

RIGAUD: But can you relate differences in the environment and different social organizations with different technological assemblages? Do you think there is a continuity between the Magdalenian and the Azilian?

BOSINSKI: I think this is a possibility.

STRAUS: It is interesting that at Gönnersdorf there were people going back to this specific spot time after time. Some returned only in the summer, building their houses, and reusing them again the next summer. And then, a few meters away, there are these houses that were being reused again and again, but only in winter. Why would they come back there to that same spot? Is it possible that there is a microstratigraphic separation between these?

BOSINSKI: I think not.

SACKETT: I'm worried about your reconstruction of the lifeways in the Alleröd forest. Your measure of the economic potential of the forest seems to be a reflection of the archaeology rather than the environment.

BOSINSKI: Perhaps I overstated the case. But I do think that life was much easier for grassland peoples.

ROLLAND: You mentioned that very interesting comparison between Pincevent and Gönnersdorf, suggesting that Pincevent might be a satellite site and Gönnersdorf a residential settlement. Would you consider relating the two sites as part of the same group? In other words, were the same people spending some time at Pincevent and then some time at Gönnersdorf?

BOSINSKI: No, this was too large an area.

MARKS: I thought I heard you say that the fact that the various structures had different raw materials proves that they were different groups. In other words, there is a one-to-one correlation between raw materials and residential groups. But let us imagine that we are talking about a period of 20 or 30 years. One group moves in, builds a house, and exploits an area up to the northwest, coming back seasonally. But after some years something happens in that area, perhaps a new group moves in, or perhaps the house is getting old and smelly. So these people construct a new house some 30 m away. And at the same time they start exploiting in the other direction, with different kinds of fauna. Could this explain the variability that you see?

BOSINSKI: I do not think that it is that easy.

RIGAUD: I would like to know if there is any indication of the seasonality in the way they build the houses.

BOSINSKI: They are the same, with one exception.

RIGAUD: Therefore, there is really no difference in the way they build summer and winter houses. The only difference is in terms of the contents of the houses.

COMMENTS

OTTE: La nature des roches utilisées à Gönnersdorf indique des relations vers le nord (moraine) mais aussi vers l'ouest, soit le Bassin mosan en Belgique. Cependant, il ne semble pas exister de relations inverses. Les sites magdaléniens de Belgique ne manifestent pas jusqu'ici la présence de matériaux d'origine rhénane. Par contre, certains témoins (matériaux et, surtout coquilles) indiquent des relations entretenues vers le sud, soit vers le Bassin parisien. En admettant donc le modèle d'habitats d'importance variée selon leur fonction proposé par G. Bosinski, on pourrait proposer l'existence de "camps de base" du type de grande densité de matériel très varié dans leurs fonctions (outils domestiques et outils de chasse), une faune très abondante témoignant de passages répétés et des oeuvres d'art mobilier. Les camps de chasse provisoires du type Pincevent se trouveraient donc ainsi complétés par des sites d'habitat d'occupation plus dense et plus systématique. Il est vraisemblable qu'une partie des sites magdaléniens de l'est de la Belgique (tel Fonds de Forêt, Bassin de la Vesdre) se soit trouvés davantage en relation avec les sites rhénans tel Gönnersdorf. Leur exploitation est cependant encore trop peu avancée pour être assuré à cet égard.

Le modèle d'exploitation d'un même territoire à la fin du Paléolithique peut être enrichi en comparant les installations dans les Ardennes belges du Creswellien aux affinités britanniques et le Magdalénien, plus proche des sites français. Ces deux cultures sont contemporaines (fin du Bölling) et exploitent le même environnement. Aucun témoin d'échange inter-culturel n'est cependant visible et leur équipement technique est très différent (armatures à cran et à dos anguleux d'un côté, lamelles à dos et sagaies osseuses de l'autre). Les contacts devaient donc être très limités peut-être à la fois par les aires d'occupations extérieures très différentes (Angleterre et Bassin parisien) et par les courtes durées d'installation épisodiques dans les zones de recouvrement. Les fouilles actuellement en cours dans les sites principaux (Presle, Creswellien; Chaleux, Magdalénien) fourniront bientôt de plus amples données sur ces différences comportementales.

XXV

The Gravettian Peopling of Southwestern France

Taxonomic Problems

Jean-Philippe Rigaud

The passage from the Middle Paleolithic to the Upper Paleolithic has always been associated with the replacement of *Homo sapiens neanderthalensis* by *Homo sapiens sapiens*, but the technological and typological discontinuity that one observes between Mousterian and Upper Paleolithic tools does not coincide exactly with this anthropological discontinuity. The discovery at St. Césaire of Neandertal remains associated with a Castelperronian industry shows clearly that Neandertal man was, from the beginning of the Recent Würm, on the route to "leptolithization," and that he had reached a techno-typological level appropriate to the Upper Paleolithic by the time the first Aurignacians reached the Perigord; the latter group are also known to have reached this techno-typological level.

As a result, several questions are raised, chiefly:
—Were the carriers of the Aurignacian "culture" new arrivals in the northeast of Aquitaine?
—What were the anthropological characteristics of the first Aurignacians?

It seems necessary to reject a local origin for the Aurignacians, in spite of some resemblances of a stylistic order (for example, the scalariform retouch called *Quina retouch* in the Mousterian and *Aurignacian retouch* in the Aurignacian). Aside from this common trait, one does not find in the latest Quina Mousterian the slightest technological or typological character indicative of a leptolithization that would lead to the Aurignacian. In the absence of new data bearing on this point, one cannot therefore sustain the hypothesis of a Quina Mousterian-Aurignacian link in Aquitaine.

If the human remains associated with Aurignacian industries are clearly indicative of *H. sapiens sapiens*, one must note that, in the great majority of cases, such industries are attributable to a Middle and not an Archaic Aurignacian. We do not know the anthropological characteristics of the first Aurignacians, those who occupied the Perigord contemporaneously with the Castelperronians.

From 30,000 B.P. on, Neandertals had disappeared from the Aquitaine, replaced by *H. sapiens sapiens*, carriers of an industry which—by its technological and typological characteristics—is fully Upper Paleolithic. Bone technology had reached an exceptional level, and personal adornment, the first artistic manifestations, and the organization of habitation space were developing. Until a date close to 27,000 B.P., the Aurignacian in the Perigord underwent a considerable florescence, if we are to judge by the number of sites occupied and by the richness of the archaeological levels. The diachronic modifications in Aurignacian toolkits between 33,000 and 27,000 B.P. have been described at length by Peyrony (1930) following his work at La Ferrassie and by de Sonneville-Bordes (1961), and I have recently shown that the "evolutionary model" proposed by these authors should be reconsidered in light of the recent excavations such as those of Le Flageolet I (Rigaud 1982a, b).

After 27,000 B.P., we witness an abrupt abandonment of the Perigord by the Aurignacians and a rapid development of the Gravettian. The existence of an Aurignacian contemporary with the late Gravettian (Laville 1971) about 20,000 B.P. could be represented by the Aurignacian V of Laugerie Haute, but certain authors would make this a cultural entity distinct from the Aurignacian or the Perigordian (Demars

1985). For my part, I see in this assemblage similarities to the Aurignacian which justify its attachment to that industry more than to any other culture, but it will be necessary to await new data on the Aurignacian contemporary with the Gravettian to confirm (or reject) this hypothesis.

THE ORIGIN OF THE GRAVETTIANS

The hypothesis upheld by Bordes of a link between the Castelperronian and the Gravettian has recently been contradicted by the discovery at St. Césaire and, in the absence of new arguments, it is necessary to admit that there are no industries that could be considered typologically and chronologically intermediate between the Castelperronian and the Gravettian (Bordes 1968b). If one rejects the hypothesis of a local origin, one must then admit that the Gravettian populations of the Perigord came from elsewhere. The Iberian Peninsula and Northern Europe can be excluded because they have not yet yielded industries that could be at the origin of the Gravettian of the Perigord.

By contrast, in Central Europe, industries with backed pieces existed from 30,000 B.P. (Kozlowski and Kozlowski 1979: 33) and one can see there a possible origin for the Gravettian assemblages of Western Europe. This is, in any case, the most probable original Gravettian population. Its migration toward the west could have had multiple and complex causes. It coincided, however, with the climatic degradation that succeeded the Würm Interstadial and that led, approximately 19,000 B.P., to pleniglacial conditions in the Perigord (Laville, Raynal, and Texier 1986).

The first Gravettian occupations in the Perigord (= Perigordian) are not very well known, on the one hand because of the rarity of sites where they have been found and on the other hand because of the poor quality of the excavations at the eponymous site of La Gravette.

The cultural sequence of the initial stages of the Perigordian has undergone, since Peyrony, several rearrangements, especially following the work of de Sonneville-Bordes, which can be consulted for more details. Let us simply recall that the Perigordian I of Peyrony became the Castelperronian; the Perigordian II, Aurignacian; and the Perigordian III, Perigordian VI. The first Gravettian stage in the Perigordian is thus the old "Perigordian IV."

THE "PERIGORDIAN IV"

The rockshelter of La Gravette (Bayac, Dordogne) yielded a stratigraphic sequence in which, above an Aurignacian level, were found a Perigordian ensemble subdivided in two: at the base, a level of *fléchettes* and rare Gravette points; at the top, a level with numerous Gravette points. The industry from the basal level, with numerous *fléchettes*, is sometimes designated by the term "Bayacian" (Lacorre 1960; Delporte 1972; see below).

At the Abri Pataud, the recent excavations by Movius uncovered, above a long Aurignacian sequence, an Ensemble 5 that contained a Perigordian V industry dated by carbon-14 between 26,000 ± 260 and 28,150 ± 225 B.P. (Movius 1972), dates confirmed recently by the Oxford Laboratory (26,000 ± 1000 and 28,400 ± 1000) (Mellars 1986a, b). In spite of a stratigraphic uncertainty between the levels in front of the shelter and those at the back (Movius 1975) that could justify the gap separating these dates, the lithics from Ensemble 5 at the Abri Pataud can be considered representative of the Perigordian IV (Bricker 1976). They will be described below.

At the Roc de Combe, the excavations of Bordes and Labrot revealed a Bed 4 attributable to the Perigordian IV, which Laville places in Phase V of his chronoclimatic system.

In the cave of Maldidier, our own excavations uncovered two beds of Upper Perigordian: Bed 2, which was too poor for a more precise attribution, and Bed 3, which was a bit richer (74 objects) and which corresponds, on the basis of its typological composition, to the industries of the Perigordian IV. According to Laville, Bed 3 belongs at the end of Phase IV in his chronological scheme.

Phase IV of the Abri du Facteur at Tursac, in spite of recent excavations, has yielded only Aurignacian and an ambiguous "Aurignaco-Perigordian" assemblage (Delporte 1968).

Several sites in the Perigord have yielded lithics attributed by de Sonneville-Bordes to the Perigordian IV. We do not share the opinion of de Sonneville-Bordes concerning the attribution of the series from the Roque Saint Christophe, excavated successively by Peyrony and P. Fitte, to the Perigordian IV. The series collected by Fitte includes several Noailles burins, and in the Peyrony series, now in the Musée des Eyzies, there are some Raysse (= Bassaler) burins, some of which also appear in de Sonneville-Bordes's (1960: fig. 112, nos. 10, 11, 12) plate of material from that site. In my opinion, the presence at the Roque Saint Christophe of a Perigordian with Noailles burins is indisputable, while that of a Perigordian IV remains to be established.

At the Abri Vignaud, a series at the Institut de Paléontologie Humaine (de Sonneville-Bordes 1960) would seem to show resemblances to the lithics from La Gravette, but neither Peyrony in 1941 nor Geneste (1982) found a level assignable to the Perigordian IV.

At the Trou de la Chèvre, at La Ferrassie, and at Le Flageolet I, the levels contemporary with Laville's Phase IV have yielded Aurignacian industries (Arambourou and Jude 1964; Delporte 1978; Rigaud 1982a, b).

TYPOLOGICAL CHARACTERISTICS OF THE PERIGORDIAN IV

While taking into account the reservations required when dealing with assemblages collected in a less than systematic fashion, we can summarize the typological characteristics of the Perigordian IV as follows: burins and endscrapers appear in very variable proportions (for example, in the eight subdivisions of Ensemble 5 from Pataud, the ratio of IG to IB is reversed several times and, as a result, cannot be considered characteristic of the Perigordian IV). *Fléchettes* seem to be associated with the initial stage of the Perigordian. Gravette and microgravette points are always present, but in variable numbers; the triangles to which de Sonneville-Bordes (1960) attaches a chronological significance are reported from the Roque Saint Christophe, the Abri Labattut, the cave of Font-Robert, and Le Flageolet I, where they are present in Beds VII, VI, and V in association with industries postdating the Perigordian IV. Triangles seem thus to be a (rare) component of Perigordian assemblages *sensu lato*.

Perigordian shouldered points, whose rarity makes them, too, a poor director fossil, are ambiguous artifacts. For certain authorities, shouldered points are simply Gravette points in the process of production and, for this reason, they do not appear as shouldered points in the typological inventories.

This enumeration of typological characteristics of the Perigordian IV is incomplete and imprecise because it does not include recent data. It should be developed in light of the results of modern excavations. The term "Bayacian," used by certain authors to designate the Perigordian IV (Lacorre 1960), designates only badly excavated, badly described, and badly dated lithic assemblages, and should therefore be banished from our terminology.

THE PERIGORDIAN V

On the basis of technology and typology, Peyrony placed the industries from Beds J, K, and L of La Ferrassie after "the upper level of La Gravette" (= Perigordian IV). But it was not until the excavation of the Abri Pataud that a level with Gravette points (Perigordian IV, Bed 5) and a level likewise containing Gravette points, but also with abundant Noailles burins (Perigordian V, Bed 4), were observed together in stratigraphic position. A similar superposition may have existed elsewhere—at the Abri Vignaud at the Roque Saint Christophe—but the rudimentary nature of the excavations made it impossible to distinguish them. Generally, the Perigordian V appears at the end of an Aurignacian sequence: La Ferrassie, the Roc de Combe, Le Flageolet I, etc. It was on the basis of the sequence at La Ferrassie that Peyrony defined the Perigordian V and its subdivisions, which, in spite of some reservations, were maintained in de Sonneville-Bordes's (1960) schema. From bottom to top:

—Perigordian Va (or V1) with Font-Robert points,
—Perigordian Vb (or V2) with truncated elements,
—Perigordian Vc (or V3) with Noailles burins.

For Peyrony (1948), the Perigordian with Noailles burins was culturally distinct from the Perigordian with Font-Robert points and followed it, as the sequence at La Ferrassie showed. As for the Perigordian with truncated elements, it seems to have been the object of little interest on the part of taxonomists.

It was only after 1960 that this "classification" was challenged by Alaux's (1973) excavations at Les Battuts (Tarn), Bordes's and Labrot's (1967) excavations at the Roc de Combe (Lot), and our own work at Le Flageolet I (Dordogne) (Rigaud 1969, 1982a, b).

These recent excavations showed that the schema proposed by Peyrony and confirmed by the recent excavations of Delporte could not serve as a reference and that the director fossils of the Perigordian V (Font-Robert points, truncated elements, and Noailles burins) do not have the chronological significance that Peyrony attributed to them, because they could, in fact, appear repeatedly in association (Rigaud 1976b). It was thus necessary to find another explanation for the presence of these objects in Perigordian V assemblages, since Peyrony's chronological hypothesis was no longer tenable.

Several recent works on the Perigordian V, however, do not seem to have taken into account these recent data (David 1973, 1985; David and Bricker 1985; Delporte and Tuffreau 1973, 1984; Mellars 1986a, b), and we are thus led to repeat here certain elements of our interpretation that have been expounded at length elsewhere (Rigaud 1969, 1976b, 1978, 1982a, b). In response to various issues raised in these works, we shall discuss the following points:

—Variability in the Perigordian V: typological and chronological data;
—Fontrobertian and Noaillian: typological realities, functional or cultural facies;
—The unity of the Gravettian: Perigordian, Protomagdalenian, and their post-Solutrean continuation.

THE CHRONOLOGICAL LIMITS OF THE PERIGORDIAN V

The Perigordian V is generally considered contemporaneous with Phase VII of the Recent Würm in the collectively developed chrono-climatic system (Laville et al. 1983). This is the palynologists' "Tursac Oscillation," corresponding to a mild, humid climate interrupted quite systematically by a brief return of cold conditions (Laville 1975; Laville and Thibault 1967).

It must be noted, however, that the first industries assignable to the Perigordian V appear slightly before this oscillation under still relatively cold climatic conditions: in Bed 3 of the Roc de Combe, in Bed VII of Le Flageolet I, in Bed 3 of Les Jambes, and in Bed 4 of the Abri Pataud, which is placed by Laville (1975) in Phase VI.

When climatic conditions deteriorated once more in Phase VIII, most of the rockshelters of the Perigord attained their equilibrium profiles and the sedimentary processes that contributed to filling them were interrupted. This was the case at the Roc de Combe, La Ferrassie, Le Facteur, the Trou de la Chèvre, Les Jambes, and, a bit later perhaps, Le Flageolet I. Only in the shelters of Laugerie Haute and Pataud did new deposits form.

Recent series of C-14 dates enable us to place the Perigordian V industries in a period between 23,000 and 27,000 B.P. (Laville, Delpech, and Rigaud 1985; Mellars 1986a, b). These dates come essentially from the shelters of Pataud and Le Flageolet I. We have grouped them in Table 25.1, which makes several points apparent:

—The Oxford dates from Bed IV of the Abri Pataud confirm the Groningen date and indicate a probable age between 27,000 and 26,500 B.P.
—At Le Flageolet I, the Perigordian levels with Noailles burins (Beds VII to IV) are distinctly more recent.

TABLE 25.1

Pataud—Bed 4 (after Movius 1972 and Mellars 1986a)

GrN 4280	27,060 ± 370 B.P.
OxA 168	26,900 ± 1000 B.P.
OxA 374	26,300 ± 900 B.P.
OxA 167	26,500 ± 980 B.P.

Le Flageolet I

Ly 2723	26,150 ± 600 (Bed VII)
Ly 2722	24,280 ± 500 (Bed VI)
OxA 579	26,500 ± 900 (Bed VI)
Ly 2721	22,520 ± 500 (Bed V)
OxA 447	25,700 ± 700 (Bed V)
Ly 2186	22,950 ± 500 (Bed IV)
OxA 596	23,250 ± 500 (Bed IV)

Let us remember that for Laville, Bed 4 of the Abri Pataud belongs to Phase VI while Beds VI, V, and IV of Le Flageolet I correspond to variations of Phase VII. The C-14 dates thus confirm this interpretation and contradict the proposition formulated by David and Bricker (1985).

TYPOLOGICAL FLUCTUATIONS

We showed in 1973 that the typological composition of industries with Noailles burins was a function of three typological poles (Laville and Rigaud 1973b):
—Noailles burins
—Gravette and microgravette points
—Raysse burins.

In addition to the foundation common to all Upper Paleolithic assemblages, the industries of the Perigordian V appear in the form of a mixture of these three components, with a clear predominance of one or two of them over the other(s).

We have proposed therefore the following distinctions:

—industries very rich in Noailles burins, poor in Raysse burins and Gravette points:

Roc de Gavaudun (Monméjean, Bordes, and de Sonneville-Bordes 1964);
Le Facteur 10-11 (Delporte 1968);
probably also the lower levels of Bed 4 of the Abri Pataud (David 1973).

—industries with numerous Gravette and microgravette points, poor in Noailles and Raysse burins:

Le Flageolet I, Beds VI and VII (Rigaud 1982a, b);
Roc de Combe, Beds 1, 2, and 3 (Bordes and Labrot 1967).

—industries with numerous Raysse burins, poor in Noailles burins and in Gravette and microgravette points:

Les Jambes, Beds II and III;
Le Flageolet I, Beds IV and V;
probably the top of Bed 4 of the Abri Pataud and, by extension, the industry from the middle of this bed.

At Le Flageolet I, as at the Abri Pataud, one sees the progressive replacement of Noailles burins by Raysse burins. This transformation could have a chronological significance, but the relative and absolute chronological data indicate otherwise, since there is a significant difference between the sequences at Pataud and Le Flageolet I. It is moreover for this reason that David and Bricker (1985) reject Laville's chronological conclusions and cite an identical conclusion by Farrand which we would like to see confirmed here.

We must admit certain difficulties in accepting that such a well-defined transformation in the lithic assemblages could take place independently and in parallel manner in two sites separated by less than 20 km.[1]

FONTROBERTIAN AND NOAILLIAN
TYPOLOGICAL REALITIES, FUNCTIONAL FACIES OR CULTURAL MYTHS?

The well-marked typological characteristics of Perigordian V industries have led certain authors to see in them the manifestation of a cultural individuality.

On the basis of the simple idea that the typological composition of an assemblage has "cultural tradition" as its only determining factor, Movius, David, Bricker, and Delporte proposed assigning the different facies of the Perigordian to more or less independent cultural entities of the Perigordian (David 1966; David and Bricker 1985; Delporte and Tuffreau 1973).

What can we retain of these propositions after having objectively analyzed all the data available to us?

THE PERIGORDIAN WITH FONT-ROBERT POINTS AND THE "FONTROBERTIAN"

This industry is known primarily as the result of Peyrony's excavations at La Ferrassie. It corresponds to the assemblage from Bed J analyzed by de Sonneville-Bordes, but following this author, we accept the quantitative data with some caution (de Sonneville-Bordes 1960; Rigaud 1969). Delporte's excavations made it possible to find Peyrony's Bed J—the ensemble E1, D2, and D3 (Delporte and Tuffreau 1973). In spite of the serious reservations concerning the quantitative data for the lithic assemblages at La Ferrassie that are prompted by the very small size of Delporte's excavations,[2] certain tendencies do appear:

—the index of endscrapers is higher than that of burins;
—Gravette and microgravette points are abundant (E1: 31.3%; D3: 28.4%; and D2: 25.3%);
—there is a sporadic presence of rare Noailles burins;
—the frequency of Font-Robert points is variable (from 13.8% to 6.8%).

Following a very rapid and superficial comparative study with the contemporaneous industries from Les Battuts, the Roc de Combe, and Le Flageolet I, but also from Laussel, Mas Nègre, Font-Robert, Les Vachons, Laraux, and the Cirque de la Patrie, Delporte came to see the existence of two subfacies of the Perigordian V1 (Delporte and Tuffreau 1973):

The Perigordian V1a, with very numerous endscrapers, rare burins, abundant Gravette and microgravette points, and numerous Font-Robert points. These are the characteristics of the industries of Levels E1, D3, and D2 at La Ferrassie.

The Perigordian V1b, which, according to Delporte, adheres to some extent to the statistical norms of the Perigordian: burins more numerous than endscrapers, dihedral burins predominant over those on truncations, and uncommon Font-Robert points associated with truncated elements and Noailles burins. Roc de Combe Bed I and Le

Flageolet I Bed VII would belong to this subfacies.

In the La Ferrassie monograph, Delporte and Tuffreau (1984) designate the Perigordian V1a by the term "Perigordian V1, La Ferrassie variant," probably for the simple reason that it exists only at La Ferrassie, and the Perigordian V1b by the term "Perigordian V1, Roc de Combe (Bed 1) variant." The industry of Bed VII of Le Flageolet I was excluded from the subfacies by Delporte and Tuffreau in 1984, probably because of its typological characteristics published in 1982: IG = 22.1, IB = 14.5, IBd = 6.9, IBt = 6.03. We do not envisage the creation of another subfacies of the Le Flageolet I type, but we emphasize here that the Roc de Combe type does not seem to have real typological identities.

As for the V1a facies, called the La Ferrassie type, Delporte proposed to distinguish it because of its typological peculiarities: "The Perigordian V1a seems to be an especially distinctive ensemble and rates being distinguished under the name of Fontrobertian, for example. From numerous perspectives it is clearly separate from the Upper Perigordian" (Delporte and Tuffreau 1973: 117).

It seems to us audacious to create an additional term to designate an industry that exists only at the site of La Ferrassie and whose "definition" does not permit one to group with it industries that are typologically very similar. The industries of the Perigordian V with Font-Robert points have a variability that does not exclude them from the Perigordian ensemble. The term "Fontrobertian" should thus also be excluded from our taxonomic vocabulary.

THE PERIGORDIAN WITH NOAILLES BURINS AND THE "NOAILLIAN"

Following a path very similar to that of Delporte, David proposed in 1966 the isolation of the Perigordian with Noailles burins under the term "Noaillian," thus considering it to be a cultural entity distinct from the Perigordian (David 1973; David and Bricker 1985). In justification of their point of view, these authors relied upon differences of a typological order (richness in Noailles burins and then of Raysse burins, for example), but also on the results of subtypological analyses (attribute analyses) which, according to them, "permit one to see beyond the presence or absence of traditional director fossils" (David and Bricker 1985: 7).

The Traditional Director Fossils

Table 25.2 shows the distribution of these specimens in the levels of Perigordian with Noailles burins in the Abri Pataud and Le Flageolet I.

This table makes it clear that, in spite of important fluctuations, the Gravettian character is a fundamental constant in these industries; that Noailles burins are also consistently present; that Raysse burins progressively replace Noailles burins; and that truncated elements, like Font-Robert points, are archaeologically associated with Noailles burins and Gravette points. An identical association was found at the site of Le Caillou (Dordogne) (Boyer, Geneste, and Rigaud 1984). One of the levels of Le Flageolet I even exhibits the association of all the "traditional director fossils" of the Perigordian. We do not see in this distribution

TABLE 25.2

	Pataud			Le Flageolet I			
	L	M	U	VII	VI	V	IV
Gravette and microgravette points	0.65	0.42	0.29	10.94	4.53	0.40	1.72
Noailles burins	37.60	9.14	2.44	1.09	1.30	2.77	0.57
Raysse burins	0.30	23.40	30.30		0.48	6.52	3.44
Font-Robert points				0.87	0.48		
truncated elements			0.76	4.36	0.59		

any good reason for inferring cultural diversity; all these industries are Gravettian by virtue of the presence of Gravette and microgravette points.

Subtypological Analysis

According to David and Bricker (1985), this typological refinement permits one to distinguish differences of a techno-typological order between the Perigordian and the so-called Noaillian.

Aside from the fact that these authors assert these differences without demonstrating them with the results of their analyses, the significance of this difference may be questioned. Is it, as David and Bricker believed, of a "cultural" order or only the reflection of individual technological variations?

In the absence of a conclusive argument relative to this point, we prefer basing our arguments on more concrete and systematic typological arguments. In addition, we need not evoke an entirely hypothetical "process of acculturation" in order to explain the consistent presence of a Gravettian component in the "Noaillian" (David 1973).

INTERPRETATION OF VARIABILITY IN LITHIC ASSEMBLAGES OF THE PERIGORDIAN WITH NOAILLES BURINS

If one considers all assemblages of the Perigordian with Noailles burins, and not a selection of industries that fit a subjective model from which certain assemblages are excluded, we have shown (Laville and Rigaud 1973b) that there is a significant degree of variability. In order to explain this variability, we have proposed a functional hypothesis that contrasts with Peyrony's and de Sonneville-Bordes's chronological hypothesis and with David's cultural interpretation. We believe we have shown that the typological compositions of assemblages with Noailles burins were in large part determined by activity (Rigaud 1978).[3] Thus we have shown, using an example from Le Flageolet Bed VII, that on one occupation surface different activity areas (fire area, interior domestic activities, exterior, dump, etc.)

contained different lithic assemblages whose composition was closely comparable to that of various assemblages of Perigordian with Noailles burins. Intersite variability could therefore have the same cause as intrasite variability. In other words, typological variations observed among the various sites studied may be attributed to the relative importance of certain activities (which have yet to be identified). Let us note, in addition, that in 1966 David proposed a functional explanation of this kind to explain the variability he was unable to deny within the "Noaillian," going so far as to propose the application of an ethnographic model (Gubser 1965) which was also familiar to us but which we had judged to be unsuitable. Finally, if we were to admit the existence of an independent "Noaillian" culture which, in the Perigord, was influenced by contact with the Perigordians (David 1973), we would need to find an origin, a center of diffusion, for this culture. We know of no such center, however, in Western Europe. Would this "Noaillian" heartland have been associated with mythic Atlantis?

Moreover, how can one conceive of the coexistence of "Noaillian" and Perigordian groups during the whole of climatic Phase VII, almost 3000 years, in a region as limited as the Perigord without the inevitable contacts between them having more profoundly affected the tools?

If one accepts the functional argument to explain the variability among Perigordian industries with Noailles burins, one is forced, ipso facto, to reject the "Noaillian" and its cultural implications.

To conclude on this point, we return to the evidence: following the Perigordian with Gravette points (Bed 5 of the Abri Pataud), Gravettian industries developed that were characterized by Noailles burins and Raysse burins in their later phase, by Font-Robert points in their earlier phase; and the variations that one observes in the proportions of Noailles and Raysse burins and microgravette points reveal, in our opinion, the existence of functional facies rather than of cultural entities.

THE UPPER AND FINAL PERIGORDIAN

The development of Gravettian industries continued in the Perigord after 22,000 B.P. For some (Bricker and David 1984), this development is discontinuous with regard to the preceding Noaillian. The Perigordian VI appears totally discontinuous typologically. According to David and Bricker (1985), the Perigordian VI has much stronger affinities with the Perigordian IV than with the Perigordian V. But if we share this last point of view and accept a continuity between the Perigordian IV and the Perigordian VI, we do not agree that there was a discontinuity between the Perigordian V and the Perigordian VI.

In Table 25.3, we have calculated several typological indices for lithic assemblages from the Abri Pataud and Le Flageolet I, after having removed Raysse and Noailles burins from the typological inventories. These two typological categories, which manifest a clear inflation, mask in certain levels the relative proportions that exist among the other typological categories. We have therefore calculated the weighted indices.

The table shows clearly a certain consistency in the weighted indices, and the proportions of Gravette and microgravette points are confirmed, although it is a matter of a Perigordian constant that one finds in the Perigordian IV, V, and VI.

In the industries that are rich in Noailles and/or Raysse burins, one observes a relative diminution of the percentages of Gravette and microgravette points. The return in the Perigordian VIa of more "Gravettian" assemblages is confirmed as well by the data from Corbiac (Bordes 1968b), where one also sees an inversion at the level of burin types: in the Noailles and/or Raysse industries, the index of burins on a truncation (Noailles and Raysse excluded) is generally greater than that of dihedral burins.

PROTOMAGDALENIAN OR PERIGORDIAN VII?

At Laugerie Haute, D. Peyrony described, above the Perigordian VI (i.e., his Perigordian III), an industry in which Gravette points were extremely rare but which he linked, rather, to the Gravettian (Peyrony and Peyrony 1938). Bordes and de Sonneville-Bordes (1966) later confirmed this attribution and proposed designating the Protomagdalenian by the term Perigordian VII.

The Perigordian character is very attenuated, but it is evident that this assemblage from Laugerie Haute has the typological proportions of the Gravettian; it also has the same technological characteristics. If the Protomagdalenian industry is related to an earlier industry, it is certainly the Perigordian. But, as Peyrony remarked, it already has certain *Magdalenian* characteristics and, as de Sonneville-Bordes emphasized, these characteristics are those of the Upper and not the "Early" Magdalenian.

In fact, we have proposed the hypothesis of a cultural affiliation between the Protomagdalenian and the Magdalenian *sensu stricto* (Rigaud 1976b), that is to say, the Middle and Upper Magdalenian. We are, in effect, convinced that the Badegoulian (the old "Early Magdalenian") more closely resembles the Aurignacian typologically and technologically than it does the Perigordian. If we do not limit our analysis to "unique" industries that are, in fact very poorly known, the debitage and the typology of the Badegoulian do not have the very laminar character of the Protomagdalenian and of the Middle and Upper Magdalenian. As for the "reciprocal influences" between the Badegoulian and the Magdalenian, they too often have an exceptionally anecdotal character. Unfortunately, the period of the Protomagdalenian-Magdalenian transition is obliterated by the Solutrean phenomenon.

TABLE 25.3

Indices	P.V	P.IV l	P.IV m	P.IV u	P.III	F.VII	F.VI	F.V	F.IV	F.I/III	Corbiac
I.G.	19.30	14.40	17.10	13.40	13.70	22.30	13.90	8.90	8.90	11.40	6.19
I.B.	20.90	43.90	59.30	64.30	31.30	13.20	17.40	49.40	56.20	31.60	
I.Bd.	12.01	26.30	23.50	19.20	7.30	7.20	10.40	23.09	22.16	13.70	20.30
I.Bt.	4.70	13.30	27.60	39.30	18.40	5.20	6.14	23.90	31.10	16.09	10.60
Gravettes and microgravettes	25.03	3.20	0.60	0.50	20.30	11.06	4.40	0.40	2.40	2.30	9.90
Presence of Noailles and Raysse burins	?	*	*	*	?	*	*	*	*	—	?

P: Abri Pataud
F: Abri Le Flageolet I

NOTES

1. This is not the first time that we have established differences of this order in the stratigraphic and cultural sequences of two neighboring sites, and one may wonder if there are not differences between the sites in conditions affecting the conservation of C-14.

2. We have developed this argument elsewhere (Rigaud 1982a, b). Let us repeat simply that the area excavated by Delporte (1/200 of the probable extent of the site) does not in any way correspond to the demands of a representative sample. One may therefore question the use of elaborate statistical methods to analyze such poor samples (Djindjian 1980, especially since Delporte himself recognizes the lack of a representative sample (Delporte 1984: 273).

3. David and Bricker (1985) appear to be unaware of this publication (in English).

DISCUSSION

OTTE: I think that in order to understand the phylogenetic relation between Middle Paleolithic and the Upper Paleolithic cultures, we have to widen our point of view and take into account what happens in Belgium or Germany at the same time. This is also true for the Upper Paleolithic. For example, when we argue about the meaning and the implications of the so-called Noaillian, that is, whether it is a functional distinction or a chronological phase, we need also to consider the geographical distribution. As you know, we find shouldered points in Belgium, Germany, northern France, and East Germany, but no Noailles burins. The Noaillian is mainly in southeastern Europe, southeastern France at least, and Italy. To understand the end of the Upper Perigordian or Gravettian, Bordes's stage 6 or 7, we will also have to take into account what happened in Central Europe. In thinking about the origins of these cultural phases, we need to consider the possibility of polymorphic and polycentric developments.

BOSINSKI: I tried to propose that the so-called Gravettian is the result of the invention of inserted projectile points—backed bladelets, microbladelets. This invention was so useful that it spread to many groups in a relatively short time. Thus, the Gravettian is not a people coming from somewhere.

FREEMAN: The industry from Level 10 at Cueva Morín, which is one of the Chatelperronian horizons, is unlike many French Chatelperronian industries. This level is at the base of the Upper Paleolithic sequence but above an early, primitive Aurignacian. At El Pendo, as in Morín, the same kind of primitive Aurignacian occurred right above the Chatelperronian. That archaic Aurignacian, if it has any similarities at all, has them with the Aurignacian zero. But perhaps this Chatelperronian is not the same thing that we are calling Chatelperronian in other places. For example, it has no blade technology to speak of.

RIGAUD: I agree with the notion that the Castelperronian, especially the Castelperronian from St. Césaire, should be considered as derived from the Mousterian. But the fact that it does have a well-developed blade technology shows that the cultural discontinuity between the Middle Paleolithic and the Upper Paleolithic is not based solely on the introduction of blade technology.

MONTET-WHITE: Perhaps the Chatelperronian should not be regarded as a culture, or even an industry, but only as the spread of a hafting technique and backed blades.

RIGAUD: This backing technique has been used by different kinds of Mousterian before, so the only change in the backing technique is the Castelperronian knives.

STRAUS: Is it not a question of semantics? You speak of population change while others speak of the rapid spread of a technological invention.

RIGAUD: I agree with the fact that we could change the name, but it is not going to help. I did not see the difference between Aurignacian and Perigordian as a functional difference. There are all kinds of technological as well as stylistic differences between the Aurignacian and the Perigordian.

FREEMAN: That's right as long as you are talking about the later phase, and I have no doubt about the real dissimilarity between these two. But I wonder if less differentiation is apparent for the earlier phases.

KOZLOWSKI: I think that the most important argument against continuity between Castelperronian and Perigordian is the observation of internal dynamics of the long Castelperronian sequence which in its later stages does not develop toward the Gravettian. I think it would be very useful to re-excavate

La Gravette and to examine again the layer with *fléchettes*, because it is crucial for the understanding of the origin of the Upper Perigordian in France.

MÜLLER-BECK: What do we know about human remains associated with the Aurignacian?

RIGAUD: Not much.

STRAUS: But is the Aurignacian a distinct population, or a widely distributed technocomplex, or a series of technological inventions?

FARRAND: My comments are on the chronology and the sequence at Pataud relative to those at La Ferrassie and Le Flageolet: Level 4 at Pataud should be viewed as equivalent to Phase 7a of Laville, dated between 25,000 and 27,000. The tripartite nature of the Tursac Oscillation provides a nice correlation across the board for all these sites. Couche 3 at Pataud is 23,000 and Perigord 5 at Le Flageolet is 23,000.

RIGAUD: It seems that the Noaillian from Pataud is not contemporary with the Noaillian of some other sites including Flageolet, which raises some archaeological problems.

COMMENTS

OTTE: La compréhension des faciès gravettiens, comme de tous les phénomènes paléolithiques en Europe, exige d'ouvrir le champ d'étude au-delà du Périgord et même au-delà du territoire de la France. Toutes les composantes techniques et typologiques présentes dans les stades du "Périgordien supérieur" se retrouvent sous des formes variées dans le Gravettien européen et leur répartition changeante permet de mieux saisir leur sens que lorsqu'elles sont rassemblées dans un seul gisement d'Aquitaine.

Les "fléchettes" caractéristiques du "Bayacien" ou du Périgordien IV se trouvent en une trainée de sites au sud de l'Europe centrale: Geissenklösterle, Billenhöhle (Jura Souabe), Mauern (Bavière) et Willendorf (Autriche). Arrivant apparemment comme un moment en Périgord, elles correspondent en fait à une tendance d'extension beaucoup plus vaste et de signification culturelle distincte (groupe ethnique particulier, mode de chasse?).

De la même manière, on retrouve du "Laugérien" (H. L. Movius) ou Périgordien VII en Rhénanie à Sprendlingen et à Mayence. Les pointes pédonculées ("Font-Robertien", H. Delporte) sont d'expression plus septentrionale encore, de la Belgique à la Thuringe en passant par le Bassin parisien et semblent clairement plus anciennes dans ces régions "périphériques". Les pointes à cran du type Kostenki constituent apparemment leur équivalent fonctionnel dans les régions plus orientales lors des phases récentes.

C'est dans cette perspective qu'il faut considérer le cas du Noailles dont les traces à l'extérieur de la France sont très discutables (Belgique) si ce ne sont celles reconnues en Italie. Considérée largement, il semble donc bien se dessiner une "province" méridionale occupée par ce faciès Ve de D. Peyrony et les indices inter-stratifications des différents "fossiles directeurs" semblent bien limités à la région où chacun des faciès régionaux se sont un jour trouvés en contact, qu'il s'agisse d'échanges d'idées ou de contaminations de matériel dans des strates en voie de formation.

XXVI
Le Magdalénien ancien en Gironde

Conditions de gisement, variabilité typologique et technique

Michel Lenoir

Située en marge du Périgord, la région des basses vallées de la Dordogne et de la Garonne en constitue le prolongement occidental et s'ouvre sur l'océan atlantique. C'est une région de faible altitude où règne actuellement un climat océanique et se développe une végétation de caractère atlantique soumise à quelques influences méditerranéennes.

Du point de vue géologique, cette région qui appartient à un bassin sédimentaire voit affleurer des formations cénozoïques, marines ou lacustres, revêtues de formations quaternaires d'origine éolienne (sable des Landes), fluviatile (dépôts alluviaux) ou colluviale.

Le réseau hydrographique, relativement dense, est responsable d'un compartimentage net entre Dordogne et Garonne, dans le secteur de l'Entre-Deux-Mers. Les cours d'eaux principaux (Dordogne, Isle, Garonne) et leurs nombreux affluents ont constitué des voies de pénétration et permis ainsi une meilleure implantation des groupes humains, liée à la présence d'abris naturels creusés dans les abrupts rocheux du calcaire à Astéries et du calcaire de Castillon, aux points hauts et aux versants exposées au midi, outre l'abondance de gîtes de matière première et de ressources animales. Des buttes résiduelles de calcaire lacustre ou de hauts niveaux alluviaux sur les lignes de crête, constituent des accidents topographiques siège d'occupations répétées au cours du Pléistocène.

Il existe dans le Bazadais et à l'est de la Garonne, dans la région interne de la Gironde, des gîtes de matière première siliceuse (accidents siliceux du calcaire lacustre aquitanien et du calcaire lacustre de Castillon) ou des sources de matière allochtone (silex sénoniens sous forme de galets dans les dépôts alluviaux de la basse vallée de la Dordogne et de l'Isle) où l'homme préhistorique s'est approvisionné.

Les recherches anciennes, notamment de Daleau dans le Bourgeais et sur le littoral médocain, Labrie dans l'Entre-Deux-Mers, Conil et Morin en pays foyen, outre l'essai de synthèse de Ferrier (1938) pour l'ensemble du département ont mis en évidence dans cette région une occupation préhistorique de plein air et sous abri.

Les recherches ultérieures de nombreux préhistoriens amateurs qui ont effectué des récoltes de surface et fouilles programmées (Abri Houleau: Sireix; Saint-Germain-la-Rivière: Trécolle) ont apporté de nouvelles données qui ont servi de base à nos propres travaux dont nous avons récemment présenté les résultats (1983). Depuis cette date, de nouvelles découvertes plus particulièrement dans la partie orientale de l'Entre-Deux-Mers (Boireau, Obry) et dans le Bazadais (Obry) ont complété le cadre établi et fait de plus en plus apparaître l'étroite relation entre la localisation des sites et celle des gîtes de matière première.

Si l'occupation la plus ancienne est attestée dès le Mindel (Moisan 1978) ce n'est qu'à partir du Riss qu'elle s'accentue sans nette solution de continuité postérieure.

De plein-air pour le Paléolithique ancien et moyen à l'exception des niveaux moustériens de la grotte de Pair-Non-Pair, cette occupation se fixe davantage sous abri au Paléolithique supérieur parallèlement à un habitat de plein-air particulièrement développé pour la phase ancienne du Magdalénien.

Ces gisements de Magdalénien ancien de plein-air excepté un site sous abri (abri Houleau) se situent dans le Bourgeais de part et d'autre de la vallée du Moron affluent de la rive droite de la Dordogne et en Entre-Deux-Mers (Fig. 26.1), où ils apparaissent plus dispersés, outre la récente découverte d'une station dans le Bazadais. D'importance inégale tant par leur étendue que par l'abondance des vestiges lithiques, ces gisements se placent pour la plupart sur des points hauts, buttes résiduelles de calcaire lacustre ou hautes terrasses alluviales.

Les sites du Bourgeais et du Cubzadais sont connus surtout par des découvertes anciennes (découvertes de Daleau, Maziaud) ou des prospections récentes (Dupuy, Fredon). Ils ont livré des séries plus ou moins abondantes, d'inégale homogénéité, avec cependant une composante clairement attribuable au Magdalénien ancien par la présence d'outils caractéristiques (raclettes, pièces esquillées, burins transversaux) parfois en grand nombre ou de types spéciaux (pièces de La Bertonne) particulièrement abondants dans le site éponyme découvert par Daleau qui y récueillit une riche série complétée par les découvertes récentes de Fredon. Tandis que l'industrie de Viaud à Pugnac, relativement laminaire, apparaît comme un Magdalénien ancien assez classique, riche en raclettes, celle de La Bertonne—riche en pièces esquillées mais dépourvue de raclettes typiques—se singularise par la présence d'outils spéciaux déjà abondamment décrits (Daleau 1910; Lenoir 1976, 1983, 1987) qui portent sur la face inférieure des enlèvements lamellaires plus ou moins parallèles et obliques qui recoupent ceux d'une troncature retouchée inverse (Fig. 26.2). Ces pièces signalées par Daleau (1910) comme "silex à retouches anormales" puis postérieurement par Leysalles et Noone (1949) comme "grattoirs de Saint Sourd" sont communes dans certains faciès de Magdalénien ancien (Lenoir 1983, 1987). Outre La Bertonne, nous les connaissons en Gironde dans quelques gisements de l'Entre-Deux-Mers (Le Gouillard, Casevert, Gregeons, Pellegrue).

Toujours dans le Bourgeais l'industrie de Croûte Charlus sans raclette mais riche en burins transver-

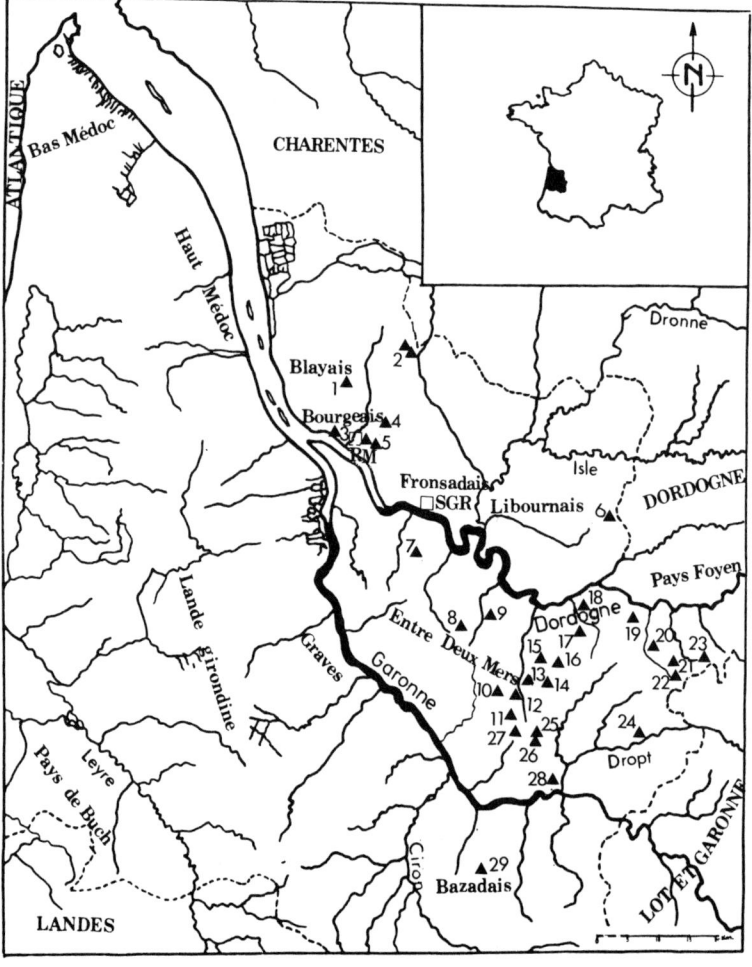

Figure 26.1 Carte de répartition des gisements de Magdalénien ancien en Gironde.

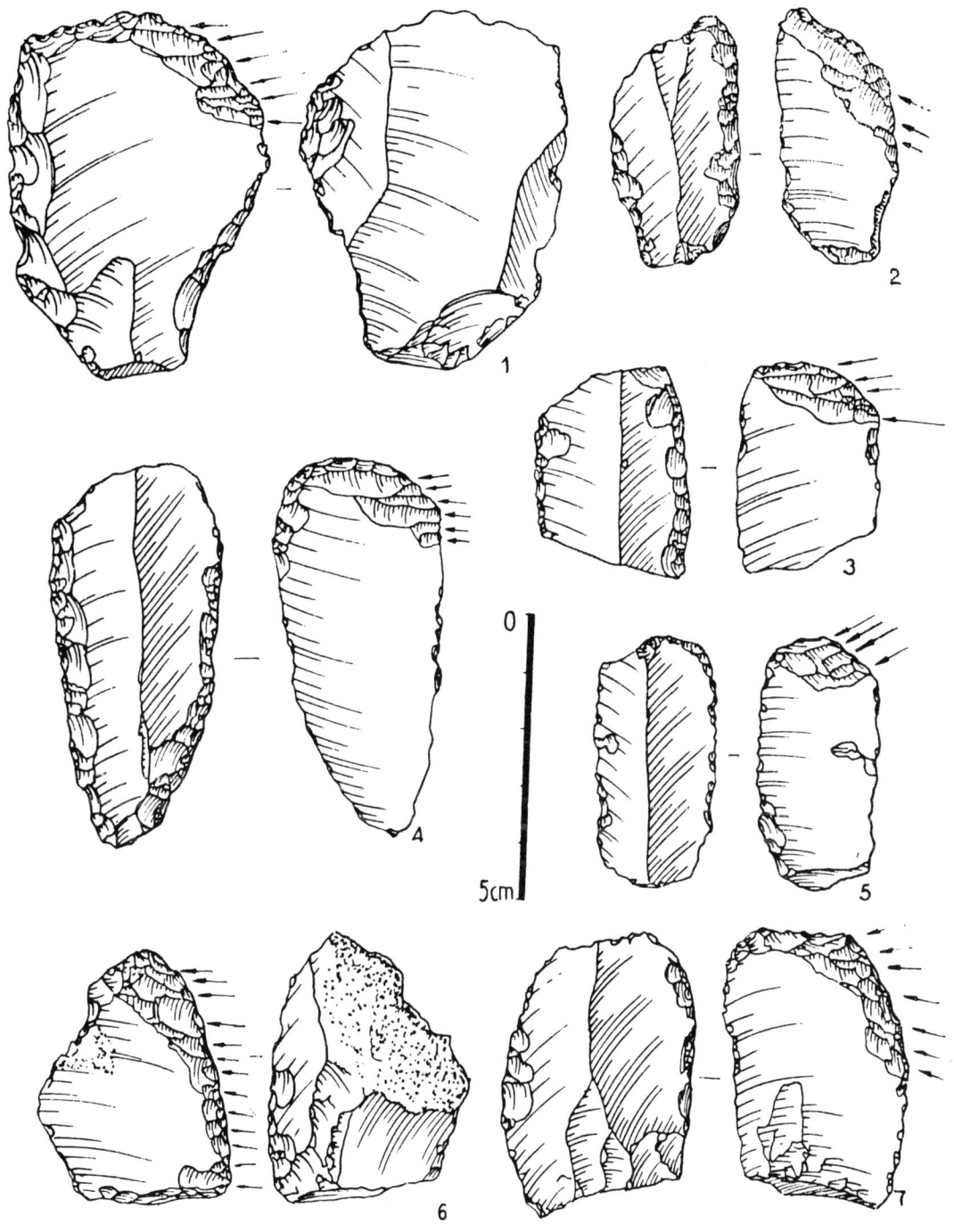

Figure 26.2 Pièces de La Bertonne du site éponyme de La Bertonne à Peujard, Gironde (coll. Daleau, Musée d'Aquitaine).

saux pourrait appartenir à un stade archaïque du Magdalénien ancien comparable au Magdalénien O de Laugerie Haute (Bordes 1958) de même que la petite série provenant du site de Viaud à Pellegrue, dans la partie est de l'Entre-Deux-Mers. Si les séries recueillies par A. Dupuy sur le plateau proche de Pair-Non-Pair et du Roc de Marcamps ne montrent pas de parfaites garanties d'homogénéité, elle comportent cependant une composante clairement attribuable au Magdalénien ancien par la présence de raclettes, de burins transversaux, l'allure générale de l'outillage et le mode de débitage à éclats. Au Roc de Marcamps, les niveaux datés de la phase de Lascaux ont livré une industrie à lamelles à dos identique à celle des niveaux du Dryas ancien sus-jacents. Plus au nord dans le secteur de Cavignac en limite des Charentes des découvertes inédites de Magdalénien à raclettes témoignent de sa présence aux confins du département girondin.

Toujours en rive droite de la Dordogne, quelques pièces attribuables au Magdalénien ancien proviennent de récoltes de surface sur le site de Camp de la Hire dans le Castillonnais ne se prêtent pas à une étude statistique parce que sporadiques et mêlées à des séries plus abondantes de Paléolithique ancien et de Périgordien supérieur. L'industrie des couches inférieures (C3, C4) du talus de Saint-Germain-la-Rivière (fouilles Trécolle) semble être contemporaine des débuts du Dryas ancien. Cette industrie d'allure grossière associe à un outillage sur éclat de petites lamelles à dos d'un type particulier où le dos généralement peu épais est opposé à un bord non retouché le plus souvent convexe. Dépourvu de raclette, de pièce de La Bertonne typique, de perçoir multiple, l'outillage commun, surtout sur pièces supports épaisses issues d'un débitage désordonné, comporte des grattoirs épais, carénés ou à museau, des denticulés massifs, des burins peu typiques le plus souvent nucléiformes, le tout associé à des nucléus informes ou des nucléus à lamelles sur éclat avec tous les termes de passage aux burins et aux grattoirs à retouches lamellaires. Cette industrie très particulière, très aurignacoïde d'aspect diffère nettement de celle des niveaux de Magdalénien moyen sus-jacents et du Magdalénien ancien le plus classique. Elle est associée à une faune steppique riche en Antilope saïga. Nous disposons d'une date pour la couche 4: Gif 5479 = 16,200 ± 600 B.P.

Dispersés dans l'Entre-Deux-Mers sur le bassin versant de la basse vallée de la Dordogne, la ligne de partage des eaux avec celui de la Garonne constituant leur limite méridionale de répartition, les gisements de Magdalénien ancien y montrent une grande variété dans l'étendue, l'abondance des vestiges lithiques et la composition statistique des outillages. Le gisement le plus occidental (Birac) domine la plaine alluviale de la Dordogne, au bassin de la Canodonne appartient le site de Gouillard à Camiac Saint Denis outre quelques indices recueillis sur le talus des Artigauts à Tizac de Curton. Plusieurs gisements se placent de part et d'autre de la vallée de l'Engranne et les autres se répartissent entre la Dordogne et le Dropt dans la partie orientale de l'Entre-Deux-Mers. Les sites les plus riches sont ceux de Birac, Pourquey, Casevert qui ont livré plusieurs milliers de vestiges parmi lesquels on compte plusieurs centaines d'outils, d'autres (Tauzin, Les Queyrons, Liobou) comportent plus d'une centaine d'outils, les autres assemblages (Pontaret, Gregeons, Moulin de Barrail, Casseuil, Pellegrue, Fougirard, Le Gouillard, Balette) possèdent moins de cent outils.

Plusieurs gisements de plein-air (Charron, François Brugier, La Chapelle, Les Vignes du Moulin, La Pibole) bouleversés par des travaux agricoles ont livré des indices très nets de Magdalénien ancien au sein d'un mélange de vestiges appartenant à plusieurs industries et pour cette raison ne peuvent être étudiés statistiquement. Sans doute existait-il dans le talus du Grand-Moulin des niveaux de Magdalénien ancien sur les couches profondes solutréennes, mais le matériel des fouilles anciennes de l'Abbé Labrie ne porte pas d'indications stratigraphiques.

Certaines séries (Birac, Pourquey, Gregeons, Abri Houleau, Les Queyrons et dans une moindre mesure Fougirard, Les Vignes du Moulin, Le Gouillard et Casevert) sont riches en raclettes tandis que les autres en sont mal pourvues. La plupart de ces séries (Tabl. 26.1) sont nettement plus riches en burins qu'en grattoirs exceptée celle de Tauzin qui possède un fort pourcentage de grattoirs épais de type aurignacien de même qu'à Pourquey et Birac III (Fig. 26.3). Les perçoirs et les becs sont en faibles pourcentages sauf à La Bertonne où ils comptent pour près de 5% de l'outillage. Les perçoirs multiples en étoile ne sont connus que dans ce site outre un perçoir triple à Birac. Les burins très nombreux à Casevert y comportent un fort pourcentage de burins transversaux sur éclat. Les pièces tronquées constituent près de 20% de l'outillage à Casevert, 12% à Viaud dans le Bourgeais et moins de 6% dans les autres séries. Abondantes à Viaud (près de 13%), les lames retouchées sont en pourcentage plus faible partout ailleurs. Les pièces esquillées sont abondantes dans le Bourgeais dans les

TABLEAU 26.1
RACLETTES ET OUTILS

Site	Nombre de Raclettes	Nombre Total d'Outils
Bourgeais		
Viaud (Pugnac)	45	22
Bel-Air	3	20
Coudet	1	mélange d'industries
La Bertonne	5 (atypiques)	672
Mauran 1	8	64
Mauran 2	72	69
Castillonnais		
Camp de la Hire	18	mélange d'industries
La Bernarderie	1	mélange d'industries
Entre-Deux-Mers		
Birac II	17	48
Birac II bis	3	14
Birac III	224	608
Le Gouillard	5	47
Beauregard	4	19
Les Queyrons	25	131
François-Brugier	4	mélange d'industries
Pourquey	216	?
Grand-Moulin	2	mélange d'industries
Pontaret	4	59
Casevert	45	893
Charron	20	78
Abri Houleau	1	mélange d'industries
Vignes du Moulin	16	mélange d'industries
Moulin de Barrail	2	35
Gregeons	17	84
Le Tauzin	3	143
Liobou	3	14
Bazadais		
Beauregard (Mazères)	2	124

sites de Viaud et de La Bertonne (10,5%). Les pièces de La Bertonne n'atteignent jamais, lorsqu'elles sont représentées, de pourcentage aussi élevé que dans le site éponyme tandis que le fort taux de racloirs de certaines séries peut être dû à un mélange avec du Moustérien. Les microlithes sont rares ou absents excepté à Gregeons (près de 5% de l'outillage).

Dans l'ensemble ces séries montrent une forte proportion d'outils sur éclat cependant accompagnés d'outils sur lame, une série est nettement laminaire (Pontaret) mais dans ce cas précis peut être mélée à du Périgordien (Lenoir 1983), une autre (Gregeons) apparaît relativement lamellaire et possède des microlithes tandis que l'industrie récemment découverte à

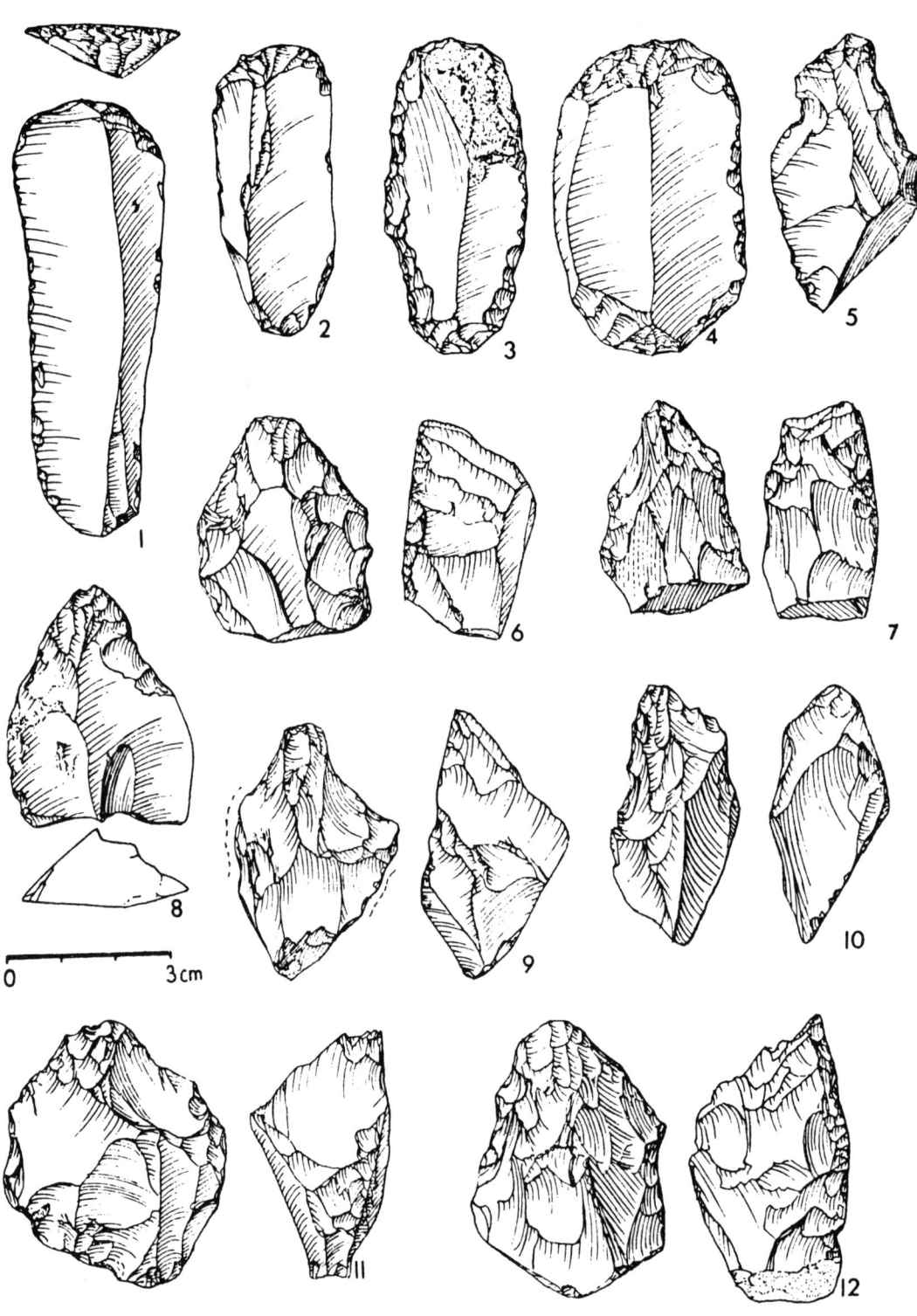

Figure 26.3 Birac III, grattoirs.

Balette apparaît relativement laminaire. Les chutes de burins sont nombreuses dans les riches séries de La Bertonne et de Birac et leur abondance y peut être mise en parallèle avec celle des burins. Les nucléus montrent des fréquences variables toujours inférieures à 16% de la totalité des produits de débitage. Ils sont particulièrement bien représentés à Liobou où abondent aussi les éclats corticaux. Certaines séries (Birac, Pourquey, Gregeons) sont riches en petits éclats plats (Fig. 26.4) extraits de nucléus à tendance discoïde connus à plusieurs exemplaires dans le gisement de Mauran dans le Bourgeais.

Très marginal par sa position géographique en rive gauche de la Garonne dans le Bazadais, le gisement de Beauregard à Mazères récemment découvert par Obry utilise le silex lacustre local et se singularise par la prédominance des grattoirs, souvent épais, sur les autres types d'outils, outre la présence de nombreux racloirs, de denticulés, de pièces esquillées et de quelques raclettes. Jusqu'ici l'occupation du Magdalénien ancien n'était connue en bordure de l'axe garonnais que plus en amont en Agenais (Le Tensorer 1981).

Ces industries dans l'ensemble peu laminaires, pauvres en lamelles, riches en petits éclats associés à des nucléus le plus souvent épuisés, globuleux ou informes, plus rarement prismatiques, parfois discoïdes avec un outillage plus ou moins diversifiés comportant des outils spéciaux présentent un même air de famille, différent de celui du Magdalénien classique à tel point que certains auteurs (Vignard 1965; Allain 1968; Schmider 1971; Trotignon 1984) ont exclu le Magdalénien ancien (Badegoulien) de la lignée magdalénienne. Leur variabilité typologique et technique suggère l'existence de faciès chronologiques ou géographiques encore mal définis. L'allure périgordienne de certaines séries (Pontaret, François Brugier) pourrait témoigner d'une appartenance à un faciès spécial si elle n'est pas imputable à des mélanges d'industries, tandis que les autres séries présentent plutôt des traits aurignacoïdes.

Il existe de fortes similitudes entre l'industrie de Birac (coll. Crochet) et celle de Pourquey (coll. Sireix). Comme cette dernière est inédite nous n'avons pu effectuer de comparaisons statistiques entre ces deux séries numériquement importantes. Par sa structure typologique l'industrie de Birac rappelle également celle du gisement de Maubin en Lot-et-Garonne (Tabl. 26.2; Le Tensorer 1981).

Ces séries riches en burins, avec une dominance des burins dièdres comportent un fort pourcentage de

TABLEAU 26.2

	Birac III	Maubin
Grattoirs	9,53	6,25
Grattoirs aurignaciens	4,58	1,14
Outils composites	2,96	4,55
Perçoirs et becs	2,13	5,68
Burins	28,12	30,68
Burins dièdres	19,24	18,78
Burins/troncature	4,76	9,09
Burins transversaux	1,15	3,41
Lames à dos	0,32	0,00
Lames tronquées	2,46	2,27
Outils divers	49,34	43,75
Raclettes	36,84	37,50
Pièces esquillées	0,98	1,14
Microlithes	0,32	0,00
n:	608	176

raclettes, tandis que les pièces esquillées sont rares, les microlithiques sporadiques ou absents, peut être en partie parce qu'il s'agit de séries recueillies en surface. Les grattoirs aurignaciens sont cependant mieux représentés à Birac qu'à Maubin, tandis que c'est l'inverse pour les outils composites et pour les perçoirs. L'industrie de Maubin apparaît un peu plus riche en burins transversaux que celle de Birac, mais malgré ces quelques divergences, ces deux gisements sont cependant assez proches par la composition générale de l'outillage.

Si on porte sous forme de diagramme triangulaire (Fig. 26.5) la représentation relative des grattoirs, des burins et des raclettes pour différentes séries de Magdalénien ancien d'après les décomptes qui en ont été publiés et d'après nos propres recherches pour les séries girondines, peuvent être faites quelques remarques. Ces remarques doivent cependant être présentées avec les réserves imposées par l'importance numérique trop faible de certaines séries de comparaison statistiquement non représentatives et données à titre indicatif et par le fait que d'autres séries recueillies dans un même site lors de fouilles anciennes se placent dans des secteurs différents du diagramme selon les collections concernées ce qui laisse supposer d'éventuelles concentrations ou un mode de prélèvement différent. Sur ce diagramme n'apparaissent pas de groupements parfaitement séparés mais des indus-

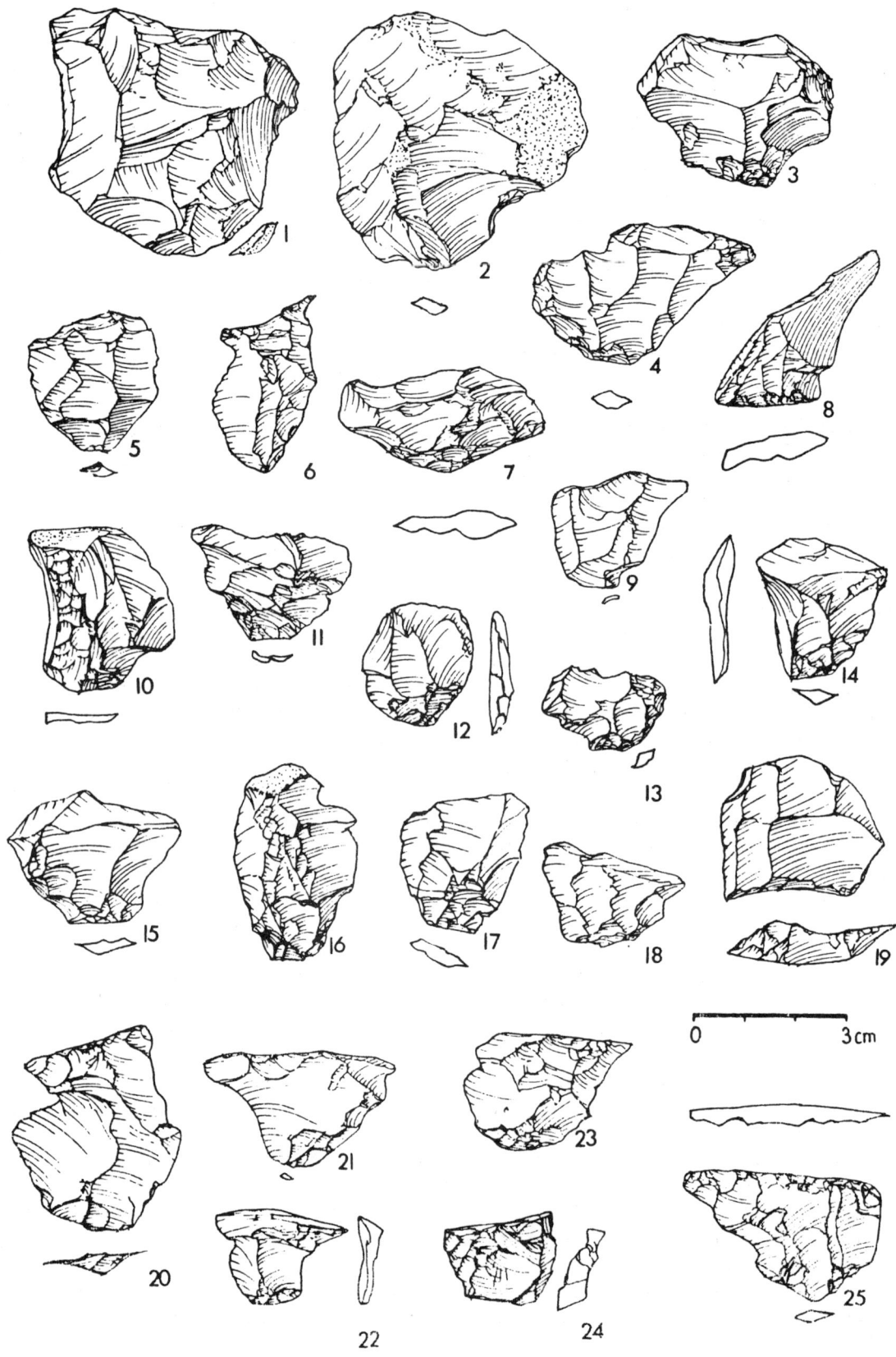

Figure 26.4 Birac III, petits éclats courts.

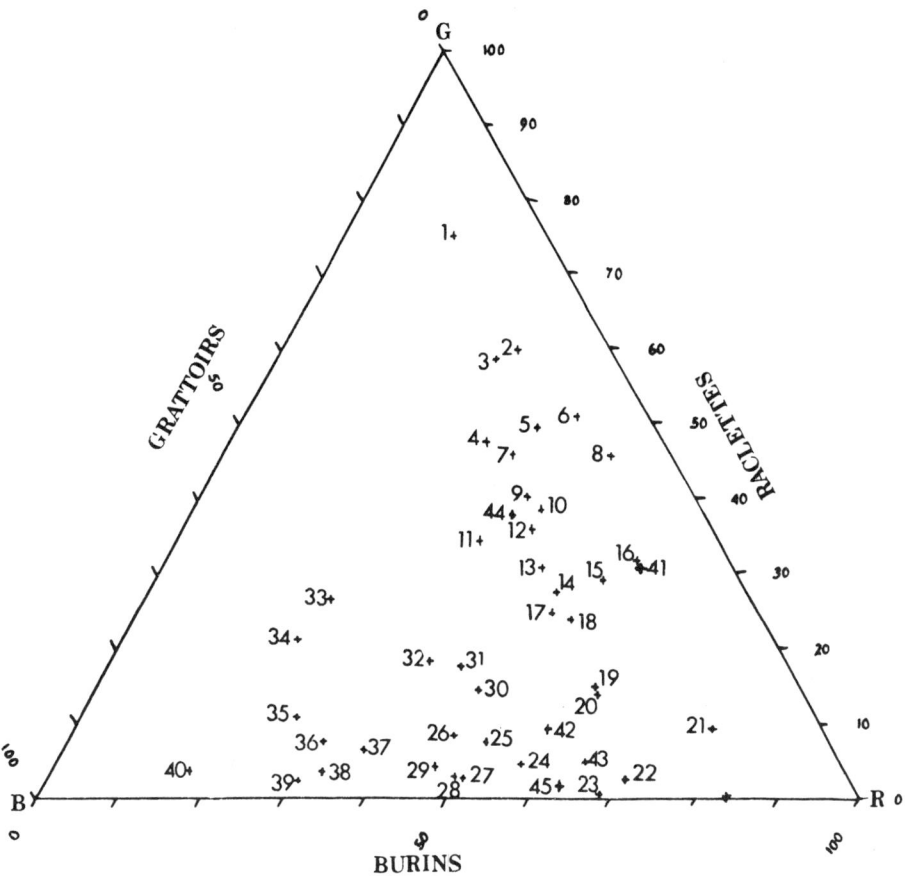

Figure 26.5 Représentation des grattoirs, burins et raclettes dans diverses séries de Magdalénien ancien.

tries riches en raclettes par rapport aux burins et aux grattoirs (Jean-Blanc, Maubin, Birac III, Badegoule C7, Solvieux, Pégourié C8, Abri Fritsch C4) s'opposent à des industries riches en burins (La Bertonne, Casevert, Guillassou, Pégourié C9, Abri Fritsch C5b, C5d, C6) avec des raclettes et des grattoirs moins abondants. Les autres assemblages appartiennent à des industries moyennement pourvues en burins, avec des pourcentages plus ou moins forts de grattoirs et de raclettes tandis que l'industrie de Mazères s'individualise nettement par son taux élevé de grattoirs. Pauvres en raclettes, les séries attribuées au Magdalénien O (Laugerie Haute Est niveau 18, Cassegros C10, Guillassou) se placent dans la partie inférieure du diagramme, celles des sites méditerranéens (Camparnaud, Lassac, La Rivière) sont groupées et il en est de même des séries du Lot-et-Garonne (Cassegros C9, Maubin, Layrac) réparties dans un secteur du diagramme où se situe également la série de Birac.

D'après Hemingway (1980), le développement du "Magdalénien initial" est marqué par le déclin du pourcentage des burins transversaux et par l'augmentation de celui des raclettes qui deviennent l'élément dominant à Badegoule (couche 7), Pégourié (couche 8), Maubin, Solvieux, aux Jean-Blancs et à Birac. Ces outils portent une retouche de plus en plus abrupte et de plus en plus étendue. Dans les stades terminaux leur pourcentage décroît au profit de celui des microlithes. Si l'on se calque sur ce schéma évolutif, l'industrie de Croûte-Charlus près de Bourg sur Gironde et celle du gisement de Viaud à Pellegrue pourraient appartenir à un stade archaïque du Magdalénien ancien (Magdalénien O ou Badegoulien ancien selon les auteurs) par l'absence de raclettes, la présence de burins transversaux et l'allure massive de l'outillage, mais ces séries pauvres en outils ne sont guère expressives. Sans raclette typique, sans microlithe mais relativement riche en burins transversaux (2,23%), l'industrie de La Bertonne pourrait se rattacher à un stade ancien de même que celle de Casevert riche en burins transversaux (7,27%) mais assez pauvre en raclettes et pauvre en microlithes. Ces deux séries possèdent des pièces de La Bertonne rares ou absentes dans les autres sites. Riche en raclettes morphologiquement diversifiées, à retouche bien caractéristique, nettement abrupte sur une grande partie des bords, les séries de Birac, Viaud (Pugnac), Pourquey, Houleau évoquent le Magdalénien ancien évolué sans que l'on puisse leur assigner un position chronologique précise. Les autres assemblages sont trop pauvres ou trop mélangés pour permettre de proposer quelque datation. Ils semblent cependant relativement riches en raclettes compte-tenu de leur faiblesse numérique et évoquent davantage le Magdalénien I que le Magdalénien O tels qu'ils ont été définis en Périgord (Bordes 1966, 1984).

D'après Hemingway, les grattoirs épais de type aurignacien ne sont pas systématiquement plus abondants dans les stades les plus anciens du Magdalénien initial et ils auraient même tendance à se développer dans les stades les plus récents. En Gironde, ils sont surtout bien représentés à Birac (IGa: 3,13), Casevert (IGa: 2,91), La Bertonne (IGa: 1,04) et Tauzin (IGa: 4,92), mais l'industrie de Beauregard à Mazères, bien que riche en grattoirs n'est pas particulièrement mieux pourvue en grattoirs de type aurignacien. Faute d'éléments de datation plus pertinents, les industries du Magdalénien ancien girondin pour la plupart recueillies hors stratigraphie dans des sites de plein-air ne peuvent être datées plus précisément.

LES RACLETTES

Très abondantes dans certains gisements, les raclettes ont plus particulièrement retenu notre attention et fait l'objet d'une analyse détaillée. Elles sont souvent bien représentées dans les industries du Magdalénien ancien et perdurent sporadiquement dans le Magdalénien plus récent.

Ce type d'outil, décrit avec précision par Cheynier (1930), a été défini par de Sonneville-Bordes et Perrot (1956) comme: éclat ou plus rarement fragment de lame, de forme variable, généralement petit et assez mince, à faces subparallèles, à retouches continues très courtes et abruptes, portant généralement sur tous les bords.

Cette définition générale nous a semblé recouvrir une multitude de modalités au sein desquelles nous avons quelque temps espéré déceler des constantes. Nous avons donc entrepris dans les années 70 une analyse d'attributs des raclettes de l'Abri Houleau et de Pourquey (coll. Sireix) et nous les avons comparées à celles des niveaux de Magdalénien I de Laugerie Haute Est (séries Bordes). Cette analyse a concerné les principales caractéristiques morphométriques de l'outil et de sa pièce support, la localisation et l'étendue de la retouche abrupte et la morphologie de la pièce, afin d'individualiser d'éventuels sous-types et d'étudier leur répartition au sein des différents assemblages. L'état de fragmentation de nombreuses pièces et les difficultés rencontrées pour délimiter l'extension et l'orientation de la retouche abrupte par rapport à l'axe de débitage de la pièce support ne nous ont pas permis d'obtenir des résultats expressifs et nous n'avons donc pas réussi à donner une interprétation de la variabilité morphologique de ce type.

Par une démarche voisine Le Tensorer (1981) a distingué trois catégories morphologiques de raclettes en fonction du rapport longueur-largeur et retenu l'existence d'une dizaine de types sans préciser si l'analyse morphométrique a concerné uniquement des pièces entières. Ces types ont été définis à partir de caractères très disparates, morphologiques et métriques ou qui concernent l'état de fragmentation. Grâce à une étude détaillée des caractères morphométriques des raclettes comparés à ceux des produits de débitage susceptible de leur servir de pièces supports et grâce à une analyse d'attributs plus spécifiquement liés à la nature de la retouche, Hemingway (1980) n'a pas observé de récurrences nettes de forme générale et de position de la retouche. Des résultats de cette analyse, il a déduit le choix de pièces supports relativement plates, sans cortex et décrit pour leur obtention un mode de débitage consistant à effectuer des enlèvements transversaux sur des nucléus pyramidaux aboutissant à des nucléus globuleux particulièrement bien représentés dans les industries du Magdalénien ancien. Cette possibilité expérimentalement suggérée par Sireix (Hemingway 1980) et décrite anciennement par Cheynier (1939) comme débitage "en tranche de saucisson" ne nous paraît pas exclusive puisque nous avons obtenu le même type de pièce support par d'autres moyens tels que le détachement d'éclats à partir de petits nucléus discoïdes ou de nucléus de formes diverses sans nette direction d'enlèvements préférentielle.

A partir d'un essai de sériation chronologique fondé sur l'analyse détaillée d'attributs et de corrélations de variables concernant la retouche de raclettes d'origine stratigraphique bien établie, Hemingway a proposé un schéma évolutif montrant l'augmentation du pourcentage de ce type d'outil, une étendue croissante de la retouche par rapport au contour général de l'objet et un taux de plus en plus élevé de pièces à retouche directe et d'exemplaires composites associant la retouche abrupte à un autre outil. En outre les raclettes recueillies dans les sites proches de la Méditerranée se révèlent en moyenne plus épaisses que celles des sites plus septentrionaux.

Bien que séduisantes, confortées par des tests statistiques et un traitement informatique des données, ces conclusions mériteraient d'être renforcées par l'examen de séries plus nombreuses bien datées.

Certains gisements girondins (Abri Houleau, Pourquey, Birac) ont livré de nombreuses raclettes (plus de 200 chacun) et d'autres (Casevert, Viaud à Pugnac) des séries plus modestes (respectivement 65 et 45 pièces) cependant suffisantes pour permettre une étude métrique. Les autres séries n'apportant guère de renseignements sur ce type d'outil trop peu abondant ou absent.

De même que Cheynier, Le Tensorer et Hemingway, nous avons noté la rareté des raclettes à retouche inverse ou alterne par rapport à celles à retouche directe. Les séries que nous avons étudiées ont des caractéristiques identiques tant pour la répartition des longueurs des pièces entières que pour celle des largeurs. Les raclettes sont généralement sur pièce support peu épaisse tandis que l'épaisseur de la retouche traduit une plus grande variabilité. La série de Viaud à Pugnac montre la plus forte épaisseur moyenne mais cette série peu abondante (27 pièces) n'est sans doute pas représentative (Tabl. 26.3).

Plusieurs catégories de raclettes ont été retenues en fonction de la délinéation de la retouche par rapport à l'axe de débitage de la pièce support et en fonction de la morphologie générale:

— pièces à retouche transversale convexe se prolongeant parfois sur les côtés et qui forme un front d'axe;
— pièces à retouche transversale convexe et retouches latérales formant un front large généralement déjeté par rapport à l'axe de percussion;
— pièces à retouche transversale non convexe sans front et sans retouches latérales;
— pièces à retouche latérale ou bilatérale associées à une retouche transversale non convexe, sans front;
— pièces à retouche uni- ou bilatérale;
— pièces à retouche formant une sorte de bec ou de grossier perçoir;
— pièces retouchées sur tout le contour de la pièce support.

Le tableau de fréquence de ces différentes catégories dans les séries statistiquement étudiables témoigne d'une assez grande variabilité de répartition. On remarque cependant une similitude assez nette entre la série de l'Abri Houleau et celle de Pourquey où la prédominance des pièces à retouches latérales, résulte peut-être de l'abondance des outils fragmentaires ou de raclettes faites sur de petits fragments. Les raclettes dont la retouche dégage un bec sont nettement plus abondantes dans ces deux gisements que dans les autres séries, tandis qu'à Casevert dominent les fronts d'axe et dans le petit lot de pièces de Viaud, les pièces à retouche transversale ne formant pas de front (Tabl. 26.4).

Pour les séries girondines apparemment homo-

TABLEAU 26.3

MOYENNE DES LONGUEURS ET DES LARGEURS MAXIMUM

	n	longueur	Sd	n	largeur	Sd
Pourquey	140	2,76	1,04	149	2,26	0,92
Houleau	143	3,03	1,00	125	2,31	0,78
Casevert	52	2,77	0,87	56	2,37	0,67
Viaud (Pugnac)	26	2,93	0,89	27	2,84	0,88
Birac III	181	2,58	0,87	213	2,15	0,76

Les nombres des pièces dont la longueur et la largeur sont mesurables diffèrent puisqu'il y a des objets fragmentaires.

TABLEAU 26.4

RÉPARTITION DES RACLETTES PAR CATÉGORIES

	Houleau	Pourquey	Birac	Casevert	Viaud	Laugerie Hte. Est (Magd. Ic)
Front d'axe	19,79%	13,63	12,50	35,70	20,00	23,93
Front large	16,75	20,45	9,50	7,14	5,71	21,36
Ret. transv.	3,04	3,97	6,00	14,28	37,14	10,25
Ret. transv. et lat.	16,24	14,20	23,00	16,07	17,14	12,82
Ret. lat.	27,41	30,68	42,50	19,64	14,28	25,64
Bec	16,24	17,04	3,50	5,35	5,71	5,98
Ret. totale	0,50	-	3,00	1,78	-	-

gènes, nous avons calculé le taux d'outils par rapport au total des outils, des produits de débitage et des chutes de burins (Tabl. 26.1-2). Abstraction faite du gisement de La Bertonne où curieusement les outils comptent pour plus de 50% (65,88% série Daleau; 55,72% série Fredon) les séries les plus riches en outils sont celles qui comportent le plus de raclettes (Birac III: 34,12%; Viaud: 38,34%; Gregeons: 30,88%), ces séries se révèlent par ailleurs riches en lames (Viaud, Birac III) ou en lamelles (Gregeons) et l'abondance relative de l'outillage dépend en grande partie de celle des raclettes. Les séries de Beauregard à Mazères, Fougirard et Liobou comptent moins de 20% d'outils et se caractérisent par un débitage peu laminaire et un outillage assez massif (Mazères, Liobou) généralement fait sur éclat, tandis que le nucléus qui y sont assez nombreux sont surtout à éclats et pour la plupart globuleux ou informes. Les éclats corticaux atteignant un pourcentage assez fort à Tauzin, Beauregard, Liobou et Gouillard, les chutes de burins sont relativement abondantes à La Bertonne, Gregeons et Birac III gisements assez riches en burins, mais pas spécialement plus que d'autres inclus dans cette étude. Très laminaire et pourvue de nucléus d'allure périgordienne, l'industrie de Pontaret évoque davantage le Périgordien que le Magdalénien ancien (Tabl. 26.5).

Parmi les séries girondines examinées certaines: Birac III, Pourquey, Gregeons, Les Queyrons, Viaud (Pugnac) évoquent un Magdalénien initial assez évolué qui bien que nanti des particularités qui caractérisent le Magdalénien à raclettes semble annoncer les industries du Magdalénien moyen synchrones du Dryas ancien et bien connues dans ce secteur grâce aux récentes fouilles dans les sites du Roc de Marcamps et de Moulin Neuf (Lenoir 1983) et à l'Abri Houleau (fouilles Sireix). D'autres séries (Mauran 1 et Mauran 2, Le Gouillard, Le Tauzin, Moulin de Barrail, La Pibole, Fougirard, Pellegrue, Casevert) trop réduites ou trop hétérogènes pour permettre une analyse fiable et des conclusions péremptoires semblent cependant par leurs caractéristiques majeures pouvoir être rattachées au groupe précèdent tandis que les industries de Mazères, Liobou et Viaud (Pellegrue) s'en démarquent par leur allure frustre de même que celle de La Bertonne très particulière par l'inflation des "pièces de La Bertonne," l'abondance des pièces esquillées et l'absence de raclette typique. Enfin, l'industrie inédite des couches inférieures (C3, C4) du talus du gisement de Saint-Germain-la-Rivière en cours d'étude (Trécolle, Lenoir) et datée pour la couche 4 (GiF 5479: 16,200 ± 600 B.P.) se singularise par son débitage d'éclats épais et de fines lamelles extraites de nucléus sur éclat, son outillage très peu diversifié et diffère nettement de celle des niveaux sus-jacents clairement attribuable au Magdalénien moyen.

Ces industries du Magdalénien initial apparaissent très polymorphes à partir des données girondines et cette variabilité se manifeste également à la plus vaste échelle de la France, seul secteur géographique où elles sont représentées. Certaines semblent bien annoncer le Magdalénien plus récent, moyen et supérieur, mais s'en démarquent quelque peu par des traits particuliers concernant la technologie (débitage non laminaire, débitage sur éclats), le style de l'outillage (outils courts sur supports épais à retouche parfois d'allure aurignacienne), la structure quantitative de l'outillage et l'inflation de certains types d'outils (raclettes, pièces de La Bertonne, pièces esquillées), toutes semblent cependant se rattacher à un même technocomplexe dont le Magdalénien classique

TABLEAU 26.5
REPRÉSENTATION DES GRATTOIRS, BURINS ET RACLETTES DANS DIVERSES SÉRIES DE MAGDALÉNIEN ANCIEN

No.	Site	Nombre d'Outils	Source Bibliographique
1.	Jean-Blanc Est	236	de Sonneville-Bordes 1960
2.	Jean-Blanc Ouest	129	de Sonneville-Bordes 1960
3.	Abri Fritsch C4	61	Trotignon 1984
4.	Badegoule niv. 7	1681	Hemingway 1980
5.	Birac III	453	Lenoir 1983
6.	Maubin	131	Le Tensorer 1981
7.	Pégourié C8	192	Hemingway 1980
8.	Solvieux Ab, locus III	1877	Hemingway 1980
9.	Cassegros C7	15	Le Tensorer 1981
10.	Beauregard 2ème Redan, Chantier I	293	Schmider 1971
11.	Cassegros C9	38	Le Tensorer 1981
12.	Lassac, locus 1, C2	128	Hemingway 1980
13.	Abri Fritsch C5a	30	Trotignon 1984
14.	Layrac	18	Le Tensorer 1981
15.	Gregeons	31	décompte Lenoir
16.	La Croix de Fer	42	Gaussen 1980
17.	Lassac (surface)	794	Hemingway 1980
18.	Laugerie Haute Est niv. 12, Magd Ic	366	Bordes 1984
19.	Guillassou	403	Gaussen 1980
20.	Pégourié C9	89	Hemingway 1980
21.	Casevert	693	Lenoir 1983
22.	Abri Fritsch C5b	37	Trotignon 1984
23.	Abri Fritsch C5d	26	Trotignon 1984
24.	Abri Fritsch C6	108	Trotignon 1984
25.	Laugerie Haute Est I' (série Peyrony)	464	de Sonneville-Bordes 1960
26.	Badegoule niv. 6	2406	Hemingway 1980
27.	Laugerie Haute Est niv. 18, Magd. 0	366	Bordes 1984
28.	Cassegros C10	42	Le Tensorer 1981
29.	Le Tauzin	72	décompte Lenoir
30.	La Chapelle St. Mesmin	204	Hemingway 1980 (d'après Nouël 1937)
31.	Camparnaud	118	Hemingway 1980
32.	Beauregard (série Daniel Est)	249	Schmider 1971
33.	Beauregard (série Daniel Sud)	86	Schmider 1971
34.	Rond du Barry F2	38	Hemingway 1980 (d'après de Bayle des Hermens 1974a,b)
35.	Badegoule (Peyrony)	161	de Sonneville-Bordes 1960
36.	Badegoule (Peyrille)	63	de Sonneville-Bordes 1960
37.	Liobou	33	décompte Lenoir
38.	Beauregard (Fouju)	105	Schmider 1971
39.	Beauregard (Soudan Lapeyre)	751	Schmider 1971
40.	Mazères	52	décompte Lenoir
41.	Les Queyrons	82	décompte Lenoir
42.	Fougirard	33	décompte Lenoir
43.	La Pibole	69	décompte Lenoir
44.	Viaud (Pugnac)	122	Lenoir 1983
45.	La Bertonne	285	Lenoir 1983

semble constituer le plus proche héritier. Quant à une éventuelle filiation avec l'Aurignacien (Rigaud 1976b; Kozlowski 1985), elle demeure très sujette à caution puisque les industries les plus anciennes du Magdalénien initial ne sont pas systématiquement les plus riches en grattoirs de type aurignacien (Hemingway 1980), de même que l'hypothèse d'une origine solutréenne (Hemingway 1980; Trotignon 1984) établie à partir de similitudes bien précaires en comparaison des différences présentées par ces deux complexes.

ACKNOWLEDGMENTS

Messieurs Aubert, P. Blanchard, N. Boireau, C. Boucher, H. Crochet, A. Dupuy, J.-F. et R. Dufaget, G. Fredon, H. Gros, D. Lapoterie, J. Obry, R. Prudhomme, M. Sireix, R. Slott-Moller, G. Trécolle nous ont aimablement donné accès à leur matériel. Le regretté professeur François Bordes, M. Sireix et A. Roussot, Conservateur au Musée d'Aquitaine, nous ont donné toutes facilités d'étude respectivement pour les raclettes de Laugerie Haute, de l'Abri Houleau et de Pourquey et pour les séries du Musée d'Aquitaine. Nous leur en sommes à tous très reconnaissant.

DISCUSSION

FERRING: This paper underlines the importance of research done on surface survey and open-air sites. It is important in terms of defining typological and technological variability in the Gironde during the Magdalenian and goes far in establishing the character of Lower Magdalenian assemblage variability so that a better appraisal of this period can be done. Having multiple sites across a landscape provides the opportunity to see more typological variability across a landscape than we might see in one place, simply because of the potential for functional variation among the sites. The graphs based on the frequencies of endscrapers, burins, and *raclettes* suggest two clusters of assemblages, one which seems to be dominated by *raclettes* and endscrapers, and the other by *raclettes* and burins. This certainly suggests some functional variation among these assemblages unless other explanations emerge. Also interesting are the apparent technological differences between some of the assemblages, for example the production of small Levallois-like flakes as opposed to the blade-like tendencies of some of the assemblages. There is also the problem of attributing the differences to time or to function. Is there a possibility that it is due to mixture?

LENOIR: At least in some cases it is not a question of mixture.

SACKETT: This work illustrates the dangers of a "type-site" kind of thinking and instead shows the kinds of variability which simply do not appear in a single site, such as Laugerie-Haute. The Lower Magdalenian is also of crucial importance because it's a sort of focus for discussing the nature of lateral variability in Upper Paleolithic, for example, what Rigaud has refered to as the schizophrenic nature of the Magdalenian. It also relates to certain questions raised by Straus concerning the nature of the Solutrean.

RIGAUD: I do not agree with the term "Lower Magdalenian" and instead prefer the term "Badegoulian." I think that there is more typological and technological similarity between the Aurignacian, Late Aurignacian and the Badegoulian, or what has been called here Lower Magdalenian, than between the Aurignacian and the Upper and Middle Magdalenian. In this industry there are a lot of carinated and nosed scrapers, and in terms of technology, there are very few blades. For these reasons, I suggested some years ago that perhaps we should refer to this as the Badegoulian or even "Epi-Aurignacian."

BOSINSKI: I agree with the term Badegoulian, but I do not think that we should be compelled to link it to the Aurignacian cultural phase, any more than we would link certain Neolithic phases that have Levallois technique with the Mousterian and Neandertal man.

RIGAUD: It also appears that there is a very low population density at this time, at least based on the evidence from caves and in terms of the numbers of sites. But is it also true that such Badegoulian assemblages in open-air sites have been sometimes called Aurignacian because of these similarities.

LENOIR: In the Gironde, there are a number of sites attributable to the Aurignacian and Perigordian; most of them are open-air sites. Certainly some Aurignacian sites were confused with Lower Magdalenian sites, but in the Gironde, most open-air examples are Lower Magdalenian, while Middle and Upper Magdalenian is usually in caves. The Perigord is different.

XXVII
Frontières européennes au Paléolithique supérieur

Enregistrements et significations—le cas du Sud-Ouest français

Denise de Sonneville-Bordes

La dynamique culturelle du Paléolithique supérieur est fondamentalement différente de celle du Paléolithique moyen. Diversifiés par des caractéristiques technotypologiques statistiquement enregistrées, des groupes distincts buissonnent dans le vaste complexe moustérien, où se distinguent difficilement des répartitions territoriales encore faiblement discernables: le Moustérien de tradition acheuléenne absent du monde méditerranéen, le Moustérien type Quina, largement véhiculés par les humanités néanderthaliennes, le Moustérien à denticulés très mal reconnu, l'importance du débitage levallois dans les Moustériens méditerranéens et un Moustérien typique encore insuffisamment défini (Bordes 1981b, 1984). Antérieurement, les seules différenciations régionales observées restent l'Acheuléen méridional et le Vasconien (Bordes 1953a, 1961a; Thibault 1970; Moisan 1978).

Avec l'émergence du Paléolithique supérieur (interstade Würm II-Würm III, début du Würm III) la dynamique évolutive des cultures se modifie en Europe. L'évolution interne des technocomplexes s'effectue avec de nouvelles modalités, et leur émergence et leur disparition s'opèrent brutalement, sans possibilité de retour, les épisodes de cultures intermédiaires aux transitions climatiques drastiques restant en cours de discussion (IS Würm II/III; Châtelperron; fin des temps glaciaires: Magdalénien final - Azilien).

L'élément nouveau est également entraîné par l'apparition de phénomènes de territorialité manifestes, ce qui introduit dans l'histoire de l'Europe une nouvelle dimension. Des frontières sont désormais discernables. Elles sont expressives évidemment des contraintes climatiques, avec interdictions de parcours et de stationnement dans les zones inaccessibles ou inhabitables (front du glacier nordique, zones d'altitude montagnardes). Mais elles signifient aussi les possibilités d'appropriation des territoires par dynamisme démographique ou par réorganisations socio-politiques, dans la mesure où elles témoignent de répartitions totalement indépendantes de la configuration des milieux naturels. Elles attestent, dans l'Europe des Origines, l'existence de forces d'expansion volontariste (diffusion, expansion, conquêtes, colonisation) qui se modifient constamment au fil des millénaires, parfois en relation avec les "frontières naturelles" (fleuves, massifs montagneux).

L'enregistrement de ces variations territoriales est en relation directe *avec la chronologie*; mais, dans le Sud-Ouest, se discutent entre autres:

—les corrélations entre le Solutréen supérieur de la Couze (Le Malpas) proposées par Laville (1975) et Texier (1973a, b), et le Magdalénien ancien de la Vézère (Laugerie-Haute Est);

—le décalage chronologique du Magdalénien supérieur à harpons à deux rangs de barbelures des sites de la Vézère et de la Chalosse (Dryas II et III, Delpech et al.) *avec la composition statistique technotypologique des outillages lithiques*, qui permet de distinguer par exemple: l'"Aurignacien germanique" de l'Europe centrale (Hahn 1977) et l'Aurignacien de la région atlantique (de Sonneville-Bordes 1960, 1966, 1981); le "Gravettien" de l'Europe centrale et balkano-méditerranéenne (Kozlowski 1985, 1986) du Gravettien ou Périgordien supérieur de l'Europe du Sud-Ouest *avec la présence ou l'absence des "outils rares"* (Hahn 1969, 1983), autrement dit des outils marqueurs ("fossiles directeurs"): ils accumulent des caractéristiques techniques et typologiques associées dans une combinaison complexe, qui exclue que se renouvelle ailleurs ou dans une autre période une rencontre analogue identique, sauf quelques exceptions ("burins de Noailles" italiens; éléments tronqués du Périgordien supérieur du Sud-Ouest français et du Magdalénien final Rhin-Danube; pointes aziliennes et châtelperrons).

Lithiques ou osseux, ce sont souvent des objets à vocation perforante: pointes en silex, châtelperrons, gravettes, Font-Robert, pointes solutréennes (face plane, feuilles de laurier, pointes à cran), pointes nordiques; pointes en os: pointes à base fendue (Aurignacien), sagaie à méplat médian (Solutréen cantabrique), sagaies et harpons (Magdalénien).

Leurs cartes de répartition les montrent 1) *exclusivement cantonnés* dans une zone restreinte: les Noailles ne dépassent pas la Loire, les Font-Robert n'existent pas en Espagne, les raclettes ne traversent pas le Rhône (sauf une découverte récente en Suisse, cf. Le Tensorer 1986); les harpons ont une densité exceptionnelle dans une région (France-Espagne cantabrique) et quelques rares exemplaires en dehors (Angleterre, Suisse, Tchécoslovaquie, Rhin); 2) largement étalés sur une vaste zone: pointes à base fendue de l'Aurignacien (de la Moravie/Pologne à l'Atlantique), pointes de la Gravette, aiguilles à chas du Magdalénien.

A ces éléments de répartition purement fonctionnels (armes, outils) s'adjoignent d'autres informations et données, notamment les manifestations artistiques:
—La frise sculptée en haut ou bas-relief est restreinte à la zone entre Loire et Pyrénées, alors que les figurations féminines s'étendent du Sud-Ouest français jusqu'à l'Ukraine, restant exclues de la péninsule ibérique et de l'Angleterre. En pays atlantique, des frontières naturelles ont délimité des cultures: principalement Châtelperron, Solutréen; des outils: Noailles, Font-Robert, raclettes, bec-de-perroquet.

Les cultures de vaste expansion européenne (Aurignacien, Magdalénien supérieur) ont tout recouvert des surfaces habitables, avec des différenciations régionales non mutilantes ou dégradantes.

Le Gravettien reste un cas à part (Kozlowski 1985, 1986). Polymorphe dans le Sud-Ouest (de Sonneville-Bordes 1960, 1966), il n'a d'autre facteur de communauté européenne que la présence de la pointe à dos dite Gravette ou microgravette: son outillage d'accompagnement est très varié. Même s'il correspond *grosso modo* à une même période chronologique, il n'est pas évident que ses manifestations représentent autre chose ou plus qu'un "moment gravettien" ou un "stade gravettien" de l'évolution paléolithique. Les territoires méditerranéens et balkaniques évoluent alors différemment du reste de l'Europe continentale.

L'interprétation de ces différenciations est difficilement à mettre au compte de facteurs naturels exclusifs, quel que soit le rôle des grands conditionnements topographiques et climatiques. Il faut supposer des comportements de groupes à fondement politique, dont les intérêts, les objectifs et les capacités ont varié au cours des temps.

La densité ou les lacunes de l'occupation des territoires sont en relation avec:
—des conditions naturelles d'interdiction: désertification des pays du bassin de Paris au début du Würm III; non-présence humaine dans les zones montagneuses Jura-Alpes jusqu'au Magdalénien supérieur;
—des implantations très structurées dans un périmètre bien délimité (Rhône-Loire), avec désert humain au-delà: Châtelperron, Solutréen;
—des expansions en nappe épisodiques, indépendantes des configurations topographiques et climatiques: Aurignacien, Magdalénien supérieur (Angleterre).

A la fin des temps glaciaires, on peut admettre que l'Europe est très largement occupée par des populations parvenues à un même niveau culturel, pratiquant entre elles des échanges (pointes nordiques au sud de la Loire), mais déjà marquées par la dégradation dans le foyer artistique principal du Sud-Ouest français.

XXVIII

The Mousterian and Its Aftermath
A View From the Upper Paleolithic

James R. Sackett

INTRODUCTION

Well before the end of this conference, two highly significant points had clearly emerged. The first is that, though long eclipsed by the remarkable results of "Early Man" investigations in Africa, Upper Pleistocene archaeology in Western Eurasia has regained much of the excitement and importance it enjoyed during the formative years of Paleolithic research. There are many reasons for this, including renewed appreciation of the sheer wealth and variety of our archaeological record for the Middle and Upper Paleolithic, the degree of resolution with which its permutations can be followed over space and time, and the fact that we—unlike students of more remote periods—can feel reasonably assured that the contents of our sites are the artificial products of hominid rather than natural agencies. A final, and particularly intriguing, element is the realization that somewhere within its bounds the Upper Pleistocene archaeological record presumably saw hominids emerging into what is generally considered to be a fully "human" ecological niche.

The second point is how greatly our knowledge of Middle and Upper Paleolithic times has been augmented just during the course of the past decade or so. The fact becomes tellingly obvious simply if one compares the contents of this volume to the literature that emerged in the 1960s and early 1970s at the time of the now-classic debate between François Bordes and Lewis Binford over the significance of Upper Pleistocene variability (e.g., Bordes and de Sonneville-Bordes 1970; Binford 1973). The fundamental issues they raised concerning how ethnicity and activity are reflected in the archaeological record remain as viable as ever. But the actual terms in which the debate was argued—that is, the assumptions both participants made regarding the nature of industrial patterning involved and its variation over space and time—now seem rather simplistic. Obviously the conduct of the inquiry into Middle and Upper Paleolithic variability and the nature and meaning of its geographic and temporal permutations is being fundamentally transformed.

What follows are several reflections concerning the present state and possible future direction of that transformation. It should be stressed that they constitute my own viewpoint (though I by no means claim originality for the bulk of the individual ideas of which it is formed). For regardless of what the title of this essay might imply, I am speaking not for Upper Paleolithic research as such but instead simply as one who happens to find himself working in that block of the archaeological record. Equally to be stressed is that my concern here will fall nearly exclusively upon lithic industrial variability, grounded solidly in the traditional lithic archaeologist's perspective that—at least in the mind's eye—regards stone tools as no less significant monuments in their own right than, say, menhirs (see Fig. 28.1). Despite its restricted scope, the discussion should nonetheless serve to highlight the issues in an idiom familiar to the journeyman prehistorians who actually deal with them on an empirical basis.

Finally, it should be noted that, while numerous, my references to the work and thought of others will largely be restricted to those researchers who participated in the conference (whether represented by their articles in this volume or by previous publications that document the views they expressed in the course of our discussions). In no way is this intended to slight the contributions of our many highly valued colleagues in Middle and Upper Paleolithic research who were not present. Rather, I am adopting this measure simply as a means of giving at least some amount of coherence to what follows, to complement what the reader has already encountered in previous chapters, and to provide a sampling of the form and thrust of what happened to be a most profitable synod of Upper Pleistocene specialists. It will be seen that

Figure 28.1 To the lithic archaeologist, stone tools are no less significant monuments than menhirs. (*Drawing by Susan Sackett*)

not the least of our accomplishments was that we succeeded in identifying as many issues upon which fully reasonable and qualified observers can, and do, differ as ones upon which there seems to be general agreement.

THE MIDDLE PALEOLITHIC

Let us begin with a brief glance over our shoulder at the Mousterian. It seems to have lost its monolithic quality both figuratively and literally. We now see that there are indeed major geographic variations in its expression as we pass over Western Asia and in turn proceed across Europe; equally important, the tempo and mode of its development over time seem to have taken somewhat different forms from one region to the next (see chapters by Marks, Kozlowski, Müller-Beck; Dibble 1983). In keeping with the temporal boundaries of this conference, the significance of this newly appreciated variability has been discussed, for the most part, in terms of how the Mousterian relates to the Upper Paleolithic. There have been several hints, however, that the nature of its connections with industries predating the Upper Pleistocene is an equally intriguing problem. André Debénath's discussion (ch. 4) of the assemblages from La Chaise cannot help but remind one that the list of so-called "Premousterian" industries dating to what are referred to as Rissian times in France is becoming rather long. As some conferees noted during our discussions, apart from the style of their handaxes, later Acheulian industries themselves may differ little if at all from what is seen in the Middle Paleolithic. Attempting to grasp the meaning of the Mousterian as such, therefore, requires our asking if we have only grabbed the Upper Pleistocene tail of an animal that stretches into much more remote time periods.

Of greatest immediate interest, however, is the methodological revolution that has taken place in the manner in which Mousterian variability is being studied. Two complementary developments are crucial here. One is the factoring out of the principal typological elements responsible for the quantitative structures that lie behind the conventionally recognized industrial types—an achievement for which we seem to be particularly indebted to Nicolas Rolland (e.g., Rolland 1981). The other is, of course, a shift in emphasis from a static view of typological variation to a dynamic one, or—as Mark Baumler puts it—from product to process (ch. 15). We have come to realize that to a considerable degree the standard type-list monitors Mousterian lithics not as technological systems in action, but more likely as ones in a state of exhaustion; in other words, our conventional systematics do not so much inventory viable tool complexes as they depict landscapes of lithic discard. Hence tackling Mousterian industrial variation calls for understanding its entire reduction sequence: procurement of raw material, its conversion into utilizable tool blanks, their transformation in turn into tools, the subsequent modification of these tools through use-wear and/or rejuvenation, and, finally, their abandonment. Significantly, every Mousterian researcher who participated in the conference in one sense or another seems to be involved in this effort.[1] I myself found the point brought home most vividly by Anthony Marks's treatment (ch. 16) of the life-histories of Mousterian technology in the Negev and by Harold Dibble's archetypal example of Mousterian scraper reduction sequences (ch. 10). It hardly needs to be added that that when reflecting today on either reduction sequences or the question of the statistical infrastructure of Mousterian variability, one gains greater appreciation and understanding of what Arthur Jelinek (ch. 11) has been talking about these past several years.

The results of this methodological revolution have brought in many respects a degree of clarity, indeed simplicity, to Mousterian variability that was not there before. Nonetheless, an outsider like myself cannot help but be jarred by many of the conclusions that I heard and read during the conference. To cite but one example, Dibble (ch. 10) informs us that the type A Mousterian of Acheulian Tradition more closely approximates the Typical Mousterian industry, and that the MTA-B is much more like the Denticulate, than either is to the other. Surely such statements imply that Mousterian systematics is in need of a fundamental overhaul, both in general and with respect to its specific regional manifestations. This need is so pressing as seemingly to negate in the meanwhile fruitful discussion of some of the most basic issues. Do distinct industrial types in the Bordesian sense of discrete, recurring assemblages of artifact clusters in fact exist? If so, how do they equate, say, with climatic conditions, site types, and faunal remains? And, most basic of all, how do they pattern over time: is diachronic sequencing akin to that which Paul Mellars (1973) advocates really present or, on the contrary, do the assemblages really present a picture of interstratifying "alternating" industries? Until a revised systematics is available, such questions must be held in abeyance.

Interestingly enough, despite Jelinek's rigorous call for such a revision (ch. 11), I have sensed a general reluctance among Middle Paleolithic specialists to confront the challenge. The reasons are no doubt manifold. Certainly one could fairly invoke the principle of unripe time: there is simply too much groundwork yet to be done and the effort would be premature. This view I can appreciate if not necessarily condone. Other reasons are more basic. For one thing, I perceive considerable confusion and uncertainty regarding the theoretical issues that the enterprise would entail. Once one abandons static artifact classifications and attacks lithic archaeology in dynamic terms, traditional distinctions such as that between "technology" and "typology" or between "style" and "function" no longer seem to hold. They cease to be elements inherent in formal variation that call for isolation and become instead something quite different and much more slippery—organizing concepts that channel the manner in which we approach variation itself (detailed airing of this somewhat enigmatic statement will be found in Sackett 1988b).

The sheer technical problems posed by a new systematics would also be great. Obviously, as Jelinek points out, manifold, cross-cutting typologies are called for. This in practice means restructuring the data and codifying them into attribute systems, manipulating them within analytic frameworks that are equipped to reveal interaction among nominally scaled variables as well as ordinal and interval ones, and developing the habit of thinking of lithic variation in alternative classificatory idioms—only some of which approximate in either form or philosophy the type-lists to which we are now accustomed. Such issues of methodology are by no means virgin territory, and many researchers happen to have given them much thought. It may be found, for example, that the analytic framework for "dynamic typology" being employed on the Solvieux collections (Sackett 1988a, forthcoming) is directly applicable to exploring many aspects of Mousterian variability, and at least a point of departure for approaching many others.

Finally, to be frank, I sense a certain timidity in approaching the new systematics due to what might be called, for want of a better term, the "Bordesian block." It was François Bordes who literally created the Mousterian as we know it, and it is perhaps not unreasonable to speculate that an unconscious fear of revisionism constitutes an honest, if somewhat inverted, manner of paying tribute to our mentor. Yet for the spirit of discipleship to take this form is neither rational nor realistic. Bordes was indeed a great innovator, but he also in many respects marked the culmination of the traditional school of thought (see Sackett 1981: 94-97). Type-list systematics, even if continuously updated and adapted to the peculiarities of individual regional sequences, still serves in a sense to hold the data at a distance, if only because it constitutes a static codification of what we need to regard in dynamic terms and because it tends to obscure the alternative, cross-cutting patterns inherent in artifactual variation. It bears noting in this connection that, when not provoked into a schematic frame of mind in debating Binford, Bordes himself clearly regarded the type-list in highly pragmatic terms, not so much as a model of archaeological reality but as a vehicle for imposing manageable order upon artifact samples as simply a prelude to their detailed analysis (e.g., Bordes 1981b). In any event, the greatest homage we can pay to him is to acknowledge our debt, honor his memory, and then resolve to stand on his shoulders rather than in his shadow.

UPPER PALEOLITHIC TYPOLOGICAL VARIATION

Let us now turn to the issues raised by Upper Paleolithic variability. We begin with the question of its definition, which not only is of great interest in its own right but serves as the frame of reference against which Middle Paleolithic variability is defined by means of contrast. It is presumably because of the latter that the most explicit generalizations on the subject proffered during the conference came from Mousterian researchers, whose need to characterize variability in the ensemble is one not felt by those who must cope with its fragmentary manifestations in the field and laboratory. At any rate, according to what might fairly be labeled the "received" view, the Upper Paleolithic can be summarized as follows.

Apart from an obvious shift in quantitative emphasis away from certain typological forms, such as sidescrapers, that characterize Mousterian industries, towards certain hitherto rare ones, in particular endscrapers and burins, Upper Paleolithic variability is supposedly characterized by distinct trends that contrast markedly with what went before. Tools are now predominately made upon blades and display great proliferation in the number and variety of their typological forms, whose standardized shaping bears witness to a specificity in type design and manufacture that is unseen in the Mousterian. A particularly striking element here is presented by the *fossiles directeurs*, especially distinctive but relatively short-lived forms that represent more often than not alternative stylistic variants of the same generic functional categories. The industries into which the tools combine are equally specific in the twofold sense of being relatively undifferentiated in their internal typological makeup and correspondingly marked in their contrasts with one another. As a result they segregate fairly cleanly from one another over both space and time. Patterning in the latter dimension can be particularly dramatic, presenting a picture of industrial succession that is as marked by the diachronic contrasts it displays as by the relative rapidity with which it takes place.

While the above may be somewhat overdrawn for purposes of exposition, it does represent a fair collation of the views that have been expressed in more piecemeal fashion by many conferees. How accurate is it? I believe it is reasonable to say that, if the Upper Paleolithic itself is regarded in equally piecemeal fashion, at least much of it can be said to be true. For example, the Middle Magdalenian assemblages recovered from the Neuvic sector (ch. 3) may very possibly constitute a distinctive industrial block characterized typologically by relative internal homogeneity, noticeable differences from quasi-contemporaneous industries in other regions, and even greater diachronic contrasts with the industries that precede and succeed it within its own.

Nonetheless, I believe it safe to say that most Upper Paleolithic specialists would be most uncomfortable in accepting the above characterization as valid for their block of the archaeological record in any collective sense, and would point out in addition certain key points that it overlooks altogether. We shall now turn to these issues in some detail, treating firstly the nature of Upper Paleolithic typological variation itself, and secondly the way it behaves in determining the formal makeup of industries. Coming from an unreconstructed Perigordcentric, my remarks will be illustrated mainly by data recovered within a 50-km radius of Les Eyzies, especially featuring the Neuvic materials whose analysis I have only recently completed (ch. 3). A simplified chart of the Upper Paleolithic traditions of the Perigord is provided as an anchor for those readers whose familiarity with its classic sequence may be rusty (Fig. 28.2). Although I believe most of my points have fairly general validity for the Upper Paleolithic world, other regions will be referred to only in those instances where they have provided my fellow conferees with particularly apposite examples.

To begin with, by no means all Upper Paleolithic typologies are dominated by blades, and even if there exists a trend toward increasingly laminar technologies over time, the exceptions are numerous. A particularly telling example is the so-called Magdalenian "0" (or Early Badegoulian), whose strong flake element contrasts markedly both with the relatively elegant blade technology of many earlier industries, such as that of the Protomagdalenian (or Perigordian VII), and with that often encountered in the later Magdalenian phases that succeed it. Equally important, techniques of blank production themselves may vary greatly within one and the same industry. In the Neuvic group, for example, the strongly laminar 3-A assemblage of Solvieux Centre assigned to the Early (stage I or "Raclette") Magdalenian contrasts markedly with the pseudo-Levallois technique that dominates the same industry at the nearby site of La Croix de Fer and that Michel Lenoir has described for related sites downstream in the neighboring department of the Gironde (ch. 26).

Particularly striking in this connection is that the two principal Raysse Perigordian (Vc) assemblages which derive from contiguous sectors of Solvieux itself employ altogether different reduction strategies on the two flint types that abound in the vicinity of the site and dominate all of its industries. In one, the 2-III assemblage from Solvieux Centre, the relatively large nodules of brown Bergerac flint are converted into robust if irregular blades, while the smaller nodules of black gravel flint are crudely reduced to quite amorphous cortical flakes. In the other, the 6-M assemblage from Solvieux Est, somewhat thick but nonetheless regular and metrically indistinguishable smallish blades are obtained from both.

An interesting byproduct of this difference is that, whereas the quantitative distributions of tool classes

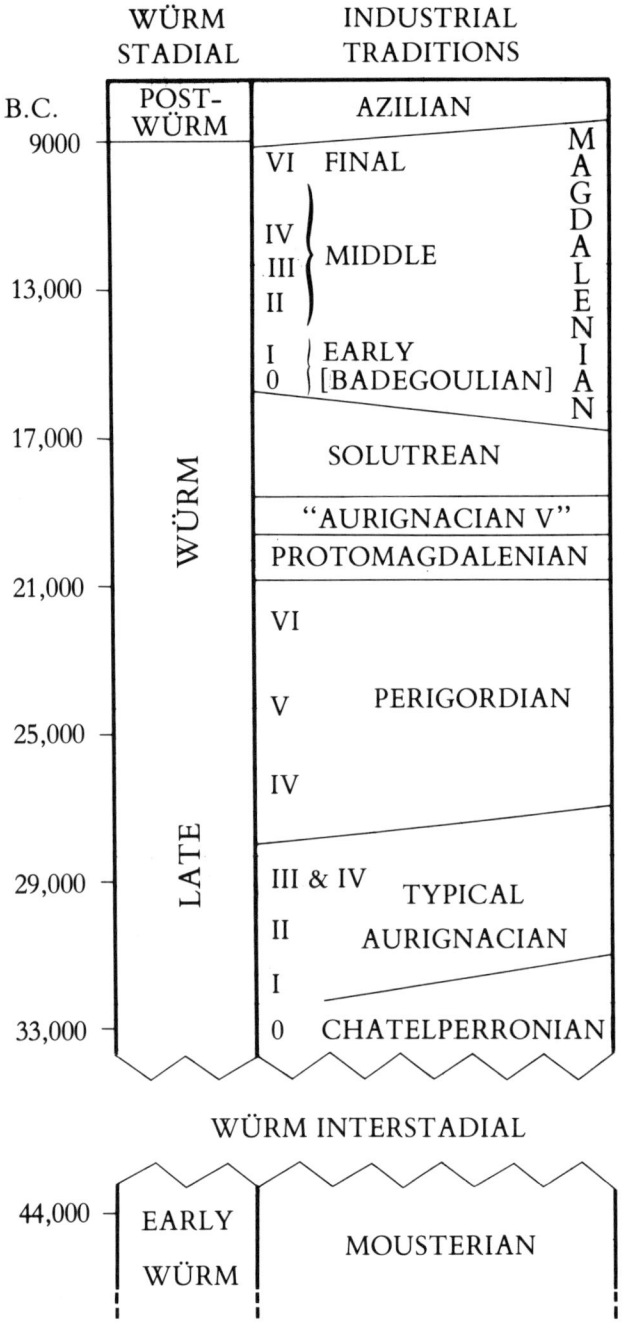

Figure 28.2 *Upper Paleolithic sequence of the Perigord.*

within the primary typological groups (such as the dihedral, truncation, and break types that compose the "standard" burin family) are statistically identical in the two assemblages, those aspects of typological variation that are mechanically or geometrically contingent upon the properties of the blank vary significantly. Thus with respect to the outline profiles described by the working end (trigon) of its burins, the 6-M sample more closely approximates the much later Middle Magdalenian industry (assemblages 1-I and 1-II) from the site, which employs a comparable if somewhat more elegant version of the same blank-production strategy, even though its burin classes themselves exhibit an entirely different pattern of relative popularity. To make matters even more complex, the site's Magdalenian I (3-A) assemblage, which falls intermediate in time between the above two industries, employs still a third strategy wherein blades are obtained from both flint types but display quite distinct metrical distributions commensurate with the difference in size of the original nodules from which they derive. Such examples, it may be added, tend perhaps to make Upper Paleolithic specialists somewhat less prone than their colleagues working in the Middle Paleolithic to search for simple, straightforward parallels between specific reduction strategies and variations in the raw materials to which they are applied.

Secondly, typological variation in Upper Paleolithic industries by no means consistently displays a high degree of artifact standardization that segregates cleanly into distinct types. Again, as in the case of reduction strategies, a time trend in this direction may be present, but again as well there are many exceptions. The Perigordian VI industry, for example, would appear to exhibit much narrower tolerances in the expression of type-design than are seen in much of the Solutrean and at least the pre-Middle phases of the Magdalenian industries that follow it (see Bricker and David 1984). And in some the amount of intergradation between types is so great as to frustrate even the most experienced typologist. A particularly telling example is the Typical Aurignacian, especially with respect to its large component of tools bearing multiple lamellar retouch—which easily accounts for more than half of any given sample. The type-list categories into which such forms are ordered—carinate scrapers, muzzled scrapers, busked burins, and so forth—are in reality no more than idealized nodal points on what amounts to a multidimensional block of continuous formal variation that may exhibit little in the way of obvious typological planes of cleavage. Furthermore, this block is by no means neatly segregated from artifact classes that the type-list places outside its boundaries: rounded carinate scrapers pass by imperceptible degrees into simple elevated endscrapers, just as the line between busked burins and more ordinary polyhedric asymmetric dihedral burins can only be arbitrarily drawn.

An equally important point often closely allied to the above is that Upper Paleolithic tools—just like those of the Mousterian—are frequently heavily subjected to what Jelinek calls the "Frison effect," and may be strongly modified during the course of their use-life by breakage and subsequent rejuvenation, whether by continued use or intentional reworking or both. The distinction between Aurignacian carinate and muzzled scrapers noted above is a particularly good case in point, as inspection of the latter very often suggests a tool that began its career as a rounded carinate and only subsequently assumed a nosed form as a result of heavy use and breakage. In at least one Upper Paleolithic example, the Frison effect is expressed with a ferocity that may surpass anything yet reported for the Mousterian itself. For, as I understand it, such use-reduction, as in Dibble's scraper example, is the product of continually employing a given tool for essentially one and the same function. Yet in the case of even "typical" Solvieux truncations of the Beauronnian industry (Fig. 3.12), at least three quite different kinds of use-wear and breakage suggesting rather different functions can appear singly or in combination on any given piece. Moreover, it seems to have been standard practice among Beauronnian artisans to employ exhausted truncations both as endscrapers and as blanks that could be spalled in such a fashion as to achieve what in most Upper Paleolithic industries would be regarded as a fairly standard form of truncation burin (no matter how out-of-place it may appear in the context of most Beauronnian burins).

In short, Upper Paleolithic typological variation as often as not fails to display the neat segregation of highly standardized forms postulated by received opinion. Instead, just like its Mousterian counterpart, the Upper Paleolithic type-list often monitors a morphological landscape lacking much specificity of type-design and marked by an exhausted technology whose components may be dramatically changed from their pristine condition.

An interesting footnote to this point is that not only the degree of tolerance with which type-design is expressed but also the degree of use-modification that is admissible before artifacts are discarded may be fairly industry-specific. If quarter-century-old memories dating back to my stint at the Abri Pataud and subsequent dissertation research serve me well, a Perigordian IV or VI industry should tend to exhibit considerably more standardization, and probably less use-modification, than do any phases of the Typical Aurignacian. Moreover, to judge from my findings at Solvieux, these particular attributes seem to cross-cut the blank-production strategies mentioned earlier. Thus, even though its blanks closely approach those of the Middle Magdalenian assemblages, whose tools exhibit a relatively high degree of standardization and relatively little use-wear, the 6-M Raysse Perigordian sample displays essentially the same lax standards of type-design and tolerance for heavy usage that are seen in its considerably less laminar 2-III industrial counterpart.

Finally, some comments are in order regarding the frequently misunderstood topic of Upper Paleolithic *fossiles directeurs*. The notion is a flexible one indeed and essentially connotes no more than artifact types that have particular diagnostic value for identifying and segregating lithic industries because they happen to possess more or less distinctive morphologies and tend to have restricted distributions over space and time. They constitute the unstable or mutable element in Upper Paleolithic typological variation, which is—as is often overlooked—for the most part highly stable and immutable. The basic, so-called *banal*, tools that dominate Upper Paleolithic industries—such as simple endscrapers and dihedral and truncation burins—changed very little during the course of Late Würm times. The contrast in behavior between *fossile* and *banal* forms must be stressed, because it is the only thing that distinguishes the former as a group. They otherwise share no consistent features and, as a result, few if any of the generalizations often made about them really obtain.

For example, it is by no means true that the Upper Paleolithic *fossiles* by nature usually constitute specific stylistic variations upon a single generic artifact class. The claim is likely true in the case of the alternate forms of Solutrean bifacially flaked leaf points, and it may also prove correct that Raysse burins and even Noailles burins in some sense had functions that were ordinarily carried out by the more *banal* types of truncation burins. But it does not hold for the successions of most *fossiles* that follow one another across the major industrial boundaries. Thus the sequence of forms running from Aurignacian carinate scrapers in turn through Upper Perigordian Gravette points, Solutrean leaf points, Early Magdalenian *raclettes,* Middle Magdalenian backed bladelets, and Final Magdalenian parrot-beaked burins can hardly be viewed as any kind of functional continuum.

Another common misapprehension is that the distinctiveness of form exhibited by *fossiles* is necessarily the product of considerable artisanal investment with respect to both design and execution. Such investment is indeed reflected in the bifacial flaking borne by a willow-leaf point, the backing of a Gravette point, or the ventral spalling of a Raysse burin; but it is not seen in many equally diagnostic *fossiles,* such as Aurignacian carinate and muzzled scrapers, Azilian points, and Solvieux truncations. In the case of one of the most distinctive *fossiles* of all, the Early Magdalenian *raclette,* what little uniformity exists is imposed only by the mechanical contingencies of flint technology itself. The aim in manufacturing a *raclette* is solely to obtain an abruptly retouched edge whose thickness is uniform and also falls within rather stringent metrical limits. But the overall size and outline shape seem to be of little or no importance, and the variation in both exhibited by *raclettes* is so great as to tax the classificatory powers of even the most carefully designed descriptive or analytic framework.

Mention of this last tool reminds us that we are far from understanding the enigma presented by some of the *fossile* forms. The *raclette* in particular happens to be puzzling, given the fact that it can occur in such great absolute and relative frequencies during its comparatively short lifespan and yet appear only sporadically before or after. What special purpose could it have served that required its manufacture in such numbers for only a brief segment of Upper Paleolithic times? Or, if the need was of a more generic nature that was met by another tool or tools at other times, whey did the *raclette* appear at all? Or again, once on the scene, why did it disappear so quickly despite its obvious popularity? To my knowledge, these questions have so far failed to elicit even suggestive guesswork.

UPPER PALEOLITHIC INDUSTRIAL VARIATION

Let us now turn from Upper Paleolithic typological variation as such to the manner in which it expresses itself at the level of the industry. Here my first point rather strikingly contradicts the received view: in short, despite the length and seeming complexity of the Upper Paleolithic type-list, the number of truly distinct artifact classes that make up any given industry tends to be relatively small. A reasonable estimate might be that most industries are composed of something on the order of from only five to ten basic classes. If considerably more type-categories happen to figure in their inventory counts, inspection will reveal that these mostly represent relatively minor permutations on the generic classes, reflecting more often than not either successive stages in the progressive modification of a single tool (as, for example, often accounts for the distinction between *becs* and *perçoirs*) or minor alterations in form arising from variations in blank morphology (which, we have seen, is at least partly responsible for the alternative profile types into which dihedral and truncation burins are subdivided).

It bears stressing in this connection that the seeming specificity of morphological detail represented by the type-list is in large part a pragmatic accommodation to the larger sample sizes and greater resolution of the archaeological record available in Upper Paleolithic times. Were its assemblages less common, numerically smaller, and dispersed over greater intervals of space and time, it is very likely that much of this apparent detail would not be formally recognized, but instead simply dismissed as typological "noise." One cannot help but speculate that the lack of specificity that purportedly characterizes Middle Paleolithic industries, along with the concomitant use of a shorter type-list of more generically defined categories, reflects at least in part the fact that Mousterian researchers work with smaller samples and a considerably coarser-grained archaeological record. This theme provides a disturbing *leitmotif* that echoes continually in Rolland's most interesting search for time-trends in the French Mousterian (ch. 9).

Also pertinent to the question of the relative lack of typological diversity in Upper Paleolithic industries is the fact that their tool samples are numerically dominated by only a few artifact classes. This is clearly illustrated by the Solvieux assemblages. For example, 70% of the 2-III Raysse Perigordian sample is contributed just by truncation burins, Raysse burins, and simple endscrapers, the second of these alone accounting for one-third of the total. In the Middle Magdalenian 1-I sample dihedral burins, endscrapers, and backed bladelets make up 80% of the total, of which the first category alone is responsible for 54%. Even in our largest and typologically most heterogeneous assemblage, the Early Magdalenian 3-A, six classes—dihedral and truncation burins, simple endscrapers, marginally retouched pieces, retouched bladelets, and *raclettes*—compose 87% of the total, somewhat more than a third of which (727 specimens!) involves the last class alone. Finally, 47% of the enigmatic Beauronnian assemblage consists solely of Solvieux truncations, and its remainder is dominated by a family of burins that is somewhat heterogeneous but still based upon a common plan that essentially ignores the conventional dihedral-truncation burin distinction (Fig. 3.11).

While the above facts are not cited in an attempt to argue that Upper Paleolithic industries are really no more complex than Middle Paleolithic ones, they do indicate that the proliferation of typological variation often attributed to them by received opinion has been considerably exaggerated. In this light it is especially intriguing to note the fact that, regardless of the industrial polymorphism discussed below, it nonetheless appears that the Perigord could be occupied by but a single Upper Paleolithic industry at a time. The consequences of this fact are rather startling when it is recalled that the Middle Paleolithic industries supposedly interstratify so as to suggest that they more often than not coexisted in the region side by side. For if, as is frequently argued, they actually represent alternative functionally specific technologies produced by one people, it follows that at least some Mousterian artisans produced a considerably broader range of industrial variation than did at least some of their Upper Paleolithic successors!

A second point of considerable interest is that it is becoming increasingly clear that Upper Paleolithic industries are by no means relatively undifferentiated in their internal makeup. As Michel Lenoir's work in the Gironde particularly well illustrates (ch. 26), our picture of industrial variation is progressively moving away from one of standardization to one of polymorphism. To a considerable extent this may be the product of a change in excavation strategies. In the Perigord, for example, traditional research concentrated upon "rich" rockshelters, whose stereotypically homogeneous tool samples derived from thick and artifactually charged levels. The latter, when viewed in retrospect, seem likely to have comprised palimpsests that intermixed, and consequently "averaged out," the remains of several distinct occupations. Today, excavation tends more to concentrate upon "weak" shelters, which—as Jean-Philippe Rigaud (1982b) has shown at sites like Le Flageolet and Abri Vaufrey—often display considerably greater occupational integrity. Assemblages recovered from such excavations tend to show considerably greater variation in the relative frequencies of the major tool families, suggesting functionally significant variations in site use or at least in the horizontal distribution of activities over occupation surfaces. This finding is of course not restricted to the Perigord. Thus in Cantabrian Spain seemingly nondirectional frequency changes are reported for both the Magdalenian (Freeman et al., ch. 1) and Solutrean (Straus 1978).

It is important to note that, apart from the indications furnished by the presence or absence of *fossiles directeurs*, the industrial distinctiveness of such assemblages is not correspondingly weakened so much as it is simply expressed in a somewhat different manner than was appreciated by traditional prehistorians. This is because, regardless of even major differences from one assemblage to the next in the representation of a given typological family in the global tool sample, the specific types that constitute its internal makeup may nonetheless display a high degree of patterning when their relative frequencies are calculated as "restricted" proportions of the family sample alone. This may take the form of either remarkable consistency from one assemblage to the next or directional shifts that lend themselves to seriation. In fact, in those industries represented at Solvieux by more than one occupation, simple restricted-sample comparisons of just the dihedral, break, and truncation forms that make up the *banal* "standard" burin family virtually ubiquitous in all Upper Paleolithic traditions yield measures of inter-assemblage similarity or difference as accurate as more complex comparisons that take their entire tool inventories into account.

As was noted in an earlier chapter's discussion of the Neuvic group (ch. 3), open-air sites even more than rockshelters have served to enhance our appreciation of industrial polymorphism. Here the degree of what seems to be functional specialization is particularly marked. An especially striking example is presented by Le Cerisier, whose tool sample is restricted to heavily use-modified burins accompanied by a strong component of notches and denticulations. While Le Cerisier's burin morphology at least suggests affiliation with the Middle Magdalenian, there exist two additional Neuvicois assemblages—the Beauronnian at Solvieux and the tool sample recovered from the single-occupation site of Lacaud—that defy comparison with any known industry. Their uniqueness is indisputable regardless of whether ultimately they prove to represent highly specialized functional variants of a known industrial tradition or truly new ones that have hitherto gone unrecognized. In any event, they demonstrate that we have yet to sample the full range of Upper Paleolithic industrial variability even in an area as heavily culled archaeologically as the Perigord.

This brings us to the third and final point that needs to be made on the topic of Upper Paleolithic industrial variability. It is that the conventional systematics and even the philosophical basis upon which it is grounded no longer hold. Apart from the fact that none of the traditional problem areas of industrial classification have been resolved, many of the conclusions that once enjoyed general acceptance are now clouded with doubt. To mention only a few of the examples raised during the course of conference discussion, the question of affiliation between the Chatelperronian and the later "Gravettian" block of Perigordian phases remains an issue of debate; the degree of distinctiveness and even culture-historical integrity of the various industries that fall into what was traditionally labeled the Perigordian "V" complex is hotly argued; and even the unity of the Magdalenian itself is seriously questioned. A major catalyst to this atmosphere of doubt and dispute has of course been the emerging picture of industrial polymorphism noted above, which—while not necessarily blurring the lines between the industrial complexes themselves—has greatly complicated the task of giving them clear definition. Another concerns the meaning and utility of many of the long-cherished *fossiles directeurs*. A prime example here is whether "Final" Magdalenian *fossiles* such as Azilian and Laugerie-Basse points are really trustworthy chronological indicators or instead simply functionally specific tool types that may or may not appear as if by chance in what otherwise would be labeled Middle Magdalenian assemblages (Rigaud 1977).

Lurking in the background of nearly all of these controverted questions is the issue of time. Observers often fail to appreciate that the belief in Upper Paleolithic industrial variation as inherently successional in nature has been based as much upon theoretical expectations as upon solid empirical evidence. As I have discussed at some length elsewhere (Sackett 1981), traditional Paleolithic research was grounded in the assumption that the archaeological record conformed to what was essentially an "organic" model of diachronic change. Among other things, this meant that the expression of any given industry in the archaeological record should be invariant at any given time (like that of any given fossil species of animal in the paleontological record), and consequently that any significant variations were automatically assumed to have temporal significance. The assumption has of course collapsed under the weight of the demonstration of clearly synchronous industrial polymorphism. It now appears that at least many temporal horizons of the Late Würm are likely to have encompassed an appreciable range of industrial variability.

This appreciation of synchronous polymorphism, however, raises a crucial new question of the degree-versus-kind genre. Does it merely entail "lateral" variability *within* the industrial traditions or does it in fact *cross-cut* them in such a way that the traditions themselves can be seen to overlap in time? The question is vital because, if the latter happens to be true, we immediately find ourselves confronted with two additional questions of supreme interest. Firstly, instead of the straightforward successional model implied by traditional thought, does Upper Paleolithic variability to at least a significant degree suggest an alternating model of interstratifying industrial traditions akin to that seen in the standard Bordesian view of the Mousterian? Secondly, to what extent do the traditions themselves represent functionally distinct activity complexes that at any given time might have been pursued by a single group of people rather than discrete culture-historical lineages of ethnicity that remained distinct from one another (irrespective of whatever functional specificity they still might possess)?

That the traditions might in reality constitute interstratifying, functionally specific technocomplexes is in some respects a seductive notion. For example, to regard the Aurignacian and Perigordian traditions as alternative toolkits, so to speak, would account both for the marked contrast in their respective typological characters and for the fact that what little directional diachronic change they do exhibit fails to correlate in any obvious way with the major shifts in climate and ecology that so rapidly succeeded one another during their lifespans. It would also seemingly account for the apparent typological simplicity that I previously noted tends to characterize individual lithic industries. Any given industry could be viewed in this light simply as one segment of a much broader typological repertory that was actually being employed by a single human group at the time.

The current evidence, though, seems to line up against an interstratification model for the Upper Paleolithic traditions, at least as they are currently defined. For one thing, the findings of modern chronostratigraphic research like that represented in the present volume by the contributions of Henri Laville (ch. 8) and William Farrand (ch. 19) largely fail to support it. It is true that Chatelperronian and early Typical Aurignacian industries do appear to interstratify in the initial phase of Late Würm in the Perigord, and several thousand years later there follows a significant span of time when late Typical Aurignacian and early "Gravettian" Perigordian (IV) may coexist (see Laville, Rigaud, and Sackett 1980: fig. 8.2). There is also evidence for at least some temporal overlap in the region between late Solutrean and initial Magdalenian (Laville, Rigaud, and Sackett 1980: fig. 9.7). Even though parallel examples can be found in other regions of Western Europe, however, chronostratigraphy for the most part reveals that the traditions as wholes seem to retain their integrity as distinct, temporally segregated blocks of industrial variability.

It is important to note in this connection that the apparent lack of consistent interstratification among the Upper Paleolithic traditions is not to be explained away as an artifact of systematics, as some have claimed (e.g., Binford 1982: 180-181). In other words, it is not true that they happen to be defined at such a high level of specificity as to obscure the more basic patterns in the mode of their diachronic evolution. At least my own experiments have failed to reveal either more instances or greater degrees of interstratification when I have attempted to reorder the industrial succession using more "generalized" traditions, defined in terms of a type-list whose categories are as generic as those used in the Middle Paleolithic list. The reasons are twofold and refer to points I have already touched upon. For one thing, most of the apparent proliferation or "detail" of the Upper Paleolithic list in fact represents not so much greater specificity of type-design as it does simply variation around essentially generic types produced by use-wear and their mechanically contingent accommodations to blank morphology. For another, most *fossiles directeurs*—which account for the bulk of the diachronic segregation of the traditions—are sufficiently distinctive in form as to defy merging with the generic categories. Hence, even when defined in a more "generalized" fashion, the traditions exhibit the same essential typological makeup and diachronic patterning that they display when defined in more "specific" fashion, and consequently behave in the same way with respect to one another.

We ought not to abandon the issue without noting that many researchers nonetheless see a deeper level of patterning in the Perigord sequence than that suggested by its conventional systematics. According to this view, the traditions themselves may be grouped into two more-comprehensive industrial *ur*-types or lines that in some yet-unexplained fashion coexisted as parallel phyla down through much, if not all, of Upper Paleolithic times. Understanding the argument calls for a fairly sophisticated control of regional systematics (of which Rigaud 1976a provides an excellent summary). Suffice it to state that the model begins by recognizing a basic division between the Chatelperronian and Typical Aurignacian, then in turn accepting Denis Peyrony's (1933) thesis of continuity between the former and the "Gravettian" Perigordian IV-VI industries (as did Bordes himself [e.g., 1968b]), and again in turn simultaneously regarding the Protomagdalenian as their offshoot ("Perigordian VII") and the somewhat enigmatic "Aurignacian V" as a descendant of the Typical Aurignacian (I-IV) block. At this point we arrive at the advent of the Solutrean, by which time the Upper Paleolithic had already run two-thirds of its course. The Solutrean seems to interrupt both phyla but, at least in the view of some specialists, they resume at its close with the "Aurignacian" line culminating in the Early Magdalenian (0 and I), or Badegoulian, and the "Perigordian" line in the Magdalenian *sensu stricto* (III-IV).

Many researchers, including me, find it difficult to regard the parallel-phyla model itself as anything more than an interesting speculation. Nonetheless, it serves a useful purpose in keeping before us the possibility that a hitherto unexpected pattern of industrial succession is waiting to be found, one that would entail a much greater degree of interstratification among the conventionally recognized traditions than is now appreciated, as well as raise altogether new questions about the nature of their culture-historical or "ethnic" significance. It also bears noting that an analogous model of parallel industrial lines has recently been proposed for Cantabrian Spain by Straus (1986b), whose discussion of the theoretical issues involved is particularly enlightening and provocative.

Finally, it should be kept in mind that the issue of time concerns the tempo as much as the mode of Upper Paleolithic industrial evolution. And here again, what we have termed the received view requires at least some amount of correction. In short, the Upper Paleolithic is by no means as dynamic as the supposedly rapid turnover of *fossiles directeurs* might suggest. Some *fossiles* in fact were quite long-lived: the carinate-muzzled scrapers persisted in the Typical Aurignacian block alone for a span equal to that which separates our time from the birth of civilization in Sumer. More importantly, the *banal* tools that more often than not form the typological backbone of Upper Paleolithic industries changed little if at all, and continued to play an important role even in many post-Pleistocene lithic industries.

CONCLUSIONS

The overall picture of Upper Paleolithic variability that emerges from the last two sections differs from received opinion in several respects. In brief, the typological basis of industrial variation is considerably simpler than is often assumed.[2] The tool categories as a rule do not present themselves in as standardized a fashion as many have inferred from the type-list, and much of their supposed proliferation of form simply expresses a combination of broad tolerance in the execution of type-design and heavy use-wear. Apart from the *fossiles directeurs,* most basic types change little if at all over time, and even some of the *fossiles* prove to be enduring. In addition, the specific forms assumed by any given industry, as well as the typological differences that distinguish it from other industries, tend to be dictated by only a handful of tool categories.

Industrial variation itself is nevertheless subtle and complex indeed, exhibiting considerably more in the way of synchronous polymorphism and considerably less in the way of distinct diachronic phasing than is commonly believed. This is not to argue that clear successional patterns of replacement of one industrial tradition by another do not exist, or that later industries do not in some respects more closely approach the idealized notion of what an Upper Paleolithic industry should look like than earlier ones. But the Upper Paleolithic system is indeed a noisy one that sees both considerable overlapping of industries that were once thought to be distinct, and often glaring exceptions to every diachronic trend.

All this seems to point to two rather obvious conclusions. The first is that, just like the Middle Paleolithic, the Upper Paleolithic in no sense constitutes a monolithic entity that lends itself to generalization much above the level of truism. One might even go so far as to say simply that the only thing Upper Paleolithic industries have in common is a propensity for endscrapers and burins plus the fact that they happen to be ordered in terms of a common type-list. The second conclusion is that, once one looks behind the apparent dissimilarities that are in part imposed by the difference in design of their respective type-lists, Upper Paleolithic variability resembles—more closely than is generally realized—what Mousterian specialists inform us is typical of the Middle Paleolithic. The differences between the two involve matters of degree more than of kind. As a consequence, I find myself in sympathy with those conferees who have warned us against viewing the passage from one to the other as an event rather than as a drawn-out process. Perhaps we are in reality wrestling with an evolutionary trend within what amounts to an unbroken culture-historical continuum, whose change was purely incremental in nature but whose rate of acceleration could have entailed some sort of exponential function that, in the foreshortened perspective of the archaeological record, gives the false appearance of abrupt transitions.

It seems to follow from the above that the practice of using the interstadial that separates Early and Late Würm to draw the line between the Middle and Upper Paleolithic may be justified only on the basis of pragmatic convention. (The point seems to be reinforced by the recent discovery of a Neandertal on the wrong side of the line, so to speak, in a Chatelperronian context at Saint-Césaire, Charente-Maritime [Levêque and Vandermeersch 1981].) It in fact introduces an unnecessary element of obfuscation into the business of tracing the nature of the transition, by dictating that industries that precede the interstadial will be inventoried and compared in terms of a typelist different in design from the one used for industries that succeed it. In any event, apart from the issues of method and theory involved, a strong case can be made on industrial grounds themselves either for drawing the line at a much later point in time, or for regarding it as an entirely arbitrary measure.

In the Perigord, for example, the Chatelperronian is generally seen as exhibiting definite affiliations with the Mousterian of Acheulian Tradition Type B that lies on the other side of the interstadial. Somewhat less appreciated is the affinity that some have pointed out between the Quina Mousterian, which already displays such Aurignacian elements as carinate scrapers, and the so-called Castanet type of Typical Aurignacian. The latter possesses only neglible numbers of burins but retains sidescrapers, *limaces,* voluminous denticulations, and heavy scaliform retouch that is as reminiscent of the Quina variety as it is of that found in most Typical Aurignacian assemblages (e.g., de Sonneville-Bordes 1960: vol. 1, 148). For what it is worth, seriations based upon an attributal analysis of several Aurignacian assemblages are consistent with the conclusion that the Castanet industry may be the initial phase of the Typical Aurignacian block (Sackett 1966). The possible Mousterian ancestry of these initial Late Würm industries gains added interest when it is recalled that many researchers simply view them as temporal segments of two great lines of industrial evolution that continued down through much, if not all, of Upper Paleolithic times in the Perigord.

Apart from those who may advocate the parallel-phyla model specifically, there are several conferees who either trace important continuities across the Early/Late Würm Interstadial or actually postulate that the Mousterian ended only long after what is usually recognized as the beginning of Upper Paleolithic times. The continuities are by no means restricted to the lithic dimension of archaeological variability alone. Thus Philip Chase argues that, contrary to much current opinion, what have been postulated as typically Upper Paleolithic hunting practices were already well established in the Mousterian (ch. 13). The work of Jan Simek and Lynn Snyder, in turn, suggests that the significant shifts in economic strategies that did take place during the Upper Pleistocene were not to occur until the Upper Perigordian became installed (ch. 20). Such statements have not been restricted to the Perigord alone. Leslie Freeman and his colleagues (ch. 1) maintain that the Aurignacian and Perigordian in Cantabrian Spain continue subsistence and settlement strategies along lines already known in the Mousterian; that their industrial differences from the Middle Paleolithic are the products of gradual innovation; and that an abrupt transition to new lifeways and technologies appears only with the Solutrean and Magdalenian traditions during the last ten millennia of the Upper Pleistocene. Lawrence Straus makes essentially the same argument for the Franco-Cantabrian region as a whole (ch. 2, 1983a).

Given the present state of our knowledge, all such arguments call for heightened empirical investigation and testing rather than prolonged debate. But the fact that they are being put forth by researchers whose firsthand knowledge of the data allows them to speak with authority is of great significance. Perhaps this holds for my own arguments as well, even though they—along with the so-called "received" view against which they have been contrasted—have perhaps been overschematized for purposes of exposition. In any event, it remains true that the question of the date and character of the transition from the Middle to the Upper Paleolithic is far from settled.

A final word is in order concerning what remains the question or questions for Upper Pleistocene archaeologists: whether and, if so, how the transition from the Middle to Upper Paleolithic reflects the emergence of fully human culture from some more primitive state of "protoculture." To suggest as I have that the transition at least in Western Europe came much later than is conventionally assumed, and very possibly constituted an incremental process rather than an abrupt historic event, complicates matters sorely for those researchers who feel the need to associate it with the emergence of humanness itself. For it adds an additional note of ambiguity and, indeed, disharmony to the attempt to find clear-cut associations between lithic industrial evolution and such other crucial Upper Pleistocene phenomena as the replacement of Neandertals by racially modern *Homo sapiens sapiens* and the appearance of supposedly human symbolic behavior as reflected in personal ornament, evidences of ritual, and self-conscious art.

Our colleagues working in the Near East have already learned to live with the ambiguity (Marks, ch. 16; Dibble 1983). There, it would seem, the relevant hominid fossil evidence and lithic change simply fail to correlate in what might seem a logical fashion, nor do evidences of "human" symbolic behavior necessarily accompany what are indisputably Upper Paleolithic industries. The picture may well assume a different form in Western Europe. Yet I would still argue that in the realm of lithic industrial evolution, the changes that took place there in Upper Pleistocene times largely involved matters of degree and not of kind. I therefore view with considerable skepticism the claims made by some conferees that Middle and Upper Paleolithic industries reflect inherently different mental capabilities for conceiving, producing, and using stone tools (Jelinek, ch. 11; Chase and Dibble 1987). But at this point we must stop, as the issues involved concern the role played by symbolic behavor in lithic technology, which is much too tangled a question for us to venture into here. The reader who may wish to accompany me into this particular thicket will have to trouble to undertake the journey at another time and place.

NOTES

1. It is of course being pursued with equal vigor by many Upper Paleolithic researchers, as is reflected in this volume by the contributions of Montet-White (ch. 23) and Lanzinger and Cremaschi (ch. 6).

2. A corollary of this, as my Mousterian colleagues are well aware, is that the issues of method and theory involved are correspondingly more challenging than our predecessors seem to have realized.

DISCUSSION

MARKS: There is a parallel in the Levant to the idea that a more significant change or break took place within the Upper Paleolithic than occurred between the Middle and Upper in terms of the appearance of symbolism, bone tools, complicated typologies, etc. These really tend to occur about halfway through the Levantine sequence, not at the beginning.

STRAUS: Perhaps the notion of mosaic evolution is relevant here, where changes in biology and some innovations in technology take place early, and then in the late Upper Paleolithic there is a vast elaboration and application of that potential. We cannot talk about any one point where a major change occurs, but it's important to see the order in which things happened.

KOZLOWSKI: In this regard, F. Bordes's notion of *évolution buissonnante* is very important.

HOWELL: There is a dominance of the Perigord in prehistory, but it is vital that this region be put in some kind of other perspective. The UP, for example, is a vast thing covering large chunks of time, with lots of recognizable subdivisions and different kinds of expressions. You cannot find this, however, by sitting on the banks of the Vézère—you have to pass through all the places to get a real appreciation for what it means. So, this dominance is terribly important only in the perspective that it is part of the bigger whole. The same is true for a particular site type, i.e., open-air versus shelter or cave sites.

PARTICIPANTS IN THE SYMPOSIUM

Mark Baumler
Department of Anthropology
University of Arizona
Tucson, AZ 85721
USA

Gerhard Bosinski
Forschungsstelle Altsteinzeit
Jagdhaus Monrepos
D-545 Neuwied 13
FEDERAL REPUBLIC OF GERMANY

Philip G. Chase
University Museum
University of Pennsylvania
Philadelphia, PA 19104
USA

Richard Davis
Department of Anthropology
Bryn Mawr College
Bryn Mawr, PA 19010
USA

André Debénath
Institut du Quaternaire
UA 133 CNRS
Université de Bordeaux I
Talence
FRANCE

Harold L. Dibble
Department of Anthropology
University of Pennsylvania
Philadelphia, PA 19104
USA

William Farrand
Museum of Anthropology
University Museums Bldg.
The University of Michigan
Ann Arbor, MI 48109
USA

C. Reid Ferring
Institute of Applied Sciences
North Texas State University
Denton, TX 76203
USA

Leslie G. Freeman
Department of Anthropology
1126 E. 59th Street
University of Chicago
Chicago, IL 60637
USA

F. Clark Howell
Department of Anthropology
University of California, Berkeley
Berkeley, CA 94720
USA

Arthur J. Jelinek
Department of Anthropology
University of Arizona
Tucson, AZ 85721
USA

Janusz Kozlowski
Instytut Archeologii
Uniwersytet Jagiellonski
Ul. Golebia 11
Krakow
POLAND

Michele Lanzinger
Istituto de Geologia dell'Università
Corso Ercole 1 d'Este 32
44100 Ferrara
ITALY

Henri Laville
Institut du Quaternaire
UA 133 CNRS
Université de Bordeaux I
Talence
FRANCE

Michel Lenoir
Institut du Quaternaire
UA 133 CNRS
Université de Bordeaux I
Talence
FRANCE

Anthony E. Marks
Department of Anthropology
Southern Methodist University
Dallas, TX 75275
USA

Anta Montet-White
Department of Anthropology
University of Kansas
Lawrence, KS 66045
USA

Hansjürgen Müller-Beck
Institut für Urgeschichte
Schloss D-7400 Tübingen 1
FEDERAL REPUBLIC OF GERMANY

Marcel Otte
Université de Liège
Département de Préhistoire
Place du XX Août 7
B-4000 Liège
BELGIUM

Jean-Philippe Rigaud
Direction des Antiquités Préhistoriques
28 Place Gambetta
Bordeaux
FRANCE

Nicolas Rolland
Department of Anthropology
University of Victoria
Victoria, BC V8W 2YZ
CANADA

James Sackett
Department of Anthropology
University of California, Los Angeles
Los Angeles, CA 90024
USA

Jan Simek
Department of Anthropology
University of Tennessee
South Stadium Hall
Knoxville, TN 37996-0720
USA

Lawrence G. Straus
Department of Anthropology
University of New Mexico
Albuquerque, NM 87131
USA

OTHER CONTRIBUTORS TO THIS VOLUME

Sylvie Beyries
URA 28 du Centre de Recherche
 Archéologique du CNRS
Sophia-Antipolis
06565 Valbonne
FRANCE

Mauro Cremaschi
CNR—Centro per la Stratigrafia e
 Petrografia delle Alpi Centrali
Milan
ITALY

William T. Crowe
Department of Botany
Field Museum
Chicago, IL
USA

Jean-Marcel Evrard
Université de Liège
Service de Préhistoire
Place du XX Août 7
B-4000 Liège
BELGIUM

Miklós Gábori
H-1053 Budapest
Karolyi U. 16.
HUNGARY

Veronika Gábori-Csánk
H-1053 Budapest
Karolyi U. 16.
HUNGARY

Joaquín González Echegaray
Director, Museo Etnográfico de
 Cantabria
Muriedas, Cantabria
SPAIN

Richard G. Klein
Department of Anthropology
1126 E. 59th Street
University of Chicago
Chicago, IL 60637
USA

Alain Mathis
Université de Liège
Service de Préhistoire
Place du XX Août 7
B-4000 Liège
BELGIUM

Alan Mann
Department of Anthropology
University of Pennsylvania
Philadelphia, PA 19104
USA

Carmel Schrire
Department of Human Ecology
Cook College
Rutgers University
New Brunswick, NJ 08903
USA

Lynn M. Snyder
Department of Anthropology
University of Tennessee
South Stadium Hall
Knoxville, TN 37996-0720
USA

Denise de Sonneville-Bordes
Institut du Quaternaire
UA 133 CNRS
Université de Bordeaux I
33405 Talence
FRANCE

ABBREVIATIONS

AA	*American Anthropologist*
AAASH	*Acta Archaeologica Academiae Scientarum Hungaricae*
AAC	*Acta Archaeologica Carpathica*
AFEQ	Association Française pour l'Etude du Quaternaire
AGSO	Association des Géologues du Sud-Ouest
AIPH	Archives de l'Institut de Paléontologie Humaine
AK	*Archäologisches Korrespondenzblatt*
AmAnt	American Antiquity
ARA	*Annual Review of Anthropology*
ASPR	American School of Prehistoric Research
ASU	Arizona State University
AV	Archaeologica Venatoria
BAFEQ	*Bulletin de l'Association Française pour l'Etude du Quaternaire*
BAR	British Archaeological Reports
BIGBA	*Bulletin de l'Institut Géologique du Bassin de l'Aquitaine*
BJ	*Bonner Jahrbücher*
BPH	Bibliotheca Praehistorica Hispana
BSAHC	*Bulletin de la Société Archéologique et Historique de la Charente*
BSB	*Bulletin de la Société de Borda*
BSPA	*Bulletin de la Société Préhistorique de l'Ariège*
BSPF	*Bulletin de la Société Préhistorique Française*
CA	*Current Anthropology*
CIMA	Centro de Investigación y Museo de Altamira
ČMM	*Časopis Moravského Muzea*
CNRS	Centre National de la Recherche Scientifique
CNSS	Congrès National des Sociétés Savantes
CQ	Cahiers du Quaternaire
CRASP	*Comptes rendus de l'Académie des Sciences de Paris*
ČSAV	Československé Akademie Věd
EP	*Etudes préhistoriques*
EQ	Etudes quaternaires
ERAUL	Etudes et Recherches Archéologiques de l'Université de Liège
FNRS	Fonds National de la Recherche Scientifique
GP	*Gallia préhistoire*
INQUA	International Union for Quaternary Research

IPH	Institut de Paléontologie Humaine
IPI	Institute for Prehistoric Investigations (Chicago and Santander)
IPUB	Institut Préhistorique de l'Université de Bordeaux
JAA	*Journal of Anthropological Archaeology*
JAR	*Journal of Anthropological Research*
JAS	*Journal of Archaeological Science*
JFA	*Journal of Field Archaeology*
JHE	*Journal of Human Evolution*
JRGZM	*Jahrbuch des Römisch-Germanischen Zentralmuseums Mainz*
LPHP	Laboratoire de Paléontologie Humaine et de Préhistoire (Université de Provence)
LT	*Lithic Technology*
MIPUB	Mémoires de l'Institut Préhistorique de l'Université de Bordeaux
MSPF	Mémoires de la Société Préhistorique Française
NATO	North Atlantic Treaty Organization
NSF	National Science Foundation
OJA	*Oxford Journal of Archaeology*
PPS	*Proceedings of the Prehistoric Society*
QR	*Quaternary Research*
QRA	*Quarterly Review of Archaeology*
RA	*Revue anthropologique*
RAST	*Réunion de l'Association des Sciences de la Terre*
RSP	*Rivista di scienze preistoriche*
SAA	Society for American Archaeology
SAAB	*South African Archaeological Bulletin*
SciAm	*Scientific American*
SJA	*Southwestern Journal of Anthropoplogy*
SMU	Southern Methodist University
SPB	Studia Praehistorica Belgica
SPF	Société Préhistorique Française
UCLA	University of California at Los Angeles
UISPP	Union International des Sciences Préhistoriques et Protohistoriques
UM	Urgeschichtliche Materialhefte
UNESCO	United Nations Educational, Scientific, and Cultural Organization
WA	*World Archaeology*

BIBLIOGRAPHY

Abramova, V. A.
1984a   Paléolithique inférieur dans le territoire asiatique d'URSS. Pp. 135-160 in *Paléolithique d'URSS*, ed. P. I. Boriskovski. Moscow: Nauka. (in Russian)
1984b   Paléolithique supérieur dans le territoire asiatique d'URSS. Pp. 302-346 in *Paléolithique d'URSS*, ed. P. I. Boriskovski. Moscow: Nauka. (in Russian)

Ackerley, N. W., and Bayham, F. E.
1984   Comment. *CA* 25:85-86.

Adam, K.
1951   Der Waldelefant von Lehringen: eine Jagdbeute der diluvialen Menschen. *Quartär* 5:75-92.

Ait-Fora, A.
1986   Recherches sur les faunes du Würm récent en Périgord: le gisement du Flageolet I. Thesis, Université de Bordeaux.

Alaux, J. F.
1973   Pointes de la Font-Robert en place dans le Périgordien à burins de Noailles de l'abri des Battuts (commune de Penne, Tarn). *BSPF* 70:33-39.

Allain, J.
1968   A propos du Badegoulien: méthode et typologie. *BSPF* 65:36-38.

Allain, J., and Fritsch, R.
1967   Le Badegoulien de l'abri Fritsch aux roches de Pouligny Saint-Pierre (Indre). *BSPF* 64:83-84.

Allen, R. G. D.
1966   *Statistics for Economists*. London: Hutchinson.

Allsworth-Jones, P.
1986   *The Szeletian and the Transition from Middle to Upper Palaeolithic in Central Europe*. Oxford: Clarendon Press.

Alpysbaev, X. A.
1979   *Pamyatniki Nizhnego Paleolita Yuzhnogo Kazakhstana*. Alma Ata: Fan.

Altuna, J.
1972   Fauna de mamíferos de los yacimientos prehistóricos de Guipúzcoa, con catálogo de los mamíferos cuaternarios del Cantábrico y del Pireneo occidental. *Munibe* 24:1-464.

Altuna, J.; Baldeón, E.; and Mariezkurrena, K.
1985   Cazadores magdalenienses en Erralla (Cestona, Pais Vasco). *Munibe* 37:1-206.

Altuna, J., and Merino, J. M., eds.
1984   *El yacimiento prehistórico de la cueva de Ekain (Deba, Guipúzcoa)*. Eusko-Ikaskuntza B1. San Sebastian: Sociedad de Estudios Vascos.

Anderson, P. C.
1979   A Microwear Analysis of Selected Flint Artefacts from the Mousterian of Southern France. *LT* 9:32.
1980   A Testimony of Prehistoric Tasks: Diagnostic Residues on Stone Tool Working Edges. *WA* 12:181-194.

Anderson-Gerfaud, P.
1981   Contribution méthodologique à l'analyse des micro traces d'utilisation sur les outils préhistoriques. Thesis, Université de Bordeaux.

Anderson-Gerfaud, P., and Helmer, D.
1984   Détermination et signification possible d'emmanchements moustériens de certains outils. Pré-tirages du Colloque de Lyon (November).

App, V.; Campen, I.; Dombek, G.; and Hahn, J.
1987   Eine altsteinzeitliche Fundstelle auf dem Schwalbenberg bei Remagen, Lkr. Ahrweiler. *Archäologie an Mittelrhein und Mosel* 1:85-102.

Arambourou, R.
1978   *Le gisement préhistorique de Duruthy à Sorde-l'Abbaye*. MSPF 13. Paris: SPF.

Arambourou, R., and Jude, P. E.
1964   *Le gisement de la Chèvre à Bourdeilles (Dordogne)*. Périgueux: R. & M. Magne.

NOTE: Citations of works as "in press" or "n.d." may reflect information available as of late 1986 or 1987—when the papers were being prepared for the symposium—not as of this volume's publication date of 1988.

Arambourou, R.; Straus, L.; and Merlet, J.-C.
1985   Les recherches de préhistoire dans les Landes en 1984. *BSB* 110:451-474.

Arambourou, R.; Straus, L.; and Normand, C.
1986   Les recherches de préhistoire dans les Landes en 1985. *BSB* 111:121-140.

Ashton, N., and Cook, J.
1986   Dating and Correlating the French Mousterian. *Nature* 324:113.

Assassi, F.
1986   Recherches sédimentologiques sur la climatologie du Würm ancien et de l'interstade würmien en Périgord. Thesis, Université de Bordeaux.

Bahn, P. G.
1977   Seasonal Migration in South-west France during the Late Glacial Period. *JAS* 4: 245-257.
1982   Inter-site and Inter-regional Links during the Upper Palaeolithic: The Pyrenean Evidence. *OJA* 1:247-268.
1984   *Pyrenean Prehistory*. Warminster: Aris & Phillips.

Barandiarán, I.; Freeman, L.; González Echegaray, J.; and Klein, R. G.
1987   *Excavaciones en el yacimiento magdaleniense de "El Juyo."* Vol. 1: *El entorno natural*. Santander: CIMA.

Bartolomei, G.; Broglio, A.; Cattani, L.; Cremaschi, M.; Guerreschi, A.; Montovami, E.; Peretto, C.; and Sala, B.
1982   I depositi würmiani del riparo tagliente. *Annali dell'Università Ferrara* n.s. 15:61-105.

Bartolomei, G.; Broglio, A.; Cattani, L.; Cremaschi, M.; Guerreschi, A.; and Peretto, C.
1984   Il Paleolitico superiore e Mesolitico. Pp. 233-243 in *Il veneto nell'antichità—preistoria e protostoria*, ed. A. Aspes. Verona.

Bar-Yosef, O., and Belfer, A.
1977   The Lagaman Industry. Pp. 42-84 in *Prehistoric Investigations in Gebel Maghara, Northern Sinai*, eds. O. Bar-Yosef and J. Phillips. Qedem 7. Jerusalem: Institute of Archaeology, Hebrew University.

Bar-Yosef, O.; Vandermeersch, B.; Goldberg, P.; Laville, H.; Meighen, L.; Rak, Y.; Tchernov, E.; and Tillier, A. M.
1986   New Data on the Origin of Modern Man in the Levant. *CA* 27:63-64.

Basler, D.
1961   Londža-Makljenovac, Paleolitska Stanića. *Arheološki Preglev* 3:8-10.
1962   Paleolitsko Nalaziste Visoko Brdo u Lupljanici. *Glasnik Zemaljskog Muzeja Arheologija* 17:5-13.
1971   Luščić: station paléolithique. Pp. 63-64 in *Epoque préhistorique et protohistorique en Yougoslavie: recherches et résultats*, ed. G. Novak. 8e Congrès International de l'UISPP. Belgrade: Société Archéologique de Yougoslavie.
1976   Ein Vierteljahrhundert der Paläolithforschung in Nordbosnien (1949-1974). *Golisnjak* 13:27-32.
1979   (ed.) *Praistorija Jugoslavenskih Zemalja*. Vol. 1: *Paleolitske i Mesolitske Doba*. Sarajevo: Zemaljski Muzej.

Bastin, B.
1986   Analyses palynologiques aux grottes de Sclayn. *BAFEQ*: 168-177.

Bastin, B.; Levêque, F.; and Pradel, L.
1976   Mise en évidence de spectres polliniques interstadiaires entre le Moustérien et le Périgordien ancien de la grotte des Cottés (Vienne). *CRASP* 282:1261-1264.

Baumler, M. F.
1987   Core Reduction Sequences: An Analysis of Blank Production in the Middle Paleolithic of Northern Bosnia, Yugoslavia. Ph.D. dissertation, University of Arizona. Ann Arbor: University Microfilms.

Baumler, M.; Dibble, H.; Speth, J.; and Holdaway, S.
1986   A Reevaluation of the Zagros Mousterian: New Data from Old Collections. Paper presented at 51st Annual Meeting of the SAA (New Orleans, April).

Bayle des Hermens, R. de
1974a Note préliminaire sur le Magdalénien ancien de la couche F2 de la grotte du Rond-du-Barry. *L'Anthropologie* 78:17-36.
1974b Vue d'ensemble sur les niveaux préhistoriques de la grotte du Rond du Barry, fouilles 1966-1973. *BSPF* 71:130-132.

Beaulieu, J. L. de, and Reille, M.
1984   The Pollen Sequence of Les Echets (France): A New Element for the Chronology of the Upper Pleistocene. *Géographie physique et quaternaire* 38:3-9.

Beaune, S. de; Roussot, A.; and Sackett, J. R.
1986   Les lampes de Solvieux (Dordogne). *L'Anthropologie* 90:107-119.

Bégouën, R., and Clottes, J.
1982   Des ex-votos magdaléniens? *La recherche* 13:518-520.

Belfer-Cohen, A.
1986   The Evolution of Symbolic Expression through the Upper Pleistocene in the Levant as Compared to Western Europe. Pp. 125-128 in *L'homme de Néandertal* (preprints), ed. M. Otte. Liège: Université de Liège.

Belfer-Cohen, A., and Bar-Yosef, O.
1981   The Aurignacian at Hayonim Cave. *Paléorient* 7(2):19-42.

Bernaldo de Quirós Guidotti, F.
1980   *Notas sobre la economia del Paleolítico superior cantábrico.* Monografía 1. Santander: CIMA.
1982   *Los inicios del Paleolítico superior cantábrico.* Monografía 8. Santander: CIMA.

Beyries, S.
1984   Approche fonctionelle de l'outillage provenant d'un site paléolithique moyen du nord de la France: Corbehem. Pp. 219-224 in *Actes du Colloque de Lille* (September). Paris: AFEQ.
1986   Approche fonctionelle des industries lithiques de la couche 10 de Marillac (Charente). *Actes du 3ème CNSS* (Poitiers), Pré- et protohistoire: 145-150.
1987   *Variabilité de l'industrie lithique au Moustérien: approche fonctionelle sur quelques gisements français.* BAR International Series 328. Oxford: BAR.
in press   Quelques exemples d'emmanchements observés sur des outils du Paléolithique moyen. In *Manches et emmanchements préhistoriques* (Colloque de Lyon, November 1984). Paris: AFEQ.

Beyries, S., and Boëda, E.
1983   Etude technologique et traces d'utilisation des "éclats débordants" de Corbehem (Pas-de-Calais). *BSPF* 80:275-279.

Binford, L. R.
1973   Interassemblage Variability: The Mousterian and the "Functional" Argument. Pp. 227-254 in *The Explanation of Culture Change*, ed. C. Renfrew. London: Duckworth.
1977   Forty-seven Trips: A Case Study in the Character of Archaeological Formation Processes. Pp. 24-36 in *Stone Tools as Cultural Markers*, ed. R. Wright. Canberra: Australian Institute of Aboriginal Studies.
1978   *Nunamiut Ethnoarchaeology.* New York: Academic Press.
1979   Organization and Formation Processes: Looking at Curated Technologies. *JAR* 35:255-273.
1981   *Bones: Ancient Men and Modern Myths.* New York: Academic Press.
1982   Comment on "Rethinking the Middle/Upper Paleolithic Transition." *CA* 23:177-181.
1983a   The Challenge of the Mousterian. Pp. 79-94 in *In Pursuit of the Past*, by L. R. Binford. New York: Thames & Hudson.
1983b   *In Pursuit of the Past: Decoding the Archaeological Record.* New York: Thames & Hudson.
1983c   *Working at Archaeology.* New York: Academic Press.
1983d   Working at Archaeology: The Mousterian Problem—Learning How to Learn. Pp. 65-69 in *Working at Archaeology*, by L. R. Binford. New York: Academic Press. demic Press.
1983e   Working at Archaeology: The Mousterian Problem—Learning How to Learn. Pp. 65-69 in *Working at Archaeology*, by L. R. Binford. New York: Academic Press.
1984   *Faunal Remains from the Klasies River Mouth.* New York: Academic Press.
1985   Human Ancestors: Changing Views of Their Behavior. *JAA* 4:292-327.

Binford, L. R., and Binford, S. R.
1966   A Preliminary Analysis of Functional Variability in the Mousterian of Levallois Facies. *AA* 68:238-295.

Binford, S. R.
1968a   Early Upper Paleolithic Adaptations in the Levant. *AA* 70:707-717.
1968b   A Structural Comparison of Disposal of the Dead in the Mousterian and the Upper Paleolithic. *SJA* 24:139-154.

Bleich, K. E.
1975   Die Sedimente des Mauerner Tals. *Quartär* 26:100-106.

Bliss, L. C., and Richards, J. H.
1982   Present-Day Arctic Vegetation and Ecosystems as a Predictive Tool for the Arctic-Steppe Mammoth Biome. Pp. 241-257 in *Paleoecology of Beringia*, eds. D. M. Hopkins et al. New York: Academic Press.

Blumenschine, R. J.
1986   *Early Hominid Scavenging Opportunities.* BAR International Series 283. Oxford: BAR.

Boëda, E.
1986   Approche technologique du concept levallois et évaluation de son champ d'application: étude de trois gisements saaliens et weichséliens de la France septentrionale. Thesis, Université de Paris.

Boëda, E., and Pelegrin, J.
1979-80 Approche technologique du nucléus levallois à éclat. *EP* 15:41-48.

Bogaard, P. v. d., and Schmincke, H.-U.
1984   The Eruptive Center of the Late Quaternary Laacher See Tephra. *Geologische Rundschau* 73:933-980.

Bohmers, A.
1951   Die Höhlen von Mauern, Teil I: Kulturgeschichte der altsteinzeitlichen Besiedlung. *Palaeohistoria* 1:1-107.

Bolus, M.
in press Steinartefakte. In *Das Endpaläolithikum von Andernach*. Neuwied: Schriftenreihe Monrepos.

Bonifay, E.
1962   *Les terrains quaternaires dans le Sud-Est de la France.* MIPUB 2. Bordeaux: Delmas.
1964-65 Moustérien et Prémoustérien de la grotte de Rigabe (Artigues, Var). *Quartär* 15-16:61-78.
1981   Les plus anciens habitats sous grotte découverts à Lunel-Viel (Hérault). *Archaeologia* 150:30-42.

Bordes, F.
1947   Etude comparative des différentes techniques de taille du silex et des roches dures. *L'Anthropologie* 51:1-29.
1948   Les couches moustériennes du gisement du Moustier (Dordogne): typologie et techniques de taille. *BSPF* 45:113-126.
1950a   L'évolution buissonnante des industries en Europe occidentale: considérations théoriques sur le Paléolithique ancien et moyen. *L'Anthropologie* 54:393-420.
1950b   Principes d'une méthode d'étude des techniques de débitage et de la typologie du Paléolithique ancien et moyen. *L'Anthropologie* 54:19-34.
1953a   Essai de classification des industries "moustériennes." *BSPF* 50:457-466.
1953b   Levalloisien et Moustérien. *BSPF* 50:226-235.
1953c   Notules de typologie paléolithique I: outils moustériens à fracture volontaire. *BSPF* 50:224-226.
1953d   Notules de typologie paléolithique II: pointes levalloisiennes et pseudolevalloisiennes. *BSPF* 50:311-313.
1953e   Station de la Chaise, grotte Suard: les industries moustériennes—premiers résultats. *BSAHC* 1952-53:17-18.
1954a   *Les limons quaternaires du bassin de la Seine.* AIPH Mémoire 26. Paris: Masson.
1954b   Notules de typologie paléolithique III: pointes moustériennes, racloirs convergents et déjetés, limaces. *BSPF* 51:336-339.
1955   Le Paléolithique inférieur et moyen de Jabrud (Syrie) et la question du pré-Aurignacien. *L'Anthropologie* 59:486-507.
1957   Préface. Pp. 5-6 in *Les industries moustériennes et pré-moustériennes du Périgord*, by M. Bourgon. AIPH Mémoire 27. Paris: Masson.
1958   Nouvelles fouilles à Laugerie Haute Est: premiers résultats. *L'Anthropologie* 62:205-244.
1960   Evolution in the Palaeolithic Cultures. Pp. 99-110 in *Evolution after Darwin: The University of Chicago Centennial*, Vol. 2, ed. S. Tax. Chicago: University of Chicago.
1961a   Mousterian Cultures in France. *Science* 134:803-810.
1961b   *Typologie du Paléolithique ancien et moyen.* 2 vols. MIPUB 1. Bordeaux: Delmas.
1962   Le Moustérien à denticulés. *Arheološki Vestnik* 13:43-49.
1965   A propos de la grotte de la Chaise: une rectification. *L'Anthropologie* 69:602-603.
1966   *Cours polycopié de préhistoire.* Bordeaux: Institut du Quaternaire, Université de Bordeaux I.
1968a   *The Old Stone Age.* London: Weidenfeld & Nicolson.
1968b   La question périgordienne. Pp. 59-70 in *La préhistoire: problèmes et tendances*, ed. D. de Sonneville-Bordes. Paris: CNRS.
1969   Livret-guide de l'excursion A5—Landes—Périgord. *Proceedings of the 8th INQUA Congress*: 38-87.
1970   Réflexions sur l'outil au Paléolithique. *BSPF* 67:199-202.
1971   Physical Evolution and Technological Evolution in Man: A Parallelism. *WA* 3:1-5.
1972   *A Tale of Two Caves.* New York: Harper & Row.
1973   On the Chronology and Contemporaneity of Different Palaeolithic Cultures in France. Pp. 217-226 in *The Explanation of Culture Change*, ed. C. Renfrew. London: Duckworth.

1978 Typological Variability in the Mousterian Layers at Pech de l'Azé I, II, and IV. *JAR* 34:181-193.

1980 Le débitage levallois et ses variantes. *BSPF* 77:45-49.

1981a La préhistoire "nouvelle" et quelques-uns de ses problèmes. *Scripta Ethnologia Caea* 6:61-66. (Repr. as pp. 429-437 in *Leçons sur le Paléolithique*, Vol. 2, by F. Bordes [1984]. Paris: CNRS.)

1981b Vingt-cinq ans après: le complexe moustérien revisité. *BSPF* 78:77-87.

1984 *Leçons sur le Paléolithique*. Vol. 2: *Le Paléolithique en Europe*. CQ 7. Paris: CNRS.

Bordes, F., and Bourgon, M.
1951 Le complexe moustérien: Moustérien, Levalloisien et Tayacien. *L'Anthropologie* 55:1-23.

Bordes, F., and Crabtree, D.
1969 The Corbiac Blade Technique and Other Experiments. *Tebiwa* 12:1-21.

Bordes, F.; Debénath, A.; Kervazo, B.; Laville, H.; Le Tensorer, J.-M.; Texier, J.-P.; and Thibault, C.
1980 Les dépôts quaternaires en Aquitaine. Pp. 250-267 in *Problèmes de stratigraphie quaternaire en France et dans les pays limitrophes*, ed. J. Chaline. *BAFEQ* Supplément n.s. 1. Dijon: AFEQ.

Bordes, F.; Fitte, P.; and Blanc, S.
1954 L'abri Armand Chadourne. *BSPF* 51:229-254.

Bordes, F., and Gaussen, J.
1970 Un fond de tente magdalénien près de Mussidan (Dordogne). Pp. 312-329 in *Frühe Menschheit und Umwelt*, Vol. 1, eds. K. Gripp, R. Schütrumpf, and H. Schwabedissen. Fundamenta A2. Cologne: Hermann Böhlau.

Bordes, F., and Labrot, J.
1967 La stratigraphie du gisement de Roc-de-Combe (Lot) et ses implications. *BSPF* 64:15-28.

Bordes, F.; Laville, H.; and Paquereau, M.-M.
1966 Observations sur le Pléistocène supérieur du gisement de Combe-Grenal (Dordogne). *Actes de la Société Linnéenne de Bordeaux* 103:3-19.

Bordes, F., and Prat, F.
1965 Observations sur les faunes du Riss et du Würm I en Dordogne. *L'Anthropologie* 69:31-46.

Bordes, F.; Rigaud, J.-P.; and Sonneville-Bordes, D. de
1972 Des buts, problèmes et limites de l'archéologie paléolithique. *Quaternaria* 16:15-34.

Bordes, F., and Sonneville-Bordes, D. de
1966 Protomagdalénien ou Périgordien VII? *L'Anthropologie* 70:113-122.

1970 The Significance of Variability in Palaeolithic Assemblages. *WA* 2:61-73.

Boriskovski, P. I., ed.
1984 *Paleolit SSSR (Paléolithique d'URSS)*. Moscow: Nauka.

Borziak, I. A.; Grigorieva, G. V.; and Ketraru, A. N.
1982 *Poseleniya Drevnekamennogo Veka na Severo-Zapade Moldavii*. Kishinev: Stiintsa.

Bosinski, G.
1967 *Die Mittelpaläolithischen Funde im Westlichen Mitteleuropa*. Fundamenta A4. Cologne: Hermann Böhlau.

1969 Der Magdalénien-Fundplatz Feldkirchen-Gönnersdorf, Kreis Neuwied: Vorbericht über die Ausgrabungen 1968. *Germania* 47:1-38.

1978a Adlerquelle. Pp. 107-109 in *Alt- und mittelsteinzeitliche Fundplätze des Rheinlandes*, ed. S. Veil. Cologne: Rheinland-Verlag.

1978b Wildscheuer IV. P. 107 in *Alt- und mittelsteinzeitliche Fundplätze des Rheinlandes*, ed. S. Veil. Cologne: Rheinland-Verlag.

1978c Wildscheuer V. P. 128 in *Alt- und mittelsteinzeitliche Fundplätze des Rheinlandes*, ed. S. Veil. Cologne: Rheinland-Verlag.

1978d Wildweiberlei. Pp. 126-128 in *Alt- und mittelsteinzeitliche Fundplätze des Rheinlandes*, ed. S. Veil. Cologne: Rheinland-Verlag.

1979 *Die Ausgrabungen in Gönnersdorf 1968-1976 und die Siedlungsbefunde der Grabung 1968. Der Magdalénien-Fundplatz Gönnersdorf* 3. Wiesbaden: Franz Steiner.

1982a *Das Eiszeitalter in Ruhrland*. Ruhrlandmuseum Essen, Heft 2. Cologne: Rheinland-Verlag.

1982b *Die Kunst der Eiszeit in Deutschland und in der Schweiz*. Kataloge vor- und frühgeschichtlicher Altertümer 20. Bonn: Rudolf Habelt.

1983a *Eiszeitjäger im Neuwieder Becken*. 2d ed. Archäologie an Mittelrhein und Mosel 1. Koblenz: Landesamt für Denkmalpflege Rheinland-Pfalz.

1983b Die jägerrische Geschichte des Rheinlandes: Einsichten und Lücken. *JRGZM* 30:81-112.

1984a The Mammoth Engravings of the Magdalenien Site Gönnersdorf (Rhineland, Germany). Pp. 295-322 in *La contribution de la* zoologie et de l'ethologie à l'interprétation de l'art des peuples chasseurs préhistoriques, eds. H.-G. Bandi et al. 3ème Colloque de la Société Suisse des Sciences Humaines (Fribourg, 1979). Fribourg: Editions Universitaires.

1984b   Paläolithische Funde in den Höhlen Nordrhein-Westfalens. *Kölner geographische Arbeiten* 45:371-398.

Bosinski, G.; Bosinski, H.; Cziesla, E.; Lanser, K. P.; Neuffer, F.-O.; Preuss, J.; Spoerer, H.; Tillmanns, W.; and Urban, B.

1985   Sprendlingen: ein Fundplatz des mittleren Jungpaläolithikums in Rheinhessen. *JRGZM* 32:5-91.

Bosinski, G.; Braun, R.; Turner, E.; and Vaughan, P.

1982   Ein spätpaläolithisches Retuscheurdepot von Niederbieber/Neuwieder Becken. *AK* 12:295-311.

Bosinski, G., and Fischer, G.

1974   *Die Menschendarstellungen von Gönnersdorf der Ausgrabung von 1968.* Der Magdalénien-Fundplatz Gönnersdorf 1. Wiesbaden: Franz Steiner.

1980   *Mammut- und Pferdedarstellungen von Gönnersdorf.* Der Magdalénien-Fundplatz Gönnersdorf 5. Wiesbaden: Franz Steiner.

Bosinski, G.; Kröger, K.; Schäfer, J.; and Turner, E.

1986   Altsteinzeitliche Siedlungsplätze auf den Osteifel-Vulkanen. *JRGZM* 33:97-130.

Bouchud, J.

1975   Etude de la faune de l'abri Pataud. Pp. 69-153 in *Excavation of the Abri Pataud, Les Eyzies (Dordogne)*, ed. H. L. Movius. ASPR Bulletin 30. Cambridge, MA: Peabody Museum Press.

Bourgon, M.

1957   *Les industries moustériennes et prémoustériennes du Périgord.* AIPH Mémoire 27. Paris: Masson.

Bourlon, M.

1905   Une fouille au Moustier (Dordogne). *L'homme préhistorique* 7:293-304.

1910   L'industrie des foyers supérieurs au Moustier. *Revue préhistorique* 5:157-167.

1911   Industrie des niveaux moyens et inférieurs de la terrasse du grand abri du Moustier. *Revue préhistorique* 6:283-300.

Bowman, S. G. E., and Sieveking, G.

1983   Thermoluminescence Dating of Burnt Flint from Combe-Grenal. *PACT 9: Third Specialist Seminar on TL and ESR Dating* (July 1982): 253-268.

Boyer, M.; Geneste, J.-M.; and Rigaud, J.-P.

1984   Le Périgordien supérieur du site de plein air du Caillou, Rouffignac de Sigoulès (Dordogne). *BSPF* 81:302-310.

Bradley, B.

1975   Lithic Reduction Sequences: A Glossary and Discussion. Pp. 5-13 in *Lithic Technology: Making and Using Stone Tools*, ed. E. Swanson. The Hague/Paris: Mouton.

1982   Review of *Rock Shelters of the Perigord*, by H. Laville, J.-P. Rigaud, and J. Sackett. *AmAnt* 47:246-247.

Bradley, B., and Sampson, C. G.

1986   Analysis by Replication of Two Acheulian Artefact Assemblages from Caddington, England. Pp. 29-45 in *Stone Age Prehistory*, eds. G. N. Bailey and P. Callow. Cambridge: Cambridge University Press.

Brande, A.

1975   Vegetationsgeschichtliche und pollenanalytische Untersuchungen zum Paläolithikum von Mauern und Meilenhofen (Fränkische Alb). *Quartär* 26:73-106.

Breuil, H.

1912   Les subdivisions du Paléolithique supérieur et leur signification. *Comptes rendus du 14ème Congrès International d'Anthropologie et d'Archéologie Préhistorique* (Geneva): 165-238.

1932   Les industries à éclats du Paléolithique ancien, I: Le Clactonien. *Préhistoire* 1:125-190.

Breuil, H., and Dubalen, P.

1901   Fouilles d'un abri à Sordes en 1900. *Revue de l'Ecole d'Anthropologie de Paris* 8:251-268.

Breuil, H., and Kelley, H.

1956   Les éclats acheuléens à plan de frappe à facettes de Cagny-la-Garenne (Somme). *BSPF* 53:174-191.

Breuil, H., and Lantier, R.

1959   *Les hommes de la pierre ancienne.* Paris: Payot.

Brewer, R.

1976   *Fabric and Mineral Analysis of the Soil.* New York: Kriger.

Brézillon, M.

1968   *La dénomination des objets de pierre taillée.* Paris: CNRS.

Bricker, H. M.

1973   The Perigordian IV and Related Cultures in France. Ph.D. dissertation, Harvard University.

1976   Upper Palaeolithic Archaeology. *ARA* 5: 133-148.

1981 Review of *Rock Shelters of the Perigord*, by H. Laville, J.-P. Rigaud, and J. Sackett. *AmSci* 69:680-681.

Bricker, H. M., and David, N. C.
1984 *Excavation of the Abri Pataud, Les Eyzies (Dordogne): The Perigordian VI (Level 3) Assemblage*. ASPR Bulletin 34. Cambridge, MA: Peabody Museum Press.

Brunnacker, K., ed.
1978 *Geowissenschaftliche Untersuchungen in Gönnersdorf. Der Magdalénien-Fundplatz Gönnersdorf 4*. Wiesbaden: Franz Steiner.

Brunnacker, K.; Fruth, H.; Juvigné, E.; and Urban, B.
1982 Spätpaläolithische Funde aus Thür, Kreis Mayen-Koblenz. *AK* 12:417-427.

Butzer, K. W.
1981 Cave Sediments, Upper Pleistocene Stratigraphy and Mousterian Facies in Cantabrian Spain. *JAS* 8:133-183.

Cabrera, V.
1984 *El yacimiento de la cueva de "El Castillo" (Puente Viesgo, Santander)*. BPH 22. Madrid: Instituto Español de Prehistoria/Universidad de Madrid.

Cahen, D.
1985 Fonction, industrie et culture. Pp. 39-51 in *La signification culturelle des industries lithiques*, ed. M. Otte. Actes du Colloque de Liège (October 1984). SPB 4; BAR International Series 239. Oxford: BAR.

Cahen, D.; Keeley, L. H.; and Van Noten, F.
1979 Stone Tools, Toolkits, and Human Behavior in Prehistory. *CA* 20:661-683.

Cahen, D., and Moeyersons, J.
1977 Subsurface Movements of Stone Artifacts and Their Implications for the Prehistory of Central Africa. *Nature* 266:812-815.

Callow, P.
1986 The Saalian Industries of La Cotte de St. Brelade, Jersey. Pp. 129-140 in *Chronostratigraphie et faciès culturels du Paléolithique inférieur et moyen dans l'Europe du nord-ouest*, eds. A. Tuffreau and J. Sommé. *BAFEQ* Supplément 26. Paris: AFEQ.

Campbell, J. B.
1986 Hiatus and Continuity in the British Upper Palaeolithic: A View from the Antipodes. Pp. 7-42 in *Studies in the Upper Palaeolithic of Britain and Northwest Europe*, ed. D. A. Roe. BAR International Series 296. Oxford: BAR.

Chase, P. G.
1983 The Use of Animal Resources in the Mousterian of Combe Grenal, France. Ph.D. dissertation, University of Arizona.
1986 *The Hunters of Combe Grenal: Approaches to Middle Paleolithic Subsistence in Europe*. BAR International Series 286. Oxford: BAR.

Chase, P. G., and Dibble, H. L.
1987 Middle Paleolithic Symbolism: A Review of Current Evidence and Interpretations. *JAA* 6:263-296.

Cheynier, A.
1930 Un outil magdalénien nouveau en silex à Badegoule: la raclette. *BSPF* 27:483-488.
1939 Le Magdalénien primitif de Badegoule: niveaux à raclettes. *BSPF* 36:354-396.
1951 Les industries proto-magdaléniennes. *BSPF* 48:190-192.
1954 Note complémentaire à l'article de H. Breuil sur le Magdalénien. *BSPF* 51:64-66.
1963 Description des outillages. Pp. 61-173 in *La cirque de la Patrie*, eds. A. Cheynier, R. Daniel, and E. Vignard. MSPF 6. Paris: SPF.

Clark, G. A., and Straus, L. G.
1983 Late Pleistocene Hunter-Gatherer Adaptations in Cantabrian Spain. Pp. 131-148 in *Hunter-Gatherer Economy in Prehistory: A European Perspective*, ed. G. Bailey. Cambridge: Cambridge University Press.

Clark, G. A., and Yi, S.
1983 Niche-width Variation in Cantabrian Archaeofaunas: A Diachronic Study. Pp. 183-208 in *Animals and Archaeology*, Vol. 1, eds. J. Clutton-Brock and C. Grigson. BAR International Series 163. Oxford: BAR.

Clark, J. D.
1958a Certain Industries of Notched and Strangulated Scrapers in Rhodesia: Their Time Range and Possible Use. *SAAB* 13:56-66.
1958b Some Stone Woodworking Tools in Southern Africa. *SAAB* 13:144-151.

Clark, J. G. D.
1969 *World Prehistory: A New Outline*. Cambridge: Cambridge University Press.

Clot, A.
1984 Faune de la grotte préhistorique du Bois du Cantet (Espèche). *Munibe* 36:33-50.

Clottes, J.
1976 Les civilisations du Paléolithique supérieur dans les Pyrénées. Pp. 1214-1231 in *La*

préhistoire française, Vol. 1, ed. H. de Lumley. Paris: CNRS.

1983 La caverne des Eglises à Ussat: fouilles 1964-1977. *BSPA* 38:23-81.

Collins, M. B.
1975 Lithic Technology as a Means of Processual Inference. Pp. 15-34 in *Lithic Technology*, ed. E. Swanson. The Hague/Paris: Mouton.

Combier, J.
1962 Chronologie et systématique du Moustérien occidental: données et conceptions nouvelles. *Atti del VI Congresso Internazionale delle Scienze Preistoriche e Protostoriche* (Rome) 1:77-96.
1967 *Le Paléolithique de l'Ardèche dans son cadre paléoclimatique*. Bordeaux: Delmas.

Conkey, M. W.
1980 The Identification of Prehistoric Hunter-Gatherer Aggregation Sites: The Case of Altamira. *CA* 21:609-630.

Copeland, L.
1975 The Middle and Upper Paleolithic of Lebanon and Syria in the Light of Recent Research. Pp. 317-350 in *Problems in Prehistory*, eds. F. Wendorf and A. Marks. Dallas: SMU Press.
1983 Levallois/Non-Levallois Determinations in the Early Levant Mousterian: Problems and Questions for 1983. *Paléorient* 9:15-25.
1986 Introduction to Volume 1. Pp. 1-19 in *Ksar Akil, Lebanon*. Vol. 1: *Levels XXV-XII*, by I. Azoury, eds. C. Bergman and L. Copeland. BAR International Series S289. Oxford: BAR.

Corchón, M. S.
1971 *El Solutrense en Santander*. Santander: Institución Cultural de Cantabria.

Cordy, J.-M.
1982 Biozonation du Quaternaire postvillafranchien continental d'Europe occidentale à partir des grands mammifères. *Annales de la Société Géologique de Belgique* 105:303-314.

Cotterell, B., and Kamminga, J.
1979 The Mechanics of Flaking. Pp. 97-112 in *Lithic Use-Wear Analysis*, ed. B. Hayden. New York: Academic Press.

Crabtree, D.
1972 *An Introduction to Flintworking*. Occasional Papers of the Idaho State University Museum 28. Pocatello: Museum.

Crabtree, D., and Davis, E. L.
1968 Experimental Manufacture of Wooden Implements with Tools of Flaked Stone. *Science* 159:426-428.

Cremaschi, M.
1979 The Loess in the Central Po Valley. *Proceedings of the 15th Plenary Meeting of the Commission on Geomorphological Survey and Mapping, International Geographical Union* (Modena-Catania, November). Modena: Istituto Geologico dell'Università di Modena.
1987 Paleosols and Vertisols in the Central Po Plain (Northern Italy): A Study in Quaternary Geology and Soil Development. Thesis, University of Amsterdam.

Cremaschi, M., and Lanzinger, M.
1983 La successione stratigrafica e le fasi pedogenetiche del sito epigravettiano di Andalo, i loess tardiglaciali della Val d'Adige. *Preistoria alpina* (Memoria del Museo Tridentino di Scienze Naturali) 19:179-187.
in press Aspetti geomorfologici e pedostratigrafici dell'area circostante il sito tardo paleolitico-mesolitico di Terlago (Trento): loess ed evoluzione dei suoli tra Tardiglaciale ed Olocene in Trentino. *Acta geologica* (Memoria del Museo Tridentino di Scienze Naturali).

Crew, H.
1975 An Evaluation of the Relationship between the Mousterian Complexes of the Eastern Mediterranean: A Technological Perspective. Pp. 427-437 in *Problems in Prehistory*, eds. F. Wendorf and A. E. Marks. Dallas: SMU Press.
1976 The Mousterian Site of Rosh Ein Mor. Pp. 75-112 in *Prehistory and Paleoenvironments in the Central Negev, Israel*, Vol. 1, ed. A. E. Marks. Dallas: SMU Press.

Crochet, J.-Y.
1967 Le Magdalénien I de Birac, commune de St. Sulpice et Cameyrac (Gironde). *BSPF* 64:100-106.

Crowe, W.
n.d. Paleolithic Seeds from El Juyo, Spain. In preparation.

Daleau, F.
1910 Silex à retouches anormales de la station de la Bertonne ou la Rousse, commune de Peujard (Gironde). *Société Archéologique de Bordeaux* 31:31-48.

Daniel, G. E.
1975 *A Hundred and Fifty Years of Archaeology*. 2d ed. London: Duckworth.

David, N. C.
1973 On Upper Palaeolithic Society, Ecology and Technological Change: The Noaillian Case. Pp. 277-303 in *The Explanation of Culture Change*, ed. C. Renfrew. London: Duckworth.
1985 *Excavation of the Abri Pataud, Les Eyzies (Dordogne): The Noaillian (Level 4) Assemblages and the Noaillian Culture in Western Europe.* ASPR Bulletin 37. Cambridge, MA: Peabody Museum Press.

David, N. C., and Bricker, H.
1985 Perigordian and Noaillian in the Greater Perigord. Paper presented at 50th Annual Meeting of the SAA (Denver, May).

Davis, R. S.; Ranov, V. A.; and Dodonov, A. E.
1980 Early Man in Soviet Central Asia. *SciAm* 243:130-137.

Debénath, A.
1965 Recherches sédimentologiques sur le remplissage des grottes-abris de la Chaise de Vouthon (Charente). Thesis, Université de Bordeaux.
1974 Recherches sur les terrains quaternaires des Charentes et les industries qui leur sont associées. Thesis, Université de Bordeaux.
1977 The Latest Finds of Antewürmian Human Remains in Charente (France). *JHE* 6:297-302.
1980 Die altsteinzeitlichen Fundstellen von La Chaise de Vouthon (Charente, Frankreich): Geologie, Formenkunde, Paläontologie. *AK* 10:5-8.
1983 Quelques particularités techniques et typologiques des industries de la Chaise de Vouthon (Charente). *Actes du 105ème CNSS* (Caen, 1980): 239-247.

Debénath, A., and Duport, L.
1971 Os travaillés et os utilisés de quelques gisements charentais (Paléolithique ancien et moyen). *BSAHC*: 189-201.

Debénath, A.; Raynal, J.-P.; and Schwarcz, H.
1980 Remarques sur l'édification des planchers stalagmitiques quaternaires. Pp. 149-161 in *Cristallisation, déformation, dissolution des carbonates: Actes de la réunion organisée par le Groupe d'Etude des Systèmes Carbonatés.* Bordeaux: Société Géologique de France and Société Française de Minéralogie et Cristallographie.

Delpech, F.
1979 Les faunes de la fin des temps glaciaires dans le Sud-Ouest de la France. Pp. 169-176 in *La fin des temps glaciaires en Europe*, ed. D. de Sonneville-Bordes. Colloques Internationaux du CNRS 271. Paris: CNRS.
1983 *Les faunes du Paléolithique supérieur dans le Sud-Ouest de la France.* CQ 6. Paris: CNRS.
1984 La Ferrassie: carnivores, artiodactyles et périssodactyles. Pp. 61-90 in *Le grand abri de la Ferrassie: fouilles 1968-1973*, ed. H. Delporte. EQ 7. Paris: LPHP.
1985 La réponse des ongulés du Pléistocène supérieur aux changements climatiques en Aquitaine. Paper presented at Réunion Annuelle de l'Association des Paléontologistes Français (Marseille).
1986 Les rennes du grand abri de Laugerie-Haute en Dordogne (fouilles F. Bordes). *Arqueologie* (Porto) 13:66-71.
in press Les grands mammifères de la grotte Vaufrey, à l'exception des Ursidés. In *La grotte XV dite Grotte Vaufrey, à Cenac-et-Saint-Julien (Dordogne)*, ed. J.-P. Rigaud. MSPF.

Delpech, F., and Laville, H.
in press Climatologie et chronologie de la Grotte Vaufrey: confrontation des hypothèses et implications. In *La grotte XV dite Grotte Vaufrey, à Cenac-et-Saint-Julien (Dordogne)*, ed. J.-P. Rigaud. MSPF.

Delpech, F.; Laville, H.; and Paquereau, M.-M.
1986 Chronostratigraphie et paléoenvironnements du Paléolithique moyen en Périgord. Paper presented at "L'homme de Néandertal: centenaire de la découverte de l'homme de Spy," Colloque de Liège (December).

Delpech, F.; Laville, H.; and Rigaud, J.-P.
in press Chronologie et environnement climatique du Paléolithique supérieur dans le Sud-Ouest de la France. *Actes des Travaux de la Commission 10 de l'UISPP: Réunion de Leone (Espagne)* (March 1983).

Delpech, F., and LeGall, O.
1983 La faune magdalénienne de la grotte des Eglises (Ussat, Ariège). *BSPA* 38:91-118.

Delpech, F., and Prat, F.
1980 Les grands mammifères pléistocènes du Sud-Ouest de la France. Pp. 268-297 in *Problèmes de stratigraphie quaternaire en France et dans les pays limitrophes*, ed. J. Chaline. *BAFEQ* Supplément n.s. 1. Dijon: AFEQ.

Delporte, H.
1968 L'abri du Facteur à Tursac (Dordogne). *GP* 11:1-112.

1972	L'Aurignacien et le "Bayacien" de la Gravette. *BSPF* 69:337-346.
1978	Etat actuel de l'analyse de l'Aurignacien de la Ferrassie. *BSPF* 75:65.
1984	(ed.) *Le grand abri de la Ferrassie: fouilles 1968-1973*. EQ 7. Paris: LPHP.

Delporte, H., and Tuffreau, A.
1973	Les industries du Périgordien supérieur de la Ferrassie. *Quartär* 23-24:93-123.
1984	Les industries du Périgordien V et de la Ferrassie. Pp. 235-247 in *Le grand abri de la Ferrassie: fouilles 1968-1973*, ed. H. Delporte. EQ 7. Paris: LPHP.

Demars, P.-Y.
1982	Origine proche ou lointaine des silex au Paléolithique supérieur: une réponse à Annie Masson. *BSPF* 79:266-267.
1985	La signification de l'Aurignacien V dans l'évolution des cultures lithiques au Paléolithique supérieur en France. Pp. 328-336 in *La signification culturelle des industries lithiques*, ed. M. Otte. Actes du Colloque de Liège (October 1984). SPB 4; BAR International Series 239. Oxford: BAR.

Dennell, R.
1983	*European Economic Prehistory*. London: Academic Press.

Dibble, H. L.
1983	Variability and Change in the Middle Paleolithic of Western Europe and the Near East. Pp. 53-71 in *The Mousterian Legacy*, ed. E. Trinkaus. BAR International Series 164. Oxford: BAR.
1984a	Interpreting Typological Variation of Middle Paleolithic Scrapers: Function, Style, or Sequence of Reduction? *JFA* 11:431-436.
1984b	The Mousterian Industry from Bisitun Cave (Iran). *Paléorient* 10:23-34.
1985a	Raw Material Variability in Levallois Flake Manufacture. *CA* 26:391-393.
1985b	Technological Aspects of Flake Variation: A Comparison of Experimental and Prehistoric Flake Production. *American Archeology* 5:236-240.
1987a	Comparaisons des séquences de réduction des outils moustériens de la France et du Proche-Orient. *L'Anthropologie* 19:189-196.
1987b	Direct Measurement of Artifact Provenience with an Electronic Theodolite. *JFA* 14:249-254.
1987c	The Interpretation of Middle Paleolithic Scraper Morphology. *AmAnt* 52:109-117.
1987d	Reduction Sequences in the Manufacture of Mousterian Implements of France. Pp. 33-44 in *The Pleistocene Old World: Regional Perspectives*, ed. O. Soffer. New York: Plenum Press.

Dibble, H. L., and Whittaker, J. C.
1981	New Experimental Evidence on the Relation between Percussion Flaking and Flake Variation. *JAS* 6:283-296.

Djindjian, F.
1980	Les faciès chronologiques aurignaciens et périgordiens à la Ferrassie (Dordogne). *Dossiers de l'archéologie* 42:70-74.

Dobosi, V.
1987	Discontinuity in the Paleolithic of Hungary. Paper presented at symposium, "Rhin et Danube au Paléolithique supérieur et final," UISPP Congress (Mainz, September).

Dodonov, A. E., and Ranov, V. A.
1977	Stupeni v Kammennyy Vek. *Znaniye-Sila* 601:20-23.
1984	Antropogen Sredney Aziy: Stratigrafiya, Korrelyatsiya, Paleolit. Pp. 67-81 in *Chetvertichnaya Geologiya i Geomorfologiya, 27-i, Mezhdunarodnii Geologicheskiy Kongress*. Moscow: Nauka.

Drozdowski, E.
1980	Chronostratigraphy of the Vistulian Glaciation on the Lower Vistula River. *Quaternary Studies in Poland* 2:13-20.

Dunnell, R. C.
1980	Evolutionary Theory and Archaeology. Pp. 35-99 in *Advances in Archaeological Method and Theory*, Vol. 3, ed. M. B. Schiffer. New York: Academic Press.

Ericson, J. E., and Purdy, B. A.
1984	*Prehistoric Quarries and Lithic Production*. New Directions in Archaeology. Cambridge: Cambridge University Press.

Farrand, W. R.
1975a	Analysis of the Abri Pataud Sediments. Pp. 27-68 in *Excavation of the Abri Pataud, Les Eyzies (Dordogne)*, ed. H. L. Movius. ASPR Bulletin 30. Cambridge, MA: Peabody Museum Press.
1975b	Sediment Analysis of a Prehistoric Rockshelter: The Abri Pataud. *QR* 5:1-26.
1981	Pluvial Climates and Frost Action during the Last Glacial Cycle in the Eastern Mediterranean: Evidence from Archaeological Sites. Pp. 393-410 in *Quaternary*

	Palaeoclimate, ed. W. C. Mahaney. Norwich, Eng.: Geoabstracts Ltd.
1982	Environmental Conditions during the Lower/Middle Paleolithic Transition in the Near East and the Balkans. Pp. 105-108 in *The Transition from Lower to Middle Palaeolithic and the Origin of Modern Man*, ed. A. Ronen. BAR International Series 151. Oxford: BAR.
in prep.	Sedimentology of the Abri Pataud. In a monograph on the Abri Pataud excavations, ed. H. M. Bricker, to be pub. in Bordeaux.

Faulkner, A.
1972 Mechanical Principles of Flintworking. Ph.D. dissertation, Washington State University. Ann Arbor: University Microfilms.

Fedoroff, N., and Goldsberg, P.
1982 Comparative Micromorphology of Two Late Pleistocene Paleosols. *Catena* 9:227-251.

Ferrier, J.
1938 *La préhistoire en Gironde*. Le Mans: Monnoyer.

Ferring, C. R.
1976 Sde Divshon: An Upper Paleolithic Site on the Divshon Plain. Pp. 199-226 in *Prehistory and Paleoenvironments in the Central Negev, Israel*, Vol. 1, ed. A. E. Marks. Dallas: SMU Press.
1977 The Late Upper Paleolithic Site of Ein Aqev East. Pp. 81-118 in *Prehistory and Paleoenvironments in the Central Negev, Israel*, Vol. 2, ed. A. E. Marks. Dallas: Department of Anthropology, SMU.
1980 Technological Variability and Change in the Late Paleolithic of the Negev. Ph.D. dissertation, SMU. Ann Arbor: University Microfilms.

Feustel, R.
1973 *Technik der Steinzeit: Archäolithikum, Mesolithikum*. Veröffentlichungen des Museums für Ur- und Frühgeschichte Thüringens 4. Weimar: Hermann Böhlau.
1986 *Mündliche Mitteilung zur Neubearbeitung des Schädels von Weimar durch Vlček*. Cologne: Herbst.

Fish, P. R.
1979 *The Interpretive Potential of Mousterian Debitage*. ASU Anthropological Research Papers 16. Tempe: ASU.

Flenniken, J. J.
1984 The Past, Present and Future of Flintknapping: An Anthropological Perspective. *ARA* 13:187-203.
1985 Stone Tool Reduction Technologies as Cultural Markers. Pp. 265-276 in *Stone Tool Analysis: Essays in Honor of Don E. Crabtree*, eds. M. G. Plew, J. C. Woods, and M. G. Pavesic. Albuquerque: University of New Mexico Press.

Flenniken, J., and Raymond, A.
1986 Replication Experimentation and Technological Analysis. *AmAnt* 51:603-614.

Floss, H.
1985 *Das Magdalénien von Andernach: Rohmaterial und Bearbeitungstechnik der Steinartefakte*. Magisterarbeit Köln. Cologne: Universität Köln.

Floss, H., and Terberger, T.
1986 Das Magdalénien von Andernach: Ausgewählte Beispiele von Zusammensetzungen der Steinartefakte. *AK* 16:245-250.

Fosse, G.; Cliquet, D.; and Vilgrain, G.
1984 Le Moustérien du Nord-Cotentin (département de la Manche): premiers résultats de trois fouilles en cours. Pré-tirages du Colloque de Lille (September).

Franken, E., and Veil, S.
1983 *Die Steinartefakte von Gönnersdorf*. Der Magdalénien-Fundplatz Gönnersdorf 7. Wiesbaden: Franz Steiner.

Freeman, L. G.
1973 The Significance of Mammalian Faunas from Paleolithic Occupations in Cantabrian Spain. *AmAnt* 38:3-44.
1975a Acheulean Sites and Stratigraphy in Iberia and the Maghreb. Pp. 661-743 in *After the Australopithecenes*, eds. K. Butzer and G. Isaac. The Hague: Mouton.
1975b By Their Works You Shall Know Them: Cultural Development in the Paleolithic. Pp. 234-361 in *Hominisation und Verhalten*, eds. G. Kurth and I. Eibl-Eibesfeld. Stuttgart: Gustav Fischer.
1980 The Development of Human Culture. Pp. 79-86 in *The Cambridge Encyclopedia of Archaeology*, ed. A. Sherratt. New York: Crown/Cambridge University Press.
1981 The Fat of the Land: Notes on Paleolithic Diet in Iberia. Pp. 104-165 in *Omnivorous Primates*, eds. R. S. O. Harding and G. Teleki. New York: Columbia University Press.
1982 Review of *Rock Shelters of the Perigord*, by H. Laville, J.-P. Rigaud, and J. Sackett. *AA* 84:440-442.

Freeman, L. G., and González Echegaray, J.
1981a El Juyo: A 14,000 Year Old Sanctuary from Northern Spain. *History of Religions* 21:1-19.
1981b La máscara del santuario de la cueva del Juyo. Pp. 251-265 in *Altamira Symposium*, ed. M. Almagro. Madrid: Ministry of Culture.
1983 Magdalenian Mobile Art from El Juyo (Cantabria). *Ars Praehistorica* 1:161-167.
1984 Magdalenian Structures and Sanctuary from the Cave of El Juyo (Igollo, Cantabria, Spain). Pp. 39-49 in *Upper Paleolithic Settlement Patterns in Europe*, eds. H. Berke, J. Hahn, and C.-J. Kind. Tübingen: Institut für Urgeschichte, Universität zu Tübingen.
in press Possible Dice or Divining Pieces from the Spanish Magdalenian. *Miscellanea of the IPI*.

Freeman, L. G.; Klein, R.; and González Echegaray, J.
1983 A Stone Age Sanctuary. *Natural History* 92:46-53.

Frenzel, B.
1980 Klima der letzten Eiszeit und der Nacheiszeit in Europa. *Veröffentlichungen der Joachim Jungius Gesellschaft* 44:9-46.

Fruth, H.-J.
1979 Ein spätpaläolithischer Fundplatz bei Mühlheim-Dietesheim, Kreis Offenbach. *AK* 9:261-266.

Gábori, M.
1964 New Data on Palaeolithic Finds in Mongolia. *Asian Perspectives* 7:105-112.
1976a *Les civilisations du Paléolithique moyen entre les Alpes et l'Oural: esquisse historique*. Budapest: Akadémiai Kiadó.
1976b Die neuesten Paläolithforschungen in Mittelasien. Pp. 68-85 in *Festschrift für Richard Pittioni zum siebzigsten Geburtstag*. Vienna: Franz Deuticke.
1979 Type of Industry and Ecology. *AAASH* 31:239-248.
1984 Le Paléolithique moyen en Europe orientale: synthèse et perspectives. Pp. 233-257 in *Scripta Praehistorica: Francisco Jorda, Oblata*. Salamanca: Ediciones Universidad de Salamanca.

Gábori, M., and Gábori, V.
1957 Etudes archéologiques et stratigraphiques dans les stations de loess paléolithiques de Hongrie. *AAASH* 8:3-73.

Gábori-Csánk, V.
1983 La grotte Remete "Felsö" et le "Szelétien de Transdanubie." *AAASH* 35:249-285.

Gamble, C. S.
1986 *The Palaeolithic Settlement of Europe*. Cambridge: Cambridge University Press.
1987 Man the Shoveler: Alternative Models for Middle Pleistocene Colonization and Occupation in Northern Latitudes. Pp. 81-98 in *The Pleistocene Old World: Regional Perspectives*, ed. O. Soffer. New York: Plenum Press.

Garrod, D.
1953 The Relations between South-west Asia and Europe in the Later Paleolithic Age. *Journal of World History* 1:13-38.
1954 Excavations at the Mugharet el-Kebara, Mount Carmel, 1931: The Aurignacian Industries. *PPS* 22:155-192.

Gaussen, J.
1964 *La grotte ornée de Gabillou, près Mussidan (Dordogne)*. MIPUB 3. Bordeaux: Delmas.
1977 Le peuplement magdalénien dans la vallée de l'Isle (secteur Mussidan - St.-Astier): forme des habitats et choix des emplacements. Pp. 425-434 in *La fin des temps glaciaires en Europe*, ed. D. de Sonneville-Bordes. Colloques Internationaux du CNRS 271. Paris: CNRS.
1980 *Le Paléolithique supérieur de plein air en Périgord: secteur Mussidan - Saint Astier, moyenne vallée de l'Isle*. GP Supplément 14. Paris: CNRS.
1982 Le Paléolithique supérieur de plein air dans la moyenne vallée de l'Isle en Périgord: l'aménagement des sols d'habitat. Pp. 180-191 in *Les habitats du Paléolithique supérieur*, Vol. 1, ed. J. Combier. Paris: CNRS.
1986 La Croix de Fer: patines et âges. *BSPF* 83:7-9.

Gaussen, J., and Moissat, J.-C.
1985 Lacaud: habitat magdalénien ancien de plein air (vallée de l'Isle en Périgord). *BSPF* 82:350-376.

Gaussen, J., and Sackett, R.
1984 La pierre gravée de Solvieux. *L'Anthropologie* 88:655-660.

Gaussen, J., and Texier, J.-P.
1974 Le Périgordien ancien de La-Côte et son contexte géologique. *L'Anthropologie* 78:499-528.

Geneste, J.-M.
1982 Les Eyzies de Tayac: abri Vignaud. In Informations archéologiques: circonscription d'Aquitaine, ed. J.-P. Rigaud. *GP* 25:415-416.

1985 Analyse lithique des industries moustériennes du Périgord: une approche technologique du comportement des groupes humains au Paléolithique moyen. Thesis, Université de Bordeaux.

1986 Zonation économique du milieu et organisation spatiale des vestiges dans sites moustériens du Sud-Ouest de la France. Pp. 170-175 in *L'homme de Néandertal* (preprints), ed. M. Otte. Liège: Université de Liège.

Gilead, I.
1977 Lagama X. Pp. 102-114 in *Prehistoric Investigations in Gebel Maghara, Northern Sinai*, eds. O. Bar-Yosef and J. Phillips. Qedem 7. Jerusalem: Institute of Archaeology, Hebrew University.
1981 Upper Paleolithic Tool Assemblages from the Negev and Sinai. Pp. 331-342 in *Préhistoire du Levant*, eds. J. Cauvin and P. Sanlaville. Colloques Internationaux du CNRS 598. Paris: CNRS.
1986 Is the Term "Epipaleolithic" Relevant to Levantine Prehistory? *CA* 25:227-228.

Gilead, I., and Grigson, C.
1984 Far'ah II: A Middle Paleolithic Open-Air Site in the Northern Negev, Israel. *PPS* 50:71-97.

Girard, C.
1974 Les industries moustériennes de la grotte de l'Hyène à Arcy-sur-Cure (Yonne). Thesis, Université de Paris.
1978 *Les industries moustériennes de la grotte de l'Hyène à Arcy-sur-Cure (Yonne)*. GP Supplément 11. Paris: CNRS.

Girard, C., and David, F.
1982 A propos de la chasse spécialisée au Paléolithique moyen: l'exemple de Mauran (Haute-Garonne). *BSPF* 79:11-12.

Girard-Farizy, C.
1982 Problèmes méthodologiques liés à la fouille d'un habitat de plein air du Paléolithique moyen. Pp. 192-193 in *Les habitats du Paléolithique supérieur*, Vol. 1, ed. J. Combier. Paris: CNRS.

Gladilin, V. N., and Ranov, V. A.
1986 Ot Pamira do Karpat. *Znaniye-Sila* 704: 29-31.

Goldberg, P.
1976 Upper Pleistocene Geology of the Avdat/Aqev Area. Pp. 25-55 in *Prehistory and Paleoenvironments of the Central Negev, Israel*, Vol. 1, ed. A. E. Marks. Dallas: SMU Press.
1983 The Geology of Boker Tachtit, Boker, and Their Surroundings. Pp. 39-62 in *Prehistory and Paleoenvironments in the Central Negev, Israel*, Vol. 3, ed. A. E. Marks. Dallas: Department of Anthropology, SMU.

Goldberg, P., and Brimer, B.
1983 Late Pleistocene Geomorphic Surfaces and Environmental History of Avdat/Havarim Area, Nahal Zin. Pp. 1-14 in *Prehistory and Paleoenvironments in the Central Negev, Israel*, Vol. 3, ed. A. E. Marks. Dallas: Department of Anthropology, SMU.

González Echegaray, J., and Barandiarán, I., eds.
1981 *El Paleolítico superior de la cueva de Rascaño (Santander)*. Monografía 3. Santander: CIMA.

González Echegaray, J., and Freeman, L. G.
1978 *Vida y muerte en Cueva Morín*. Santander: Institución Cultural de Cantabria.

González Echegaray, J.; Freeman, L. G.; Barandiarán, I.; Apellaniz, J. M.; Butzer, K. W.; Fuentes Vidarte, C.; Madariaga, B.; González Morales, J. A.; and Leroi-Gourhan, A.
1980 *El yacimiento de la cueva de "El Pendo" (excavaciones 1953-57)*. BPH 17. Madrid: Instituto Español de Prehistoria/Universidad de Madrid.

González Sainz, C., and González Morales, M.
1986 *La prehistoria en Cantabria*. Santander: Ediciones Tantin.

Gordon, B.
1986 Of Men and Reindeer Herds in French Magdalenian Prehistory. In *The Pleistocene Perspective*, Vol. 1, comps. M. Day and R. Folley. Preprint of Proceedings of the World Archaeological Congress (Southampton, September). London: Allen & Unwin.

Goring-Morris, N.
1985 Terminal Pleistocene Hunter/Gatherers in the Negev and Sinai. Ph.D. dissertation, Hebrew University.

Grahmann, R., and Müller-Beck, H.
1967 *Urgeschichte der Menschheit*. Stuttgart: Kohlhammer.

Gralyuk, B.
1979 Pečine, Klašnice, Banja Luka: Paleolitska Stanica. *Arheološki Pregled* 21:9-14.

Grayson, D. K.
1984 *Quantitative Zooarchaeology*. New York: Academic Press.

1985 Review of *Faunal Remains from the Klasies River Mouth*, by L. R. Binford. *Science* 228: 869-870.

Grootes, P. M.
1977 Thermal Diffusion Isotopic Enrichment and Radiocarbon Dating beyond 50,000 Years BP. Dissertation, Rijksuniversiteit Groningen.

Gubser, N. J.
1965 *The Nunamiut Eskimos: Hunters of Caribou.* New Haven: Yale University Press.

Guichard, G.
1976 Les civilisations du Paléolithique inférieur en Périgord. Pp. 909-928 in *La préhistoire française*, ed. H. de Lumley. Paris: CNRS.

Guilaine, J., et al.
1985 La Balma Margineda: aux origines du peuple andorran; [etc.]. *Histoire et archéologie* 96:10-33.

Gupta, S. P.
1979 *Archaeology of Soviet Central Asia and the Iranian Borderlands*. 2 vols. Delhi: B. R. Publishing Company.

Haesaerts, P.
1984 Le Quaternaire: problèmes, méthodologie et cadre stratigraphique. Pp. 17-25 in *Peuples chasseurs de la Belgique préhistorique dans leur cadre naturel*, eds. D. Cahen and P. Haesaerts. Brussels: Institut Royal des Sciences Naturelles de Belgique.

Haesaerts, P. and Sirakova, S.
1979 Le Paléolithique moyen à pointes foliacées de Mousselievo, Bulgarie. Pp. 35-64 in *The Middle and Early Upper Palaeolithic in the Balkans*, ed. J. Kozlowski. Krakow: Nakladem Uniwersytetu Jagiellonskiego.

Hahn, J.
1969 Gravettien-Freilandstationen im Rheinland: Mainz-Linsenberg, Koblenz-Metternich und Rhens. *BJ* 169:44-87.
1977 *Aurignacien: das ältere Jungpaläolithikum in Mittel- und Osteuropa*. Fundamenta A9. Cologne: Hermann Böhlau.
1983 Eiszeitliche Jäger zwischen 35000 und 15000 Jahren vor heute. Pp. 273-330 in *Urgeschichte in Baden-Württemberg*, ed. H. Müller-Beck. Stuttgart: Konrad Theiss.

Harrold, R.
1980 A Comparative Analysis of Eurasian Palaeolithic Burials. *WA* 12:195-211.

Heinzelin de Braucourt, J. de
1962 Manuel de typologie des industries lithiques. *Sciences* (Brussels) 14:1-72.

Hemingway, M. F.
1980 *The Initial Magdalenian in France*. 2 vols. BAR International Series 90. Oxford: BAR.

Hietala, H.
1983 Boker Tachtit: Intralevel and Interlevel Spatial Analysis. Pp. 217-282 in *Prehistory and Paleoenvironments in the Central Negev, Israel*, Vol. 3, ed. A. E. Marks. Dallas: Department of Anthropology, SMU.
1984 Variations on a Categorical Data Theme: Local and Global Considerations with Near-Eastern Paleolithic Applications. Pp. 44-53 in *Intrasite Spatial Analysis in Archaeology*, ed. H. Hietala. Cambridge: Cambridge University Press.

Hietala, H., and Stevens, D.
1977 Spatial Analysis: Multiple Procedures in Pattern Recognition Studies. *AmAnt* 42: 539-559.

Hofman, J. L.
1981 The Refitting of Chipped-Stone Artifacts as an Analytical and Interpretive Tool. *CA* 22:691-693.

Honea, K.
1983 *Lithic Technology: An International Annotated Bibliography 1725-1980*. *LT* Special Publications 2. San Antonio, TX: Center for Archaeological Research.
1986 Dating and Periodization: Strategies in the Romanian Middle and Upper Paleolithic. In *The Pleistocene Perspective*, Vol. 1, comps. M. Day and R. Folley. Preprint of Proceedings of the World Archaeological Congress (Southampton, September). London: Allen & Unwin.

Horowitz, A.
1983 Boker Tachtit and Boker: The Pollen Record. Pp. 63-68 in *Prehistory and Paleoenvironments in the Central Negev, Israel*, Vol. 3, ed. A. E. Marks. Dallas: Department of Anthropology, SMU.

Hours, F., and Karlin, C.
1982 L'organisation de l'espace dans la couche XII de la grotte du renne à Arcy-sur-Cure (Moustérien à denticulés). P. 93 in *Les habitats du Paléolithique supérieur*, Vol. 1, ed. J. Combier. Paris: CNRS.

Inizian, M. L.; Roche, H.; and Texier, J.-P.
1975-76 Avantages d'un traitement thermique pour la taille des roches siliceuses. *Quaternaria* 19:1-18.

Isaac, G. L.
1969　Studies of Early Culture in East Africa. *WA* 1:1-28.
1975　Stratigraphy and Patterns of Cultural Change in the Middle Pleistocene. *CA* 15:508-514.

Ivanova, I. K.
1969　Etude géologique des gisements paléolithiques de l'URSS. *L'Anthropologie* 73:5-48.

Ivanova, S.
1979　Cultural Differentiation in the Middle Paleolithic on the Balkan Peninsula. Pp. 13-33 in *The Middle and Early Upper Paleolithic in the Balkans*, ed. J. Kozlowski. Krakow: Nakladem Uniwersytetu Jagiellonskiego.

Jacobsen, T. W.
1973a　Excavation in the Franchthi Cave, 1969-1971, Part I. *Hesperia* 42:45-88.
1973b　Excavation in the Franchthi Cave, 1969-1971, Part II. *Hesperia* 42:253-283.
1976　17,000 Years of Greek Prehistory. *SciAm* 234:76-87.

Janssens, P., and González Echegaray, J.
1958　*Memoria de las excavaciones de la cueva del Juyo (1955-1956)*. Santander: Patronato de las Cuevas Prehistóricas.

Jelinek, A. J.
1975　A Preliminary Report on Some Lower and Middle Paleolithic Industries from the Tabun Cave, Mount Carmel (Israel). Pp. 279-316 in *Problems in Prehistory*, eds. F. Wendorf and A. E. Marks. Dallas: SMU Press.
1976　Form, Function, and Style in Lithic Analysis. Pp. 19-33 in *Cultural Change and Continuity: Essays in Honor of James Bennett Griffin*, ed. C. E. Cleland. New York: Academic Press.
1977　The Lower Paleolithic: Current Evidence and Interpretations. *ARA* 6:11-32.
1981　The Middle Paleolithic of the Levant: Synthesis. Pp. 299-302 in *Préhistoire du Levant*, eds. J. Cauvin and P. Sanlaville. Paris: CNRS.
1982a　The Middle Paleolithic in the Southern Levant, with Comments on the Appearance of Modern *Homo sapiens*. Pp. 57-101 in *The Transition from the Lower to Middle Palaeolithic and the Origin of Modern Man*, ed. A. Ronen. BAR International Series 151. Oxford: BAR.
1982b　The Tabun Cave and Paleolithic Man in the Levant. *Science* 216:1369-1375.
1984a　Mousterian Variability and Reduction Intensity: A Comparison of Levantine and Perigordian Industries. Paper presented at 49th Annual Meeting of the SAA (Portland, OR, April).
1984b　New Data on the Middle Pleistocene of France. *QRA* 5:1.

Jelinek, A. J.; Debénath, A.; and Dibble, H. L.
1986　A Preliminary Report on Evidence Related to the Interpretation of Economic and Social Activities of Neanderthals at the Site of La Quina (Charente), France. Paper presented at "L'homme de Néandertal: centenaire de la découverte de l'homme de Spy," Colloque de Liège (December).

Jochim, M. A.
1976　*Hunter-Gatherer Subsistence and Settlement: A Predictive Model*. New York: Academic Press.
1979　Breaking Down the System: Recent Ecological Approaches in Archaeology. Pp. 77-119 in *Advances in Archaeological Method and Theory*, ed. M. B. Schiffer. New York: Academic Press.
1981　*Strategies for Survival: Cultural Behavior in an Ecological Context*. New York: Academic Press.
1983　Palaeolithic Cave Art in Ecological Perspective. Pp. 212-219 in *Hunter-Gatherer Economy in Prehistory*, ed. G. Bailey. Cambridge: Cambridge University Press.

Jones, M.; Marks, A. E.; and Kaufman, D.
1983　Boker: The Artifacts. Pp. 283-329 in *Prehistory and Paleoenvironments in the Central Negev, Israel*, Vol. 3, ed. A. E. Marks. Dallas: Department of Anthropology, SMU.

Julien, M.
1982　*Les harpons magdaléniens*. GP Supplément 17. Paris: CNRS.

Kantman, S.
1970a　Esquisse d'un procédé analytique pour l'étude macrographique des "encoches." *Quaternaria* 13:269-280.
1970b　Essai d'une méthode d'étude des "denticulés" moustériens par discrimination des variables morpho-fonctionnelles. *Quaternaria* 13:281-294.
1970c　"Raclettes moustériennes": une étude expérimentale sur la distinction de retouche intentionnelle et les modifications du tranchant par utilisation. *Quaternaria* 13:295-304.

Keeley, L. H.
1974 Technique and Methodology in Microwear Studies: A Critical Review. *WA* 5:323-336.
1975 Microwear Flint: Some Experimental Results. *Nederlande geologische Vereriging, No. 3: 7ème Symposium International du Silex*: 49-51.
1977 The Functions of Paleolithic Flint Tools. *SciAm* 237(5):108-126.
1980 (ed.) *Experimental Determination of Stone Tool Uses: A Microwear Analysis*. Chicago: University of Chicago Press.
1981 Reply to Holley and Del Bene. *JAS* 8:348-352.
1982a Hafting and Retooling: Effects on the Archaeological Record. *AmAnt* 47:798-809.
1982b Les villages d'hiver des chasseurs-ceuilleurs: pour une alternative aux modèles explicatifs courants des comportements socio-économiques des Magdaléniens. Pp. 201-210 in *Les habitats du Paléolithique supérieur*, Vol. 1, ed. J. Combier. Paris: CNRS.

Kelley, H.
1949 Prise de date. *BSPF* 46:405.
1954 Contribution à l'étude de la technique de la taille levalloisienne. *BSPF* 51:149-169.

Kervazo, B.
1973 Recherches sur les formations superficielles en Périgord Noir. Thesis, Université de Bordeaux.

Kervazo, B., and Laville, H.
in press Etude stratigraphique et analyse physico-chimique des dépôts de la grotte Vaufrey. In *La grotte XV dite Grotte Vaufrey, à Cenac-et-Saint-Julien (Dordogne)*, ed. J.-P. Rigaud. MSPF.

Ketraru, N. A.
1973 *Pamiatniki Epokh Paleolita i Mezolita*. Kishinev: Stiintsa.

Kintigh, K. W.
1984 Measuring Archaeological Diversity by Comparison with Simulated Assemblages. *AmAnt* 49:44-54.

Klapchuk, M. N.
1976 Pozdneashel'skoye Mestonakhozhdeniye Zhaman-Aybat 4 v Tsentral'nom Kazakhstane (Le site acheuléen tardif de Jaman Aïbat 4 [région centrale du Kazakhstan]). *Sovetskaya Arkheologiya* no. 3:176-190.

Klein, R. G.
1969 The Mousterian of European Russia. *PPS* 35:77-111.
1975 Middle Stone Age Man-Animal Relationships in Southern Africa: Evidence from Die Kelders and Klasies River Mouth. *Science* 190:265-267.
1976 The Mammalian Fauna of the Klasies River Mouth Sites, Southern Cape Province, South Africa. *SAAB* 31:75-98.
1980 Later Pleistocene Hunters. Pp. 87-95 in *The Cambridge Encyclopedia of Archaeology*, ed. A. Sherratt. New York: Crown/Cambridge University Press.
1982 Review of *Rock Shelters of the Perigord*, by H. Laville, J.-P. Rigaud, and J. Sackett. *JAS* 9:307-315.
1986 Review of *Faunal Remains from the Klasies River Mouth*, by L. R. Binford. *AA* 88:494-495.

Klein, R. G.; Allwarden, K.; and Wolf, C.
1983 The Calculation and Interpretation of Ungulate Age Profiles from Dental Crown Heights. Pp. 47-57 in *Hunter-Gatherer Economy in Prehistory*, ed. G. Bailey. Cambridge: Cambridge University Press.

Klein, R. G., and Cruz-Uribe, K.
1984 *The Analysis of Animal Bones from Archaeological Sites*. Chicago: University of Chicago Press.

Klein, R. G.; Wolf, C.; Freeman, L.; and Allwarden, K.
1981 The Use of Dental Crown Heights for Constructing Age Profiles of Red Deer and Similar Species in Archaeological Samples. *JAS* 8:1-31.

Koenigswald, W. von; Müller-Beck, H.; and Pressmar, E.
1974 *Die Archäologie und Paläontologie der Weinberghöhlen bei Mauern (Bayern): Grabungen 1937-1967*. AV 3. Tübingen: Institut für Urgeschichte, Universität zu Tübingen.

Kolosov, I. G.
1978 *Spetsifitcheskiye Typy Orudiy Akkayskoy Stoyanki Musterskoy Kultuy v Krymu*. Orudia Kamennogo Veka. Kiev: Naukova Dumka.

Kopper, J. S.
1981 Palaeolithic Tools: Some Design Considerations. *Expedition* 24:49.

Kozlowski, J. K.
1982 (ed.) *Excavations in the Bacho Kiro Cave (Bulgaria)*. Warsaw/Krakow: Panstwowe Wydawnictwo Naukowe.
1984 Earliest Upper Palaeolithic Habitation Structures from Bacho Kiro Cave. Pp. 109-129 in *Jungpaläolithische Siedlungsstrukturen in Europa*, eds. H. Berke, J. Hahn, and

C.-J. Kind. UM 6. Tübingen: Archaeologica Venatoria.

1985 Sur la contemporanéité des différents faciès du Magdalénien. *Jahrbuch des Bernischen Historischen Museums* 63-64:211-216.

1986 The Gravettian in Central and Eastern Europe. Pp. 131-199 in *Advances in World Archaeology*, Vol. 5, eds. F. Wendorf and A. E. Close. New York: Academic Press.

Kozlowski, J. K., and Kozlowski, S. K.

1979 *Upper Palaeolithic and Mesolithic in Europe: Taxonomy and Palaeohistory*. Prace Komisji Archeologicznej 18. Wroclaw: Polska Akademia Nauk.

1981 Paléohistoire de la grande plaine européenne. *Archaeologia Interregionalis* 1:143-162.

Kozlowski, J. K.; Laville, H.; and Sirakov, S.

in press La grotte Temnata près de Karlukovo: une importante séquence géologique et archéologique aux Balkans. *L'Anthropologie*.

Kozlowski, J. K.; Manecki, A.; Rydlewski, J.; Valde-Nowak, P.; and Wrzak, J.

1981 Mineralogico-Geochemical Characteristics of Radiolarites Used in the Stone Age in Poland and Slovakia. *AAC* 21:172-210.

Kukla, G.

1978 The Classical European Glacial Stages: Correlation with Deep-Sea Sediments. *Transactions of the Nebraska Academy of Sciences* 6:57-93.

Labeyrie, J.

1984 Le cadre paléoclimatique depuis 140,000 ans. *L'Anthropologie* 88:19-48.

Lacorre, F.

1960 *La Gravette: le Gravétien et le Bayacien*. Laval: Barnéoud.

Lanzinger, M.

1986 Risultati preliminari delle ricerche nel sito aurignaziano del Campon di Monte Avena (1430 m) nelle Alpi feltrine. *RSP* 34:287-299.

in press Mining and Chipping-Stone Activity in the Mount Avena Aurignacian Open-Air Site (East-Alps): Preliminary Report. In *International Conference on Flint Mining and Raw Material Identification in the Carpathian Basin* (Sümeg, 1986). Budapest: Institute of Geology.

Laquay, G.

1981 Recherches sur les faunes du Würm I en Périgord. Thesis, Université de Bordeaux.

Larson, P., and Marks, A. E.

1977 Two Upper Paleolithic Sites in the Har Harif. Pp. 173-189 in *Prehistory and Paleoenvironments in the Central Negev, Israel*, Vol. 2, ed. A. E. Marks. Dallas: Department of Anthropology, SMU.

Lartet, E., and Christy, H.

1864 Cavernes du Périgord. *Revue archéologique* 1:233-267.

Lautensach, H.

1967 *Geografía de España y Portugal*. Barcelona: Vicens Vives.

Laville, H.

1964 Recherches sédimentologiques sur la paléoclimatologie du Würmien récent en Périgord. *L'Anthropologie* 68:1-48, 219-252.

1969a L'interstade Würm II—Würm III et la position chronologique du Paléolithique supérieur ancien en Périgord. *CRASP* 269D:10-12.

1969b Paléoclimatologie du Würm ancien en Périgord: données sédimentologiques. *Proceedings of the 8th INQUA Congress* 1:513-518.

1971 Sur la contemporanéité du Périgordien et de l'Aurignacien: la contribution du géologue. *BSPF* 68:171-174.

1973a Climatologie et chronologie du Paléolithique en Périgord: étude sédimentologique des dépôts en grottes et sous abris. Thesis, Université de Bordeaux.

1973b The Relative Position of Mousterian Industries in the Climatic Chronology of the Early Würm in the Perigord. *WA* 4:323-329.

1975 *Climatologie et chronologie du Paléolithique en Périgord: étude sédimentologique de dépôts en grottes et sous abris*. EQ 4. Marseille: LPHP.

1979 Chronostratigraphie des dépôts de la fin du Würm en Périgord. Pp. 159-167 in *La fin des temps glaciaires en Europe*, ed. D. de Sonneville-Bordes. Colloques Internationaux du CNRS 271. Paris: CNRS.

1982 On the Transition from "Lower" to "Middle" Palaeolithic in South West France. Pp. 131-135 in *The Transition from Lower to Middle Palaeolithic and the Origin of Modern Man*, ed. A. Ronen. BAR International Series 151. Oxford: BAR.

Laville, H.; Delpech, F.; and Rigaud, J.-P.

1985 Sur la zonation pollinique du Pléistocène récent: les précisions du domaine aquitain. Pp. 245-257 in *Actes du Colloque sur Palynologie Archéologique*. Notes et Monographies Techniques du Centre de Recherche Archéologique 17. Paris: CNRS.

Laville, H.; Paquereau, M.-M.; and Bricker, H.
1985 Précisions sur l'évolution climatique de l'interstade würmien et du début du Würm récent: les dépôts du gisement castelperronien des Tambourets (Haute-Garonne) et leur contenu pollinique. *CRASP* 301: 1137-1140.

Laville, H.; Raynal, J.-P.; and Texier, J.-P.
1984 Interglaciaire . . . ou déjà glaciaire? *BSPF* 81:8-11.
1985a Le dernier interglaciaire et le cycle climatique würmien dans le Sud-Ouest et le Massif Central français. Paper presented at the Colloque de l'AFEQ, "Oscillations climatiques entre 125,000 ans et le maximum glaciaire" (Rennes, June).
1985b Signals, Thresholds and Rhythms during the Past 150 Ky: Examples from South-West and Massif Central of France. Paper presented at "Abrupt Climatic Change," NATO/NSF Workshop (Biviers, October).
1986 Le dernier interglaciaire et le cycle climatique würmien dans le Sud-Ouest et le Massif Central français. *BAFEQ* 25-26: 35-46.

Laville, H., and Rigaud, J.-P.
1973a L'abri inférieur du Moustier (Dordogne): précisions stratigraphiques et chronologiques. *CRASP* 276:3097-3100.
1973b The Perigordian V Industries in Perigord: Typological Variations, Stratigraphy and Relative Chronology. *WA* 4:330-338.

Laville, H.; Rigaud, J.-P.; and Sackett, J. R.
1980 *Rock Shelters of the Perigord: Geological Stratigraphy and Archaeological Succession.* New York: Academic Press.

Laville, H.; Rigaud, J.-P.; and Texier, J.-P.
1986 *Quaternaire et préhistoire en Périgord.* Livret-guide de l'excursion de l'AFEQ, 8-10 mai. Paris: AFEQ.

Laville, H., and Texier, J.-P.
1972 De la fin du Würm III au début du Würm IV: paléoclimatologie et implications chronostratigraphiques. *CRASP* 272D:329-332.

Laville, H., and Thibault, C.
1967 L'oscillation climatique contemporaine du Périgordien supérieur à burins de Noailles, dans le Sud-Ouest de la France. *CRASP* 264:2364-2366.

Laville, H., and Tuffreau, A.
1984 Les dépôts du grand abri de la Ferrassie: stratigraphie, signification climatique et chronologie. Pp. 25-50 in *Le grand abri de la Ferrassie*, by H. Delporte. EQ 7. Paris: LPHP.

Laville, H.; Turon, J.-L.; Texier, J.-P.; Raynal, J.-P.; Delpech, F.; Paquereau, M.-M.; Prat, F.; and Debénath, A.
1983 Histoire paléoclimatique de l'Aquitaine et du Golfe de Gascogne au Pléistocène supérieur depuis le dernier interglaciaire. Pp. 151-161 in *Paléoclimats: actes du Colloque de l'AGSO* (Bordeaux, May). CQ no. hors série; BIGBA 34. Paris: CNRS.

Lenoir, M.
1976 Etude typologique et technique des "pièces à retouche anormale" de la station de la Bertonne, commune de Peujard (Gironde). *BSPF* 73:43-47.
1983 Le Paléolithique des basses vallées de la Dordogne et de la Garonne. 2 vols. Thesis, Université de Bordeaux.
1986 Un mode d'obtention de la retouche "Quina" dans le Moustérien de Combe-Grenal (Domme, Dordogne). *Bulletin de la Société Anthropologique du Sud-Ouest* 21:153-160.
1987 Les pièces de la Bertonne, "fossile directeur" du Magdalénien ancien? *BSPF* 84: 167-171.

Leroi-Gourhan, A.
1956 La galerie moustérienne de la grotte du renne (Arcy-sur-Cure, Yonne). *Congrès préhistorique de France*: 1-16.
1961 Les fouilles d'Arcy-sur-Cure (Yonne). *GP* 4:3-16.
1963 Châtelperronien et Aurignacien dans le nord-est de la France. *Bulletin de la Société Méridionale de Spéléologie et de Préhistoire* 6-9: 75-84.
1966 *La préhistoire.* Paris: Presses Universitaires de France.
1968 Le petit racloir châtelperronien. Pp. 275-282 in *La préhistoire: problèmes et tendances*, ed. D. de Sonneville-Bordes. Paris: CNRS.
1972 Vocabulaire. Pp. 321-327 in *Fouilles de Pincevent*, eds. A. Leroi-Gourhan and M. Brézillon. Paris: CNRS.
1982 La grotte du renne à Arcy-sur-Cure. Pp. 235-240 in *Les habitats du Paléolithique supérieur*, Vol. 1, ed. J. Combier. Paris: CNRS.

Leroi-Gourhan, A., and Brézillon, M.
1966 L'habitation magdalénienne no. 1 de Pincevent près Montereau (Seine-et-Marne). *GP* 9:263-385.

1972 (eds.) *Fouilles de Pincevent: essai d'analyse ethnographique d'un habitat magdalénien (la section 36)*. GP Supplément 7. Paris: CNRS.

1983 (eds.) *Fouilles de Pincevent: essai d'analyse ethnographique d'un habitat magdalénien (la section 36)*. GP Supplément 7. Paris: CNRS. [repr. of 1972 ed.]

Leroi-Gourhan, Arl.
1977 Les climats, les plantes et les hommes: Quaternaire supérieur d'Europe occidentale. *Studia Geologica Polonica* 52:249-261.

Leroi-Gourhan, Arl., and Renault-Miskovsky, J.
1977 La palynologie appliquée à l'archéologie: méthodes, limites et résultats. Pp. 35-49 in *Approche écologique de l'homme fossile*, eds. H. Laville and J. Renault-Miskovsky. BAFEQ Supplément 47. Paris: Laboratoire de Géologie I, Université Pierre et Marie Curie.

Le Tensorer, J.-M.
1978 Le Moustérien type Quina et son évolution dans le sud de la France. *BSPF* 75:141-149.
1981 *Le Paléolithique de l'Agenais*. CQ 3. Paris: CNRS.
1986 L'homme de Néandertal et le mythe du culte de l'ours en Europe occidentale: état de la question. Paper presented at "L'homme de Néandertal: centenaire de la découverte de l'homme de Spy," Colloque de Liège (December).

Levêque, F., and Vandermeersch, B.
1980 Les découvertes des restes humaines dans un horizon castelperronien de Saint-Césaire (Charente-Maritime). *BSPF* 77:35.
1981 Le Néandertalien de Saint-Césaire. *La recherche* 12:242-244.

Lévi-Strauss, C.
1958 *Anthropologie structurale*. Paris: Plon.

Levine, M. A.
1979 Archaeozoological Analysis of Some Upper Pleistocene Horse Bone Assemblages in Western Europe. Ph.D. dissertation, Cambridge University.
1983 Mortality Models and the Interpretation of Horse Population Structure. Pp. 23-46 in *Hunter-Gatherer Economy in Prehistory*, ed. G. Bailey. Cambridge: Cambridge University Press.

Lewontin, R. C.
1974 *The Genetic Basis of Evolutionary Change*. New York: Columbia University Press.

Leysalles, G., and Noone, H. V. V.
1949 Le Pech Saint Sourd. *L'Anthropologie* 53:247-251.

Liubin, V. P.
1984 Pervonachal'noye Zaseleniye Sredney Azii. *Priroda* 1:90-93.

Löhr, H.
1974 Ein neuentdeckter Magdalénien-Fundplatz bei Alsdorf, Kreis Aachen-Land. *AK* 4:293-297.
1978a Abri "Katzensteine," Gemeinde Mechernich, Kreis Euskirchen. P. 137 in *Alt- und mittelsteinzeitliche Fundplätze des Rheinlandes*, ed. S. Veil. Cologne: Rheinland-Verlag.
1978b Barmen. P. 141 in *Alt- und mittelsteinzeitliche Fundplätze des Rheinlandes*, ed. S. Veil. Cologne: Rheinland-Verlag.
1978c Kinzweiler. P. 139 in *Alt- und mittelsteinzeitliche Fundplätze des Rheinlandes*, ed. S. Veil. Cologne: Rheinland-Verlag.
1978d Urbar. Pp. 131-132 in *Alt- und mittelsteinzeitliche Fundplätze des Rheinlandes*, ed. S. Veil. Cologne: Rheinland-Verlag.
1978e Vom Altpaläolithikum bis zum Mittelalter: die Grabungen des Jahres 1977 am Kartstein, Gemeinde Mechernich, Kreis Euskirchen. *Rheinische Landesmuseum Bonn, Sonderheft*: 40-46.
1979 Der Magdalénien-Fundplatz Alsdorf, Kreis Aachen-Land: ein Beitrag zur Kenntnis der funktionalen Variabilität jungpaläolithischer Stationen. Thesis, Universität Tübingen.

Löhr, H., and Brunnacker, K.
1974 Metternicher und Eltviller Tuffhorizonte im Würm-Löss am Mittel- und Niederrhein. *Notizblatt hessisches Landesamt für Bodenforschung* 102:168-190.

Loftus, J.
1982 Ein verzierter Pfeilschaftglätter von Fläche 64/74—73/78 des spätpaläolithischen Fundplatzes Niederbieber/Neuwieder Becken. *AK* 12:313-316.

Loftus, R.
1984 *Der spätpaläolithische Fundplatz Niederbieber, Fläche 33/32—38/39*. Magisterarbeit Köln. Cologne: Universität Köln.

Lucchita, B. K., and Ferguson, H. M.
1986 Antarctica: Measuring Glacier Velocity from Satellite Images. *Science* 234:1105-1108.

Lumley, H. de
1965 La grande révolution raciale et culturelle de l'Inter-Würmien II-III. *Cahiers ligures de préhistoire et d'archéologie* 14:133-135.
1969 *Le Paléolithique inférieur et moyen du Midi méditerranéen dans son cadre géologique*. Vol. 1: *Ligurie-Provence*. Paris: CNRS.

1972 *La grotte de l'Hortus (Valflaunès, Herault).* EQ 1. Marseille: LPHP.

McBurney, C. B.
1960 *The Stone Age of Northern Africa.* Harmondsworth: Pelican.
1975 Current Status of the Lower and Middle Palaeolithic of the Entire Region from the Levant through North Africa. Pp. 411-425 in *Problems in Prehistory*, eds. F. Wendorf and A. E. Marks. Dallas: SMU Press.

McCullough, M.
1971 Perigordian Facies in the Upper Paleolithic of Cantabria. Ph.D. dissertation, University of Pennsylvania. Ann Arbor: University Microfilms.

Madeyska, T.
1982 The Stratigraphy of Paleolithic Sites of the Cracow Upland. *Acta Geologica Polonica* 32:3-4.

Mai, D. H.; Mania, D.; Nötzold, T.; Toepfer, V.; Vlček, E.; and Heinrich, W. D.
1983 *Bilzingsleben II:* Homo erectus—*seine Kultur und Umwelt.* Berlin: VEB Deutscher Verlag der Wissenschaften.

Mania, D.; Toepfer, V.; and Vlček, E.
1980 *Bilzingsleben I:* Homo erectus—*seine Kultur und Umwelt.* Berlin: VEB Deutscher Verlag der Wissenschaften.

Mania, D., and Weber, T.
1986 *Bilzingsleben III:* Homo erectus—*seine Kultur und Umwelt.* Berlin: VEB Deutscher Verlag der Wissenschaften.

Margalef, R.
1968 *Perspectives in Ecological Theory.* Chicago: University of Chicago Press.

Markovic-Marianovic, J.
1964 Le loess en Yougoslavie. In *Proceedings of the 6th INQUA Congress* (Warsaw, 1961) 4.

Marks, A. E.
1976a Ein Aqev: A Late Levantine Upper Paleolithic Site in the Nahal Aqev. Pp. 227-291 in *Prehistory and Paleoenvironments in the Central Negev, Israel*, Vol. 1, ed. A. E. Marks. Dallas: SMU Press.
1976b (ed.) *Prehistory and Paleoenvironments in the Central Negev, Israel.* Vol. 1: *The Avdat/Aqev Area, Part 1.* Dallas: SMU Press.
1977 (ed.) *Prehistory and Paleoenvironments in the Central Negev, Israel.* Vol. 2: *The Avdat/Aqev Area, Part 2, and the Har Harif.* Dallas: Department of Anthropology, SMU.
1981a The Middle Paleolithic of the Negev. Pp. 287-298 in *Préhistoire du Levant*, eds. J. Cauvin and P. Sanlaville. Paris: CNRS.
1981b The Upper Paleolithic of the Negev. Pp. 343-352 in *Préhistoire du Levant*, eds. J. Cauvin and P. Sanlaville. Paris: CNRS.
1983a The Middle to Upper Paleolithic Transition in the Levant. Pp. 51-98 in *Advances in World Archaeology*, Vol. 2, eds. F. Wendorf and A. E. Close. New York: Academic Press.
1983b (ed.) *Prehistory and Paleoenvironments in the Central Negev, Israel.* Vol. 3: *The Avdat/Aqev Area, Part 3.* Dallas: Department of Anthropology, SMU.
1985 The Levantine Middle to Upper Paleolithic Transition: The Past and Present. In *Studi di paletnologia in onore di Salvatore M. Puglisi*, eds. M. Liverani, M. Palmieri, and R. Peroni. Rome: Università di Roma "La Sapienza."

Marks, A. E., and Ferring, C. R.
1976 Upper Paleolithic Sites near Ein Avdat. Pp. 141-198 in *Prehistory and Paleoenvironments in the Central Negev, Israel*, Vol. 1, ed. A. E. Marks. Dallas: SMU Press.

Marks, A. E., and Freidel, D.
1977 Prehistoric Settlement Patterns in the Avdat/Aqev Area. Pp. 131-158 in *Prehistory and Paleoenvironments in the Central Negev, Israel*, Vol. 2, ed. A. E. Marks. Dallas: Department of Anthropology, SMU.

Marks, A. E., and Volkman, P.
1983 Changing Core Reduction Strategies: A Technological Shift from the Middle to the Upper Paleolithic in the Southern Levant. Pp. 13-33 in *The Mousterian Legacy*, ed. E. Trinkaus. BAR International Series 164. Oxford: BAR.
1986 The Mousterian of Ksar Aqil: Levels XXVIA through XXVIIB. *Paléorient* 12:5-20.
1987 Technological Change Seen from Core Reconstructions. Pp. 11-20 in *The Use of Flint and Chert: Papers from the Fourth International Flint Symposium*, eds. G. Sieveking and M. Newcomer. Cambridge: Cambridge University Press.

Martini-Jacquin, A.
1984 Considérations sur les faunes du Riss dans le Sud-Ouest de la France. P. 382 in *10ème RAST* (Bordeaux). Paris: Société Géologique de France.

Martinson, D. G.; Pisias, N. G.; Hays, J. D.; Imbrie, J.; Moore, T. C.; and Shackleton, N. J.
1987 Age Dating and the Orbital Theory of the

Ice Ages: Development of a High-Resolution 0 to 300,000-Year Chronostratigraphy. *QR* 27:1-29.

Masson, A.
1982 Circulations paléolithiques: une question de longueur. *BSPF* 79:197.

Medoev, A. G.
1982 *Geokhronologiya Paleolita Kazakhstana*. Alma Ata: Nauka.

Mellars, P. A.
1964 The Middle Palaeolithic Artifacts at Kokkinopilos. *PPS* 30:229-244.
1965 Sequence and Development of Mousterian Tradition in Southwestern France. *Nature* 205:626-627.
1969 The Chronology of Mousterian Industries in the Perigord Region of South-west France. *PPS* 35:134-171.
1970 Some Comments on the Notion of "Functional Variability" in Stone Tool Assemblages. *WA* 2:74-89.
1973 The Character of the Middle-Upper Palaeolithic Transition in Southwest France. Pp. 255-276 in *The Explanation of Culture Change*, ed. C. Renfrew. London: Duckworth.
1982 Review of *Rock Shelters of the Perigord*, by H. Laville, J.-P. Rigaud, and J. Sackett. *Antiquity* 56:68-70.
1986a A New Chronology for the French Mousterian Period. *Nature* 322:410-411.
1986b A New Chronology for the French Mousterian Period. Pp. 28-29 in *L'homme de Néandertal* (preprints), ed. M. Otte. Liège: Université de Liège.
1986c Reply to "Dating and Correlating the French Mousterian," by N. Ashton and J. Cook. *Nature* 324:113-114.

Miskovsky, J.-C.
1974 *Le Quaternaire du Midi méditerranéen: stratigraphie et paléoclimatologie*. EQ 3. Marseille: LPHP.

Moisan, L.
1978 Recherches sur les terrasses alluviales du Libournais et leurs industries préhistoriques. Thesis, Université de Bordeaux.

Monméjean, F.; Bordes, F.; and Sonneville-Bordes, D. de
1964 Le Périgordien supérieur à burins de Noailles du Roc de Gavaudun (Lot-et-Garonne). *L'Anthropologie* 68:253-316.

Montet-White, A.
1982a (ed.) *Le Malpas Rockshelter: A Study of Late Paleolithic Technology in Its Environmental Setting*. University of Kansas Publications in Anthropology 4. Lawrence: University of Kansas Press.
1982b Modèle typométrique d'une industrie gravettienne d'Europe Centrale. Pp. 217-229 in *Aurignacien, Périgordien et Gravettien*, fasc. 2. ERAUL 13. Liège: Service d'Archéologie Préhistorique et Centre Interdisciplinaire de Recherches Archéologiques.
in press Raw Material Economy in the Paleolithic of Northern Bosnia. In *International Conference on Flint Mining and Raw Material Identification in the Carpathian Basin* (Sümeg, 1986). Budapest: Institute of Geology.

Montet-White, A., and Basler, D.
1977 Industrie gravettienne en Bosnie du Nord. *BSPF* 74:532-544.

Montet-White, A., and Johnson, A. E.
1976 Kadar: A Late Gravettian Site in Northern Bosnia. *JFA* 3:408-424.

Montet-White, A.; Laville, H.; and Lézine, A.-M.
1986 Le Paléolithique en Bosnie du Nord: chronologie, environment et préhistoire. *L'Anthropologie* 90:29-88.

Mörner, N.-A.
1979 The Grande Pile Paleomagnetic/Paleoclimatic Record and the European Glacial History of the Last 130,000 Years. Pp. 19-24 in *International Project on Paleolimnology and Late Cenozoic Climate*, No. 2, ed. S. Horie. IPPCCE Newsletter 2. Kyoto: Institute of Paleolimnology and Paleoenvironment on Lake Biwa, Kyoto University.

Mortillet, G. de
1883 *Le préhistorique: antiquité de l'homme*. Paris: C. Reinwald.

Moure Romanillo, J. A.
1974 Magdaleniense superior y Aziliense en la región cantábrica española. Thesis, Universidad de Madrid.
1975 *Excavaciones en la cueva de "Tito Bustillo" (Asturias): campañas de 1972 y 1974*. Oviedo: Instituto de Estudios Asturianos.

Moure Romanillo, J. A., and Cano Herrera, M.
1976 *Excavaciones en la cueva de "Tito Bustillo" (Asturias): trabajos de 1975*. Oviedo: Instituto de Estudios Asturianos.

Movius, H. L., Jr.
1950 A Wooden Spear of Third Interglacial Age from Lower Saxony. *SJA* 6:139-142.
1953 Palaeolithic and Mesolithic Sites of Soviet

Central Asia. *Proceedings of the American Philosophical Society* 97:383-421.
1966   The Hearths of the Upper Perigordian and Aurignacian Horizons at the Abri Pataud, Les Eyzies (Dordogne), and Their Possible Significance. *AA* 68:296-325.
1972   Radiocarbon Dating of the Upper Palaeolithic Sequence at the Abri Pataud, Les Eyzies (Dordogne). Pp. 253-260 in *The Origin of* Homo sapiens: *Proceedings of the Paris Symposium* (September 1969), ed. F. Bordes. Paris: UNESCO.
1975   (ed.) *Excavation of the Abri Pataud, Les Eyzies (Dordogne).* ASPR Bulletin 30. Cambridge, MA: Peabody Museum Press.
1977   *Excavation of the Abri Pataud, Les Eyzies (Dordogne): Stratigraphy.* ASPR Bulletin 31. Cambridge, MA: Peabody Museum Press.

Müller, H.
1974   Pollenanalytische Untersuchungen und Jahresschichtzählungen an der eemzeitlichen Kieselgur von Bispingen/Luhe. *Geologische Jahrbuch* 21:149-169.

Müller-Beck, H.
1956   Das Obere Altpaläolithikum in Süddeutschland. Teil I: Text. Thesis, Universität Tübingen.
1967   Vorbericht über die Grabung 1966 am Speckberg. *Bayerische Vorgeschichtsblatt* 32: 148-153.
1982   Late Pleistocene Man in the Northern Eurasia Mammoth-Steppe Biome. Pp. 329-352 in *Paleoecology of Beringia*, eds. D. M. Hopkins et al. New York: Academic Press.
1987   (ed.) *Das Faustkeilpaläolithikum von Şehremuz bei Samsat am Euphrat.* Tübinger Monographien zur Urgeschichte. Stuttgart: Kohlhammer.

Munday, F. C.
1976   Intersite Variability in the Mousterian of the Central Negev. Pp. 113-140 in *Prehistory and Paleoenvironments in the Central Negev, Israel*, Vol. 1, ed. A. E. Marks. Dallas: SMU Press.
1977   Nahal Aqev (D35): A Stratified, Open-Air Mousterian Occupation in the Avdat/Aqev Area. Pp. 35-60 in *Prehistory and Paleoenvironments in the Central Negev, Israel*, Vol. 2, ed. A. E. Marks. Dallas: Department of Anthropology, SMU.
1979   Levantine Mousterian Technological Variability: A Perspective from the Negev. *Paléorient* 5:87-104.

Musil, R.
1980-81   Ursus spelaeus: *der Höhlenbar.* Weimarer Monographien zur Ur- und Frühgeschichte 2. Weimar: Museum für Ur- und Frühgeschichte Thüringens.

Neter, J.; Wassermann, W.; and Kutner, M. H.
1985   *Applied Linear Statistical Models.* 2d ed. Homewood, IL: Richard D. Irwin.

Newcomer, M. H.
1974   Study and Replication of Bone Tools from Ksar Akil (Lebanon). *WA* 6:138-158.
1975   "Punch Technique" and Upper Paleolithic Blades. Pp. 97-102 in *Lithic Technology*, ed. E. Swanson. The Hague/Paris: Mouton.

Newcomer, M. H., and Watson, P.
1984   Bone Artifacts from Ksar 'Aqil (Lebanon). *Paléorient* 10:143-148.

Niederlender, A.; Lacam, R.; Cadiergues, D.; and Bordes, F.
1956   Le gisement moustérien du Mas-Viel (Lot). *L'Anthropologie* 60:209-235.

Nobis, G.
1979   Der ältest Haushund lebte vor 14.000 Jahren. *Umschau* 79 19:610.

Nouël, A.
1937   Une station du Paléolithique supérieur à La-Chapelle-Saint-Mesmin (Loiret). *BSPF* 34:379-387.

Okladnikov, A. P.
1966   Paleolit i Mezolit Sredney Aziy. Pp. 11-75 in *Srednyaya Aziya v Epokhu Kamnya i Bronzi*, ed. V. M. Masson. Moscow: Nauka.

Oliva, M.
1979   Die Herkunft des Szeletien im Lichte neuer Funde von Jezeřany. *ČMM* 64:45-78.
1984   Le Bohunicien, un nouveau groupe culturel en Moravie: quelques aspects psycho-technologiques du développement des industries paléolithiques. *L'Anthropologie* 88: 209-220.

Osole, F.
1979   Rad na Istrazivanju Paleolitskog i Mesolitskog Doba u Sloveniji. Pp. 129-135 in *Praistorija Jugoslavenskih Zemalja*, Vol. 1, ed. A. Benac. Sarajevo: Svjetlost.

Otte, M.
1979   *Le Paléolithique supérieur ancien en Belgique.* Brussels: Royal Museums of Art and History.
1985   (ed.) *La signification culturelle des industries lithiques.* Actes du Colloque de Liège (October 1984). SPB 4; BAR International Series 239. Oxford: BAR.

Otte, M., and Gob, A.
1983 Datations radiométriques à la grotte de Sclayn (prov. Namur, Belgique). Archéométrie, groupe de contact FNRS, prétirages de la Réunion de Gand (December).

Otte, M.; Schneider, A. M.; and Gautier, A.
1983 Fouilles aux grottes de Sclayn (Namur). *Hélinium* 23:112-142.

Paquereau, M.-M.
1974-75 Le Würm ancien en Périgord: étude palynologique. *Quaternaria* 18:67-159.
1975 Flores des deux derniers interglaciaires dans le Sud-Ouest de la France. *L'Anthropologie* 80:201-225.
1978a Analyses palynologiques de l'abri Duruthy. Pp. 96-109 in *Le gisement préhistorique de Duruthy à Sorde-l'Abbaye*, ed. R. Arambourou. MSPF 13. Paris: SPF.
1978b Flores et climats du Würm III dans le Sud-Ouest de la France. *Quaternaria* 20:123-164.
1979 Documents palynologiques du Pléistocène moyen dans le Sud-Ouest de la France. *Quaternaria* 21:17-44.
1980 Chronologie palynologique du Pléistocène dans le Sud-Ouest de la France. Pp. 298-306 in *Problèmes de stratigraphie quaternaire en France et dans les pays limitrophes*, ed. J. Chaline. *BAFEQ* Supplément n.s. 1. Dijon: AFEQ.
1984 Etude palynologique du gisement de la Ferrassie (Dordogne). Pp. 51-59 in *Le grand abri de la Ferrassie*, by H. Delporte. EQ 7. Paris: LPHP.
n.d. Abri Dufaure: analyses palynologiques. Unpub. ms. in possession of the author.

Paquereau, M.-M., and Texier, J.-P.
1972 L'interglaciaire Riss-Würm du Breuil (Dordogne). *CRASP* 276D:2769-2771.
1973 La séquence würmienne et interglaciaire Riss-Würm du Breuil. *Quaternaria* 15:321-330.

Patou, M.
1984 *Contribution à l'étude des mammifères des couches supérieures de la grotte du Lazaret (Nice, A.M.)*. Paris: Muséum National d'Histoire Naturelle.

Păunescu, A.
1965 Sur la succession des habitats paléolithiques et post-paléolithiques de Ripiceni-Izvor. *Dacia* 9:5-31.

Payne, S.
1982 Faunal Evidence for Environmental/Climatic Change at Franchthi Cave (Southern Argolid, Greece), 25,000 BP to 5,000 BP: Preliminary Results. Pp. 133-137 in *Palaeoclimates, Palaeoenvironments and Human Communities in the Eastern Mediterranean Region in Later Prehistory*, eds. J. L. Bintliff and W. van Zeist. BAR International Series 133(i). Oxford: BAR.

Perlès, C.
in press *Les industries lithiques taillées de Franchthi. Vol. 1: Présentation générale et industries paléolithiques*. Bloomington: Indiana University Press.

Petraglia, M.
1987 Site Formation Processes at Abri Dufaure: An Upper Paleolithic Rockshelter and Hillslope in Southwestern France. Ph.D. dissertation, University of New Mexico.

Peyrille, L., and Blanc, S.
1952 Le gisement de Beaufort, près Saint-Louis-en-l'Isle (Dordogne). *Bulletin de l'Association Préhistorique des Amis des Eyzies* 2:28-29.

Peyrony, D.
1930 Le Moustier: ses gisements, ses industries, ses couches géologiques. *RA* 1:48-76, 155-176.
1933 Les industries aurignaciennes dans le bassin de la Vézère: Aurignacien et Périgordien. *BSPF* 30:543-549.
1934 La Ferrassie: Moustérien, Périgordien, Aurignacien. *Préhistoire* 3:1-92.
1948 Le Périgordien, l'Aurignacien et le Solutréen en Eurasie d'après les dernières fouilles. *BSPF* 45:305-328.

Peyrony, D., and Peyrony, E.
1938 *Laugerie-Haute*. AIPH 19. Paris: Masson.

Pielou, E. C.
1975 *Ecological Diversity*. New York: John Wiley & Sons.

Pope, K. O., and van Andel, T.
1984 Late Quaternary Alluviation and Soil Formation in the Southern Argolid: Its History, Causes and Archaeological Implications. *JAS* 11:281-306.

Poplin, F.
1976 *Les grands vertébrés de Gönnersdorf: fouilles 1968. Der Magdalénien-Fundplatz Gönnersdorf 2*. Wiesbaden: Franz Steiner.

Pradel, L., and Pradel, J. H.
1970 La station paléolithique de Fontmaure, commune de Velleches (Vienne). *L'Anthropologie* 74:481-526.

Prat, F., and Suire, C.
1971 Remarques sur les cerfs contemporains des deux premiers stades würmiens. *BSPF* 3: 75-79.

Ranov, V. A.
1965 *Kamenyy Vek Tadzhikistana* (*L'âge de la pierre de Tadjikhistan*). Dushanbe: Akademii Nauk Tadzhikskoy SSR. (in Russian)
1972 Le peuplement préhistorique de la Haute-Asie. *L'Anthropologie* 76:5-20.
1976 The Palaeolithic Industries of Central Asia. *Pré-tirages du 9ème Congrès de l'UISPP* (Nice, September): 91-129.
1984 Neue Forschungen zur Altsteinzeit: Zentralasien. *Forschungen zur allgemeine und vergelcheinde Archäologie* 4:299-343.

Ranov, V. A., and Davis, R. S.
1979 Toward a New Outline of the Soviet Central Asian Palaeolithic. *CA* 20:249-270.

Ranov, V. A., and Nesmeyanov, S. A.
1973 *Paleolit i Stratigraphiya Anthropogena Sredney Azii* (*Le Paléolithique et stratigraphie anthropogène de l'Asie centrale*). Dushanbe: Donish. (in Russian)

Ranov, V. A., and Zhukov, V. A.
1982 Raboty Otryada po Izucheniyu Kamennogo Veka v 1976 g. Pp. 9-30 in *Arkheologicheskiye Raboty v Tadzhikstanye 1976*. Dushanbe: Donish.

Raynal, J.-P.; Paquereau, M.-M.; Daugas, J.-P.; Miallier, D.; Fain, J.; and Sanzelle, S.
1985 Contribution à la datation du volcanisme du Massif Central français par la thermoluminescence des inclusions de quartz et comparaison avec d'autres approches: implications chronostratigraphiques et paléoenvironnementales. *BAFEQ* 4:183-207.

Richter, J.
1981 Der spätpaläolithische Fundplatz bei Gahlen, Ldkr. Dinslaken. *AK* 11:181-187.

Rieder, K. H.
1983 Kritische Analyse alter Grabungsergebnisse aus dem Hohlen Stein bei Schambach aus der Sicht der Profiluntersuchungen 1977-1982: Aspekte zur Geschichte der Höhlenverfüllung, ihrer Paläontologie und Archäologie. Thesis, Universität Tübingen.

Riek, G.
1934 *Die Eiszeitjägerstation am Vogelherd im Lonetal.* Vol. 1: *Die Kulturen.* Tübingen: Heine.

Rigaud, J.-P.
1969 Note préliminaire sur la stratigraphie du gisement du "Flageolet I" (commune de Bézenac, Dordogne). *BSPF* 66:73-75.
1970 Etude préliminaire de l'industrie magdalénienne de l'abri du "Flageolet II" (commune de Bézenac, Dordogne). *BSPF* 67:456-474.
1976a Les civilisations du Paléolithique supérieur en Périgord. Pp. 1257-1270 in *La préhistoire française*, Vol. 1, ed. H. de Lumley. Paris: CNRS.
1976b Données nouvelles sur le Périgordien supérieur en Périgord. Pp. 53-65 in *L'évolution de l'Acheuléen en Europe* (Pré-tirages du 9ème Congrès de l'UISPP [Nice, September]). Paris: CNRS.
1978 The Significance of Variability among Lithic Artifacts: A Specific Case from Southwestern France. *JAR* 34:299-310.
1979 A propos des industries magdaléniennes du Flageolet. Pp. 467-469 in *La fin des temps glaciaires en Europe*, ed. D. de Sonneville-Bordes. Colloques Internationaux du CNRS 271. Paris: CNRS.
1982a Données nouvelles sur l'Aurignacien et le Périgordien en Périgord. Pp. 289-324 in *Aurignacien et Gravettien en Europe*. Actes de la 10ème Commission de l'UISPP (Krakow-Nitra 1980); ERAUL 13. Liège: Service d'Archéologie Préhistorique et Centre Interdisciplinaire de Recherches Archéologiques.
1982b Le Paléolithique en Périgord: les données du Sud-Ouest sarladais et leurs implications. 2 vols. Thesis, Université de Bordeaux.
1984 Circonscription d'Aquitaine. Dordogne. *GP* 27:274.
in press Analyse typologique des industries de la grotte Vaufrey. In *La grotte XV dite Grotte Vaufrey, à Cenac-et-Saint-Julien (Dordogne)*, ed. J.-P. Rigaud. MSPF.

Rigaud, J.-P., and Simek, J.
1987 "Arms Too Short to Box with God": Problems and Prospects for Paleolithic Prehistory in Dordogne, France. Pp. 47-61 in *The Pleistocene Old World: Regional Perspectives*, ed. O. Soffer. New York: Plenum Press.

Rigaud, J.-P., and Texier, J.-P.
1981 A propos des particularités techniques et typologiques du gisement des Tares, commune de Sourzac (Dordogne). *BSPF* 78:109-117.

Rindos, D.
1986 The Evolution of the Capacity for Culture: Sociobiology, Structuralism, and Cultural Selectionism. *CA* 27:315-332.

Ringer, A.
1982 *Babonyen, eine mittelpaläolithische Blattwerkzeugindustrie in Nordostungarn.* Dissertationes Archaeologicae, Vol. 11, Ser. II. Budapest: Instituto Archaeologico Universitatis Rolando Eötvös.

Rogachev, A. N.
1962 Osnovniye Itogi i Zadachi Izucheniya Paleolita Russkoy Ravniny (Principal Results and Problems in the Study of the Paleolithic of the Russian Plain). *Kratkiya Soobshcheniya Instituta Arkheologii* 92:3-11.

Rogers, R. A.
1973 Faunal Remains. Pp. 36-40 in *Le Malpas Rockshelter*, ed. A. Montet-White. Lawrence: University of Kansas Press.

Rognon, P.
1983 Essai de définition et typologie des crises climatiques. Pp. 151-164 in *Paléoclimats: actes du Colloque de l'AGSO* (Bordeaux, May). CQ no. hors série; BIGBA 34. Paris: CNRS.

Rolland, N.
1972 Etude archéometrique de l'industrie moustérienne de la grotte de l'Hortus. Pp. 489-508 in *La grotte de l'Hortus (Valflaunès, Herault)*, ed. H. de Lumley. EQ 1. Marseille: LPHP.
1975 The Antecedents and Emergence of the Middle Palaeolithic Industrial Complex in Western Europe. Thesis, Cambridge University.
1977 New Aspects of Middle Palaeolithic Variability in Western Europe. *Nature* 266:251-252.
1981 The Interpretation of Middle Palaeolithic Variability. *Man* 16:15-42.
1986 Recent Findings from La Micoque and Other Sites in South-western and Mediterranean France: Their Bearing on the "Tayacian" Problem and Middle Palaeolithic Emergence. Pp. 121-151 in *Stone Age Prehistory*, eds. G. N. Bailey and P. Callow. Cambridge: Cambridge University Press.

Rust, A.
1950 *Die Höhlenfunde von Jabrud (Syrien).* Neumünster: Karl Wachholtz.

Sacchi, D.
1986 *Le Paléolithique supérieur du Languedoc occidental et du Roussillon.* GP Supplément 21. Paris: CNRS.

Sackett, J. R.
1966 Quantitative Analysis of Upper Paleolithic Stone Tools. *AA* 68:356-394.
1973 Style, Function, and Artifact Variability in Palaeolithic Assemblages. Pp. 317-325 in *The Explanation of Culture Change*, ed. C. Renfrew. London: Duckworth.
1981 From de Mortillet to Bordes: A Century of French Palaeolithic Research. Pp. 85-99 in *Toward a History of Archaeology*, ed. G. Daniel. London: Thames & Hudson.
1982 Approaches to Style in Lithic Archaeology. *JAA* 1:59-112.
1985 Style, Ethnicity, and Stone Tools. Pp. 277-282 in *Status, Structure and Stratification: Current Archaeological Reconstructions*, eds. M. Thompson, M. T. Garcia, and F. J. Kense. Proceedings of the 16th Annual Chacmool Conference. Calgary: Archaeological Association of the University of Calgary.
1986 Style, Function, and Assemblage Variability: A Reply to Binford. *AmAnt* 51:628-634.
1987 New Approaches to Upper Paleolithic Industrial Variability. Paper presented at Lithic Analysis Conference (University of Tulsa, June).
1988a New Approaches to Stone Age Lithic Variability. Revised version of paper presented at Lithic Analysis Conference (University of Tulsa, June 1987). Unpub. ms. in possession of the author.
1988b Style and Symbolism in Paleolithic Stone Tools: A Reply to Chase and Dibble (1987). Unpub. ms. in possession of the author.
forthcoming *The Archaeology of Solvieux: Excavations and Industries.* Monumenta Archaeologica. Los Angeles: Institute of Archaeology, UCLA.

Sackett, J. R., and Grimm, L.
1987 Un site de plein air du Paléolithique supérieur de la moyenne vallée de l'Isle en Dordogne: Solvieux. In *Les habitats du Paléolithique supérieur*, Vol. 2, ed. J. Combier. Paris: CNRS.

Saint-Périer, R. de
1920 Les migrations des tribus magdaléniens des Pyrénées. *RA* 30:136-140.

Sarntheim, M.; Stremme, H. E.; and Mangini, A.
1986 The Holstein Interglaciation: Time-Stratigraphic Position and Correlation to Stable-Isotope Stratigraphy of Deep-Sea Sediments. *QR* 26:283-298.

Schaller, G. B., and Lowther, G. R.
1969   The Relevance of Carnivore Behavior to the Study of Early Hominids. *SJA* 25:307-341.

Schild, R.
1976   Flint Mining and Trade in Polish Prehistory as Seen from the Perspective of the Chocolate Flint of Central Poland: A Second Approach. *AAC* 16:147-177.

Schild, R., and Sulgostowska, Z.
1986   The Middle Paleolithic of the Northern European Plain at Zwolen. Paper presented at "L'homme de Néandertal: centenaire de la découverte de l'homme de Spy," Colloque de Liège (December).

Schmider, B.
1971   *Les industries lithiques du Paléolithique supérieur en Ile-de-France.* GP Supplément 6. Paris: CNRS.

Schneider, A.-M.
1983   Premiers résultats de l'étude palynologique. *Hélinium* 23:134-137.

Schönweiss, W., and Werner, H.-J.
1986   Ein Fundplatz des Szeletien in Zeitlarn bei Regensburg. *AK* 16:7-12.

Schvoerer, M.; Rouanet, J. F.; Navailles, H.; and Debénath, A.
1977   Datation par thermoluminescence des restes humains antéwürmiens de l'abri Suard, à la Chaise de Vouthon (Charente). *CRASP* 284:1979-1982.

Schwarcz, H. P., and Blackwell, B.
1983 ^{230}Th/^{234}U Age of a Mousterian Site in France. *Nature* 301:236-237.

Schwarcz, H. P.; Blackwell, B.; and Debénath, A.
1983   Absolute Dating of Hominids and Palaeolithic Artefacts in the Cave of La Chaise de Vouthon (Charente), France. *JAS* 10:493-513.

Semenov, S. A.
1964   (ed.) *Prehistoric Technology: An Experimental Study of the Oldest Tools and Artefacts from Traces of Manufacture and Wear.* New York: Barnes & Noble; London: Cory, Adams & Mackay.
1966   Etude technologique des outils du Paléolithique ancien, trs. J. Gaudey and C. R. A. Valbonne. *7ème Congrès International de Préhistoire: rapport et communiqué des archéologues d'U.R.S.S.*: 21-37.
1970   The Form and Function of the Oldest Tools. *Quartär* 21:1-20.

Séronie-Vivien, M.
n.d.   L'étude de quelques silex préhistoriques provenant de l'abri Dufaure. Unpub. ms. in possession of the author.

Sevink, J.
1974   *Landscape Evolution and Soils in South-Western Velay (France).* Fysisch Geographisch en Bodemkundig Laboratorium. Amsterdam: Universiteit van Amsterdam.

Shackleton, N. J., and Opdyke, N. D.
1973   Oxygen Isotope and Paleomagnetic Stratigraphy of Equatorial Pacific Core V28-238: Oxygen Temperatures and Ice Volume on a 105 Years and 106 Years Scale. *QR* 3:39-55.
1976   Oxygen Isotope and Paleomagnetic Stratigraphy of Pacific Core V28-239: Late Pliocene to Latest Pleistocene. *Geological Society of America Memoirs* 145:449-464.

Shackleton, J. C., and van Andel, T.
1986   Prehistoric Shore Environments, Shellfish Availability, and Shellfish Gathering at Franchthi, Greece. *Geoarchaeology* 1:127-143.

Shannon, C. E.
1948   A Mathematical Theory of Communications. *Bell System Technology Journal* 27:379-423, 623-656.

Sheets, P.
1975   Behavioral Analysis and the Structure of a Prehistoric Industry. *CA* 16:369-391.

Simek, J. F.
1987   Spatial Order and Behavioural Change in the French Palaeolithic. *Antiquity* 61:25-40.

Simonnet, R.
1985   Le silex du Magdalénien final de la grotte des Eglises dans le bassin de Tarascon-sur-Ariège. *BSPA* 40:71-97.

Singer, C.
1975   The Non-Flint Tools and Other Lithic Artifacts from Solvieux: A Preliminary Analysis. M.A. thesis, UCLA.

Sirakov, N.
1983   *Reconstruction of the Middle Palaeolithic Flint Assemblages from the Cave Samuilitsa II (Northern Bulgaria) and Their Taxonomical Position Seen against the Palaeolithic of South-Eastern Europe.* Folia Quaternaria 55. Krakow: Polska Akademia Nauk.

Skinner, J. H.
1965   The Flake Industries of Southwest Asia: A Typological Study. Ph.D. dissertation,

Columbia University. Ann Arbor: University Microfilms.

Smith, P.
1966 *Le Solutréen en France.* MIPUB 5. Bordeaux: Delmas.

Sonneville-Bordes, D. de
1960 *Le Paléolithique supérieur en Périgord.* 2 vols. Bordeaux: Delmas.
1961 *L'âge de la pierre.* Paris: Presses Universitaires de France.
1966 L'évolution du Paléolithique supérieur en Europe occidentale et sa signification. *BSPF* 63:3-34.
1981 Cultures et milieux d'*Homo sapiens sapiens* en Europe. Pp. 115-129 in *Les processus de l'hominisation*, ed. D. Ferembach. Colloques Internationaux du CNRS 599. Paris: CNRS.

Sonneville-Bordes, D. de, and Perrot, J.
1956 Lexique typologique du Paléolithique supérieur: outillage lithique. *BSPF* 53:408-412.

Souleimanov, R. H.
1972 *Etude statistique de la civilisation de la grotte Abi-Rakhmat.* Tashkent: Fan. (in Russian)

Speth, J. D.
1972 Mechanical Basis of Percussion Flaking. *AmAnt* 37:34-60.
1975 Miscellaneous Studies in Hard-Hammer Percussion Flaking: The Effects of Oblique Impact. *AmAnt* 40:203-207.
1981 The Role of Platform Angle and Core Size in Hard-Hammer Percussion Flaking. *LT* 10:16-21.

Speth, J. D., and Spielmann, K. A.
1983 Energy Source, Protein Metabolism and Hunter-Gatherer Subsistence Strategies. *JAA* 2:1-31.

Stampfuss, R., and Schütrumpf, R.
1970 Harpunen der Allerödzeit aus Dinslaken, Niederrhein. *BJ* 170:20-35.

Stefánsson, V.
1962 *My Life with the Eskimo.* New York: Collier Books (orig. pub. 1913).

Stodiek, U.
1987 Fussgönheim—zwei spätjungpaläolithische Fundplätze in der Vorderpfalz. *AK* 17:31-41.

Straus, L. G.
1975 ¿Solutrense o Magdaleniense inferior cantábrico? Significado de las "diferencias." *Boletín del Instituto de Estudios Asturianos* 86:781-790.
1977 Of Deerslayers and Mountain Men: Paleolithic Faunal Exploitation in Cantabrian Spain. Pp. 41-76 in *For Theory Building in Archaeology*, ed. L. R. Binford. New York: Academic Press.
1978 Variabilité dans les industries solutréennes de l'Espagne cantabrique. *BSPF* 75:276-280.
1983a From Mousterian to Magdalenian: Cultural Evolution Viewed from Vasco-Cantabrian Spain and Pyrenean France. Pp. 73-111 in *The Mousterian Legacy*, ed. E. Trinkaus. Oxford: BAR.
1983b *El Solutrense vasco-cantábrico: una nueva perspectiva.* Monografía 10. Santander: CIMA.
1986a The Azilian of Abri Dufaure: A Preliminary Note. *Mesolithic Miscellany* 7:1-7.
1986b A Comparison of La Riera Assemblages with Those from Contemporary Sites in Cantabrian Spain. Pp. 219-236 in *La Riera Cave*, by L. G. Straus and G. A. Clark. ASU Anthropological Research Papers 36. Tempe: ASU.
1986c Late Würm Adaptive Systems in Cantabrian Spain: The Case of Eastern Asturias. *JAA* 5:330-368.
in press Chronostratigraphy of the Pleistocene-Holocene Transition: The Azilian Problem in the Franco-Cantabrian Region. *Palaeohistoria* 27.

Straus, L. G.; Altuna, J.; Clark, G.; González Morales, M.; Laville, H.; Leroi-Gourhan, Arl.; Menéndez de la Hoz, M.; and Ortea, J.
1981 Paleoecology at La Riera (Asturias, Spain). *CA* 22:655-682.

Straus, L. G., and Clark, G. A.
1986 *La Riera Cave: Stone Age Hunter-Gatherer Adaptations in Northern Spain.* ASU Anthropological Research Papers 36. Tempe: ASU.

Straus, L. G., and Petraglia, M.
1985 Abri Dufaure Prehistoric Project. *Old World Archaeology Newsletter* 9:10-13.

Straus, L. G., and Spiess, A.
1985 Le Magdalénien final de l'abri Dufaure: un aperçu de la chronologie et de la saison d'habitation humaine. *BSPA* 40:169-184.

Street, M.
1986 Ein Wald der Allerödzeit bei Meisenheim, Stadt Andernach (Neuwieder Becken). *AK* 16:13-22.
in press Grosstierfauna. In *Das Endpaläolithikum von*

Andernach. Neuwied: Schriftenreihe Monrepos.

Stremme, H. E.
1986 Die Korrelation quartärer Paläoböden in Nordwest-Deutschland. *Zeitschrift für Geomorphologie* N. F. Suppl. 61:89-100.

Svoboda, J.
1980 *Křemencová Industrie z Ondratic: K Problému Počátků Mladého Paleolitu*. Studie Archeologickeho Ústavu ČSAV v Brně 9. Prague: Academia.
1985 Neue Grabungsergebnisse von Stránská Skála, Mähren, Tschechoslowakei. *AK* 15:261-268.

Swanson, E., ed.
1975 *Lithic Technology: Making and Using Stone Tools*. The Hague/Paris: Mouton.

Targullian, D.; Biridina, A. G.; Kulikov, T. A.; Solokova, T. A.; and Tselischeva, L. K.
1974 Arrangement, Composition and Genesis of Podsolic Soils Derived from Mantles Loam. *Transactions of the 10th International Congress of Soil Scientists* (Moscow) 6:564-589.

Taute, W.
1968 *Die Stielspitzen-Gruppen im nördlichen Mitteleuropa: ein Beitrag zur Kenntnis der späten Altsteinzeit*. Fundamenta A5. Cologne: Hermann Böhlau.

Tavoso, A.
1984 Réflexion sur l'économie des matières premières au Moustérien. *BSPF* 81:79-82.

Tchernich, O. P. [or Chernysh, A. P.]
1961 *Paleolitichna Stoianka Molodone V*. Kiev: Naukova Dumka.

Terán, M. de; Barceló y Pons, B.; Bosque Maurel, J.; García Fernández, J.; Llobet Reverter, S.; López Gómez, A.; Mensua Fernández, S.; Solé Sabarís, L.; and Vilá Valenti, J.
1969 *Geografía regional de España*. Esplugues de Llobregat: Ariel.

Terberger, K.
1986 Das Lahntalpaläolithikum. Thesis, Universität Köln.

Terberger, T.
1985 *Das Magdalénien von Andernach: die retuschierten Steinartefakte*. Magisterarbeit Köln. Cologne: Universität Köln.

Texier, J.-P.
1973a Etude sédimentologique du gisement du Malpas, commune de Bourniquel (Dordogne). *L'Anthropologie* 77:35-55.
1973b Sedimentological Analysis. Pp. 25-31 in *Le Malpas Rockshelter*, ed. A. Montet-White. Lawrence: University of Kansas Press.
1980 Recherches sur les formations superficielles du bassin de l'Isle. Thesis, Université de Bordeaux.
1982 *Les formations superficielles du bassin de l'Isle*. CQ 4. Paris: CNRS.

Texier, J.-P.; Raynal, J.-P.; Laville, H.; Paquereau, M.-M.; Prat, F.; Debénath, A.; and Delpech, F.
1983 Histoire paléoclimatique de l'Aquitaine du Pléistocène ancien au dernier interglaciaire. Pp. 207-217 in *Paléoclimats: actes du Colloque de l'AGSO* (Bordeaux, May). CQ no. hors série; BIGBA 34. Paris: CNRS.

Thibault, C.
1970 Recherches sur le terrain quaternaire du bassin de l'Adour. Thesis, Université de Bordeaux.

Thoma, A.
1972 Contribution to the Discussion of K. Valoch's Report. Pp. 161-170 in *The Origin of* Homo sapiens: *Proceedings of the Paris Symposium* (September 1969), ed. F. Bordes. Paris: UNESCO.

Tinnes, J.
1984 *Die Knochen-, Geweih- und Elfenbeinartefakte des Magdalénien-Fundplatzes Gönnersdorf*. Magisterarbeit Köln. Cologne: Universität Köln.

Torke, W.
1981 *Fischreste als Quellen der Ökologie und Ökonomie in der Steinzeit Südwest-deutschlands*. UM 4. Tübingen: Archaeologica Venatoria.

Torti-Zannoli, C.
1983 Contribution à l'étude paléogéographique du Massif Central au Paléolithique moyen et supérieur. *BSPF* 80:300-307.

Toth, N. P.
1982 The Stone Technologies of Early Hominids at Koobi Fora, Kenya: An Experimental Approach. Ph.D. dissertation, University of California at Berkeley. Ann Arbor: University Microfilms.

Tozzi, C.
1970 La grotta di San Agostino (Gaeta). *RSP* 23:3-87.

Trinkaus, E., ed.
1983 *The Mousterian Legacy: Human Biocultural Change in the Upper Pleistocene*. BAR International Series 164. Oxford: BAR.

Tromnau, G.
1982 Kaiserberg in Duisburg. P. 61 in *Das*

Eiszeitalter in Ruhrland, ed. G. Bosinski. Ruhrlandmuseum Essen, Heft 2. Cologne: Rheinland-Verlag.

Trotignon, F.
1984 Les industries lithiques badegouliennes. Pp. 1-100 in *Etudes sur l'abri Fritsch (Indre)*, by F. Trotignon, T. Poulain, and Arl. Leroi-Gourhan. *GP* Supplément 19. Paris: CNRS.

Tuffreau, A.
1971 Quelques aspects du Paléolithique ancien et moyen dans le nord de la France (Nord, Pas-de-Calais). *Bulletin de la Société Préhistorique du Nord* 8:1-99.
1972 Les industries moustériennes du nord de la France (Nord, Pas-de-Calais). *Septentrion* 1:37-45.
1978 Les industries acheuléennes de Cagny-la Garenne (Sommes). *L'Anthropologie* 82:37-40.
1979a Le gisement de Corbehem (Pas-de-Calais). *GP* 22:371-389.
1979b Recherches récentes sur le Paléolithique inférieur et moyen de la France septentrionale. *Bulletin de la Société Royale Belge d'Anthropologie* 90:161-177.

Tuffreau, A., and Sommé, J., eds.
1986 *Chronostratigraphie et faciès culturels du Paléolithique inférieur et moyen dans l'Europe du nord-ouest*. BAFEQ Supplément 26. Paris: AFEQ.

Turner, J., and Greig, J. R. A.
1975 Some Holocene Pollen Diagrams from Greece. *Review of Palaeobotany and Palynology* 20:171-204.

Turon, J. L.
1984 Direct Land/Sea Correlations in the Last Interglacial Complex. *Nature* 309:673-676.

Turq, A.
1982 Moulin du Milieu. In Informations archéologiques: circonscription d'Aquitaine, ed. J.-P. Rigaud. *GP* 25:420-421.
1985 Le Moustérien de type Quina du Roc de Marsal (Dordogne). *BSPF* 82:46-51.

Ulrix-Closset, M.; Otte, M.; and Cattelain, P.
1986 Le "trou d'Abîme" à Couvin (province de Namur, Belgique). Pp. 316-326 in *L'homme de Néandertal* (preprints), ed. M. Otte. Liège: Université de Liège.

Utrilla Miranda, P.
1981 *El Magdalenense inferior y medio en la Costa Cantábrica*. Monografía 4. Santander: CIMA.
1982 El yacimiento de la cueva de Abauntz (Arraiz, Navarra). *Trabajos de arqueología de Navarra* 3:203-345.

Valladas, H.; Geneste, J.-M.; Joron, J.-L.; and Chadelles, J.-P.
1986 Thermoluminescence Dating of Le Moustier (Dordogne, France). *Nature* 320:452-454.

Valoch, K.
1966 Die altertumlichen Blattspitzindustrien von Jezeřany. *ČMM* 51:XXX-XXX.
1982 Neue paläolithische Funde von Brno-Bohunice. *ČMM* 67:31-48.
1986 Stone Industries of the Middle/Upper Paleolithic Transition. In *The Pleistocene Perspective*, Vol. 1, comps. M. Day and R. Folley. Preprint of the Proceedings of the World Archaeological Congress (Southampton, September). London: Allen & Unwin.

Valoch, K., and Oliva, M.
1985 Das Frühaurignacien von Vedrovice II und Kuparovice I in Südmähren. *Anthropozoikum* (Prague) 16:107-203.

van Andel, T. H., and Lianos, N.
1984 High-Resolution Seismic Reflection Profiles for the Reconstruction of Postglacial Transgressive Shorelines: An Example from Greece. *QR* 22:31-45.

Vandermeersch, B.
1981 *Les hommes fossiles de Qafzeh (Israel)*. Paris: CNRS.

Van Vliet, B., and Langhor, R.
1981 Correlations between Fragipans and Permafrost with Reference to Silty Weichselian Deposits in Belgium and Northern France. *Catena* 8:137-155.

Van Vliet, B., and Lanoe, B.
1985 Frost Effects in Soils. Pp. 117-158 in *Soils and Quaternary Landscape Evolution*, ed. J. Boardman. New York: John Wiley & Sons.

Veil, S.
1978a (ed.) *Alt- und mittelsteinzeitliche Fundplätze des Rheinlandes*. Kunst und Altertum am Rhein 81. Cologne: Rheinland-Verlag.
1978b Muffendorf. Bad Godesberg. Pp. 111-112 in *Alt- und mittelsteinzeitliche Fundplätze des Rheinlandes*, ed. S. Veil. Cologne: Rheinland-Verlag.
1978c Ziegenberg bei Altenrath. Pp. 133-135 in *Alt- und mittelsteinzeitliche Fundplätze des Rheinlandes*, ed. S. Veil. Cologne: Rheinland-Verlag.

1982a   Drei Frauenstatuetten aus Elfenbein vom Magdalénien-Fundplatz Andernach, Rheinland-Pfalz. *AK* 12:119-127.

1982b   Der späteiszeitliche Fundplatz Andernach-Martinsberg. *Germania* 60:391-424.

1984   Siedlungsbefunde vom Magdalénien-Fundplatz Andernach: Zwischenbericht über die Grabungen 1979-1983. Pp. 181-193 in *Jungpaläolithische Siedlungsstrukturen in Europa*, eds. H. Berke, J. Hahn, and C.-J. Kind. UM 6. Tübingen: Archaeologica Venatoria.

Verworn, M.; Bonnet, R.; and Steinmann, G.
1919   *Der diluviale Menschenfund von Oberkassel bei Bonn.* Wiesbaden: J. F. Bergmann.

Veyrier, M.; Beaux, E.; and Combier, J.
1951   Grotte de Neron, à Soyons (Ardèche): les fouilles de 1950—leurs enseignements. *BSPF* 48:70-78.

Vignard, E.
1965   Le Badegoulien. *BSPF* 62:262-263.

Villa, P.
1975-76   Sols et niveaux d'habitat du Paléolithique inférieur en Europe et au Proche-Orient. *Quaternaire* 19:107-134.

1982   Conjoinable Pieces and Site Formation Processes. *AmAnt* 47:276-290.

Vitaliano, C. J.; Taylor, S. R.; Farrand, W. R.; and Jacobsen, T. W.
1981   Tephra Layer in Franchthi Cave, Peleponnesos, Greece. Pp. 373-379 in *Tephra Studies*, eds. S. Self and R. S. J. Sparks. Amsterdam: Riedel.

Volkman, P. W.
1983   Boker Tachtit: Core Reconstructions. Pp. 127-190 in *Prehistory and Paleoenvironments in the Central Negev, Israel*, Vol. 3, ed. A. E. Marks. Dallas: Department of Anthropology, SMU.

Waechter, J. d'A.
1968   The Evidence of the Levallois Technique in the British Acheulian and the Question of the Acheulio-Levallois. Pp. 491-497 in *La préhistoire: problèmes et tendances*, ed. D. de Sonneville-Bordes. Paris: CNRS.

Wagner, E.
1983   *Das Mittelpaläolithikum der Grossen Grotte bei Blaubeuren (Alb-Donau-Kreis).* Forschungen und Berichten zur Vor- und Frühgeschichte in Baden-Württemberg 16. Stuttgart: Konrad Theiss.

Waterbolk, H. T.
1971   Radiocarbon Dates from the Palaeolithic Sites in Western Europe, Compared with the Climatic Curve of the Netherlands. Pp. 245-252 in *The Origin of Homo sapiens: Proceedings of the Paris Symposium* (September 1969), ed. F. Bordes. Paris: UNESCO.

Weiss, G.
1978   Magdalenahöhle. Pp. 104-105 in *Alt- und mittelsteinzeitliche Fundplätze des Rheinlandes*, ed. S. Veil. Cologne: Rheinland-Verlag.

Welten, M.
1978   Gletscher und Vegetation im Laufe der letzten hundert tausend Jahre. Vorläufige Mitteilung. *Jahrbuch der schweizerischen naturforschung Gesellschaft, wissenschaftlicher Teil*: 5-18.

1981   Verdrängung und Vernichtung der anspruchsvollen Gehölze am Beginn der letzten Eiszeit und die Korrelation der Frühwürm-Interstadiale in Mittel- und Nordeuropa. *Eiszeitalter und Gegenwart* 31: 187-202.

1982   *Pollenanalytische Untersuchungen im Jüngeren Quartär des nördlichen Alpenvorlandes der Schweiz.* Beiträge zur Geologische Karte der Schweiz N.F. 156. Bern: Stämpfli & Cie.

Wendorf, F., and Schild, R.
1974   *A Middle Stone Age Sequence from the Central Rift Valley, Ethiopia.* Warsaw: Wydawnnictwo Polskiej Akademii Nauk.

Whallon, R.
n.d.   Unconstrained Clustering for the Analysis of Spatial Distributions in Archaeology. Unpub. ms. in possession of the author.

White, R.
1982   Rethinking the Middle/Upper Palaeolithic Transition. *CA* 23:169-192.

Winter, D.
1986   *Der spätpaläolithische Fundplatz Niederbieber, Fläche 50/14—56/20.* Magisterarbeit Köln. Cologne: Universität Köln.

Winterman, R.
1975   Problems in the Horizontal Analysis of Archaeological Remains from Upper Paleolithic Sites. M.A. thesis, UCLA.

Wobst, M.
1979   Computers and Coordinates: Strategies for the Analysis of Paleolithic Stratigraphy. Pp. 61-68 in *Computer Graphics in Archaeology*, ed. S. Upham. ASU Anthropological Research Papers 15. Phoenix: ASU.

Woillard, G. M.
1978   Grande Pile Peat Bog: A Continuous

Pollen Record for the Last 140,000 Years. *QR* 9:1-21.

1979 The Last Interglacial-Glacial Cycle at Grande Pile in Northeastern France. *Bulletin de la Société Belge de Géologie* 88:51-69.

1980 The Pollen Record of Grande Pile (NE France) and the Climatic Chronology through the Last Interglacial-Glacial Cycle. Pp. 95-103 in *Problèmes de stratigraphie quaternaire en France et dans les pays limitrophes*, ed. J. Chaline. *BAFEQ* Supplément n.s. 1. Paris: AFEQ.

Woillard, G. M., and Mook, W. G.
1982 Carbon-14 Dates at Grande Pile: Correlation of Land and Sea Chronologies. *Science* 215:159-161.

Wynn, T.
1986 Archaeological Evidence for the Evolution of Modern Human Intelligence. In *The Pleistocene Perspective*, Vol. 1, comps. M. Day and R. Folley. Preprint of Proceedings of the World Archaeological Congress (Southampton, September). London: Allen & Unwin.

Yellen, J.
1977 *Archaeological Approach to the Present: Models for Reconstructing the Past.* New York: Academic Press.

Young, D. E., and Bonnichsen, R.
1984 *Understanding Stone Tools: A Cognitive Approach.* Orono: Center for the Study of Early Man, University of Maine.
1985 Cognition, Behavior, and Material Culture. Pp. 91-129 in *Stone Tool Analysis*, eds. M. G. Plew, J. C. Woods, and M. G. Pavesic. Albuquerque: University of New Mexico Press.

Zagwign, W. H., and Paepe, R.
1968 Die Stratigraphie der weichselzeitlichen Ablagerungen der Niederlande und Belgiens. *Eiszeitalter und Gegenwart* 19:129-146.

Zar, J. H.
1984 *Biostatistical Analysis.* 2d ed. Englewood Cliffs, NJ: Prentice-Hall.

Zeist, W. van, and Bottema, S.
1982 Vegetational History of the Eastern Mediterranean and the Near East during the Last 20,000 Years. Pp. 277-321 in *Palaeoclimates, Palaeoenvironments and Human Communities in the Eastern Mediterranean Region in Later Prehistory*, eds. J. L. Bintliff and W. van Zeist. BAR International Series 133 (ii). Oxford: BAR.

Zotz, L. F.
1955 *Das Paläolithikum in den Weinberghöhle bei Mauern.* Bonn: Quartär-Bibliothek.

With the exception of some special characters, this book has been set in Bembo Multi-Language. This typeface is named for Pietro Bembo (1470-1547), a Venetian-born cleric, scholar, and poet who served as secretary to Pope Leo X and librarian of St. Mark's Basilica before his elevation to the rank of cardinal. Apart from his contributions to Renaissance literature, theology, and historiography, he is perhaps best remembered for his 16-year courtship of Lucrezia Borgia.

The paper in this book meets the guidelines for permanence and durability of the Committee on Production Guidelines for Book Longevity of the Council on Library Resources.

Grotte des Eyzies.